The Purpose and Practice of Buddhist Meditation

The Purpose and Practice of Buddhist Meditation

A SOURCE BOOK OF TEACHINGS

Sangharakshita

Ibis Publications

Published by Ibis Publications
The Annexe
Coddington Court
Ledbury
Herefordshire
HR8 1JL

© Sangharakshita 2012
Reprinted 2015.

Cover illustration: 'Head, 1981' by Cecil Collins (1908-89). Many thanks to the Monnow Valley arts centre in Herefordshire, the Cecil Collins estate and the Tate Gallery for permission to use the image.

Printed by Berforts Information Press in the UK.
Reprinted by Bell & Bain Ltd., Glasgow.

British Library Cataloguing in Publication Data
A catalogue record for this book is available from the British Library

ISBN 978-0-9574700-0-2
The right of Sangharakshita to be identified as the author of this work has been asserted by him in accordance with the Copyright, Designs and Patents Act 1988

Contents

Editor's Preface   *xviii*

PART ONE: INTRODUCTION

1 What is meditation?

     1. 'Meditation proper'   3
     2. The five main stages of meditation   5
     3. What meditation really is   11

2 A system of meditation

     1. A successful experiment   25
     2. Underground meditation   26
     3. A complete meditation practice   28
     4. An organic, living system   29
     5. Where do these meditation practices come from?   36
     6. An unbroken meditation tradition?   36
     7. Laying a good foundation   40
     8. The path of irregular steps   41
     9. The five great stages   43

3 Motivations and misunderstandings

     1. Motivations for meditation   47
     2. The route to human development   48
     3. What does concentration mean?   49

4. Meditation is more ...   50
5. Why does a Bodhisattva meditate?   51
6. The possibilities of human experience   51
7. Two essential practices   52
8. Meditation and the Bodhisattva spirit   53
9. It's quality that counts   54

PART TWO: MINDFULNESS

1 *The mindfulness of breathing*

1. How to do the practice   58
2. The origins of the mindfulness of breathing   59
3. Why do you get distracted?   64
4. Meditation by numbers   65
5. The point of concentration   66
6. A glowing feeling   67
7. Isn't the mindfulness of breathing a bit boring?   68
8. The mindfulness of breathing and Insight   69

2 *General mindfulness*

1. Knowing what is going on   72
2. Why are we so easily distracted?   74
3. The Japanese tea ceremony   76
4. Mindfulness and pleasure   77
5. Doesn't mindfulness take too much time?   78

3 *Walking meditation*

1. A useful practice?   81
2. The aim of walking and chanting   82
3. A very pleasant practice   85
4. An undesirable way to do it   86
5. Walking and reflecting   87

4 *Clear thinking*

1. The role of clear thinking   88

5 Alienated awareness

1. Integrating our total being	96
2. Is it possible to become too mindful?	98
3. Levels of experience and awareness	99
4. Does meditation cause alienation?	106

PART THREE: THE DEVELOPMENT OF POSITIVE EMOTION

1 The mettā-bhāvanā: introduction

1. The antidote to anger and hatred	109
2. Buddhism was never as individualistic as people think	111
3. *Mettā*: active by definition	113
4. May all beings be happy!	119

2 Mettā for oneself

1. All is not lost	123
2. Why is it hard to love oneself?	125
3. No escape from the *mettā-bhāvanā*	126
4. Do you give yourself what you really need?	127
5. Do you understand what *mettā* means?	128

3 Mettā for a friend

1. Isn't it rather exclusive?	129
2. *Mettā* and erotic feelings	131
3. Can the Buddha be your friend?	133

4 Mettā for a 'neutral person'

1. Love that breaks out	135
2. Drifting away from the practice	138
3. The charms of the neutral person	139

5 Mettā for an 'enemy'

1. Getting a grip on *mettā* — 140
2. Try not to feel discouraged — 145
3. Is *mettā* unconditional love? — 146
4. Directing *mettā* — 149
5. A tinge of dislike — 149

6 Mettā for everyone

1. The whole world of beings — 151
2. Why care? — 153
3. Isn't *mettā* a bit boring? — 155
4. Is there a place for parents and teachers? — 157
5. Specific people in the fifth stage — 159

7 Mettā: further reflections

1. An airy and weightless joy — 160
2. The love mode — 163
3. Not just an elementary little meditation — 164
4. Just as the sun shines — 165
5. Everyday emotions — 166
6. Praise everything — 167
7. The essential characteristic of *mettā* — 170
8. Reflection in the *mettā-bhāvanā* — 173
9. *Mettā* and nostalgia — 174
10. *Mettā* and non-violence — 174
11. *Mettā* for the dying — 177
12. Can *mettā* reach the dead? — 178
13. How can I develop more feeling? — 183
14. Pure *mettā* — 185
15. Dimensions of *mettā* — 186
16. Can *mettā* take me all the way to Enlightenment? — 189
17. *Mettā* and the *bodhicitta* — 190

8 The brahma-vihāras: introduction

1. The sublime abidings — 192

2. *Mettā* must be the basis 196
3. Happiness with its causes 197

9 *The karuṇā-bhāvanā*

1. A natural response 199
2. Is compassion enough? 200
3. 'The extrovert jolliness which is so irritating ...' 201
4. A hierarchy of compassion? 203

10 *The muditā-bhāvanā*

1. A shock and a pleasure 204
2. Joy and compassion 205

11 *The upekṣā-bhāvanā*

1. The practice of equanimity 207
2. Beyond likes and dislikes 208
3. Pure awareness and positivity 210
4. Equanimity doesn't exclude happiness 212
5. The power of peace 213

12 *The brahma-vihāras: further reflections*

1. The basis of it all 215
2. Are the *brahma-vihāras* a path to Insight? 216
3. An alternative route to Enlightenment 217
4. The Illimitables 219
5. Going beyond *mettā* 220

PART FOUR: LEVELS OF CONCENTRATION

1 Samādhi

1. Clearing the decks for action 223
2. A concentrated mind is a happy mind 225

3. Is meditation making the mind a blank? (revisited)   228
4. Neighbourhood concentration   230

2 The dhyānas

1. 'To pass through the door of the mind ...'   231
2. The nature of *dhyāna*   237
3. The characteristics of *dhyāna*: five factors   242
4. The release of blocked energy   245
5. Total saturation   247
6. A very mysterious body of experiences   250
7. What do you get out of the spiritual life?   251
8. The best way of living   253
9. The radiant lamp dispelling the darkness   260
10. Staying in *dhyāna*   260
11. *Dhyāna* outside meditation   263
12. The great difference between *dhyāna* and *prajñā*   264
13. *Dhyāna* approached through different methods   265
14. Can anything 'shade into' the Transcendental?   266
15. The other-regarding aspects of *dhyāna*   269
16. A balancing trick   270
17. Drugs and *dhyāna*   270
18. Consult your own experience   275
19. How does one enter into the *arūpā dhyānas*?   277
20. How do you know when you're in the second *dhyāna*?   279
21. Why bother getting into the higher *dhyānas*?   280

PART FIVE: WORKING IN MEDITATION

1 Preparing to meditate

1. A spontaneous expression of the way you are   283
2. Virtually meditating already ...   285
3. The secret lies in the preparation   289
4. The way you live has an effect on your mind   290
5. The benefits of collective practice   290
6. Sitting down in a state fit for meditation   293
7. Is there a wrong time to meditate?   295

8. Make your meditation independent of conditions 296
  9. 'Do not force your mind or body' 300
  10. Colours for a meditation space 303
  11. Take a deep breath 303
  12. A straight back 304
  13. Cushion-fluffing 305
  14. Getting up early 306

2 Ending the meditation

  1. Don't just throw it away 308
  2. You must be on your guard 310
  3. Communication without chattering 311

3 Identifying hindrances to meditation

  1. The five mental poisons 313
  2. Destroying the bandits' hideout 314
  3. Keep the initiative 318
  4. Sailing into the *dhyānas* 325
  5. Know the enemy 325
  6. Drowsiness and distraction 331
  7. The sensation of waking up 334
  8. An unwillingness to make up one's mind 336
  9. Have faith that you really can 338
  10. Floating thoughts 339
  11. Subtle fetters 342
  12. What would life be like without the hindrances? 344
  13. Out of gladness is born joy 345

4 Antidotes to the hindrances

  1. Cultivating the opposite 346
  2. Why on earth am I doing this? 349
  3. Stand up to Māra 352
  4. The Vajrayana approach to the hindrances 355
  5. Very difficult to resist 356
  6. If all else fails 357

5 Keeping a meditation diary

1. Fresh hope — 359
2. Meditation is a serious business — 360
3. First of all, get a good big notebook! — 361

6 Dangers and difficulties in meditation

1. The gravitational pull — 363
2. Coping with fear in meditation — 366
3. Extreme meditation experiences — 369
4. Is meditation dangerous? — 370
5. The protest of hastily departing notions — 372

7 Discipline in meditation

1. To do it and want to do it — 376
2. No need to meditate with clenched teeth — 378
3. Really enjoy it — 379
4. The problem with the word 'meditation' — 380
5. Regularity is very important — 381
6. How much meditation is good for you? — 382
7. A trace of joy — 384

8 Talking about meditation

1. 'What do you think I experienced this morning?' — 387
2. Becoming aware of the details of one's practice — 391

9 Reflections on effort in meditation

1. That last delicate, subtle effort — 390
2. A strong determination — 391
3. With mindfulness, strive — 394
4. The degree of effort needed — 394
5. Growing naturally — 395
6. The mind almost wants to be distracted — 397

PART SIX: INSIGHT AND ITS RELATIONSHIP WITH DHYĀNA

1 Insight

1. Tangible realities	401
2. 'With mind thus composed …'	401
3. A direct intuitive perception	403
4. Watching a leaf fall	403
5. The aim of all Buddhist practice is ultimately Insight	405
6. Seeing through conditioned existence	406
7. A different sort of mental activity	409
8. Thought-processes are of three kinds	413
9. A calm and gentle aura	415
10. Intellectual understanding and Insight	417
11. A total experience	419
12. Certain changes are going to take place	420
13. Won't Insight arise naturally?	424
14. When can one stop meditating?	421
15. How much concentration is enough?	422
16. Just sitting quietly	423

2 The relationship between Insight and dhyāna

1. *Dhyāna* is essentially a skilful mental state	427
2. Really putting meditation into practice	428
3. The Bodhisattva way of life	431
4. The classical approach	432
5. Insight is the fundamental thing	433
6. Is *dhyāna* a detour?	438
7. Insight and Stream-entry	440
8. You can't worry your way to Insight	441
9. It all seems so self-obsessed …	444
10. A glimmering of Insight	444
11. The *arūpa dhyānas* and Insight	445
12. A key to successful meditation	446
13. The vital point of mind	447
14. Make your mind pliable	452
15. 'Dry' Insight	455
16. Is *vipassanā* more difficult than *samatha* meditation?	456

17. Insight experiences cannot be lost   457
18. It's not enough to meditate; we do have to study   458

PART SEVEN: VIPASSANĀ PRACTICES

1 Impermanence

1. Keeping one's awareness fresh and alive   463
2. No big secret   464
3. One must remember the principle of the thing   469
4. Estimate how much you can take   470

2 The six element practice

The Six Elements Speak   472
1. Nothing really belongs to us   474
2. A very effective practice   477
3. Sources of the practice   480
4. Different forms of element practice   482
5. Infinite consciousness   484
6. The six element practice and the blue sky   486
7. How Buddhism sees the elements   488

3 The chöd practice

1. Egoism is not an entity, but an attitude   496

4 The unpleasantness of the body

1. Restoring a balance   499
2. A very positive kind of detachment   507
3. Surely contemplating 'loathsomeness' can only be off-putting? 508

5 The nidāna chain

1. The truth of conditionality   511
2. How we make ourselves what we are   512
3. You can't find any absolute first beginning   514

6 Śūnyatā meditations

    1. A springboard for the experience of Insight   516
    2. How do you meditate on *śūnyatā*?   521
    3. Just a mode of looking at things   521
    4. Exploring *śūnyatā*   522

PART EIGHT: VISUALIZATIONS AND RECITATIONS

1 The foundation yogas

    1. Introducing the four foundation yogas   525
    2. The foundation yogas and the system of meditation   541
    3. Don't skimp the basics   542
    4. The relevance of the foundation yogas   543
    5. Offering the mandala   544
    6. Preliminary practices   548
    7. Total withdrawal, total engagement   549
    8. The arising of the *bodhicitta*   552
    9. The purification of the mind   556

2 Visualization exercises: kasiṇa and stūpa visualizations

    1. A disc of light   559
    2. A stepping-stone to the visualization practices   561
    3. How can focusing on a sense-object lead beyond the senses?   563
    4. *Stūpa* visualization: the release of psycho-spiritual energy   565

3 The visualization of Buddhas and Bodhisattvas

    1. A Tantric visualization practice: Green Tārā   568
    2. An embodiment of Reality itself   579
    3. The ultimate depths of one's being   580
    4. The whole teaching distilled into a single figure   581
    5. Delicate, tender, subtle   583
    6. That which you're trying to become   584
    7. Two aspects of visualization   585
    8. The relationship between *mettā* and visualization   585

9. Can visualization cure illness?	587
10. Visualization and *dhyāna*	588
11. A deeply spiritual meaning	590
12. Visualization and emptiness	593
13. There's no point in putting off Enlightenment	595
14. Light through a stained glass window	596
15. Choose *mettā*	602
16. You're just supposed to do it!	603
17. 'Western' visualizations	604
18. The relationship between visualization practices	604
19. Difficulty in visualizing	606
20. This is what I want to be like	607
21. An important distinction	609
22. Don't force it	611
23. Falling in love with a Bodhisattva	612
24. The *yidam* and sexual desire	614
25. The right one	615
26. Why visualize an Enlightened being?	616
27. Why bother visualizing at all?	618
28. Making a start	618

4 Mantras

1. What compassion would sound like if we could hear it	620
2. Which is more important, visualization or mantra?	623
3. Attend to the sound	625

PART NINE: INDIRECT METHODS, RETREATS, AND TAKING MEDITATION FURTHER

1 Indirect methods

1. Is meditation the only way?	629
2. Writing instead of meditating?	630
3. Insight in daily life	631
4. I'm afraid that when the big moment comes I will miss it	633
5. Can you enter *dhyāna* through reading a novel?	635
6. An uninterrupted flow	638

7. Physical labour and meditation — 642
8. Wouldn't it be better to open a soup kitchen? — 644
9. Meditation and activity: two sides of the same coin — 645
10. A very dynamic state — 645
11. Meditation in a busy life — 647
12. Are there places that meditation doesn't reach? — 648
13. Meditation versus psychotherapy — 649

2 Going on solitary retreat

1. Can you get by on your own? — 662
2. Consult your own experience — 663
3. It's not just what you do, it's the way that you do it — 666
4. Is going on solitary retreat escapism? — 670
5. Sleepiness in solitude — 673
6. Being sure you are really an individual — 675
7. Do you need solitude to practise *dhyāna*? — 676
8. The whole art of life — 676
9. In a way quite simple — 677

3 Progress in meditation

1. Can you tell if meditation is changing you? — 680
2. 'More advanced practices' — 682
3. Press on — 683
4. No need to worry about the next step — 685
5. Beginner's mind — 685
6. The rhythm of the spiritual life — 687
7. When meditation begins to bite — 689
8. Letting go — 691
9. With mindfulness, strive (revisited) — 692
10. Never lose sight of your objective — 695

Editor's preface

Although Sangharakshita first came across Buddhism in his native England, it was in India that he learned to meditate. Not initially in an ashram or a vihara; this was not the 1960s but the 1940s, and he made his first attempts to meditate sitting on his bunk in the army quarters he shared with his fellow conscripts. At the end of the war, he set out with a friend as a homeless wanderer, seeking spiritual instruction and advice on meditation wherever he could find it. He was eventually ordained in the Theravāda Buddhist tradition, and settled in the Himalayan town of Kalimpong, where he made contact with many Tibetan refugees, among them lamas who became his friends and teachers, and from them he learned much about Tibetan Buddhist practices. He also spent many hours discussing meditation with Mr C.M. Chen, a Zen practitioner who lived as a hermit in the Kalimpong bazaar. (Notes were taken of these discussions, and they are now available on line at www.yogichen.org.)

During the twenty years he lived in India, Sangharakshita learned many meditation techniques and methods, but the mainstays of his practice were the mindfulness of breathing and the development of loving kindness (*mettā-bhāvanā*), and it was these two practices that he taught when he returned to England in the 1960s. In the decade that followed, in addition to the basis of mindfulness and *mettā* he taught more practices, to create a system of meditation which he first outlined specifically in a seminar given to members of the Western (now Triratna) Buddhist Order in 1976. He elaborated further in a talk given in 1978, which was later published in *A Guide to the Buddhist Path*. More details of the story of how Sangharakshita began to practise meditation and how his system of meditation system evolved are included in the introductory section of this book. (For an excellent presentation of the system of meditation, see the work of Cittapala, who has devoted much time and creative energy to a synthesis of it, the results of which can be found at www.cittapala.org.)

The rest of the book is a collection of some of Sangharakshita's writings and teachings on meditation, some of it taken from previously published works, but much of it edited from previously unpublished seminar transcripts. In the 1970s and 1980s in particular, Sangharakshita spent many hours in discussion with the men and women who had joined, or wanted to join, the Buddhist order he founded in 1968 – then known as the Western Buddhist Order, now renamed as the Triratna Buddhist Order. The seminars were usually based on a text from the Buddhist tradition, whether a sutta from the Pāli canon, a Mahāyāna sutra or one of the songs of Milarepa, but the discussion would be wide-ranging, and whatever the ostensible subject, conversation would often turn to how everybody was getting on with their meditation practice. Full transcripts are available at www.freebuddhistaudio.com; for this book Shantavira and I have sifted through the millions of words to find material specifically on the subject of meditation, and we present some of it here. There is more buried treasure; one of my hopes for this book is that it will bring awareness to the wealth of teaching contained in these transcripts.

For the purpose of this book, seminar extracts have been lightly edited, with the aim of focusing on topics specifically relating to meditation. I decided to keep to the question and answer format simply because I found it heartening, and thought others might as well, to read the questions and insights of the seminar participants, as well as Sangharakshita's answers. It's a reminder that teaching is a communication, which depends on students as well as a teacher. The names of the participants have been replaced simply by 'Q' for question. I hope no one will be troubled by this. The names are not always given in the transcripts anyway, but I hope the effect of 'Q' is to help one as a reader to feel that one might be asking the question oneself – Q being a sort of Everyman or Everywoman – especially when the question is a heartfelt wail along the lines of 'But this is so boring!' or 'Isn't this all horribly self-obsessed?' or 'I'm having trouble understanding …' We can be grateful to those who blurted out the kind of question that others might have hesitated to ask. Of course, some of the questioners then have by now been distinguished meditation teachers themselves for decades, and some have written their own books about meditation. Some have helped to found and run meditation retreat centres, some have spent years on solitary retreat, and some have found entirely other ways to live out their commitment to spiritual life.

It's entirely possible that one or two have scarcely looked at a meditation cushion from that day to this.

Almost all of the seminars and lectures on which this book is based took place during the time when Sangharakshita was in full flow as a teacher and adviser, a role which over time others have been able to share. This means that some of the themes, topics and controversies about meditation that have exercised the Order in more recent times are only minimally represented here – perhaps to the disappointment of some readers. I'm aware that during this time Sangharakshita has spoken in all kinds of contexts, recorded in all kinds of media, and there is sure to be more to be included in a future second edition, or perhaps a second volume. If you're aware of something that you feel should be included, please get in touch.

Of the topics tackled in this book, some are covered much more fully than others, depending on the material available, though I have tried to include at least something about all the areas of the subject that Sangharakshita has mentioned over the years. Some aspects of meditation and Buddhist practice (Insight, for example) have particularly interested or puzzled seminar participants over the years, while Sangharakshita himself has repeatedly drawn attention to themes he clearly considers especially important (*mettā* being one clear example).

What has struck me in reading all these seminars is how much effort Sangharakshita has always made to make sure that those in a discussion are making sense of what was being said, hence his often-repeated question: 'Do you see what I mean?', which could have been an alternative title for the book. Although most discussions of the kind are rather too long for inclusion, I've included at least a few exchanges in which Sangharakshita is asking the questions, trying to draw out answers people didn't even know they knew. Quite often he says, in answer to a query, 'Well, consult your own experience.' On other occasions, though, it is the Buddhist tradition to which we are referred. The seminars are based on Buddhist texts from a wide variety of sources, and the source text has been quoted in this book where appropriate; so the teachings here come from many Buddhist schools and traditions. Endnotes have been added to help you find source material.

I should mention that Sangharakshita and Subhuti (who was himself 'Q' in some of the earliest exchanges recorded here) have very recently produced an illuminating series of essays which reveal new thinking on various aspects of the themes of this book. In particular, the question of visualization and *sādhana* practice receives detailed consideration in a paper on 'Re-imagining the Buddha' which has profound implications for how some of the material in the section of this book on visualization should be approached – an example of how this body of teaching has evolved over the years, and is still evolving.

I think there may be a general impression that Sangharakshita has never published – or perhaps even given – much meditation teaching. It's not really so; Windhorse Publications' *Living with Awareness* and *Living with Kindness* are important commentaries on the Triratna community's two key practices, the mindfulness of breathing and the *mettā-bhāvanā*, and there is much material in many other books – *A Guide to the Buddhist Path*, for example. But Sangharakshita himself was surprised to see quite how much material Shantavira and I have managed to gather for this book, and I know is very pleased to see it appear.

Everyone will find something new here, I would think – after all, it tackles a very wide range of subjects, everything from whether the Buddha needed to keep meditating to the best techniques for meditation cushion-fluffing – but a lot of it will be familiar ground to some, and almost all the topics addressed have certainly been covered in other books (Q in his/her various persons having been a prolific writer over the years). There's a degree of repetition – justified, I felt, on the ground that it's interesting and even illuminating to view the same thing from different angles. But there is only one passage (as far as I'm aware) that is included twice; a prize to the person who spots it first! I hope that you'll find the book useful either to dip into as a reference work or a kind of handbook, or to read cover to cover if you have world enough and time. My sense of the cumulative effect of all this material collected together – on this reader, anyway, and I hope it will be true for you too – is that it gives a clear sense of the purpose of Buddhist meditation, and a feeling of confidence that it's possible for us (yes, even us) to attempt to achieve it, whether at this moment we consider ourselves to be meditators or not. It is, as the Dharma always is, *ehipassiko* – 'of the nature of a personal invitation'.

Notes on the text
This book has been designed along the lines of Wisdom Publications' *The Essential Sangharakshita*, as a sort of companion volume. The source is noted at the end of each extract, and there's a list of books and seminars quoted at the back of the book. The page numbers for seminars refer, rather quaintly you may feel, to the paper versions of them still available in some Buddhist centre libraries. (Some of the copies I have myself date back to

the days of *Mitrata*, a periodical which used to publish edited seminar extracts; I remember with gratitude my days working with Srimala and the team of women who produced it in Norwich in the 1980s. The style of this book is in part inspired by that of *Mitrata*.) Almost all the seminar material is also available at freebuddhistaudio.com, where the pagination is different.

The transcripts were produced by dint of great effort by many transcribers over many years, quite a feat given the state of the recording art when the recordings were made. As well as giving intriguing glimpses of what it was like to be trying to work out how to live a Buddhist life in a particular time and place, they are often fun to read, especially the asides ('laughter', 'rattle of teacups', 'jet plane drowns out speech'). My favourite misheard transcription has always been a valiant attempt at the title of a book called *Kindly Bent to Ease Us*: 'Kindly Bent Tweezers'.

Some of the endnotes are from the original sources and some give references to the texts on which commentaries are based. Some of the source material had diacritics for Pali and Sanskrit words, and some didn't; I have attempted to add diacritics where necessary and standardize throughout.

Acknowledgements

Many thanks to Shantavira, who has given many hours to researching source material and proofreading the trial version of the book. Readers of Sangharakshita's books owe a great deal to Shantavira's dedicated work over many years. Thanks also to Shantipala and Ananda, who read the text thoroughly and thoughtfully, and gave very useful and encouraging feedback, and to Satyalila for inspiring the first version of the cover. Many thanks to Dhammarati for the beautiful cover, and for all his kindness and support. Thanks also to Dharmashura for his help with the Birmingham launch on Sangha Day 2012, to Kalyanaprabha, my fellow Ibis Publications editor for her support, and to Priyananda and Windhorse Publications for permission to quote from their published works and for all their help with distribution. Thanks to my husband for all his help with the technical aspects of the book, and his patience as I disappeared repeatedly into the strange world of italics and diacritics. And of course, thanks above all to Sangharakshita himself, for all he has done to encourage and inspire generations of Dharma practitioners in our meditation practice.

Vidyadevi
Herefordshire, November 2012

1 Introduction

1 What is meditation?

Here perpetual incense burns;
The heart to meditation turns,
And all delights and passions spurns.

A thousand brilliant hues arise,
More lovely than the evening skies,
And pictures paint before our eyes.

All the spirit's storm and stress
Is stilled into a nothingness,
And healing powers descend and bless.

Refreshed, we rise and turn again
To mingle with this world of pain,
As on roses falls the rain.

(1947)

1. 'MEDITATION PROPER'

One is living in a different world, and is indeed a different person, at least to some extent.

The word meditation is used, even misused, in all sorts of ways, but properly speaking it has three meanings that correspond to three successively higher levels of spiritual experience. To begin with, there is meditation in the sense of concentration of mind, the withdrawal of one's attention from the external world. You no longer see anything – well, your eyes are closed. But you no longer hear anything either, or taste anything, or smell anything. You don't even feel the meditation cushion on which you are seated, or the clothes you are wearing. Your attention is withdrawn from the senses, and therefore also from the corresponding sense objects, and you become centred within. All your psychophysical energies too are no longer scattered and dispersed but drawn together, centred on one point, vibrating, even, on one point.

Next there comes what we could perhaps call 'meditation proper'. Attention has been withdrawn from the senses, from the external world. The energies have been concentrated within, unified, integrated. Then, at this second stage, the energies start to rise, and there is a gradual raising of the whole level of consciousness, the whole level of being. One is carried up, away from one's ordinary physical body, away out of the ordinary, physical, material universe that one knows. One ascends in one's inner experience up to successively higher states or stages of 'superconsciousness'.

As one becomes more and more concentrated, more and more peaceful, more and more blissful, the world becomes more and more distant. Even mental activity fades away, until only stillness and silence is left, within which one begins to see with the inner vision and hear with the inner hearing. These stages of superconsciousness are known in Buddhism as the four *dhyāna* states. This is 'meditation proper': not just unification of one's psychophysical energies but the raising of them to ever higher levels of consciousness and being, so that one is living in a different world, and is indeed a different person, at least to some extent.

Finally, there comes meditation in the highest sense of all: contemplation – turning this unified, elevated state of being in the direction of the Unconditioned, of reality itself. One sees it, or at least has a glimpse of it, and one begins to move towards it, flow towards it, gravitate towards it. One's unified, elevated consciousness begins to come into contact with the very depths and the very heights of existence and being and consciousness.

From *What is the Dharma?* (1998, p.94)

2. THE FIVE MAIN STAGES OF MEDITATION

These stages are not rigidly demarcated; like the colours of the rainbow, one fades into another by imperceptible degrees.

Meditation, or *dhyāna*, is an important aspect of all Buddhist traditions. Whether one examines the Theravāda teachings or those of the Mahāyāna, whether Indian or Far Eastern, whether one looks at the Tendai school or the Shin school, one finds that meditation in one form or another is an important aspect of each and every one of them. This isn't surprising, because from the very beginnings of Buddhism, if we go right back to the Buddha's own teaching, so far as we can make that out, it seems that a very great emphasis was placed upon meditation. For example, the last three stages of the Buddha's Noble Eightfold Path – Perfect Effort, Perfect Awareness, and Perfect Samadhi – are all concerned with meditation. If we go to that other great formulation of the Path, the path of the Bodhisattva, the path of the six or the ten perfections or transcending virtues, we find that the fifth *pāramitā*, the fifth perfection, is meditation (Sanskrit *dhyāna* or *samādhi*). And if we look among the schools of Buddhism we see that although some concentrate on metaphysics, others – and among them one of the most famous of all Buddhist schools, the Ch'an or Zen school – specialize, as it were, in meditation. So meditation occupies an integral place in the whole Buddhist tradition as exemplified by all schools.

Broadly speaking (it isn't easy to generalize in matters of experience of this sort), regardless of the method we pursue and the specific meditative path which we follow there are five main stages of what we may call the meditation experience. These stages are not rigidly demarcated; like the colours of the rainbow, one fades into another by imperceptible degrees. The first of these five stages is the stage of what we may describe as withdrawal of the mind from the senses. This is why when we meditate we choose a quiet, secluded place in which there will be a minimum of interference from the external world. We shut out as far as possible all external stimuli. Very often we sit cross-legged, fold our hands in our lap, and close our eyes, to shut out all sights, all visual objects. We withdraw the mind, withdraw the consciousness, not just from visual objects, but from sounds, tangibles, tastes, sensations of every kind coming from or through the senses. We try to shut out the external world, and withdraw within. So this is the first stage of all meditation practice: a withdrawal within, a turning away of the mind from the external world and from the senses. This is the first step, but it certainly does not mean that withdrawal or turning away from the world is the aim of meditation. But in this first stage of our meditation experience, the mind or the consciousness is withdrawn from the physical senses and poised as it were in itself. Sometimes if we are practising intensively, the external world does as it were just disappear. We don't perceive it any more, we don't see anything, we don't hear anything, we don't smell, or taste, or touch anything. We are just fully absorbed and concentrated within. This is the first stage in the meditation experience.

The second stage is traditionally called the suppression of the five hindrances. The five hindrances are five unhealthy, negative psychological states, especially emotional states. In this second stage of meditation experience, there is no possibility of eradicating the hindrances, but they have to be temporarily suppressed if further progress is to be made. The first of these hindrances is what we call desire or thirst or craving for sensuous experience. You may for a while shut out the external world, but as you sit there, concentrated as you are, a little sort of tremor may arise in your mind, based on a recollection of a previous experience. That will lead the mind as it were insensibly back towards the original sense object, and along with that will arise a desire for the experience of, the enjoyment of, that sense object. This is very difficult to get rid of, because it goes deep down into the unconscious mind, right down to the roots of the mind as it were.

The second hindrance is ill will: anger or hatred or antagonism in any of its forms. If while you're sitting there trying to concentrate there's any residue in your conscious mind of antagonism towards anybody, if you're irritated or upset, you will not be able to make any further progress in your meditation. So the hindrance of ill will also has to be suppressed, has to be held in abeyance as it were.

The third hindrance is what we call sloth and torpor. This is a very terrible hindrance indeed; it probably holds people back much more than either the desire for sensuous experience or ill will. As you sit there trying to meditate you may find that your mind is quite free from desire for anything; you don't want a cup of tea or to be more warm and cosy. Likewise, you may not be conscious of any ill will towards anybody, or at least you may not be feeling murderous! – you may be feeling moderately affectionate. But sloth and torpor is quite a different proposition, and it may overwhelm you. In Pāli sloth and torpor are called *thīna-*

middha, and the distinction between them is quite interesting. *Thīna* or sloth is a sort of physical sluggishness, while *middha* is a psychological inertia, a stagnation of both body and mind, a dullness, a deadness, a stiffness, a lack of resilience, a sort of force which is pulling you down and preventing you from making any further progress. So this also is a hindrance to be overcome.

The fourth hindrance is the opposite of sloth and torpor. It is restlessness and anxiety, hurry and flurry. If you do manage to get out of the state of sloth and torpor, you'll probably find that you get restless and start worrying; in other words, you fly from one extreme to the other. In a state of restlessness and anxiety, you are on edge, nervy, anxious, looking at things with a furrowed brow as it were, wondering what on earth is going to happen next, what disaster or tragedy is going to strike you down. The effect of this in meditation is that you can't settle down. One thought chases after another, and you're anxious. But if you want success in meditation, you must be calm, you must be peaceful, you must settle down, you mustn't worry about anything. Just leave your worries outside the door of the meditation room. In India, when people enter a temple or a shrine they leave their shoes outside the door, and this is said to symbolize the leaving outside of all one's cares and worries. If your wife or your husband is sick, or if your children aren't doing too well at school, try to forget about it for one hour. Just put it down, just drop it. Anyone who knows anything about Zen will find that the little phrase 'putting it down' has all sorts of meaningful associations.

The fifth and last hindrance is doubt (Pāli *vicikicchā*) – not doubt in the sense of wondering whether something is true or false, but doubt in the sense of indecisiveness, unwillingness to commit oneself. You wonder at the time of the meditation, 'Is this going to do me any good?' or 'Is there any meaning in meditation?' or 'Am I really going to get anywhere?' or 'Am I wasting my time?' You may think that you're rather a fool just sitting there with your legs crossed. This sort of thing is doubt, indecision, and it is suppressed, or held in abeyance, by a firm determination that as a result of the practice you are going to get somewhere. This *vicikicchā*, this doubt, this indecisiveness, has been placed last on the list for a definite reason: it's probably the last hindrance you get rid of. Sometimes people come to me and say, 'I've been meditating for a year. I suppose I'm doing quite well, but I do sometimes wonder why on earth I do it. I can't help wondering whether I'm wasting my time, whether I'd be better reading books on Buddhism, or even giving up

Buddhism altogether.' This is the lurking presence of doubt and indecisiveness. So this also is a hindrance to be overcome. If it is present at the time of meditation, no further progress is possible; it just undermines you.

So this is the second stage of meditation experience: at least temporary freedom from these five hindrances. Of course, when you come along to meditation class at the end of a busy day, in the course of which no doubt your mind has been in turmoil of one kind or another, it isn't easy to settle down and allow these five hindrances to die away. It takes time. Sometimes people say, after meditating for an hour, or at least sitting there for an hour, that when the bell rings to mark the end of the session, they feel that they're just about ready to begin, because it's only then that all these hindrances have died down. This is one of the reasons why retreats are so helpful. If you can get away for a weekend, or even a week, when you are living in a pleasant, natural environment, when you see trees every day and hear birds singing every morning, when it's peaceful and you don't hear the traffic, and with a bit of luck there are no planes roaring overhead, and when you're with people who share your ideals and with whom you can talk on Buddhism, and you do a little reading and some meditation, then you find that these hindrances die away of their own accord almost, so that when you sit for meditation, they are just not there, they've already gone, and you can get on with your meditation.

The third stage of the meditation experience consists in elimination of discursive thought. Very often people think that meditation consists in getting rid of thoughts, and in a sense this is correct, with the proviso that you don't sit there just as it were throwing out the thoughts or trying not to think thoughts. Trying not to think thoughts is rather like trying not to think of a monkey: the more you try not to think of it, the more it comes to mind. You don't make the mind free from thoughts by setting to work on each individual thought and thinking how to get rid of it. You eliminate thoughts by forgetting about thoughts altogether. You take a particular concentration technique, a particular object of concentration, and without thinking about the wandering thoughts, without thinking about the discursive mental activity, you concentrate all your attention on that object of concentration. For instance, when you're practising the mindfulness of breathing, your object is the breath itself, and you're concentrating on the breath; you're trying to be aware of the breath in different ways. If you start thinking about the thoughts that are interrupting your practice, you lose whatever gains you've made. So you have to ignore the thoughts – not try to get rid of them directly, but just concentrate on the object of your concentration, whatever it is. Just concentrate on that, forgetting all about thoughts, and then you'll find – or rather, you won't find, because you won't notice, perhaps – that the thoughts are no longer there.

So this is the third stage, the attainment of no discursive thought. Obviously, there are different degrees. At first, when you practise, you just manage to hang on, like grim death almost, to your concentration object, and you're vaguely conscious of a swarm of thoughts swirling all around you. But gradually you can relax your grip on that concentration object. You don't need to hang on to it, it's there, you're getting more and more absorbed in it, and you feel rather than see that the wandering thoughts are subsiding. They become faint and indistinct, and eventually they die away altogether. You're not thinking about the day's work tomorrow; you're not thinking of anything that has happened today; you're not thinking about your job, or your family, or yourself, you don't even know who you are. You're not thinking about anything. But at the same time, you're not thinking that you're not thinking about anything. As soon as the thought occurs to you, 'Oh, look, I'm not thinking about anything', at that moment all your concentration slides away, and you have to start all over again, or practically all over again. This stage of absence of discursive thought is emphatically not a state of unconsciousness; it's not a blank state. Often people talk about meditation in terms of emptying the mind, or making the mind a blank, but this is nonsense. You don't make the mind a blank by removing discursive thought because when discursive thought is removed, awareness is left, and awareness is something very positive. The mind in its purity begins to be revealed. When you eliminate discursive thought, what results is not just a blank; you're not in a psychological vacuum. At that point the fullness of the mind, the purity of the mind, can begin to manifest itself. So this is the third stage; negatively, the elimination of discursive thought; positively, the emergence of the pure mind, which is above and beyond discursive thought.

That brings us to the fourth stage, the development of higher states of awareness, new levels of consciousness, new levels of mind. This comes almost of its own accord as concentration deepens, as one becomes more and more absorbed in one's concentration object, and eventually unified with it, so that in a sense there is no longer any concentration object.

You're concentrated, but you're not concentrating on anything in particular, you're just concentrated. With this experience of concentration there comes an experience of purity, repose, peace, happiness, joy, bliss, and so on. Sometimes in this stage we have a sensation of being carried out of ourselves, or flowing out of ourselves, or being swept beyond ourselves or above ourselves.

Sometimes when this sort of experience comes, people resist it. They become afraid that they're dissolving, disintegrating, being swept away, and they don't know where. It's as though they have become caught up in a mighty rushing river which is carrying them to some destination, some ultimate goal, the nature of which they don't fully understand; so they resist. If you start resisting, eventually the experience passes away and you return to a lower stage. But don't resist, just let go. Don't worry about what is going to happen to you or whether you are losing yourself or whether your ego is dissolving. Just trust the nature of the experience itself. Surrender yourself to the experience and let it carry you whithersoever it will.

The fifth stage is the stage of the arising of what we call Insight. This stage represents a sort of knowing of Reality, Ultimate Reality, or even a suffusion of our whole being with Reality, in such a way that it is transformed and transfigured. At this point in our meditation experience, quantitative change – increase of concentration and so on – becomes qualitative, and something quite different happens. We start seeing into the heart of things: not in the sense of seeing apparitions or anything of that sort, but seeing things as they are, seeing things more clearly than we have ever seen them before. At first, we see just by flashes. Coleridge wrote that to see the actor Edmund Kean acting was like reading Shakespeare by flashes of lightning. These flashes of Insight are rather like that: they light up the whole intellectual and spiritual landscape just for a instant. But eventually the Insight becomes more stable. The flashes last longer, and you start taking in more and more of the spiritual landscape which is revealed. Eventually it's as though a continuous light starts dawning, and you never altogether lose that. In this way, in the course of years or decades or lifetimes of practice, eventually Enlightenment dawns.

So this is the way in which our meditation experience unfolds, at least in outline, through these five progressive stages, starting with withdrawal of the mind from the senses, and then continuing with suppression of the five hindrances and elimination of discursive thought, then going to development of higher states of awareness and consciousness, and culminating in the arising of Insight into Reality itself. These features seem to be common to all kinds of meditation practice and experience, but there are many possible variations, and it's possible to pass through these stages in a number of different ways.

From 'The Four Foundation Yogas' in a lecture series on Tibetan Buddhism; an edited version appears in *Tibetan Buddhism* (1996), pp.87-9

3. WHAT MEDITATION REALLY IS

To reach an understanding of the true nature and purpose of meditation, we need to bear in mind the gap between the ideal and the real, between the Enlightened human being, or Buddha, and the unenlightened, ordinary human being.

Not so very long ago, meditation had hardly been heard of in the West, and knowledge about it or interest in it was for the most part confined to obscure groups and eccentric individuals. These days, by contrast, the term meditation is almost a household word. But this does not mean that what the word represents – what meditation means – is at all well understood. So many times I have heard people say, 'Meditation means making the mind a blank, making the mind empty.' Others seem to think that meditation simply means sitting and doing nothing. That may be a fine thing to do, or not do, but it is not meditation. Again, sometimes you hear people say, or you read, that meditation means sitting and gazing at your navel, possibly squinting as you do so, or that it means 'going into some kind of trance'. Other people think that meditation means just sitting quietly and thinking about things, turning things over in one's mind. Others again think that meditation means getting yourself into a sort of self-induced hypnotic state. These are just a few of the more widespread misunderstandings.

Why there should be these misunderstandings seems fairly obvious. Meditation is comparatively new in the West, or at least the modern West. There has not been anything quite like it within the range of our experience. We do not even have the proper words, the specialized terms, to describe meditation states and processes. It is only natural, therefore, that at first there should be some misunderstanding.

We must remember that meditation is essentially something one does or experiences, and one can't really know what it is like from hearsay or even reading a book. In the West today there is a boom in spiritual things in general, and at least a modest boom in meditation. Quite a number of people are dissatisfied with their ordinary, everyday lives, their conventional way of living and doing things. People cannot accept a purely scientific explanation of life, despite the great success of science in dealing with the material world, while at the same time they find themselves unable to accept the traditional, mainly Judaeo-Christian, explanation of things. They therefore begin looking for something which will satisfy them more deeply, more permanently, more creatively, and more constructively. Some people look in the direction of the Eastern spiritual traditions, and especially in the direction of meditation. They want to know about it and learn how to practise it, and in this way a demand for meditation teaching is created – and there are only too many people who are ready to fulfil that demand. Some of them are quite well qualified to teach meditation, but others are not, and in this way, misunderstandings arise. Quite often meditation is identified with a particular kind of meditation, or a particular concentration technique. It is not always understood that there are many kinds and methods of meditation. Sometimes people who just know one, or who practise just one, tend to identify the whole practice of meditation exclusively with that particular method. They may claim that their method is the best, or even that it is the only one, and that you are not meditating at all unless you meditate in that particular way. It becomes all the more important, therefore, to clear up the confusion, to resolve the misunderstandings. It becomes important to understand what meditation really is.

To reach an understanding of the true nature and purpose of meditation, we need to bear in mind the gap between the ideal and the real, between the Enlightened human being, or Buddha, and the unenlightened, ordinary human being. The Buddha represents a mode of being and consciousness for which we have no equivalent in Western thought, and therefore no equivalent term. 'Buddha' does not mean God, the supreme being, the creator of the universe, or God incarnate. Neither is the Buddha a human being in the ordinary sense. We can best think of the Buddha in evolutionary terms, as a human being but a very special kind of human being, a more developed human being – in fact an infinitely developed human being, a human being who has reached, and realized fully, the state of spiritual perfection that we call Enlightenment. This is what 'Buddha' means. And 'Buddhism' is whatever helps us to close the gap between the ideal and the real, whatever helps to transform the unenlightened person into the Enlightened man or woman; whatever helps us to grow, to evolve, to develop. This transformation involves a tremendous change, perhaps the greatest human development that can take place. And it is this that we call the spiritual life, or the process of what I sometimes like to call the Higher Evolution.

But what is it that changes? Obviously it is not the physical body, because physically the Enlightened human being and the unenlightened one look very much alike. The change that takes place can only be a purely mental one – using the word mental in its widest sense. It is consciousness that develops, and this is the great difference between the Higher Evolution and the lower evolution.

What I mean by the lower evolution corresponds to the whole process of development from amoeba up to the ordinary or unenlightened human being: a predominantly biological process, though it becomes psychological towards the end. And the Higher Evolution corresponds to the whole course of development which leads from unenlightened humanity up to Enlightened humanity, a purely psychological and spiritual process, which may eventually become entirely dissociated from the physical body.

Levels of consciousness
Traditional Buddhism speaks in terms of four grades or levels of consciousness, each one higher than the one preceding. First of all there is consciousness associated with the plane, or 'world', of sensuous experience (the *kāmaloka*). Secondly there is consciousness associated with the plane, or 'world', of mental and spiritual form – the plane or world of archetypes (*rūpāloka*). Then there is consciousness associated with the formless plane or 'world' (*arūpāloka*), and finally, consciousness associated with the Transcendental Path, which is to say, with the path leading directly to Nirvāṇa, Enlightenment, or Buddhahood, as well as with Nirvāṇa, Enlightenment, or Buddhahood itself.

But there is another classification which may be more helpful. This too has four stages, or four levels, of consciousness, although they do not correspond very exactly to the four already enumerated. First of all comes sense-consciousness – that is, consciousness associated with objects experienced through the physical senses, sometimes called simple consciousness or animal consciousness. It is the consciousness we share with members of the animal kingdom. Secondly, there is self-consciousness: not in the colloquial sense of the term, but in the sense of awareness of being aware, knowing that we know. This is sometimes called reflexive consciousness because here, consciousness so to speak bends back upon itself, knows itself, experiences itself, is aware of itself. We may say, perhaps, that this self-consciousness, or reflexive consciousness, is human consciousness in the full sense of the term. Thirdly, there is Transcendental consciousness: consciousness of, or even direct personal contact with, Reality – Ultimate Reality – experienced as an object 'out there'. Finally, there is Absolute Consciousness, in which the subject-object relation is entirely dissolved, and there is a full realization of Ultimate Reality as transcending altogether the subject-object duality.

In both these classifications, the first consciousness enumerated is that of the ordinary unenlightened person, the man or woman who is not even trying to develop spiritually. And the fourth consciousness, in both cases, is that of the Enlightened human being. We can now begin to see in what the spiritual life essentially consists. It consists in a continual progression from lower to higher, and ever higher, states of being and consciousness: from the world of sensuous experience to the world of mental and spiritual form, from the world of mental and spiritual form to the formless world, and from the formless world to Nirvāṇa, or Enlightenment; or, from sense-consciousness to self-consciousness, self-consciousness to Transcendental consciousness, Transcendental consciousness to Absolute Consciousness.

We can now begin to see what meditation really is. Indeed, we shall see it all the more clearly for having gone a little way into these fundamentals first. There is, however, just one more point to be made. Spiritual life consists in the development of consciousness, and Buddhism, the Dharma, the teaching of the Buddha, is whatever helps in that development. But there are two different ways in which consciousness can be developed, two different methods of approach: the subjective and the objective, or the direct and the indirect. Meditation is the subjective or direct way of raising the level of consciousness. In meditation we raise the level of consciousness by working directly on the mind itself.

But there are also 'objective' or indirect methods of raising the level of consciousness. Some people appear to think that meditation is the only way there is to raise the level of consciousness, as if to say that consciousness must be raised directly, by working on the mind itself, or not at all. Such people therefore identify meditation with the spiritual life, and the spiritual life exclusively with meditation, and say that if you are not meditating you cannot possibly be leading a spiritual life. But this is far too narrow a view. It makes us forget what the spiritual life really is – which is to say, the raising of the level of consciousness – and it sometimes makes us forget what meditation itself really is. It is true that the raising of the level of consciousness by direct methods is at least as important as raising it by indirect methods; we might even say that it is perhaps more important. But we should not forget that other methods do exist; if we did forget this, our approach to the spiritual life would be too one-sided, and we might even exclude from it certain kinds of people – people of certain temperaments, for example – who were not particularly interested in meditation.

Indirect methods

One indirect, non-meditative method of raising the level of consciousness is changing one's environment. We do this quite consciously as an indirect means of changing, and hopefully raising, our level of consciousness when we go away on retreat – perhaps into the country, to a retreat centre. There we spend a few days, or even a few weeks, in more pleasant, more congenial surroundings, perhaps not even doing anything in particular. This is often more helpful than people realize, and it suggests that the environment in which we normally live and work may not be particularly good for us, may not help in the raising of the level of our awareness. It really does seem as if, for most people, a positive change of environment leads quite naturally to a raising of their level of consciousness – even without any further effort.

Another practical and simple indirect method of raising the level of consciousness is what we call in Buddhism Right Livelihood. Practically everybody has to work for a living. Quite a lot of us do the same kind of work every day, five days a week, fifty weeks of the year. We may do it for five, ten, fifteen, twenty, twenty-five, or thirty years, until we come to the age of retirement. All this has a continuous effect on our state of mind. If our work is unhealthy in the mental, moral, and spiritual sense, the effect on our minds will also be unhealthy. So in Buddhism, we are advised very strongly to practise Right Livelihood, which means earning our living in a way that does not lower our state of consciousness or prevent us raising it, and which does no harm to other living beings. In Buddhist tradition there is a list of occupations which are seen as unhelpful: the work of a butcher, of a trader in arms, of a dealer in liquor, and so on. Simply changing our means of livelihood (assuming that at present it is not quite right) – changing what we do, where we do it, who we work with, the sort of thing that we have to do every day – will have a positive and helpful effect on our level of consciousness, or at least it will not prevent it from rising.

Then, to become more specific, there is the leading of a regular and disciplined life: something which apparently is becoming less and less popular. This may consist in the observance of certain moral precepts and principles, in having regular hours for meals, for work, for recreation, and for study, or in observing moderation in such things as eating, sleeping, and talking – perhaps even in fasting occasionally, or observing silence for a few days or weeks. In its fully developed form this more regular, disciplined life is what we call the monastic life. Among those who are leading such a regular, disciplined life, even without any meditation, over a period of years, one can see quite clearly a change taking place in their state of consciousness.

There are other indirect methods, such as Hatha Yoga or yoga in the more physical sense. Especially there are what are called yogic *asanas*, which affect not only the body, but the mind as well. They affect the mind through the body, and even people who meditate regularly sometimes find these asanas very helpful. Sometimes even the experienced meditator may be a bit too tired at the end of a day's work, or a bit too worried, to meditate properly. At such times he or she may practise a few *asanas* until his or her mind becomes calmer and more concentrated. The effect can be almost as refreshing as meditating. Then again there are the various Japanese Do or 'Ways' – like ikebana, flower arrangement. It might seem a very simple and ordinary thing, just to arrange a few flowers in a vase in a traditional way, but people who engage in this over a period of years are definitely changed in their minds, changed in their consciousness. One can also think of things like T'ai Chi Ch'uan and so on. These all have an effect upon the mind. They are all indirect ways of raising the level of consciousness. Likewise, the enjoyment of great works of art – poetry, music, and painting – often helps to raise the level of consciousness, if the works in question are truly great, if they really do issue from a higher state of consciousness in the artist, if they actually are an expression of a higher state of consciousness than we usually experience.

On a more practical level, there is simply helping other people. We might devote ourselves to helping the sick, the destitute, and the mentally disturbed, as well as to visiting people in prison. We might do these things very willingly and cheerfully, disregarding our own comfort and convenience – might do them without any personal, selfish motive. This is what in the Hindu tradition is called *nishkama karma yoga*, or the yoga of disinterested action. This too is an indirect means of raising our state of consciousness.

Then there is association with spiritually minded people, especially those who are more spiritually advanced than ourselves – if we are able to find them. Such association is regarded in some traditions, or by some teachers, as the most important of all the indirect methods. It is what is referred to again and again in Indian religious and spiritual literature as *satsangh*. *Sat* means true, real, authentic, genuine, spiritual – even Transcendental – while *sangh* means association, or communion, or fellowship. *Satsangh* is simply a getting together – often in a very happy, carefree spirit – with people who are on the spiritual path and whose predominant interest is in spiritual things. This rubs off on oneself, almost without any effort on one's own part. Thus *satsangh* too is an indirect means of raising the level of consciousness. It is what in Buddhism we call *kalyāna mitratā*.

Then again, there is chanting and ritual. Ritual is sometimes looked down upon today, especially by the more 'intellectual' sort of person, but it is a time-honoured method of raising the level of consciousness. Even if we simply offer a few flowers, or light a candle and place it in front of an image or picture, all this has an effect upon the mind, and sometimes people are surprised to find how much effect it does have. You may read lots of books about the spiritual life, you may even have tried to meditate – or even have succeeded in meditating – but sometimes you may find that the performance of a simple but meaningful symbolic ritual action helps you far more.

There are many more indirect methods that could be mentioned, and these methods can of course be combined with each other. Some of them can be combined with the direct method, with the practice of meditation. Good though these indirect methods are, some of them at least will not carry us very far – certainly not through all the levels of consciousness. But since for most of us it will be quite a while before we do pass on to the higher levels of consciousness, the indirect methods will be useful to us for a long time. However, if by means of such methods we do succeed in getting anywhere near those higher levels then, in order to progress further, we shall have to have greater and greater recourse to meditation. We shall have to start working directly on the mind itself.

Working on the mind directly

How do we do this? In what does this direct working on the mind consist? So far I have been using the very general term 'meditation', because this is the one that has gained currency in the West, at least in the English-speaking countries. But the English word 'meditation' does not correspond to any one Buddhist term. It covers three different ways of working directly on the mind – three different stages, even, in the development of consciousness – and for each of these three things, Buddhism, like other Indian spiritual traditions, has quite separate terms. In plain English, 'meditation' comprises Concentration, Absorption, and Insight.

The Stage of Concentration

Concentration is of a twofold nature, involving both a narrowing of the focus of attention and a unification of energy. As such, it can be described in terms of integration, which is of two kinds, the 'horizontal' and the 'vertical', as I shall call them. Horizontal integration means the integration of the ordinary waking consciousness within itself, or on its own level, while vertical integration means the integration of the conscious mind with the subconscious mind, a process which involves the freeing of blocked somatic energy as well as the tapping of deeper and ever deeper energies within the psyche.

Horizontal integration corresponds to what is generally known as mindfulness and recollection. This English word 'recollection' is rather a good one, because it means just what it says – re-collection. It is a collecting together of what has been scattered, and what has been scattered is ourselves, our conscious selves, or so-called conscious selves. We have become divided into a number of selves, or part-selves, each with its own interests, its own desires, and so on, each trying to go its own way. At one time one self is uppermost, at another time another, so that sometimes we hardly know who we are. There is a dutiful self and there is a disobedient self. There is a self that would like to run away from it all, and there is a self that would like to stay at home and be a good boy or girl, and so on. We hardly know, very often, which of these selves we really and truly are. Each of them is our self, and yet none of them is our self. The truth is that we do not really have a self at all. It has not yet come into existence. It has not yet been born. The self – the overall self, as it were – comes into existence only with the practice of mindfulness and recollection, when we 'collect' all these selves together.

Mindfulness, or recollection, in Buddhist tradition is of three kinds. Firstly, there is mindfulness of the body and its movements: knowing exactly where the body is and what it is doing. Here we make no unmindful movements, no movements of which we are unaware. When we speak, too, we are mindful, knowing what we are saying and why we are saying it. We are fully alert, composed, aware.

Secondly, there is mindfulness of feelings and emotions. We become quite clearly conscious of our passing, changing moods, of whether we are sad or happy, pleased or displeased, anxious, afraid, joyful, or excited. We watch, we see it all, we know exactly how we are. This does not mean standing back from our feelings and emotions like a sort of spectator, looking at them in a very external, alienated way. It means experiencing our feelings and emotions – being 'with' them, not cut off from them – but at the same time being always mindful of them and observing them.

Thirdly and lastly, there is mindfulness of thoughts: knowing just what we are thinking, just where our mind is from instant to instant. As we know, the mind wanders very easily. We are usually in an unconcentrated, unrecollected state as regards our thoughts. For this reason we have to practise being mindful of our thoughts, aware of what we are thinking from moment to moment.

If we practise in this way, then horizontal integration is achieved. We are brought together, and a self is created. When this is properly and perfectly done, we develop complete self-consciousness: we become truly human. But concentration is not only horizontal; it is also vertical. The conscious mind must now be integrated with the subconscious mind. This is achieved by having recourse to an object of concentration – an object on which one learns to concentrate one's whole attention, and into which the energies of the subconscious are allowed to be gradually absorbed.

At this point, as a meditator, or would-be meditator, you have reached a crucial stage. You are about to make a very important transition, from the plane or world of sensuous experience to the plane or world of mental and spiritual form. But you are held back by what are known as the five mental hindrances, which have to be suppressed before the stage of Absorption can be entered upon. (This suppression is temporary. The five mental hindrances are permanently eradicated only when Insight has been attained.) First of all, there is the hindrance of desire for sensuous experience through the five physical senses, desire, that is, for agreeable visual, auditory, olfactory, gustatory, and tactile sensations – especially those connected with food and with sex. So long as desires of this sort are present in the mind, no transition to the stage of Absorption is possible, since while they are present the meditator cannot really occupy himself with the concentration-object.

Secondly, there is the hindrance of hatred, which is the feeling of ill will and resentment that arises when the desire for sensuous experience is frustrated – a feeling that is sometimes directed towards the object of the desire itself. Thirdly comes the hindrance of sloth and torpor, which keeps one on the plane of sensuous desire, on the ordinary, everyday level of consciousness. It is a sort of animal-like stagnation, both mental and physical. Fourthly, there is the opposite hindrance to sloth-and-torpor, the hindrance of restlessness and worry. This is the inability to settle down to anything for very long. It is a state of continual fussing and bothering, never really getting anything done. Fifthly and lastly, there is the hindrance of doubt – not an honest intellectual doubt, but something more like indecision, or even unwillingness to make up one's mind, to commit oneself. Basically, it is a lack of faith, a lack of trust: a reluctance to acknowledge that there is a higher state of consciousness for human beings to achieve.

These, then, are the five mental hindrances which must be allowed to subside, or which must even be suppressed, before we take up the concentration-object and prepare to enter upon the stage of absorption. For a mind obscured by the five mental hindrances, as our minds so often are, there are five traditional similes, in each of which the mind itself is likened to water. The mind which is contaminated by desire for sensuous experience is likened to water in which various bright colours have been mixed. It may be pretty, but the purity and translucency of the water has been lost. The mind which is contaminated by hatred is, we are told, like water that has been brought to the boil, and is hissing and bubbling and seething. The mind contaminated by sloth-and-torpor is said to be like water choked with a thick growth of weeds, so that nothing can get through it. The mind contaminated by restlessness-and-worry is like water which has been whipped up into waves by the wind, even by a great storm. Lastly, the mind which is contaminated by doubt, by uncertainty, is like water full of mud.

When the five hindrances are suppressed, the conscious mind becomes like pure water – cool, calm and clear. It is now ready to take up an object of concentration. These objects of concentration, even in the Buddhist tradition alone, are of very many kinds: some rather ordinary and everyday, and others rather extraordinary. First of all there is the breath, our own breath, as it comes in and goes out; there are various forms of this practice. Another object of concentration, a very important one, is sound, especially the sacred sound called mantra. Or we can take as an object of concentration a disc of very pure, bright colour – red or blue or green, etc., according to temperament. Again, we can make our object of concentration a piece of human bone, preferably a sizable piece to provide a good solid object of concentration. Alternatively we can take an idea, a concept, or a particular virtue to be cultivated, such as generosity. And again – to take something quite ordinary and mundane – we can concentrate on the flame of a lamp or a candle. We can also concentrate on the various psychic centres within our own body, or on a mental image or picture of the Buddha, or of a great Bodhisattva or teacher. In all of these objects, the mind can become absorbed, even deeply absorbed.

We do not have to practise concentration with each and every one of these objects, though several different concentration-objects are combined in sequence in some systems or traditions of meditation practice. The different objects of concentration can also be combined with some of the indirect methods of raising the level of consciousness, particularly with chanting and ritual.

Now if we proceed in this manner – if we integrate the conscious mind with itself, and then integrate the conscious mind with the subconscious mind, and if we suppress the five mental hindrances and take up an object or objects of concentration, and if our deeper energies start flowing more and more powerfully into the object of concentration – then a great change will take place. Our level of consciousness will definitely start rising from the plane or world of sensuous experience to the plane or world of mental and spiritual form. In other words, we will begin to pass from the first to the second stage of meditation, from meditation in the sense of concentration, to meditation in the sense of absorption.

The Stage of Absorption
Absorption, the second level of meditation, is generally divided into four levels, throughout which the process of vertical integration, begun at the stage of concentration, continues. At this stage there is no question of integrating the conscious and the subconscious mind, for that has already been done. Now the purified, integrated conscious mind is itself integrated with the superconscious, and the energies of the superconscious – energies, that is to say, which are purely spiritual – begin to be tapped. Absorption therefore represents the unification of the mind on

THE PURPOSE AND PRACTICE OF BUDDHIST MEDITATION

higher and ever higher levels of consciousness and being. As this process continues, our cruder mental states and functions are refined, and our energies are absorbed into higher states and functions.

In the first level of absorption (*dhyāna*) there is a certain amount of mental activity present. We are still thinking about this and that, perhaps thinking subtle thoughts about worldly matters, or even about our meditation practice itself. From the second level of absorption onwards, mental activity of this kind is entirely absent. Thinking as we know it entirely disappears. You might think that if we are not thinking, we will become dead and inert, but this would be a great mistake. One might even say that because we are not thinking, consciousness becomes clearer, brighter, more intense and more radiant than ever. But since thinking does not occur at the second and higher levels, it is important not to think about these levels of absorption too much, or preferably not at all. Instead, we should try to get some feeling of what they are like, proceeding not analytically, not intellectually, but with the help of images, symbols, and similes. We can best do this with the help of the four traditional similes for the four states of absorption – similes which go back to the Buddha's own personal teaching.

The simile for the first level of absorption is that of soap powder and water. The Buddha asks us to imagine that a bath-attendant takes some soap powder in one hand – apparently they had soap powder in ancient India – and some water in the other. He mixes the two together in a platter in such a way that all the water is fully absorbed by the soap powder, and all the soap powder is thoroughly saturated by the water. There is not a single speck of soap powder unsaturated, and not a single drop of water left over. The first stage of absorption, the Buddha says, is just like that. In it, the entire psycho-physical organism is completely saturated with feelings of bliss, of ecstasy, of supreme happiness, and these feelings are all contained. At the same time, the whole being is saturated. There is no part of one's being, physical or mental, left unsaturated, and yet there is nothing left over. Thus there is no inequality, no imbalance. It is all calm and steady, stable and firm: naturally concentrated.

Describing the second level of absorption, the Buddha asks us to imagine a great lake of water, very pure, calm and still. This lake is fed by a subterranean spring, so that all the time in the very heart of the lake there is a bubbling up of pure water from a great depth. The second level of absorption is like this. It is calm and clear, it is peaceful, pure, translucent, but from an even greater depth there is something even more pure, bright and wonderful, bubbling up all the time. This 'something' is the higher spiritual element, the higher spiritual consciousness, by which we are now as it were infiltrated, by which we are inspired.

The third level of absorption, the Buddha says, is like the same lake, the same body of water, only with lotus blossoms growing in it. These lotus blossoms are standing right in the water, soaked and pervaded by it. They are thoroughly enjoying the water, you could say. Similarly, in the third level of absorption, we are, so to speak, bathing in that higher spiritual element, that higher spiritual consciousness – soaking in it, permeated by it within and surrounded by it without. This, the Buddha said, is what the third level of absorption is like.

In the case of the fourth and last level of absorption, the Buddha asks us to imagine a man who, on a very hot day, has a bath in a great tank of water. Having washed himself clean, he comes out, and then wraps his whole body in a sparklingly white, clean, new sheet, so that he is swathed in it, and it completely covers him. The fourth level of absorption, the Buddha says, is like that. We are insulated by that higher spiritual consciousness from the contact, and from the influence, of lower states and levels. It is as though we are surrounded by a powerful aura. It is not that we immerse ourselves in that state, but rather that the state has descended into us, permeated us. Furthermore, it has started radiating outwards from us so that we have a sort of aura of meditation extending from us in all directions. In this state we cannot be easily influenced or affected, although we can easily influence and affect other people.

These, then, are the four levels of absorption. If we want to recall them, and get the feeling of them, perhaps we should just recollect the four beautiful similes given by the Buddha to illustrate them. Having traversed, at least in imagination, these four levels of absorption, we can now come on to the third and last stage of meditation.

The Stage of Insight
By Insight we mean the clear vision, the clear perception, of the true nature of things – of what in traditional Buddhist terminology is called things 'as they really are'. In other words, to use more abstract, more philosophical phraseology, it is a direct perception of Reality itself. This is what meditation at its height is – this is what Insight really is. Such perception is twofold. It is Insight into the conditioned, which is to say, the 'world', or whatever is mundane, transitory, and so on; and it is Insight into the Unconditioned, that which transcends the world: the Absolute, the Ultimate.

The former, Insight into the conditioned, has three aspects. We see first of all that conditioned things, worldly things, by their very nature cannot give permanent and lasting satisfaction. For that we have to look elsewhere. Secondly, we see that all conditioned things are impermanent. We cannot possess any of them for ever. And thirdly and lastly, we see that all conditioned things are only relatively existent. They do not possess permanent, ultimate reality.

Insight into the Unconditioned consists, in one formulation, of what are known as the Five Knowledges, or the Five Wisdoms. This is not knowledge in the ordinary sense, but something far beyond that. First of all there is what we can only describe as knowledge of the totality of things, not in their particularity, but in and through their ultimate depths and spiritual essence, in the light of their common unifying principle. Then there is the knowledge of all things, conditioned and Unconditioned, without the slightest trace of subjective distortion. This is sometimes called the Mirror-like Knowledge, so called because it is like a great mirror which reflects everything just as it is – without subjectivity, or prejudice, or dimming, or clouding, or obscuration. In it everything is seen just as it is. Thirdly, there is the knowledge of things in their absolute sameness and identity – seeing everywhere one mind, one reality, one Sunyata. Fourthly, there is the knowledge of things in their difference. The absolute unity does not wipe out the absolute difference. There is no one-sidedness. We see things in their absolute unity, but we also see them in their absolute multiplicity, their absolute uniqueness. We see them in both ways at once. And then, finally, there is the knowledge of what is to be done for the spiritual welfare of other living beings.

These Five Knowledges, or Five Wisdoms, are symbolized in Buddhist iconography by what we call the Mandala of the Five Buddhas. Visualizing this mandala, we see first of all a vast expanse of blue sky, very deep and very brilliant. At the centre of this expanse we see appearing a pure white Buddha figure, holding a brilliant golden wheel. Then in the east we see a deep, dark blue Buddha holding a vajra, a 'diamond sceptre'. In the south we see a golden yellow Buddha holding a brilliantly shining jewel. In the west we see a deep red Buddha holding a red lotus. And in the north we see a green Buddha, holding two 'diamond sceptres' crossed.

When all the Five Knowledges dawn, Enlightenment has been attained. We become ourselves the embodiment of all five Buddhas. Insight has been fully developed, meditation has been practised to the very limit, and we have understood for ourselves what meditation really is.

From *Human Enlightenment* (1993, pp.32-55)

INTRODUCTION

2 A system of meditation

1. A SUCCESSFUL EXPERIMENT

I feel strongly that there is a great need for a wider and more intensive practice of the 'classical' systems of meditation.

When I came back to England in 1964, a high proportion of Western Buddhists seemed interested in meditation, and it was significant that at the Summer School there were four different meditation sessions a day, all of them well attended. In view of the alarmingly high incidence of mental strain and disorder this interest was natural, I observed in an article I wrote at the time, adding that it was always to be borne in mind that the significance of Buddhist meditation was not merely psychological but primarily spiritual: its goal was Enlightenment. The article continued:

> Some people at the Summer School, however, regretted that a wider range of meditation practices were not available. As one of them told me, 'We aren't attracted by Zen, and we don't like Vipassanā, and there doesn't seem to be anything in between.' Actually there is very much 'in between'. At the 9.30 meditation sessions I conducted an experiment in what I afterwards called Guided Meditation, the class progressing from one stage to another of *Mettā-Bhāvanā* (Development of Love) practice as directed at five-minute intervals by the voice of the instructor. Verbal directions were gradually reduced to a minimum until, in

the last session, transition from one stage to the next was indicated merely by strokes on the gong. The experiment seemed successful, and it may be possible to apply the same technique to the teaching of other types of meditation. In any case, I feel strongly that there is a great need, among English Buddhists, for a wider and more intensive practice of the 'classical' systems of meditation, such as Mettā Bhāvanā and Ānāpāna Sati (Respiration-Mindfulness), which are common to all Yānas and which constitute the indispensable foundation of the more advanced techniques. I also feel that less attention is paid than might be to the devotional side of the Buddha's Teaching. As the formula of the Five Spiritual Faculties reminds us, Faith (*śraddhā*) and Wisdom (*prajñā*), Energy *(vīrya)* and Meditation (*samādhi*), must be in perfect equilibrium: Mindfulness (*smṛti*) 'is always useful'.

The Vipassanā that some people at the Summer School didn't like was the controversial Burmese 'insight meditation' that Ananda Bodhi had been teaching. My experiment in Guided Meditation was an experiment in the sense that I had not taught meditation in this way before, and as the experiment was successful it did prove possible to apply the same technique to the teaching of types of meditation other than *mettā-bhāvanā*. Guided *Group* Meditation, as I now called it, came to be the standard way in which I taught *mettā-bhāvanā* and *ānāpāna-sati* to beginners in meditation both at the Vihara and elsewhere. This served to encourage the practice of the 'classical' systems of meditation among English Buddhists, some of whom were inclined to hanker after more 'advanced' methods of development.

From *Moving Against the Stream* (2004, pp.28-9)

2. UNDERGROUND MEDITATION

Quite soon, people attending these classes regularly were becoming noticeably calmer, clearer, and happier – as was only to be expected.

When in 1967 I founded a new Buddhist movement, I did so with few preconceived ideas of how Buddhism might be introduced most effectively into this – as it seemed to me then – quite strange society. My initial point of interaction was meditation. I started conducting weekly meditation classes in a tiny basement room in central London. This setting was, I feel now, quite appropriate for my earliest forays into alien territory, into a culture devoted to values that are largely inimical to my own. In some sense one had to work below the surface, as an underground movement, rather like the early Christians in Rome who are supposed to have met in the Catacombs to take refuge from persecution. We are very fortunate in the West that we are not subject to overt persecution; but modern values which are antipathetic to religious faith of any kind – like materialism, consumerism, and relativism – are enforced in subtle but pervasive ways that make them all the more difficult to resist.

In these 'underground' meditation classes, I taught two methods of meditation: the mindfulness of breathing, known in Pāli as *ānāpānasati*, and the cultivation of universal loving kindness, the *mettā-bhāvanā*. Quite soon, people attending these classes regularly were becoming noticeably calmer, clearer, and happier – as was only to be expected. There are many ways of defining meditation, but in very simple terms we can say that it enables the mind to work directly on itself in order to refine the quality of one's conscious experience, and in this way to raise one's whole level of consciousness. This process may be augmented by various indirect methods of raising consciousness, such as Hatha yoga, T'ai chi Ch'uan, and similar physical disciplines, together with the practice and appreciation of the arts. Thus the integration of Buddhism into Western society begins with at least some members of that society raising their levels of consciousness both directly through meditation, and indirectly through various other disciplines.

After a few months, we held our first retreat in the countryside, for just one week. It was attended by fifteen or twenty people who had been coming along regularly to these weekly meditation classes. On this retreat we meditated together, engaged in various devotional practices together, and discussed the Dharma together. Some of the retreatants were there to deepen their experience of meditation, and this they were able to do. But all of them discovered that simply being away from the city, away from the daily grind of work and home life, and being in the company of other Buddhists, with nothing to think about except the Dharma, was sufficient to raise their level of consciousness. So here was another point of interaction: changing the environment, changing the conditions in which people lived. That is, consciousness can be raised, at least to some extent, by changing society.

The integration of Buddhism into Western society therefore involves changing Western society. Inasmuch as our level of consciousness is affected by external conditions, it is not enough for us to work directly on the mind itself through meditation. We cannot isolate ourselves from society or ignore the conditions in which we and others live. We must make it easier for anyone within that society who wants to live a life dedicated to the Dharma to do so. To the extent that Western society has not been changed by Buddhism, to that extent Buddhism has not been integrated into Western society. In order to change Western society it is necessary to create Western Buddhist institutions and Western Buddhist lifestyles.

From *What is the Sangha?* (2001, pp.243-5)

3. A COMPLETE MEDITATION PRACTICE

Is that all in one sitting?

Sangharakshita: If one wanted a more or less complete and systematic meditation practice, one could start off with the mindfulness of breathing, and get quite a lot of experience of that, then take up the *mettā-bhāvanā*, which would develop one's emotional positivity and refine one's being. Then one could go on to the six element practice, which would develop some Insight into the egolessness of the person, the individual, and then to the *śūnyatā* practice of the Mahāyāna, and the visualization practice of the Vajrayāna, which represents the birth of the new as it were Enlightened personality. This would give a quite comprehensive practice.

Q: Is that all in one sitting?

S: Oh, no. Well, you could do it in one sitting, but no, I'm thinking of one's whole practice throughout one's whole life. You could spend a day, especially on solitary retreat going through these practices in this order, or they could be done on an intensive retreat, but essentially they are practices spread over one's whole lifetime. You start off with mindfulness, you learn to be very mindful. It may take you several years to get any real improvement. Then – I say then, but that is thinking in terms of the path of regular steps, you don't have to wait until your mindfulness is perfect before you

ⓦ indhorse Publications

life changing books

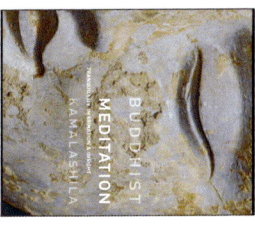

Windhorse Publications is a Buddhist charitable company based in the UK. We place great emphasis on producing books of high quality that are accessible and relevant to those interested in Buddhism at whatever level. We are the main publisher of the works of Sangharakshita, the founder of the Triratna Buddhist Order and Community. Our books draw on the whole range of the Buddhist tradition, including translations of traditional texts, commentaries, books that make links with contemporary culture and ways of life, biographies of Buddhists, and works on meditation.

As a not-for-profit enterprise, we ensure that all surplus income is invested in new books and improved production methods, to better communicate Buddhism in the 21st century. We welcome donations to help us continue our work – to find out more, go to
www.windhorsepublications.com

KEEP UP-TO-DATE WITH THE LATEST NEWS AT WINDHORSE PUBLICATIONS

Become part of the Windhorse Publications community by engaging with our latest videos and articles on Buddhism

Find out about the stories behind our books with our monthly author features

Share the books you love by posting reviews on our website

And **be inspired to read new books** on the recommendations of others:

'The clear and simple words were revelatory. Inherent in these lines is everything we need to know about what it means to live a Buddhist life.'
– Bodhipaksa on the *Dhammapada*

SIGN UP FOR OUR EMAIL NEWSLETTERS AND FOLLOW US ONLINE

www.windhorsepublications.com/newsletters
www.blog.windhorsepublications.com

take up *mettā* – but then you perfect your positive emotions, not only *mettā*, but *karuṇā*, *muditā*, *upekkhā*. So far these have all been samatha practices. But then you can take up *vipassanā*, especially the six element practice, which will in a sense disintegrate the old self and pave the way for the birth of the new self, so to speak. Then one can get further into that by practising the Mahāyāna *śūnyatā* meditation, and then the Vajrayāna stages of generation and perfection. This would give one a complete meditation practice from beginning to end, in a very simplified form. And this is essentially the path that we follow in our Buddhist movement.

From a seminar on Nāgārjuna's *Precious Garland* (1976, p.707)

4. AN ORGANIC, LIVING SYSTEM

Buddhism grew out of meditation ...

Buddhism grew out of meditation; it grew out of the Buddha's meditation under the bodhi tree 2,500 years ago. It grew therefore out of meditation in the highest sense: not simply concentration, nor even the experience of higher states of consciousness, but contemplation – a direct, total, all-comprehending vision and experience of ultimate Reality. It is out of this that Buddhism grew, and out of this that it has continually refreshed itself down through the ages.

Of the many methods of meditation developed within the Buddhist tradition, in my own teaching I have taken a few to form what can be called, perhaps a trifle ambitiously, a system: not a dead, mechanical, artificially created system, but an organic, living system. These methods are: the mindfulness of breathing; the *mettā-bhāvanā*, or the development of universal loving-kindness; the just sitting practice; the visualization practice (the visualization of a Buddha or a Bodhisattva, together with the recitation of the mantra of that Buddha or Bodhisattva); the recollection of the six elements; and the recollection of the *nidāna* chain.

According to another arrangement of the five basic methods of meditation outlined by my teacher Mr Chen, each meditation is the antidote to a particular mental poison. Meditation on impurity (the 'corpse meditation') is the antidote to craving. The *mettā-bhāvanā* is the antidote to hatred. Mindfulness, whether of the breathing process or of any other physical or mental function, is the antidote to doubt and distraction of mind. Recollection of the *nidāna* chain is the antidote to ignorance.

Recollection of the six elements is the antidote to conceit. If you get rid of these five mental poisons, then you are well on your way indeed; you are, in fact, quite close to Enlightenment. In this arrangement, however, the relationship between the practices is, as it were, spatial (they are all on the same level, arranged like a sort of pentad), not progressive. What we need is a progressive arrangement of the methods of meditation, a definite cumulative sequence that takes us forward step by step.

The mindfulness of breathing
In such a series, first comes the mindfulness of breathing. There are various reasons why it comes first. It is a 'psychological' method, in the sense that the newcomer can look at it psychologically; one does not need to know any distinctively Buddhist teaching to practise it. And it is the starting point for the development of mindfulness with regard to all the activities of life. We start by being mindful of our breath, but we have to try to extend this until we are aware of all our bodily movements and exactly what we are doing. We must become aware of the world around us and aware of other people. We must become aware, ultimately, of Reality itself. But we start with the mindfulness of breathing.

The development of mindfulness is also important because it is the key to psychical integration. When we first learn to meditate, we are usually just a bundle of conflicting desires, both conscious and unconscious, even conflicting selves, loosely tied together with the thread of a name and an address. Even the limited mindfulness developed by practising the mindfulness of breathing helps to bind them together; it at least tightens the string a little bit, to make a more recognizable, identifiable bundle of these different desires and selves.

To carry it a bit further, the practice of mindfulness helps to create harmony between the different aspects (as they have now become) of ourselves. It is through mindfulness that we begin to create true individuality. Individuality is essentially integrated; an unintegrated individuality is a contradiction in terms. Unless we become integrated, unless we are really individuals, there is no real progress, because there is no commitment. Only an integrated person can commit himself, because all his energies are flowing in the same direction; one energy, one interest, one desire, is not in conflict with another. Mindfulness, at so many different levels, is therefore of crucial importance – it is the key to the whole thing.

But there is a danger that in the course of our practice of mindfulness we develop what I have come to term 'alienated awareness'. This arises when we are aware of ourselves without actually experiencing ourselves. Therefore, as well as practising mindfulness, it is very important that we establish contact with our emotions, whatever they are. Ideally we will establish contact with our positive emotions, if we have or can develop any, but for the time being, we may have to establish contact with our negative emotions. It is better to establish real, living contact with our negative emotions (which means acknowledging them and experiencing them but not indulging them) than to remain in that alienated state and not experience our emotions at all.

The mettā-bhāvanā
It is here that the *mettā-bhāvanā* and similar practices come in: not just *mettā* (Sanskrit *maitrī*), loving-kindness, but also the other *brahma-vihāras*: *karuṇā*, *muditā* and *upekṣā* (Pāli *upekkhā*) (compassion, sympathetic joy, and equanimity respectively), as well as *śraddhā* (Pāli *saddhā*), faith. All of these are based on *mettā*, loving-kindness, friendliness; this is the fundamental positive emotion. As the years go by, as I come into contact with more and more people, I see more and more clearly the importance of positive emotions in our lives, both our spiritual lives and our worldly lives. I would say that the development of positive emotions is absolutely crucial for our development as individuals. We are not kept going by abstract ideas. It is our positive emotions that keep us going on the spiritual path, giving us inspiration and enthusiasm, until such time as we can develop Perfect Vision and be motivated by that.

The six element practice
But suppose you have developed mindfulness and all these positive emotions, suppose you are a very aware, positive, responsible person, even a true individual, what is the next step? The next step is death. The happy, healthy individual you now are – or were – must die. In other words, the subject-object distinction must be transcended; the mundane individuality, pure and perfect though it may be, must be broken up. Here the key practice is the recollection of the six elements. There are other practices that help us to break up our present individuality: the recollection of impermanence, the recollection of death, and the *śūnyatā* meditations, including the meditation on the *nidāna* chain. But the *śūnyatā* meditations can become rather abstract, not to say intellectual. The recollection of the six elements – involving the giving back of the elements in us to the elements in the universe, relinquishing in turn

earth, water, fire, air, space, even our individualized consciousness – is the key practice for breaking up our sense of relative individuality. We can even say that it is itself a *śūnyatā* meditation, because it helps us to realize the emptiness of our individuality – it helps us to die. There are many translations for the word *śūnyatā*. Sometimes it is translated 'voidness', sometimes 'relativity'; H.V. Guenther renders it 'nothingness'. But it could well be rendered 'death', because it is the death of everything conditioned. It is only when the conditioned individuality dies that the unconditioned Individuality begins to emerge. In meditation, as we go deeper and deeper, we often experience a great fear. Sometimes people shy away from it, but it is good to allow oneself to experience it. The fear occurs when we feel what may be called the touch of *śūnyatā*, the touch of Reality, on the conditioned self. The touch of *śūnyatā* feels like death. In fact, for the conditioned self it *is* death. So the conditioned self feels – *we* feel – afraid. The recollection of the six elements and the other *śūnyatā* meditations are *vipaśyanā* (Pāli *vipassanā*) or Insight meditations, whereas the mindfulness of breathing and the *mettā-bhāvanā* are *samatha* (Pāli *samatā*) or pacification-type meditations. *Samatha* develops and refines our conditioned individuality, but *vipaśyanā* breaks down that individuality, or rather it enables us to see right through it.

Visualization
When the mundane self has died, what happens next? In not very traditional language, out of the experience of the death of the mundane self the Transcendental self arises. It arises in the midst of the sky – in the midst of the Void – where we see a lotus flower. On the lotus flower there is a seed in the form of a letter – what we call a *bīja mantra* – which is transformed into a particular Buddha or Bodhisattva figure. Here, obviously, we have come on to the visualization practices.

The visualized figure before you, the figure of a Buddha or Bodhisattva, sublime and glorious though it may be, is, in fact, you: the new you – you as you will be if only you allow yourself to die. In some forms of visualization practice, we recite and meditate first of all upon the *śūnyatā* mantra: *om svabhāva suddhah sarvadharmah svabhāva suddho 'ham*, which means 'all things are pure by nature; I too am pure by nature'. Here pure means pure of all concepts, pure of all conditionality, because we cannot be reborn without passing through death. To be a little elliptical, there is no Vajrayāna without Mahāyāna, and the Mahāyāna is the *yāna* of the experience of *śūnyatā*. This is why my old friend and teacher, Mr C.M. Chen, the Ch'an hermit in Kalimpong, used to say, 'Without the realization of *śūnyatā*, the visualizations of the Vajrayāna are only vulgar magic.'

There are many different Buddhas, Bodhisattvas, *ḍākas*, *ḍākinīs* and *dharmapālas* to visualize, but the general significance of visualization practice comes out with particular clarity in the Vajrasattva *sādhana*. Vajrasattva is a Buddha appearing in Bodhisattva form. He is white in colour: white for purification. Here the purification consists in the realization that in the ultimate sense you have never become impure: you are pure from the beginning, the beginningless beginning, pure by nature, pure essentially; in the depths of your being you are pure of all conditionality, or rather you are pure of the very distinction between conditioned and Unconditioned. For anyone brought up in a guilt-ridden culture like ours in the West, this sort of statement must surely come as a great revelation – a great, positive shock.

Vajrasattva is also associated with death: not only spiritual death, but physical death. There is a connection here with the *Tibetan Book of the Dead*. In Tibetan, the (so-called) 'Book of the Dead' is called *Bardo Thödol*, which means 'liberation by hearing in the intermediate state' (that is to say, by hearing the instruction of the Lama seated by your erstwhile body and explaining to you what is happening to you in the intermediate state after your death). The intermediate state is intermediate between physical death and physical rebirth. But meditation is also an intermediate state, because when we meditate – in the true sense – we die. In the same way, physical death is a meditative state, a state of enforced meditation, enforced *samādhi*. In both intermediate states – the one between death and rebirth and the one that occurs in meditation – we can see Buddhas and Bodhisattvas, even mandalas of Buddhas and Bodhisattvas. These are not outside us; they are the manifestation of our own True Mind, the manifestation of the *Dharmakaya*, and we can, as it were, identify with them and thus be spiritually reborn in a Transcendental mode of existence. If we do not succeed in identifying in this way, then we are simply reborn in the ordinary sense – we fall back into the old conditioned self.

The four stages
So that's the system of meditation, at least in outline. The first of the four great stages is the stage of integration, achieved mainly through practice of the mindfulness of breathing, with the help of mindfulness and awareness in general. In this stage, we develop an integrated self.

The second stage is the stage of emotional positivity, achieved mainly through the development of *mettā*, *karuṇā*, *muditā*, and so on. Here the integrated self is raised to a higher, more refined, more powerful level, symbolized by the beautiful blooming white lotus flower.

Then there is the third stage: spiritual death, achieved mainly through the recollection of the six elements, but also through the recollection of impermanence, the recollection of death, and the *śūnyatā* meditations. Here the refined self is seen through, and we experience the Void, experience *śūnyatā*, experience spiritual death.

And fourthly, there is the stage of spiritual rebirth, achieved through the visualization and mantra recitation practice. Abstract visualization (the visualization of geometric forms and letters) also helps. This, in broad outline, is the system of meditation.

Where do ordination, the arising of the bodhicitta and Just Sitting fit in?
'Ordination' means Going for Refuge; Going for Refuge means commitment; and commitment is possible on different levels. Theoretically, one could be ordained without ever having practised meditation, but that's highly unlikely. One cannot commit oneself unless one is reasonably integrated; otherwise you commit yourself today and tomorrow you withdraw the commitment, because your total being was not involved. You also cannot commit yourself unless you have a certain amount of emotional positivity; otherwise you've nothing to keep you going. And there should also be at least a faint glimmer of Perfect Vision, or the reflection of a glimmer. Ordination would therefore seem to come somewhere in between the second and third of the main stages of the system of meditation. One might say that it comes when one has just begun to enter the stage of spiritual death, or when one is at least open to that possibility. This, of course, is according to the path of regular steps; we know that there is also a path of irregular steps.

And where does the arising of the *bodhicitta* come in? *Bodhicitta*, the will to Enlightenment, is not an egoistic will; it's more of the nature of a supra-individual aspiration, and it arises only when the individuality in the ordinary sense has been destroyed or seen through, to some extent at least. The *bodhicitta* is the aspiration to gain Enlightenment for the benefit of all. Not that – as Mahāyāna Buddhists would point out – there is a real individual seeking to gain Enlightenment for the sake of real others. The *bodhicitta* arises, we may say, *beyond* self and others, though not *without* self and others. It arises when the mundane self is destroyed or seen through, but before the 'Transcendental self' has emerged; when one is no longer seeking Enlightenment for the so-called self, but has not yet fully dedicated oneself to gaining it for the so-called other. The *bodhicitta* therefore arises in between the third and the fourth stages; that is, between the stage of spiritual death and the stage of spiritual rebirth. The *bodhicitta* is indeed the seed of spiritual rebirth. There is an anticipation of this at the time of the private ordination when one receives the mantra; the mantra is in a sense the seed of the *bodhicitta*. After all, one's ordination is a Going Forth. One has gone forth from the group, at least psychologically if not physically; one aspires to Enlightenment. And surely one aspires not just for one's own sake but for the sake, ultimately, of all. It isn't surprising, therefore that at that time some faint reflection of the *bodhicitta* should arise, at least in some cases.

And thirdly, what about the Just Sitting practice? Well, what about it? It's difficult to say anything about it, because when one Just Sits, well, one just sits! But at least one can say that there are times when one just sits and there are times when one does not just sit – times, that is to say, when one is doing other things. One of the times when one does not just sit is when one is practising meditations other than Just Sitting (if Just Sitting can be described as a meditation practice) – that is to say, when one is practising meditations such as the mindfulness of breathing, the *mettā-bhāvanā*, or the six element practice. In all of these, conscious effort is required. But one must be careful that this effort does not become too willed, even too wilful, and to guard against this possibility, one can practise Just Sitting. In other words, there is a period of activity, during which you are practising, say, the mindfulness of breathing or the *metta-bhavana*, and then a period of, as it were, passivity, receptivity. So in this way we go on: passivity, activity; activity, passivity. Mindfulness – Just Sitting. Metta – Just Sitting. Six Elements – Just Sitting. Visualization – Just Sitting. In this way we can develop a rhythm: taking hold of; letting go; grasping; opening up; action; non-action. Thus we achieve a perfectly balanced practice of meditation, a perfectly balanced spiritual life, and the whole system of meditation becomes complete.

> Slightly edited from *A Guide to the Buddhist Path* (1990, pp.145-50), which came from the talk 'A System of Meditation', given in 1978

5. WHERE DO THESE MEDITATION PRACTICES COME FROM?

It seems that many of the later practices are just elaborations of earlier forms of meditation.

As far as we can tell, the mindfulness of breathing practice goes back to the Buddha himself. Whether the *mettā-bhāvanā* was practised in the Buddha's time in the specific way that we do it now is difficult to say; but certainly the systematic development of *mettā* was a practice of major importance. They might not have done it in five stages in earlier times, they might have done it in seven, or whatever, but the meaning and the purpose of the practice was the same. The recollection of impermanence, the recollection of death, and the five or six element practice were all in use in the Buddha's own time, and so was the *kasiṇa* practice, the visualization of coloured discs as a means of concentrating your mind. It seems that many of the later practices are elaborations of these earlier forms of meditation.

From a seminar on the *Ratana Sutta* (1980, p.25)

6. AN UNBROKEN MEDITATION TRADITION?

If you have got just a few glowing embers you can blow them into a fire. So to that extent there is continuity of tradition.

Q: Is there an unbroken meditation tradition in any of the Theravāda countries?

Sangharakshita: It is impossible to know. You may know that you have a particular experience, but how can you know that it is the same as somebody else's experience in the past? There may well be an unbroken chain of experience, but you can't know that unless you have some Transcendental faculty. Even if there had been historical records of some such thing, there could have been misunderstandings, and actually the continuity could have been broken. Bhikkhu A might have given a teaching to Bhikkhu B, but what is the guarantee that the spirit and the realization are transmitted? In some parts of the Buddhist world, there is an uninterrupted transmission of the words, but we cannot really know whether the words invariably had an experiential counterpart.

Q: Having been ordained into the Theravāda tradition, did you have to revive meditation for yourself?

S: As regards the mindfulness of breathing, I didn't, because in Singapore I met Bhikkhu Soma, who was a great advocate of the way of mindfulness. I got my first idea about it, and to some extent instruction in it, from him. He referred me to one or two books written by people of the same tradition as himself, and that further deepened my understanding. Then I started practising it; it's quite a simple method. So I didn't discover it for myself. I think I could say that to some extent I had to discover the *mettā-bhāvanā*, because though many people spoke of it, in a way, it wasn't taken all that seriously. I can't say that the practice had altogether died out, so that I had to revive it. It was more that it was extant in a very mild form, and perhaps I intensified it and took it a bit more seriously. There may well have been bhikkhus here and there who quite spontaneously developed a higher degree of intensity of *mettā* without committing any of their experiences to writing.

It's quite an easy practice to do, once you get started, and you naturally feel like developing and intensifying it more and more. Almost anyone who at least gets a hint about the nature of *mettā* from the Pāli canon could do that, and in Buddhaghosa there are quite elaborate instructions as to how to proceed, and they are quite simple to follow; there is nothing abstruse or esoteric. So probably the tradition of *mettā-bhāvanā* has never died out entirely, even the experiential tradition, at least in a diluted form, and if it exists in a diluted form, you can always intensify it, just as if you have got just a few glowing embers you can blow them into a fire. So to that extent there is continuity of tradition.

Q: What were the circumstances that led you to take up the *mettā-bhāvanā* practice?

S: I can't remember. I think I took it up somewhat later than I took up the mindfulness of breathing, but I can't remember now. It's a bit like how some people come to play an important part in your life, but you don't remember the first meeting or how you met. It seems quite strange. Maybe as a result of my general reading I came to know something about it, and gradually intensified my practice and came to be aware that it counterbalanced the mindfulness of breathing.

Q: Is there any parallel development in Tibetan Buddhism for the system of meditation you've developed: mindfulness of breathing, *mettā-bhāvanā*, just sitting, visualization and Insight?

S: I would say not, unless it was in some obscure sect, or in the teachings of a particular lama. Somebody like Tsongkhapa would explain *samatha* and *vipassanā*, but I think in general practice there certainly wasn't a system of meditation of that kind. It seems that on the whole they jump straight into Vajrayāna methods, visualizations and so on. Mr Chen, who taught me a great deal about meditation, used to criticize the Tibetan Buddhists, including Tibetan lamas, very vehemently for not actually practising the four *brahma-vihāras*, but just reciting a little verse which summarized them, and then going straight on to the Vajrayāna.

Q: So the system you have outlined is quite a distinctive innovation?

S: Yes, I think one could say that. I think it grew to some extent out of my numerous and lengthy discussions about meditation with Mr Chen. It owes quite a lot to him, though the final systematization was my own.

Q: In your account in your memoirs you seemed to spend quite a long time establishing your meditation practice without ongoing instruction from a teacher. How well did you fare in discovering for yourself the principles of effective meditation, and what would you say was the guiding principle that you followed in evolving your own system of meditation?

S: I had access to literature, and I got a lot of inspiration from that. And later on I had contact with Tibetan lamas, and with regard to discussing and talking over meditation, I had very extensive contact with Mr Chen. I think probably my contact with him was the most useful in this respect.
    But I think I can say that from the beginning I was very self-motivated. Once I had taken up a particular form of meditation, apart from the occasional feeling of laziness and reluctance to get up early in the morning, I found that I was able to persist with it, and I can't recollect that I had any serious difficulties or any experiences that troubled me. Somewhat later I did have the sort of experiences that many meditators report – intense existential fear and things of that sort – but by that time I had a general understanding of the Dharma and I also had some spiritual friends, so I was able to push on despite such experiences. I seem

always to have had a deep innate conviction, or if you like, faith, that all would be well, I just had to carry on.

Q: Was that in the meditation experience itself or outside?

S: I think it was mostly in the meditation experience itself, but sometimes at night in dreams too. Many people who meditate have had the experience of something quite overpowering and overwhelming. You can't do anything about it, you just have to bow your head before the storm as it were, and wait until it blows over, which may take some time. If it is really existential, there is no way of grappling with it, or coping with it, you just have to endure it. Well, even the word endure isn't quite appropriate, you are not even in a state to endure sometimes, but nonetheless you have to! You have no alternative. But you come through in the end. I must have had several dozens of such experiences over a period of two or three years, after which they tapered away.

Q: For how many years did you practise just *mettā-bhāvanā* and mindfulness of breathing?

S: In my two years of wandering life, and then a year in Benares (during which time I don't think I practised so intensively), and then in Kalimpong up to 1956, when I was given my first visualization initiation which was that of Green Tārā, I was just practising the mindfulness of breathing. I think it was after taking up that Green Tārā practice that I started practising the *mettā-bhāvanā* regularly. There might have been some connection between the two, but I can't remember now.

Q: So that's about ten years of just mindfulness of breathing.

S: I was very concerned with the whole issue of mindfulness. I was very conscious that I was not always mindful in my behaviour and walking and speaking. I used to find that the situation in which I most easily lost my mindfulness was discussion. I just got carried away. Although it was a discussion about Buddhism perhaps, I realized afterwards that I had lost my mindfulness in the sense of losing track of my overall purpose in engaging in the discussion. I found it quite difficult to bring this under control; I eventually succeeded, but it took some years, and I used to be quite, not exactly remorseful because it wasn't exactly a sin, but certainly quite regretful or disappointed that yet again I had lost mindfulness of the purpose for which I was engaging in discussion, and just got carried away.

I was very concerned for years together about general mindfulness, about speaking mindfully, sitting mindfully, walking mindfully, eating mindfully. I was not just practising the mindfulness of breathing; I was concerned with a general *satipaṭṭhāna* practice. I think I did get a bit one-sided, and that was one of the reasons I was very glad to take up a visualization practice and later on the *mettā-bhāvanā*. I don't say I was too mindful or practised too much mindfulness, but I think it probably wasn't balanced sufficiently. Probably what saved me was that I kept up my interest in, and practice of, poetry, I think that was a balancing factor, but I think I also needed the *mettā-bhāvanā*. Looking back, in some ways it is surprising how much importance I attached to the mindfulness of breathing and to mindfulness in general. What I often think nowadays is that I was not nearly mindful enough in ordinary everyday matters.

From a seminar on *The Forest Monks of Sri Lanka* (1985, pp.234-7)

7. LAYING A GOOD FOUNDATION

One should not rush ahead. One should proceed step by step so far as meditation is concerned.

Q: How did you come across the *mettā-bhāvanā*?

Sangharakshita: I was familiar with it in theory from the Pāli texts for many years before I started practising it. From my Theravāda contacts and reading, I was then under the impression that the *mettā-bhāvanā* was not of any great importance, whereas the practice of mindfulness was very much stressed by Theravādins I met and texts I read. There was a whole book written on the mindfulness practice in the broad sense, *The Heart of Buddhist Meditation*, but there was no similar book, hardly an article, written about the practice of the *mettā-bhāvanā*. So, in a sense, it escaped my notice, which is a great pity, and tells one quite a lot about attitudes among many Buddhists at that time. Certainly there was nothing to cause me to think that it was of any great importance until I came into contact with the visualization practices, and found that the practice of the visualization was to be preceded by the practice of the four *brahma-vihāras*. Then I started thinking about *mettā* more seriously. Certainly I can remember a point when I seemed to be taking the *mettā-bhāvanā* more seriously, practising it myself and also teaching it to others. But I can't remember exactly how or when it began.

Q: You practised the mindfulness of breathing for a very long time before taking up the visualization practice. Is there a lesson there for us?

S: Not necessarily, because in my case it was due to lack of opportunity and lack of proper guidance that I didn't take up those practices earlier. But as a general rule, perhaps one could say that one should not rush ahead. One should proceed step by step so far as meditation is concerned. That is why, in our own Buddhist movement, we don't give visualization practices to people who are not ordained, because we consider that the necessary basis of commitment and determination needs to be developed.

From a seminar on the Noble Eightfold Path (1982, pp.363-4)

8. THE PATH OF IRREGULAR STEPS

You could be given simply the teaching that, as a novice, you should sweep up the leaves in the courtyard. You wouldn't be taught anything more than that.

Q: In the lecture 'A System of Meditation' you said that a meditator passes through the stage of integration before going on to the stage of spiritual death and finally spiritual rebirth. I took this to mean that one has to have extensive experience of meditation before going on to what you describe as spiritual death and spiritual rebirth. You connected each of these stages with certain meditation practices. Integration – *samatha* practices, spiritual death – six element practice and contemplation of the *nidāna* chain, spiritual rebirth – visualization practices. In practice, however, people in the [Triratna] community do not seem to follow this path of regular steps. For instance, every Order member [that is, every member of the Triratna Buddhist Order] has a visualization practice. Could you please clarify the situation?

Sangharakshita: I would say that in the Order people do follow the path of regular steps. But one must remember that the spiritual path is a spiral, in more ways than one. One of the characteristics of a spiral is that it traverses the same ground, so to speak, again and again but each time at a higher level. So all right, you practise *samatha* meditation. You have some experience, let's say, of the *dhyānas*, and then, having practised *samatha*, having become relatively integrated, you experience 'death' through the practice of the six element meditation. You experience it to some extent and then through the visualization practice you experience rebirth – again, to some extent. So it isn't as though you go through one stage, perfecting that, and then through the next, perfecting that. That would be following the path of regular steps very strictly, as it were. But that is not what actually happens. You go round and round, again and again, but each time hopefully on a higher level. Having been reborn, you are able to be more integrated. Being more integrated, you die to an even greater extent. Dying to an even greater extent, you're reborn more truly. But having been reborn again more truly, you go round again as it were. It's as though you go round and round the spiral of the spiritual life, of these three kinds of practice, these three levels, but each time you go round on a higher level so that you have a greater experience of the *dhyānas*. You become more and more integrated. You have a deeper and deeper experience of spiritual death and a more and more overwhelming experience of spiritual rebirth. You go on in this way until, eventually, you have the full experience of integration followed by the full experience of spiritual death, followed by the full experience of spiritual rebirth.

Nowadays it is difficult to do things in any other way because you can't keep people from accessing theoretical knowledge of the higher stages. Formerly you could, because teachings were transmitted purely orally or they existed in handwritten manuscripts which were kept under lock and key, so you could be given simply the teaching that you needed at a particular time. As a novice, you could be given the practice of sweeping up the leaves in the courtyard. You wouldn't be taught anything more than that. You wouldn't know what the bhikkhus were doing or the teachers were doing. Your job would be to sweep up the leaves in the monastery courtyard and you might be concentrating on that for two or three years. At the end of that period, perhaps you'd be given a very small teaching and you'd be told to practise that, and that's all you would know. In this way you would proceed, step by step, and stage by stage.

But that isn't possible any more. People have read all sorts of books about Theravāda, Mahāyāna, Zen, esoteric Tantric practices, perhaps they've even had half a dozen high-grade Tantric initiations from travelling Tibetan lamas, and they sometimes get very confused in the process. You can't keep things from them, they know that there are these higher stages; so the only possible pattern is to go through these successive stages again and again, on higher and higher levels, each time round deepening your experience of that particular level until finally you experience each level to the full. In a way you're following the path of irregular steps but you're following that path in a regular way that amounts, one might say, to following the path of regular steps.

From Q&A on a Mitra retreat (1985, pp.25-6)

9. THE FIVE GREAT STAGES

If you just try to do these five things, you can forget all about making progress or where exactly you are along the path. Just intensify your effort in those five directions all the time – then you simply can't go wrong.

In Buddhist texts one finds different descriptions of the path, and some of them are very inspiring, but they don't always agree. Sometimes, in fact, they're very different, though at times they overlap. Some of these descriptions are very detailed and it's possible to get rather lost in the detail. You can't help wondering exactly where you are and what you have to do to get to the next stage or substage or even sub-substage. So I thought it might be useful to outline the main stages so far as we're concerned, and indicate some connections with some of the traditional formulations of the path. It seems to me that we can regard the spiritual path as consisting of five great stages. They very roughly correspond to the five paths of the Indian Buddhist tradition but I won't go into that comparison. I just want to give a straightforward account in terms of our own needs and our own experience.

The first stage is the stage of mindfulness and awareness. One can think in terms of the four foundations of mindfulness or the four dimensions of awareness, but that is a detail. The main point is that the first thing that one has to do is to develop awareness, especially self-awareness, which in turn means self-integration. We bring all our scattered bits together, we integrate ourselves, we overcome conflict and disharmony within ourselves. We get ourselves functioning as a smoothly working whole, not a jumble of bits and pieces, or a heap of fragments of selves all jostling for supremacy. You can begin to see that this is quite a big task in itself. But this is the first stage: giving birth to oneself as an integrated person, a self-aware individual.

Then comes the stage of positive emotion: friendliness, compassion, joy, equanimity, faith and devotion. Because positive emotion is something that moves, not something static, this is also the stage of energy. In this stage one tries to make oneself as emotionally positive as possible, one overcomes all negative emotions. One tries not only to develop one's emotions but to refine them, developing not simply positive emotions but even spiritual emotions. Here the whole subject of spiritual beauty becomes important. So in this stage one develops emotions to a very high pitch of intensity indeed. This is also the stage of meditation – *samādhi* – because these positive emotions and the energies that you generate carry you through all the levels of *dhyāna*. But it's not simply about sitting in meditation. It's being emotionally positive whatever you are doing, whether you are sitting and meditating, or working, or talking, or just being quietly by yourself.

The third stage is the stage of vision. One sees the truth – not, of course, regarding truth as a thing 'out there' to be seen like an ordinary object. This is the stage of openness to truth. Guenther talks in terms of the dimension of openness of Being with a capital B, by which he means *śūnyatā*; though his phrase is a bit roundabout, it's quite expressive. This is the stage of openness in the direction of ultimate reality, not holding back on the process of expansion; not opening up so far but then refusing to open up any further. It's indefinite openness to the ultimate or, in terms of sight, a vision of reality, a vision of truth. This is also the stage of death – spiritual death, the death of the old self, the death of the ego however much refined, and the birth of, if you like, the seed of Buddhahood. In a sense that seed was there already, but it has now become visible, and from it the new being, the Buddha, will eventually develop. When you see the truth you die, as it were; or perhaps one could say that when you die, you see the truth. Among meditation practices this is covered by the six element practice and the meditation on *śūnyatā*. Again, you don't meditate on *śūnyatā* as though it were a thing 'out there' on which you are meditating. That would just be an idea, a concept, a vague image of *śūnyatā*, not *śūnyatā* itself. So that's the stage of vision, or reality, or death, or spiritual rebirth – whatever you like to call it.

Then comes the stage of transformation, when the vision that you have seen or your experience of reality starts, as it were, descending and transforming every aspect of your being. It is not just in the head, not even in your spiritual being; it pervades all parts of your being, all parts of, as it were, your spiritual body. This is also a stage of meditation – not the meditation with the help of which you gain that initial visionary experience but the meditation that you practise after it. In this stage, the practice of meditation is dwelling on that visionary experience, that glimpse of reality, so as to deepen and broaden it and bring it down, as it were, so that it pervades and transforms all the different aspects of one's being.

And fifth and lastly there's what we may call the stage of compassionate activity. Having completely transformed oneself in accordance with one's vision of reality, one is in a position really to help others. This is also the stage of true spontaneity. You don't think about what you're going to do to help others – at least not in the ordinary way. You just spontaneously function, you do what needs to be done. There's a sort of overflow of your Enlightened being.

These five stages form a series, and if one traverses them, one traverses the whole spiritual path. But there is a path of regular steps and there is also a path of irregular steps. You could conceivably start work on the first stage, the stage of mindfulness and integration, complete that and then go on to the next stage, that of positive emotion, complete that and then go on to the third stage, and so on. But I think very few people would function in this way. Most people, for some time at least, will have to follow the path of irregular steps, working now on one and now on another of these stages. One could even go so far as to say that one can think in terms of working on all five stages simultaneously. The first would be perfected first, the second would be perfected second, and so on – that's where the path of regular steps comes in. You can work on all of them simultaneously so that the first becomes perfected and then you are just working on four; the second becomes perfected and you're just working on three; the third becomes perfected and you're just working on two; the fourth becomes perfected and you're working on one; the fifth becomes perfected, and you're perfected then.

What does this mean? It means that all the time, every day, you have got five things to practise as best you can. You keep up the effort to be mindful and aware, and to be as together as possible, as integrated as possible. You remain in as positive a mental state as you possibly can. You don't lose sight of your ultimate goal at any time. You try to practise at every level whatever you've realised or discovered or seen on the highest level of your being. And you do what you can to help people. This is your spiritual life and this is your spiritual practice. These are the things with which you are basically concerned. You can forget about all the other formulations, all about the Four Noble Truths and the Eightfold Path. On the practical side, this is all that you really need to think in terms of. Whatever has been said by all the different Buddhist teachers in the course of hundreds of years of development is contained in this, in principle. Whatever they've had to say about the different stages of the path – as I said, you can get some very elaborate descriptions indeed, which may confuse you or even mislead you – this is basically what it's all about.

You can also think of these five stages in terms of the Five Spiritual Faculties. The first stage corresponds to the faculty of mindfulness, the second to the faculty of faith, the third to the faculty of wisdom, the fourth to the faculty of meditation, and the fifth to the faculty of *vīrya*. If you want to think of any particular Buddhist virtue and understand its place in the total scheme of things, you can allocate it to one of these five stages. For instance, where does *dāna*, generosity, come in? It clearly comes in stage two, because when you're overflowing with love and joy, your natural tendency is to give; you can't help it. You're giving yourself all the time, you're flowing out all the time. Perhaps I need not multiply examples. Just think in terms of these five principal stages. These are the aspects of the spiritual path that you will be cultivating all the time. If you just try to do these five things, you can forget all about making progress or where exactly you are along the path. Just intensify your effort in those five directions all the time – then you simply can't go wrong.

You may notice that stages three and four correspond to the path of vision and the path of transformation as described in connection with the Eightfold Path, but unless you've got a scholarly mind you need not worry too much about these sorts of connections. Just get a sense of this general understanding of the path, and don't worry if the traditional descriptions don't seem to square very closely with your own experience or your own needs.

From a seminar on Nāgārjuna's *Precious Garland* (1976, pp.337-41)

INTRODUCTION

3 Motivations and misunderstandings

1. MOTIVATIONS FOR MEDITATION

The basic motivation for meditation is the search for peace of mind.

Motivation is an important and constant element in determining how effective one's meditation practice is, and even whether one continues to meditate at all. Having known a great many meditators, I would say that there are basically two types of motivation or approach. These may be provisionally designated as the 'psychological' approach and the 'spiritual' approach.

The basic psychological motivation for meditation is the search for peace of mind. People who are not particularly interested in Buddhism or philosophy or religion, or even in psychology, may still be looking for something that they call peace of mind. They find that the hurry and bustle, the wear and tear, of day-to-day living is a bit too much for them. The various strains and tensions to which they are subjected – financial pressures, personal difficulties, problems with relationships, even perhaps degrees of neurotic anxiety – all add up to a general feeling of unhappiness. They hear that meditation can give you peace of mind, and they have the impression that Buddhists are happy, tranquil people, so in this way they come to Buddhist meditation, looking for some inner tranquillity, for the peace which, it seems, the world cannot give.

As for the spiritual motivation for meditation, this is at root the desire or aspiration for Enlightenment. In wider terms, it encompasses the desire to understand the meaning of existence itself, the desire to come to some sort of intelligible terms with life, or even, more metaphysically, to know reality, to see the truth, to penetrate into the ultimate nature of things. In this way meditation may be approached as a stepping-stone to something higher – to an awareness, an understanding, an experience even, of ultimate reality itself.

These two approaches – the psychological and the spiritual – are not, of course, mutually exclusive. You can take up meditation with a psychological motivation, and then find that imperceptibly the sheer momentum of your practice carries you beyond the boundaries of the psychological into a world of spiritual experience. And on the other hand, even if your motivation is spiritual from the word go, you will still need to establish a healthy psychological foundation for your practice, which may well involve a purely psychological approach in the early stages.

Indeed, it is not easy to draw a hard and fast line between the realm of the psychological and the realm of the spiritual. They shade into each other in such a way that you cannot always be sure which realm your experience and approach falls into. There is an overlap, a sort of common ground, between them. In terms of expanding consciousness, we could say that the psychological approach represents a partial and temporary expansion of consciousness, whereas the spiritual approach stands for a total and permanent expansion of consciousness. There is a difference of degree (in a certain sense), rather than a difference of kind, between the two. However, they are, in the end, quite distinct approaches or motivations, and they should not be confused with each other more than we can help. If we identify the spiritual with the psychological, then we will be setting unnecessary limits on our practice and what we are capable of achieving with it.

From *What is the Dharma?* (1998, pp.183-4)

2. THE ROUTE TO HUMAN DEVELOPMENT

However active you might be in all sorts of external areas – political, social, educational, or whatever – if you are not trying to develop yourself, you are not going to be able to make any truly positive contribution to anything or anyone.

Human development essentially consists in the development of the mind, the raising of consciousness to ever higher levels of awareness, and for most people the route to achieving this is through meditation.

The practice of meditation essentially involves three things. Firstly, it involves concentration, the integration of all our energies, conscious and unconscious. Secondly, it involves the raising of consciousness to suprapersonal states, leaving the ego-realm for higher, wider, even cosmic dimensions. And thirdly, it involves contemplation: the direct insight of the uncluttered mind – the mind in a state of higher consciousness – into the ultimate depths of existence, the seeing of reality face to face. Meditation is concerned with achieving all this. There are many different methods; you just need to find a teacher who will introduce you to one or two of them. After that, you stick with the methods and practise them regularly. That's all there is to it, really.

The more demanding aspect of self-development consists in what one does with the rest of one's life in order to support one's meditation practice. One will look after one's health. One will simplify one's life as far as possible, dropping all those activities, interests, and social contacts which one knows to be a waste of time. One will try to base one's life, and in particular one's livelihood, on ethical principles. One will make time – perhaps by working part-time – for study; for study of the Dharma, of course, but also for study of other subjects of general human interest: philosophy, history, science, comparative religion. Finally, one will find opportunities to refine and develop one's emotions, especially through the fine arts. Self-development always comes first. However active you might be in all sorts of external areas – political, social, educational, or whatever – if you are not trying to develop yourself, you are not going to be able to make any truly positive contribution to anything or anyone.

From *What is the Sangha?* (2001, pp.239-40)

3. WHAT DOES CONCENTRATION MEAN?

One shouldn't be too ambitious to get hold of some very esoteric difficult practice which nobody else has got.

Q: Would you regard sitting watching a fire as meditation?

Sangharakshita: You might get into a highly concentrated state but it's very doubtful whether you'd get any further than that. It's all right as far as it goes but I wouldn't call it meditation.

Q: Should you try to concentrate?

S: Well, you begin with concentration. You can't really meditate unless you're concentrated. But what does concentration mean? It doesn't mean forcibly fixing the mind on something. It means a gradual unification of one's energies so that they naturally remain on a single point. It requires quite a bit of practice and skill to get to such a point. You have to coax yourself a bit but not force yourself. You also have to prepare. You can't just sit down and make the mind concentrated. You have to remember at least an hour or two before that you're going to be sitting and concentrating and meditating so that when you do sit all your energies are pulling together, there's no distraction and there's a definite energy. You're not just dull and blocked. There's an aware energy which gradually comes together, you've settled down on whatever subject of meditation you have chosen, and then you can meditate.

There are many forms of meditation; there are several hundred in Buddhism. In the Buddhist movement I founded we concentrate to begin with on just a very few, like the mindfulness of breathing and the *mettā-bhāvanā* – just a few very simple but effective practices. One shouldn't be too ambitious to get hold of some very esoteric difficult practice which nobody else has got. That's a waste of time and it's the wrong way to do it anyway. Just take up a single meditation, a simple concentration exercise.

From Q&A in Christchurch (1979, p.20)

4. MEDITATION IS MORE …

It's quite important to think of meditation not only in terms of becoming more and more concentrated.

I think it's quite important to think of meditation not only in terms of becoming more and more concentrated but in terms of becoming more positive, more creative, more outward-going, more reflective, more contented, more happy to be on one's own, more full of energy, more playful. Meditation is equally all those things.

From Q&A in New Zealand (1975, p.30)

5. WHY DOES A BODHISATTVA MEDITATE?

The perfection of meditation ...

The Bodhisattva practises not just meditation but *dhyāna pāramitā*, the perfection of meditation. In other words, he or she practises meditation not for peace of mind (though that certainly does come) nor to get to heaven (though even that may come if desired). He or she practises meditation as one aspect of the path which will lead one day to Enlightenment for the benefit of all.

From *The Bodhisattva Ideal* (1999, p.163)

6. THE POSSIBILITIES OF HUMAN EXPERIENCE

The range of our potential experience extends far beyond what we usually consider to be possible.

Dr Conze says that one of the 'avenues of approach to the spiritual' is 'to regard sensory experience as relatively unimportant'. The key word here is 'relatively'. It does not mean that there is only sensory experience, but that it's *relatively* unimportant – relatively because there are whole spheres of experience to which we can have access which have got nothing to do with the physical senses or the lower mind. The range of our potential experience extends far beyond what we usually consider to be possible, and through meditation, chiefly, we have access to these other, higher realms of experience. It's crucially important to understand that the possibilities of human experience far transcend what those possibilities are usually considered to be. Or put it this way: our possible experience far transcends our actual experience, and the way into that other or higher experience is meditation.

Despite the many disadvantages of the drug culture, at least the experience of taking drugs has made one thing clear to a number of people: that there is a possibility of experience beyond what we usually do experience. That has made it much easier to talk to quite a lot of people in terms of some experience other than, higher than, what we usually know through the senses and the ordinary mind. At least there is a way in, an analogy, which perhaps wasn't available before. Dreams provide another useful point of entry.

So 'to regard sensory experience as relatively unimportant' doesn't mean a depreciation of sensory experience, or a dismissing of it as something evil. It simply means that sensory experience and the experience of the lower mind occupies a very narrow band in the total spectrum of human experience, and that one can have access to these other higher spheres through meditation. If one wants to have a comprehensive view even of conditioned existence, not to speak of the Unconditioned, one has to take all these different bands of the total spectrum into consideration.

Buddhism certainly does this, and probably most spiritual traditions do. There are many traditions which point out that sense experience and experience through the lower mind is only part of the total spectrum of possible human experience. This was certainly known to the ancient Greeks, to Plato, and to the Neoplatonists and the Gnostics. In India it was known to the Hindus, especially to the yogins, and in China it was known to the Taoists. Among the Muslims it is known to the Sufis. So here there is a certain amount of common ground. And in another way, everybody who has taken drugs knows that there are other levels, other dimensions of experience possible.

From a Buddhist point of view, the main avenue, if you like, to these other dimensions is meditation, and this is one of the reasons why meditation is so important. It enlarges one's perspective in this sort of way. One of the terms for the *dhyānas* in the Abhidhamma is *mahaggata*, which means 'that which has become great, or which has expanded'. So the meditative consciousness is an expanded consciousness, a consciousness that has expanded beyond the ordinary sensory and mental levels. It doesn't negate those levels; it transcends them and includes them. But they are lower levels; there is no doubt about that. The meditative levels are higher in the sense that they are more integrated, more blissful, and, in a manner of speaking closer to Reality.

From a seminar on Edward Conze's *Buddhism* (1976, pp.22-3)

7. TWO ESSENTIAL PRACTICES

They really do work, and they're not too difficult to do.

Q: I've heard that Buddhist meditation blanks the mind.

Sangharakshita: No, Buddhism doesn't teach blanking the mind. I don't think any form of Buddhist meditation advises that. In the Buddhist movement I founded, we teach mainly two methods. One of them is the mindfulness of breathing, in which, far from blanking the mind, you concentrate on the process of respiration. The aim of the practice is to unify one's energies. People are often rather scattered, so the mindfulness of breathing brings them together. You become quiet, serene, and – I'd rather say 'integrated' than 'concentrated'. Your whole being becomes more integrated. And the other method we teach is the *mettā-bhāvanā*, which is the development of an attitude of love and kindness towards all living beings. This again is a definite technique. We cultivate loving kindness first towards ourselves, then towards a near and dear friend, then towards a neutral person, then towards an 'enemy', then towards all four simultaneously, then we go out in widening circles until we envelop all living beings. This is not just an exercise; it is something which people actually experience. Some have some difficulty getting into it, but others manage quite easily. But the result is that you end up in a positive emotional state, and transcending your usual self-interest. So these are the two basic practices we teach. They really do work, and they're not too difficult. Most people can do them after a few sessions quite successfully.

From questions and answers in New South Wales (1979, p.12)

8. MEDITATION AND THE BODHISATTVA SPIRIT

Meditation is brought into existence, but it isn't anybody's property. It's just as much yours as mine.

There is a very strong sense in the Mahāyāna of devoting oneself to the promotion of good, and getting rid of sorrow and suffering, without so much reference to one's personal situation. In a way it doesn't matter whether you call it mine or yours: there is this mass of suffering to be got rid of, and there is this mass of joy which can be brought into existence. We are all affected by the 'cloud of suffering', so let's all get rid of it, without bothering too much which bit is 'mine' and which bit is 'yours'. It's the same with the cloud of joy, and even with the cloud of Enlightenment; just try to bring it into existence. I might do a bit more than you, or you might do a bit more than me, but we will all benefit in the end: we will all share it; we will all enjoy it. There's a little story in this connection about the Buddha's disciple Sāriputta. He had been meditating in the forest one day, and when he emerged from meditation, his friend Moggallāna asked him how it was that his face was shining with such unusual radiance. Sāriputta replied, 'All day I've been meditating in the forest, but there never came to me the thought "I am meditating".' In this little episode there's a bit of the Mahāyāna spirit. Meditation is brought into existence, but it isn't anybody's property. It's just as much yours as mine. A higher state of consciousness has been brought into existence. I'm not saying it's mine; it's yours too. That's the spirit of the Bodhisattva also, at his own much higher level. 'Some good is being brought into existence – some higher states of being, some happiness, some joy – but it's not mine, it's everybody's.' That's the attitude behind the Bodhisattva's so-called renunciation of a personal Nirvāna. He knows it isn't 'his', anyway. It's there to be shared by all.

From a seminar on *The Endlessly Fascinating Cry* (1977, p.238)

9. IT'S QUALITY THAT COUNTS

To meditate for two hours is not necessarily twice as good as meditating for one hour.

Q: Could you say something about growth in the context of meditation?

Sangharakshita: It's very difficult to generalize. People's experience seems to be very different. It isn't just a question of spending more and more time on it. I think we have to be very careful about that. To meditate for an hour is good; to meditate for two hours is good; to meditate for three hours is good. But to meditate for two hours is not necessarily twice as good as meditating for one hour. One mustn't think of progress in meditation or spiritual life as necessarily coming about in that sort of way. It's very much a question of the quality of the meditation, though provided that the quality can be maintained or even enhanced, the length of time you spend meditating does play its part. Essentially growth in meditation is a question of remaining in contact with higher states of consciousness more and more – though that may or may not be correlated with longer and longer periods of sitting – and to do everything in or with that state of consciousness. One also finds more and more energy being liberated.

From the Western Buddhist Order's first convention (1974, p.5)

2 Mindfulness

1 The mindfulness of breathing

Producing a slender booklet on anapana-sati, *or mindfulness of the process of respiration, which I had bought in Ceylon, I asked Bhikkhu Soma if he could recommend the method it described. His reply was unhesitating. It was the best of methods, he said, the method employed by the Buddha on the eve of his Enlightenment. In fact, having himself derived great benefit from it, he had translated the canonical text in which it was expounded into English, together with its commentary. A copy of this work, together with two or three other books he had published, he presented to me.*

That night, for the third time since leaving England, I sat beneath my mosquito net meditating while others slept. This time success was immediate. My mind became at first buoyant, then filled with peace and purity, and finally penetrated by a 'quintessential, keen, ethereal bliss' that was so intense I had to break off the practice. Obviously, the conditions under which I was then living were not ideal for meditation. I therefore resolved to continue the practice later, when they had become more favourable. This resolution I kept. Though the Theravāda sectarianism of Bhikkhu Soma and the author of the slender booklet was the antithesis of my own acceptance of the entire Buddhist tradition, in all its ramifications, I remain grateful to them for having introduced me to a practice which was for long the sheet-anchor of my spiritual life.

From *The Rainbow Road* (1997, pp.138-9)

1. HOW TO DO THE PRACTICE

The point is not to *think* about the breath, or do anything about it at all, but simply to be aware of it.

The mindfulness of breathing is the antidote to the mental poison of distractedness because it eliminates wandering thoughts. This is one of the reasons why it is generally the first practice to be learned; no other method can be practised until some degree of concentration has been mastered.

This practice is not about concentration in the sense of a narrow, willed application of the attention to an object. It involves gradually unifying the attention around one's own natural breathing process, integrating all one's mental, emotional, and physical faculties by means of gently but persistently bringing the attention back to the experience of the breath, again and again. The point is not to *think* about the breath, or do anything about it at all, but simply to be aware of it. There are four stages to the practice. For beginners, five minutes to each stage is about right.

Sitting still and relaxed, with the eyes closed, we begin by bringing our attention to the breathing. Then we start mentally to count off each breath to ourselves, after the out-breath, one to ten, over and over again. There is no particular significance to the counting. It is just to keep the attention occupied with the breathing during the early stages of the practice while the mind is still fairly scattered. The object of our developing concentration is still the breath (rather than the numbers).

In the second stage we continue to mark the breaths by counting them, but instead of counting after the out-breath we now count before the in-breath. Ostensibly there may not seem to be any great difference between these first two stages, but the idea of the second is that we are attentive right from the start of each breath, so that there is a quiet sharpening of the concentration taking place. There is a sense of anticipation; we are being aware before anything has happened, rather than being aware only afterwards.

In the third stage we drop the support of the counting and move to a general and continuous (at least, as continuous as we can manage) awareness of the whole process of the breathing, and all the sensations associated with it. Again, we are not investigating or analyzing or doing anything special with the breath, but just gently nudging the attention to a closer engagement with it. As our concentration deepens, it becomes easier to maintain that engagement, and the whole experience of the breath becomes more and more pleasurable.

In the fourth and final stage we bring the attention to a sharper focus by applying it to a single point in our experience of the breath. The point we focus on is the subtle play of sensation where we feel the breath entering and leaving the body, somewhere round about the nostrils. The attention here needs to be refined and quiet, very smoothly and intensely concentrated in order to keep continuous contact with the ever-changing sensation of the breath at this point. The practice is brought to an end by broadening our awareness again to include the experience of the whole of the breath, and then the whole of the body. Then, slowly, we bring the meditation to a close and open our eyes.

From *What is the Dharma?* (1998, pp.188-90)

2. THE ORIGINS OF THE MINDFULNESS OF BREATHING

Some say the mindfulness of breathing was the meditation the Buddha was practising when he gained Enlightenment.

> *And how, bhikkhus, does a bhikkhu abide contemplating the body as a body? Here a bhikkhu, gone to the forest or to the root of a tree or to an empty hut, sits down; having folded his legs crosswise, set his body erect, and established mindfulness in front of him, ever mindful he breathes in, mindful he breathes out.*[1]

Having laid down the four foundations of mindfulness, the Buddha goes on to recommend a particularly accessible method of developing mindfulness: the mindfulness of breathing. The fact that it is *accessible* is very important. The plain truth is – and we had better face this squarely – that awareness of any kind is not easy to develop. The Buddha's method is therefore to start by encouraging us to develop awareness of the aspect of our experience that is closest to us: the body. Even this is not as easy as one might think. The first of the four foundations may be 'mindfulness of the body', but it is hard to focus on 'the body' as a whole; it is such a complex thing, within which all sorts of processes are going on at the same time. To lead your awareness towards a broader experience of the body, it is therefore best to begin by focusing on the breath. Breathing is a simple bodily activity, providing a relatively stable object of attention that is both calming and capable of sustaining one's interest. On this basis, you can go on to become aware of your bodily sensations and even of your feelings and thoughts, which are still more subtle and difficult to follow.

The breath is available to us at every moment of our lives, and becoming aware of it has a calming effect at stressful times, as we know from the received wisdom of our own culture: 'Take a deep breath.' But it is possible to cultivate a more systematic awareness of the breathing through a meditation which is widely practised throughout the Buddhist world: the mindfulness of breathing (*ānāpāna-sati* in Pāli), which some say was the meditation the Buddha was practising when he gained Enlightenment.

The precise details of the mindfulness of breathing are not recorded in any text, perhaps because the detailed ins and outs of the practice have traditionally been handed down from teacher to pupil by word of mouth; one can see the teaching of meditation in classes or groups as a continuation of that tradition. But the best method to start with is probably the traditional Theravādin practice of *ānāpāna-sati*. This is divided into four stages, the first two of which involve counting the breaths, to stop the mind from wandering and help you become aware of the breathing's dynamic yet gentle regularity. In the first stage you count at the end of each out-breath; according to the commentaries this corresponds to the phrase in the *Satipaṭṭhāna Sutta* which describes the meditator as knowing 'I am breathing in a long breath.'

There is nothing sacrosanct about this counting – in a sense it doesn't matter what number you count to. In some traditions you don't count at all – for example, there is a Thai method whereby you prevent the mind from straying by combining the inward and outward breathing with the pronunciation of the syllables *buddh* and *dho* (*buddho* means 'awake'). Other traditions go to the opposite extreme – some Tibetan yogis count on indefinitely, even into the thousands. The *Satipaṭṭhāna Sutta* itself makes no mention of counting. But the best method for the beginner is probably to count the breaths in groups of ten, as they do in the Theravādin tradition. Counting to five or less tends to restrict the mind unnecessarily, while going beyond ten involves paying too much attention to keeping track of which number you've reached.

Although you should be careful not to become so preoccupied with counting that you forget to concentrate on the breathing itself, it is a good idea to keep counting in these early stages of the practice.

Experienced meditators may find that counting obstructs their concentration, but in that case the counting tends to fall away quite naturally. If you are going to modify the practice, you need to be able to recognize the state of concentration you have reached and what to do to deepen it, and that calls for a good deal of experience. If you are a relative beginner, you may think you are concentrating when all that has happened is that you have slipped into a light doze as your thoughts wander to and fro. Some beginners do become deeply absorbed in meditation, but it is rare to be able to stay concentrated. It is best to adopt a systematic method that will help you keep up the momentum of the practice.

Once the first stage has been established, the sutta tells us that the meditator knows that he is breathing in a short breath. This can be taken to refer to the second stage of the *ānāpāna* practice, in which you change the emphasis slightly by counting before each in-breath rather than after each out-breath. Presumably a correspondence between the sutta's instructions at this point and the first two stages of the *ānāpāna* method is made because the breath has a natural tendency to become a little longer in the first stage and a little shorter in the second. But you don't deliberately make the breaths shorter or longer – you just watch and count them as they come and go, steadily becoming more and more aware of the whole breathing process as you do so.

In the early stages of meditation, much of your effort will be taken up with drawing the disparate energies of your mind and body together, and this involves recognizing the various ways in which the mind resists the process of deepening concentration. Traditionally these forms of resistance are called the five hindrances: doubt, sensual desire, ill will, sloth and torpor, and restlessness, and one's effort in meditation is mainly directed towards avoiding them.

Buddhaghosa's commentary on the *Satipaṭṭhāna Sutta* (he was a celebrated scholar of the Pāli texts who lived in the fourth century CE) compares the mind at this stage to a calf which, having been reared on wild cow's milk, has been taken away from its mother and tethered to a post. At first, unsettled and ill at ease in its unfamiliar surroundings, the calf dashes to and fro trying to escape. But however much it struggles, it is held fast by the rope tethering it to the post. The rope of course symbolizes mindfulness. If your mindfulness holds firm, your mind will eventually be brought to a point where, like the wild calf, it finally stops trying to get away and settles down to rest in the inward and outward flow of the breath.

For all its qualities of strength and steadfastness in the face of distraction, mindfulness is neither forceful nor aggressive in its quiet taming of the wayward mind. Like the rope, mindfulness has a certain pliancy. If you fix your attention too rigidly on the object of meditation, subtle states of concentration will have little opportunity to arise. The aim is a gradual process of unification: you guide your energies firmly until they harmonize about a single point without strain or tension, and you are absorbed in the breathing for its own sake. A deep contentment will then lead quite naturally into concentration, as the traces of distraction fade away.

> *He trains thus: "I shall breathe in experiencing the whole body (of breath)"; he trains thus: "I shall breathe out experiencing the whole body (of breath)." He trains thus: "I shall breathe in tranquillizing the bodily formation"; he trains thus: "I shall breathe out tranquillizing the bodily formation." Just as a skilled turner or his apprentice, when making a long turn, understands: "I make a long turn"; or, when making a short turn, understands: "I make a short turn."* [2]

In the *ānāpāna* method the first two stages of the practice are succeeded by two more, in the course of which your awareness of the breathing becomes increasingly refined. In stage three you drop the counting altogether and give your attention to the breathing process as a whole, experiencing your breath rising and falling continuously and without effort, like a great ocean wave. You follow the breath going into the lungs, you feel it there, and you continue to experience it fully as it is breathed out.

Note that the future tense used here ('I shall breathe in') simply signifies the meditator's intention; it carries no suggestion that the breathing should be controlled in any way. Nor should the injunction to verbalize, even silently, be taken literally: if you become deeply concentrated there will be no mental activity at all. Another possible source of confusion is the expression 'whole body of breath', which means simply the whole breath, not a subtle counterpart of the physical body like the Hindu concept of *prāna*. When you are experiencing the whole breath body, it is not just an awareness from the outside, but a total experience – you are identifying yourself with the breath.

After some time this subtle stage gives way to the fourth stage of the practice, which is more subtle still. Now you bring your attention to the first touch of the breath about your nostrils or upper lip, maintaining a delicate, minutely observed awareness of the breath's texture as it enters and leaves your body. Buddhaghosa compares this to a carpenter sawing timber, who keeps his attention fixed not on the saw as it moves back and forth but on the spot where the saw's teeth are cutting into the wood.

The sutta itself provides the analogy of a skilful wood turner who knows precisely what kind of turn – long or short – he is making. For most of us the reference will be somewhat obscure, but this is the kind of rural image the Buddha often used, and it would have been immediately clear to the people of village India in his own time. The basic principle of turning remains the same to this day: the turner shapes the wood by rotating a piece of timber at speed and applying various cutting tools to the surface as it spins. In the Buddha's day this would have been a very simple process, by which a strip of wood would be peeled from the rotating timber in either a long or a short traverse. The turner's whole attention has to be concentrated on the point at which the timber revolves, and this demands steady concentration, because a hesitation would leave a mark which would be hard to remove. Likewise, by means of the meditation technique, your consciousness becomes increasingly refined and you become more keenly aware of the breathing. As you bring your physical and mental energies into a state of tranquillity and dynamic balance, you steadily identify yourself with the breath until there is only the subtlest mental activity around the breathing process. You are simply and brightly aware.

When you are just starting the practice, your experience of the breath will be more or less the same as usual, but as the meditation moves into a different gear you will perceive it more subtly and it will become much more interesting to you, as though it were an entirely new experience. This signals that you are entering the phase known as access concentration, *upacāra-samādhi*, a state in which meditation becomes lighter and more enjoyable and distractions are easier to recognize and deal with. You feel buoyant, as though you are floating or expanding, and everything flows naturally and easily.

This phase of meditation might be accompanied by experiences called *samāpatti*. These are difficult to describe because they vary so much from person to person and from one time to another. They might take a visual form – perhaps a certain luminosity before the mind's eye – or arise as a kind of symbol of your state of awareness. All such phenomena are just signs that your concentration is becoming deeper. Your aim is to concentrate all the more deeply on your breathing, leaving these experiences to look after themselves, not dwelling on them or getting too interested in them.

Gradually, if you keep your momentum, you will be able to go just a little further than access concentration, to enter full mental absorption or *appanā-samādhi*, otherwise known in Pāli as *jhāna* and in Sanskrit as *dhyāna*. In *dhyāna* you enter a crucial stage, passing beyond the psychological process of integrating the disparate aspects of yourself into true concentration. As long as you remain immersed in this state you are no longer dependent on the physical senses for anchorage – a statement which makes more sense in experience than in words, it has to be said. Absorption in *dhyāna* is inherently pleasurable. It is a highly positive state of integration and harmony, which moves consciousness, at least temporarily, into the realm of genuinely spiritual experience. It has longer-lasting effects too: it is what is sometimes called 'weighty' karma – that is, it has very powerful positive karmic consequences. It is a mistake to think of *dhyāna* as passive, mild, and restful in a pleasantly vague way – it is an active, powerful state. But for all its skilfulness, *dhyāna* is by no means the final goal of the mindfulness of breathing. Its main importance lies in the fact that it is the basis for the development of Transcendental Insight.

From *Living with Awareness* (2003, pp.25-32)

3. WHY DO YOU GET DISTRACTED?

You might be just a jumble of elements and attitudes and ideals, but meditation creates a mandala out of all those disorganised things.

> *Oh, Rechungpa, do not be proud and go astray!*
> *Let us go into the mountains and meditate in solitude.*[3]

Sangharakshita: Milarepa is always bringing Rechungpa back to the main point – which for Rechungpa is meditating in solitude. That is what he really needs. Do you think there is any special reason for this advice in Rechungpa's case? Meditation in solitude is good for everybody, surely, at least from time to time. Why is Milarepa so insistent that *Rechungpa* should meditate in solitude?

Q: Is it because Rechungpa gets distracted very easily by external things?

S: Yes. He seems to get distracted very easily. So how does meditation work to counteract that tendency? Why do you get distracted?

Q: You're not integrated.

S: Yes. Maybe part of you does want to follow the spiritual path, lead a spiritual life, but another part of you, so to speak, wants to do something else. Meditation counteracts that. It pulls all the different bits of yourself together. Among the more well-known meditation practices, the mindfulness of breathing in particular has this effect. It makes a whole, out of all the different bits and pieces. It creates a mandala, it turns you into a mandala. You might be a jumble of elements and attitudes and ideals, but meditation creates a mandala out of all those disorganised things. It's as though you had a jigsaw puzzle of a mandala, and all the pieces are just heaped up anyhow. Meditation helps you to put all the bits of the jigsaw in the right places and you get a picture of the mandala; in fact you get the mandala itself. You become the mandala, because it is you who were originally that heap of bits and pieces. Meditation gives you a centre around which the rest of the mandala can be arranged. First you establish the centre. Meditation helps you to do that. You find what you really want to do, the thing that is the most important thing for you. You clarify that, and then you organize the rest of your personality, the rest of your being, around that. In that way you create the mandala.
From a seminar on Milarepa's *Story of the Yak Horn* (1980, p.105)

4. MEDITATION BY NUMBERS

In the mindfulness of breathing, when you are counting the stages it sometimes helps to visualize the figures one to ten.

Sangharakshita: In the mindfulness of breathing, when you are counting the stages it sometimes helps to visualize the figures one to ten. You can even make the numbers different colours, according to your taste or temperament. You can imagine that it is like having a block calendar with one date for each day, and you tear them off, one to ten, one by one. You say 'in out one' and you see this red figure one flashing against a white background. Then, 'in out two', the one disappears and you see then two. This can certainly help improve concentration.

Q: Whenever I have mentioned this, people have become rather distracted by it. They start making the letters all fancy and illuminated.

S: Oh dear! It's because we have all these artists in the group, isn't it? But for those who are not artistically inclined it might be useful, though from the sound of it artists should take care not to get distracted. It can certainly steady concentration. Perhaps if you visualize numbers at all, you should visualize quite stark figures, very plain and functional, like the figure on the date pad. Red against a white background is quite good.
From a seminar on *The Tibetan Book of the Dead* (1979, pp.362-3)

5. THE POINT OF CONCENTRATION

One shouldn't rush from an absorbed concentrated state straight into doing something else. Give yourself time. Have a little break.

Q: In the fourth stage of the mindfulness of breathing, why focus attention on the nose/mouth area?

Sangharakshita: The reason for focusing the attention on the point where the in-and-out breath enters the body, and making that your object of concentration, rather than the in-and-out breath itself, is that it's a very fine point, just that sensation, so the concentration that you achieve at that stage is quite refined. In some traditions one concentrates on the rise and fall of the abdomen but that's a much larger object of concentration, obviously! The sensation at the tip of the nose made by the breath coming and going is a much finer point, so you achieve a better concentration by concentrating on that. It's not so much the nose/mouth area, it is just that sensation at the tip of the nostrils made by the breath coming in and going out.

Q: Isn't ending the practice with the experience of single-pointedness like this a bit abrupt? Some meditation teachers end by leading the meditator into a more expansive sense of the environment around them. Is that advisable?

S: Well, if as a result of concentrating on the sensation at the tip of the nostrils you do become really concentrated, it can even seem that the breath has stopped and that there's no sensation and you're just absorbed. You may have a *dhyānic* experience. Obviously you must not make too abrupt a transition back into the world, as it were. But I think most people take care of that automatically. After you've been in that very concentrated state for a little while, you usually find after a minute or two that your breath is becoming a little harsher, and your concentration then becomes less refined because the object of concentration is less refined. So you gradually come down. Usually that happens quite naturally.

If some meditation teachers do suggest that one just becomes aware of the environment, there's nothing wrong with that. Usually what happens is that people are meditating with their eyes closed, and when the meditation has come to an end they open their eyes. Even if you don't look around, if you open your eyes after a period of concentrated meditation, you become aware of your environment anyway, automatically. You may sometimes find that you see it in a very clear way because you see it without any thoughts. And then of course gradually the thoughts start coming back and you start thinking about the next thing to do.

So I don't think usually any special sense of the environment needs to be cultivated. The general point is, as you're implying, that one shouldn't rush from an absorbed concentrated state straight into doing something else. Give yourself time. Have a little break. Just sit on just for a few minutes before you get up from your seat and carry on with whatever else it is that you have to do.

From Q&A at Dhanakosa (1993, pp.7-8)

6. A GLOWING FEELING

A useful practice for those who are in their heads, so to speak ...

Q: In the last stage of the mindfulness of breathing, we tend to focus on the nostrils, the place where the breath enters and leaves the body. If you tend to be a 'head person', wouldn't you be better focusing lower down in your body?

Sangharakshita: Yes, there is a technique of concentrating not on the in and out breath but on the rise and fall of the abdomen. Sometimes this has a calming and steadying effect in the case of the person who is concentrated more in his head. In the fourth stage you could concentrate not on the breath coming and going within the nostrils but on the very gentle, as it should be by that time, rise and fall of the diaphragm. That will pull the consciousness down, so to speak, you can develop a warm, comfortable, glowing feeling doing that.

Q: There is a Japanese meditation practice where you focus on the hara.

S: Yes. It's quite a useful practice for those who are in their heads, so to speak, the more brainy, intellectual, conceptualizing types, to sometimes sink the consciousness down to the *tantien*, as it's called in T'ai Chi, or just to concentrate on the rise and fall of the diaphragm instead of the point in the nostrils where the breath strikes as it comes in and goes out.

From a seminar on *The Tibetan Book of the Dead* (1979, pp.361-2)

7. ISN'T THE MINDFULNESS OF BREATHING A BIT BORING?

It does seem that if one isn't very careful, the mindfulness of breathing tends to be a bit cold or dry.

Q: I find that the mindfulness of breathing can become uninteresting. I think I remember you once suggesting trying to visualize flowers in a blue sky instead. Have I got that right?

Sangharakshita: I think that unless you were relatively concentrated you couldn't really do that. Your mind would wander. You might be initially interested but I think most people's minds would wander after a while. Perhaps you could do that sort of thing after at least the first three stages of the mindfulness of breathing, even if you abbreviate them a bit. You could spend five minutes on each in turn, then take up the visualization practice when you get to the fourth stage. I think it's not wise to skip the mindfulness of breathing altogether; the danger would be that you would employ the mind with this pretty picture for a few minutes and then you would start wandering, because there would be no concentration.

Q: But sometimes you can have some concentration without your emotions being all that involved, and that's where the need for more interest comes in.

S: It's very important to get the emotions involved – this should of course be the case with the *mettā-bhāvanā* right from the beginning – but it does seem that if one isn't very careful, the mindfulness of breathing tends to be a bit cold or dry. If you do the practice regularly, it can be quite good to go into a visualization-type practice, or at least mantra recitation, instead of the fourth stage of the mindfulness of breathing.

Q: Sometimes I get quite concentrated in the fourth stage, but then I just don't feel like carrying on; I lose interest.

S: As though there's nothing much to do. At that point one can very well take up one of these other exercises or practices.
From a seminar on *Milarepa's Meeting at Silver Spring* (1976, pp.12-13)

8. THE MINDFULNESS OF BREATHING AND INSIGHT

You realize in a very immediate way that just as you are breathing in and out, so too are other beings.

One tends not to think of the mindfulness of breathing as an insight practice, but in principle it is, just as much as practices more usually designated '*vipassanā*'. The *Satipaṭṭhāna Sutta*'s description of the practice certainly suggests that it is. *Vipassanā* is presented here as a stage of meditation – that stage of meditation which follows on naturally from the concentration and tranquillity established by the mindfulness of breathing. As this section of the sutta moves beyond the technical description of the establishment of concentration around the breath, it goes into a series of more general reflections concerning the nature of breathing: the contemplation of the breath internally and externally, and of the origination and dissolution factors of the breath. Through these reflections – this is the intention – you eventually come to grasp the essential fragility of the breathing process.

So it is possible to take a reflective attitude to the breath as well as dwelling on the physical experience of breathing. Although these reflections are suggested here in the *Satipaṭṭhāna Sutta*, such a reflective attitude is seldom mentioned in the Theravādin tradition, while in the Mahāyāna, *vipassanā* practices such as the six element practice may take over where the mindfulness of breathing leaves off.

No doubt the six element practice could be said to provide a more comprehensive method of channelling the same kinds of reflection. But to reflect on the nature of the breath is in essence to reflect on what the Buddhist tradition calls the three *lakṣaṇas* (Pāli: *lakkhaṇas*), the three characteristics or 'marks' of mundane existence: that it is impermanent, unsatisfactory, and insubstantial – and what could be more directly related to Insight than that? The sutta instructs the practitioner to live 'contemplating in the body its arising factors, or its vanishing factors'. The meaning of this is quite straightforward: you contemplate all the factors or conditions that go to produce the breathing process, and in the absence of which it does not take place. It is essentially a recognition of the breath's contingent nature. As well as bringing to mind the physiological conditions affecting the rise and fall of the breath, you can also reflect that the breathing, as an intrinsic part of the body as a whole, is ultimately dependent upon the ignorance and craving that, under the law of karma, have brought that body into existence.

The very impermanence of the body, you can further reflect, gives rise to its unsatisfactoriness. This is the second of the three 'marks' of conditioned existence: the truth that all conditioned things are unsatisfactory, even potentially painful, because they cannot last for ever. The breath, like the body, arises and passes away, and one day our breathing – and our life – will come to an end. To bring this reflection home, you can call to mind the inherent fragility of the breathing. Like the body, it is a delicate, vulnerable thing that is always susceptible to the unpredictable forces of the natural world.

This inherent instability is something we share with all sentient beings, indeed with everything, which is presumably what is meant in the sutta by the exhortation to contemplate the body 'externally' as well as 'internally'. It could conceivably mean looking at the body from the outside as well as experiencing it subjectively from within, but it is usually taken to mean contemplation of the physical experience of others. In the later stages of the mindfulness of breathing, when you might be concentrating more on the development of Insight, you can recollect that just as you are breathing, so too are all other living beings (or at least those that do breathe). In this way you cultivate a feeling of solidarity with all other forms of life. As far as I know, this sort of reflection forms no specific part of the mindfulness of breathing as it is usually practised, but it is the natural result of sustained practice: you realize in a very immediate way that just as you are breathing in and out, so too are other beings. The mindfulness of breathing practised in this way thus provides a corrective against an alienated or one-sided approach to spiritual life. It seems a shame that it is not standard practice.

In reflecting that we share with all breathing beings the same body of air and the same material elements, we approach the third mark of conditioned existence – the fact that the distinction we make between ourselves and others is quite arbitrary. This is the truth of insubstantiality – the fact that the discrete and permanent self is only an illusion. We depend on other people for our existence and we are very much like them. And when we die, the material elements of which we are all composed will disperse across the universe once more. The sutta thus refers to the monk's body not as 'his' body but as 'the' body. There is no question here of 'I' or 'mine'; it's just a body. Reflecting in this way is not meant to alienate you from your body; you are trying to see it as an impersonal process, part of the universal rise and fall of things. It is another move towards a sense of solidarity with other beings.

In this way the sutta leads the meditator through the *samatha* stages of calming and integrating consciousness around the breathing, through the various levels of absorbed concentration, and on to the contemplation of the inherent truths of conditioned existence, in preparation for the arising of Transcendental Insight.

From *Living with Awareness* (2003, pp.33-5)

2 General mindfulness

1. KNOWING WHAT IS GOING ON

'You are not yet ready to practise meditation. First you need to learn mindfulness.'

The spiritual life, one could say, begins with awareness: simply knowing what is happening, knowing what is going on. Not that it is simple to do this. Four kinds of awareness are usually distinguished. In the first stage we are aware of what we are doing – that is, we are aware of bodily movement, and also of what we are saying. We are rarely fully aware of what we are doing; very often we don't really know what we are saying either, because our minds are elsewhere – but this is a crucial aspect of awareness.

Then, we also need to know what we are feeling: whether we are happy or sad, greedy or contented, angry or loving. And we also need to become aware of what we are thinking. At first it may not be obvious that we need to make an effort to do this; surely we know what we're thinking, at least most of the time? But very often we don't. At this very moment, even, you may not really know what you are thinking. You may think you are fully absorbed in what you are reading – but are you? Or are you thinking about what you need to do next, or what you did yesterday, or what to have for supper? Unless we know what we are thinking from moment to moment, the mind will be scattered and confused. The fourth kind of awareness to be practised is awareness of the Dharma. Once we know – at least intellectually – the truth of how things really are, we must try never to forget it. Whatever we do, we must keep the Dharma in mind.

But we can start with the basics. We may find it impossible to keep the Dharma in mind much of the time. We may find it hard to stay aware of what we are thinking and feeling. But we can begin by at least trying to stay aware of what we are saying and doing. There's a story that illustrates the fundamental importance of this level of mindfulness. It's about a young Japanese Buddhist who wanted to learn meditation. Deciding he needed a meditation teacher, he searched for some months, and travelled many hundreds of miles, until he came to a temple where – so he had heard – a great meditation teacher lived. Having been granted an interview, the young man entered the teacher's room. First, though, he folded up the umbrella he was carrying, and put it to one side of the door.

The teacher asked him what he wanted, and he said, 'I want to learn to meditate. Please teach me.' The teacher said, 'All right. But first I want to ask you one or two questions.' The young man was quite pleased to hear this, thinking that he would be questioned about the theory of meditation. But the teacher asked, 'When you arrived just now, was it raining?' The young man replied, 'Yes, it was raining quite heavily.' Then the guru asked, 'Did you come carrying an umbrella?' The young man thought this rather an odd question. Why wasn't the teacher asking him anything about meditation? But anyway, he thought he'd better reply. 'Yes,' he said. 'I was carrying an umbrella.' Then the teacher asked, 'When you came into my room, on which side of the door did you leave it?' Try as he might the young man couldn't remember. There was nothing he could say. So the teacher said, 'You are not yet ready to practise meditation. First you need to learn mindfulness.' And away the young man had to go.

Of course, we need not really put off learning to meditate until we have learned to be mindful. Indeed, meditation – especially the mindfulness of breathing – will help us to cultivate mindfulness. But our practice need not be – *should* not be – restricted to when we're sitting in meditation. We can practise mindfulness in all situations. Whatever we do, we should do it carefully, with proper thought. We may be studying, or cooking, or sweeping the floor, or mending the car, or driving, or talking with our friends – but whatever it is, we can try to do it with a clear mind, with *smṛti*, with recollection and awareness.

From *What is the Dharma?* (1998, pp.132-3)

2. WHY ARE WE SO EASILY DISTRACTED?

Why are we so half-hearted? It is because we have no continuity of purpose.

Suppose you are writing a letter, an urgent letter that must go off by the next post. But, as so often happens in modern life, the telephone rings, and on the other end is a friend of yours who wants a little chat. Before you know where you are, you are involved in quite a lengthy conversation. You go on chatting perhaps for half an hour, and eventually, the conversation completed, you put down the phone. You have talked about so many things with your friend that you have quite forgotten about the letter, and you have talked for such a long while that you suddenly feel quite thirsty. So you wander into the kitchen and put the kettle on for a cup of tea. Waiting for the kettle to boil you hear a pleasant sound coming through the wall from next door, and realizing it is the radio, you think you might as well listen to it. You therefore nip into the next room, switch on the radio, and start listening to the tune that's playing. After that tune is finished there comes another, and you listen to that too. In this way more time passes, and of course you've forgotten all about your boiling kettle. While you are in the midst of this daze, or trance-like state, there is a knock at the door. A friend has called to see you. Since you are glad to see him, you make him welcome. The two of you sit down together for a chat, and in due course you offer him a cup of tea. You go into the kitchen and find it full of steam. *Then* you remember that you had put the kettle on some time ago, and *that* makes you remember your letter. But now it is too late. You have missed the post.

This is an example of unmindfulness in everyday life. Indeed everyday life consists, for the most part, of this sort of unmindfulness. We can all no doubt recognize ourselves in the portrait, and may have to admit that this is the chaotic, unmindful fashion in which, for the most part, we live our lives. Now let us analyze the situation, to give ourselves a better understanding of the nature of unmindfulness. First of all in our example we see the plain and simple fact of forgetfulness, which is a very important element of unmindfulness. We forget about the letter which we are writing when we are talking on the phone, and we forget the kettle which is boiling for tea when we are listening to the radio.

Why do we forget so easily? Why do we so often lose sight of something we ought to be bearing in mind? The reason is that we are very easily distracted; our minds are very easily turned aside. It often happens for instance that I am giving a lecture or talk of some kind. Everybody is paying close attention, and there is a pin-drop silence. But then the door opens, and someone comes in. And what happens? Half the heads swivel round as though they had all been pulled by the same string. People are as easily distracted as that. Sometimes it is a bluebottle buzzing against the window-pane, or the dropping of a sheet of my notes that distracts people. Such things show how easily we are distracted, which is why we tend to forget in the affairs of everyday life

Why is it that we are so easily distracted? How does it happen? It is because our concentration is weak. Usually we attend to what we are doing or saying or thinking only in a half-hearted way. But why is our concentration so weak? Why are we so half-hearted? It is because we have no continuity of purpose. There is no one overriding purpose that remains unchanged in the midst of all the different things that we do. We switch from one thing to another, one wish to another, all the time, like the character in Dryden's famous satire who

> *Was everything by starts, and nothing long;*
> *But in the course of one revolving moon*
> *Was chymist, fiddler, statesman, and buffoon.*[4]

Because we have no continuity of purpose, because we are not bent on one main thing all the time, we have no real individuality. We are a succession of different people, all of them rather embryonic. There is no regular growth, no real development, no true evolution.

Some of the main characteristics of unmindfulness should now be clear. Unmindfulness is a state of forgetfulness, of distraction, of poor concentration, of an absence of continuity of purpose, of drift, and of no real individuality. Mindfulness, of course, has just the opposite characteristics: it is a state of recollection, of undistractedness, of concentration, of continuity and steadfastness of purpose, and of continually developing individuality.

From *Vision and Transformation* (1999, pp.124-6)

3. THE JAPANESE TEA CEREMONY

We should do everything on the same principle as the Japanese tea ceremony, with mindfulness and awareness, and therefore with stillness, quietness and beauty, as well as with dignity, harmony and peace.

On the face of it the Japanese tea ceremony revolves around a very ordinary act which we do every day: the making and drinking of a cup of tea. This is something we have all done hundreds and thousands of times. But in the Japanese tea ceremony, it is done in a quite different way, because it is done with awareness. With awareness the kettle is filled with water. With awareness it is put on the charcoal fire. With awareness one sits and waits for the kettle to boil, listening to the humming and bubbling of the water and watching the flickering of the flames. Finally with awareness one pours the boiling water into the teapot, with awareness one pours out the tea, offers it, and drinks it, all the time observing complete silence. The whole act is an exercise in awareness. It represents the application of awareness to the affairs of everyday life.

This attitude should be brought into all our activities. We should do everything on the same principle as the Japanese tea ceremony, with mindfulness and awareness, and therefore with stillness, quietness and beauty, as well as with dignity, harmony and peace.

But if the Japanese tea ceremony represents a certain level of awareness in everyday life and a certain type of spiritual culture – that of Far Eastern Buddhism, especially Zen – what analogous ceremony or institution is there which represents the attitude of the West today? What do we have that breathes the whole spirit of our commercial culture? After turning this question over in my mind, I have come to think that what is characteristic of our culture is the business lunch. In the business lunch you are trying to do two things at the same time: trying to have a good meal, and trying to pull off a good deal. This sort of behaviour, where one is trying to do two contradictory things at once, is quite incompatible with any true, real or deep awareness. It is also very bad for the digestion.

Awareness of the body and its movements will, if practised continually, have the effect of slowing these movements down. The pace of life will become more even and more rhythmical. Everything will be done more slowly and deliberately. But that does not mean that we will do less work. That is a fallacy. If you do everything slowly because you are doing it with awareness and deliberation, you may well accomplish more than someone who looks very busy, someone who is always dashing around and whose desk is piled high with papers and files, but who is in fact not busy but just confused. If you are really busy, you go about things quietly and methodically, and because you don't waste time in trivialities and fuss, and because you are aware, in the long run you get more done.

From *Vision and Transformation* (1999, pp.130-1)

4. MINDFULNESS AND PLEASURE

In the effort to preserve your mindfulness you shouldn't eliminate pleasure, and in your determination to experience pleasure you shouldn't forget about mindfulness.

One of the things I noticed on many of our early retreats was that people would come on retreat and, what with the meditation and silence and everything, they'd gradually become more mindful, but quite often as they became more mindful they'd become a bit less joyful, so you'd have to ease things up a bit and give them a bit more scope. Then they'd be more lively and jolly, but then they'd tend to get a bit carried away and become a bit unmindful. It's as though it's very difficult to combine the two. If you're experiencing joy and pleasure very intensely, it tends to conduce to loss of mindfulness; and if you're preserving your mindfulness quite carefully, you can get a bit out of touch with your emotions – not that that need be the case. So you have to try and bring the two things together, so that you can experience even intense delight at the same time as equanimity and mindfulness, all brought together. In short, in the effort to preserve your mindfulness you shouldn't eliminate pleasure, and in your determination to experience pleasure you shouldn't forget about mindfulness. You need both.

From a seminar on the *Samaññaphala Sutta* (1982, p.161)

5. DOESN'T MINDFULNESS TAKE TOO MUCH TIME?

One can have one's moments of just looking, even in the course of the busiest life.

Q: The trouble with mindfulness is that it leaves you with so many decisions. It is such a responsibility. If you notice things that need doing, you've got to make the decision either to do them or not to do them.

Sangharakshita: On the contrary, in some ways I think awareness relieves you of decisions, because you can just be aware of things that otherwise you might worry about.

Q: How do you mean? I don't quite understand,

S: Well, awareness is in a way non-reactive. Suppose you're aware that it's raining. If you're mindful, you don't think, 'Oh, what a pity, it's raining. Shall I go out or not? Shall I risk getting wet, or would I get wet if I went out?' You're just aware of the fact that it's raining. It's true that if you are aware of your surroundings, you may be aware that there are a lot of things to be done. But then you should even take that calmly and in a sensible way, realizing that you can't do everything all at once, and that some things are more important than others.

Q: There's a conflict between developing the ability to just look and having a busy life. Does this matter in one's spiritual development?

S: Just looking takes time, but it doesn't always take very much time. Even if you're living in the city, you can have a walk in the park, with or without company, and you can be aware of the trees and the flowers. One can have one's moments of just looking, even in the course of the busiest life. One doesn't necessarily have to look at trees and flowers, though that is pleasant; one can just look at the wall opposite, or the demolition work that is in progress outside. The important thing is to be aware of one's surroundings, and aware of other people. You can be quite simply aware of their bodily presence: what they're wearing, whether they've shaved that morning, whether they've combed their hair, whether they've left some jam around their mouth. There's always scope for awareness: whether the surface of your desk is dusty, whether a picture on the wall is askew. So long as your eyes are open, you can practise just looking. You can take a few minutes off from the furious race of thoughts and the frantic planning.

Maybe in between different kinds of work, you can pause, just for two or three minutes. This has quite a beneficial effect. For instance, if you've written something and you are going to type it up, don't jump up and start typing as soon as you've written it. Just pause. Just sit for a couple of minutes, do nothing, think nothing, have a complete break, and then start on your typing. And as soon as the typing is finished, don't jump up and put a stamp on it and dash straight to the post office, but again pause, give yourself a break for a minute or two – even one minute is enough – and then carry on. In this way you won't remain too long divorced from that state of more pure awareness.

Q: Presumably, if you paused like that, it would have an effect on the continuity of your mindfulness through the day.

S: Oh, yes: and also you'd refresh yourself, and prevent yourself from being too carried away by your own thoughts, from worrying, even, or becoming too hectic mentally.

From a seminar on the *Higher Evolution of the Individual*
(year unknown, pp.41-3)

3 Walking meditation

Up and down the gravel path,
Between the flowering trees,
I've walked this summer afternoon
To give my spirit ease.

I could not idly stand, nor sit
Upon the grassy ground,
For like a mill-wheel in my head
The thoughts flew round and round.

Oh thoughts of life and thoughts of death
Chased thoughts of love and pain
Like golden hawk and sable dove
Inside my reeling brain.

The withered hopes like wind-whirled leaves
Thick on my heart did come,
With dreads like shapes that dance for blood
About the sorcerer's drum.

So up and down the shadowy paths,
Between the moon-white trees,
Through pools of silver, I must walk
To give my spirit ease.

(1952)

1. A USEFUL PRACTICE?

Your breath adjusts naturally to the rhythm of your walking, so you are in a harmonious, peaceful state, and you can think calmly and quietly.

> *So the Venerable Meghiya, robing himself in the forenoon and taking bowl and robe, entered Jantu Village in quest of alms food. And after questing for alms food there, returned after his rounds and after eating his meal, went towards the bank of the river Kimikala and on reaching it, while taking exercise by walking up and down and to and fro, he saw a lovely delightful mango grove.*[5]

Q: Walking meditation is quite a common practice in the Buddhist tradition, isn't it? Is it possible to get into the first *dhyāna* doing walking meditation?

Sangharakshita: I think it's quite difficult to get into a *dhyānic* state if you're moving about. Once mental activity ceases, as it does as you enter the second *dhyāna*, it is very difficult to maintain any physical activity. You're almost obliged to sit down, lie down or recline in some way. It's as though you want to put the body aside and not have to think about it, so that you can go deeper into concentration.

It is said that Aristotle was in the habit of walking up and down. It seems as though he thought best when he was walking, and apparently he even lectured when walking up and down. This is why his philosophy is sometimes called the peripatetic philosophy – peripatetic simply meaning 'walking up and down'. It's certainly quite a common practice in Buddhism. It's still well known in Theravāda countries, and in some of the Buddhist holy places, Buddha Gaya for instance, they have a row of carved stone lotuses which are supposed to mark the spot where the Buddha walked up and down. In Europe in the Middle Ages, every monastery had a cloister. In warmer countries like Italy, the cloister gave the monks protection from extreme heat, so that they could walk up and down in the shade in the middle of the day, and in countries like England, of course, the cloister gave you protection from the rain; you could still get your daily exercise walking within the cloister, even when the weather didn't permit you to take exercise outside.

Q: There's that story of Soṇa in the Pāli canon too – that seems to point to the fact that it was a popular practice.

S: Yes. He was of course overdoing it: he walked up and down to such an extent that his feet started bleeding.

Q: Could it be a useful practice for us? – in moderation, of course.

S: Perhaps not many people have time to walk up and down. If you're working on a building site, you don't particularly want to walk up and down in your spare time. But if you lead a sedentary life, as many of the bhikkhus did, then walking up and down as a form of exercise is very useful, and it does say here that Meghiya was taking exercise by walking to and fro. And there is another passage which I recently came across where the Buddha seems to recommend exercise in the form of walking up and down, to keep the bhikkhus healthy.

Q: When I lived in the mountains in New Zealand, I did a bit of walking meditation and found it a very useful way of absorbing Dharma or what I'd read; I'd read for an hour or two, then walk up and down for a while.

S: Yes, you can reflect very easily and naturally in that way, especially if you are walking in a fairly leisurely fashion. Your breath adjusts naturally to the rhythm of your walking, so you are in a harmonious, peaceful state, and you can think calmly and quietly.

From a seminar on the *Meghiya Sutta* (pp.11-3)

2. THE AIM OF WALKING AND CHANTING

If you decide to do the walking and chanting, obviously you must do it with a clear understanding of why you are doing it.

Q: Sometimes when people walk and chant they fold their hands in front of them, while some just let their hands hang loose or clasp them behind their backs.

Sangharakshita: When I was teaching this originally, I asked people not to fold their hands, but just to let the hands move quite gently and loosely. I think one of the reasons why some people clasp their hands is not out of feelings of devotion, but because they just don't know what to do with their hands, they feel uncomfortable with them just swinging at their sides. But it's best just to allow the hands to swing – gently, not as though one is marching on the parade ground!

After you have been sitting in meditation, you can do the walking and chanting practice, partly to give you a break from the sitting posture, and partly to help you practise going back into ordinary life and movement maintaining your mindfulness. That is its twofold purpose. It is a devotional practice only in a very secondary sense, so one emphasizes the mindfulness aspect, not the devotional aspect.

Q: When you suggested the silent walking practice, you definitely suggested that people might have their hands together.

S: Well, this is the Zen practice and I think I said that by way of partial concession to the Zen tradition, and also because I saw that people used to swing their arms and that wasn't what was required. But I would rather see people just walking in a perfectly natural way. The practice is simply walking and chanting: just walking in a perfectly normal, natural way, not in a sloppy or slovenly way, but with mindfulness. It is as simple as that.

Q: Do you see silent walking as having more or less the same function?

S: Oh yes indeed!

Q: Recently some people have started doing very slow walking, because they find that they can concentrate much more if they do it very slowly, and that seems to be in fashion at the moment. What do you think of that?

S: Well, that perhaps is giving too much importance to the aspect of maintaining mindfulness. The aim of the practice is not to be as mindful as you possibly can because then you might as well sit down and carry on with the mindfulness of breathing or whatever other practice you are doing. The whole idea of the walking and chanting, or just walking, is that you learn to make the transition, or you're given some experience of making the transition from a spiritual practice back into the ordinary activities of the world, carried out with uninterrupted mindfulness –

the same mindfulness, virtually, that you had developed when you were sitting and meditating.

So the aim of walking meditation is not, at all costs, to maintain as high a level of mindfulness as possible, but to maintain as high a level of mindfulness as is compatible with physical functioning in the ordinary way. If you slow down the walking and slow it down still more, you are defeating the purpose of the practice.

Q: So there is no benefit in that?

S: Well, it may be beneficial from another point of view, but not from that point of view. If you are feeling as inclined to be mindful as all that, perhaps you should not be doing the walking and chanting practice at all, but just carrying on sitting and meditating.

If you decide to do the walking and chanting, obviously you must do it with a clear understanding of why you are doing it. So far as I am concerned, the purpose of it is to give you practice in prolonging your mindfulness into those activities of life where you are not carrying out any specific spiritual practice or exercise. So you walk in a completely normal way, not in any special way, not particularly slowly, nor particularly fast.

Q: It seems to me that perhaps the very, very slow walking would enable one to have quite a long session of meditation with breaks, so you can stretch your legs, but retain the results of the practice, disrupted as little as possible, into another session.

S: In that case you don't need to walk, you can just stand up and stretch yourself in your place. That's why you have to decide beforehand what you really want to do. If you want to carry on uninterruptedly meditating for as long as possible, just stretch yourself mindfully in your seat, or even stand up when you feel like it. But if you want to develop the practice of prolonging the mindfulness into the affairs and the activities of everyday life, then in between periods of seated meditation, you can do the walking and chanting practice, or the just walking and being mindful practice. It is a question of being clear in your mind beforehand what particular effect you want to produce, which particular aspect of the spiritual life you want to develop or cultivate.

I certainly noticed in the old days that a lot of people needed the practice of bringing meditation into their ordinary life, because more often than not they would be quite mindful in the shrine room, but the minute they got outside the shrine room, they would relapse into their previous extremely unmindful behaviour. So I saw the walking and chanting as a means of helping them to prolong mindfulness into their ordinary everyday lives. It is possible to ask whether in fact it does help one to do that, but by one means or another that is what we have to achieve. Rather than having highly mindful periods of seated meditation and very unmindful periods of doing other things, we somehow have to make the connection, and prolong the mindfulness into the midst of our ordinary life.

From a seminar on *The Forest Monks of Sri Lanka* (1985, pp.75-8)

3. A VERY PLEASANT PRACTICE

Even if one doesn't find sitting for long periods difficult, sometimes it is quite pleasant to walk up and down and meditate.

Much of the meditation is done while walking back and forth.

Q: What do you think is meant here by meditating while walking?

Sangharakshita: I imagine what is meant is the practice of *satipaṭṭhāna* – that is to say, one is mindful of the walking process, and perhaps of other bodily processes that are going on. One has attained a certain degree of concentration, not exceeding that of neighbourhood concentration, because if you go beyond that, it is difficult to carry on walking. And one is trying on that basis to develop Insight, perhaps in connection with reflection on the painful, impermanent and soulless nature of the body, the feelings, the mental process itself and so on. You can certainly do this while walking up and down.

Q: Is it possible to meditate while walking, using a *samatha* practice?

S: Well, almost any practice will carry you into neighbourhood concentration, and you can use any *samatha* practice which does that when you are walking and meditating. You can recite a mantra while walking up and down mindfully, and no doubt you would gain neighbourhood or access concentration, and would be able to reflect on the meaning of the mantra as a way of developing Insight. It is very doubtful, though, if you would be able to do elaborate visualization exercises while walking up and down.

Q: If it is possible to meditate while walking, would it be of value to develop such a practice to help people who find sitting for long periods difficult?

S: Not only that. Sometimes it is quite pleasant to walk up and down and meditate. I did quite a lot of this in Kalimpong, especially once I had my own hermitage, which had a nice long verandah. I often walked up and down there meditating, especially during the rainy season. It is a very pleasant practice, more suited to the development of Insight than to the deepening of *samatha* experience for obvious reasons, but it has a definite place, and I think we could probably make more use of it.
From a seminar on *The Forest Monks of Sri Lanka* (1985, pp.104-105)

4. AN UNDESIRABLE WAY TO DO IT

The idea of walking meditation is to cultivate mindfulness at the same time that you are moving, not chop your movement up into bits.

Q: Could you say something about the walking practice which you quite often see Theravāda monks doing, where they lift their feet and tread in a very slow manner?

Sangharakshita: It is not only that they do it slowly. This is when they practise *satipaṭṭhāna* according to the Vipassana School tradition, where they break up the continuity of movement into a number of discrete stages. I don't personally think that this has a very positive effect. If this stop-go, stop-go thing is carried on for a long time it can be quite disturbing. You know: 'I am about to lift up my hand, I have lifted my hand, now I will move my hand forward,' or, 'It is the fire element that is responsible for moving it forward'. This interruption of the continuity of the flow of energy can have a deeply disturbing effect. The idea of walking meditation is to cultivate mindfulness at the same time that you are moving, not chop your movement up into these discrete bits. So I think that this type of practice of mindfulness is not desirable.
From a seminar on *The Forest Monks of Sri Lanka* (1985, pp.153-4)

5. WALKING AND REFLECTING

The rhythmic quality characteristic of walking seems to be especially conducive to the purposive application of one's thinking to the investigation of a particular subject.

One gets the impression that, far from having time on their hands, the monks in the Buddha's day were more or less fully occupied. There is a good day's work in just making one's way through a couple of sentences of a teaching – considering what is involved, examining the operation of your own mind in the light of its analysis, and reflecting on your observations – let alone the lifetime's work of perfecting the practice. Once the monks had bathed, gone on their almsround and come back, eaten, and rested, the remainder of the day would have been spent in meditation, the sessions of seated practice would be interspersed with periods devoted to the regular, rhythmic exercise of what is called in Pāli *cankamana* – that is, walking up and down, or ambulating, as the practice is termed in the Christian tradition. (The cloisters of medieval monasteries and cathedrals were designed for this purpose.) I used to do this practice myself when I lived in Kalimpong, walking up and down the veranda every evening, and sometimes after lunch as well, to avoid the drowsiness that might have set in if I had sat down to meditate.

Cankamana not only provides physical exercise and relaxation; it is also a great aid to contemplation or reflection. The rhythmic quality characteristic of walking seems to be especially conducive to the purposive application of one's thinking to the investigation of a particular subject. This might be a doctrinal, philosophical, or spiritual question, or even some quite ordinary practical matter. A slow and measured walking pace seems to help bring one's mind to bear on that point of doctrine or that practical issue, isolating it from other concerns. *Cankamana* as a Buddhist practice involves thinking of a very different kind from the aimless, more or less involuntary mental activity of ordinary daily life. One is thinking in a highly directed and specific way about the Dharma, the truth as experienced and taught by the Buddha. To be committed to this truth involves dwelling upon it in some depth – hence the importance of developing the ability to think clearly and directly.

From *Living with Awareness* (2003, pp.114-5)

4 Clear thinking

1. THE ROLE OF CLEAR THINKING

There are always urgent matters to attend to, but these should not be allowed to push the really important questions to the margins of our consciousness.

To reflect on the Dharma is to reflect on the expression of fundamental truth in terms only barely accessible to human thought; without intellectual clarity we will be unable to grasp the essence of the teaching in all its subtlety and depth. If we are to practise Buddhism effectively, in short, we will need to learn to reflect.

It is not easy, however, to concentrate the mind and direct one's thoughts undistractedly for sustained periods. When you are engaged in a discussion or absorbed in a book, you might be able to hold your mind to a train of thought, but if you leave it to its own devices you are likely to find your attention wandering and your concentration starting to flag. You might set yourself to reflect undistractedly for an hour on, for instance, the three *lakkhaṇas*, but it takes a lot of practice to manage more than a few minutes. (Anyone who doubts this should try it and see what happens.)

Thinking should be under one's control, and when it isn't objectively necessary one just shouldn't engage in it. The Buddha used to exhort his disciples to maintain a noble silence (*ariya-mona*) rather than indulge in unprofitable talk, and one could say that the same should go for thought-processes. The alternative to clear and mindful thinking should not be idle mental chatter; one should be able to maintain inner silence. Again, it is obviously a lot easier to say this than to do it – but it is possible.

One way to improve one's ability to think in a directed way is to plan time for thinking. One can learn to take up and put down one's thinking according to one's own needs, not just circumstances. Why not plan thinking time just as you schedule other activities? This is in effect a practice of *sampajañña*, mindfulness of purpose. We all have plenty to think about but our trains of thought seldom reach a conclusion. We are forever dropping one thing and picking up another, then when we sit down to meditate, unfinished business resurfaces and hinders our concentration. Such muddled mental activity is an obstacle to action of any kind and means that we often end up making decisions on the spur of the moment rather than thinking them through. If it is necessary to make a decision it is best to sit down, apply oneself to the matter in hand, and come to a well-considered conclusion. But if we sit down to reflect at all, we often turn the matter over in our mind in such a half-hearted way that quite soon our thoughts have wandered away to irrelevant topics. Unable to come to any clear conclusion, we just make the decision on the basis of how we happen to be feeling at the time, or in response to some quite incidental external pressure. We cannot afford to do this if our decisions are going to count for anything.

We should think about things when we have time to do them justice. Just as mealtimes, meeting friends, and making time for exercise and meditation involve making definite arrangements, mental activity can also be planned. You could apportion, say, an afternoon each week for thinking about things that really matter, things that are of much more consequence than day-to-day practicalities, although they might not be so pressing. If you keep yourself free of thinking about your deeper problems until the appointed time, you might also find everyday difficulties easier to deal with. If you try this out, though, make sure you are going to be free from interruption for however long you need – half an hour or an hour, or even weeks or months together. A chain of sustained and directed thinking can be very subtle, and to have it snapped by untimely and trivial interruptions is painful. The idea of planning in a period of thinking at two o'clock on Tuesday afternoon might come as a shock, but anyone with a busy life already has to do this to some extent. There are always urgent matters to attend to, but these should not be allowed to push the really important questions to the margins of our consciousness.

Whether planned or not, the best way to improve one's directed thinking is simply to think more. Just as physical exercise is the way to become fit, so thinking is the way to improve the capacity for thought. It is a good idea to take any opportunity you get to consider views and opinions with a logical, questioning attitude. Reasoned discussion with a friend or in a small group – the smaller the better – gives different angles on an issue and brings an enjoyable stimulus to thinking. Because our views tend to be emotionally based, if you are thinking about something on your own, there is always the temptation to come to a premature conclusion and resist thinking along lines that run counter to that conclusion. Collaborative thinking forces you to be more objective, to look for a truth that does not necessarily suit you. There is something about the physical presence of another person that generates interest and a keenness to get at the truth, and if you are talking with someone whose intellect is quite active, you might find that you have to get used to organizing and articulating your thoughts more carefully, to avoid non-sequiturs and short-cuts in your argument. Your friends might convince you, or you them. You might even end up convincing yourself, if you were not sure at the outset of the discussion what you really thought. Writing also helps to develop clear thinking – your argument has to be more rigorous than when you are speaking to people you know, and you have to be more careful to make logical connections between the ideas you present.

From the point of view of learning to think clearly, argument is better than agreement. If you only ever have discussions with people whose views you share and read books you agree with, you will never be obliged to address any faulty reasoning that might underpin your view of things. A valid conclusion does not guarantee the logic of any and every argument used in its support. A statement based on a poor line of argument – or no argument at all – might go unchallenged because everyone agrees with the conclusion anyway, regardless of how it is reached. It can therefore be a good idea to seek out a bit of opposition: there is nothing like meeting criticism for improving one's ability to frame a logical argument and make it watertight. Even though sound arguments are unlikely to win over someone with a deep emotional investment in the views they hold, trying to win that person over can make you aware of the strength or weakness of your logic. On the other hand, if your arguments do hold water, the confidence this gives you will help you to be more open to new ideas, because you will know that you have the ability to sift through them without getting muddled or feeling threatened.

The capacity for directed thinking is a characteristic of the truly integrated personality, and the more highly developed an individual is, the more capable of sustained and directed thought he or she will be. All too often, falling back on a romantic view of how thoughts arise, people believe there is some special faculty that makes a certain person an originator of new ideas, a genius. This idea that you've either got genius or you haven't is of course a convenient excuse to disguise one's unwillingness to make the effort to think things through. Genius, the old saying goes, is an infinite capacity for taking pains, and chief among the qualities of someone who has it is sheer creative energy. When the whole person is integrated around a creative vision, the energy that arises can be tremendous. The works of Dickens, for example – a genius if ever there was one – are full of tremendous zest, and the same is true of those of Shakespeare, Mozart, Titian, and Rembrandt. Another quality that marks such geniuses out as special is their refusal to be caught up in the petty details of everyday life at the expense of a higher goal. Instead, they dedicate all their energies to the production of a truly great body of work.

In modern times people seem to desire to be 'original' at any cost, as though originality signified genius. But being different is not the same as being original. Original thought is always an extension of what has been thought by others in the past; originality thus requires you to interpret the tradition, and to do that you need to understand it. People would often rather not acknowledge their debt to tradition; they want to start being 'original' without troubling to master what has gone before them. But if you are really interested in a subject, you will want to know what others have had to say about it, and you might then see a way to move further in the same direction. That is the point at which original thought begins.

Most of the time, of course, our thoughts and ideas are far from original. They are also far from being directed; they arise haphazardly, stimulated by random external events and wandering from one thing to another. This kind of associative thinking does have its value. Just as your dreams – proceeding as they do by way of free association – can tell you something about yourself, so too can patterns of associative thought, if you can become aware of them. One thing leads apparently arbitrarily to another, but the connection is never as arbitrary as it seems. If you allow the mind to free-associate, it will still be choosing which direction it takes, though you will not be conscious of its choices. Wherever your thinking process starts, you will generally keep returning to much the same sequence of thoughts. To take the classic psychoanalytical scenario, you might find that your thoughts are always coming back to some aspect of your childhood, in one disguised form or another, and once you have realized this, you might be able to see a link between those early events and certain patterns of behaviour in the present. As you begin to understand your conditioning better, you free yourself from it.

Thus, associative thinking has its place in reflection, especially if you want to uncover something on an emotional level. Suppose, for example, that you are prone to anger: rather than following a strictly logical process of deduction, you might use associative thinking to feel your way closer to the source of your problem. And we are in a sense thinking associatively every time we use metaphor or symbol. Literature, especially poetry, often helps us to appreciate truths that could never be fully communicated in a logical way. But you have to keep an eye on the direction in which your thought is moving so that your associative thinking takes place within a broader sense of purpose. Despite its associative, impressionistic tone, you are not merely wool-gathering. It is still directed thinking in a sense, although it is being directed from a distance. Just as the recollected, purposeful aspect of mindfulness brings the mind back to the breath when you become distracted, so directed thinking draws your awareness back to the purpose of your mental activity. All your thinking should have an aim, even if that aim is sometimes best served by thinking associatively. Associative thought might help us to unearth resemblances and patterns hidden from rational thought, but this is only valuable if it helps us to arrive at a correct conclusion – that is to say, a true conclusion. Very often associative thinking arrives at no conclusions at all.

If your thinking has to lead somewhere, to solve a problem or explain something to someone, the connections between your thoughts must be logical, not private, arbitrary, or symbolic, however significant the latter kinds of connection might be. If you can't put an argument together, even if you are right, you will not be able to convince anyone else that you are. It is fine to pay attention to your intuition and feelings within the context of your own reflections, but it is not so reasonable then to dress up your feelings as objective facts. When someone says 'How do you know?' it is no good replying, 'Well, I just know,' however confident of your knowledge you feel. Either something is capable of demonstration or it isn't. You might have a well-developed intuitive faculty which you know you can rely on, but it is unreasonable to expect someone else to accept your views simply because you feel them to be true.

Of course, strong feeling has tremendous power to convince, especially if it is forcefully expressed, but it is all the more convincing if it is backed up by reason. For example, you could give a talk on compassion by evoking, in poetic and symbolic language, the figure of Avalokiteśvara, the Bodhisattva who is the embodiment of that sublime quality. You might paint a vivid and appealing picture in the minds of your audience, but your communication would only be fully effective if you were able to demonstrate that the image corresponded in some way to some external reality – otherwise you would be left with a kind of extra-terrestrial, science-fictional figure. There is, in other words, a big difference between a compelling image of the ideal and the reality of that ideal. The Christian evangelist falls into a similar trap if he opens up his Bible and says, 'It must be true, it's written here,' – because, of course, the fact that certain assertions are printed in a book does not prove them to be true. He will have to demonstrate that the Bible has that kind of authority, and if he cannot do so, he will have no reason to be annoyed if other people cannot accept what he says.

One way to make your case is to refer to the experience of the person you are talking to. They might never have had *dhyānic* experience, for example, but you can give them an idea of what the *dhyānas* are like by referring to experiences that *are* familiar to them. Pleasure, for instance, is part of *dhyānic* experience and everyone has experienced at least some pleasure, so if you ask the person to imagine the pleasure they have experienced magnified ten or twenty times, they will get some sense of the intense pleasure of *dhyāna*. Likewise, we have all experienced at least short periods of creativity and positivity. If we were to imagine that positivity continuing unbroken for a whole day at a time, what would it be like? Imagine waking up in the morning with that positive feeling already there, so that you were happy and cheerful, and glad to jump out of bed and begin enjoying the day ahead. That mood would grow – you would become blissful, even rapturous, and certainly inspired – and that inspiration would have all sorts of consequences. You might be inspired to write a poem, or help a neighbour, or any number of things. Then imagine what those few hours of positivity would be like extended into a whole day, and another, and another, indefinitely, into a whole lifetime, week after week, month after month of creativity, building to ever higher and more positive levels of awareness. This is the kind of life to which the

Buddhist aspires. Thus one might conclude if one were trying to describe the goal of Buddhism in terms with which someone else could identify. Starting from an everyday experience of positivity, you would use simple logic to suggest how the state of Enlightenment might be compared to it, if only very approximately. People are not always convinced by an image – metaphor and symbol hold different associations for different people – but reason is a language we all have in common.

But you don't always need to find a logical argument to show that something is true. If you have experienced the benefits of something, you can demonstrate them simply by being able to speak about them with confidence – or even just by being the way you are. For example, the fact that a Buddhist right livelihood business exists and thrives shows that it is possible to reject an economic system geared to material gain and still have a viable means of supporting oneself. If you are living contentedly in a single-sex community, this is direct evidence that true happiness does not depend upon being part of a nuclear family with the statutory number of children. The reality of your life is its own argument. This was especially true of the Buddha. If someone living at the Buddha's time had said they did not believe that the Enlightened state was possible, they only needed to observe the Buddha to see that it was indeed possible. His immense kindness, his intelligence, his very existence, was living proof of the possibility of Enlightenment.

For all its subtlety and rigour the Buddha's teaching is not in essence intellectual. For Buddhism the heart and the mind are not separate: the term *citta* refers to both, so that, for example, *bodhicitta*, the 'will to Enlightenment' which is the central aspiration of the Mahāyāna tradition, is not just a thought about Enlightenment in an abstract intellectual sense, but a heartfelt aspiration to emancipate oneself and all other beings from suffering.

In the early Buddhist tradition, wisdom is also seen not as an intellectual pursuit but a spiritual one, to be realized through reflection, meditation, and direct experience. After all, there can be no intellectual clarity without an awareness of one's emotions. Even the most rigorously intellectual disciplines are taken up on the basis of some emotional motivation, and if this goes unacknowledged any pretensions to rationality are vitiated from the outset. By the same token, you will never be able to convince someone by rational argument if you fail to take their feelings into consideration: 'He that complies against his will, / Is of his own opinion still', as Samuel Butler says.[6] This is the potential flaw in academic scholarship, even in the field known these days as Buddhist studies. Good scholarship is usually measured in terms of the strictness of its objectivity, and this is thought to mean setting aside one's own emotional responses to the material being studied – but this is not possible. There is no such thing as a 'pure' intellectual who is not influenced by the emotions. What, after all, is the reason behind one person's choice to take up, say, Tibetology while another chooses marine biology or nuclear physics? There is always some subjective element at work, and if it is not acknowledged it will make its presence felt by indirect means. Indeed, there is nothing wrong with an emotionally engaged argument, as long as those emotions are acknowledged. Problems only arise when you try to present your pet hobby-horse or deeply held conviction as unbiased logical thinking.

When it comes to mindfulness, what we are aiming for is an ability to think conceptually in a way that is infused with positive emotion. Thought cannot be separated from emotion; effective thinking is wholehearted, with the whole person focused on the activity and integrated around it – 'a man in his wholeness, wholly attending', as D.H. Lawrence wrote. As with everything, we are looking for a middle way. We don't have to be intellectuals to be Buddhists – rather the opposite. We don't have to get bogged down in the minutiae of Abhidhamma philosophy; very often those who make the most spiritual progress are those who concentrate on the basic teachings. But although the intellectual study of Buddhism has its limitations, we cannot afford to underestimate its importance to the cultivation of Insight. Whatever aspect of the teaching we decide to focus on, we must know it and practise it thoroughly, and for this a clear understanding of the tradition is essential. There is no substitute for a committed and clear effort to think things through. Any rational grasp of truth is provisional and we will have to venture beyond rational thinking in the end – but the end may be further away than we think.

From *Living with Awareness* (2003, pp.115-22)

5 Alienated awareness

1. INTEGRATING OUR TOTAL BEING

The traditional Buddhist practice of mindfulness nurtures the integration of our many 'selves', as we make the effort to maintain continuous awareness throughout the activities of daily life.

Becoming an individual is a process of integration. Somehow we have to find a way of unifying the different selves that are within us, integrating our total being, conscious and unconscious, intellectual and emotional. As well as this integration, which we could call 'horizontal', there is also 'vertical' integration to achieve: an integration with our own unrealized higher potential, which is achieved through allowing ourselves to experience our heights – and our depths. Thinking of the Buddhist life in these terms, we can see that committing ourselves to the observance of ethical precepts helps us to live in such a way that we mean what we say, and do what we mean to do; in other words, we develop integrity. The traditional Buddhist practice of mindfulness in all its forms also nurtures the integration of our many 'selves', as we make the effort to maintain continuous awareness throughout the activities of daily life.

Meditation can be described as a direct method of integrating ourselves. Firstly, it brings about 'horizontal' integration, as our scattered selves are gradually drawn together through our focus on the object of concentration. Then, on the basis of that horizontal integration, we can engage in meditation practices in the course of which we reflect on and progressively experience higher truth, in a process of 'vertical' integration. Devotional practices and Dharma studies also help us to move towards this kind of vertical integration.

But even once we have understood the need to develop awareness in all senses, and have perhaps made a start with trying to developing it through such methods, it is still not certain that we will develop it in the right way. There is a danger that we will develop instead what I think of as alienated awareness. In an age of transition, when there are no stable, universally accepted values upon which we can base our lives, many people lose any very solid sense of identity. Also, many people are conditioned to clamp down on their bodily sensations, especially those connected with sex, and to repress negative emotion, to feel what they are told they ought to feel rather than what they truly feel. So, for a variety of reasons, many of us find ourselves unable, or unwilling, to experience ourselves, especially our feelings and emotions. As a result, when we try to develop awareness, we may become aware of ourselves without actually experiencing ourselves. In a sense, we are aware of a non-experience of ourselves, of ourselves not being there.

This failure to experience ourselves is disastrous because it tends to create a split between the conscious and the unconscious, between that part of ourselves which we allow ourselves to experience continuously, and that part which we have made an unconscious decision not to experience and which we therefore experience only intermittently and partially, if at all.

But refusing to experience a certain part of oneself does not mean that the part in question has ceased to exist. Unacknowledged it may be, but it is still very much alive; and not only alive, but kicking. In one way or another, it will make its presence felt, typically in the guise of moods. Suddenly we feel depressed, or angry, or anxious; the mood seems to take possession of us, and we don't really know why. We sometimes even say, 'I didn't feel quite myself yesterday,' or, 'I don't know what's come over me today,' – almost as if we feel we are someone else for as long as that mood persists.

Unfortunately, the painful state of alienated awareness has in the past been aggravated by certain Eastern spiritual teachers who have made all sorts of statements that fail to take account of the differences between the modern Western mentality and the traditional Eastern way of seeing things. Buddhist teachers, for example, and many of their Western disciples, have been known to assert, on the authority of the Buddha's teaching of *anattā*, that we have no self, or that the self is an illusion.

Hindu teachers, meanwhile, will tell you that you are not the body, you are not the mind, you are not your feelings or emotions or thoughts; you are, in fact, God.

True awareness, integrated awareness, is developed by learning to experience yourself more fully, to be more aware of what you experience in your physical body, and in your feelings and emotions, particularly those feelings that you like to think you don't experience. One of the basic but very important functions of the Sangha is to provide a safe environment in which we may disclose ourselves to others and – in having our experience acknowledged by others – gradually learn to acknowledge more of it ourselves.

Another way the Sangha plays a big part in all this is to help us to become aware of what is going on. It is obviously very difficult for us to tell whether there are aspects of our experience that we are not allowing ourselves to be aware of, as the problem is lack of awareness itself. But our spiritual friends may well be able to see what is going on better than we can ourselves, and will find ways – kind and sympathetic ways – to draw it to our attention. And, of course, we will be able to do the same for them.

From *What is the Sangha?* (2001, pp.108-9)

2. IS IT POSSIBLE TO BECOME TOO MINDFUL?

Maybe even mindfulness has to have its phases.

Q: When trying to learn to be mindful, is it possible to become *too* mindful, at the risk of losing one's natural exuberance?

Sangharakshita: In that case, you are misunderstanding mindfulness to mean alienated awareness, not as real awareness *along with* your actions and your feelings.

Q: But doesn't bounciness means loss of mindfulness?

S: In practice it often does – but that doesn't mean you should go to the opposite extreme. There are two extremes: bounciness without mindfulness, and mindfulness without feeling, which is the alienated type of awareness. Sometimes you may have to go to one extreme, as it were, in order to balance the other, but sooner or later you have to get back to the middle position where bounciness and mindfulness are not only fully developed but thoroughly integrated with each other.

Q: Perhaps one has to be less concerned with mindfulness for a while in order to allow something repressed to emerge.

S: Indeed. Maybe even mindfulness has to have its phases. You could be very mindful for a few weeks, say, after which you allow yourself to get more into your feelings. Not that mindfulness is completely neglected, of course, but during that period you let your feelings rip and sort out the question of how mindful you were afterwards.

Q: You get a much clearer picture of what mindfulness is if you let yourself do what you want to do and just watch what's happening. Some people end up being 'good Buddhists' and not being themselves.

S: I think it's possible to get a bit sick with psychological analysis. If you're always trying to find a murky motive, if you think that someone's much more likely to be, at bottom, negative in what he's doing rather than positive, this is all rather twisted. Tutored as you are by psychology, you may find it difficult to believe that he's behaving as he does because he's happy, or because he feels friendly. Maybe there should be a bit more bouncing around and general jubilation. It would be good if we could find ways of being happy and joyful, and even dancing around, mindfully.
 From a seminar on *The Endlessly Fascinating Cry* (1977, pp.245-6)

3. LEVELS OF EXPERIENCE AND AWARENESS

Many of the old values are breaking up. We are no longer so sure what is right and what is wrong.

Briefly, we may say that alienated awareness is awareness of ourselves, without actually experiencing ourselves, especially without experiencing our feelings and emotions. In its extreme form alienated awareness is awareness of one's own non-experience of oneself, even awareness that one is 'not there', paradoxical as that may seem. Obviously this is a quite dangerous state to be in.

Alienated awareness may be accompanied by various physical symptoms, especially by severe – even excruciating – pains in the head. This is more likely to occur when one is deliberately increasing alienated awareness under the erroneous impression that one is thereby practising mindfulness. (I am not, of course, saying that *all* pains in the head encountered in the course of meditation are due to alienated awareness.)

Integrated awareness, on the other hand, is awareness of ourselves, while at the same time actually experiencing ourselves. Our experience of ourselves may be either positive or negative; we may be in either a positive or a negative mental state. But if it is a negative state that we are in, the negativity will eventually be resolved by the fact that besides allowing ourselves to experience it we are also aware of it.

Alienated awareness is therefore that awareness which is alienated *from* the experience of self, especially from the experience of the emotions; integrated awareness is that awareness which is integrated *with* the experience of self, especially with the experience of the emotions. From this the nature of the distinction between alienated awareness and integrated awareness should be at least conceptually clear.

The Three Levels of Experience and Awareness
Perhaps, however, it is still difficult for some of us to recognize the distinction in a way that accords with our actual experience. So let us approach the matter in a somewhat different way, thinking in terms of three levels, or three grades. The first level is the level of experience without awareness. This is what we have most of the time. We feel happy or sad, experience pain or joy, love or hate, but we don't really know, we are not really aware, that we are experiencing these things. There is no awareness, just the bare sensation, or feeling. We are lost in the experience. We 'forget ourselves', as when, for example, we become very angry. After we have been angry, when we recover and survey the damage, we say, 'I didn't know what I was doing. I wasn't myself. I forgot myself.' In other words, while we were identified with, even 'possessed' by, that emotion, there was no awareness. At this first level there is experience – no lack of it at all – but no awareness alongside the experience.

The second level is the level of awareness without experience. This is alienated awareness. We as it were stand back from our experience. It is as though it is not *our* experience – it is going on 'out there'. So we are not really experiencing it. We are not really feeling our feelings: we love but we don't *really* love, we hate but we don't *really* hate. We stand back and look at our experience with this alienated awareness.

The third level is that of experience plus awareness. This is integrated awareness. Here, by very virtue of the fact that we are now experiencing integrated awareness, the emotional experience tends to be a positive rather than a negative one. Here we have the experience, but also, saturating the experience, identical even with the experience, we have awareness. The awareness and the experience have come together. We might say that the awareness gives clarity to the experience, while the experience gives substance to the awareness. The awareness and the experience coalesce, without it being really possible to draw a line between the two, isolating the experience on this side and the awareness on that side. You are fully immersed in the emotion, in the sense of actually experiencing it, but at the same time, together with it, without being different from it, there is the awareness.

This is a much higher state, a state that it is difficult for us to have any idea about if we have not experienced it ourselves. It is not so much an awareness *of* experience but an awareness *with* experience. It is an awareness *in* experience, even an awareness *in the midst of* experience.

These three levels therefore are: (1) experience without awareness, which is our usual state; (2) awareness without experience, or relatively without experience, which is our state when sometimes we get on to the spiritual path and go a little astray; and (3) awareness with experience, experience with awareness, the two beautifully blended together.

How does alienated awareness arise? How do we come not to experience ourselves? To some extent it is due to the nature of the times in which we live, especially here in the West. We are often told that we are living in an age of transition. This is very true. Sometimes we do not realize how abrupt, how violent even, yet also how potentially valuable, the transition is. Many of the old values are breaking up. We are no longer so sure what is right and what is wrong. We no longer know how we ought to live, what role in life to adopt. Our sense of identity is weakened in this way, and as a result there is a widespread feeling of anxiety.

I do not want to attach too much importance to this factor of the times in which we live; I want to look more closely at some of the more immediate factors that give rise to alienated awareness. I have spoken elsewhere of three levels of awareness of self: awareness of the body, awareness of feelings and emotions, and awareness of thoughts. We can speak in the same way of three levels of experience of self and even of three levels of non-experience of self.

The Three Levels of Experience and Non-Experience of Self
First of all, there is non-experience of the body. There are several reasons for this. One of the most important is the refusal actually to experience bodily sensations, especially sensations connected with sex. Such refusal is often connected with wrong training early in life. One finds, for instance, that people are brought up with the idea, or with the vague feeling, that the body is somehow shameful, or at least that it is not so noble, or so respectable, as the mind. Similarly some people have been indoctrinated with the idea that sexual feelings are sinful. All these sorts of ideas and feelings are legacies from Christianity. Though in many ways we might have outgrown Christianity, at least outgrown Christian dogma and ecclesiastical supervision, these attitudes are very widespread and still do quite a lot of harm. We may say that it is one of the great merits of Wilhelm Reich that he went into this whole subject so very thoroughly, and showed quite clearly how inhibition in infancy of pleasurable bodily sensations can lead ultimately to a crippling negation on the part of the adult of his or her whole life force.[7]

Secondly, there is non-experience of feelings and emotions. This also comes about in various ways. For instance, we have been brought up to believe that certain emotions, especially negative emotions, are wrong and should not be indulged in. We may have been taught that it is wrong to get angry. Having been taught in this way, we feel guilty if for any reason we happen to become angry. Even when *we are* angry, we sometimes try to pretend that we are not. We refuse to recognize that we are angry. In other words, we repress the feeling: we refuse to experience it, and it goes underground.

Then again we experience an emotion but we are told by someone in an authoritative position that we do *not* in fact experience that emotion. Perhaps as a small child we don't like our little sister – a common family situation. Our mother or father, however, says, 'Of course you like her. You like her because she is your little sister.' In this situation we don't know where we stand: we experience a feeling but we are told that we don't experience it. It is not even that we are told we *ought not* to experience the feeling. We are told that we *do not* experience it.

To take another example, mother tells the small boy that he is not afraid of the dark 'because,' she says, 'brave little boys are never afraid of the dark'. Wanting, of course, to be considered a brave little boy, the child tries to push his fear out of sight – it gets repressed. He ceases to experience his fear consciously, but it may, of course, come out in dreams or nightmares. Again, the little boy sometimes blurts out, 'I want to kill daddy.' But mother says, 'No, you don't. No one would ever want to kill daddy.' Or the little boy or little girl doesn't like brown bread, but mother says, 'Of course you like brown bread. You like it because it's good for you.' In each of these cases there is confusion and repression, and the child becomes alienated from his or her own feelings.

The effects of this may continue throughout life. In fact they may not only continue but be powerfully reinforced from other sources. When we are a bit older, maybe when we are adolescent, we perhaps discover that we dislike going to parties, but we convince ourselves that we do like going, because everybody – so we tell ourselves – likes going to parties. On another level, we may discover that we are not in the least bit moved by the work of a certain famous artist – his work just leaves us cold. But we find that all our most intelligent friends are much moved by his work. In fact they are highly excited about it. So we, though we may privately think his work even deplorable, have to be highly excited too. We need not multiply examples here. The end result is that we become alienated, to a greater or lesser degree, from our own feelings and emotions.

Thirdly, there is non-experience of thoughts. Here it is not so much that we fail to experience our thoughts, but that we fail to have any thoughts at all. This is because nowadays so many agencies – parents, teachers, the various media, etc. – are telling us what to think. This is not just a case of feeding us with information, with facts – that is quite a different thing. These various agencies impart value judgements too: they tell us that 'this is right' and 'that is wrong', that 'this is good' and 'that is bad', and so on. The newspapers, radio, television give us very selective, slanted information. They make up our minds for us about all sorts of things, but we are rarely conscious of how they are doing this or even that they *are* doing this.

Having made this little survey, we can begin to see what sort of state most of us are in, at least to some extent. We are alienated from ourselves: alienated from our physical bodies, from our feelings and emotions, and from our thoughts. The world, the age, society, our parents and teachers, finally we ourselves – continuing the good work – have got us into this state. We do not experience ourselves. This is something that we really have to recognize, accept, and come to terms with. We can think in terms of an iceberg. Only the tip of an iceberg protrudes above the surface of the waves, while the greater part lies below. Similarly, our self is relatively extensive, just like the iceberg continuing underneath the water, but that part of our self which we experience, which we allow ourselves to experience, which we are allowed to experience, like the tip of the iceberg, is relatively small – in some cases it is infinitesimal.

While in this state of alienation, some of us now come into contact with Buddhism. We start learning about all sorts of wonderful things, including mindfulness. What we are taught about mindfulness seems to suggest that what we have to do is stand aloof from ourselves, especially from our negative emotions, and not experience anything; we have to just watch ourselves, as though we were watching another person. Of course, we are much impressed by this teaching because, in our alienated state, we cannot help thinking that this is just the thing for us. So we start practising mindfulness – or what we think is mindfulness. We stand back from our thoughts, back from our feelings; we push them 'out there' and just look at them. The result of this, in nine cases out of ten, is that we simply succeed in intensifying our experience of alienated awareness.

We learn other good things from Buddhism. We learn that desire, anger, and fear are unskilful states. (We are told that we must call them 'unskilful states' not 'sins' because in Buddhism there are no sins, though they seem to be just as bad as sins, if not much worse.) We learn that we have to get rid of these unskilful states. We *think* we are glad to hear this – at this stage we can't really *feel* glad. We think we are glad because this means we can continue sweeping all these emotions under the carpet, pretending that they are not really there. This too increases our alienated awareness.

Later on still, when we start reading books about Buddhism, we come across the *anātman* (Pāli *anattā*) doctrine, the doctrine of no-self. At this stage, if we are lucky, some smiling Eastern monk tells us that, according to Buddhism, there is no self, that the self is pure illusion. He says that if we could only see clearly, we would see that the self is just not there. He tells us that it is our big mistake that we think we have a self. We rather like the sound of this teaching too. This appeals to us because, as a result of practising so-called mindfulness, we have begun to feel rather unreal. To us, in our experience of our unreality, it seems as though we have begun to realize the truth of *anātman*. In other words, we start thinking that we have developed Transcendental Insight.

The same smiling Eastern monk, because he does not know anything about the mistakes that Western people can make, may encourage us to continue thinking this. The result again is that we get more and more alienated. Here the trouble is not that the teaching itself is wrong, but that we apply it wrongly, or, we may say, sometimes Eastern teachers, even in the West, unacquainted with Western psychology, apply it wrongly. The teaching is metaphysically true: in a metaphysical sense there is no individual self. We, however, don't take this metaphysically. We take it psychologically; in this way all the harm is done.

So a strange pseudo-spirituality develops in some Buddhist circles. The people there are on the whole quite mindful: they shut the door silently; if it's a rainy day they wipe their feet before they come into the house. They don't get angry – or at least they don't show it. They are very controlled and very quiet. But everything seems a bit dead; they don't seem really alive. They have repressed their life-principle and have developed a cold alienated awareness. They have not developed the true integrated awareness, in which one's awareness and one's life-principle, one's aliveness, are 'merged'.

Developing Integrated Awareness
Another question now arises: how can integrated awareness be developed? In order to develop integrated awareness, we have, first of all, to understand, at least theoretically, what has happened; we have to understand the distinction between alienated awareness and integrated awareness. We have to retrace our steps and undo the harm that we have done – or that has been done to us. We have to allow ourselves to experience ourselves. If we have once taken that wrong turning, if alienated awareness has developed to any serious degree, then we have to go back to square one and learn to experience ourselves. We have to learn to experience our own body, to experience our own repressed feelings and emotions, have to learn to think – to insist on thinking – our own thoughts.

This will not be easy, especially for those who are comparatively advanced in life, because some feelings are very deeply buried and are therefore very difficult to recover. We may even need professional help in the matter. We may even sometimes have to act out our feelings, express them externally. This does not mean that we indulge them, but that slowly and mindfully we start letting them out: we allow ourselves to experience our feelings, remaining aware of them as we are actually experiencing them.

If we do this and other things of the same nature, we shall begin to experience ourselves all over again. We shall begin to experience the whole of ourselves, ourselves in our totality: we shall experience the so-called good and the so-called bad, the so-called noble and the so-called ignoble, all as one living whole which is us. When we have done this, when we really experience ourselves in this way, fully and vividly, we can begin to practise mindfulness, because then when we practise mindfulness, it will be the real thing: it will be integrated – or integral – awareness.

From *A Guide to the Buddhist Path* (1996, pp.155-8)

4. DOES MEDITATION CAUSE ALIENATION?

If you are out of touch with your emotions, the best thing you can do is to get straight back into contact with them, and what better way is there than practising the metta bhavana?

Q: A lot of people seem to think that meditation causes alienation and blocked emotion.

Sangharakshita: Meditation in what sense? Did anyone ever hear of the *mettā-bhāvanā* causing alienation or blocked emotion? It is true that if you are in an alienated state, practising the mindfulness of breathing may not be very helpful, because if you're very alienated, it may increase your alienation. But that's no reason not to meditate. Do the *mettā-bhāvanā*. If you are out of touch with your emotions, the best thing you can do is to get straight back into contact with them, and what better way of getting back into contact with your emotions is there than practising the *mettā-bhāvanā*? I am aware that the *mettā-bhāvanā* tends to be neglected as compared with the mindfulness of breathing, which people seem to find easier on the whole. But if one starts with the mindfulness of breathing, that being as it were a more accessible technique, one should aim as soon as one can at balancing the two practices, and doing as much *mettā-bhāvanā* as mindfulness of breathing.

From a Men's Order/Mitra event at Vinehall (1981, p.19)

3 The development of positive emotions

THE DEVELOPMENT OF POSITIVE EMOTIONS

1 The *mettā-bhāvanā*: introduction

1. THE ANTIDOTE TO ANGER AND HATRED

If the potential for Buddhahood is within all of us, then the potential for *metta* certainly is.

The cultivation of universal love, or *mettā-bhāvanā*, is the antidote to anger or hatred. *Mettā*, *maitrī* in Sanskrit, is a response of care and warmth and kindness and love to all that lives, a totally undiscriminating well-wishing that arises whenever and wherever we come into contact with, or even think about, another living being.

The practice is divided into five stages. In the first stage we develop love towards ourselves, something that many people find very difficult indeed. But if one can't love oneself one will find it very difficult to love other people; one will only project on to them one's dissatisfaction with – or even hatred of – oneself. So we try to appreciate or enjoy what we can about ourselves. We think of a time when we were happy and content, or we imagine being in a situation where we would feel quite deeply happy being ourselves, and then we try to tune into that feeling. We look for and bring awareness to elements in our experience of ourselves that are positive and enjoyable.

Then, in the second stage, we develop *mettā* or love towards a near and dear friend. This should be someone of the same sex, to reduce the possibility of emotional projections – and it should be someone towards whom we have no erotic feelings, because the point of the practice is gradually to develop a focus on a very specific positive emotion that is closer to friendship than to erotic love. For the same sorts of reasons, this person should be still living and approximately the same age as oneself. So we visualize, or at least we get a sense of, this person, and we tune into the feeling they evoke in us, looking for the same response of benevolence that we have been developing towards ourselves. Usually this second stage is the easiest, for obvious reasons.

In the third stage, while maintaining the sense of an inner warmth, a sort of glow that we have generated towards ourselves and our good friend, we bring to mind in their stead a 'neutral' person. This is someone whose face we know well, whom we see quite often, but whom we neither particularly like nor dislike. It may well be someone who plays a more or less functional role in our life, like a postman, a shopkeeper, or a bank-clerk, or it may be someone we see regularly on the bus. We cultivate towards this neutral person the same benevolence and care that we naturally feel for our friend. It must be emphasized that what we are trying to develop in this type of practice is not a thought – not an *idea* – about developing a feeling, but the actual feeling itself. Some people may find this quite difficult to achieve – they feel dry and numb when they try to be aware of their emotions. It is as if their emotional life is so unconscious that it is simply unavailable to them to begin with. However, with time and practice it all starts to flow more easily.

In the fourth stage, we think of someone we dislike, even someone we hate – an enemy – someone who has perhaps done us harm or an injury – though to begin with it may be best to think of someone with whom we just don't get on. At the same time we deliberately leave our heart open to them. We resist the urge to indulge in feelings of hatred or animosity or resentment. It is not that we necessarily condone their behaviour; we may well need to criticize and even condemn it; but we stay in touch with a fundamental care for their welfare. In this way, by continuing to experience our friendly attitude even in relation to an enemy, our emotion starts to develop from simple friendliness into real *mettā*.

These first four stages are introductory. At the beginning of the fifth and last stage, we bring together in our mind all these four persons – self, friend, neutral person, enemy – and we cultivate the same love equally towards them all. Then we go a little further, we spread our vision a little wider, to direct this *mettā* towards all beings everywhere, starting with those close to us, either emotionally or geographically, and then expanding outwards to include more and more people, and excluding no one at all. We think of all men, all women, all ages, nationalities, races, religions; even animals, even beings, maybe, who are higher than human beings – angels and gods – and even beings higher than that: Bodhisattvas and spiritual teachers, whether Buddhist or non-Buddhist; whoever is eminent in good qualities. We may also expand out beyond our own planet, sending *mettā* to whatever beings may live in other parts of the universe, or in other universes. We develop the same love towards all living beings.

In this way we feel as though we are being carried out of ourselves in ever expanding circles; we forget ourselves, sometimes quite literally, becoming enfolded in an ever-expanding circle of love. This can be a very tangible experience for those who practise the *mettā-bhāvanā*, even after a comparatively short time. Not for everyone, of course: it is very much a matter of temperament. Some people take to it like ducks to water and enjoy it immensely within a matter of minutes. For others it is a struggle to get a fitful spark of *mettā* going, and the idea of radiating it seems a joke – they don't see how they are ever going to do it. But they can, and they do. In the end, with a bit of practice, a bit of perseverance, it happens, it arises. If the potential for Buddhahood is within all of us, then the potential for *mettā* certainly is.

From *What is the Dharma?* (1998, pp.190-2)

2. BUDDHISM: NEVER AS INDIVIDUALISTIC AS PEOPLE THINK

However important our subjective experience might be and however much we need to work on our own growth and development as individuals, the other-regarding aspects of Buddhist life are just as important.

Anyone can practise the *mettā-bhāvanā*. You don't have to be a scholar; you don't even have to be able to read and write. Some Theravādins, even today, tend to look down on the practice as being essentially for lay people. Even though the *Mettā Sutta* is one of the most frequently recited texts, it is not necessarily taken seriously any more than the commandment to love your neighbour as yourself is taken seriously by all Christians. Such is the effect of many hundreds of years of institutionalized religion. Although everyone might agree that loving-kindness is a good thing, it seems that the editors of the sutta did not see the need to spell out the importance of this other-regarding attitude.

But the further back you go in the history of the Buddhist tradition, the more significant this attitude seems to be. Buddhism, in other words, was never as individualistic as people sometimes think. It may well have been that the other-regarding aspect of the practice was second nature to the early Buddhists and hence did not receive so full an emphasis in the oral tradition. The *Satipaṭṭhāna Sutta* contains only the most perfunctory references to anything beyond one's experience of oneself, the fourfold establishment of mindfulness apparently having come to be regarded as an all-sufficient method.

It is easy to imagine how this might have been so. The Buddha's early followers would not have experienced the alienation from nature that characterizes the lives of so many people today. For them the natural world was ever-present, and the forest glades and parks in which the monks and nuns meditated were highly conducive to the cultivation of enthusiasm and *mettā*. These days we have to shut ourselves off from the clutter and disharmony of modern urban life, in which the cultivation of positive emotion is continually undermined, and in these circumstances we are likely to find it difficult to contact our feelings in meditation. A relatively integrated and balanced person practising the mindfulness of breathing will naturally and spontaneously feel goodwill towards other people, and for them the method of the *Satipaṭṭhāna Sutta* as it has come down to us will be quite sufficient. However, it is unlikely to be so for all of us. We have to make sure that we pay specific attention to the other-regarding aspects of spiritual practice, both for their own sake and because they involve the deeper energies that remain untapped by simple concentration. There is a dreadful lack of positivity in many people's lives, and to be positive is absolutely essential to spiritual life and growth. As modern Buddhists we need all the help we can get from devotional practices and the *mettā-bhāvanā*.

As well as meeting the needs of our own age, this approach has a sound basis in Buddhist thought. Whether or not they were part of the original teaching, the sutta's references to the external aspect of practice serve to remind us that the Buddhist path has a double emphasis. However important our subjective experience might be and however much we need to work on our own growth and development as individuals, the other-regarding aspects of Buddhist life are just as important. If your aim is ultimately to transcend the subject-object duality, you have to transcend the object just as much as the subject, the two being mutually dependent. The teaching of the Four Noble Truths is not just about getting rid of your own personal suffering; it is about getting rid of suffering itself, wherever it exists in the universe. As Śāntideva says in the *Bodhicaryāvatāra*, whether it is you that happens to be suffering or somebody else doesn't matter in the light of that aim. Any approach to the non-dual calls the whole idea of 'individualistic' versus altruistic motivation into question: the more we progress in our individual growth and development, the more positive and creative will be our effect on everyone with whom we come into contact.

From *Living with Awareness* (2003, pp.159-60)

3. METTĀ: ACTIVE BY DEFINITION

Metta is blissful, ecstatic, a naturally expansive desire to brighten the whole world, the whole universe, and universes beyond that.

Throughout the ancient scriptures of the Pāli canon it is made clear that the way to Enlightenment involves the cultivation of the emotions at every step, most often in the form of the four *brahma-vihāras* (the Pāli words can be translated as 'sublime abidings'). This series of meditations is designed to integrate and refine one's emotional experience so as to produce four different but closely related emotions: *mettā* or loving-kindness, *muditā* or sympathetic joy, *karuṇā* or compassion, and *upekkhā* or equanimity. *Mettā* is the foundation of the other three *brahma-vihāras*; it is positive emotion in its purest, strongest form. The way in which this positive emotion is to be cultivated is laid out in a text called the *Karaṇīya Mettā Sutta*.

Let us first examine the term *mettā* itself a little more closely. Of course, an emotion cannot be conveyed fully by verbal explanation, though poetry sometimes comes close to doing so. Then we have the added complexity of translation, as there is no exact English equivalent of the Pāli word *mettā*. But nonetheless, let us try to get at least a sense of the nature of this very special emotion.

An ardent good will
The Pāli word *mettā* (*maitrī* in Sanskrit) is related to *mitta* (Sanskrit: *mitra*), which means 'friend'. *Mettā* can thus be translated as friendliness or loving-kindness. Developed to its full intensity, *mettā* is a down-to-earth care and concern directed to all living beings equally, individu-

ally and without reservation. The unfailing sign of *mettā* is that you are deeply concerned for the well-being, happiness, and prosperity of the object of your *mettā*, be that a person, an animal, or any other being. When you feel *mettā* for someone, you want them to be not just happy, but deeply happy; you have an ardent desire for their true welfare, an undying enthusiasm for their growth and progress.

The friendliness of *mettā* doesn't necessarily involve actual friendship in the sense of a personal relationship with the person towards whom you are directing it. *Mettā* can remain simply an emotion; it doesn't need to become a relationship. Nevertheless, when you feel *mettā*, you will want to go out to other beings, to help them and express good will towards them in everyday, practical ways, and thus friendships can easily develop out of *mettā*. If two people develop *mettā* towards each other, their *mettā* is likely to blossom into a true friendship – a friendship with a difference. The same goes for an existing friendship into which an element of *mettā* is introduced. The *mettā* will tend to take the self-interest out of the friendship, so that it becomes something more than the cheery camaraderie or emotional dependency that is the basis of most ordinary friendships. Friendship infused with *mettā* becomes *kalyāna mitratā* – spiritual friendship – which flourishes not on the basis of what each party gets out of the relationship, but by virtue of the mutual desire for the other's well-being that flows unreservedly in both directions.

Thus there is no rigid distinction to be drawn between 'worldly' friendliness – or the worldly friendships that may come of it – and *mettā*. In its most highly developed form *mettā* is akin to Insight into the very nature of things (Insight with a capital I, as I sometimes say). But as a developing emotion it remains for a very long time more akin to ordinary friendliness. *Mettā* is friendliness as we know it, carried to a far higher pitch of intensity than we are used to. In fact, it is friendliness without any limit whatsoever. *Mettā* is present in the feeling you have for your friends, but it includes the intention continually to deepen and intensify whatever element of disinterested good will there is within it. Any friendly feeling, any friendship, contains the kernel of *mettā*, a seed that is waiting to develop when we provide it with the right conditions.

There is by definition something active about *mettā*. We call it a feeling, but it is more precisely described as an emotional response or volition rather than a feeling in the sense of a pleasant, unpleasant, or neutral sensation. (This distinction between a feeling and an emotion is a basic Buddhist teaching.) It includes the desire to act on our positive feelings, to do something practical to help the object of our *mettā* to be happy, to look after their welfare and encourage their growth and progress, so far as lies in our power. As well as friendliness, therefore, *mettā* includes the active, outgoing sense of good will or benevolence.

So why don't we translate *mettā* as love? Love, especially romantic or parental love, can have the intensity and strength to move mountains, and this vigorous concern is one of the most important characteristics of *mettā*. The problem with the word love is that it can be applied to almost anything that takes your fancy, including simple objects of appetite: you love your children or your boyfriend, but also the scent of orange blossom and many more things besides. *Mettā*, on the other hand, is directed only towards living beings.

Moreover, when it is based on appetite or possessiveness, love always has the potential to turn sour, because that appetite may be thwarted, that possession may be taken away. The feelings of jealousy or resentment that derive from romantic – that is to say, dependent – love can be more powerful than the most positive feelings of love in full bloom. Even parental love can turn bitter when it is felt to be unreciprocated – when one's child's ingratitude is 'sharper than a serpent's tooth', as Shakespeare's King Lear describes it.

An ecstatic energy
While being careful to differentiate *mettā* from all sorts of other emotions, we need not be so precious about it that we refine it out of existence. In the *Itivuttaka*, a collection of sayings from the Pāli canon, there is a passage in which the Buddha says of *mettā* that 'it burns and shines and blazes forth', suggesting that it is closer to incandescent passion than what we usually think of as 'spiritual' emotion. The English terms friendliness, loving-kindness, and good will don't come close to expressing this sort of intensity and expansive energy.

Indeed, the words we tend to use for the more spiritual emotions – that is, the more refined and positive ones – are usually understood in a rather weak sense. For example, the words refinement and purity, which refer to the quality of being free from impurities, and in that sense concentrated or powerful, suggest quite the opposite – something effete and diluted. When it comes to the more positive spiritual emotions, words seem to fail us. By contrast, our words for harmful and unrefined emotions – hatred, anger, jealousy, fear, anguish, despair – make a much more vivid and powerful impression.

Mettā, as I have described it, may seem pure but rather cool, aloof, and distant – more like moonlight than sunshine. We tend to have the same sort of idea of angels. These celestial beings, for all their purity, usually come across as rather weak and lacking in energy by comparison with devils, who tend to be both physically and spiritually powerful and full of vigour. Rather like the angelic realm, *mettā* or 'loving-kindness' is for most people ultimately just not very interesting. This is because it is difficult to imagine developing positive emotion to anything like the degree of intensity of one's experience of the passions. We rarely experience purely positive emotion that is also strong; if we do experience any really intense emotion, there is usually an element of possessiveness or aversion or fear in it somewhere.

It is not easy to get rid of emotional negativity and develop the strong and vigorous positive emotion that is true *mettā*. To do so, we have somehow to bring to the refined and balanced emotion of universal good will the degree of energy and intensity of lower, coarser emotions. To begin with, we have to acknowledge that this goes against the grain. If we are to do justice to *mettā* as an ideal, we have to be realistic about the kind of strong emotion we actually experience. It may seem strange, but this is the basis upon which a higher emotional synthesis may be achieved.

In our desire to be near the object of our passion, in our need to possess it and our longing for it to be part of us, we experience the energy and intensity that will eventually characterize our experience of *mettā*. Similarly, when we achieve the object of our passion we may for a brief moment experience the blissful calm, the balance and harmony, that also characterize the genuine *mettā* state. *Mettā* brings together the contrasting emotional reactions of dynamic energy and calm repletion into a single quality of emotion, completely transforming them in the process. Although, when it is fully developed, *mettā* is a feeling of harmony, both in oneself and with all beings, it also has a fiery, full-blooded, even ecstatic quality. Ecstasy literally means a sense of standing outside oneself, and this is how *mettā* can feel: it is marked by such an intensity of positive emotion that, when purely felt, it can carry you outside yourself. *Mettā* is blissful, ecstatic, a naturally expansive desire to brighten the whole world, the whole universe, and universes beyond that.

A rational emotion
Mettā is clearly a good thing in itself. But there is another reason to practise it, apart from its obvious merits as a very positive state of mind.

It makes clear sense in terms not only of subjective feeling, but also of objective fact. This is brought out very clearly by the philosopher John MacMurray. He distinguishes first of all between intellect and reason, designating reason as the higher, or integrated and integrating, faculty. Reason, he says, is that within us which is adequate to objective reality. When reason, thus defined, enters into intellect, you have an intellectual understanding that is adequate or appropriate to the objective situation, to reality. This definition of reason comes very close to the Buddhist understanding of *prajñā*, or wisdom.

Next, he goes on to point out that reason may be applied not only to intellectual understanding, but also to emotion. A brief example should illustrate the point. If, when you see a small spider, you fly into a panic, jump up, and run to the other end of the room, this is an irrational reaction: the emotion is not appropriate to the object, because the spider is not really harmful. But when reason, as defined above, enters into emotion, your emotional responses will be adequate or appropriate to the objective situation, the real situation.[8]

We can see *mettā* in the same way. Unlike emotions like mistrust, resentment, and fear, *mettā* is the appropriate and adequate response to other human beings when we meet or think of them. That is, *mettā* is a rational emotion. When we think of others the most reasonable response is that of *mettā*. We will wish all other beings happiness and freedom from fear, just as we wish ourselves these things. To understand that one is not so very different from any other human being, and that the world does not revolve around oneself, is an example of an intellectual understanding that is adequate to reality. To proceed from such a basis provides an appropriate foundation for our interactions with others.

Mettā is the norm or measure of our human response to others. This term 'norm' does not mean average or ordinary: it is closer in meaning to words like template or pattern or model. It is an ideal to which one seeks to conform. It is in this sense that Caroline Rhys Davids and other early western scholars of Buddhism sometimes translated Dhamma as 'the Norm'. For all its shortcomings, this translation does bring out the sense of the Buddha's teaching as being the template of the spiritual life. Likewise, in the true sense of the word normal, a normal human being is someone who accords with the norm for humanity, and a normal human response is the response to be expected from that positive, healthy, properly developed, balanced human being. *Mettā* is the response to be expected, as it were, from one human being encountering another.

There has to be that fellow feeling if we are to experience our humanity to the full. It is what Confucius called *jen* or human-heartedness: the appreciation of our common humanity, and the behaviour or activity that is based on that feeling.

Mettā is an emotional response to others that is appropriate to reality, and to that extent it has the nature of insight. That insight is likely to be fairly mundane to begin with – insight with a small i, one might say – but eventually it can become Insight with a capital I: *prajñā* or wisdom in the full sense. In other words, through the development of *mettā* you can eventually transcend the subject-object duality – and this is the ultimate goal of the wisdom-seeker.

The sublime abidings

In cultivating *mettā*, we are trying to develop what one might call the higher emotions, that is, those emotions that provide us with a means of bringing together our everyday consciousness and something more purely spiritual. Without such a possibility we have no way of approaching either the higher ranges of meditative experience – called *dhyāna* – or Enlightenment itself. It is as though *mettā* in the sense of an ordinary positive emotion stands midway between the worldly and the spiritual. First, we have to develop *mettā* in ways we can understand – just ordinary friendliness – and from there we can begin to take our emotions to a far higher degree of intensity.

As should now be clear, *mettā* in the true sense is different from ordinary affection. It isn't really like the love and friendliness we are used to; it is much more positive and much more pure. It is easy to underestimate *mettā* and think of it as being rather cosy and undemanding. It is difficult, after all, to conceive what it is really like; only when you have felt it can you look back to your previous emotional experience and realize the difference. The same goes for each of the four *brahma-vihāras*. When we begin to cultivate compassion, for example, we have to take whatever seed of it we can find within ourselves and help it to grow. As time goes by, our experience of it will deepen, and if our efforts to develop it are accompanied by a keen appetite for studying the Dharma and a willingness to bring our ideals into our everyday activity, we can come to experience a very pure, positive compassion which is quite different from what we usually understand by the term. In the same way the pure experience of sympathetic joy, *muditā*, is, because of its intensity, entirely different from the ordinary pleasure we might take in knowing that somebody else is doing well.

Upekkhā, equanimity, is a spiritual quality of a particularly elevated kind. There are traces of it in ordinary experience, perhaps in the tranquillity that can be found in nature, in the experience of standing alone in a forest when the air is still and the trees stand silently around you. But *upekkhā* goes far beyond even that kind of stillness; it has an intense, definite, even dynamic character of its own. And that is only to describe *upekkhā* in its mundane sense. The fully developed *brahma-vihāra* is peacefulness of an indescribably subtle and intense kind. Infused as it is by Insight, it is as though there is nothing but that peace. It is truly universal and utterly immovable. It is not just an absence of conflict; it has a magnitude and a solidity all of its own. Since it partakes of the nature of reality itself, no kind of disturbance can affect it in any way.

Through cultivating *mettā* you lay a strong foundation for the development of Insight. In other words, the more adequate to reality your emotional responses become, the closer you are to Insight. In the Mahāyāna this fully realized *mettā* is called *mahāmaitrī*. '*Mahā*' means 'great' or 'higher', and *maitrī* is the Sanskrit equivalent of *mettā*, so this is *mettā* made great, made into its ultimate, Enlightened form. *Mahāmaitrī* represents a Buddha's or Bodhisattva's response to the reality of sentient beings, though that response is not quite emotion as we understand it. For one thing, it is suffused with a clear and rational awareness. Sentient beings are suffering, so what reason can there possibly be not to feel sympathy? How can I not feel compassion? How can I not try to help them?

From *Living with Kindness* (2008, pp.11-19)

4. MAY ALL BEINGS BE HAPPY!

The technique of the metta-bhavana is based on the principle that the more strongly you feel metta towards one person, the easier it will be to experience the same emotion towards someone else.

> *May all beings be happy and secure, may their hearts be wholesome!* [9]

This phrase sums up the generosity, the sincere and heartfelt regard for others, in which the cultivation of *mettā* consists. We wish simply that beings may be happy and secure and that their hearts may be wholesome.

Khemino means secure, that is, free from danger, free from disturbance, free from fear. *Sukhi* simply means happy. *Sukhitattā* is translated here as 'their hearts be wholesome', but the suffix *atta* means 'self' or 'being', so the Pāli term literally means 'of happy self' or 'happy-hearted'. To be precise, the whole phrase could be translated as 'May they be those whose self is happiness.' This makes it clear that you want their happiness, their bliss, to be entirely within themselves, not dependent on external circumstances. In their essence they should be happy. Happiness is not something they should *have*, but something that they should *be*. It is happiness in this sense, together with the *mettā* that produces such happiness for oneself and wants it for others, that characterizes the spiritual community. If you don't find a greater degree of *mettā* and happiness in the spiritual community than you find in the world generally, it isn't really a spiritual community.

The wish expressed in this verse, that all beings may be happy and secure, is more than a vague hope. It introduces the section of the sutta that is concerned with the technique of meditating on loving-kindness, and thus designed to help us develop that aspiration for the well-being of others in a very real way. It is in the practice of formal meditation, when the mind is brought to bear directly on the mind, that *mettā* is cultivated most intensely.

There are many variations of the *mettā-bhāvanā* practice, including the one outlined by the Buddha here and a version contained in the *Visuddhimagga*, Buddhaghosa's fifth century exposition of the Buddha's teaching as found in the Pāli canon. But all the variations share their working method with other Buddhist contemplations and meditations for the cultivation of particular kinds of awareness or understanding. In the contemplation of impermanence, for example, you call to mind a number of things that can be identified as impermanent, some quite easily, others with a little more difficulty. This helps you to deepen a fundamental awareness of impermanence as being in the nature of all conditioned existence. The general methodology is the same in the case of the cultivation of *mettā*. Universal loving-kindness is not the easiest of emotions to cultivate, but there do exist various effective stage-by-stage ways of doing it.

The more or less standard way of practising the *mettā-bhāvanā* is in five stages, each of which takes your *mettā* deeper. First you generate *mettā* towards yourself, then towards a good friend, thirdly towards a 'neutral' person – someone whom you know but for whom you have no particularly strong feelings – and fourthly towards an 'enemy' – someone you find difficult for some reason. In the fifth stage you try to feel *mettā* for all four persons equally, then conclude the practice by radiating your *mettā* outward in wider and wider circles. The main thing is to get your *mettā* flowing; and bringing to mind the four different persons and then 'equalizing' the *mettā* seems to do that most effectively.

Thereafter, you can either go all round the world in your imagination, country by country, continent by continent, or you can take up the traditional method of dividing the globe into the four directions or quarters – north, south, east, and west – and radiating your *mettā* in each direction in turn. Another method is to consider variations on the sutta's different categories of beings – say the rich, the poor, the well, the sick, the young, the old, animals, birds, fish, and so on. You can try any combination of these approaches to the fifth and last stage. Once you have got the *mettā* flowing it doesn't really matter which method you follow, as long as you include everyone, indeed all beings, everywhere. The technique of the *mettā-bhāvanā* is based on the principle that the more strongly you feel *mettā* towards one person, the easier it will be to experience the same emotion towards someone else who is less obviously a candidate for your affection. By bringing all those categories of beings to mind, one after the other, you give yourself the best possible opportunity to amplify and deepen your experience of *mettā*.

To transform emotions we need to feel them, but in doing so we have to take into account an external reality with which our feelings and urges are not necessarily in touch. We should take care to do this especially if, as is likely, that external reality involves other people. No one can dispute that we feel what we feel. But we need to ask ourselves whether our feelings correspond to reality, whether they are adequate to the situation. From the authoritative way in which many people speak about how they feel, it would seem that they believe that invoking their feelings excuses them from considering objective reality, and that their feelings about it constitute a fully adequate assessment of the situation. Of course, no one should be allowed to get away with this. By all means have emotions – be as emotional as you like – but let them be true to the situation. Don't dress up peevishness or fury as clear thinking and straight talking. If the intellect is to support the emotions, the emotions have to return the favour and support the intellect.

When we are indulging in a subjective and perhaps negative emotion, we very often know in our heart of hearts that our response is not really true to the way things are. When we get angry with someone for a trivial reason, we know – if we are even just a little aware – that the situation does not justify that emotional reaction. When this happens, instead of thinking, 'Oh, I must get rid of my negative emotions,' ask yourself, 'What is the objective situation? Are my emotions appropriate to what is really going on?'

The harmful states that are the enemies of *mettā* can arise in many different forms, gross and subtle. If you are in a happy, upbeat mood and you mix with people who are not, they may want to share your happiness, but it is also possible that they will prefer to see you as being no less unhappy than they are themselves. They may resent your happiness and feel they have to resist it, even destroy it, as if it were an affront or a challenge to them. Perhaps they want you to show their misery a little respect, or suspect that you are feeling superior and smug. Humans are contradictory beings. How strange it is that we do not quite naturally and wholeheartedly wish others the deepest happiness and bliss! It's as if we feel that there is only so much happiness to go round and that if others are happy there is less happiness left over for us. Certainly people often feel they have a limited quantity of love, to be preserved for close friends and family. But of course the happiness of others cannot do us or them anything but good. Our task in practising the *mettā-bhāvanā* is to learn to extend our *mettā* beyond this small circle, bit by bit, until it encompasses all beings. In the five-stage version of the practice we begin very close to home indeed: with ourselves. This makes perfect sense. If, as we have seen, the enemy is within, it is within that the enemy needs to be tackled – indeed, needs to be transformed from an enemy into a friend.

From *Living with Kindness* (2003, pp.77-8, 81-2, 90-1)

2 The first stage of the *mettā-bhāvanā*: *mettā* for oneself

1. ALL IS NOT LOST

Feeling *metta* for oneself is the keystone of contentment – and when you are contented, you can maintain your equanimity no matter in what circumstances you find yourself.

You simply cannot develop much loving-kindness towards anyone else if you are on bad terms with yourself, or if you are uncomfortable with what you find out about yourself when all your external supports and comforts are removed. This is why in the first stage of the *mettā-bhāvanā* meditation you begin by cultivating *mettā* towards yourself. Most people find that this is not at all easy. Only too often the residue of hatred within us is directed towards ourselves.

The solution for many of us lies in our relationships with other people. One way to learn to feel *mettā* towards yourself is through becoming aware that someone else feels good will towards you, and in this way coming to feel it for yourself. This is rather tricky. When you don't have *mettā* for yourself, you experience an emptiness, a hunger, and you look for love from someone else to fill that void and make you feel better, at least for the time being. You clutch at love, demanding it as compensation for the unconditional acceptance that you are unable to give yourself. But this can only be a substitute for the real thing. You try to squeeze as much love as you can get out of others, even though that love is something only you can give yourself. It is as though you need them to do it for you. Being dependent on their love, you cannot care for their welfare except in relation to yourself; you cannot feel *mettā* for them because of your own neediness. For many people this is surely a depressingly familiar picture.

But if you find yourself in this situation, all is not lost. By calmly reasoning with yourself, you can begin to turn that misapprehension around, using the 'substitute' love shown by others to help you develop *mettā* towards yourself. If they can feel good will towards you, you can learn to feel the same positive emotion towards yourself, and thus gradually learn to stand on your own feet emotionally. Even though you may have begun with the assumption that you were not worth much, you learn from the other person that you were mistaken and thus begin to appreciate your own worth. You allow the knowledge that another person feels that you are genuinely worthwhile to percolate through your mind. You can learn to love yourself, in other words, by realizing that someone else really values you.

Feeling *mettā* for oneself is often simply a question of dropping the habit of self-criticism and allowing the objective reality of the situation to arise. Whatever you have done, however great your failings, the honest intention to develop *mettā* towards yourself and all living beings can be a source of happiness in itself. Feeling *mettā* for oneself is the keystone of contentment – and when you are contented, you can maintain your equanimity no matter in what circumstances you find yourself. It is a resilient, deeply-rooted state of peace, a source of energy and confidence. Contentment is, moreover, an inherently active state, with nothing of the resignation or passivity that is sometimes associated with it. The contented person is both inspired and an inspiration to others. It isn't a question of just gritting your teeth and grinding your way through some awful situation. There is a place for selflessness in Buddhism, but not for acquiescence in the face of ill-treatment or a grey and unrewarding environment. Human beings need food, light, space, periods of peace and quiet, human companionship, friendship, and so on. We are naturally geared to look for delight in the world. But if you are contented, you can find delight in the world around you, even when you don't have everything you would like.

The way to cultivate contentment is to bring a lighter touch to your experience. It is to enjoy what is enjoyable in it, but not to become attached to your pleasures, nor overwhelmed when things appear not to be going your way, in the knowledge that both the pleasures and the pains of life are impermanent. Contentment comes from being aware that as long as you depend on external objects for a sense of well-being, your happiness can never be guaranteed.

Developing *mettā* consists largely of finding contentment in oneself and living by that. Once it becomes a way of life, one stands a good chance of communicating that peace of mind to everyone with whom one comes into contact. Thus, the first stage of the *mettā-bhāvanā* practice flows naturally into the second.

From *Living with Kindness* (2008, pp.91-4)

2. WHY IS IT HARD TO LOVE ONESELF?

Human nature is very resilient and has very deep resources.

Q: Do people not love themselves because they've never really been loved – as babies, for instance?

Sangharakshita: This is what we are told, but in practice it doesn't seem always to work out like that. One does see people who don't seem to have received much care or love as babies, but who seem to love themselves and to get on well with others; and similarly one sees some people who seem to have received every care and attention when they were babies, but who have not turned out very well. So I don't think one can regard it as an absolutely decisive factor in all cases, though no doubt if you are brought up lovingly, it does help you to love yourself and to love others. I wouldn't say though that it's invariably the decisive factor, or that if you are brought up unlovingly you cannot possibly love yourself or others. Human nature is very resilient and has very deep resources.

Certainly as a mature adult, one should be able to love oneself. There should be contentment. You enjoy yourself, but not in a self-indulgent, narcissistic way. Your self-love, the pleasure you take in yourself, is a positive total experience of yourself, without dividing yourself into an object to be enjoyed and a subject that does the enjoying. There's just that healthy glow of joy in yourself, just as you can take delight in somebody else, as distinct from making them the object of your enjoyment. That is rather a different thing from just delighting in them for their own sake, for the sake of what they are. Delighting in them is more in the nature of an aesthetic experience. There's less of a grasping and grabbing. There's no desire to get your grubby little paws on the picture. You are quite content just to look at it, admire it, delight in it.

Q: Why do you think it is that people do find it so difficult to love themselves?

S: It's quite difficult to say. I think we must be careful from what samples, as it were, we are generalizing. We talk about people and human beings when usually we mean our own particular section of society in the West. I don't know that people have such difficulty loving themselves say in India or other such places.

Q: Do you think that if we're in a society that boosts and induces pleasures, that might cause lack of self-love?

S: Oh yes. If there's a habitual tendency to emphasize enjoyment of pleasures, this could discourage the development of *mettā* for self and others, yes. Perhaps one could even say that the extent to which people indulge in food and habits which disagree with their health is a measure of their lack of self-love.
From the second seminar on *Precepts of the Gurus* (1979, p.253)

3. NO ESCAPE FROM THE METTĀ-BHĀVANĀ

Usually people who have a lot of difficulty doing the *metta-bhavana* are not on good terms with themselves, and they may have to spend quite some time working out why.

I must say that after years of experience of teaching meditation in England I tend to place more and more importance on the *mettā-bhāvanā*. I regard this as quite crucial, and if anyone is having serious difficulty with it after two or three years, I really try to go into that with that person. What I usually find is that at the bottom of difficulty with the *mettā-bhāvanā* is self-depreciation. It's very difficult to have a positive attitude towards others if you don't have a positive attitude towards yourself. This seems to be the basis. You can't love others while you're hating yourself, or looking down on yourself. Usually people who have a lot of difficulty doing the *mettā-bhāvanā* are not on good terms with themselves, and they may have to spend quite some time working out why.

I don't allow people to escape from the *mettā-bhāvanā*. No! Some people try to tell me that they are full of love and kindness all the time, and they don't need to practise the *mettā-bhāvanā*, but I don't just accept that.

From Q&A in New South Wales (1979, p.13)

4. DO YOU GIVE YOURSELF WHAT YOU REALLY NEED?

It isn't easy to be kind to yourself.

> *Much more than yourself,*
> *I am concerned about the things you are doing.*[10]

Sangharakshita: This is the most significant thing that Milarepa says here. In other words, Milarepa is looking after Rechungpa better than Rechungpa is looking after himself. This is characteristic of the spiritual friend. He has your true interests at heart more than you do yourself sometimes. So he's a better friend to you than you are to yourself. Very often, you are your own worst enemy.

This reminds us of a very important point: that people often don't love themselves. They aren't really good friends to themselves. They don't have *mettā* for themselves. We know that when we do the *mettā-bhāvanā*, we start off with ourselves, and this certainly shouldn't be a formality, because good will towards ourselves is the basis of good will towards other people. But it isn't easy to be kind to yourself. Very often people are very unkind to themselves for one reason or another. They don't do what is best for themselves. It's easy to blame your parents for not doing their best by you, but what about you yourself? You yourself don't do the best that you can for yourself – how can you blame other people? They're no worse than you are yourself every day of the week, perhaps. Mother and Father perhaps didn't give you what you really needed, but do you give yourself what you really need? You blame your parents for not knowing the best way to bring you up, but do you yourself know the best way to bring yourself up now, to a higher level of maturity?

From a seminar on Milarepa's *Story of the Yak Horn* (1980, p.105)

5. DO YOU UNDERSTAND WHAT METTĀ MEANS?

I think sometimes people can't identify the state at all, because there isn't anything in their experience corresponding to it.

Q: I've heard a number of people say that they don't want to start the *mettā-bhāvanā* with themselves. They prefer to do the last stage first, because after that, they can feel *mettā* for themselves much more easily.

Sangharakshita: I am a bit suspicious. There are some people who like to play around with a practice or method, and not do it in the established way, almost to assert their independence and freedom. And I think one must be very cautious with people who claim that they can feel *mettā* towards somebody else but not towards themselves. They may have a feeling for somebody else, but that may not be *mettā* in the Buddhist sense; it may be quite projective or sentimental, or perhaps they may be a bit in love with them or something of that sort.

Q: But suppose they say it helps them feel *mettā* towards themselves?

S: It may be that they don't really understand what is meant by *mettā*. They may just identify what they think of as positive feeling as *mettā*. I think sometimes people can't identify the state at all, because there isn't anything in their experience corresponding to it. They might think *mettā* is liking someone very much, and that if you like someone very much, you have got *mettā* towards them; so they perhaps want to think first of someone that they like very much. But that isn't *mettā*.

From Study Group Leaders' Q&A on the Noble Eightfold Path
(1985, pp.34-5)

3 The second stage of the *mettā-bhāvanā*: *mettā* for a friend

1. ISN'T IT RATHER EXCLUSIVE?

A trusting and open friendship is an excellent context within which to bring our fears and antagonisms to the surface and begin to lay them aside.

In the second stage of the practice we call to mind a good friend and direct our *mettā* towards them. But if our ultimate aim is to feel *mettā* for everyone, doesn't this carry with it the danger that we will get this far and no further? Isn't it rather exclusive? Here we need to take a pragmatic approach. Although we can do our best to respond positively to everyone, if we are going to explore friendship in any great depth we can do this in practice with only a limited number of people. Friendship requires a level of trust and intimacy that can arise only through spending a lot of time with a person, becoming a significant part of their life and allowing them to become a significant part of our own. We need not think of our circle of friends as being exclusive; it is simply a fact that we cannot develop depth and intensity in our relationships without making a firm decision to deepen our friendships with just a few people. This remains true even when one has a great deal of spiritual experience. Perhaps after years of practice you will no longer experience partiality in your friendships, and will be able to be equally friendly towards anyone you happen to meet, taking life as it comes and relating to everyone equally warmly and with an equally genuine desire for their well-being. But with the best will in the world, your capacity for friendship will still be limited by the number of people with whom you are realistically able to come into contact.

Thus one can cultivate *mettā* as a universal and ever-expanding care for all beings, whether near or far, while at the same time enjoying substantial relationships of trust and affection with those with whom one has chosen to enter into a closer relationship. Committed friendship demands personal contact, and that requires both time and opportunity. But a friendly disposition is another matter. There is no limit to the number of people towards whom we can feel genuinely friendly, and with whom we could potentially be friends. And that friendliness, however strongly felt, can only improve the depth of our existing friendships.

Committed friendship obviously involves openness, and this calls for patience and empathy when what our friends reveal to us turns out to be difficult or even hurtful. A trusting and open friendship is an excellent context within which to bring our fears and antagonisms to the surface and begin to lay them aside. But if this is to happen, the friendship must have a spiritual dimension, because hatred is far more than the psychological phenomenon that we have been examining so far. Just as *mettā* is a spiritual rather than a psychological quality, so its antithesis, hatred, is not just a psychological state, but a spiritually destructive force operating within us.

It is perhaps not surprising that when we start to practise the later stages of the *mettā-bhāvanā* we can find the going difficult. We may even discover, if we are honest with ourselves, that despite our good intentions we do not as a rule experience much desire for the happiness and well-being of even our closest friends. A famous moralist once observed that 'in the misfortune of our best friends, we always find something which is not displeasing to us'. It would seem that even our friends represent some kind of threat. Perhaps this is why ex-lovers are able to do each other so much harm, and why the break-up of a marriage can be so acrimonious: both partners know each other's weak spots only too well. It is the person with whom you have fully lowered your guard who can do you the most damage if the relationship changes. It is all about power. If some misfortune befalls our friends and they are brought down a peg or two, or suffer some disappointment, they are made, as it were, less powerful in relation to us, and the threat is to some extent removed. Sometimes we cannot help finding pleasure in that, however fond of them we might be. If you are very observant and honest with yourself, you will notice these little flashes of pleasure from time to time at the adversity suffered by even your dearest friends. It is sad but true.

At the same time – and this is an encouraging thought – we don't have to act on our feelings. Our task is to experience our negative emotions and then find a way to change them. If we never get to know these emotions, if we indulge them unthinkingly or try to deny them, no transformation will be possible. One of the skills you need to develop as a meditator is therefore to learn to broaden the scope of your emotional awareness, without allowing completely unmindful expression of what you start to feel. This is by no means easy: it requires experience, patience, the clarity and kindness of your friends, and gentle persistence in the *mettā-bhāvanā* practice.

From *Living with Kindness* (2008, pp.94-6)

2. METTĀ AND EROTIC FEELINGS

It's not easy to follow a middle path between blocking and just allowing completely free, i.e. unmindful expression of what one feels.

Sangharakshita: In the second stage, it's best to choose someone (of either sex) with regard to whom you have definite feelings of friendliness and affection, without any erotic feelings. Of course, if your feelings of friendliness are invariably associated with erotic feelings, you're going to find it quite difficult to develop *mettā*, but usually there is somebody that you feel quite warmly towards without any mixture of erotic feelings. If there isn't, you're in a difficult position – not impossible, but a little difficult.

Q: I find that if I get to know somebody quite closely, erotic feelings arise quite naturally. It seems as though one can't separate them.

S: One undoubtedly has a reservoir of erotic feeling, and to some extent that erotic feeling becomes allied with feelings of affection, so that when the one arises, there is the tendency for the other to arise. Sometimes the erotic feeling comes first and the affection comes along later (or not), and sometimes the feeling of affection comes first and the erotic feeling arises later (or not). But in some cases you get both together.

Q: I'm not quite clear whether one can put somebody towards whom one does have some sort of erotic feeling in the second stage of one's *mettā* practice. Maybe one has quite a close friendship with them, with just an element in it of an erotic nature.

S: At best I think one could regard that as an intermediate stage. It is *mettā* that you are trying to develop, and that has *pema*, as it is called in Buddhism, the attachment kind of love, including sexual love, as its near enemy. You can't really experience the two together. You can experience both for the same person, but not at the same time.

Q: When we talk about this, it does seem to exclude whole classes of people from consideration, doesn't it?

S: In what way?

Q: Well, of people you consider friends, you can only choose those of your own age and sex.

S: But why is this limitation introduced?

Q: I understand wanting to get away from erotic or morbid feelings; but I don't know why you should restrict it to people in your own age group.

S: It's because people of an older generation may represent authority figures for you. You may have a fear of them, or experience a lack of openness with them, which is incompatible with the development of *mettā*. It isn't that you can't possibly have *mettā* towards someone very much older or very much younger – of course you can. But generally the difference in age does make that sort of difference.

Q: And having generated *mettā* towards easier targets, as it were, you can then extend it.

S: That's right, because you end up directing it towards all. Some traditions say specifically all men and women, for instance, because by the time you've reached that level, you transcend the level of sexual attraction and repulsion altogether, so you are able to extend the *mettā* literally towards everybody, whether they're older or younger, the same sex or a different sex, and so on. But you start with those people with regard to whom it is relatively more easy to develop *mettā*. Just as you wouldn't start off trying to develop *mettā* towards someone that you really hated – that would make it just too difficult – in the same way it would be difficult to start developing *mettā* towards someone to whom you had a powerful sexual attraction.

Q: So really in the second stage one shouldn't choose anybody to whom one is sexually attracted, whether of the same sex or the opposite sex.

S: Yes, this is the essence of the matter. It may be a question of retreating towards the easier target, so that you can then go forward to deal with the person with whom you have greater difficulty. Or you may decide to face it out. If you do, then of course what is important is that you note the sexual feelings that arise. You recognize them but you go on trying to cultivate *mettā* towards that person. You don't indulge feelings of anger or hatred or sexual feelings. You just recognize them. You note that they're there and go on trying to develop *mettā*. If you're feeling particularly heroic, you could do that. But if you feel it's too much for you, just retreat temporarily from the situation and strengthen your *mettā* towards some other person. Then, when you are relatively full of *mettā*, go back to the first person and you'll find it more easy to feel *mettā* towards them rather than some unskilful emotion.

It's not easy to follow a middle path between blocking and allowing completely free, i.e. unmindful expression of what one feels. If there are any feelings for any particular person of which you're not conscious, it is better to become conscious of them even though that may create difficulties for you for the time being. But eventually you have to go beyond that.

From a seminar on the *Karaṇīya Mettā Sutta* (1978, pp.90-3)

3. CAN THE BUDDHA BE YOUR FRIEND?

I think it probably would be better to choose an ordinary friend and keep the Buddha for the puja.

Q: Do you think it is possible to choose the Buddha as your friend in the second stage of the *mettā-bhāvanā*?

Sangharakshita: You could, I suppose, but I think you have to be rather careful here. The more appropriate emotion is faith or reverence. Just as *mettā* becomes *karuṇā*, compassion, when it encounters those who are less fortunate than you are, in the same way, *mettā* becomes faith and reverence and devotion when it encounters those who are more developed than you are. You still have to develop *mettā* first. If you have great difficulty thinking of any ordinary friend, you could choose the Buddha but you should be careful that isn't an escape from facing up to your feelings about people. I think it probably would be better to choose an ordinary friend and keep the Buddha for the puja.

From a seminar on *The Door of Liberation* (year unknown, p.291)

4 The third stage of the *mettā-bhāvanā*: *mettā* for a 'neutral person'

1. LOVE THAT BREAKS OUT

Just as the sun is not selective in the giving of its light and warmth, when you feel metta, you don't choose its recipients or keep it for those you deem worthy of it.

In the third stage of the *mettā-bhāvanā*, you direct *mettā* towards someone you know hardly at all, someone who has only a very minor walk-on part in your life – perhaps the man who sells you your newspaper in the morning, or the woman you pass in the park when you're walking your dog. To see the point of this stage, we need to examine our emotional life a little further. Although we may not like to think so, in the usual run of things our experience of what we imagine to be positive emotion is likely to be sketchy and intermittent. Whether or not we are aware of it, this is partly because we tend to limit our affection to those we deem deserving of it, usually those who are likely to return the favour. But the chief characteristic of *mettā* is that it is entirely without self-interest. It is not possessive or selfish, and has nothing to do with appetite. This is why 'friendliness', although it may seem insipid, translates *mettā* more accurately than 'love'. Being applied only to other sentient beings, and having an inherently outgoing quality, friendliness is more likely to be relatively free of self-interest.

I say 'relatively' because a great deal of what we think of as friendliness and even friendship involves a need for something in return. When we give affection we want something back, and when a little intensity develops in our friendships we can end up with a dependency that has something of the nature of an unspoken contract. The Pāli term for this mixture of honest affection and an expectation of some return is *pema* (the Sanskrit is *prema*). It is usually translated as 'affection' in the limited sense of ordinary human fellowship, and it is contrasted with *mettā*, which is the corresponding, more spiritual emotion.

Pema is often understood to be the natural affection and good will that arises within the family group, and it is undoubtedly a positive emotion. Indeed, it is the cement that holds social life together. Expressing warmth and affection to your family members and close friends is a very good thing. Through your affection for them you learn to set aside your own narrow self-interest and get a sense of yourself as being involved with other people in a real and tangible sense. But your family, your circle of friends, the supporters of your football team, the members of your ethnic or cultural group, are only a tiny fraction of the universe of living beings. What might it be like to feel the same warmth towards everyone you meet, whether known to you or not? This may seem a naive dream, a well-meaning fantasy that could never be realized, but before we give up the whole idea, we could consider the implications of one of the essential tenets of Buddhism – that in reality there is no separate self, and that we are related, directly or indirectly, to everyone else. If we reflect on this, we will come to see that unlimited friendliness is not a dream at all. It is we who are in a dream when we imagine that only our close ties with friends and family are important, while relationships between other families and other groups are of little or no consequence.

When we look at things in this way, we have to admit that our relationships contain more than a little self-interest. Indeed, the very warmth of our relationships with family members and close friends can be what makes the rest of the world seem cold, unfriendly, and uninteresting. Through our relationships we are seeking security; we want things to stay the same; we want the relationships we build to provide a refuge against the difficulties and uncertainties of life, thus guaranteeing the stability and security of our own small, inward-looking world. We need those people, those relationships, if we are not to feel terribly alone and vulnerable. We are, in other words, desperately attached to them, an attachment that is entirely bound up with *pema*.

Pema is essentially a social emotion, concerned with preserving the human group, rather than with transcending boundaries and reaching out to all life however it manifests. If *pema* is love or friendliness that expresses attachment, *mettā* is love or friendliness that is not self-referential at all. Both are positive in their own way, but *mettā* is positive in the spiritual sense whereas *pema* is a more worldly emotion. *Pema* is love and affection for others in the ordinary, human way, ranging from erotic desire to a simple warm fellow feeling, a sense of human solidarity with others.

Pema provides a useful contrast with *mettā*, as the two words are close enough in meaning to be confused with each other, so that *pema* is sometimes identified as the 'near enemy' of *mettā*. *Mettā* is much more than the warmth of good fellowship, or a gregarious feeling of togetherness. Unlike *pema*, *mettā* includes no attachment, no self-interest, no need even to be near its object, much less to possess it. *Mettā* is not necessarily a reciprocal emotion. As already mentioned, you can cultivate *mettā* or friendliness towards someone without that person knowing about it – indeed, without your having any connection with them at all. You can even express your *mettā* in practical ways – by putting in a good word for someone, say, or helping them financially – without there being any personal contact between you.

Ordinarily we feel affection more or less exclusively. Indeed, the more intense the affection, the more exclusive it tends to be. When we use the word 'love' to describe our strong feeling for someone, the someone in question is usually just that – some one: a single individual. It is a strong partiality for that one person over anyone else. But when you feel *mettā*, a strongly developed feeling of good will towards one person will tend to spread more and more widely. Being without self-interest, *mettā* is impartial. Just as the sun is not selective in the giving of its light and warmth, when you feel *mettā*, you don't choose its recipients or keep it for those you deem worthy of it. *Mettā* is love that breaks out of the narrow confines of self-referential selectivity, love that does not have a preference, non-exclusive love.

If we are going to use the word 'love' at all, we could describe *mettā* as disinterested love. It is of course 'interested' in the sense of 'concerned' – it is not *un*interested – but it is *dis*interested in the sense that when you feel it you have no thought of what you might get back in return. There are a number of English words that include a quality of disinterested love or appreciation in their meaning. Philosophy, for example, is the love of wisdom for its own sake, not for what is to be gained from it. Wisdom is essentially useless. Whatever practical purpose it might have is incidental to what it is really about: the direct realization of the truth of things. Similarly, *mettā* is concerned with its object purely for the sake of that object in itself.

There is in *mettā* no desire to impress, or to ingratiate oneself, or to feather one's nest, or to gain favours. Nor is there any expectation of emotional reciprocity. Being friendly or offering friendship to someone in the spirit of *mettā* is something you do for their sake, not just for yours. *Mettā* is not erotic love, or parental love, or the love that seeks the admiration and esteem of a particular social group. It is a cherishing, protecting, maturing love which has the same kind of effect on the spiritual being of others as the light and heat of the sun have on their physical being. We really can learn to love in this way. This is the value, and the challenge, of the third stage of the *mettā-bhāvanā*.

From *Living with Kindness* (2006, pp.96-100)

2. DRIFTING AWAY FROM THE PRACTICE

I sort of wake up and realize I haven't developed any *metta* at all …

Q: I frequently find that when I get to the neutral person, I sort of wake up and realize I haven't developed any *mettā* at all, and it's very difficult to get started with that person. Do you think one should persevere anyway, or should you maybe try to hop back a couple of stages and build up *mettā* from there?

Sangharakshita: Usually it's said that if you find difficulty with a further stage of whatever meditation practice you're doing, you should go back and do the earlier stages, to strengthen the basis, as it were, then go forward when you feel you can. One does this with the mindfulness of breathing too.

I have noticed a tendency over the years for people to drift away from the *mettā-bhāvanā*. They learn both methods but then they find that while they get on pretty well with the mindfulness of breathing, and get quite concentrated, they find the *mettā* so much more difficult that in the end they drop it altogether and just carry on with the mindfulness of breathing. Well, sometimes it's fine just to concentrate on one single meditation practice but I think in the case of most people it's advisable to cultivate both, and if you do give more importance to one, probably

it should be to the *mettā-bhāvanā*. That's the one that most people need to cultivate more.
    From a (2nd) Men's Order/Mitra event at Vinehall (1981, pp.40-1)

3. THE CHARMS OF THE NEUTRAL PERSON

They may be a very worthy person who would be worthy of your friendship, but they have no very obvious charm or attractiveness, at least as far as you are concerned.

Q: We are usually mindful that we should not choose for the second stage a person who we find sexually attractive. Could that apply also to the stage of the neutral person?

Sangharakshita: It is unlikely that you will put in the stage of the neutral person someone to whom you could easily be sexually attracted. I think it is usually someone you think of as nondescript, not very appealing, even drab; they may be a very worthy person who would be worthy of your friendship, but they have no very obvious charm or attractiveness, at least as far as you are concerned, so you tend not to have any particular reaction towards them at all.
    From Study Group Leaders' Q&A on the Noble Eightfold Path (1985, p.38)

5 The fourth stage of the *mettā-bhāvanā*: *mettā* for an 'enemy'

1. GETTING A GRIP ON METTĀ

In this stage of the practice you try to make that person the object of your metta not on account of anything they have done or not done but simply because they are there.

To practise the *mettā-bhāvanā* effectively we need to learn to detach the emotion of which we have become aware from the person towards whom we are feeling it. Success in the meditation depends in large measure on how pliant one's mind can be in this respect. You probably won't be able to do it straightaway; it takes quite a lot of practice. The challenge is particularly great in the fourth stage of the meditation, when we try to maintain our feelings of loving-kindness in the 'presence' of someone who is perhaps intent on doing us harm.

The method of the *mettā-bhāvanā* is systematically to coax the habitual reactive mind into the first glimmerings of positive emotion by concentrating one's thoughts and emotions on real individuals, with all their virtues and failings. However, sooner or later you will have to detach the emotion from these particular individuals. *Mettā* is essentially objectless, and in the course of the practice it should come to depend less and less on the nature of the object and more and more on itself. This is what it means to say that *mettā* is ultimately impersonal. It is no less an emotion, but it is less dependent on particular persons. You feel the same *mettā*, the same emotional response, towards the so-called enemy as towards the so-called friend.

This does not mean eradicating the particularity of our emotions. *Mettā* expresses itself in different ways according to the differing nature and degrees of intimacy of our different relationships. What *mettā* does is infuse our positivity with the heightened energy that previously arose when we felt anger or hatred towards an enemy. The *mettā-bhāvanā* is fundamentally a practice of transformation, not annihilation; the aim is not so much to obliterate our negative emotions as to redirect them. There is energy in anger, and if we are to attain the ultimate good – Nirvāṇa – all our energies, all our emotions, positive and not so positive, have to be released in the direction of that goal. Rather than suppress negative emotions when we can and allow them to run riot when we can't, the aim is to transform the energy in them and integrate it into the existing stream of our positive emotion, thereby making that positive stream of emotion stronger.

Here again there is an important role for reflection, as Śāntideva advises in his *Bodhicaryāvatāra* or 'Guide to the Bodhisattva's Way of Life'. Reminding us of the central Buddhist insight of conditionality, he points out that people who do us harm do so on the basis of conditioning factors over which they have no control: 'A person does not get angry at will, having decided "I shall get angry."'[11] Anger and hatred arise owing to factors outside our conscious control, and the anger with which we respond to anger is also irrational. There is no justification for anger, and no point to it. Anger and hatred are states of suffering that can lead only to further distress, so there is nothing to be gained from perpetuating them. Śāntideva goes on to encourage us to reflect on the painful consequences of our anger or hatred, and to inform our emotional life with the only rational conclusion to draw from these reflections: that unhelpful emotions should be abandoned for more positive ones. This is the only effective way to help beings, including ourselves.

Such reflections may help a little, but our emotions are rarely susceptible to reason alone. It is relatively easy to acknowledge that we feel ill will, and certainly easy to talk about turning it into love, but it is not at all easy actually to bring about the transformation. If the kind of reasoning that Śāntideva proposes is to be successful, we need to ensure that all our emotions are lined up behind our spiritual aspirations. If they aren't, anger and hatred, for example, will make their presence felt in a way that obstructs those aspirations (in the guise of 'righteous indignation', for example). We may then find that we simply cannot get started on feeling *mettā* for our enemy.

It is an unfortunate fact that our emotional life very often tends to lag some way behind our intellectual development. We can analyse our situation indefinitely, but without a fair degree of self-knowledge our feelings will tend to remain tied to their old familiar objects in an ever-recurring cycle of craving and dissatisfaction. Directed thinking is important – indeed, essential – but we also need to find a way of working directly on and with our emotions. Our task is to unlock the energy uselessly tied up in harmful feelings and channel it into positive and productive mental states.

If the object of your attention brings up intensely negative feelings, it can be difficult to get any grip on *mettā* at all. Positive emotion no longer seems even a remote possibility; just for that moment you seem to have forgotten what *mettā* might even feel like. If you are beset by strong feelings of resentment, anger, jealousy, or craving, you may feel they are just too much for you to handle at present. If you have presented your emotional positivity with too great a challenge, it may be best to withdraw temporarily and retrace your steps, dwelling for a while longer on someone towards whom your feelings are more straightforwardly positive before returning to this most difficult but vital stage.

We need to be able somehow to grapple with the very idea we have of this person as an 'enemy'. We have probably designated them as such because they have upset us in some way, and now we are maintaining this fixed view of them by dwelling on the injury they have done to us. The solution is simple: concentrate on their more attractive qualities. In order to draw your attention away from someone's irritating habit of always arriving late, for example, you can direct it towards some mitigating factor you have overlooked: they may be turning up late because they are devoted to looking after their young family, for example. You focus on their positive human qualities, or at least the problems that they face. At the very least, you can reflect that they are not always performing injurious actions, or perhaps not towards everybody. In this way you learn to paddle against the stream of your ill will.

You can even begin to like your enemy, just a little. But while such a shift in your feelings is a very positive development, it should not be taken for the arising of *mettā* itself. Liking someone is not the same as feeling *mettā* for them. Our usual attitude towards someone perceived to have harmed us – which is what an 'enemy' is by definition – is to feel hatred towards them. But in this stage of the practice you try to make that person the object of your *mettā*, not on account of anything they have done or not done but simply because they are there. Irrespective of whoever is around, or whether there is anyone around at all, you are aiming to be entirely equanimous in your attitude of loving-kindness. You are not so much feeling love for your enemy as simply being undisturbed in your attitude of *mettā* towards all beings by the thought of someone who has done you an injury.

Although *mettā* is in a sense the rational response to reality, in the end it is produced without cause or justification. When we practise the *mettā-bhāvanā*, our feelings of good will towards beings do not arise on account of anything those beings may have said or done. We simply wish them well. If it were otherwise, *mettā* would be no more than a psychological thing, coming and going in dependence on whom we bring to mind at any one time. As a spiritual quality, *mettā* is not bound by any kind of stipulation or qualification or condition. It is not meted out according to whether beings deserve it or not.

According to Buddhism, there is no entity corresponding to an unchanging self underlying all that we do and say and experience. If there were, then one might approach the fourth stage of the *mettā-bhāvanā* with the thought that underneath all the bad that one can see in someone, there is something good that is still lovable. To view a person as essentially good despite their unskilful actions suggests there is an underlying person there to begin with. Buddhism, on the other hand, sees a person not as an entity that can become sullied by unskilfulness and then cleansed of impurities, but as the sum total, and nothing more than the sum total, of their actions, bodily, verbal, and mental.

If we are trying to direct loving-kindness towards somebody of whose actions we do not approve, what is it, then, towards which we are really directing our attention? As far as Buddhism is concerned, a person is not any kind of fixed identity. There is no underlying 'self' that is somehow capable of performing actions while remaining essentially unchanged. Those actions are precisely what that human being ultimately is. Hence it is self-contradictory to speak, for example, of hating a person's actions but not the actual person, because the person includes the action that you have just said you condemn. The villain of Shakespeare's *Measure for Measure*, Angelo, who asks with rhetorical sarcasm, 'Condemn the fault and not the actor of it?' is quite right. It cannot be done.

In this penultimate stage of the *mettā-bhāvanā*, you deliberately call to mind someone who has hurt you, not in order to change your opinion of them but to test and strengthen your attitude of *mettā*. If your *mettā* is genuine, it will not be disturbed even by your thinking of a so-called enemy. Taking in their bad qualities with their good qualities, you direct *mettā* to the person as a whole, good and bad.

This is very much the sense in which we speak of the limitless compassion of the Buddhas towards living beings. A Buddha's compassion – which is the response of *mettā* to suffering – does not emerge in the form of isolated acts of loving-kindness that you somehow earn by your devotion or some other 'deserving' action. A Buddha has the same attitude of *mettā* towards beings whatever they do or don't do, because that *mettā* is beyond time and space; it exists both before and after those beings committed any action or exhibited any quality, skilful or unskilful. This is not to say that Buddhas condone unskilfulness, only that their *mettā* is unaffected by it and they do not threaten to withdraw their limitless care and concern. Indeed, as it is limitless, you will not get more of it by behaving better. A Buddha's *mettā* is rather like that of a loyal friend whose attitude does not change even though you have done something to upset them. You may apologize to your friend and beg forgiveness, but they will continue to feel – and perhaps say – that there is nothing to forgive.

The *mettā* of the Buddhas is unwavering; they are entirely compassionate, before, during, and after whatever might have taken place. For this reason we need never approach them with the slightest fear or apprehension. To sit in judgement forms no part of a Buddha's business. Nor therefore is there any need for us to ask for their forgiveness or mercy. Buddhas do not, after all, administer the law of karma. Conditionality will go on operating, come what may, and nobody, not even a Buddha, can save us from experiencing the consequences of our foolish actions.

The unconditional love of a Buddha takes place on a plane altogether beyond such concepts as 'enemy' or 'person' in the way these terms are generally understood. You can love someone unconditionally, as a Buddha does, only in so far as you believe, unconditionally, that they can change, however apparently hopeless the state they are in. This means being unconditionally willing to help them evolve, irrespective of the point at which they have now arrived. If they have abused you, you fully take in what they have done and still you wish them well. Truly loving someone does not mean seeing them as perfect or their moral weaknesses

as unimportant. Quite the opposite: the more you care about someone the more you are concerned for their spiritual welfare. With the warm and unflinching gaze of *mettā* you see them as they are, warts and all.
From *Living with Kindness* (2006, pp.100-106)

2. TRY NOT TO FEEL DISCOURAGED

This is why cultivating *metta* is such a challenge. It is an attempt to reverse our usual way of experiencing the world and ourselves.

A great deal of our latent tendency towards ill will is likely to stem from our early conditioning. It is easy to recognize people whose early life has been comparatively untroubled, as they are relatively straightforward, open, and receptive. Others are much more suspicious, reserved, and wary, and this may be a result of their early experience. It seems that many of us have a certain residual resentment, or even hatred, that lingers from our childhood and tends to attach itself to objects and people as we make our way through adult life.

Sometimes these negative feelings are found to be attached to close relatives, if we are prepared to look for them there, although many people are shocked at the idea of feeling animosity towards their nearest and dearest. When such feelings do come out into the open, the resulting family disturbance can be particularly painful. If you think there is no one you dislike, it might be revealing to try putting one of your relatives in the fourth stage of the *mettā-bhāvanā*, in which *mettā* is directed towards an 'enemy', and see what happens. If we live with someone, or work closely with them, or share a circle of friends with them, and have no particular reason to dislike them, we often fail to realize that, all the same, we do dislike them. It seems to be a sort of rule that there will always be someone we dislike among our acquaintances or colleagues. When that person leaves, another person with whom we have previously been on good terms may well take their place, to be the next object for the residue of hatred that is so difficult to shift from the human psyche. This is why removing someone from a situation of conflict rarely solves the problem in the long run.

We should try not to feel discouraged by all this. It is true that to wake up in the morning with an overwhelming wish for the happiness and bliss of absolutely everyone is highly unusual even if one aspires to do so. Even after a great deal of intense effort in meditation, a tidal wave of universal love is unlikely to sweep us off our feet and carry us away. We shouldn't really be surprised. In trying to cultivate *mettā* we are swimming against the current of our human nature as it has evolved over millions of years from its animal origins. Sometimes we simply feel like a rest. As we struggle against the stream of our habitual negativity, *mettā* seems just too much to ask of ourselves. The tendency to feel hatred for others, even for people who pose no threat, comes all too easily to us. It is a basic human trait. It should be no surprise that the world is so full of conflicts, wars, and fatal misunderstandings. As beings with reflexive consciousness, with a sense of ourselves as continuous identities moving through time, our defences are naturally directed against the threat of attack, not just upon our bodies but also upon our fragile sense of who we think we are. This is why cultivating *mettā* is such a challenge. It is an attempt to reverse our usual way of experiencing the world and ourselves.

From *Living with Kindness* (2006, pp.87-8)

3. IS METTĀ UNCONDITIONAL LOVE?

Loving someone does not mean seeing them as perfect.

Sangharakshita: Broadly speaking, Buddhism sees a person as the sum total of his actions, bodily, verbal and mental, so it is self-contradictory to speak of hating a person's actions but not hating the person himself.

Q: One could imagine a situation in which someone you love very much does something of which you strongly disapprove, but you still continue to love them very much.

S: Yes, you love them, but what does one mean by love? You wish them well, which means that you wish that they may not commit that offence again. But you don't regard that offence as not an offence just because you love them. Loving someone doesn't mean seeing them as perfect.

Q: There's this whole notion of unconditional love as a positive thing.

S: Unconditional love does not mean seeing whatever somebody does as worthy of love. If one can speak in terms of loving anyone unconditionally, it can only be that you believe in the unconditioned possibility of their changing. Perhaps one should distinguish between love which is unconditional psychologically and love which is unconditional metaphysically. You can't really love someone unconditionally on the psychological level; on that level they don't deserve it. You can only love them unconditionally on a metaphysical plane. But that is quite meaningless for ordinary purposes, so perhaps it is unwise even to mention it.

Loving someone unconditionally doesn't mean unconditionally approving of whatever they do, good, bad or indifferent; it means being unconditionally willing to help them mature spiritually regardless of the point at which they are at this present moment.

Q: I think people sometimes get an impression that that is what *mettā* is about. I've definitely heard people expressing the view that in the fourth stage you should consider that underneath what you see as bad there's something good that is lovable.

S: But the Pāli canon's description of the *mettā-bhāvanā* says no such thing. The danger of the approach you describe is that you will transform the *mettā-bhāvanā* from an emotional exercise into a psychological exercise.

Q: With someone in the fourth stage of the *mettā*, you tend to be thinking of them in terms of the bad acts that they have done. So what you have to do is to posit a possibility of ...

S: No, I think that would be a concession. You arrive at the beginning of the fourth stage in a state of *mettā*. You then conjure up the image of someone who is your enemy, as he is called: that is to say, he has done you some injury. But even the thought of that person who has done you the injury is not able to disturb your attitude of *mettā*, as normally it would. In other words, you persist in your attitude of *mettā*. You don't allow the image of that person who has done you an injury to give rise to thoughts of anger and vindictiveness, as normally it might do. You don't think about more positive aspects of his character; you can do that as a concession, but that isn't really the full practice of that fourth stage.

Q: Except that if you are in a state of *mettā* you are more likely to see him in terms of his potential than in terms of his actuality.

S: Well, that's another point. In the context of the practice, you are thinking of an enemy – that is to say, someone who has done you an injury. That is the aspect that you are directing your attention to. Why are you doing it? To test and strengthen your attitude of *mettā*, so that it is not disturbed even by such an image.

It is true that you can consider other aspects of the same person's character, but that is not this particular practice. In this practice, you are considering that he has done you an injury, which normally you would resent; but you have now arrived at a state where you do not resent it.

Q: In that case, I think the *mettā-bhāvanā* is often incorrectly taught. It's normally talked about in terms of trying to see that person in a more positive light.

S: Well, one can practise it in that way, but that is a provisional and one might even say imperfect practice. Maybe one does have to do that to begin with. If, as a result of doing the other three stages, you haven't developed a state of genuine *mettā*, you can't really practise the fourth stage fully, so you may have to practise it in a quite provisional manner by reflecting that that person isn't always performing injurious actions, at least not to everybody.

Q: Buddhaghosa recommends that you try out the fourth stage, and if you can't do it you retreat back to the stage where your *mettā* is firm, and then you push forward again. Presumably you could do that within the fourth stage by thinking of good qualities, and then push forward from there.

S: Yes, even to the extent that you can think of the injury that has been done you and still have your *mettā* not affected.

Q: So you just contemplate the bad things that you think of him as having done to you, rather than trying to develop any positive feelings towards him?

S: Well, the positive feeling is already there, inasmuch as the *mettā* is already there, towards him as well as to anybody else who happens to come within your purview. The *mettā* has already been developed, and it is, if anything, strengthened by surviving under those conditions.

From a seminar on *The Duties of Brotherhood in Islam* (1983, pp.202-4)

4. DIRECTING METTĀ

The problem ought to die of boredom because it has been talked about so much.

When you do the *mettā-bhāvanā*, do you just discharge a quantity of *mettā* into the air and hope that some of it will do some good somewhere? Is it not possible to direct one's *mettā*? Some years ago I experimented with this. If I had had any little misunderstanding with anybody, I used to try directing *mettā* towards that person, and I always found that the next time I met them, a change seemed to have taken place. The sceptic might say that the change was in me; but I don't think it was entirely in me. I did observe, or at least I thought I observed, some change in the person towards whom I had directed the *mettā*, presumably brought about by the *mettā*. So this does suggest that *mettā* can be directed.

There is a more general point that emerges here. When people have misunderstandings, or they have difficulties in getting on with other people, they tend to think in terms of talking it out, talking it through, even talking it to death – the problem ought to die of boredom because it has been talked about so much. But one could, either instead or by way of supplement, do more *mettā-bhāvanā* – saturate that person in *mettā*, and see whether that makes a difference. It ought to.

From discussion in Tuscany on the Noble Eightfold Path (1982, pp.458-9)

5. A TINGE OF DISLIKE

Very often we don't realize that we dislike someone.

Q: Sometimes people say that they can't think of someone to put in the fourth stage; they don't happen to feel animosity towards anybody at that particular time, which seems fair enough. Perhaps one could just put in another neutral person?

Sangharakshita: I sometimes say: 'If you really think there is no one that you dislike, put a close relation in the fourth stage!' – because sometimes there are disguised negative feelings in the case of close relations. Or you can put some historical person there, or some political figure that you don't like. A very left-wing person could choose a very right-wing politician. Mrs Thatcher, for example!

Q: Oh, that's OK, is it?

S: Well, why not? Surely one wishes her well, even if one does disagree with her policies?

Q: I kind of thought that someone like Margaret Thatcher had become such a figure that she wasn't really a person any more to people, she was just a big projection.

S: Well, perhaps putting her in the *mettā-bhāvanā* would help you to withdraw your projections! Obviously, one doesn't know her personally, one only forms an impression from what one reads, but a negative feeling is a negative feeling, whether directed towards an actual person or only what you think is an actual person. It still needs to be withdrawn or resolved. So you could do that. Or someone who is very right-wing could direct *mettā* towards one of the more extreme Union leaders.

Q: A friend once told me that when he first learned the *mettā-bhāvanā*, his attitude was that he had no enemies. After a week, he discovered he did have one or two. And after a month, he realized he had a dozen!

S: I think very often we don't realize that we dislike someone. We don't allow it to come to full consciousness. If you live in a community, you can ask yourself whether there isn't someone in the community that you dislike, at least slightly. If it is a reasonably large community, I am sure there is almost always someone that you have slightly negative feelings towards or that you don't particularly want to be friends with. Well, you could put them in the fourth stage. You're certainly not neutral with regard to them; there is a tinge, at least, of dislike, or a tinge almost of repulsion on a quite basic level.

From Study Group Leaders' Q&A
on the Noble Eightfold Path (1985, pp.35-6)

6 The fifth stage of the *mettā-bhāvanā*: *mettā* for everyone

1. THE WHOLE WORLD OF BEINGS

One would do well to draw up a list of one's own prejudices to make the list as inclusive as possible.

> *Whatever living beings there be: feeble or strong, tall, stout or medium, short, small or large, without exception; seen or unseen, those dwelling far or near, those who are born or those who are to be born, may all beings be happy!*[12]

The aim of any meditation practice is to train the mind and thereby to heighten and transform consciousness. In the *mettā-bhāvanā* meditation this training takes the form of various explicitly formulated aspirations and wishes for the welfare of different classes of beings, and for their abstaining from various forms of unskilful behaviour. Calling to mind those categories of beings and directing thoughts of loving-kindness towards them, you engender loving-kindness towards real people, as many of them as possible. In the course of your meditation you bring to mind all the weak, helpless beings, all the strong and healthy ones, and then beings of various shapes and sizes, right down to those beings who are too small to be seen at all – which presumably refers to microbes and single-celled organisms, as well as to those beyond human perception in other ways. You call to mind those who are as far away as you can possibly imagine, and those nearby. So this is one systematic way of developing *mettā*. In other forms of the practice you concentrate on the geographical differentiation of beings by directing your *mettā* towards all beings in the eastern quarter, all those in the south, the west, and the north, and finally all those above you and below you. You then call to mind those born and those unborn, thus reminding yourself that your *mettā* is not limited by time or by space.

In this way the sutta addresses the central problems of cultivating *mettā*. Firstly, there is the sheer scale of its reference. If you sat down to meditate and found yourself immediately full of *mettā*, you could no doubt direct that *mettā* towards any class of beings that you wished. But probably very few people would find themselves in that position. A methodical approach is therefore necessary if you are going to get anywhere with the practice. Otherwise, you would wish for all beings without number to be well and, after a brief but mind-boggling attempt to visualize them all, you would pass on to the next meditation.

The second problem is that *mettā* is impersonal in the sense that it has no specific object, while at the same time it is not at all 'woolly'. A vague sense that you wish everyone well together with a generalized impression of 'everyone' won't do. Ultimately *mettā* may be without an object, but to begin with you have to develop it in relation to actual specific persons, otherwise your emotions will not get involved. You have to begin closer to home. The same goes for other reflective practices: the contemplation of impermanence, for example.

Another practical reason for the sutta's detailed roster of the recipients of *mettā* is to counteract any irrational dislike you may have for certain categories of people. One would do well to draw up a list of one's own prejudices to make the list as inclusive as possible. You might have a prejudice against tall people or fat people, or men with beards, or blonde women. Since there is no accounting for taste, or indeed distaste, it is as well to include these formally in the practice, as well as trying to become aware of those categories of beings you have overlooked altogether.

From *Living with Kindness* (2006, pp.79-80)

2. WHY CARE?

I think in our quite justified attempt to see the relativity of things, and the lesser value of worldly things, we mustn't adopt a cynical or a depreciating attitude.

> *Inasmuch as all beings are our kindly parents, it would be a cause of regret to have aversion for and thus disown or abandon any of them.*[13]

Sangharakshita: The assumption on which this is based – a very common assumption in Tibetan Buddhism, based on the teaching about rebirth – is that all the people that we meet in this present life have, in the course of all the numberless previous lives that we've lived, at some time or other been our mother or our father. This being the case, how can we have an inimical attitude towards them?

This implies two things: one, that you actually believe that; and two, that for you the parental relationship is a positive one. You can see what the Tibetans are trying to do: to get you to develop a positive attitude towards all living beings. That's fine – it's an integral part of the spiritual life. But is this the right sort of argument to convince most modern people? That's the real question. The ideal is excellent, but the motivation, or the would-be motivation, would seem not quite to work in our case. So what is one to do about this? One accepts that we should develop this positive attitude of *mettā* towards all living beings, especially those with whom we come into immediate contact. But can we encourage ourselves to develop that attitude by saying to ourselves that they were all our mothers and fathers in previous lives? Can we really feel this? Most people find it difficult enough to love the mother and father they've got, never mind loving those who have been their mothers and fathers in the past.

Q: Couldn't you say something in terms of ecology or pollution or something like that, where you begin to see that what you do affects things on a global scale?

S: Yes, but where is the motivation for caring about that going to come from? The precept is trying to create a motivation.

Q: Perhaps to begin with you'd have to put it in terms of how developing that attitude would benefit you.

S: Very often the way we treat other people is due to lack of imagination. We don't really realize that other people have feelings too, that other people can be hurt as well as ourselves, and that we should therefore treat them just as carefully as we treat ourselves, consider them as much as we consider ourselves.

Q: Isn't there an element of gratitude in this as well? Don't you feel positive towards other beings because you're grateful?

S: Yes, that might be a useful approach. As a member of a society, you're dependent on a lot of other people. You ride about in a motor car, but who made that motor car? – a lot of people working in a factory. What about the man or woman driving the bus or the train, or selling you a ticket, or selling you things in shops? You're dependent on all these people. Shouldn't you feel grateful to them for what they're doing for you and the way in which they're making it possible for you to lead your life? They're doing all sorts of things you wouldn't like to do for yourself. They're doing these things for you, as it were – you amongst others.

Q: The usual tendency is to see how people are hindering you, as it were. 'What an awful shop that is, I had to wait for ten minutes. This bus is late.'

Q: But strictly speaking, those people are working for a wage, aren't they?

S: That's true, but you can disregard that, and just see that they are helping you, whether intentionally or unintentionally. Restrict your attention to that, as it were, and feel grateful that there is a bus service and that these people are running it. I think in our quite justified attempt to see the relativity of things, and the lesser value of worldly things, we mustn't adopt a cynical or a depreciating attitude.

So, 'inasmuch as all beings are our kindly parents, it would be a cause of regret to have aversion for and thus disown or abandon any of them'. We could paraphrase that, to say something like: 'Inasmuch as all beings contribute, in one way or another, directly or indirectly, to our own present well-being, it would be a cause of regret to have aversion for and thus disown or abandon any of them.'

People may trouble you, but they trouble you only sometimes, whereas they're sustaining your existence *all* the time. The fact that you have a house to live in, the fact that food comes to the door, or that you're able to go shopping for it; all of that is the result of other people's efforts, all the time. Any annoyance, like a strike, is only occasional. When railwaymen, for instance, go on strike, how annoyed one is: the wretched creatures wanting more money, greedy lot – two trains not running today! But when the trains do run, do you ever think of the railwaymen, or are you ever grateful to them? No, you buy your ticket, board the train and that's that. It's all part of the existing machinery. But actually people are helping you much more than they're hindering you.

From the first seminar on *Precepts of the Gurus* (1978, pp.104-109)

3. ISN'T METTĀ A BIT BORING?

The experience of metta is a far more satisfying state than this emotional up and down business.

Q: Surely, if you have the same attitude towards all people it would tend to break down the group way of looking at them, so you would tend to see them more as individuals.

Sangharakshita: Yes, that's true. In the general way of things you always belong to a particular group and the natural tendency is to like your group and dislike other groups. It certainly breaks that down, so to that extent it is a move in the direction of emphasis on individuality.

But if you treat everybody alike, it saves you a great deal of mental and emotional disturbance, doesn't it? If you've got the attitude of *mettā* towards everybody then you won't be happy if somebody wins something and unhappy if they lose. If you feel the same *mettā* towards all, it doesn't really matter who wins a football match and who loses. You'll enjoy the game but it's exactly the same to you whether one team wins or the other. You've got the same *mettā* towards both teams – and their supporters, even! So you're not upset if one team wins or elated if they lose. If you have the same *mettā* towards all, it saves you from all these emotional ups and downs.

Q: It's true; it does create less emotional disturbance if you have the same emotional response to all. But some people would say that that emotional response is what makes life exciting.

S: Yes, but what does one mean by excitement? It's the up and down, up and down. The Buddhist reply would be that the experience of *mettā* is a far more satisfying state than this emotional up and down business. Buddhism would say that if you only have a little experience of *mettā* – a positive emotional state which transcends the elation of excitement and the depression which is its inevitable counterpart – you realize that *mettā* is infinitely preferable. No doubt it's a very common and popular attitude that it's all the competitiveness and the rivalry and the excitement that gives a spice to life, and that without that, life is dull, meaningless and pointless. That's not the Buddhist point of view, but you have to be in contact with some real experience of *mettā* to be able to feel that. I think it's true to say generally that life is dull and pointless without some sort of emotional interest, but the Buddhist point of view would be that the best and most enjoyable form that that emotional interest can possible take is simply *mettā*, *karuṇā*, *muditā*, and *upekkhā*, plus *saddhā* and *bhakti* (faith and devotion).

Very often you hear that without some sort of emotional interest there's no zest, no spice in life, nothing interesting, and that's true. But the sort of emotional interest that we usually have gives us all sorts of emotional ups and downs. There's a bit of excitement, yes, but quite a lot of dullness and boredom too. A bit of elation, but also depression, anxiety, disappointment, etc., etc. The emotional interest you get out of *mettā*, *karuṇā*, and so on is infinitely better. It gives a real zest to life: a zest that doesn't ever change. If you've got *mettā* towards others and what you do is activated by that *mettā*, then despite peripheral disappointments and ups and downs, you feel very deeply contented and satisfied.

To have this same attitude of *mettā* towards all, to treat them all alike, doesn't necessarily mean to behave towards all in the same way. That would depend upon their situation and your own limitations. You may not be able to help very many people but you've got the willingness to help.

From a seminar on Edward Conze's *Buddhism* (1976, pp.27-9)

4. IS THERE A PLACE FOR PARENTS AND TEACHERS?

It doesn't really matter which method you follow once you have got the *metta* flowing.

Q: Is there a place in the *mettā-bhāvanā* for parents and teachers?

Sangharakshita: After you've done the first four stages of the *mettā-bhāvanā* and directed your *mettā* to all four people equally – yourself, your friend, the 'neutral' person and the 'enemy' – thereafter, you can either go all round the world country by country, from east to west, or you can divide the globe into north, south, east and west and direct your *mettā* to each quarter in turn. Alternatively, you can consider different categories of beings: the sick, the old, human beings and animals, and so on. I would suggest that if you want to include teachers or parents specifically, it would probably be best to include them in that fifth stage.

Having said that, it doesn't really matter which method you follow once you have got the *mettā* flowing; but I assume that most people would find it difficult to get it flowing without going through those five stages. If you sat down and found yourself immediately *mettā*ful, no doubt you could direct your *mettā* towards any class of beings that you wished. But I think very few people find themselves immediately overflowing with *mettā*.

Maybe it wouldn't be a bad idea to include your parents, because a lot of people still have residual feelings of ill will towards their parents, and those really do need to be resolved. If you are on very bad terms with your parents, you can always include them in the fourth stage of your meditation. It is unfortunate if you have to do that, but sometimes perhaps it's necessary.

If you find that your *mettā* is flowing freely towards a particular person, whether towards teacher, parents, the sick, or whoever, you can make that your starting point, without necessarily going through those first four stages. Some people are particularly stimulated by this or that person or this or that class of persons. That may provide a natural starting point.

Q: If we put our teacher into the *mettā-bhāvanā*, wouldn't we be adding an element of *śraddhā*?

S: That is true, yes.

Q: Would that be OK in the *mettā-bhāvanā*? Wouldn't it be a complicating factor?

S: It might be. Not that what you would experience would be unskilful or negative, but it might be a different kind of positive emotion. If you are intending to develop *mettā*, you should just develop *mettā*. Do you see what I mean? It is just a question of being clear as to what it is you are trying to do. Some people might regard their teacher more as just a friend; others might regard him in a very different way. Occasionally, you might regard him as an enemy. That's not unknown.

Q: Is the difference really so clear-cut between *mettā* and *śraddhā*? Defining *mettā* as an overwhelming desire for the spiritual welfare of another seems to suggest an element of something overlapping with *śraddhā*.

S: Personally, I wouldn't think of developing *mettā*, say, for someone like my teacher Dhardo Rimpoche; I would consider that to be rather inappropriate. I would definitely think in terms of *śraddhā*, not *mettā*, even though *mettā* is the basic sentiment, and when with *mettā* you look up to someone, your emotion turns into *śraddhā*, just as when you regard someone who is suffering, it turns into compassion. But I would not think in terms of developing *mettā* towards a teacher. I would think in terms of developing *mettā* to begin with, and then, if the teacher was to be brought into it at all, regarding him in such a way that the *mettā* was transmuted into *śraddhā*.

Q: Could one perhaps do a *śraddhā-bhāvanā*, including your own teacher first, and then his teachers?

S: You could, but then again you must be clear what it is you are doing: whether you are trying to develop *mettā* or *śraddhā*. Inasmuch as *śraddhā*, like compassion, is an application of *mettā*, you probably would be well advised to start off with an 'ordinary' *mettā-bhāvanā*.

Q: In a sense, in doing the puja, we are doing a kind of *śraddhā-bhāvanā*. Could one not do a formalized meditation where one thinks of one's teacher and then other teachers?

S: Well, yes, one can do the Guru Yoga, where one does exactly that. But that is not to be confused with the *mettā-bhāvanā*. It is just a question of making up your mind what you are doing. You can certainly proceed from one to the other, but you should do so deliberately and with mindfulness and awareness, not just drift around.

From Study Group Leaders' Q&A
on the Noble Eightfold Path (1985, pp.33-4, 36-7)

5. SPECIFIC PEOPLE IN THE FIFTH STAGE

Think of people whom you know or about whom you know in each country.

Q: In the *mettā-bhāvanā* practice, how important is it in the last section to go around each country by name? I sometimes find this method a bit abstract and laboured, and usually end the practice by trying to radiate out whatever *mettā* I've generated to all sentient beings, allowing the feeling to expand increasingly. Would it be better to apply this to beings country by country?

Sangharakshita: I think it is important, when first learning to practise the *mettā-bhāvanā*, to direct your *mettā* towards actual persons. This of course you do in the four stages, but you can do it in the fifth stage too. When you go round country by country, if you adopt that method, I think it's important not just to think of, say, France, Germany, Australia, etc., but to think of people whom you know or about whom you know in each country. In other words, stay with specific people. Similarly, if you are radiating out in any other way, stay with specific people for as long as feels necessary, and only expand your *mettā* when you've got a good momentum going. When you feel that your *mettā* is flowing quite strongly, it doesn't need the support of being directed towards individual beings. You can then, paradoxically, have a *mettā* which is not explicitly directed towards any living being. If you were to happen to encounter any living being in that mental state, that *mettā* would automatically be directed to them.

From discussion on a women's ordination retreat (1988, p.11)

7 *Mettā*: further reflections

1. AN AIRY AND WEIGHTLESS JOY

The expansive quality of metta is by no means confined to meditation.

> *Whether he stands, walks, sits, or lies down, as long as he is awake, he should develop this mindfulness. This they say is the noblest living here.*[14]

Mettā is not just a meditation exercise; it's a way of life. The phrase 'whether he stands, walks, sits or lies down' is found in almost identical form in the verse on mindfulness of the body in the *Satipaṭṭhāna Sutta*, the discourse on the four foundations of mindfulness. Like mindfulness, *mettā* is something you never lose sight of, and clearly this verse of the sutta envisages it as a form of mindfulness. If you really want to attain the 'noblest living', you will need to practise *mettā* in every moment of the day and night, not just when you are seated on your meditation cushion. This is *mettā* in the full or true sense.

The qualifier 'as long as he is awake' can be taken in different ways. It refers to being awake in the everyday sense, but if you are going to be truly awake in the sense of *sati*, mindfulness, then you can take such wakefulness in connection with *mettā* into your dream life. In fact, in any state of consciousness, *mettā* will stand you in good stead, as long as you remain attentive. So the phrase can refer to a physical state or a spiritual state, but it can also refer to a more general state of alertness or vigour.

Etam satim adhittheyya, which Saddhatissa translates as 'let him develop this mindfulness', could perhaps also be rendered as 'let him radiate this mindfulness', implying that by this stage of the sutta you are no longer in the process of developing the 'power' of *mettā*. That power has now been developed, and you are just extending its influence, radiating *mettā* for the benefit of all beings everywhere.

But while your *mettā* may have a powerful influence on others, an influence that you are now able to extend and to radiate, it is in no sense your own. We do speak of 'developing' *mettā*, but this is not a kind of power technique whose aim is to manipulate other people to one's own advantage. *Mettā* is certainly powerful, but it is not a coercive power. For example, if you cultivate *mettā* towards an 'enemy', there is at least a possibility that this will have a positive effect on their behaviour towards you, but you are not to think of *mettā* as a force or power, to be used so that others will have no choice but to fall under your spell and like you. This would not be *mettā*, but an assertion of your ego over that of another person. It is of course skilful to direct *mettā* towards people who seem to be trying to do us harm. But if we do so just to stop them giving us a difficult time and making a nuisance of themselves, it probably won't be the real thing. If we then start getting irritated because we have tried to be full of *mettā* towards them and they do not respond positively, then our mental state will be not unlike theirs.

Other factors being equal, your practice of the *mettā-bhāvanā* will have a positive effect on others. The expansive quality of *mettā* is by no means confined to meditation. One of the sure signs of *mettā* is that you will quite naturally have a lightening, encouraging, even tonic effect on those around you. But others must be allowed the freedom to resist that influence if they want to. In the end we are all responsible for our own mental state. A positive emotion cannot be imposed.

Just as a mother's nurturing love for her child helps the child to grow, our *mettā* for others helps them to develop, as well as being the means of our own growth and development. *Mettā* is not only expansive in itself; it is also a cause of increase and expansion in others, and of the joy that comes with such expansion. It brings a lightness to your being, taking you beyond narrow, purely personal concerns. You start to become receptive to other people, happy to open yourself up and let them in, unafraid to pay them more attention and give them more of yourself.

Mettā is not just metaphorically expansive. You *feel* expansive; you feel an airy and weightless joy. This quality is characteristic of positive emotion generally, hence expressions like 'up in the clouds' and 'walking on air', and *mettā* is the brightest and most positive of emotional states. You feel carried outside yourself, warm, sunny, uplifted. If you want to develop the joy of *mettā*, look for this sense of lightness. If your devotions are heavy and cheerless, and your faith is a dull and dismal piety, *mettā*, which has the taste of freedom and delight, will be very slow in coming.

Of course, freedom and delight are not emotions usually associated with religion, especially in Europe, where an uplifting legacy of tapering Gothic spires and sublime church music is accompanied by the whiff of brimstone and the promise of eternal damnation for the unbeliever. Anxiety and guilt may be the traditional flavours of established religion in our culture, but they are the antithesis of *mettā*. It is a dreadful pity that our emotions are so often a source of misery rather than joy. No wonder that we try to suppress, constrict and crush them! But in doing so, we compound our unhappiness. We become more and more downcast, we go about with head bowed and shoulders drooping, and of course it spreads. When we meet someone who starts to tell us about their difficulties, we can't wait to start putting in a word about our own troubles, looking for an audience for our complaints. But just as we tend to want to pass on our misery, the generosity of spirit that comes with *mettā* makes us want to confer our happiness on everyone we meet. While intention is the starting point of *mettā*, its culmination is a matter of conduct, the 'noblest living' of Saddhatissa's translation.

Friendliness and Friendship
No doubt if everyone in the world were to cultivate genuinely expansive positive emotion as a way of life, human society would be entirely transformed. But even though this is hardly feasible, at least for the time being, it should be possible to experience such a thing within the Sangha, the spiritual community. The Sangha is the expression, across time and space, of that practical commitment to transforming self and world which is inherent in the life and teaching of the Buddha. Through *kalyāna mitratā*, or spiritual friendship, through which one connects with and encourages the best in one's friends, one generates and intensifies positive emotions in a continual reciprocity of good will.

In the Sangha, everyone is committed to the cultivation of *mettā* as a way of life, *mettā* being experienced as a practical reality through friendship. You may well profess great feelings of *mettā* towards all sentient beings, and even perhaps try to put *mettā* into practice in the way you behave with colleagues and acquaintances. But how far are you really living out your ideals? If you never experience *mettā* in the closeness and reciprocity of friendships that are essentially spiritual rather than collusive, you will never experience the full possibilities of *mettā*. Spiritual friendship enables us to be true to our individuality and on that basis bring about an authentic meeting of hearts and minds. It is very difficult to develop *mettā* as a purely individual experience. You need other people.

From *Living with Kindness* (2006, pp.118-23)

2. THE LOVE MODE

In one way or another we deceive people, and ourselves, as to our real motives.

With the help of this meditation practice we can develop a friendly attitude. In other words, we shift from operating in the power mode to operating in the love mode. There are many ways of operating in the power mode – that is, focusing on getting what we want in a situation that involves other people. Usually, if we are clever enough, we don't have to use force. Subtly and indirectly we manipulate other people into doing what we want them to do, not for their good but for our own purposes. Some people are very good at this. They are so subtle, they seem so unselfish and so frank, that you hardly know that you are being manipulated, and it's so indirect that they may not even realize they're doing it. But in one way or another we deceive people, and ourselves, as to our real motives. We cheat, we lie, we commit emotional blackmail. But in *mettā*, in friendship, there is none of this, but only mutual concern for each other's happiness and well-being.

From *What is the Sangha?* (2001, pp.200-201)

3. NOT JUST AN ELEMENTARY LITTLE MEDITATION

Insight can have non-conceptual forms – this is the important point – or rather, it need not be expressed in conceptual terms.

Sangharakshita: If you have literally the same *mettā* towards others that you have towards yourself, assuming to begin with that you experience a very powerful *mettā* towards yourself, you have virtually abolished the distinction between self and others, and to that extent the experience of *mettā* amounts to Insight. Insight can have non-conceptual forms – this is the important point – or rather, it need not be expressed in conceptual terms. If you act out of *mettā*, as though there's no difference between yourself and others, if you treat others just as you treat yourself, if others are just as near and dear to you as you are to your own self, then surely you are no longer under the power of the illusion of selfhood. Even though you may not experience it in a cognitive fashion, you certainly have developed Insight, the emotional equivalent of Insight. The aim of *mettā* is to feel equally towards all living beings. If you don't discriminate between living beings at all, including yourself, if you feel the same intense *mettā* towards all living beings whatsoever, where is the feeling or the experience of self? It just disappears. So *mettā* isn't just an easy, simple, elementary, introductory little meditation. It's much more than that.

Why do you think *mettā* has been undervalued in modern times in some forms of Buddhism, and by some teachers, including some meditation teachers?

Q: They concentrate on *vipassanā* ...

S: Or on what they think of as *vipassanā*. Then there's the over-evaluation of the rational and the scholastic, and the 'intellectual'.

Q: Also there may be confusion over the idea of emotions being kind of wrong somehow. You can read in some texts the word 'emotion' classified as being wrong in itself, or unskilful.

S: Well, putting it technically, all emotion is *kleśa* – all emotion, that is to say, is defilement. But that is not the truly Buddhist view. There are positive mental events as well as negative ones.

From a seminar on the *Karaṇīya Mettā Sutta* (1978, pp.87-8)

4. JUST AS THE SUN SHINES

Eventually your *metta* becomes detached from particular persons so that it is capable of being directed towards anybody, whoever happens to fall across it.

Q: When one is trying to cultivate positive feelings towards somebody in particular, like in the early stages of the *mettā*, does one really need to *see* that person before one can feel *mettā*?

Sangharakshita: You mean seeing in the sense of really understanding?

Q: Yes. I feel that you really have to understand the person to have feelings of *mettā* and compassion for them.

S: Yes and no.

Q: Is it then valid to have feelings of *mettā* to a projection, or an idea, of the person?

S: The aim is really just to have feelings of *mettā* which can then be directed towards anyone you happen to meet or think of. But at the beginning you don't have any feelings of *mettā* at all, so how are you going to develop them? To do so, you, as it were, fool yourself, in a positive, skilful way, and you think, actually you *experience*, that you are having feelings of *mettā* towards somebody, because that is the way we usually experience things. So when you are trying to get the *mettā* going, to make a start, obviously you have to know that particular person and on the basis of your knowledge of them you can develop *mettā*.

But as you get into the *mettā* and you feel it more strongly, the experience of *mettā* becomes dissociated from any particular object. It is just *mettā* existing by itself, so that if you just happen to think of anyone, even if you don't know them at all, the *mettā* goes towards them. *Mettā* can exist without an object – you can just be experiencing it without having anybody consciously in mind – and this is in fact what should develop.

Q: So what is the point of choosing a personal friend, then a neutral person then an enemy? Why not just stick with a friend who conjures up your *mettā* more?

S: You can stick with them for the time being but then you have got to expand your *mettā*, you have got to get it away from a particular person, otherwise you are stuck, because the *mettā* has to some extent the nature of attachment. It must depend less and less upon the nature of the object and more and more upon itself. It must be more purely creative, not reactive. When you are feeling *mettā* just for a friend, not for a so-called enemy, to some extent the *mettā* is reactive. But if it is purely creative and non-reactive it is the same towards all. You have the same *mettā* towards the so-called enemy as towards the so-called friend. You start with your friend because that is easiest for you, but you should only stay with the friend just as long as is necessary to get a very definite feeling of *mettā*. Then, to practise extending your *mettā*, you take up the neutral person because that is next easiest. And eventually your *mettā* becomes detached from particular persons so that it is capable of being directed towards anybody, whoever happens to fall across it, as it were, just as the sun shines upon whatever happens to come in the way, whether it is a heap of jewels or a dung heap. So this is what is meant by saying *mettā* is impersonal ultimately. Not that it is less of an emotion, but that it is less dependent upon particular persons, or upon any person.

From a seminar on *The Door of Liberation* (year unknown, pp.290-1)

5. EVERYDAY EMOTIONS

If you have practised the *metta-bhavana*, it is to be expected that it should make some difference to your ordinary outlook on life.

Q: I have begun to feel that the *brahma-vihāras* are, in a very ordinary sort of way, permeating my life. But is this an illusion? Are they very high, metaphysical spiritual states, or can they, and do they, just sort of filter into one's everyday life?

Sangharakshita: It's a question of degree. Certainly if you practise them, it is to be expected not only that you should feel them at the time of meditation but also that something of them should percolate through at other times. This is what should happen with *mettā* especially, that being the really basic *brahma-vihāra*.

There are many different levels. You can have a full-blown experience of the *brahma-vihāras*, with feelings of overflowing love and compassion for all, and you can also have feelings of strong goodwill in the ordinary human sense – that's also *mettā* – and work on that comparatively lower, though still very worthwhile, level. Certainly, the *brahma-vihāras* are very lofty experiences, but it's not that there's just one level. There's a whole series of levels, right down to one's ordinary human feelings of goodwill and kindliness towards others. They are the link – the bridge, if you like. If you have practised the *mettā-bhāvanā*, it is to be expected that it should make some difference to your ordinary outlook on life, and your behaviour and attitude towards other people. You should be at least a bit more friendly, a bit kinder. If you're not, that's rather surprising. You don't keep it all shut up in the meditation hour.

From a seminar on *The Endlessly Fascinating Cry* (1977, pp.233-4)

6. PRAISE EVERYTHING

Positive feelings should not be left unexpressed, because there's a natural urge to express them.

One views ... others to be oceans of virtue.[15]

Sangharakshita: There's something much more elementary than viewing others as oceans of virtue, and that is, being much more appreciative of their good side. Goethe mentions this here and there, and in some of his poetry Rilke goes quite deeply into the matter, which is also linked up with the idea of thanksgiving and rejoicing in merits. The fact is that we should have a much more positive and appreciative attitude towards things and people than we do. Only too often we don't give appreciation, or else we give it halfheartedly, and that creates a lot of frustration and disappointment. We should not only see the good side of things, which is sometimes difficult enough, but also express it, and let people know we appreciate the things that they do. We are often very deficient in this respect. Yet even from a practical, psychological point of view (leaving aside spiritual considerations), appreciation is very important. If you say to someone, 'That was really good. You've done it really well' – if they have done it well, of course (and if you sincerely feel they have, why not say it?) – then it sets up good vibrations, as it were. It's not a question of a bit of back-slapping or back-scratching, but of genuine, heartfelt appreciation. Such appreciation is very useful, and moreover good in itself.

Q: Very often it can be the key to a natural, positive flow between people.

S: Yes, right. Absence of appreciation can often obstruct the flow, especially when it is withheld in situations where it would be quite natural and appropriate. Some people find it very difficult to express their appreciation. They just don't know how to do it.

Q: The chance seems to come up so quickly and go so quickly. If you're not right on the ball it's gone, and you've missed it. Really it's a matter of training yourself to do it.

S: Yes, training yourself not to withhold the appreciation that is due.

Q: It comes back to promptitude of action.

S: Yes, indeed. In the case of one's feelings, especially, one has to be quite watchful about that, because unless you express a feeling on the spot it doesn't get expressed at all and usually goes a bit sour. Positive feelings in particular should not be left unexpressed, because there's a natural urge to express them. Even if you feel you might be making yourself a bit ridiculous, never mind, say what you feel. The poet Rilke is very much concerned with this question of praise. He's always saying that praise is the great thing: you should praise everything and adopt an attitude of praise towards it. Quite a few of his poems touch on this. Rilke is rather against anything negative or dispraising. Praise nature. Praise a tree for being a tree, a human being for being a human being. Praise is the great word, and that should be the attitude. It's very much the Bodhisattva's attitude. It's also, in a way, the attitude of the Christian who praises God for the beauty of creation though here, of course, there is a theological difficulty, in that there are certain unpleasant aspects of creation, and if you believe that God is all good you wonder how he could have created those aspects too. But leaving that aside, praise is very much the attitude of, say, St. Francis when he sings his Canticle of the Sun – when he gives praise to Brother Sun, and praise to Sister Water, and so on. That seems to be his attitude. It's not just sentimentality; it goes much deeper than that. St. Francis gives praise to Brother Fire too, even when he burns him.

Q: There's such a strong tendency amongst people to run themselves down!

S: And run others down – run life down, run everything down. You notice it in politics. Nowadays politics is mainly just 'knocking'. There's rarely anything positive or constructive about it. It's all grumbling, whining, complaining and finding fault, prevaricating, carping and criticizing. There is hardly anything strong, constructive and inspiring. You find plenty of fine words and flourishing phrases, but they are empty and hollow and the people who use them don't mean them – you know that from their past behaviour, and from the way that they say them. It's just propaganda. Then there is misattribution of motives, one politician trying to make whatever the other one has said sound worse than it really was, or misinterpreting it. This goes on all the time. A great deal of our life seems to be of this captious nature. You can't even praise anything wholeheartedly, or approve of anything wholeheartedly.

Q: What should one do if one feels really negative?

S: For one thing, you mustn't inflict your negative states on others. Sometimes you may be entitled, in the positive context of friendship and mutual help, to let out negative things with people, but you must be very careful not to overdo this. Some forms of modern psychotherapy seem to encourage this sort of 'letting out' to a greater extent than is justified. People should be encouraged to be much more positive. Then, even though there may be the occasional outbreak of negativity, the negative states will be dealt with automatically. A lot of our troubles are due to the fact that we are not allowed to be positive. Only too often it is our positive feelings, not our negative ones, that get repressed by the way in which we live. A lot of negativity is positiveness just gone a bit sour: it hasn't had a chance to express itself. I'm very suspicious of the whole idea that you must let all your negative emotions out. You can go on like that for years, because the energy is there, but you just keep on giving it a negative expression. I don't think there is such a thing as negative energy or negative emotion as such. It's just that a negative twist has been given to that basically positive – I don't think I'll even say neutral – energy. You can very easily just turn the valve a bit this way, or a bit that, and it's surprising how quickly the so-called negativity turns positive – or vice versa, in some cases. Just give that tiny little twist, and it makes all the difference in the world.

From a seminar on *The Endlessly Fascinating Cry* (1977, pp.239-41)

7. THE ESSENTIAL CHARACTERISTIC OF METTĀ

Though we emphasize that metta is disinterested and it isn't attachment, it mustn't be one-sided.

Attachment may be mistaken for benevolence and compassion.[16]

Sangharakshita: Our English words sometimes don't represent the full value of the Pāli and Sanskrit terms; the words 'benevolence' and 'compassion', though positive, are not very strong. We seem to have difficulty in making that association between strength and positivity of emotion. If an emotion is strong, it tends to assume almost the character of violence; it cannot be strong and completely non-violent, completely peaceful. We seem to have difficulty in envisaging that sort of emotion. So we think of peace as something rather weak and colourless, flavourless; not as anything strong or vibrant or potent.

'Attachment' is here the kind of attachment mixed up with affection which is covered by the Pāli word *pema*, the Sanskrit equivalent of which is *prema*. The text tells us that attachment may be mistaken for benevolence and compassion, but what is the distinctive mark of this benevolence or *mettā*? How is it defined? You can define it as a desire, if you like, because we have to operate in these basic terms, but what sort of desire is it? It's quite simple and straightforward; it's desire for another person's well-being and happiness. This is the essential characteristic of *mettā*: a sincere and clear-sighted desire for the happiness, the well-being, the growth, the development, the prosperity, of the other person.

So how does that *mettā* differ from attachment? First of all, let's see what the resemblances are. With both *mettā* and *pema*, you are drawn towards something or someone, aren't you? There's an attraction, you could say. But in the case of attachment, *pema*, for whose sake is that?

Q: Your own.

S: Yes – whereas in the case of *mettā*, it's for the sake of the other person. Of course, you won't usually experience a clear-cut distinction, that your feeling is either this or that. Usually it is very mixed, and you have to sort it out, you have to purify it. But attachment is when your contact with somebody is on the whole for your sake, for the sake of some satisfaction on your part, or some sort of security, rather than for the sake of anything that you can do for the other person, whereas with *mettā*, your attraction towards the other person is for the sake of making some contribution to their happiness, their well-being, their progress, or at least – this not being an ideal world – for their sake as much as for yours, let us say, and generally not just a *quid pro quo* of satisfaction and gratification. That means that you see the other person clearly to some extent. How can you make any contribution to their well-being, their happiness, until you can see them clearly and see what they need? So a certain clear-sightedness is implied. But is that clear-sightedness necessarily present when you approach somebody simply for the sake of whatever is in it for you? No, you may not see that person at all. You may even see them in a completely different way from how they really are. You may, in common psychological parlance, just project something on to them, and be attracted by what you've projected rather than by the real person.

But do you think it is possible to be attracted to somebody simply and solely so that you can make some contribution to their happiness? And if it is possible, do you think that it is a good thing? I wonder whether it is really a good thing to allow anybody else to be in the position of only receiving from you, and never being expected to do anything for you. Is that necessarily a very positive human situation? It could be that your *mettā* is then a kind of mothering. That is right and proper where those concerned are children, but if the other person is an adult, while you must certainly have *mettā* towards them, and do what you can for their happiness, from another point of view, it is in their interest that they should develop that sort of *mettā* towards you. Though we emphasize that *mettā* is disinterested and it isn't attachment, it mustn't be one-sided. *Mettā* should spark off *mettā*. You mustn't encourage the other person to be simply a passive recipient of your *mettā*, because then you put them in a childlike position. If you are virtually treating them like a child, and doing everything for them and trying to make them happy, the chances are that this wouldn't even be *mettā*. It would be a form of attachment, because you have a need for a child to look after, or to be a Lady Bountiful, or whatever it might be.

Even though one person might be a little ahead of the other, or contributing more than the other, *mettā* should be mutual, should be reciprocal, where adults are concerned. But you don't expect a return from children, not until they begin to grow up. You expect that it's going to be one-sided; being a parent is a one-sided business, as some of you know.

So 'attachment can be mistaken for benevolence and compassion'. What is the difference between benevolence and compassion, *mettā* and *karuṇā*? Is there any essential difference?

Q: When you're benevolent, open, you begin to see that there are things going on which are not very beneficial to anybody, and it's really quite difficult to handle. You can be quite overwhelmed, in rather subtle emotional ways.

S: Yes. This begins to get near to it. It's said in Buddhist tradition that as regards the emotion itself there's really no difference between *mettā* and *karuṇā*. You start off with the *mettā*: that's the basic positive emotion, a desire or an aspiration for the happiness and well-being of others. But if you become aware of the fact that others, far from being happy as you would like them to be, are suffering, your *mettā* is transformed, so to speak, into *karuṇā*. *Karuṇā* is not an independent emotion; it is the colouring that your *mettā* receives when it comes into contact with suffering on the part of those whom you would wish to be well and happy. *Karuṇā* is difficult to handle, one could say, only to the extent that it isn't real *karuṇā*, only to the extent that it causes distress to yourself. If it is pure *karuṇā*, it doesn't do this, because in a way you're not concerned with yourself. Whatever feeling you have, even painful feeling, is for the sake of those other people. In a sense you even welcome the painful feeling because it keeps you constantly aware that other people are suffering and that something needs to be done about it. It's not something that you want to get rid of so that you can feel less uncomfortable. This is very often the spirit in which people contribute money to famine relief appeals and things of that sort. No doubt the contribution does good objectively, but a large part of the motivation is very often to get rid of that uncomfortable feeling, and then they can forget all about it.

In a way the truly compassionate person wants to go on feeling that pain and suffering for as long as the pain and suffering exists for the other person. So there isn't really a separate emotion of *karuṇā*. *Karuṇā* is what happens to the emotion of *mettā* when it comes up against human suffering.

In the same way, to bring in another of the *brahma-vihāra*s, *muditā*, sympathetic joy, is what happens to *mettā* when you become aware that other people are happy, that they're getting on well, that they're progressing. That makes you feel happy and joyful. It's not a separate emotion. It's just a response of your *mettā* to that situation. And in the same way, *upekṣā*, the fourth *brahma-vihāra*, arises when you become aware that you have the same *mettā* equally towards all. It's not an absence of positive emotion, it's the complete equalization of the positive emotion.

From the fourth seminar on *Precepts of the Gurus* (1980, pp.11-15)

8. REFLECTION IN THE METTA-BHĀVANĀ

There is quite a strong element of reflection in the *metta-bhavana* practice.

Q: You have talked at times of Insight arising from the development of *mettā*.

Sangharakshita: Yes.

Q: Where would the conceptual element be there?

S: When, for instance, you reflect that your *mettā* is boundless, that there is no limitation. There is quite a strong element of reflection in the *mettā-bhāvanā* practice. In a way you consciously make it boundless.

Q: What I had understood you to be saying was that the Insight consisted in your capacity to transcend the subject-object distinction, to be able to feel *mettā* for others in that sort of way.

S: Yes.

Q: That doesn't seem to imply a conceptual element – more that the Insight was the change that had taken place.

S: I think you would find that in experiencing *mettā* in that way, you were reviewing what was happening in subtle mental terms and in that way providing a bridge between the experience itself and your 'normal' experience, so that the one could influence the other. I suppose it depends on the degree of subtlety of the mental process.

From Q&A on the *Mitrata Omnibus* (1981/2, Part 2, Session 2, pp.34-5)

9. METTĀ AND NOSTALGIA

You must have some feeling somewhere ...

Sangharakshita: I must say I am somewhat surprised that so many people seem to find the *mettā-bhāvanā* so difficult. Something that one might try is to put oneself into touch with one's feelings, by whatsoever means – even by way of a daydream or fantasy in the sense that you recall a situation in which your feelings were very much alive, very much awake, very much stirred. You should avoid thinking of a sexual situation because that's quite different. Think of a situation in which your feelings have been very much stirred and as it were dwell on that feeling and try to develop it. This will certainly flow through into the practice of the *mettā-bhāvanā*. Just dwell upon those aspects of your life where there is a very strong positive emotion and put yourself in touch with that, recapture that, revive that, experience that. You must have some feeling somewhere.

Q: What about nostalgia?

S: I think one has to be a bit careful about nostalgia in the ordinary sense. If one can positively and happily recall and recapture positive experiences of the past in such a way that a positive feeling is created in the present, that is quite in order. But if your nostalgia consists in dwelling upon the pleasures of the past in such a way that you feel sadness in the present that those pleasures are past, that's different. Usually nostalgia is tinged with sadness because there are feelings of regret that that happiness is past.

From Q&A on the *Mitrata Omnibus* (1981/2, Part 2, Session 20, pp.3-4)

10. METTĀ AND NON-VIOLENCE

It is not that you just sit on your meditation mat radiating *metta* towards the world but keeping well out of the way of the world.

Q: In *The Ten Pillars of Buddhism*, you say that even the word *maitri* is not altogether satisfactory to express the positive counterpart of non-killing or non-violence.

Sangharakshita: I'm not sure what I had in mind at the time, but I rather think that I felt that the word *maitrī* (Pāli *mettā*) did not have a strong enough connotation of non-violent action. It is not that you just sit on your meditation mat radiating *mettā* towards the world but keeping well out of the way of the world. It is that *mettā* enters into your action and expresses itself in terms of non-violent action for the benefit of others. I think this connotation is not sufficiently present in the term *maitrī*; perhaps it is to some extent in the Mahāyāna *mahāmaitrī*, as practised by the Bodhisattva. I think this may be what I had at the back of my mind. If you want the literal counterpart of non-killing or non-violence, it must be preserving life, protecting life, furthering life, caring for people; and *maitrī* does not fully convey that, I think.

Q: In *The Ten Pillars*, you say that *mettā* is essentially the vigorous expression of an imaginative identification with others.

S: This gets a little closer, doesn't it?

Q: What implications does it have for the practice of the *mettā-bhāvanā*?

S: I think perhaps we should talk in terms of *mettā*'s representing the normal human response to others, the response which corresponds to reality, the response which is to be expected, as it were, from one human being to another. There should be that fellow feeling: what Confucius called human-heartedness, *jen*, which is a very important term in Confucianism: the feeling, the appreciation, of your common humanity and the reciprocal mutual behaviour that is based upon that feeling.

Q: Could you clarify what you mean by the 'normal' human response? It is obviously not normal in the sense of usual.

S: When I say 'normal', I don't mean the average or the ordinary. The norm is, in a way, the ideal, that to which you should conform. So a normal human response would be the response which could be expected from a positive, healthy, properly developed, balanced human being. Such a human being is the norm for humanity, not normal in the sense of ordinary or what usually happens. Most people are not normal! It is not so much normal as norm-oriented or norm-expressing. You may remember that Mrs Rhys Davids and others sometimes translate *dhamma* as 'norm', 'the Norm'. That brings out the aspect of the Dharma as something to be accorded with. So a normal human being is a human being who accords with the norm of or for all humanity.

Q: People often do the *mettā-bhāvanā* as it were staying within themselves, towards someone else, another human being. Your definition of *mettā* seems to suggest that you should much more put yourself in the position of the other person in order to develop *mettā*.

S: This comes out more obviously in the case of the *karuṇā-bhāvanā*: you are feeling with that person, you are as it were putting yourself in that other person's shoes; you are empathizing. It is not sympathy but empathy. So perhaps there should be more of that imaginative identification. Otherwise, even *mettā* can seem a little aloof. You are radiating it from a safe distance; you are not actually getting involved with other people in a positive way. There is no use practising the *mettā-bhāvanā* quite effectively, and then when you go out of the meditation room, behaving in a cold and inhuman or even angry way. You have to try and bring that warmth into your actual relations with people. That reminds me of one of my little stories; perhaps you'll have heard it before! Apparently there was a very worthy Sri Lankan gentleman who was practising the *mettā-bhāvanā* every morning; and usually, just as he finished his meditation, his servant would come in with a cup of tea. So he was meditating away, radiating *mettā*, and the servant came in with a cup of tea and happened to trip over the carpet. The cup smashed, and the gentleman was roused from his *mettā-bhāvanā*. Saying 'You fool! you idiot!', he seized a stick, and gave the boy a few blows. 'What do you mean, interrupting me when I am practising *mettā-bhāvanā*?'

Kindness to others needs to be cultivated not just within one's own mind in the meditation room, but in one's everyday dealings with people. I think very often we don't have enough faith in the path of *mettā*. It is as though we very easily forget it, just leave it in the shrine room and walk away without it, though we may have quite genuinely experienced it while we were meditating.

From Q&A at Guhyaloka (1988, pp.27-9)

11. METTĀ FOR THE DYING

Let them feel your presence in a very supportive manner, let them feel that you really are with them, that you are concerned for them, that your metta is being directed towards them.

Q: How can one help friends and relations who aren't Buddhist but don't have any other religious convictions to die in as positive a mental state as possible? What can we do if anything to help them gain a rebirth in which they come into contact with the Dharma?

Sangharakshita: The one-word answer to this is simply *mettā*. That's the best thing you can do. If you can't speak directly about the Dharma to them because they aren't interested or don't have any religious conviction, if you are in contact with them at the time or the moment of death just be as positive as you can. Let them feel your presence in a very supportive manner, let them feel that you really are with them, that you are concerned for them, that your *mettā* is being directed towards them. Not in a clinging way; don't encourage that. Just say, 'The time has come to die. There's nothing to it. Just let go, calmly, quietly, easily. You're all right. Everything's all right.' Just give this sort of reassurance so that they are peaceful and collected and depart with some sense of somebody's *mettā*. And of course, after death according to Tibetan tradition one can remain in contact with them. They are still in contact with you, perhaps. Perhaps they can even sense you, even see you and hear you with subtle senses, so continue to direct thoughts of *mettā* towards them. This is the best thing you can do, and it's a very great deal. If they feel somebody's *mettā* that will surely have a soothing effect on them, and a positive effect as regards any future possible rebirth. And depending on the circumstances of the person you can aspire, or even pray, as it were, or wish very intensely that they may come in contact with the Dharma. Or you may wish that you may be together in a future life, so that you may be able to communicate to them the Dharma which you've not been able to do in this life. You can express in a very heartfelt way some such prayer, some such aspiration, after they are gone. This, inasmuch as thought is a force, will surely help.
From the Western Buddhist Order convention (1978, pp.9-10)

12. CAN METTĀ REACH THE DEAD?

You may not know what the deceased person is going through, but if you can genuinely bear them in mind with powerful thoughts of metta, that must have some beneficial effect.

> *You should pray for him as you pray for yourself, making no distinction at all between you and him.*[17]

Sangharakshita: Christians and Muslims believe that you can pray for material blessings, but does the *mettā-bhāvanā* work like that? Do you think, for instance, that in the same way that this text is encouraging you to pray to God to give your brother riches, you could direct *mettā* towards someone in such a way that he does actually become richer? Does it work that way, or is it simply a question of affecting his mental state?

It seems that certain yogis and holy men and Sufis have possessed quite remarkable mental powers, even apparently to the extent of being able to invoke material blessings on people. It's as though their mental power is such that they can exercise it over a whole field of conditions and circumstances, not just in respect of one individual person.

Q: Does that correspond with your own experience?

S: I can't say that I've any personal experience of this. Certainly no one has ever blessed me that I may attain riches! Or at least if they have, the blessing has not been very efficacious. But I have read many accounts of such things, which in some cases seem plausible, if not actually credible. I wouldn't be prepared to press the point.

I think in any case the emphasis needs to be on the inculcation by direct mental means of a positive mental state in the other person. That is the most important thing of all. And in the *mettā-bhāvanā* it does seem that we concentrate on that. When we say 'May they be well, may they be happy', what we really mean is 'May they enjoy a *dhyānic* or semi-*dhyānic* mental state. May they progress spiritually, may they develop Insight.' Those are our wishes for them, rather than that they may have many children or be successful in their business affairs.

It does seem that one mind can act directly upon another, and that therefore *mettā-bhāvanā*, for instance, is not simply for your own subjective benefit, but for the objective good and benefit of the person or persons to whom it is directed.

Q: Would you say there is any particular key to developing that capacity?

S: I think it depends on two things. First of all, your energies need to be unified so that you can send a concentrated stream of *mettā* in the direction of the other person – which you can't do if your energies are scattered and fragmented or weak. And secondly, you must have the genuine good will towards that person which causes you to wish to direct your unified energies towards him in that way.

Q: That's rather interesting. I think I have a tendency to think of the *mettā-bhāvanā* as being a less concentrated meditation technique than the mindfulness of breathing.

S: In a sense, it is; but only in a sense. Perhaps you think of it as less concentrated because by the very nature of the practice it is more outward-going.

Q: I suppose the big difficulty in considering whether the *mettā-bhāvanā* has an objective effect is the lack of verification possible.

S: I think that sometimes there can be a verification. Sometimes you can direct your *mettā* towards someone with whom you haven't been getting on very well, and you find that, without your having said or done anything, they seem to have a change of attitude towards you, which would seem to be due – though you can't prove it conclusively – to your changed attitude towards them, or your special efforts with regard to them. This is perhaps the underlying philosophy of prayers to God on behalf of someone else. It is not necessarily that God answers your prayers, or that there is in fact a God to do so, but that by thinking of the person in that positive way, you bring a certain influence to bear upon him, perhaps without his realizing it, to which he responds, which results in a change of attitude on his part towards you.

Q: But how do the mechanics work? If somebody is living a hundred miles away, do you somehow contact him by envisaging him present, conjuring up a mental image, perhaps, or getting a feeling for him?

S: Physical distance doesn't make any difference, does it? It would seem that if you think about someone, if you form a mental image of them, you are in fact in contact with them.

Q: But there's surely a difference between being in contact with them and being in contact with your idea of them.

S: No, because your idea of them, if you know them or have any knowledge of them at all, corresponds to them.

Q: So when you are in their physical presence, are you only in contact with a strong idea of them?

S: One could even say that. You are only in contact with them through the medium of your own perception, one could say. Perhaps it's only an assumption on our part that we are closer to someone when we are physically in contact with them than when we are not. Perhaps it is possible to be equally close, if not even closer, when we are merely, as we would say, in non-physical contact with them.

Q: How do you distinguish between what is subjective and what is objective on the mental plane? Or is there no distinction to be drawn?

S: Well, everything that is subjective is objective to some extent. Even a so-called subjective thought is objective in the sense that you do actually have a subjective thought. That subjective thought is objectively part of your mental furniture, part of your thinking. So is anything ever completely subjective? Or is anything ever completely objective? The minute we start thinking about it, it ceases to be completely objective, which begins to suggest that the distinction between subject and object isn't quite so hard and fast as we had perhaps supposed.

But all this is bringing us on to the question of the dead. Can we help the dead? If you do not believe that the death of the physical body ends it all, you believe in some process still going on, which can still be meaningfully spoken of as that particular person, at least as meaningfully as you spoke of them during their so-called lifetime. If you can be in telepathic communication with someone in the absence of their physical body, can you not be in contact with them after death – which is the permanent absence of the physical body, whereas parting or separation was only the temporary absence of the physical body? And if you can be in contact with them, can you not therefore help them? Can you not induce positive mental states in them? That would seem to follow logically.

So if you have a duty to pray for your brother, to go back to the terms of the text, during his lifetime, you have equally a duty to pray for him after his death. In the same way, if you have a duty, to use that term, to direct your *mettā* towards the living, surely you have a duty also to direct your *mettā* towards the dead. The dead, too, can be included in your *mettā-bhāvanā*; and perhaps you will want to include them.

Q: Except that one's idea of them will grow weaker over time.

S: Ah, but will it? Why is that?

Q: I was thinking that the person who has died is going to be undergoing changes, and you will have no way of keeping up – unless you are very receptive – with the changes that are taking place.

S: During their lifetime people undergo changes too. Sometimes you just don't know what the other person is going through, or only in the most general way. Sometimes even someone in the same house or office as you can be going through all sorts of things of which you are unaware. So there isn't really all that much difference between the two states. But nonetheless, even if you have a general attitude of good will towards someone, that will help; you don't need to go into all the details of their particular problems and difficulties. Perhaps sometimes it's better if you don't. Likewise, you may not know what the deceased person is going through, but if you can genuinely bear them in mind with powerful thoughts of *mettā*, that must have some beneficial effect.

Q: Do you mean immediately after their death, or a long time afterwards, when they might possibly have been reborn?

S: Well, all the time, one might say, just as in the case of a person who is living. Your thoughts of *mettā* in either case will be particularly helpful in any crucial situation, and for the person who has just died, the few days after death are said to be especially crucial. But no doubt your thoughts of *mettā* will still be helpful to them later on. What usually happens, of course, is that people forget after a while, but we need not do so, just as in the case of physical absence. The great classical example, within the marital context, is Penelope, who waited faithfully for Ulysses for twenty years and didn't forget her husband.

After all, even if someone does go through the bardo, let us say, in the orthodox way, and is reborn. Well, someone exists in human form somewhere, and no doubt our *mettā* can benefit that person in just the same way as it can benefit someone with whom we are in contact in this life. No one goes beyond the sphere of your *mettā*, because physical distance, if that is involved, is of no significance. Someone might have been reborn on a distant planet or in a different solar system, even a different galaxy, but that wouldn't make the slightest difference.

If, when doing the *mettā-bhāvanā*, you choose to remember deceased friends and relations, that would be quite in order. Perhaps if any relation or friend does die, and there is something between you which was left unresolved, it would be a good thing to think of that person with thoughts of *mettā*.

Q: Buddhaghosa recommends that one doesn't do *mettā* towards somebody who is dead.

S: That is true, within the context of the five-stage *mettā-bhāvanā*, because if you are a beginner in the practice there is the danger that the thought of your loss in respect of that person will induce feelings of sadness. But when your *mettā* is sufficiently strong, and maybe when the person has been dead a sufficiently long time – and also if you have a sufficiently vivid sense of their still in some sense being present or being around – then it will be possible for you to develop *mettā* towards someone who is dead without its giving rise to any feelings of sadness or loss.

Q: He seems to give different grounds. He seems to say it's almost impossible to feel *mettā* towards somebody who is dead. He gives the example of a bhikkhu who is doing *mettā* and couldn't get it to work, so he went to his teacher, and his teacher said: 'seek out the object of your *mettā*.' And he discovered that the person towards whom he had been directing *mettā* was dead; and then he started doing it towards somebody else, and it was all right. It's as if Buddhaghosa is assuming that it was the physical existence of the other person that made the *mettā* possible.

S: Well, if you are in the same physical world as somebody else, perhaps that is a bond which is not there in the case of someone who is no longer in the same physical world as you. But nonetheless, surely it should be possible for your *mettā*, which is after all a mental state, to transcend physical boundaries, at least in the long run and when it is sufficiently strong. Perhaps we shouldn't make the hard and fast distinction between the physical and the mental that we usually do. There are degrees or levels of interconnection, some more gross and some more subtle. If you are unable to operate, so to speak, on the more subtle level you must come down to the grosser level and operate there, just as you need some degree of physical contact with someone over a certain length of time for it to be possible for you to launch, so to speak, from that to an experience of them mentally when they are no longer physically present.

From a seminar on *The Duties of Brotherhood in Islam* (1983, pp.222-7)

13. HOW CAN I DEVELOP MORE FEELING?

You have to tell yourself that you do deserve to be happy; every human being deserves to be happy.

Q: Could you give me some indication as to how I can develop a greater awareness of feeling in the *mettā-bhāvanā*? I seem only to be able to experience it on a sort of head level, and I understand that the energy of true *mettā* seems to come from further down somewhere?

Sangharakshita: From further down? I'm not so sure about that if one takes it too literally. I would say that what is important is in every stage of the practice to try to establish contact with an actual feeling of some sort. For instance, suppose you're in the first stage and you're directing or trying to direct *mettā* towards yourself. Well, what does that mean? *Mettā* means the ardent wish that someone should be happy. So, if you're not able very easily to summon up that feeling of *mettā* towards yourself, you could think of some skilful situation in which you've been really happy. Suppose you've been happy walking over the Downs on a lovely sunny day. Well, think of that occasion and try to recapture the feeling of happiness and joy that you had then, and then think, 'May I always be like that. May I always be happy.' Then you'll find that the feeling of goodwill towards yourself will come. But you have to establish contact with some actual feeling of being happy and joyful within your experience.

It's the same when you think of a friend and try to develop *mettā* towards them. If you don't find it easy to summon up *mettā* immediately, imagine yourself back in some situation when you were very happy together and had good communication or an enjoyable time, obviously in a skilful way. Then mentally recreate that and wish him well, and build up the *mettā* in that way. 'May he always be like that. Whether we're together or not, wherever he is, may he be happy.' By that time you should have built up sufficient momentum so that when you think of the neutral person, the *mettā* from the previous stages will spill over. It's very difficult to start with a neutral person if you're not naturally full of *mettā*, and still more difficult to summon up *mettā* towards the inimical person.

Q: But you don't think there's anything wrong with feeling as if it's all around one's head, so to speak, and not particularly coming from, say, one's heart?

S: So long as it's around your head and you are merely *thinking* of developing *mettā* towards people without actually feeling anything, to that extent you're not doing the practice. You're just mentally rehearsing without feeling anything. That's why it's important to establish contact with an actual feeling, especially during stages one and two because it's those stages that get you going and carry you through the remaining ones. Do you see what I'm getting at?

I think most people, if they think back, can recollect occasions on which they were really happy. You should initially try to establish contact with a positive feeling by recreating that situation and dwelling on it and recapturing the feeling and then enlarging it.

Q: Quite often I can remember occasions when I was happy, but it's quite difficult to relive the moment because in a sense I wasn't aware of being happy. I was just completely lost in the feeling at the time.

S: I don't think it is difficult in practice to recapture that, if you just dwell on it a bit. Maybe it's a question of imagination or just forgetting about the present and allowing oneself to go back. Maybe sometimes we're a bit too preoccupied with the present. It's not easy to get back into that past state if we're too caught up in the present state, which may be very dissimilar. If your present mental state is one of sadness or irritability, say, it's not very easy to recapture those moments of happiness. I think we have to try to ensure that when we sit for the meditation we are in a calm, unirritated, at least mildly pleased mood, if not actually happy – not in a disgruntled, sour or bitter mood, not tired and so on. Otherwise it's quite difficult to recapture positive experiences and develop *mettā*.

Some people have told me that they find it very difficult to develop *mettā* towards themselves because they feel that they're so wicked that they don't deserve to be happy. They deserve to be punished, in fact. Some people feel quite genuinely that they don't deserve happiness. If you feel like that, you've got to go into the whole question of guilt and recognize its irrationality and try to get free from it. You have to tell yourself that you do deserve to be happy; every human being deserves to be happy.

From a Men's Order/Mitra event at Vinehall (1981, pp.39-40)

14. PURE METTĀ

It might be more useful to think in terms of developing just *metta*, rather than tying yourself into metaphysical knots by developing *metta* towards beings who you are also trying to convince yourself are not really there at all.

Q: In the case of the *mettā-bhāvanā*, Gampopa makes the point that while you may start off developing *mettā* to what you think of as all sentient beings, as time goes on you see them increasingly as processes. In the *mettā-bhāvanā*, how far is it useful or appropriate to go from developing feeling for sentient beings whom perhaps you may start off seeing as quite real to then setting up a subtle train of thought to the effect that they aren't really solid inherently existent beings, they are more a process? And if you do that, and having perhaps felt compassion for them because they see themselves as solid existing beings, do you then go back to the *mettā* and work in that way?

Sangharakshita: But who are those 'they' that see themselves as solid, existing beings? One can ask oneself that, too. But I know what you mean. One can proceed in this way, but I don't know that it is the best way. I think it would be best, if one was on retreat, say, to do the *mettā-bhāvanā* at certain times during the day and interweave that with the six element practice, which would have the same general effect. Something from the six element practice would percolate through into the period of *mettā-bhāvanā* and vice versa. That would be a better way of approaching it.

But there is another way. After you have been doing the mettā-bhāvanā for some time within a particular session, you should be able to stop thinking about any particular person or persons, but at the same time be able to sit there experiencing exactly the same degree of mettā that you were experiencing when you were thinking of people. In a way, that would be mettā without any object. I think it might be more useful to think in terms of developing that, just mettā, rather than tying yourself into metaphysical knots by developing mettā towards beings who you are also trying to convince yourself are not really there at all. Either alternate the mettā-bhāvanā with the six element practice, or try to prolong the experience of mettā beyond the period when you are thinking of anybody in particular, or directing mettā towards them. I would suggest those two approaches.

Q: Doesn't it naturally happen as you become more concentrated in the *mettā-bhāvanā*, that the people almost recede and you are just left with the pure experience of *mettā*?

S: Yes, this is probably what naturally happens, especially when you have done a whole session of *mettā-bhāvanā*. Maybe you have directed *mettā* towards each of the four people, then towards all four of them equally, and then perhaps you have gone all round the world. By the time you have done all that for fifty minutes or an hour, you should have developed a quite powerful *mettā*, which should persist when you stop thinking about anybody in particular. That is 'objectless' *mettā*; you are just in a state of *mettā* without its being specifically directed towards anybody. One should perhaps aim at that, but I don't think you can do it straight off. You will have to get it going with the support of reflecting on, or being aware of, a whole sequence of individual people.

From a seminar on the *Jewel Ornament of Liberation* (1985, pp.299-300)

15. DIMENSIONS OF METTĀ

The distinction of self and others is contained within a wider framework as a result of which the tension between self and others is lessened.

Sangharakshita: While most people can manage a quite positive experience of *mettā* in the course of their practice of the *mettā-bhāvanā*, it isn't easy to keep it up in the midst of contact with other people. But when you can be at least reasonably positive towards other people much of the time, you could say that you are at least approaching becoming a novice bodhisattva. In Theravāda Buddhist terms one could say it is tantamount to Stream-entry. If your *mettā* is constant and there is never any reaction, you've virtually entered the Stream. So you can see how big a thing it is to be positive towards others most of the time, in spite of all their failings and your own failings, in spite of all the complications that may arise.

> *Benevolence with reference to sentient beings is found in Bodhisattvas who have just formed an enlightened attitude; with reference to the nature of the whole of reality in Bodhisattvas who live practising good; and without reference to any particular object in Bodhisattvas who have realized and accepted the fact that all entities of reality have no origin.*[18]

Bodhisattvas who are practising the first six or seven stages of the Bodhisattva path are capable of *mettā* 'with reference to the nature of the whole of reality'. You begin by developing *mettā* towards all sentient beings, which is difficult enough, but you've still got the conception of them as being separate from yourself. But at this second stage, that feeling of separateness begins to be overcome. It's not that you reduce everything to a monistic metaphysical oneness, but the sense of difference and separateness definitely lessens. It's quite difficult to describe, naturally, because one can only use words derived from dualistic experience. But it's as though without there being a cancelling out of self and others, the experience of self and others begins to be permeated by something which transcends both, without negating them on their own level. The distinction of self and others is contained within a wider framework as a result of which the tension, so to speak, between self and others is lessened. At the beginning there might be a conflict: 'Shall I buy this for myself or shall I give it to him?' In the end, with a tremendous effort you may decide to be really noble and give it to the other person. But when you reach this level there isn't that sort of conflict. You feel, 'Give it to myself, give it to the other person, what difference does it really make?' In the end it comes to the same thing, so you just give it quite freely and happily. You don't feel any conflict because you don't feel that there is a real difference between you and the other person. It's more like that. Not that you're both reduced to a sort of blank. It's just that there's not such an element of conflict or choice or sacrifice in it.

Then the text refers to benevolence 'without reference to any particular object' found in 'Bodhisattvas who have realized and accepted the fact that all entities of reality have no origin'. This occurs in the eighth of the ten Bodhisattva *bhūmis* or stages and it is very, in a way, metaphysical. It's *anutpaticca-dharma-kṣānti*, the patient acceptance of the non-arisenness of dharmas. You see that in reality there is no conditionality, no causality, and you patiently accept that. You are spiritually receptive to that realization, even though it goes against all your suppositions. It's connected with seeing the whole of existence as being, in a way, like a mirage. A mirage does not really come into existence and therefore it doesn't really go out of existence. Nonetheless, you're all the more compassionate. But this is quite difficult even to think about.

So there are these three different stages. First, there's the stage where you're benevolent and compassionate towards sentient beings, seeing them as sentient beings. Very often, there's a tension between you and others, a conflict of interest which you try to overcome. Then, on the second level, the distinction between oneself and others is considerably relaxed, so preferring other's interests to your own isn't nearly so difficult, becomes much more natural. In the third level you've arrived at a different experience altogether. All worldly conventions and ways of looking at things are transcended and your compassion becomes something which is very difficult to describe, because you see the whole of existence in a completely different way. The categories of self and others are transcended. They're part of the dream, part of the mirage. It's better not to think too much about that stage because it's really, for most people, quite academic, but Gampopa lists all three for the sake of completeness, so that we shouldn't think that benevolence and compassion for sentient beings as we experience them now are the last word on the subject. There are dimensions of experience beyond, waiting for us when we're ready for them.

Q: So in the second stage you prefer other people's needs to your own?

S. It's not that you actually prefer their needs to your own, but if there's an objective need to do so, you can do it quite spontaneously. If the occasion arises you are quite relaxed about it because you don't feel that there's all that much difference between your getting an extra slice of cake and their getting it. You could put it analogously in terms of a mother and her children. If there's an extra piece of cake, the mother usually gives it automatically to the children. She doesn't feel all that much difference between herself and her children, for obvious reasons. Analogously, the Bodhisattva in the second level feels rather like that.

From a seminar on The Jewel Ornament of Liberation, *Benevolence and Compassion (1980, pp.21-4)*

16. CAN THE METTĀ-BHĀVANĀ TAKE ME ALL THE WAY TO ENLIGHTENMENT?

Positive spiritual emotion is so important in the spiritual life. There's really no spiritual life without it.

Q: I've heard that the *mettā-bhāvanā* practice could take one all the way to Enlightenment. Would you say something about that?

Sangharakshita: That is not the Theravāda view. The traditional Theravāda view is that the *mettā-bhāvanā* can take you only a short distance, but that does not seem to be what the Buddha actually taught. It does seem to me more and more that you can perhaps go all the way with the *mettā-bhāvanā* because *mettā* leads naturally into *karuṇā*, *muditā* and even *upekkhā* and even into a sort of Insight.

One of the things that you have to do with the *mettā-bhāvanā* is to make it unlimited. You remember that in the fifth stage, first of all you think of self, friend, neutral person, enemy, and you try to devote the same *mettā* equally to all four. You try to remove the barriers which are usually present between yourself and other people. If you can really do this, what does it mean? It means you've overcome egotism. And what is Insight if not that? Do you see what I mean? And then you go on to develop *mettā* towards all living beings. If you can feel that for even an instant, then that is surely equal to an instant of Insight.

If you can go on developing that, as far as I can see, you could develop into a fully-fledged Bodhisattva without recourse to any other practice. It's all included in this one, if you practise the *mettā* in sufficient depth. I feel more and more that the *mettā-bhāvanā* has been very much undervalued in Buddhism, especially in modern Buddhism.

I've heard people say that you're wasting your time doing the *mettā-bhāvanā*, that it's a silly, sentimental little practice, just suitable for beginners. 'Real' meditation was *vipassanā* – this is what one used to hear. But it seems to me that positive spiritual emotion is so important in the spiritual life. There's really no spiritual life without it. It almost doesn't matter that you don't know the details of the doctrinal teachings, if you have an abundance of this positive spiritual emotion. It's so important. There's virtually no progress without it, I would say.

Q: I'm trying to get to *mettā* by being open ...

S: I don't like this word 'open' very much. It suggests a sort of passivity: just laying yourself open to whatever happens to come along, just taking it in. *Mettā*, by contrast, is definitely outward-going. You have a positive effect on other people, a positive effect on circumstances. If you're just sitting around being open, perhaps you don't have any effect on anything!

Q: I mean 'receptivity' more ...

S: Even receptivity suggests something coming from the other person, whereas with *mettā*, there's something coming from you, though it certainly doesn't preclude something coming from another person – far from it! I'd say that *mettā* by implication includes openness and receptivity. Openness by itself has an almost deprived feel to it, as though you're waiting for something you haven't got, rather than contributing something you have, and at the same time being open to receiving somebody else's contribution. *Mettā* is the more inclusive word. Unfortunately, we don't have a proper equivalent in English. 'Love' is overused and misunderstood.

From a seminar on *The Jewel Ornament of Liberation*,
The Motive (1982, pp.179-80)

17. METTĀ AND THE BODHICITTA

Metta is the wish that all living beings should be happy. But what is the highest happiness? Enlightenment.

The four *brahma-vihāra*s figure prominently in the *Mahāgovinda Sutta* of the *Dīgha-Nikāya*, and very often in Mahāyāna practice the development of the *bodhicitta* is preceded by the practice of the four *brahma-*

*vihāra*s. One could regard the *mettā-bhāvanā* in particular as a sort of seed out of which the *bodhicitta* developed. After all, what is *mettā*, essentially? *Mettā* is the wish that all living beings should be happy. But what is the highest happiness? Enlightenment. So, if your *mettā* is complete, you'll wish that others will gain Enlightenment, that being the highest happiness, and if your wish is sincere, you'll do all that you can to further that. In a way, the *mettā-bhāvanā* implies the *bodhicitta*, and you could therefore regard the *mettā-bhāvanā* as supplying the seed for the development of the *bodhicitta*, or what came to be regarded in the Mahāyāna as the *bodhicitta*. Perhaps the *Mahāgovinda Sutta*, especially the practice of the *mettā-bhāvanā* in that, might be regarded as indicating the shape of things to come in the form of the Mahāyāna.

From Q&A on the Bodhisattva Ideal (Tuscany 1984, p.73)

8 The *brahma-vihāras*: introduction

1. THE SUBLIME ABIDINGS

The Buddha says that if one only has compassion for the sufferings of other living beings, then in due course all other virtues, all other spiritual qualities and attainments, even Enlightenment itself, will follow.

The first of the four *brahma-vihāras* (literally 'sublime abidings') is *mettā* in Pāli, *maitrī* in Sanskrit, and – approximately – 'love' in English. The Sanskrit word *maitrī* is derived from *mitra*, which means friend. According to the Buddhist texts, *maitrī* is that love one feels for a near and dear, very intimate, friend. The English words 'friend' and 'friendship' nowadays have a rather tepid connotation, and friendship is regarded as a rather feeble emotion. But it is not like that in the East. There *maitrī* or friendship is a powerful and positive emotion, usually defined as an overwhelming desire for the happiness and well-being of the other person – not just in the material sense but in the spiritual sense too.

Again and again one is exhorted, in Buddhist literature and Buddhist teaching, to develop this feeling of friendship which we have for a near and dear friend towards all living beings. This feeling is summed up in the phrase *sabbe sattā sukhī hontu* or 'May all beings be happy!' which represents the heartfelt wish of all Buddhists. If we really do have this feeling in a heartfelt way, not just thinking about the feeling but experiencing the feeling itself, then we have *maitrī*.

In Buddhism the development of *maitrī* is not just left to chance. Some people indeed think that either you have got love for others or you haven't, and that if you haven't that's just too bad, because there's nothing you can do about it. But Buddhism does not look at it like this. In Buddhism there are definite exercises, definite practices, for the development of *maitrī* or love: what we call *maitrī-bhāvanā*. As some of those who have tried to practise them will know, they are not very easy. We do not find it very easy to develop love, but if we persist, and if we succeed, we find the experience a very rewarding one.

Karuṇā
Secondly, *karuṇā* (Sanskrit and Pāli), or compassion. Compassion is of course closely connected with love. Love, we are told, changes into compassion when confronted by the suffering of a loved person. If you love someone, and you then suddenly see them suffering, your love is all at once transformed into an overwhelming feeling of compassion. According to Buddhism *karuṇā*, or compassion, is the most spiritual of all the emotions, and is the emotion that particularly characterizes all the Buddhas and Bodhisattvas.

Certain Bodhisattvas, however, especially embody compassion; for instance Avalokiteśvara, 'The Lord Who Looks Down (in Compassion)', who among the Bodhisattvas is the principal 'incarnation' of compassion, or the compassion archetype. There are many different forms of Avalokiteśvara. One of the most interesting of these is the eleven-headed and thousand-armed form which, though it may look rather bizarre to us, from a symbolical point of view is very impressive. The eleven heads represent the fact that compassion looks in all eleven directions of space, i.e. in all possible directions, while the thousand arms represent his ceaseless compassionate activity.

There is an interesting story about how this particular form arose – a story that is not just 'mythology' but based upon the facts of spiritual psychology. Once upon a time, it is said, Avalokiteśvara was contemplating the sorrows of sentient beings. As he looked out over the world, he saw people suffering in so many ways: some dying untimely deaths by fire, shipwreck, and execution, others suffering the pangs of bereavement, loss, illness, hunger, thirst, and starvation. So a tremendous Compassion welled up in his heart, becoming so unbearably intense that his head shivered into pieces. It shivered, in fact, into eleven pieces, which became the eleven heads looking in the eleven directions of space, and a thousand arms were manifested to help all those beings who were suffering. Thus this very beautiful conception of the eleven-headed and thousand-armed Avalokiteśvara is an attempt to express the essence of compassion, or to show how the compassionate heart feels for the sorrows and suffering of the world.

Another beautiful Bodhisattva figure embodying compassion, this time in feminine form, is Tārā, whose name means 'The Saviouress' or 'The Star'. A beautiful legend relates how she was born from the tears of Avalokiteśvara as he wept over the sorrows and miseries of the world.

We may think of these legends as being just stories, and the sophisticated may even smile at them a little, but they are not just stories – not even illustrative stories. They are of real, deep, symbolical, even archetypal significance and represent, embodied in very concrete form, the nature of Compassion.

In the Mahāyāna form of Buddhism, that is to say in the teaching of the 'Great Way', the greatest possible importance is attached to Compassion. In one of the Mahāyāna sūtras, in fact, the Buddha is represented as saying that the Bodhisattva, i.e. the one who aspires to be a Buddha, should not be taught too many things. If he is taught only Compassion, learns only Compassion, this is quite enough. No need for him to know about Conditioned Co-production, or about the Mādhyamika, or the Yogācāra, or the Abhidharma – or even the Eightfold Path. If the Bodhisattva knows only Compassion, has a heart filled with nothing but Compassion, that is enough. In other texts the Buddha says that if one only has compassion for the sufferings of other living beings, then in due course all other virtues, all other spiritual qualities and attainments, even Enlightenment itself, will follow.

This is illustrated by a moving story from modern Japan. We are told there was a young man who was a great wastrel. After running through all his money, and having a good time, he became thoroughly disgusted and fed up with everything, including himself. In this mood he decided there was only one thing left for him to do, and that was to enter the Zen monastery and become a monk. This was his last resort. He didn't really *want* to become a monk, but there was just nothing else left for him to do. So along to the Zen monastery he went. I suppose he knelt outside in the snow for three days, in the way that we are told applicants have to kneel. But in the end the abbot agreed to see him. The abbot was a grim old soul. He listened to what the young man had to say, not saying very much, but when the young man had told him everything, he said, 'Hmm, well – is there *anything* you are good at?' The young man thought, and finally said, 'Yes, I'm not so bad at chess.' So the abbot called his attendant and told him to fetch a certain monk. The monk came. He was an old man, and had been a monk for many years. Then the abbot said to the attendant, 'Bring my sword'. So the sword was brought and placed before the abbot. The abbot then said to the young man and the old monk, 'You two will now play a game of chess. Whoever loses, I will cut off his head with this sword.' They looked at him, and they saw that he meant it. So the young man made his first move. The old monk, who wasn't a bad player, made his. The young man made his next move. The old monk made his. After a little while the young man felt the perspiration pouring down his back and trickling over his heels. So he concentrated; he put everything he had into that game, and managed to beat back the old monk's attack. Then he drew a great breath of relief, 'Ah, the game isn't going too badly!'

But just then, when he was sure he would win, he looked up and saw the face of that old monk. As I have said, he was an old man, and had been a monk for many years – maybe twenty or thirty, or even forty years. He had undergone much suffering, had performed many austerities. He had meditated very much. His face was thin and worn and austere. The young man suddenly thought, 'I've been an absolute wastrel! My life is no use to anybody. This monk has led such a good life, and he's going to have to die.' So a great wave of compassion came up. He felt intensely sorry for the old monk, just sitting there and playing this game in obedience to the abbot's command, and now being beaten and going to have to die. So a tremendous compassion welled up in the young man's heart, and he thought, 'I can't allow this.' So he deliberately made a false move. The monk made a move. The young man deliberately made another false move, and it was clear that he was losing, and was unable to retrieve his position. But suddenly the abbot upset the board, saying, 'No one has won, and no one has lost.' Then to the young man he said, 'You've learned two things today: concentration and compassion. Since you've learned compassion – *you'll do*.'

Like the Mahāyāna sūtras, this story teaches that all that is needed is compassion. The young man had led such a wretched, wasteful life, yet since he was capable of compassion there was still hope for him. He was even ready to give up his own life rather than let the monk sacrifice his – there was so much compassion deep down in the heart of this apparently worthless man. The abbot saw all this. He thought, 'We've got a budding Bodhisattva here,' and acted accordingly.

Muditā
Thirdly, *muditā* (Sanskrit and Pāli), or sympathetic joy. This is the happiness we feel in other people's happiness. If we see other people happy, we should feel happy too, but unfortunately this is not always the case. A cynic has said that we feel a secret satisfaction in the misfortunes of our friends. This is often only too true. Next time someone tells you of a stroke of bad luck that they have had, just watch your own reaction. You will usually see, if only for an instant, that little quiver of satisfaction; after which, of course, the conventional reaction comes and smothers your first, *real* reaction. This is the sort of thing that happens. It can be eliminated with the help of awareness, and also by means of a positive effort to share in other people's happiness. Speaking generally, we may say that joy is a characteristically Buddhist emotion. If you are not really happy and joyful, at least on some occasions, you can hardly be a Buddhist.

Upekṣā
The fourth *brahma-vihāra* is *upekṣā* (Pāli *upekkhā*). *Upekṣā* is tranquillity or, more simply, peace. We usually think of peace as something negative, as just the absence of noise or disturbance, as when we say, 'I wish they would leave me in peace.' But really peace is a very positive thing. It is no less positive than love, compassion, or joy – indeed even more so, according to Buddhist tradition. *Upekṣā* is not simply the absence of something else, but a quality and a state in its own right. It is a positive, vibrant state which is much nearer to the state of bliss than it is to our usual conception of peace.
From *A Guide to the Buddhist Path* (1990, pp.159-62)

2. METTĀ MUST BE THE BASIS

Q: Do you think one should try to perfect the *metta-bhavana* first, before doing the other three? S: Well, that's going to take one a long time, isn't it?

Q: Are there any reasons why people *shouldn't* practise all four *brahma-vihāras*? Do you view them as particularly advanced practices?

Sangharakshita: It's certainly true that even the *mettā-bhāvanā* isn't practised much by Buddhists in the East, let alone the other three *brahma-vihāra*s. But I see no reason why they should not be practised. In fact, I would go so far as to say it was desirable, especially in the case of the *upekṣā-bhāvanā*, which is traditionally regarded as carrying one a little further than the other three. If anybody wanted to extend their practice of the *brahma-vihāra*s, I would certainly encourage them to do that. But they must keep the *mettā-bhāvanā* as their basis all the time.

Q: Do you think one should try to perfect the *mettā-bhāvanā* first, before doing the other three?

S: Well, that's going to take one a long time, isn't it?

Q: So if your *mettā-bhāvanā* practice is in a reasonable state, you can do the others?

S: Yes. Buddhaghosa gives instructions in the *Visuddhimagga*; one could read those. His instructions on those three *brahma-vihāra*s are much shorter and simpler than those on the *mettā-bhāvanā*, for obvious reasons.

Q: And there are no dangers in practising these?

S: Not if they are based on the practice of the *mettā-bhāvanā*. If you were to practise, say, the *karuṇā-bhāvanā*, without a firm basis in the *mettā-bhāvanā*, you could be overcome by depression. Or if you were to practise the *muditā-bhāvanā* without a firm basis in *mettā*, you could get into a slightly hysterical state, a frothy, bubbly sort of state; and similarly if you were to practise the *upekkhā-bhāvanā* without a basis in the *mettā-bhāvanā*, you could develop a sort of indifference. Those are all the near enemies of those states. So *mettā* must be the basis.
From Study Group Leaders' Q&A on the Noble Eightfold Path (1985, p.40)

3. HAPPINESS WITH ITS CAUSES

In a way there is only one *brahma-vihara*.

> *May sentient beings possess happiness with its causes.*[19]

Sangharakshita: This is the aspiration that others may have happiness – but why add 'with its causes'? That's a very important qualification.

The reason is that when you wish happiness for others you wish that they may cultivate those skilful actions which will inevitably give them happiness. You wish that they may follow the spiritual path. You are not just wishing that happiness may fall down on them from heaven, that they may be happy just through luck, accident, good fortune – no. You are wishing that they may perform skilful actions, and thus be happy. This is your aspiration – that all beings may perform skilful actions and be happy. This is the practice of the *mettā-bhāvanā*.

And then you wish that they may be parted from all grief with its causes. Here your compassion comes in. This is the *karuṇā-bhāvanā*. You wish that all their sorrows and sufferings may be removed, and this means removing the cause, which only too often is their own greed, hatred and delusion. You also wish that they may not become parted from the happiness wherein no grief is, that they may continue to enjoy the happiness which they have at present without any admixture of grief. You rejoice in that. You've no jealousy, you don't want to take their happiness away from them. In other words you practise *muditā-bhāvanā*, sympathetic joy. And finally you wish that all may dwell in the condition of equanimity. If you wish that all may equally dwell in the condition of equanimity, well, you yourself are in a state of equanimity then. You don't distinguish between others. You wish that they may all equally enjoy equanimity.

Q: : But is it relevant to do any of the *brahma-vihāra*s other than *mettā*?

S: In a way it isn't necessary. In a way there is only one *brahma-vihāra*. There's only the *mettā-bhāvanā*, but when, feeling *mettā*, you happen to come in contact with pain and suffering, the *mettā* is spontaneously transformed into *karuṇā*. When it comes in contact with the joy of others it is transformed into sympathetic joy, and similarly when your *mettā* is extended equally towards all, there is equanimity. Look after the *mettā* and the other three will look after themselves. You don't have to think about them. They depend upon circumstances.

From a seminar on the *Mañjughoṣa Stuti Sadhana* (1977, p.22, 25)

9 The *karuṇā-bhāvanā*

1. A NATURAL RESPONSE

The purpose of calling to mind that there are people who suffer is not to strengthen your *mettā*, but to strengthen your determination to be of help.

Q: What is the *karuṇā-bhāvanā* practice?

Sangharakshita: The practice is really quite simple. The procedure is to do the *mettā-bhāvanā* in the usual way. Then, to develop *karuṇā*, you just think of people that you know of, with whom you are in contact, directly or indirectly, who are in difficulties, even suffering, and whom you could help; and you express your determination that you will help them. If you are feeling *mettā*, when you call to mind the suffering of other beings, *karuṇā* should be your natural response. So in a sense a *karuṇā* practice isn't really needed. If you've got *mettā*, as soon as you see suffering, the *mettā* is spontaneously transformed into *karuṇā*. The purpose of calling to mind that there are people who suffer is not to strengthen your *mettā* – that would be there as a basis – but to strengthen your determination to be of help. You could do *karuṇā-bhāvanā* with regard to people in your immediate circle who are sick or who are experiencing difficulties of various kinds. You could think of Buddhist friends in India, some of whom, perhaps at the very time that you are meditating, are being attacked or murdered or raped. This is all still going on, and that can strengthen your determination to help them; maybe to raise funds to send out to them. Do you see what I mean? I think that the point isn't just to develop *karuṇā* for the sake of *karuṇā* – that could be a bit self-indulgent – but to develop *karuṇā* in order to motivate oneself actually to relieve suffering.

Q: Would it be correct to call *karuṇā* a reflex?

S: In a way, provided that one doesn't understand reflex as something that happens mechanically. In the same way, if you're full of *mettā* and you call to mind people who are happy, people who are getting on well, you're spontaneously really happy too. You share their happiness, you rejoice in their merits. For instance, you can think of our friends in India who are working so well and so hard and you can rejoice in their merits. And you can think of the happiness of people who are meditating or of people who are on retreat, and feel happy for them; happy that they are able to be there and have that experience. You can make yourself emotionally positive in so many ways. Far from trying to eliminate emotions from the spiritual life, we should cultivate positive emotions as much as we possibly can. This is also where *kalyāna mitratā* (spiritual friendship) comes in, because through *kalyāna mitratā* you generate and intensify positive emotions in a continual reciprocity of good will. It seems such a pity that our emotions are usually of the afflicted variety, a source of misery rather than a source of joy.

From a seminar on *The Jewel Ornament of Liberation*,
The Motive (1982, pp.182-4)

2. IS COMPASSION ENOUGH?

You would perhaps get around to everything else simply via compassion.

Q: You quote the Buddha as saying that developing compassion is enough; there's no need to study, say, *pratītya-samutpāda*. Can you explain that a bit?

Sangharakshita: This is a quotation from a Mahāyāna text which is cited in the *Śikṣā-Samuccaya* in which the Buddha is represented as saying that a Bodhisattva needs to be taught only one thing: compassion. A standard figure of speech in Indian literature, discussed by Hindu commentators in connection with Vedic texts, is *prasamsa*, which means 'eulogy'. A certain topic, or quality, or action is eulogized in order to draw attention to its extreme importance, but the eulogy is not intended to be taken perfectly literally. So I think this is a question of eulogy. The Buddha is not to be taken as literally saying that you need only think in terms of doing the *mettā-bhāvanā* and can neglect all other practices and all other approaches. He is not saying that; he is drawing attention to the supreme importance of compassion in the life of the Bodhisattva.

This is not to say that if someone were to take up the practice only of *karuṇā*, then he would not eventually arrive at all other aspects of the Buddha's teaching. If you are determined to practise *karuṇā*, clearly you will have to be non-violent because you couldn't compassionately take people's lives. You will have to practise non-stealing, not taking what is not given, because stealing is not a very compassionate activity. And you'd have to speak the truth out of compassion. You'd have to preach the Dharma out of compassion, so you'd have to know the Dharma, so therefore you'd have to study the Dharma. So you would perhaps get around to everything else simply via compassion.

So it might not be wrong to take that statement quite literally – at least it would not lead you astray to take it literally – but I think that it is intended to be a eulogistic statement, drawing attention to the overriding importance of compassion in the life of the Bodhisattva.

From Q&A on the Noble Eightfold Path (Tuscany 1983, p.7)

3. 'THE EXTROVERT JOLLINESS WHICH IS SO IRRITATING …'

You must be very careful not to hit people over the head with your so-called positivity.

Sangharakshita: We speak of the Buddha more as compassionate than as full of *mettā* because in the midst of the world the Buddha sees everybody as suffering, from the *brahmalokas* downwards. His *mettā* is almost totally suffused with the suffering of others and therefore is experienced as *karuṇā*. In our case there's not such a great possibility of *karuṇā* because we cannot appreciate the subtle suffering of the *brahmalokas*. To us it looks like just bliss. It's only a Buddha who can see it as suffering. We can only experience compassion for people who are experiencing very obvious suffering. It's very difficult for instance for us to feel compassion for the rich. We're more likely to feel envy and jealousy, or at best contempt, which is the near enemy of compassion.

Q: Contempt?

S: Yes. When you are compassionate you look down on others because they're suffering, but if you look down on others and feel sorry for them without any real basis of *mettā* then this becomes akin to a sort of contempt. Sometimes you meet people who are very enthusiastic about their own happiness – 'Oh how happy I am, tra la, tra la' – and it's a form of superiority complex. It enables them to look down on others who are miserable. Thinking 'I'm so positive, I'm always on top of the world', they can adopt a patronizing attitude to those wretched and unfortunate people who aren't as happy as they are. That is not *karuṇā*.

Q: Is it what you would describe as pity?

S: You could reserve the term pity for that. There's a good example of this sort of thing in Shaw's play *Candida*, where the do-gooder clergyman has very much this attitude – 'Oh, I'm the happiest man in the world, therefore I've got to help others' et cetera. By evening time, after three acts, he's changed his tune, but that's how he starts off in the morning. He's so happy that he just wants to make everybody else happy, but clearly it isn't a *mettā*-based compassion. He is just full of himself, full of self-satisfaction and complacency, and does things for others out of that sense of superiority.

So you must be very careful not to hit people over the head with your so-called positivity. If you come across someone who is a bit sad or a bit down, it's no good saying, 'Feeling sad, on a lovely day like this? I'm feeling so happy! Come on!' That can sometimes be, if not sadistic, certainly so thoughtless as to amount to being quite unkind. You are just plugging your own positivity at somebody else's expense, or showing off your positivity. Real positivity doesn't show itself off in this sort of way. If real *mettā* came anywhere near you and you were feeling sad, that *mettā* would be transformed into *karuṇā*, not the sort of extrovert jolliness which is so irritating when you feel a bit down.

From a seminar on the *Mañjughoṣa Stuti Sadhana* (1977, p.25)

4. A HIERARCHY OF COMPASSION?

The Bodhisattva is not a sentimentalist, far from it.

Q: It strikes me that most of what we experience as compassion isn't compassion in the Transcendental sense, but a refined sort of sentimentality. Do you think it is useful to think in terms of a hierarchy of emotions associated with compassion, with sentimentality at one end and compassion at the other, and (say) romanticism between the two, where romanticism would be defined as those emotions which have elements of both true compassion and sentimentality to different degrees?

Sangharakshita: Hmm. I think one could establish a hierarchy of this kind, but I think one could put romanticism not only between sentimentalism and compassion, but also between sentimentalism and love, in the higher sense. In the Mahāyāna itself there is a hierarchy of compassion: there's compassion which has beings for its object, compassion which has dharmas for its object, and compassion which has *śūnyatā* for its object. A hierarchy of compassion is in principle thereby established, but there's no reason why there shouldn't be other hierarchies too. It is probably a matter of distinguishing near enemy and far enemy. You could say that sentimentality is the near enemy of compassion, and even that romanticism, in another sense, is a near enemy of compassion, though I don't think the term romanticism is usually considered to have an element of compassion in it. It would be perhaps just a question of usage.

But certainly sentimentality is not the same thing as compassion in the Buddhist sense. The Bodhisattva is not a sentimentalist, far from it. Very often in modern pseudo-traditional Buddhist art, the Bodhisattva is represented sentimentally agonizing over the sorrows of the world, wringing his hands in ineffectual despair. If you have ever seen a good reproduction of the Padmapani Bodhisattva from Ajanta, and certainly if you've seen the original, you'll realize the difference at once.

From Q&A on the Bodhisattva Ideal (1984, pp.79-80)

10 The *muditā-bhāvanā*

1. A SHOCK AND A PLEASURE

It's quite extraordinary to find yourself responding to someone else's good fortune in a wholly positive way. It seems to go completely against the grain.

Sangharakshita: If you can feel envy of your brother, there is some lack in your sense of brotherhood. You should feel as happy at any good that befalls him as if it had befallen you. This is where *muditā* comes in, sympathetic joy; and this is why *muditā* is based on *mettā* – no *mettā*, no brotherhood, no sympathetic joy. If there is no sympathetic joy there is envy. If there is no *mettā*, there is envy. So that is the test: if you feel envy there is not really – completely, at least – *mettā*.

Q: I don't think I ever really had a glimpse of that until I found the Dharma. And even now, when I feel that *muditā*, it's such a shock and a pleasure. It's quite extraordinary to find yourself responding to someone else's good fortune in a wholly positive way. It seems to go completely against the grain.

S: Well, in a way it does: against the worldly grain, as it were. Perhaps that is a quite simple way of telling, as to whether feelings of *mettā* have really been established: that you feel no envy if any good fortune befalls the person who is supposedly the object of your *mettā*. You feel just as happy as though whatever it is had been given to or achieved by yourself.
From a seminar on *The Duties of Brotherhood in Islam* (1983, p.242)

2. JOY AND COMPASSION

There are some people who are deeply moved by the sufferings of others ...

Q: The traditional order of the *brahma-vihāra*s is *mettā*, *karuṇā*, *muditā* and *upekṣā*. In practice, it seems more appropriate to do the practices in the order *mettā*, *muditā*, *karuṇā* and *upekṣā-bhāvanā*. Can you comment?

Sangharakshita: Well, why does it seem more appropriate?

Q: It seems that the transition from *mettā* to *muditā* is easier than that from *mettā* to *karuṇā*. The practice of the *karuṇā-bhāvanā* seems more difficult.

S: In what does the difficulty consist?

Q: I think there's the danger of falling into sadness.

S: So, in other words, are you saying that sadness or even pity, in the sense of contempt, is a near enemy to which one can more easily fall victim than the near enemy of *muditā*, which is exhilaration?

Q: Yes.

S: It's an interesting point. It depends, I suppose, to a great extent, on the individual practitioner's temperament, perhaps as much as on the degree of their spiritual development or the extent of their meditation practice. There are some people who are deeply moved by the sufferings of others, and who could make perhaps the transition from the *mettā-bhāvanā* to the *karuṇā-bhāvanā* more easily than the transition from the *mettā-bhāvanā* to the *muditā-bhāvanā*. Some people may experience great difficulty in rejoicing in the happiness of others, and would therefore perhaps find it more easy to reflect on their sorrows and sufferings and develop *karuṇā*. Do you see what I mean? But the point is interesting, because it suggests that the two are reversible.

I think one has to see the first three *bhāvanā*s as on the same level, and the *upekṣā-bhāvanā* as being on a higher level, so it's clear that *upekṣā* should come last, and I think you have to start with the *mettā*, because that in a way is the basic sentiment: *mettā* becomes *karuṇā* when confronted by suffering, and *muditā* when confronted by happiness. But I don't think in principle there would be any objection to changing the order of *karuṇā* and *muditā*, depending on what was appropriate for a certain type of person. The question has never been raised in Buddhist tradition before, to my knowledge, but I see no reason why those two should not be reversed. I don't think it matters in principle whether you go from *mettā* to *muditā* and then to *karuṇā*, or from *mettā* to *karuṇā* and then to *muditā*. So, yes, I am quite open to there being a little experimentation in this respect – not for the sake of experimentation, but to see what is really suited to different people.

From Q&A at Guhyaloka (1988, pp.19-20)

11 The *upekṣā-bhāvanā*

1. THE PRACTICE OF EQUANIMITY

We're so riddled by our preferences, our likes and dislikes, especially where people are concerned. We really need to watch ourselves and try to develop metta towards all and treat all alike.

Q: How do you do the *upekṣā-bhāvanā*?

Sangharakshita: It depends very much on the practice of *mettā* and the other *brahma-vihāras*. You develop *mettā* equally towards all and you do the same with *karuṇā* and *muditā*. You feel compassion equally towards people who are suffering, whether they're friends of yours or enemies, and it's the same with people's happiness; you rejoice in that, whether they're people who are against you or people who are for you. So you develop equanimity by stressing and developing this aspect of sameness of the positive emotions – that you feel the same positive emotions towards all. You don't pick and choose. It's not that you feel positive emotions towards your friends and not towards those who are not your friends. *Upekṣā* emerges when rather than feeling positive emotions towards your friends and not towards those who are not your friends, you feel the same *mettā* towards all.

Of course it's difficult. You know very well what happens. Suppose you suddenly meet a couple of people, one of whom is a very good friend of yours while the other is not a friend at all. What is your reaction in that situation?

Q: To discriminate and choose to communicate with the person that you like.

S: Yes. Suppose they both invite you to go for a walk. What's your natural reaction? To go with the one you like. But if you've developed real *mettā* towards all, you feel the same towards both of those people. When they both invite you to go for a walk and you've got to choose which, there's no conflict. You're equally happy to go with either, so you just decide according to circumstances – who'd benefit more or something of that sort. You don't feel the emotional conflict that you would feel if you wanted to go with one and not with the other. So *mettā* felt equally towards all conduces to equanimity and therefore to absence of conflict. We're so riddled by our preferences, our likes and dislikes, especially where people are concerned. We really need to watch ourselves and try to develop *mettā* towards all and treat all alike.

From a seminar on *The Jewel Ornament of Liberation*,
The Motive (1982, pp.183-4)

2. BEYOND LIKES AND DISLIKES

If you like all circumstances equally, if you welcome the rain as well as the sunshine, you're equally happy whatever happens.

Sangharakshita: Sometimes *upekṣā* or *upekkhā* is misunderstood. It's sometimes translated as indifference, but that is not meant to suggest any lack of feeling. Equanimity does not exclude *mettā*, but you develop *mettā* equally towards all, so you don't prefer one to another. You're even minded in your attitude. Then equanimity inevitably results.

Suppose you like someone very much and you're expecting to see him but instead, somebody else whom you don't like comes through the door. What happens to your equanimity?

Q: It vanishes.

S: Yes. But suppose you feel the same towards both those people. If the one that you were expecting doesn't turn up but the one that you weren't expecting does, if you feel the same towards them both, where's the disappointment? You're just as glad to see the one as the other, so there's equanimity. When you feel the same *mettā* towards all, your balance of mind cannot be disturbed in respect of persons. The same can be true in respect of circumstances. If you like all circumstances equally, if you welcome the rain as well as the sunshine, you're equally happy whatever happens.

You may work to make things go right in a skilful way but you won't be upset by the failure of your skilful actions. That doesn't mean that you just settle down and say, 'Oh it doesn't matter what happens, no need to do anything!' – that's quite wrong. In the same way, having equanimity towards people doesn't mean not caring who comes because you couldn't care less anyway. It isn't that. The aim is to feel *mettā* towards all equally. You're equally positive towards them all, so it doesn't matter who turns up.

Q: So there's a balance inside yourself. The equanimity is inside you.

S: Yes, right. But suppose one day you're waiting for your favourite girlfriend to turn up. You've been looking forward to that all the evening, but instead of her, some other person turns up. Well, what a disappointment! Why? Because your attitude to the two people is different.

Q: But surely a person who's developed equanimity would still have likes and dislikes.

S: Not really. He will see differences – he will see that one person is behaving badly and another person is behaving well, but he won't like one and dislike the other. He may even be able to see that one is better than another or more developed than another, but still there's no liking or disliking.

Q: From my own experience it's almost like two things going on at the same time. One thing is my personal likes and dislikes, and I don't even want to lose them, and at the same time there's something else going on, something that overrides …

S: Well, clearly both are functioning at the same time. The likes and dislikes are there but you can see quite objectively at the same time. What usually happens is that we're in that intermediate state for quite a while, but after a while we not only see equally but we feel equally. We see the inequalities but we don't feel them in the way that we used to.

Q: Does that mean that you can feel friendliness for someone, but if you see faults you don't condone them necessarily?

S: Exactly, yes. Unfortunately people very often can't take it like that. If you point out a fault, they take it that you don't like them, and that your pointing out of the fault is an expression of dislike and rejection on your part. They take it like that very often because of their own insecurity. Occasionally of course it may be an expression of dislike, that but it certainly need not be like that. You can point out the fault of someone that you really do like – maybe you point it out because you like them.

Q: Maybe you can only point out faults if you do like somebody.

S: Well, put it this way. If you don't like someone, be very careful about pointing out his faults to him, because he will pick up on the dislike, no doubt, people being sensitive, and almost use that as an excuse for ignoring or not taking into consideration the fault you have pointed out. You can be much more confident pointing out the faults of people you like and who know that you like them. It doesn't feel like pointing out a fault. It's just a friendly drawing of attention to something.
From a seminar on the *Mañjughoṣa Stuti Sadhana* (1977, pp.22-4)

3. PURE AWARENESS AND POSITIVITY

Perhaps we need to reconsider this whole idea of awareness.

I think the practice of pure awareness and mindfulness is perfectly valid provided it is an integrated awareness and not an alienated awareness. This is why it is so important to develop the various positive emotional factors – because we are in a process of transition from alienated awareness to integrated awareness. If your awareness is integrated, if all those highly positive emotional factors are present and operating, when you look out over the world and remain purely aware, it is possible for Insight to arise. But if you do the same thing with an alienated awareness, then Insight is not possible.

But perhaps we need to reconsider, even revalue, this whole idea of awareness. We tend to think of it as a bit dry, a bit abstract, a bit empty, but integrated awareness isn't like that. It really does contain a very powerful emotional component – though not emotion as we usually understand it. It is very sensitive, it is very alive. It contains the element of *mettā*. It is perhaps analogous to equanimity, *upekkhā*, because there is a danger of equanimity being regarded as indifference.

Years ago, Lama Govinda was invited to a conference, some sort of parliament of religions, to represent Tibetan Buddhism. Also present was a very pleasant young Nepalese monk whom I subsequently also got to know. In the course of the discussion in one of the sessions the question arose as to whether love was higher than indifference or indifference higher than love. The young Nepalese monk jumped up and said – or meant to say – that according to Buddhism, *upekkhā* was higher than *mettā*. But he was speaking in English, so he said that indifference, according to Buddhism, was much higher than love. Then all the Catholic theologians present, according to Lama Govinda, smiled, because that was just what they wanted to hear. And then, of course, they proceeded to say that in Christianity love, charity, was far higher than indifference. It was very interesting to hear that the highest virtue of Buddhism was indifference. Yes. They had suspected as much ... They had thought all along that Buddhism was selfish and individualistic and valued indifference much more highly than love. Then of course, Lama Govinda had to explain that it was not really quite like that. Upekkha was not in fact indifference; *upekkhā* was equanimity.

But even that is not sufficient explanation. Because what happens? First of all one develops *mettā*, and one develops *mettā* towards all living beings equally. This is the important point. In the practice one develops *mettā* equally to the self, the near and dear friend, the neutral person and the enemy, and feels *mettā* equally intensely towards all four. It's the same with regard to *karuṇā*: whoever is suffering, whether it's you yourself, a near and dear friend, a neutral person, or an enemy, you feel the same *karuṇā*. And similarly with *muditā*, sympathetic joy, whether it's your own well being, or a friend's, or an enemy's, you rejoice equally.

How do you develop *upekkhā*? *Upekkhā* is developed when you concentrate on the element of equality. Your *mettā* is the same for all, your *karuṇā* is the same for all, your *muditā* is the same for all – you dwell on and develop an equal attitude towards all. But – and this is the important point – you do not leave behind the experience of *mettā*, *karuṇā* and *muditā*. They are all subsumed in the equanimity. So equanimity is not to be seen as excluding *mettā* or excluding *karuṇā* or excluding *muditā*. It includes them, at their highest possible development. It's quite incorrect to translate *upekkhā* as 'indifference', and it is even problematic to translate it as equanimity. It is much more than that – it is a quite different sort of experience. It goes far beyond even equanimity. It is important to remember that.

So the experience of the *brahma-vihāras* can lead to something that begins to look rather like Insight. Not influenced by any subjective considerations of like and dislike, you are seeing all beings equally, without that subjective distortion, and therefore, at least to some extent, you are seeing them as they really are. And it is in seeing things as they really are that Insight consists.

From Q&A on the *Mitrata Omnibus* (1981/2, Part 2, Session 13, pp.10-3)

4. EQUANIMITY DOESN'T EXCLUDE HAPPINESS

Usually when we experience happiness in the ordinary sense, it becomes a bit too important to us.

> *Further, Maharaja, the bhikkhu, from the giving up of ease and dis-ease, from having set down any former happiness or unhappiness, without dis-ease, without ease, in equanimity, mindful and entirely pure, attains to and remains in the fourth jhanic state. He remains sitting, having pervaded his body with purity of heart till no part of it remains unsuffused therewith.*[20]

The term translated as 'ease' is *sukha*. It's usually translated as happiness, or even pleasure; and dis-ease, of course, is *dukkha* – usually translated as pain or suffering. So here, equanimity is considered as a higher value even than pleasure, even than happiness. One must be careful to see equanimity not as excluding happiness, but in a sense as carrying happiness to a higher level. There's an antithesis between happiness and unhappiness, so when you're just happy, just joyful, there's, in a way, an element of disturbance, even unbalance, but with equanimity the happiness becomes stable. It's not separate, not distinct, not something that stands out by itself. It's merged in the equanimity. Not that when you reach the stage of equanimity, you're no longer happy. Equanimity represents a stabilization of happiness. Usually when you're happy, there's always the possibility of unhappiness. But in the case of equanimity, happiness is there, but there's no possibility of its being disturbed.

This is quite a difficult state to achieve. Usually when we experience happiness in the ordinary sense, it becomes a bit too important to us. If circumstances change, we can have a strong reaction to the opposite – that is to say, unhappiness. With the development of equanimity this is much less likely to happen. But the really important point is that equanimity doesn't exclude happiness, just as equanimity as the fourth *brahma-vihāra* doesn't exclude *mettā*, *karuṇā*, and *muditā*. They're all present but they're much more integrated, carried to a higher level.
From a seminar on the *Samaññaphala Sutta* (1982, pp.162-3)

5. THE POWER OF PEACE

We don't often think of Peace, as it were with a capital 'P', as an idea or goal, do we?

Not peacefulness in the sense of the love and light experience we have just been talking about, but of complete encompassing peace, immovable, invincible peace, the peaceful state that cannot be challenged, that has no age, no end, no beginning.[21]

Trungpa is very rightly concerned to point out here what peacefulness really is. It isn't that the Buddha is just gentle and calm, even a bit soft. Peace is very powerful. I don't mean powerful in the sense that we speak of the group being based upon power, but in the sense of a quality, even a spiritual experience, which has a very definite nature of its own. It's as though the peacefulness is so intense that if you came in contact with it, it could give you a sort of electric shock. It is not merely the absence of noise, the absence of disturbance, the absence of war. It is peace in a very positive, even powerful sense; a vibrant peace. This is the sort of peace that normally one experiences only in connection with meditation. Perhaps it isn't quite synonymous with *upekṣā*, the fourth of the four *brahma-vihāra*s, but *upekṣā* can give us some idea of it – not a complete idea, because *upekṣā* is still a mundane quality, and the peace described here is a Transcendental quality, but even the mundane state of *upekṣā* is very difficult for us to conceive of.

Let's take it step by step. If you haven't had any experience of *mettā*, it is very difficult for you to conceive what *mettā* is like as an emotional experience. It is much more positive and pure than what one might call everyday experiences of love, affection, warmth and friendliness. It is only when you have had some experience of *mettā* that you can look back to your previous experience of warmth, love, and friendliness and see the difference. Going on from there, you can have an experience of a very pure, very positive *karuṇā* or compassion, which is very different from your usual sentimental pity. In the same way there can be a very positive, pure experience of sympathetic joy, *muditā*, much more intense than your ordinary pleasure that somebody else is getting on well. Then you come to *upekṣā*, which is not just the peacefulness that you enjoy when there isn't much noise or disturbance, when things are pretty quite in the house and there aren't many people around, when the wind isn't blowing and the trees are still. It goes far beyond that. It is much more intense, it has a definite and even dynamic character of its own.

That is only mundane *upekṣā*, and here we are talking about peacefulness on a Transcendental level. So how much further does that go? It is this that Trungpa is trying very hard to convey, and this is why he says, 'not peacefulness in the sense of the love and light and experience we have just been talking about, but completely encompassing peace'. It is as though there is nothing but that peace, it is all around, it is immovable. It seems rather strange to say that peace is immovable, but it is like a solid block as it were, it has got such a definite, strong nature of its own. It is not just the absence of something else. Because 'invincible peace' is Transcendental, what can overcome it, what can disturb it? No amount of noise, no amount of disturbance can affect it in any way. It is 'the peaceful state which cannot be challenged'; in its proximity there is no question of anything except peace. It 'has no age, no end, no beginning'. it isn't even a temporal phenomenon, it is Transcendental, it exists outside space, outside time.

> *The symbol of peace is represented in the shape of a circle; it has no entrance, it is eternal.*

We don't often think of Peace, as it were with a capital 'P', as an idea or goal, do we? We think of Enlightenment, we think of truth, we might even think of the Absolute, but we don't usually think of peace as a goal.
From a seminar on *The Tibetan Book of the Dead* (1979, pp.215-6)

12 The *brahmā-vihāras*: further reflections

1. THE BASIS OF IT ALL

According to the modern Tibetan tradition, there can be no development of *bodhicitta* without a very thorough cultivation and experience of the four brahma-viharas.

It seems to me that the *brahma-vihāras* have to be upgraded from the position they usually occupy in standard Theravāda tradition. One can understand why in the Mahāyāna tradition and the Vajrayāna tradition the cultivation of the four *brahma-vihāras* is a preliminary to the arising of the *bodhicitta* itself. They are the basis. According to the modern Tibetan tradition, there can be no development of *bodhicitta* without a very thorough cultivation and experience of the four *brahma-vihāras*. And if you haven't developed the *bodhicitta*, if the *bodhicitta* has not arisen, if you are not a Bodhisattva, how can you possibly enter upon the practice of the Vajrayāna? When one finds that neither Tibetan lamas, Tibetan teachers, nor their pupils have extensively practised the four *brahma-vihāras*, in fact have not practised them at all, one cannot help wondering, 'Where is their *bodhicitta*, and what is their practice of the Vajrayāna?' The four *brahma-vihāras* are the basis of it all, just as the Refuges are the basis of the *brahma-vihāras*.
From Q&A on the *Mitrata Omnibus* (1981/2, Part 2, Session 13, pp.13-4)

2. ARE THE BRAHMA-VIHĀRAS A PATH TO INSIGHT?

If Buddhas and Bodhisattvas are characterized by *mahamaitri*, then surely the development of *maitri* can be a way to Enlightenment.

Q: In what way are the *brahma-vihāras* a path to Insight?

Sangharakshita: My personal interpretation would be that they become means to Insight through the fourth *brahma-vihāra*, *upekkhā*. If you go through the four *brahma-vihāras*, you develop *mettā*, *muditā*, and *karuṇā*, and *upekkhā* arises when you develop *mettā*, *karuṇā* and *muditā* equally towards all. This seems to come very near to the Mahayanic *samatā-jñāna*, the wisdom of sameness, corresponding to the Buddha Ratnasambhava. I would say that *upekkhā* is very similar to that; and clearly *samatā-jñāna* is a Transcendental awareness embodied by a particular Buddha, which is usually understood as an aspect of *śūnyatā*. If your *mettā* is the same towards all living beings, if you are not distinguishing between yourself and other living beings, then surely you have transcended all distinctions between subject and object, and that is tantamount to Insight. We can therefore regard *upekkhā* as an emotional equivalent of Insight. This is further confirmed by the sequence of the seven *bodhyangas*, the culmination of which is *upekkhā*.

So I would say that the four *brahma-vihāras* become means to the development of Insight as equal *mettā* or equal *karuṇā* or equal *muditā* towards all living beings is developed. In that way, the distinctions between beings are transcended. If you could really feel the same *mettā* towards all living beings, quite literally, without making any distinction, it is inconceivable that you should not be Enlightened.

Q: Is this point made traditionally anywhere?

S: Well, the Theravādins seem not to regard the *brahma-vihāras* very highly, though there are a few indications to the contrary – in Buddhaghosa, for example, where the *brahma-vihāras* are also called the Four Infinitudes, the *apramāṇas*, meaning they are to be developed infinitely towards living beings, and that would surely suggest a going beyond, as it were.

But nowadays in Theravāda circles, *mettā* – they never seem to refer to the other three *brahma-vihāras* – is regarded as a simple little exercise for very ordinary people. You do a couple of minutes of '*mettā* radiation' every day, and this is all the value they place on it. They sometimes call for two minutes' *mettā* radiation before a public meeting. Very few people in the Theravāda tradition take the *mettā-bhāvanā* seriously; it's regarded as a very elementary little practice.

On the other hand, in the Mahāyāna it is frequently said that the Buddha and the Bodhisattvas are characterized by *mahāmaitrī*. They don't always make the connection between the practice of the *mettā-bhāvanā* and the *mahāmaitrī* of the Buddhas and Bodhisattvas, but obviously they should. If Buddhas and Bodhisattvas are characterized by *mahāmaitrī*, then surely the development of *maitrī* can be a way to Enlightenment.

Q: Is there any reference in the scriptures to the Buddha or his immediate disciples doing the practice of the *mettā-bhāvanā*?

S: Yes, I believe it is Subhuti who is referred to in the scriptures as being especially good at the *mettā-bhāvanā*. The Buddha is frequently referred to as surveying beings with compassion – with compassion rather than *mettā* for obvious reasons, but if *karuṇā* is there, surely *mettā* is there also.
From a seminar on the Noble Eightfold Path (1982, pp.106-108)

3. AN ALTERNATIVE ROUTE TO ENLIGHTENMENT

The overall picture is very clear: a hierarchy of worlds corresponding to a hierarchy of spiritual states, with the dichotomy between subject and object, state and world, becoming more and more subtle the higher you go.

Q: How do the four *brahma-vihāra*s relate to the *dhyānas*?

Sangharakshita: Studying the Pāli canon, it does seem that the *brahma-vihāra*s are, at least to some extent, envisaged as an alternative route to Enlightenment. There are some scholars, notably Mrs Rhys Davids, who believe that the four *brahma-vihāra*s were not part of original Buddhism and were incorporated at a later stage, albeit perhaps by the Buddha himself. I am not quite sure about that, but it is a fact that, though the *brahma-vihāra*s feature very prominently in the Pāli canon, they are not included in quite a number of the important numerical lists. What all that adds up to is really quite difficult to say, but at the very least, one could say that the *brahma-vihāra*s represent a parallel – or, even better, a convergent path. No doubt some Abhidharmika has correlated the *dhyāna*s and the *brahma-vihāra*s, but nonetheless it does seem that they do represent an approach in their own right.

To find out whether there's a correlation, consult your own experience. Do the *brahma-vihāra*s, do the *mettā-bhāvanā* or the *karuṇā-bhāvanā*, and compare your experience with your experience when you practise concentration and enter the *dhyāna*s. Are there any similarities? What are you doing in the one case that you are not doing in the other? Or are you basically doing the same thing?

This is one of the interesting problems relating to the Buddha's teaching which will have to be cleared up sooner or later. I think these two paths do overlap to some extent, but it isn't easy to see exactly how. There must be a certain amount of common ground, because there are certain common positive mental factors. One of my theories – though it is only a provisional one – is that the *brahma-vihāra*s may belong to an earlier phase of the Buddha's teaching, a phase in which there was more emphasis on worlds attained than on states experienced. Do you see what I mean? We do find in Buddhism on the one hand a hierarchy of states and on the other a hierarchy of worlds, and the two are correlated. There are a number of texts where it is said that the way to the *brahmaloka* is through the *brahma-vihāra*s. So it would seem that perhaps at that time one thought more in terms of entering or dwelling in a brahmaloka than in terms of achieving a certain *dhyāna*. As I say, this is just a theory of mine at the moment, something that requires further investigation.

Q: Can the *brahma-vihāra*s be Transcendental?

S: Again, this is something that requires investigation. Generally in Buddhism they are taken to be mundane; this is the standard tradition. But there are certain passages in Pāli texts which point to the possibility of their originally having been understood as Transcendental – well, not so much themselves Transcendental but approaches to the Transcendental, avenues to the Transcendental. To look into this further will require quite a comprehensive survey of Buddhist literature, especially the canonical literature in Pāli and Sanskrit, and quite a bit of reflection, and quite a lot of comparison with one's own experience and perhaps with the experience of other people, too.

But the overall picture is very clear: a hierarchy of worlds corresponding to a hierarchy of spiritual states, with the dichotomy between subject and object, state and world, becoming more and more subtle the higher you go. Perhaps one should stick firmly to that and leave the details to work themselves out little by little, in the course of time.

Q: In what sense are the *brahma-vihāra*s avenues of approach to the Transcendental?

S: There is a particular text where someone practises the *brahma-vihāra*s and as a result he has a vision of a particular Brahma, Sanankumara, and Sanankumara gives him a teaching pertaining to Insight.[22] So the avenue of approach was the *brahma-vihāra*, but what or who is it that was approached? It was that particular Brahma, Sanankumara, corresponding perhaps to Mañjuśrī or Manjughoṣa, and one gains, or one is given, as it were, a teaching pertaining to Insight, pertaining to the Transcendental.

From a seminar on the *Jewel Ornament of Liberation*
(Tuscany 1985, pp.279–81)

4. THE ILLIMITABLES

One of the essential characteristics of the brahma viharas is that they are constantly expanding.

Mettā and *karuṇā* are the first two of the four *brahma-vihāra*s, which are also called the 'Illimitables' because their essential nature is not to stop anywhere. Obviously you can't start off with unlimited *mettā* or *karuṇā*. Whatever your aspiration may be, your actual *mettā*, your actual *karuṇā*, is limited to a certain number of people – those, or some of those, with whom you are in contact. But the aspiration should be that it should be expanding all the time. You cannot feel *mettā* towards an infinite number of people, except in the abstract, which doesn't count. You can only feel *mettā* towards a finite number of people, but the point is that that finite number should be illimitable. It should not come to a stop anywhere. You shouldn't say, 'I'm not going any further. That is my ration.'

But that is in effect what people usually do. Usually, of course, the limit is the family. It is not wrong that you should love your family, obviously, but it is wrong that your love should be limited to the family. Even though for practical purposes your responsibility may have to be given to your family, you should be willing to go beyond that. One of the essential characteristics of benevolence and compassion is that they are boundless. 'Boundless' isn't meant to suggest actual boundlessness, but a continued expansion. It is very active, not only with regard to the people who are its objects, but constantly taking in more and more people. That is its nature. It doesn't wish to stop anywhere, with any one particular circle of people. This is why our Buddhist movement must expand if it is the real thing. Otherwise it would mean that you're limiting your *mettā* just towards the people within the movement, or this centre or that centre, or, dare I say it, just women or just men.

From a seminar on *The Jewel Ornament of Liberation*,
Benevolence and Compassion (1980, p.23)

5. GOING BEYOND METTĀ

If you're on a solitary retreat or a meditation retreat you could practise all four brahma viharas.

Q: Do you recommend that we practise all four *brahma-vihāras*?

Sangharakshita: If you can, yes. We emphasize the *mettā-bhāvanā* so much because that is the basis. You can't practise *karuṇā-bhāvanā* or *muditā-bhāvanā* unless you've got a solid basis of *mettā*. But perhaps if you're on a solitary retreat or a meditation retreat you could practise all four *brahma-vihāras*: a session of *mettā-bhāvanā* and then, maybe after a break, a session of the *karuṇā-bhāvanā*, then a session of the *muditā-bhāvanā*, finishing up with *upekkhā-bhāvanā*. One could distribute them through the day, with maybe mindfulness of breathing or mantra recitations in between. This would be very good practice. I don't mean to suggest that we confine ourselves to the *mettā-bhāvanā*. The *mettā-bhāvanā* is what we teach in our meditation centres and classes, rather than the other *brahma-vihāras*, because *mettā* is the basis of them all.

From a seminar on *The Jewel Ornament of Liberation*,
The Motive (1982, p.178)

4 Levels of Concentration

1 *Samādhi*

1. CLEARING THE DECKS FOR ACTION

The states of mind we have produced through our actions during the day and during the course of our life in general, whatever they are, will be the states of mind we have to address in our meditation.

A lot of Buddhist practice can seem very self-absorbed and in a way it is. But there is no healthy alternative, if one is to be effective in the world. Buddhist meditation is a clearing of the decks for action, a transforming of unskilful and unexamined mental states into integrated and refined energy, for a purpose beyond self-absorption.

As the Buddha states in the Pāli canon, *samādhi*, concentration, is the natural outcome of spiritual bliss. It increases with pleasure, and as pleasure turns into rapture and then bliss, this process of deepening and refining pleasure has the effect of deepening one's concentration even more. *Samādhi* is thus inseparable from *sukha*. *Samādhi* is what arises naturally when you are perfectly happy; when you are not, you go looking for something to make you happy. In other words, to the extent you are happy, to that extent you are concentrated. This is a very important characteristic of *samādhi*, and should be clearly distinguished from the forcible fixing of attention that is often understood by the term 'meditation'.

It's a question of motivation. If you are looking for an experience of pleasure or excitement or bliss in meditation, the result is going to be as superficial as the motive. Probably this was what the Buddha realized when, recollecting his childhood experience of spontaneously entering the first *dhyāna*, he came to understand that this was the key to Enlightenment. This is a turning point in the story of his quest for Enlightenment. Having tried all kinds of methods and practices, having meditated and fasted and performed austerities, the Buddha-to-be remembered an experience he had as a boy. He had been sitting under a rose-apple tree out in the fields when he had spontaneously entered a state of meditative concentration. He sat there all day, absorbed and happy. It was the recollection of this when he was on the very threshold of Enlightenment that gave him the clue he needed. One might wonder what such an elementary spiritual attainment might signify to one who had advanced in meditation even as far as the formless *dhyānas* under the guidance of his teachers. But he knew that he had still not attained the goal to which he aspired, and now he understood why. What he realized was that his previous mastery of meditation had been forced, however subtly; this was why it was in the end useless. Progress had been made but only part of him had been involved in that progress, because it had been produced through sheer will-power. It was not so much the first *dhyāna* itself that was the answer, but the natural manner in which he had entered into that state. The answer was to allow a natural unfolding of the whole being to take place, through the steady application of mindfulness.

We too can make use of this important insight. The states of mind we have produced through our actions during the day and during the course of our life in general, whatever they are, will be the states of mind we have to address in our meditation. Meditation is not about pushing parts of yourself away in order to force yourself into a superficially positive mental state. If you are distracted, unreflective, self-indulgent and reactive in your everyday life, you might as a novice meditator force yourself in the opposite direction to some short-term effect, but in the long run meditation is about transforming mental states, not suppressing or ignoring them.

With the integration and calming of all bodily sensations, as your consciousness becomes clearer, you enjoy states of increasing brightness, expansiveness, and harmony. But if you are to proceed to the goal of the Buddhist path, the blossoming of Insight into the nature of reality, the practice of *samādhi* has to be understood as far more than the cultivation of *dhyāna*. The intensely positive experience of *dhyāna* has to be invested with the clear recollection of your purpose, so that this intense experience of well-being can be refined still further, to produce a firm foundation for the final stage in this series of Enlightenment factors: equanimity.

From *Living with Awareness* (2003, pp.144-6)

2. A CONCENTRATED MIND IS A HAPPY MIND

It's really no use thinking that concentration can be gained by force of will; although, of course, a lot of people do think this.

In the sequence of positive mental states called the twelve positive *nidānas*, the sixth stage, arising in dependence upon *sukha*, intense happiness, is *samādhi*. The word has several different meanings, but here it means concentration. This does not mean a forcible fixation of the mind on a single object, but a concentration which comes about quite naturally when, in that state of intense happiness, all one's emotional energies are flowing in the same direction. In other words, when we are completely happy, when all our emotional energies are unified, we are concentrated in the true sense. A concentrated person is a happy person, and a happy person is a concentrated person. The happier we are, the longer we shall be able to stay concentrated; and conversely, if we find it difficult to concentrate for very long, the reason will be that we are not happy with our present state. If we were truly happy we wouldn't need to do anything else – we could just stay still. But we are unhappy, dissatisfied, so we get restless and go searching for this or that, looking for some distraction, some diversion.

This connection between happiness and concentration is illustrated by a story from the scriptures. We are told that one day there was a discussion between a certain king and the Buddha. The king came to the Buddha to ask him about his teaching, and as they talked a question cropped up – the question of which of them was happier. Was the Buddha happier than the king, or was the king happier than the Buddha? Of course, the king was quite sure that he was the happier of the two by far. He said, 'Well, look, I've got all these palaces, I've got this army, I've got this wealth, I've got all these beautiful women. I'm obviously happier than you. What have *you* got? Here you are sitting underneath a tree outside some wretched hut. You've got a yellow robe and a begging-bowl, that's all. Obviously I'm far happier than you.'

But then the Buddha said, 'Well, let me ask you a question. Tell me, could you sit here perfectly still for an hour, enjoying complete and perfect happiness?' The king said, 'Yes, I suppose I could.' Whereupon the Buddha said, 'All right. Could you sit here without moving, enjoying complete and perfect happiness, for six hours?' And the king said, 'That would be rather difficult.' Then the Buddha said, 'Could you sit for a whole day and a whole night, without moving, absolutely happy the whole time?' And the king had to admit, 'No, that would be beyond me.' Then the Buddha said, 'Well, I could sit here for seven days and seven nights without moving, without stirring, all the time experiencing complete and perfect happiness without any change, without any diminution whatsoever. So I think I must be happier than you.'[23]

The Buddha's happiness arose out of his concentration, and his concentration arose out of his happiness. Because he was happy he was able to concentrate; because he was able to concentrate he was happy. And the fact that the king could not concentrate showed that the king was not really as happy as he had thought, certainly not as happy as the Buddha.

This relates closely to the practice of meditation. We know that meditation begins with concentration, but many of us find this very difficult. It's really no use thinking that concentration can be gained by force of will; although, of course, a lot of people do think this. It's quite usual to experience a train of thought along the lines of 'Here I am. This is my time for meditation. I've got a concentration technique I can use. My mind is buzzing, full of idle thoughts. There's traffic going up and down outside. I'm sure there's going to be a knock on the door at any minute. But I'm going to concentrate. I don't particularly want to, but I've made up my mind to do it, so I will.' Most people's approach to meditation is more or less like this. We try to fix the mind forcibly on a certain point, but then all sorts of disturbances arise – we get distracted – because there is a split within us, and our emotional energies are not integrated. But meditation is not just a question of the application of techniques, not even the right techniques. It's much more a matter of gradual growth.

It has to be said that the Buddhist scriptures don't always seem to bear this out. They recount many instances in which a monk goes along to see the Buddha, the Buddha says a few words, and the monk – or sometimes the lay person – becomes Enlightened. Or they describe a monk living in the forest who sees a leaf fall from a tree, and from that gains an intense realization of impermanence which leads almost immediately to his becoming Enlightened. So why doesn't this kind of thing happen to us? Why don't the Buddha's words, or the falling leaves, affect us in this way?

Partly, at least, it's because the ground has not been prepared. It's full of rocks and stones and weeds and garbage. Even if a few seeds are scattered haphazardly here and there, they don't stand a chance, even before considerations of rain and light come into play. So the ground must have been prepared. Faith, satisfaction, delight, rapture, and so on must be cultivated (both within and without the meditation practice) before any concentration technique can be really fruitful. If concentration doesn't grow in this natural, spontaneous way, if we insist on making it a business of the forcible fixation of the mind on an object, the unregenerate or unsublimated portions of our psyche are liable to react against what we are doing.

We may manage through force of will deliberately, consciously, to hold the mind on a certain object – the breath, or an image of the Buddha, or a mantra. We may even succeed in keeping the mind on that object for a while. But we've done it with the energy of the conscious mind. The unconscious mind isn't co-operating, and sooner or later there's going to be a reaction, or even a sort of breakdown.

This doesn't mean that concentration exercises are not useful; they are. But they're much more effective when the ground has been cleared. To refer to the preceding stages in the sequence of positive *nidānas*, if we haven't really stopped to think about the unsatisfactoriness of life, if no faith has arisen, if there isn't much joy, and certainly not much rapture or calm or bliss or anything like that, there's not much possibility of real concentration. It's significant that concentration in the sense of *samādhi* arises only at the sixth stage, halfway up the path. It's only then that we can really begin to concentrate, because our emotional energies have been unified, and we are now, perhaps for the first time in our lives, happy. So really one's whole life needs to be a preparation for meditation.

It is also important to prepare well for each individual meditation session – the same gradual approach applies here, although the time scale is different. You can't just sit down and switch your mind on to the object of concentration; you have to pave the way. First of all, you have to disengage your energies from other things, and direct them into one channel; then, when your preparations for meditation are complete, the concentration exercise – the mindfulness of breathing or whatever it is – will just put the finishing touch, and you're away.

But however elevated our meditation practice, however concentrated we are, at this point we are still on the level of the mundane. We're on the spiral but we're still subject to the gravitational pull of the round. However, with the arising of the next stage in the series we come to the second part of the spiral, which is purely Transcendental and from which there is no possibility of regression.

Although this stage represents a radical change, it still arises in dependence on the previous stage of the path. There's a saying of the Buddha that comes into its own here: 'The concentrated mind sees things as they really are.'[24] When the mind is full of thoughts, when it isn't calm or harmonized or balanced, but pulled this way and that, it can't see things as they really are. But the concentrated mind – not the mind which is straining to stay on an object of concentration, but the mind which is naturally concentrated, with or without the help of a concentration exercise – is able to see the true nature of things.

From *What is the Dharma?* (1998, pp.117-20)

3. IS MEDITATION MAKING THE MIND A BLANK? (REVISITED)

There is, of course, such a thing as cessation of thought-processes, which does occur in the course of meditation, but one has to be quite clear about what one means by that expression.

Cessation of thought-processes may be mistaken for the quiescence of infinite mind, which is the true goal.[25]

Sangharakshita: In a general way, one might say that this represents a misunderstanding about the nature of meditation. One popular misunderstanding is that meditation means making the mind a blank. This is what some people think – that meditation means sitting down and wiping out all thoughts, and presumably going into a sort of unconscious state. This precept has some connection with that. There is, of course, such a thing as cessation of thought-processes, which does occur in the course of meditation, but one has to be quite clear about what one means by that expression. So in what sense is there a cessation of thought-processes?

Q: It comes when you are really concentrating on the breath or visualization practice.

S: It is really a sign of the transition from the first *dhyāna*, as it's called, to the second. In the first *dhyāna*, you are concentrated, your energies are flowing more or less together, you are in an emotionally positive state, you are balanced and calm. But there's a certain amount of discursive mental activity. You may even just be thinking about the meditation practice itself; you may say to yourself, 'It's going all right', or 'Oh, I'm starting to become concentrated'. But eventually, with practice, that discursive mental activity, which is called *vitarka-vicāra* in Pāli, subsides, and as it subsides you pass, as it were, from the first *dhyāna* to the second. This is the mark of the distinction between them. From the second *dhyāna* onwards, there are no discursive mental activities; you are not thinking about anything. All the energy of the psyche is fully absorbed by the practice. There's no energy, so to speak, left over for discursive mental activity.

So this is a stage, but it's only a stage. The important thing to bear in mind is that it isn't a blank state. Although there is no discursive mental activity, that doesn't mean that you pass into a state of unconsciousness. People tend to make the assumption that you become in some way unconscious when thought processes cease because they are identifying thought processes with consciousness and vice versa, and cannot envisage a mental state in which there are no thought processes, but in which you remain conscious. That goes beyond the experience of the ordinary person, so he or she naturally thinks that when thought processes cease, when you're not thinking about anything, the mind just becomes a blank; you become as it were unconscious. But in fact that is not what happens. Thought processes cease, but you remain fully conscious, fully aware; if anything, more so than ever.

But even that is still only a stage. As the text says, 'cessation of thought processes may be mistaken for the quiescence of infinite mind, which is the true goal'. One shouldn't take this expression 'infinite mind' too literally. In a sense, you could say there's then not a mind there at all. An infinite mind, so far as we are concerned, is a contradiction in terms, because we are acquainted only with finite mind – with my mind and your mind, and so on. It is important not to identify thought processes with consciousness, consciousness with thought processes, and not to identify even the conscious thought-free mental state with anything of a higher, Transcendental nature. It's only a stage on the way, even when one has reached that state in which thought processes have ceased; because Insight has yet to arise.

From the fourth seminar on *Precepts of the Gurus* (1980, pp.16-7)

4. NEIGHBOURHOOD CONCENTRATION

Neighbourhood or access concentration is halfway between your ordinary, relatively distracted state of mind and the full concentration that you get when you enter upon the first dhyana.

Q: What is neighbourhood or access concentration?

Sangharakshita: This is quite simple and straightforward. Neighbourhood or access concentration, *upacāra-samādhi*, is halfway to *apana-samādhi* or full absorption, which is synonymous with the *dhyāna* states. You could say that neighbourhood or access concentration is halfway between your ordinary, relatively distracted state of mind and the full concentration that you get when you enter upon the first *dhyāna*. In terms of the *kasiṇa* exercise, say, you are concentrating on that red disc which is external to you, a material red disc made of material flowers. The concentration that you get when you are gazing at that with your eyes open is just ordinary concentration, ordinary waking-state concentration. But if you then close your eyes and manage to reproduce that red disc in your mind's eye, you visualize it, and then you become fully concentrated upon that, disregarding all external stimuli and with no wandering thoughts, that is access concentration. When, out of that visualized red disc, there arises say a luminous disc, and you become much more intensely concentrated on that and all sorts of positive mental events start arising, that is the beginning of full concentration. So access or neighbourhood concentration comes halfway between the ordinary, waking-state type of concentration and the full absorption or the full concentration of the *samādhi* or *dhyāna* state.
From the Western Buddhist Order convention (1978, pp.21-2)

2 The *dhyānas*

1. 'TO PASS THROUGH THE DOOR OF THE MIND ...'

Dhyana, in the sense of the experience of superconscious states, is a natural thing. Ideally, as soon as one sits down to meditate, one should go straight into dhyana. It should be as simple and natural as that.

The Sanskrit word *dhyāna* (Pāli *jhāna*) is derived from the verbal root *dhyai* which means 'to think of', 'imagine', 'contemplate', 'meditate on', 'call to mind', 'recollect'. The term later developed quite a different meaning, and I think Dr Marion Matics put his finger on it when he said that the goal of *dhyāna* is 'to pass through the door of the mind to other regions of experience than those provided by the common faculties of thought and sense perception'.[26] This is a good general definition. We can consider *dhyāna* as comprising two things: higher or supernormal states of consciousness – states of consciousness above and beyond those of our ordinary everyday waking minds – and the various practices leading to the experience of those higher states of consciousness.

The Buddhist tradition has a number of ways of describing the different levels within, or different dimensions of, the higher consciousness. Here we will look at two lists: the four *dhyānas* of the world of form (*rūpā dhyānas*) and the four formless (*arūpā*) *dhyānas*.

The four dhyānas of the world of form
Usually four *dhyānas* are enumerated, but sometimes five, which reminds us not to take these classifications too literally. The four *dhyānas* repre-

sent successively higher stages of psychic and spiritual development, which in reality are one continuous, ever unfolding process.

Traditionally there are two ways of describing these four *dhyānas*: in terms of psychological analysis and in terms of images. In terms of psychological analysis, the experience of the first *dhyāna* is characterized by an absence of negative emotions, such as lust, ill-will, sloth and torpor, restlessness and anxiety, and doubt – in other words, the 'five mental hindrances'. Unless all negative emotions are inhibited, suppressed, suspended, unless the mind is clear not only of the five mental hindrances but of fear, anger, jealousy, anxiety, remorse, guilt, at least for the time being, there is no entry into higher states of consciousness. It is quite clear therefore that if we want to practise meditation seriously, our first task must be to learn to be able to inhibit, at least temporarily, at least the grosser manifestations of all these negative emotions.

Dhyāna, in the sense of the experience of superconscious states, is a natural thing. Ideally, as soon as one sits down to meditate, as soon as one closes one's eyes, one should go straight into *dhyāna*. It should be as simple and natural as that. If we led a truly human life, this would happen. In our practice we have to strive, struggle, and sweat, not to meditate, not to get into the *dhyāna* states, but to remove the obstacles which prevent us entering those states. If we could only remove these obstacles, we would go sailing into the first *dhyāna*.

On the positive side, the first *dhyāna* is characterized by a concentration and unification of all our psychophysical energies. Our energies are usually scattered, dispersed over a multiplicity of objects; they leak away and are wasted; or they are blocked. But when we take up the practice of meditation all our energies are brought together: those energies which were blocked are released; those which were being wasted are conserved. Our energies come together: they are concentrated, they are unified, they flow together. This flowing together, this heightening of energy, is characteristic of the first *dhyāna* (it is in fact characteristic, in increasing degrees, of all four *dhyānas*).

This concentration and unification of the energies of our total being is experienced in the first *dhyāna* as something intensely pleasurable, even blissful. These pleasurable sensations are of two kinds: there is a purely mental aspect and there is a physical aspect. The physical aspect is often described as rapture (Pāli *pīti*, Sanskrit *prīti*). It manifests in various ways. It may manifest for instance in the experience of one's hair standing on end. Some people when they practise meditation may find themselves weeping violently. This also is a manifestation of rapture on the physical level, and it is a good, healthy and positive manifestation, though it does pass away after some time.

The first *dhyāna* is also characterized by a certain amount of discursive mental activity, if only about the meditation experience itself, though it will not be enough to disturb one's concentration. After a while it may seem as though this discursive mental activity recedes to the fringes of one's experience, but it is still present.

In the second *dhyāna* the discursive mental activity fades away with increased concentration. The second *dhyāna* is therefore a state of no thought. When one speaks in terms of no thought, people often become a little afraid. They imagine that when there is no thought one almost ceases to exist – perhaps one goes into a sort of trance, or even into a sort of coma. It must be emphasized that in the second *dhyāna* there is simply no *discursive* mental activity: one is, at the same time, fully awake, one is aware, one is conscious. In fact, if anything, one's whole consciousness, one's whole being, is heightened: you are more alert, more awake, more aware, than you normally are. Even though the discursive mental activity fades away, even though the mind is no longer active in that sense, still a clear, pure, bright state of awareness is experienced.

In the second *dhyāna* one's psychic energies become still more concentrated and unified, with the result that the pleasurable sensations (both mental and physical) of the first *dhyāna* persist.

In passing from the first *dhyāna* to the second *dhyāna* discursive mental activity is eliminated. In passing from the second *dhyāna* to the third *dhyāna* it is the pleasurable physical sensations that disappear. The mind is blissful, but consciousness is increasingly withdrawn from the body and these pleasurable, even blissful physical sensations are no longer experienced. In fact in this stage bodily consciousness may be very peripheral indeed. It is as though you are conscious of your body a great way away, on the periphery of your experience – not right at the centre of it, as is usually the case. In the third *dhyāna* the other factors remain as before, except that they are further intensified.

In the fourth *dhyāna* even the mental experience of happiness disappears. Not, of course, that one becomes unhappy or uneasy in any way, but rather the mind passes beyond pleasure and pain. This is something which is rather difficult for us to understand; we cannot help thinking of such a state – which is neither pleasure nor pain – as being a neutral grey state, rather lower than either pleasure or pain. But it is not like that. In the fourth *dhyāna* the mind passes beyond pleasure, beyond pain, beyond even the mental bliss of the previous *dhyānas*, and enters a state of equanimity. To be paradoxical, one may say that the state of equanimity is even more pleasant than the pleasant state itself. (It is not true to say, however, that it is also more painful than the painful state.) In the fourth *dhyāna* all one's energies are fully integrated, so that this fourth *dhyāna* is a state of perfect mental, perfect spiritual, harmony, balance, and equilibrium.

The four *dhyānas* thus represent progressively purer and clearer states of superconsciousness, which are attained as one's energies progressively become more and more unified. They are usually described, especially by scholars, in rather a dry, analytical manner; all one gets, very often, is a catalogue of different mental functions. This is unfortunate, because it does need to be emphasized that these are actual experiences attainable by living human beings like you and me. The spirit, the human experience, of these higher or more unified states of consciousness is brought out very well by the Buddha himself in four appropriate and even delightful similes:

> *As an expert bath attendant, or bath attendant's apprentice, puts soap powder into a dish, soaks it with water, mixes and dissolves it in such a manner that its foam is completely permeated, saturated within and without with moisture, leaving none over, even so the monk suffuses, pervades, fills, and permeates his body with the pleasure and joy arising from seclusion, and there is nothing in all his body untouched by the pleasure and joy arising from seclusion ...*
>
> *As a lake with a subterranean spring, into which there flows no rivulet from east or from west, from north or from south, nor do the clouds pour their rain into it, but only the fresh spring at the bottom wells up and completely suffuses, pervades, fills, and permeates it, so that not the smallest part of the lake is left unsaturated with fresh water, even so the monk ... permeates his body with the pleasure and joy arising from concentration ...*
>
> *As in a lake with lotus plants some lotus flowers are born in the water, develop in the water, remain below the surface of the water, and draw their nourishment from the depths of the water, and their blooms and roots are suffused, pervaded, filled,*

and permeated with fresh water, even so the monk ... permeates his body with pleasure without joy ...

As a man might cloak himself from head to foot in a white mantle, so that not the smallest part of his body was left uncovered by the white mantle, even so the monk sits having covered his body with a state of extreme equanimity and concentration. ...[27]

One can see from these four similes that there is a definite progression as one passes from one *dhyāna* to the next. In the first simile there is water and there is soap powder, in other words there is a duality; but there is a resolution of that duality in their being kneaded together until you have a ball of soap absolutely saturated with water, so that there is not a single speck of soap powder that is still dry, and not a single drop of water trickling free of the ball. Thus, in the first *dhyāna* there is a complete unification of the energies of the conscious mind on the conscious level. (By the way, this soap would have come – this may come as a surprise – from a soap tree: the tree has a large fruit that would have been dried and powdered, as it still is in parts of southern India, and used as soap.)

For the second *dhyāna*, the Buddha proposes the image of a pool of perfectly clear, pure water, being constantly refreshed and replenished by a subaqueous spring. So the second *dhyāna* is a clear pure state of consciousness into which rapture and joy are bubbling up all the time from deep within you. The simile describes the trickling in, the percolating through, perhaps finally the pouring in, as a source of inspiration, of the superconscious energies, once one's energies have been unified on the level of the conscious mind.

As for the third *dhyāna*, this is likened to lotus flowers immersed in a pond of fresh water: their stalks, their leaves, flowers, blossoms, seed-pods, the whole plant is immersed in the water, permeated by the water, but still separate and distinct from it. Similarly we experience our consciousness as completely pervaded and fed by an all-encompassing bliss. The simile of the lotuses permeated by water describes the energies of the conscious mind permeated and transformed by the superconscious energies.

Finally, the Buddha comes at the fourth level of higher consciousness through another typically Indian image. He invites you to imagine that in the heat of the day, when you are very hot and dusty, you go and bathe in a pool or a river, and then, on emerging from the clear fresh water, you wrap yourself in a clean, cool, white sheet, and you just sit there like that, enveloped from head to toe. In the same way, in the fourth *dhyāna* you wrap yourself in a purified consciousness that insulates you from all harm. The dust of the world cannot touch you. The simile describes the superconscious energies not only permeating, but dominating, enclosing, and enfolding the energies of the conscious mind. In the second *dhyāna*, the superconscious energies in the form of the water flowing in from the subterranean spring are contained within the unified conscious mind (the lake). In the fourth *dhyāna*, it is the conscious mind which is contained within the superconscious energies (the white mantle). The situation has been completely reversed.

The Four Formless Dhyānas
The four formless (*arūpā*) *dhyānas* consist of the experience of objects of ever-increasing degrees of subtlety and refinement. The first of these four states of higher consciousness associated with the formless world is known as the Sphere of Infinite Space, or the Experience of Infinite Space. Here one's experience is devoid of all objects. One may recollect that by the time one reaches the fourth *dhyāna* of the world of form one leaves behind the body consciousness. If one abstracts oneself from the senses through which objects in space are perceived, one is left with the experience of infinite space – space extending infinitely in all directions, all of which is everywhere. It is not just a sort of visual experience of looking out into infinite space from a certain point *in* space; it is a feeling of freedom and expansion, an experience of one's whole being expanding indefinitely.

The second formless *dhyāna* is known as the Sphere of Infinite Consciousness. One reaches this by 'reflecting' that one has experienced infinite space; in that experience there was a consciousness of infinite space. That means that, conterminous with the infinity of space, there is an infinity of consciousness: the subjective correlative of that objective state or experience. Abstracting or subtracting from the experience of space and concentrating on the experience of consciousness, the infinity of consciousness, one experiences infinite consciousness, once again extending in all directions, but not from any one particular point – consciousness which is all present everywhere.

The third formless *dhyāna* is even more rarefied, though still mundane. This state of superconsciousness is known as the Sphere of

No-thingness, the Sphere of Non-particularity. In this experience one cannot pick out any one thing in particular as distinct from any other thing. In our ordinary everyday consciousness we can pick out a flower as distinct from a tree, or a man as distinct from a house, but in this state there is no particular thingness of things. One cannot identify this as 'this' and that as 'that'. It is not as though they are confused and mixed up together, but the possibility of picking out does not exist. This is not a state of nothingness but of no-thingness.

The fourth formless *dhyāna* is the Sphere of Neither Perception nor Non-perception. One has passed from the infinite object to the infinite subject, and now one goes beyond both. One reaches a state in which one cannot say – because in a sense there is no one to say – whether one is perceiving anything or whether one is not perceiving anything. One is not fully beyond subject and object, but one can no longer think or experience in terms of subject and object.

From *A Guide to the Buddhist Path* (1990, pp.163-7)
and *What is the Dharma?* (1998, pp.153-4)

2. THE NATURE OF DHYĀNA

Once you start radiating, you're doing pretty well ...

Sangharakshita: It is said that the fourth *dhyāna* is the basis for the development of the *iddhi* (that's the Pāli word, the Sanskrit is *siddhi*), in the sense of supernormal powers or magical powers. So why do you think that is? To consider this, we need to consider the nature of *dhyāna*. In English one can describe the four *dhyānas* as the stages of integration, inspiration, permeation, and radiation. But why these particular terms? If we go into this a little, we can come back to the link with supernormal powers.

The Buddha says the first *dhyāna* is like somebody taking a quantity of soap powder and mixing it together with water so that a sort of ball is produced, and in this ball, every single drop of the dry soap powder is saturated with water and all the water is fully absorbed into the soap powder so that no drop of water is left over. What does this suggest?

Q: Integration.

S: Integration, but what is being integrated?

Q: The emotions.

S: The emotions, energies, conscious and unconscious. According to the more analytical accounts the first *dhyāna* consists of five *dhyānāṅgas*, five *dhyāna* factors. This is quite a basic teaching. First of all there is *ekāgratā* (Sanskrit; Pāli *ekaggatā*), which is usually translated as concentration, but literally means one-pointedness. *Aga* means a peak or a pinnacle, or the gable of a house, the point where the two sides of the roof converge, so when you speak of the mind being *ekagga*, it is not just with one point, it is with one peak, a common peak up towards which everything converges. This is what we translate as concentration, but concentration doesn't give the full flavour of it. The suggestion is that all your energies are not only flowing together but flowing up towards a peak or pinnacle of convergence. Sometimes the term *cittas-ekaggatā*, which means one-pointedness of the mind or heart or consciousness, is used. This is, as it were, the spearhead of the whole process of integration. It is not just the one-pointedness of the conscious mind but the integration of the whole psychic contents, one could say. Then there is *sukha*, which is happiness; *prīti* which is rapture; then *vitarka*, (Sanskrit; Pāli *vitakka*) which is thinking *of* an object; and *vicāra,* which is thinking *about* an object. These five factors are all present in the first *dhyāna*.

As your energies are integrated, as your interest centres at higher and higher levels, you naturally feel very happy because there's an absence of conflict, especially between your conscious and unconscious 'interests'. The energy which was in the unconscious is now flowing though into the conscious mind. Hence you get that sensation of *prīti* or rapture. At the same time there is mental activity, especially with regard to the object of your practice – say, the breathing process. You think of it and you think about it, in other words *vitarka* and *vicāra*.

We can see from this analytical account of the first *dhyāna* that it is very much a process of the coming together of energies with the result of happiness and rapture, though with a certain amount of mental activity, especially with regard to the object of concentration. The Buddha's image of the soap and the soap powder is quite an apt illustration of this. It represents a coming together, a blending, a harmonization, an integration. So therefore I call the first *dhyāna* the stage of integration.

I sometimes speak also of horizontal integration and vertical integration. Horizontal integration means the integration of emotion and reason on the conscious level. Vertical integration is the integration of conscious with unconscious. A complete integration is both horizontal and vertical, and this is the nature of the first *dhyāna*. Obviously this is very important. Do you see the connection between happiness or bliss and the integration of one's energies? When you feel unhappy you are divided, but when all of your energies are flowing together in the same direction you feel happy. So a state of concentration or state of integration is also a state of happiness; it couldn't be anything else.

Q: Can one say that happiness is integration?

S: One could say that happiness is integration, and integration is happiness. To be integrated is to be happy. To be happy is to have become integrated.

All right, what about the illustration for the second *dhyāna*, bubbles coming up into a lake from an underground stream. What do you think is the point of this illustration?

Q: The unconscious is welling up into the conscious mind.

S: Perhaps it is more than just the unconscious, unless you use the word unconscious in a very broad sense indeed. In a sense, at least up to a point, the unconscious has already been integrated with the conscious. But it is as though something is welling up from an even deeper level, almost from a spiritual level. From very deep down, certainly from some other dimension, something is coming up. Or – we mustn't be misled by words or figures of speech – it can be experienced as coming from above. Indeed, although sometimes we speak of the depths, and sometimes we speak of the heights, presumably you could even imagine it or feel it coming in sideways, from some other direction. You don't really know which direction it comes from, you just find it there. It hasn't come from anywhere that you are conscious of. It just appears, out of the blue, mysteriously. But very often you do have the experience of something bubbling up from the depths, something which is quite different from your whole, even integrated state of mind. Or you experience it as coming from above, like a ray of light coming down from the heavens.

Q: Is it a Transcendental experience?

S: It's not Transcendental at this stage. Well, that's not impossible, it could be, but within the context of the four *dhyānas* as such, no. It isn't ruled out, but it would be in a way more than a *dhyāna* then. This is also the stage of pure and authentic artistic inspiration. When inspiration comes into the mind, sometimes it's little feeble flashes or just the odd bubble bubbling up, but sometimes it is very powerful indeed, quite overwhelming. But within the *dhyānic* context the experience wouldn't be quite overwhelming because the inspiration would come up within the already integrated mind. Do you get the picture? This is the stage of inspiration, for want of a better term. Inspiration of course literally means breathing into, or blowing into.

And then there's the stage of permeation. What is the illustration here?

Q: Doesn't it have a lotus flower above the water?

S: Well, the point of the illustration is that the lotus flowers are *soaked in* the water, permeated by the water, thoroughly immersed in the water. What does this suggest in terms of one's *dhyāna* experience?

Q: One's whole being is permeated by spiritual influences.

S: Yes. First of all you've got this inspiration welling up, but this eventually fills the whole area and you're completely immersed in it and soaked in it. You feel as though you're living in some new, different element. In whatsoever direction you move you are still in that and that is still in you. This is the characteristic feature of the experience, one could say. It's like swimming, except that the water is not only outside you but permeating all the way through you too. Of course, if that literally happened you'd drown ... but you get the idea? This is what the third *dhyāna* is like. This becomes more and more difficult to understand, obviously.

Q: So you are, as it were, soaked in inspiration?

S: Yes, and surrounded by inspiration. You don't feel any limitations, you feel as though you can expand and flow in any direction. This is a state which some mystics seem to experience and in which they feel that they're one with God, though from the Buddhistic point of view it is simply the experience of the third *dhyāna*. But you can understand how people could interpret this experience in that sort of way, because it is a very vivid, powerful experience, very real and certainly completely authentic. It's easy to understand how one might misinterpret it and overvalue it.

Then, what about the stage of radiation? What is the illustration for this?

Q: A man after a bath wrapped in a sheet?

S: Yes, so what does this suggest?

Q: Complete insulation.

S: Yes, but I didn't call this the stage of insulation, I call it the stage of radiation. So why is that?

Q: When you're full of inspiration it's as though you can't help but give it out.

S: It's as though the *dhyāna* state has become so strong that it begins to affect your environment. You, as it were, are stronger than it. You begin to have an effect on your environment, you begin to create an atmosphere. As you know, if you use a certain room for meditation, an atmosphere builds up which other people, even people who don't meditate, can perceive when they come in.

In this state, your *dhyāna* state can't be dispersed by your surroundings. Not only that; you can affect your surroundings, hence radiation. You've built up a very positive, very powerful mental state or spiritual state – so much so that you can start working changes in your environment. You can even start affecting other people's thoughts, other people's minds. Other people pick up things from you, even at a distance, even without seeing you. And here you begin to get the so-called supernormal faculties coming into operation. Do you see the connection now? So, for this reason, it is said that the fourth *dhyāna*, the stage of radiation, is the basis for the development of the *iddhis*, these supernormal powers or faculties.

When you meditate, in the sense of trying to develop the *samatha* side of your spiritual experience, this is what you are trying to do. First of all you are trying to integrate all your energies and emotions. Then you are trying to open yourself to inspiration from higher or deeper or other levels. Then you are trying to get into a state in which you are completely pervaded by a higher element, as it were, and live and move and have your being in it. And then you are trying to increase your psychic positivity to such an extent that it will radiate in all directions and affect others, either through your words and actions, or even without words or actions, as well as providing you with a natural insulation against all negative psychic forces. Incidentally, this is why *mettā* is said to be the best means of keeping ghosts and spirits at bay. It just naturally keeps them away or neutralizes their power if your own positivity is of sufficient intensity.

So do you get a clearer picture about these four *dhyāna* states and what you are trying to do when you cultivate them? When you meditate – leaving aside the question of Insight – you are essentially trying to get into what are called the *dhyānas*, sometimes called the superconscious states. The more you get into them the more you are integrated, inspired, permeated, and radiant. And once you start radiating, well, you're doing pretty well ...

From a seminar on the Great Chapter of the *Sutta-Nipāta* (1976, pp.376-86)

3. THE CHARACTERISTICS OF DHYĀNA: FIVE FACTORS

Before you even get into the first *dhyana* you are already in a quite highly developed mental state.

In the first *dhyāna*, there are five mental factors. First of all, the mind is still active – there are the two factors of *vitarka-vicāra*. *Vitarka* is the apprehension of an object, and *vicāra* is the more detailed investigation of that object. So these two different kinds of mental activity are both present in the first *dhyāna*. Mental activity, at least of a subtle nature, is not yet altogether stilled. Also, of course, it must be remembered that before you even enter upon that first *dhyāna* all thoughts of craving, anger, sloth and torpor, and hurry and worry, and indecision and doubt must have subsided. So before you even get into the first *dhyāna* you are already in a quite highly developed mental state.

Then there is *sukha*, which means 'happiness'. This is twofold: physical and mental. In its physical aspect, the physical body feels very much at ease. It's not merely that you're sitting comfortably, but all your physical energies are in a state of composure. Your body feels in a state of ease and well-being. And *sukha* is also happiness in the mental sense; you feel calm and happy, and at peace with yourself.

The fourth factor is *prīti*, which is the intense blissful experience that bubbles up as you become more concentrated and your energies become unified. As the unification of energy begins to extend from the conscious to the unconscious, all your blocked energies start being liberated. And as the blocked energies bubble up, this is experienced as intensely pleasurable, and this is *prīti*, which is usually translated as 'rapture' or 'ecstasy' or 'exhilaration', and is experienced to various degrees of intensity. So this is the fourth mental factor present in the first *dhyāna*.

And the fifth factor is *citta-ekagata*, which means 'unification of the whole mind'. Sometimes it is translated as 'concentration', but it's more than that. It's the coming together of all the different aspects of one's mind, all one's energies. Hence the simile of the soap powder and the water coming together: not a drop of water too much, and at the same time not a single speck of the soap powder unsoaked in water, they are completely unified.

So this is the first *dhyāna* state. It's a state in which there is a certain amount of mental activity, at least with regard to the object of concentration of your meditation, a state of physical ease and mental lightness and happiness, a rapturous experience due to the released energies that are bubbling up within you, and an overall experience of unification. Though I am using all these quite ordinary words, one must understand them in a heightened sense, when applied to the first *dhyāna*.

The second *dhyāna* develops when, as you become more concentrated on the particular object of your concentration, whether that may be breath or mantra, even the subtle mental activity dies away. There is no mental activity left. You are not thinking about or of anything in particular in the discursive sense, so you become still more unified. The experience of ease and happiness becomes intensified, and the *prīti* experience also becomes much more intense. That is the second *dhyāna*.

You reach the third *dhyāna* when *prīti* begins to die away. *Priti* is a sort of bubbling feeling which you can experience on different levels. But when all of your blocked energies have been released and absorbed, the bubbling subsides. All that you have, therefore, in the third *dhyāna* is an experience of intense psycho-physical happiness amounting to bliss, together with an even greater degree of unification and integration of one's being – one's psycho-physical energies and so on – at an even higher level. This is the third *dhyāna*.

In the fourth *dhyāna* you have an even higher degree of unification, or integration, and the experience of bliss and happiness is replaced by equanimity. So there is an experience of equanimity conjoined, as it were, with integration.

Although again I'm using ordinary words, they are to be understood in a very much heightened sense. For instance 'equanimity' doesn't just mean being a bit calm, a bit quiet. It's a very much more positive and powerful state. Equanimity is the fourth of the four 'illimitable' states, usually called *brahma-vihāras*. One must be very careful to understand that 'equanimity' is not an unemotional state. The great danger is to mistake 'equanimity' for 'indifference', or vice versa. It's said that first of all you practise the *mettā-bhāvanā* in the usual way, ending up by developing *mettā* towards all beings equally, impartially, and by dwelling upon the impartiality of *mettā*, you make the transition to equanimity: not by excluding *mettā*, not by excluding feeling or emotion, but making that particular emotion the same towards all beings.

So equanimity, far from being separated from positive emotion, is the culmination of it. It shows that the positive emotion, whether *mettā* or *karuṇā* or *muditā*, has reached its apogee, as it were: it's been fully developed, which means that it has been developed equally towards all living beings. You're not more attached to one or less attached to another; you've equal *mettā*, equal *karuṇā*, equal *muditā* towards all, as the occasion requires, and this gives you your emotional stability, your equanimity. It's equanimity in this sense that is developed in connection with the fourth *dhyāna*, and conjoined with unification, or integration, or *citta-ekagata*.

In his book about the Buddha, Trevor Ling describes the Buddha's meditation experience just before he gained Enlightenment thus:

> *This consisted first of his entry into and progress through four successively deeper stages of meditation; the emphasis here lies upon the purification of the mind which was necessary.*[28]

But that doesn't really convey the full import of the Buddha's experience, when he passed through those four *dhyānas*, thus achieving purification of the mind, which expression refers to the fourth *dhyāna*. Though the words of the tradition have been reproduced quite faithfully, there seems to be no understanding in this sentence of what the words really signify. The text goes on: 'In this way he is said to have achieved concentration, equanimity, and dispassion' – which makes it sound a very ordinary sort of experience indeed! These terms need to be understood in – I won't say in a necessarily 'spiritual' sense, but in their more heightened sense, as they are experienced in the course of meditation.

From a seminar on Trevor Ling's *The Buddha* (1976, pp.229-31)

4. THE RELEASE OF BLOCKED ENERGY

Buddhists would say that levitation isn't a very important phenomenon or experience.

Many years ago I happened to be passing through a place called Kharagpur in India. Kharagpur is near a big railway junction, and I'd gone there from Calcutta to give a lecture. The lecture was scheduled for about eleven o'clock at night – they like to have their lectures late in those parts – so I was waiting for the one o'clock morning train to take me back to Calcutta. I was waiting on the station platform among a crowd of people, and we all got talking to pass the time until the train arrived. And, as it happened, the train was late.

After a while someone brought forward a certain individual, an ordinary looking man in ordinary Indian dress, from the crowd, and they said 'This man has a problem.' I thought perhaps his wife had run away, or his son hadn't passed an examination, or something of that sort. But they said, 'No. The trouble is that he levitates.' So I said 'Do you mean that he literally levitates?' They said 'Yes. He's a Kabirapanthi.' A Kabirapanthi is someone who follows the sect founded by Kabir, the great medieval Hindu-cum-Muslim yogi. And apparently every morning this man was practising certain breathing exercises, as a result of which he would just float up a few inches, or even a few feet, above the ground.

Naturally I said to these people, a little suspiciously, 'Has anyone seen this happening?' They said, 'Oh yes, we've all seen it every day. He just can't control it. He wants to meditate, but this levitation gets in the way. As soon as he does his breathing exercises he just starts going up into the air. So what should he do? How should he stop?' This, of course, is the sort of question one might be asked at any time in India.

I said, 'According to Buddhism levitation is brought about by excess of *prīti* – that is, rapture. So what one must do is cultivate the mental faculty of equanimity or tranquillity, *upekṣā*. If one does that, there will be a sort of counterbalancing force to the *prīti*, and levitation will not occur.' I never went to Kharagpur again, so I never heard whether the prescription was successful, but let us hope that it was.

I met another levitator when I was living in Kalimpong, up in the Himalayas. I was once entertaining to lunch an American couple and a Tibetan lama, rather a distinguished one. In the course of the lunch the American man said, with a rather knowing smile, 'I suppose you haven't heard of anyone who can levitate?' So the lama said modestly 'Yes. In fact, I do a little myself.' At this the two Americans nearly fell off their chairs. They said, 'You can do it *yourself*?' He said 'Yes. I don't think I could do it right now, but if I spend about six months meditating alone in the jungle, or in a secluded monastery, at the end of that time I can levitate.'

He was not really unusual – although my visitors certainly thought so. I have met a number of Tibetans who have either seen levitation done or who can do it themselves. It is all said to be due to an excess of *prīti*, or rapture, when one's experience, especially in meditation, becomes so intense that the body is quite literally lifted up. One finds records of this sort of thing not only in Buddhist life and literature, but also in the lives of some comparatively recent Christian mystics. But Buddhists would say it isn't a very important phenomenon or experience. This is still only the third stage of the path – it's essentially a mundane experience. If it happens one shouldn't take too much notice of it. It just means that one has accumulated rapture of sufficient intensity to produce this particular psychophysical effect.

To use modern terminology, one could say that rapture comes about as a result of the release of blocked energy – energy that is short-circuiting itself, as it were, or as if locked up. In the course of one's spiritual life, especially when one practises meditation, these blocks get dissolved. One digs down, one uncovers certain depths within oneself; little complexes are resolved, so that the energy locked up in them is released and surges up. It's due to this upsurge of energy, felt throughout the nervous system as well as in the mind, that one experiences *prīti*.

From *What is the Dharma?* (1998, pp.114-5)

5. TOTAL SATURATION

Concentration, and hence the first *dhyana*, does involve a process of bringing together reason and emotion, at least to some extent.

Q: The similes for the first and third *dhyānas* both seem to suggest a state of total saturation. Could you explain how they are to be distinguished?

Sangharakshita: In the case of the simile for the first *dhyāna*, you have got two elements: the soap powder and the water. So what corresponds to which? The dry soap powder corresponds to you in your unintegrated state, and the water corresponds to the higher state of consciousness which is bringing together, so to speak, all those scattered particles, so that in the end there is a complete harmony between them. On account of the growth of concentration, all the scattered particles are brought together, so they are in a sense saturated by some higher element, bound together by that higher element; so, in a sense, completely saturated. But what is completely saturated is the previous unintegrated consciousness. But in the third *dhyāna*, whose simile is the lotus completely saturated in water, it is the integrated consciousness which is saturated by a state still higher.

Comparisons have their limitations; you can't have a *dhyāna* state apart from a mind which experiences the *dhyāna* state. But the soap powder represents the unintegrated mind, and the *dhyāna* state represents the integrated mind. The water gradually mixing with the soap powder represents the fact that the mind is gradually becoming more integrated, and therefore more concentrated. So it is a total process, in the sense that all the particles become saturated in or absorbed into that higher state, which is of course non-different from themselves – one must again remember the limitations of the analogy. Even though we say that the grains of soap powder represent the mind in its unintegrated state, it is not that the water represents something other than the mind, because the *dhyāna* is itself a mental state. To put it more simply, in the third *dhyāna* the mind attains an even higher level of integration. Nonetheless, one should be careful not to obliterate the distinction between the first and the third *dhyānas* by appearing to use more or less the same kind of language for both of them.

Q: Can't the first *dhyāna* be seen in terms of the integration of reason and emotion?

S: Yes, because in a sense reason, as ordinarily understood, is alienated, analytic, devoid of emotion, dry, just as the soap powder is dry, whereas emotion could be thought of as something moist. So one can look at it in that way. Also, why are you not concentrated? Because your interest is not involved, your emotions are not involved. So concentration, and hence the first *dhyāna*, does involve a process of bringing together reason and emotion, at least to some extent. I think it is therefore quite legitimate to speak of the attainment of the first *dhyāna* in terms of a bringing together of reason and emotion, and of the introduction of an emotional element into one's spiritual life.

Q: Would you consider that to be a sufficient way of describing the first *dhyāna*?

S: Oh no. But I think it is quite an important element of it. Of course, it also depends on a certain definition of reason and a certain definition of emotion, especially on a definition of reason as a cold, analytical, slightly alienated thing; not reason in the sense, say, that Milton uses the term.

Q: I had understood the simile to refer to one's awareness, the water, fully permeating the object of concentration, the soap powder.

S: What do you mean by consciousness permeating an object? Being fully concentrated upon it?

Q: Yes.

S: I suppose it does imply that, though I think the simile brings out more than that. One does speak sometimes of the absorption of the consciousness in the object, to the exclusion of any other object. That introduces an element of feeling, because you can't really become absorbed in something unless you have some feeling for it. Concentration necessarily involves an element of feeling, even an element of emotion. So it would still be a coming together of reason and emotion. Instead of having just an idea of the object, you would have a feeling for it, gradually become absorbed in it.

Q: Does the fragmentary nature of the soap powder also bring out something about dry reason, do you think?

S: Well, reason, you could say, is desiccated. It is emotion that binds things together, isn't it? A friend of mine once described the work of a particular Pāli Buddhist scholar as 'the last ounce of dust in desiccation'. The soap powder conjures up much the same sort of image – something very dry and crumbled into innumerable tiny particles. If one wanted to be epigrammatic, one could say that reason is analytic and emotion is synthetic.

You find that when you are writing. If you have just got a lot of ideas, it is very difficult to write, but if you have a strong feeling for the subject you are writing about, the feeling binds together all the items of information, and then you can write. But if you have just got the ideas or the information without that very strong feeling, it is almost impossible to write in any genuinely literary sense. Luther used to say that he wrote best when he was in a rage; for him, rage was the binding factor – his mind became very sharp and clear, and he could write furiously. When he had to reply to something Erasmus had written, he found it very difficult, because Erasmus, by his pseudo-meekness, had given him no opportunity or excuse for getting into a rage.

Q: Does the first *dhyāna* represent horizontal integration, or vertical integration, or both?

S: It is more horizontal than vertical, because it takes place more or less in a normal state of consciousness. The external world does not begin to fade away, as it were, as it does more or less completely in the fourth *dhyāna*. There are degrees or levels of intensity within each of the *dhyānas*, in any case. It is not that you are either definitely in the first *dhyāna* or definitely not. And there is traditionally an intermediate level, neighbourhood concentration.

From Q&A on the Noble Eightfold Path (1983, pp.140-2)

6. A VERY MYSTERIOUS BODY OF EXPERIENCES

One has to be quite careful to relate what one experiences oneself in the course of meditation to what one reads in Buddhist texts, canonical and otherwise.

> *The first three Infinities have received their respective names through an act of deliberation at the time of their realization (samāpatti) but later when this realization has been overcome there is no thought with which to make a judgement.*[29]

Q: The text refers to an 'act of deliberation' in the first three of the formless *dhyānas*. In what sense is there subtle conceptual thought in the higher *dhyānas*?

Sangharakshita: This raises the whole question of the general nature of these *arūpā-dhyānas*. They are a very mysterious body of experiences. Yogis don't have very much to say about them, it seems, not in modern times, and scholars also don't really know what to make of them. Perhaps it is one of those aspects of Buddhism that need re-evaluation. Gampopa, whether following Sarvastivada tradition or not, seems to think that there is something that requires explanation, because he mentions that the sphere of infinite space is called the sphere of infinite space, but at the same time he makes it clear that that is only the way in which we think of it prior to entering upon it. So one might ask, what is it, and from what level does one enter upon it? Does one, for instance, in the first *dhyāna*, think: 'I will enter upon the sphere of infinity of space,' and then proceed through the other *rūpā dhyānas* and only then enter that particular *arūpā dhyāna*? Is that what happens? It isn't clear. One can only try to consult, eventually, one's own experience and see what happens.

While we are on the subject, one has not only the analytical psychological accounts of the *dhyānas*, but also the Buddha's similes. Personally, I am inclined to pay more attention to the similes, on the basis that they are perhaps more representative of what actually happens than the psychological analysis. One can only try to make connections in one's own experience. For instance, in the second *dhyāna*, do you actually have an experience of something rather like a subterranean spring arising in the depth of your being? Is this what you experience? Or, one might ask, is that a standard experience? It would seem to be, judging from the fact that the Buddha gives that simile. Or can one have a sort of approximation to that? Can one experience it in a different way – for instance, the arousing of the kundalini, or something of that kind?

I think one has to be quite careful to relate what one experiences oneself in the course of meditation to what one reads in Buddhist texts, canonical and otherwise. Sometimes it will require quite a bit of thought and reflection before one sees the way in which things actually hang together. Also, one must not forget that the analysis of the different *dhyānas* into their constituent psychological factors is not complete. It is not that the *dhyānas* contain only those particular mental factors. One has to get the whole picture, and one can do that best, no doubt, by consulting the appropriate Abhidharma analysis. For instance, in the case of a *dhyāna*, you will have all the mental factors which are present in all states of consciousness anyway, and then all those which are present in all skilful states of consciousness, and then those which are present only in that particular *dhyāna*. One has to take the whole picture into consideration, all the different factors, and then try to evaluate them and perhaps translate them in terms of the corresponding simile that the Buddha gives. Then you can compare them with your own experience, see whether, as your experience of meditation deepens, you do in fact experience things in that way.

From a seminar on the *Jewel Ornament of Liberation* (1985, pp.264 5)

7. WHAT DO YOU GET OUT OF THE SPIRITUAL LIFE?

If your life was properly organized, you'd end up in the first or second *dhyana* almost without having to make an effort.

In the *Samaññaphala Sutta*, this is the Maharaja's question: whether there is a fruit of the life of a recluse, a *samana*, one devoted to the spiritual life, 'belonging to this life, and perceptible here and now'. And the Buddha says, 'Yes! You experience this *dhyānic* state.'

Someone might ask you, 'What do you get out of the spiritual life? What do you get out of doing all the things that you do?' Well, what *do* you get out of it? What is really the answer in the long run? It's not anything external. It's some transformation within yourself, some personal experience. It's the fact that you are more of a human being, you have attained a higher mental state. That is a fruit which can be visible not only to you but to other people. Other people can see that you are happier than you were. Maybe people who knew you years ago, in your unregenerate days, can't help admitting that there's a change. Even your relations can see that you've changed. You just seem so much happier, more positive. And maybe in the end they grudgingly admit that it may have something to do with the fact that you meditate.

It's as though the *dhyāna* state is just as tangible, just as concrete, as the things that are made by the potter and the carpenter. If anything, it's more concrete – it's part of you, part of your own experience of yourself.

> *Further, Maharaja, the bhikkhu, from ceasing to apply and sustain his thought with regard to objects external and ideational, attains to that serenity of mind, that singleness of purpose, which is devoid of application to any object. He enters into and remains in the ease and joy produced by concentration and one-pointedness of mind, which are of the second jhanic state. With these qualities he pervades his body till no part of it remains unsuffused with them. This, Maharaja, is a fruit of the life of a recluse, belonging to this life and more advanced and more excellent than the preceding fruits.*[30]

Here we pass from the first *dhyāna* to the second *dhyāna*, the main difference between them being the absence of mental activity. One could say that the mental activity which still takes place in the first *dhyāna* suffices to give one a purpose and direction, but by the time you reach the second *dhyāna* that purpose and that direction are so firmly established, and the whole trend of your being is so definitely in that direction that you don't need the support of any conceptual framework. Do you see what I mean? You don't need to reflect upon Enlightenment and the purpose of human life. You're actually moving in that direction, so you can stop thinking about it and just move to an even more positive mental and emotional state. You don't need conceptual support – not for the time being. You can get on without it. You see how gradual and natural the whole process is? It's as though if your life was properly organized, you'd end up in the first or second *dhyāna* almost without having to make an effort.

Some people find that when they go on retreat, their whole mental state seems to alter after a while, without their even making much of an effort, just on account of the difference in their surroundings. So suppose the whole of life, the whole of society, the whole of civilization, was organized to make it easier for you to meditate. You probably would then meditate very easily. Suppose noise was abolished, suppose there were no aircraft flying overhead, no radios blaring in the distance … I think people could make it much easier for one another, because a lot of our irritations and difficulties and disturbances do come from other people. Certainly within a spiritual community, people should try to make it easy for one another and help one another – even just by taking everybody tea in the morning to help them get up for meditation. But you can only encourage. You can't force people to lead a spiritual life. You can't even force them to discipline themselves. They've got to want to do it.

From a seminar on the *Samaññaphala Sutta* (1982, pp.158-60)

8. THE BEST WAY OF LIVING

Surely the longer you spend in dhyanic states, the less time you can spend helping other sentient beings?

> *Rechungpa bowed down at the Jetsun's feet and made many good wishes. Then he set out for Weu, and the Jetsun returned to the Belly Cave.*[31]

Sangharakshita: Milarepa always seemed to go back to his cave, back to his meditation, whatever anybody else might be doing.

Q: I'm rather surprised to find quite often in Buddhist texts that Enlightened beings apparently continue to meditate. I would have thought that meditation was a means to getting Enlightened and that once you'd got there you wouldn't have to bother.

S: So why did the Buddha continued to meditate? What happens when an Enlightened being meditates?

Q: It's not so much carrying out the mindfulness of breathing or particular practices as just enjoying his Enlightened state.

S: Enjoying his Enlightened state? Do you mean that at other times he does not enjoy it? How is that possible? His meditation has got nothing to do with his Enlightened state. He is Enlightened. If even *vipassanā* is a permanent achievement, what can be said of Enlightenment? It is not something that you experience, and then you drop out of it from time to time and you go back to it when you meditate. So what does happen when an Enlightened being meditates?

Q: Is he always in a state of meditation?

S: Not according to the Pāli scriptures. Sometimes the Buddha meditated, sometimes he didn't, but he was always the Buddha, he was always Enlightened. That suggests a distinction between Enlightenment and meditation. So when we say that the Buddha meditated, what do we mean? We don't mean that he temporarily recaptured his Enlightenment experience, because that by definition as it were is permanent; he is always the Buddha. So when he meditates what happens, if he is not recapturing that Enlightenment experience?

Q: He's experiencing the *dhyānas*.

S: Yes. But why does a Buddha bother to experience the *dhyānas*? After all, he's Enlightened! They are not a means to Enlightenment any more.

Q: Do they help him when he is in the world, when he is not meditating?

S: No. In a way they hinder him, because if you are in the *dhyānas* you are not much use so far as the world is concerned. You are oblivious to the world, even.

Q: Does the fact that the Buddha is in *dhyāna* states somehow help other beings?

S: No, the *dhyānas* in themselves are purely mundane states. He's probably much more helpful to other beings when he is not in the *dhyāna* states and when he is meeting them and talking and teaching.

Q: Is he setting an example?

S: You could say that, certainly in Milarepa's case. But what if there is not even a question of setting an example? Suppose there is nobody around to set an example to?

Q: He just enjoys *dhyāna*.

S: Yes, he just enjoys *dhyāna*! After all, it's an extremely pleasurable state. It's really as simple as that. The Buddha gives a clue in the Pāli scriptures, where he says in his extreme old age that the only time when he is free from bodily pain is when he withdraws into *dhyāna* states.[32] This suggests that even when you are an Enlightened being you still have to experience painful bodily sensations, just because your Enlightened mind is linked with a physical body. But if you are a master of the *dhyānas*, you can withdraw from your body consciousness into the *dhyāna* states, and by so withdrawing you will not experience those painful bodily sensations. So to dwell in *dhyāna* states is a more comfortable way of living. And why should you not live more rather than less comfortably, or blissfully?

Q: But does this not contradict the Bodhisattva vow? Surely the longer you spend in *dhyānic* states, the less time you can spend helping other sentient beings?

S: Well, suppose you are a Buddha, and suppose you spend quite a lot of your time teaching and preaching. You may get physically tired, and you may need to withdraw into the *dhyāna* states to refresh yourself, as it were, so that you have more physical and mental energy with which to communicate your Enlightenment experience. But if there's nobody around, and there's no possibility of communicating with anybody, why not enjoy the *dhyāna* states? In fact you will tend to do that quite naturally, you won't have to make any particular effort. After all, you've no craving to draw your attention out into the external world, so if there's nothing in the external world particularly occupying your mind, your natural tendency will be just to withdraw and experience *dhyāna* states. So left to himself, as it were, a Buddha withdraws into the *dhyāna* states, but the Enlightenment experience itself doesn't change. When he is drawn out of those *dhyāna* states to do something or speak to people, he is no longer enjoying *dhyāna*, but the Enlightenment experience remains constant. The Insight remains constant, the freedom from the *asravas* remains constant, the wisdom remains constant, the compassion remains constant, although the *dhyāna* states are not being experienced.

There was a discussion among the early schools as to whether the Buddha was always in a state of *dhyāna*. Some schools believed that he was but the Theravādins, apparently reflecting the Buddha's own statements, maintained that he was not always in the *dhyāna* states. But of course he was always the Buddha. His Insight and his Enlightenment remained constant; they were permanent.

Q: Can anybody who is Enlightened move freely through all the *dhyānas*?

S: Well, traditionally a Buddha came to be regarded as having special equipment, as it were, to fit him to become a Buddha – that is to say, to rediscover the path at a time when it wasn't known at all. The Buddha is therefore especially proficient in all sorts of ways that others don't need to be, and it seems he did have the proficiency of staying in any *dhyāna* state as long as he wished and emerging from it only when he wished to do so. Many of his disciples had that proficiency too, but not all of them had it in an equal degree. Some were merely Enlightened! – just as not all Enlightened people can paint or compose music. That doesn't affect their Enlightened state. Some can, some can't, that's all. Some Enlightened beings have the capacity to move freely among the *dhyānas*, and others don't. Perhaps it's a matter of temperament. Some Enlightened beings develop supernormal powers, others don't. Perhaps they don't have enough interest; perhaps being Enlightened is enough for them! But although that is the Theravāda tradition, it seems to me that an Enlightened mind, associated with the ordinary mundane psycho-physical organism, left to itself, so to speak, would tend to dwell in *dhyānic* rather than in non-*dhyānic* states. Just as most people need to make an effort to get into *dhyānic* states, the Enlightened being would need to make an effort to get out of *dhyānic* states, or would move out of them only when he wanted to for a definite purpose – to communicate with other living beings; well, other living beings in the *kāmaloka*, because it's said that on *dhyānic* levels you can communicate with non-human beings i.e. with devas of various kinds.

Anyway, how did we get on to that?

Q: We were wondering why Enlightened beings need to meditate.

S: It's the best way of living. Even if you are Enlightened, presumably to dwell in *dhyānic* states is preferable to dwelling in non-*dhyānic* states. Also, perhaps we can say that in Milarepa's case, he was setting an example, and had been instructed by his guru to pass his time in that way.

Q: Could you not also say that if you are dwelling in *dhyāna*, particularly fourth *dhyāna*, you are radiating a positive influence?

S: Yes, I am sure you could say that. I am sure that you are contributing to the general positivity of the world, of the universe almost. To give a very gross analogy, it is like a very wealthy man who has got enough money to live on for the rest of his life but who still goes on making money so that it can be put into circulation for the benefit of more and more people.

There is a possibility of a little misunderstanding in connection with what's just been said. I mentioned that a Buddha would dwell in a *dhyānic* state in preference to dwelling in a non-*dhyānic* state, because it was more blissful, but that his Enlightenment experience, his Insight, would remain constant. This almost suggests that the Enlightenment experience itself is not blissful, or that Insight is not blissful, but this is not in fact the case. It is said in the Pāli text that *nibbānam paramam sukham*, 'Nirvāṇa is the supreme bliss',[33] and in the context of the Vajrayāna there is the description of Enlightenment in terms of *mahāsukha*, again great bliss, although a different word for bliss is used. So how is this? Is the bliss of the *dhyānas* the same as the bliss of Enlightenment?

Buddhist tradition, especially the Pāli tradition, says that there is a definite difference, the distinction being that mundane bliss – and the *dhyānas* are still mundane even though mundane in a very refined way – is the product of the contact of a sense organ (either physical sense organ or mental sense organ) with a particular pleasurable object, but Transcendental bliss is not based on any kind of contact between sense organ and sense object. It is a non-dual bliss, as the Mahāyāna and Vajrayāna might say. So it is bliss in a quite different sense. From the mundane point of view we can't really have any conception about it. That is why, for the Buddha, for the Enlightened being, the experience of Transcendental bliss is so intense that any variation with regard to mundane pleasure and pain is very marginal and insignificant indeed. But nonetheless, bliss is better than non-bliss, pleasure is better than pain, even on the mundane level, and even from the standpoint of an Enlightened being.

This suggests on the part of Buddhism a quite different attitude to pleasure, mundane as well as Transcendental, from what we usually find in Western religious tradition. Pleasure is wholly good, in a sense. Even if you are Enlightened and you enjoy Transcendental bliss, it is natural to dwell as well in states which are blissful in a mundane sense rather than in states which are painful. I won't say painful in a mundane sense, because in Transcendental states there is no possibility of painfulness at all. I didn't want to leave you with the impression that Insight or Enlightenment is colourless or neutral, or any feeling that while it's certainly not suffering, perhaps it isn't bliss. It *is* bliss, but of a totally different order, a bliss based on freedom from contact between subject and object, because the subject-object distinction has been transcended, rather than based on the contact of subject with object, sense organ with sense object.

To go a little further, you can classify people in different ways. For instance, if you are an ordinary unenlightened person who does not lead a spiritual life at all, or even try to, what is your experience? You have of course no experience of Transcendental bliss, and you have no experience of the bliss of the *dhyānas*, which is much more intense than pleasure experienced on the ordinary level of consciousness. On the ordinary level of consciousness you have some experience of pleasure of a very mediocre nature, and some experience also of pain, sometimes considerable pain. That is the ordinary person's experience. Then, if you are on the spiritual path, but not yet on the Transcendental path, you continue to experience pleasure and pain on the *kāmaloka* level, but you also have some experience, maybe quite a limited experience, of *dhyānic* bliss. That *dhyānic* bliss is still mundane, but it's mundane in a more refined way, so you have a more pleasurable life than the ordinary worldly person. Also, even on the level of ordinary conscious experience, because your attachments have been loosened and you have fewer disappointments and frustrations, you have more pleasurable experience than painful experience, so you are better off in that respect too.

An advanced spiritual aspirant has a considerable experience of *dhyānic* bliss, and perhaps, having developed a little Insight, just a taste of Transcendental bliss. If you are spending much of your time in blissful *dhyāna* states, you don't dwell on the ordinary conscious level much anyway, so there is not much possibility of your encountering painful experiences on that level. Your experience is usually pleasurable. So you have a much more pleasurable and blissful existence even than the beginner in the spiritual life.

Then, going very much further, the Buddha experiences Transcendental bliss all the time. In addition he can experience, if he so wishes, the mundane bliss of the *dhyānas*, even though that is very much less than Transcendental bliss. On those occasions when he is functioning in ordinary waking consciousness, usually his state is pleasurable because of his positive mental attitude, his freedom from the *āsravas*. He experiences painful bodily sensations only as a result of illness or old age or other people's bodily attacks upon him. When the Buddha dies, when he gains Parinirvāṇa, when he no longer has a physical body or any contact with the physical world, his experience, if you can speak of his continuing to exist at all, is entirely blissful, and the bliss is entirely Transcendental. It's not even the mundane bliss of the *dhyānas*.

So you can look at these different classes of beings according to the extent to which they enjoy bliss, whether mundane or Transcendental. The important point is that the more you develop spiritually, the more blissful your life is. It is not that you should go after bliss, but bliss is the natural result, the natural by-product. The more spiritually developed you are, other factors being equal, that is to say if you have no serious illness and so on, the more blissful you will be. This is quite a thought.

Lama Govinda has made this point quite strongly in his book *The Psychological Attitude of Early Buddhist Philosophy*. He says that according to the Abhidharma there are more possibilities of blissful experiences than painful experiences in the universe, and the higher you go, the more blissful your experience is. This is rather different from the Christian perspective, where even saints go through all sorts of tortured experiences. You get the impression that they really tie themselves into knots, and that to be a saint means to tie yourself into a bigger and more elaborate knot than anybody else. But in the case of Buddhism, as you develop spiritually you become more and more integrated, more and more simple, more and more clear, more and more free from thoughts and also more and more blissful. In fact, you enter upon a bliss of a quite different order. The more you develop spiritually, the more pain and suffering are eliminated. Pain and suffering, according to Buddhism, are ultimately due to craving. No craving, no suffering. That doesn't mean just a cessation of suffering but a positive experience of bliss, both mundane and Transcendental, and eventually only Transcendental. This is why in the *Dhammapada* the bhikkhus chant, 'The disciples of the Buddha, happily we live'.[34] If you are not living happily, you can hardly say that you're a Buddhist. You have got to live happily, whether you like it or not! Well, some people find it quite difficult to live happily; they think maybe it's not quite right, it's not really very spiritual.

From a seminar on 'Rechungpa's Journey to Weu', *Songs of Milarepa* (1980, pp.114-7)

9. THE RADIANT LAMP DISPELLING THE DARKNESS

You don't feel so crushed and overwhelmed by the world. You feel more powerful than your surroundings.

In the midst of many manifestations,
I felt as if I were a radiant lamp;
All instructions thus became clearer than ever before.[35]

Usually we are bombarded by all sorts of influences and impressions, which have an unfortunate effect upon us. But when we meditate, we are generating very powerful, very positive, very skilful states, so it's as though we start taking the offensive. We become active, rather than passive. Do you see what I mean? We not only become positive, we become bright; not only bright, but clear. It's as though we are no longer under the influence of the things that surround us, but that they are under our influence. We are like the radiant lamp dispelling the darkness. In the light of that radiant lamp, 'all instructions thus become clearer than ever before'. There is a heightened positivity, and a stronger experience of individuality. You don't feel so crushed and overwhelmed by the world. You feel more powerful than your surroundings. The lamp is not overwhelmed by the darkness. Do you understand the sort of state that Milarepa is describing?

From a seminar on Milarepa's *Story of the Yak Horn* (1980, p.162)

10. STAYING IN DHYĀNA

Even the *samadhis*, lofty states though they are from the mundane point of view, in comparison with Wisdom, seem no more than dreams.

When the Wisdom shone bright from within,
I felt as if awakened from a great dream –
I was awakened from both the main and ensuing Samādhis;
I was awakened from both 'yes' and 'no' ideas.[36]

Sangharakshita: Even *dhyāna* states are still mundane. *Samatha* is still a mundane experience,[37] even though incredibly refined. So, 'when Wisdom shines bright from within', you awaken from conditioned existence as such. Even the *samādhi*s, lofty states though they are from the mundane point of view, in comparison with Wisdom, seem no more than dreams. Though *samādhi*, *dhyāna*, is immensely important, indispensable, the basis for the development of Insight, for the development of Wisdom, nonetheless, Wisdom infinitely transcends it.

'I was awakened from both 'yes' and 'no' ideas'.' What does that mean?

Q: Duality.

S: Duality. He's awakened from the duality of existence and non-existence, being and non-being, affirmation and negation; he's awakened from all intellectual and conceptual limitations – concepts as ends in themselves. In other words, all limitations, whether intellectual or emotional, are removed by the experience of Wisdom.

Q: I don't quite understand about the 'ensuing *samādhi*s'.

S: The 'ensuing *samādhi*' is the *samādhi* which you continue to experience after you've finished meditating, in the midst of the activities of daily life. It's not just an after-effect because you do try to keep it up, even though it's now under more difficult conditions. This is a regular or standard procedure. Say you sit in the shrine room for an hour doing the mindfulness of breathing practice, and perhaps you have an experience of a *dhyāna* state. When the period of meditation comes to an end, when you get up from your meditation cushion and you take up some other work – maybe you're chopping wood – there is some trace of the *dhyāna* experience you had while sitting on your cushion persisting still, and you can try to stay in contact with that experience, even while you're chopping wood. The experience of *dhyāna* you have sitting on your cushion is called the main *samādhi*. The experience of the trace of *samādhi* that you have while you're chopping wood is called the 'ensuing *samādhi*'. The function of the 'ensuing *samādhi*' is to link up different main *samādhi*s. If you're practising meditation seriously, you have periods of practice sitting on your cushion, and in between you're doing other things, but during the intermediate period, you try to maintain the *dhyāna* experience as long as you possibly can. When you have another period of sitting meditation, you're not starting entirely from scratch, because you haven't completely lost the benefits from last time. Do you see what I mean? If you're taking meditation seriously, even when you're not actually meditating, you're very careful to see you don't stray too far away from the *dhyāna* experience that you had sitting on your cushion.

It's probably only on retreat that you'll be able to practise seriously in this way. In daily life, you might have a good meditation in the morning, but even if you stay positive during the day, you probably won't have any trace of *dhyāna* left. You'll probably have to start all over again. But if you sit to meditate a number of times during the day, and you're very mindful about what you do in between, especially if you engage in very simple physical activity and don't talk much, you can keep the *dhyāna* experience for practically the whole day. It may fluctuate – it may go up a bit when you're sitting and down a bit when you're not – but it will be more constant than our usual experience, which is likely to be that we get into *dhyāna* in the morning and then our state goes downhill until the evening, when we may have the chance to start again with another session of seated meditation. It doesn't have to be like that, but usually it is – depending on what you're doing in between the two periods of meditation. It can make quite a difference if you can introduce a third sit just before lunch, or just before tea, to give your sagging *dhyāna* line a hoist.

Q: I've heard it said that you can function in the outside world in the first and second *dhyānas*.

S: You can certainly function in the first *dhyāna*, because discursive mental activity is still continuing, but it is quite difficult, even so.

Q: Do you think it is even desirable?

S: You shouldn't try to stay in two worlds or two mental states at the same time. If you try that, you'll get splitting headaches.

Q: So if your work involves using your head a bit, is it pointless to try to stay in a *dhyāna* state?

S: If your work involves a very simple repetitive physical movement, you can keep that up while remaining in a *dhyānic* state, but if you have to

think things out, then it becomes virtually impossible. You can chop wood in a *dhyānic* state but if you have to think in terms of selling the wood, and calculating the price, and finding a buyer, and making arrangements for transport – then it's impossible to stay in the *dhyānic* state.
From a seminar on Milarepa's *Story of the Yak Horn* (1980, pp.187-9)

11. DHYĀNA OUTSIDE MEDITATION

The experience is the thing, not the conditions under which it takes place.

Q: Can you get into the *dhyānas* through communication?

Sangharakshita: I think you can. I won't be completely sure about this, but I think on some occasions people might even get into second *dhyāna* through intense communication in which ordinary mental activity just stops.

Q: Presumably you wouldn't actually be talking?

S: Well, even in the course of fairly ordinary communication, sometimes you feel that you don't need to say any more. You understand each other without words. I don't want to romanticize or sentimentalize that sort of thing too much, but yes, that can happen. Then if the communication has been very intense, when you've stopped talking and even stopped thinking, you can enter, at least momentarily, a *dhyānic* state – even perhaps as far as the second *dhyāna*. Perhaps it's similar when you have been listening to music – when the sounds have died away and you're still completely absorbed in the music. You can almost hear the echo in your mind, but you're not thinking about anything else. Your mind hasn't started functioning again, just as after meditation.

So even though one usually has *dhyāna* experiences within the framework of formal meditation practice, one should not suppose that such experiences are necessarily confined to that framework – though one has to be quite careful not to claim that one can have meditation experiences without meditating. One experiences *dhyāna* states outside the framework of formal meditation only at one's very best moments. Maybe you have heard a wonderful symphony concert or you have been watching a wonderful sunset or had particularly good communication with somebody. You might not get such experiences more than two or three times a year. We don't even perhaps have *dhyāna* experiences very often within the framework of meditation. But one mustn't be rigid. The experience is the thing, not the conditions under which it takes place, even though normally the experience will take place under a particular set of conditions, i.e. in the shrine-room while you are meditating sitting on your cushion. But it's not confined to that. It can take place, at least occasionally, on other occasions too.

From a seminar on Milarepa's *Story of the Yak Horn* (1980, pp.187-9)

12. THE GREAT DIFFERENCE BETWEEN DHYĀNA AND PRAJÑĀ

You can have many delightful experiences of the abeyance of the ego, but from those experiences you come back to the ego ...

Sangharakshita: The great difference between *dhyāna* and *prajñā*, or between *samatha* and *vipassanā*, is that *dhyāna* is impermanent. In the *dhyāna* experience – especially higher *dhyāna* experience – there can be an abeyance of thought activity, of the rational mind: there can be an abeyance of the empirical self. But when you come out of the experience, you come back to the self; you find him waiting for you, ready to take over – ready, even, to appropriate your so-called spiritual experience. The only way you can get rid of him is through Insight and wisdom. That's the difference. Only *prajñā* brings permanent freedom and peace, which is to say, the understanding – not just the conceptual understanding – of *śūnyatā*. Thus Buddhism makes quite a lot of this distinction between *samatha* and *vipassanā*, *samādhi* and *prajñā*. You can have many delightful experiences of the abeyance of the ego, but from those experiences you come back to the ego, and your ego even tries to take over your experiences of non-ego. It's only *prajñā* which finally undermines the ego and the whole ego-based superstructure of psychic experience.

Q: What is the difference between the ego in the psychological sense and the ego in the Buddhist sense?

S: In a way, there's not much difference at all. Paradoxically, you can't get rid of the ego until you've got an ego to get rid of. It's as though the individual consciousness is the next stage up from the pre-individual consciousness, but from the individual consciousness the next stage up is what we can only describe as – not even the higher *dhyāna* consciousness, but the 'Transcendental' consciousness, and that comes about by way of the negation of the individual consciousness as a self-contained entity, complete and sufficient in itself. It's not that that particular structure of consciousness is broken down, but rather that a different sort of energy now works through it: it's no longer working under its own steam. So long as you are an embodied being, you've got to have the structure there for the higher energy to work through, as it were; otherwise you just couldn't function.

Consequently it's a healthy, positive thing for that psychological ego, i.e. that ego-structure, to be there, but not for it to be trying to function under its own steam. All we have to do is to make sure that the higher consciousness – the Transcendental consciousness, – functions through it. Even after his Enlightenment the Buddha apparently still functioned as an ordinary human being. The ego-structure remained intact, but the Enlightenment experience was functioning through it. Just as, after Enlightenment, the body's still there, but it becomes an instrument for Enlightenment, it is similar with the ego-structure. It thinks, forms ideas, philosophizes, etc., but all under the direction and inspiration of the Enlightened consciousness. You are not out to smash the ego. All you need to do is change its present state of functioning under its own energy, its own power. Hence, paradoxically, you have first of all got to build up your ego and then go beyond it.

From a seminar on *The Endlessly Fascinating Cry* (1977, pp.187-8)

13. DHYĀNA APPROACHED THROUGH DIFFERENT METHODS

In a sense, there is no such thing as a pure, abstract *dhyana* which you enter independently of the type of practice or method by means of which you entered it.

Q: Is there a qualitative difference in the experience of *dhyāna* if you have entered the *dhyānic* states through different meditation practices – say, through the mindfulness of breathing or the *mettā-bhāvanā*?

Sangharakshita: In principle no, because *dhyāna* is *dhyāna*. Nonetheless, I would personally say – and I don't know that tradition says anything about this – that in practice, the *dhyāna* experience must be suffused by a carry-over from the method by means of which you have approached it. I would say that is inevitable. In a sense, there is no such thing as a pure, abstract *dhyāna* which you enter independently of the type of practice or method by means of which you entered it. That is what seems reasonable to me. I don't know whether tradition has discussed this.

From the *Jewel Ornament of Liberation* (Tuscany 1985, p.262)

14. CAN ANYTHING 'SHADE INTO' THE TRANSCENDENTAL?

One should not think of the *dhyanas* as being as it were too rigidly stratified. It is not quite like ascending to the different floors of a house and then descending. In fact it is not at all like that.

Q: Are the four *arūpa-dhyānas* four higher and progressive stages beyond the *rūpa-dhyānas*, or are they four dimensions of the fourth *dhyāna*?

Sangharakshita: In a sense, they are both. They are usually presented in traditional Buddhism as forming a continuous series with the four *rūpa-dhyānas*. At the same time, it is made clear, especially in the Abhidharma, that the four *arūpa-dhyānas* are so many variations of the fourth *rūpa-dhyāna*. In terms of the customary analysis, only *samādhi*, *citta-ekaggata*, and *upekkhā* are the special characteristics of that state. In the same way, one-pointedness of mind and equanimity are the special features of the four *arūpa-dhyānas*. So, in that sense, they are variations of the fourth *rūpa-dhyāna*, or explorations of its different dimensions.

Q: Do the higher *dhyānas* shade into the Transcendental?

S: Well, can anything 'shade into' the Transcendental? Is anything mundane any nearer to the Transcendental than any other mundane thing? In other words, are you really any nearer to the Transcendental whether you are in the first *dhyāna*, the second, third, fourth, fifth, sixth, seventh, eighth, or in no *dhyāna* at all? The mundane is the mundane, so, in the strict sense if you like, in the ultimate sense, you don't get any nearer. You become more refined, you become less mundane, but you don't become more Transcendental! This is looking at it from one point of view. So I don't think one can speak, in the strict sense, of the *arūpa-dhyānas* shading into the Transcendental. But the whole nature, the whole position in the total scheme of Buddhist spiritual life, of the *arūpa-dhyānas*, is quite strange, quite mysterious. I have been looking into various Pāli and Sanskrit texts with this in mind for some time, without coming to any very definite conclusions; except that we can say that, in early Buddhism, one has, it would seem, originally, a set only of four *rūpa-dhyānas*, to which the set of four *arūpa-dhyānas* seems to have been added subsequently. But we can't be completely sure even about that.

Q: Going back to this question of whether the mundane can shade into the Transcendental, if you move generally to states of more and more awareness, as you move from cyclical conditioning to spiral conditioning, could you not see that in a sense as a move away from the mundane towards this whole idea of progressive, open-ended spiral conditioning?

S: Only in a manner of speaking. I was speaking from a strictly logical point of view. For instance, suppose some world, is infinitely far away. If you go a billion miles in its direction, are you any nearer to it? That was the sort of point of view I was adopting.

Q: Does that correspond to – I hesitate to say 'the facts'?

S: Well, again, it depends upon the point of view that you adopt. If you use the terminology of the conditioned and the Unconditioned, the mundane and the Transcendental, as many Buddhist texts do, you cannot think in terms of getting any nearer to the Transcendental by simply refining the mundane. Practically speaking, yes, you are nearer; but not in the absolute sense, not in the ultimate sense, not logically.

I certainly see what you are getting at, and if you think too rigidly in terms of a mundane and a Transcendental, though much of Buddhism does that, certain logical difficulties do arise. In fact, you can't explain how one can become Enlightened. But, one might say, is it possible to explain that? How can you explain how you cover that distance between yourself and infinity? Perhaps there is no logical explanation of it; it ought to be impossible, but actually it isn't. Logically it is, but in practice it isn't. Perhaps it is better and safer to go back to the familiar, well-worn terminology of 'in dependence upon A, B arises'.

Q: It seemed to me you were saying that you can't attain the Transcendental from the higher *dhyānas*, strictly speaking, because Insight requires the cognitive faculty. Is that due to the fact that you are using a logical model?

S: Oh no, the model is definitely psychological, if one can even speak of a model. One is giving, according to Buddhist tradition, just a description of what happens, of the psychological facts, as it were. But one has to be careful not to think too literally. It is not that, having explored the higher *dhyānas*, you abandon them completely and – bonk! – down you come to the first *dhyāna*, with its cognitive processes, its intellection and so on. It isn't really like that, because there is that background of the experience of the higher *dhyānas*. That, in a sense, is still with you; you don't completely lose it. But against that background, while you are very still and very concentrated and very integrated, there arises a subtle, delicate cognitive process, rather different from what we usually experience; and it is in dependence upon that that one develops Insight.

Q: So are you suggesting that there is a middle ground where you can maintain, say, the third *dhyāna* but also have ...

S: Not exactly maintain it, not in its fullness, because in its fullness it is incompatible with mental activity. Perhaps what I am saying amounts to this: that one should not think of the *dhyānas* as being as it were too rigidly stratified. It is not quite like ascending to the different floors of a house and then descending. In fact it is not at all like that. In 'descending' to a lower *dhyāna* you don't lose everything that you gained by ascending to the higher *dhyāna*. Nonetheless, there is some difference between being fully 'in' the higher *dhyāna* and 'descending' and allowing that subtle cognitive process to start up, to become the basis for one's development of Insight.

Q: Are you saying that it is not possible to obtain Insight if you are fully immersed in the higher *dhyānas*?

S: You could probably summarize it like that, yes. But you are not therefore to think that, in order to develop Insight, you have completely to abandon those higher *dhyānas*. In that sense it is, as you said, a sort of middle ground, though again you mustn't take that literally and try to draw up a more elaborate scheme of the *dhyānas* incorporating this middle ground as a separate level or even as a series of levels.

Q: I was just puzzled, because it seems that the traditional description of Insight has almost an inordinate emphasis on the cognitive mental faculties; whereas one would have thought that the emphasis would be on emotion.

S: Yes, that is true. One must not forget that the language of Indian Buddhism, including Pāli Buddhism, is very cognitive, even intellectual. It is very easy to misunderstand that. When one speaks of Insight as arising in dependence on a certain cognitive process or on a certain intellectual understanding, one must not think of that as being one-sidedly cognitive, or one-sidedly intellectual. If that was really the case, it is very doubtful whether any Insight would arise at all. So one should not take the language of some of the Indian Buddhist texts too literally. There is an understanding, yes; but that understanding, by its very nature, almost, contains a definitely emotional component.
From the *Jewel Ornament of Liberation* (Tuscany 1985, pp.268-71)

15. THE OTHER-REGARDING ASPECTS OF DHYĀNA

If you experience the *dhyanas* you become very sensitive, you become quite aware, you see things more clearly, not in terms of Insight but in terms of observation.

Q: Does one's experience of the *dhyānas* have any other-regarding aspect?

Sangharakshita: This is an interesting point. It must have, because the *mettā-bhāvanā* has a *dhyānic* aspect to it. If you experience the *dhyānas* you become very sensitive, you become quite aware, you see things more clearly, not in terms of Insight but in terms of observation, and you become more sensitive to other people, more sensitive to their reactions and their mental states. Therefore you treat them differently, you relate to them more gently, more tactfully, more subtly. So it does affect your relations with other people; you become more gentle, and you also become firmer, more confident, more decisive, less scattered.
From a seminar on 'The Stages of the Path', *The Three Jewels* (1977, p.94)

16. A BALANCING TRICK

If you haven't prepared a basis for *dhyana* experience, you are holding yourself in an unnatural position.

Q: Presumably the Buddha had considerable will power. You've said that he attained the *dhyānas* before his Enlightenment as a result of that.

Sangharakshita: But could an experience of the *arūpā-dhyānas* be brought about by sheer will power? That would seem to be very doubtful. Perhaps one could get by will power into the first or even the second *dhyāna*, but one wouldn't be able to stay there very long; there would be too many opposing factors. In fact, I doubt whether one could get very far at all in a wilful fashion. One can fixate one's attention wilfully, but is that concentration in the full sense? Is not a feeling of ease, of *sukha*, inseparable from such concentration?

Q: Does that mean that some concentration techniques are ineffective?

S: It's like a balancing trick. You can learn to balance yourself on the tip of your big toe, but it's a very unstable position, and you can't maintain it for very long. If you haven't prepared a basis for *dhyāna* experience, if you are getting up to, say, first *dhyāna* by means of a forcible exertion of will, you are holding yourself in an unnatural position, one for which you are not prepared, for which there is no base.

So I am inclined to doubt my own explanation, which was admittedly provisional, of the Buddha's experience of all eight *dhyānas* before his Enlightenment as having been a result of a certain amount of wilful striving. I rather doubt whether that could have been possible.

From a seminar on the Noble Eightfold Path (1982, pp.395-6)

17. DRUGS AND DHYĀNA

Is it appropriate to talk of taking LSD and getting into a dhyanic state?

Q: If you get into *dhyāna* during meditation, that is a positive weighty karma. Would similar states which you happen upon through more artificial means, say through taking psychedelic drugs, equally be positive weighty karma?

Sangharakshita: No, they wouldn't, by definition, because they would be *vipākas* rather than *karmas*. They would represent pleasurable sensations, simply; not pleasurable experiences which arose within the context of willed action. For instance, if someone touches you, that may be a pleasurable sensation, but it is a *vipāka*, so the fact that you experience that pleasurable sensation has no karmic significance. What has karmic significance is your reaction to it, whether grasping or whatever. If you take a drug which gives you a pleasurable sensation, that's just a *vipāka*, and there is no question of its having a *vipāka* of its own. It only has a *vipāka* to the extent that on the basis of that pleasurable experience you develop a certain attitude in which there is an element of will. Even then it's not the pleasurable experience that is followed by a *vipāka* but your attitude towards that experience.

Q: In *Peace is a Fire*, you talk about *dhyāna* being not so much a state that you get into but a way in which you reorganize your being. Is it appropriate to talk in terms of getting into a *dhyāna* state other than by making an effort of will to reorganize your being?

S: You can get into a *dhyāna* state on the basis of an effort of will, but only very briefly. So it's not enough just to snatch at *dhyāna* experiences in a happy-go-lucky way, leaving the rest of your life unorganized, because you will be unable to sustain that experience, and it will be of a slightly schizophrenic character. What you need to do is to reorganize your whole way of life, your whole being, your attitude towards life, in such a way that *dhyāna* is the natural result of that, so that you are dwelling in *dhyāna* in a consistent way.

Q: Is it appropriate to talk of taking LSD and getting into a *dhyānic* state?

S: I think it's quite misleading. The analogy between the two is quite superficial, inasmuch as the *dhyāna* state is one of intense volition, whereas the psychedelic experience, the drug experience, is pure *vipāka*, though it no doubt very quickly gives rise to various reactions which may constitute karma.

Q: You were just talking about *dhyāna* as a concentrated act of volition, almost, and not a passive state, not a *vipāka*, not the result of some outside experience. In my limited experience of *dhyāna*, it often seems to happen quite unexpectedly, obviously during meditation, but it seems that it builds up over quite a long period. Then, without seeming to have put a lot more effort into that meditation than any other, I find myself in *dhyāna*. And once in *dhyāna*, it seems to require a very subtle effort of maintaining concentration to remain in it for a while. How does this tie in with *dhyāna* being a very intense effort of will, or at least of volition?

S: I suppose it depends how we think of will. The word has perhaps the wrong connotations, because we think of something very effortful. But if you are doing something which you very much want to do and which you enjoy doing, you can be putting a lot of energy into it without any sense of strain or exertion. Your experience of the *dhyānic* state eventually becomes like that. It becomes so enjoyable that in a sense you don't need to make an effort, but nonetheless, your energies are going into it, as into any other activity that you find intensely pleasurable.

It's a bit like being in an aeroplane: you look out of the window and it seems as though you're standing still, even when you are going at 500 miles an hour. Have you noticed that when you enjoy doing something, you are not conscious of effort, even though you are expending a lot of energy in that activity? Perhaps only subsequently you realize that you feel tired. You may even feel that you are gaining energy from that activity, rather than expending it.

Q: So, just to make sure I've got this clear: *dhyāna* definitely can't be a passive state that you can be sort of catapulted into by circumstances?

S: Well, some people would disagree with this, because some would say that you can, for instance, be catapulted into a *dhyānic* state by the touch of some spiritual master. There is no doubt that other people can give you experiences, but whether they are *dhyānic* experiences I am far from being sure. Drugs can give you experiences of various kinds; alcohol can give you experiences; even a cup of strong tea can give you an experience. But that experience is not necessarily of a *dhyānic* nature, inasmuch as you are passive in respect of it. In a sense, it is not your experience, it is not an expression of you, so to speak.

Q: Would you say that the effects of using a drug such as LSD could be said to be an altered state of consciousness, and if so, would it be a higher state of consciousness, or where in the scale of things would it be?

S: That depends very much upon the person. The term 'altered state of consciousness' is quite precise, quite satisfactory, because that is what happens; your state of consciousness is altered. Whether it is higher or lower, or whether altered for the better or for the worse, is entirely another matter. Those who have had experience of such matters, and I have known in the past people who have had several hundred trips, as they used to call them, used to say that what happened was that the drug put your mental state under a microscope; it greatly magnified it, so that you experienced far more intensely whatever you normally experienced, good, bad or indifferent. If you had a slight feeling of paranoia, in the LSD experience that could be magnified a thousand times into a quite horrific experience. And if you were an affectionate person, that could be magnified a thousand times also. That would seem to be a leading feature of that type of experience. Your consciousness is not even just altered, but magnified, so that you can see what is actually there. There are other kinds of LSD experience of a more visionary nature, but that might depend on the nature of the person taking the drug.

Q: I remember reading an article by Lama Govinda on these drugs, in which he suggested that they essentially do expand your consciousness, but without strengthening it, so it is as if it is shattered into small pieces, there is no integrating factor there to hold it together. He compares this with meditation, which he says also expands the consciousness but in a gradual and regular way, sort of strengthening it as it goes. Would you say that that is a sensible way of looking at the effect of some of these drugs?

S: I suppose it depends what one means by expanding. What I describe as 'blowing up' could be regarded as a kind of expansion. There is no doubt that meditation expands the consciousness. In fact, we have the term in Pāli, 'expanded consciousness', *mahaggata-citta*, which is an Abhidhamma term. *Mahaggata* means 'become great', i.e. expanded. It is the exact equivalent. And the *mahagata-cittas* are, of course, the *dhyānas*; so the *dhyānas* are expanded states of consciousness, according to Buddhism.

I am not quite sure what to say about expansion as characteristic of altered states of consciousness in the sense that Lama Govinda seems to be using the term. If there is any element of disintegration or non-integration in that kind of experience, I suppose it is inasmuch as the experience is thrust upon one, chemically induced, does not grow out of one's personal development, doesn't grow out of the exercise, so to speak, of one's own will at higher and higher levels. It's therefore something that you can't possibly assimilate, so it may even have a disintegrating effect. We know that some people at least who regularly take drugs do almost literally disintegrate; that is true not only of LSD, but of alcohol too.

Q: I think also in that article he talked about blowing psycho-physical energy; the experience, because it was drug-induced, was just wasting energy, whereas the *dhyānic* state was containing and concentrating it.

S: It seems a far cry from the drug culture of the sixties, when one thinks back to what people used to say in those days about those things.

Q: I had a friend who killed himself, indirectly because of bad drug experiences, and he told me before his mental illness got worse that he had an experience which I can only put in the category of *vipassanā*. He had taken quite a strong drug, and it was almost as if a bolt of brilliant light came out and sort of split him in two, and yet he was still in the body, so to speak. I was wondering if you can have a bad *vipassanā* experience on drugs, whereas you don't get that in meditation.

S: I don't think you can have a *vipassanā*-type experience of that sort beyond a certain point. I don't think, without a good measure of integration, you can have a genuine *vipassanā*-type experience at all. You can certainly have abnormal experiences, which have a shattering effect; but not every experience which has a shattering effect is a *vipassanā*-type experience. It just doesn't sound like the same sort of thing at all.

Q: Could you have a *vipassanā*-type experience on a drug like LSD?

S: I would say you definitely couldn't, because by the very nature of the drug experience, it is passive, something that's almost imposed upon you; whereas Insight is *your* Insight. Of course, while the drug-induced experience is passive, if you remain in control of the situation, you can adopt a definite attitude towards the drug experience, and you can even utilize it as the basis for something further of your own, as it were, which can be useful. If you've had previous training in meditation you might even be able to lead it in the direction of *vipassanā*, but that would presuppose that you remain in control and conscious, and separate as it were from the drug experience, not totally overwhelmed by it. You would be treating it then just as you would treat any other powerful experience, including the experience you had in a dream, while remaining as it were still conscious.

But for you to be in control in that way presupposes two things: one, that you already have a strongly integrated personality, which many people who take drugs don't have; and two, that you don't take the drug in such a dose that you are completely overwhelmed. Other drugs can be taken in that way; opium can be taken in that way. You can remain in, as it were, control of the experience.

Q: Can you think of any situation where it might be advisable to do so?

S: I can't, because the question is in the abstract, and therefore the answer has to be in the abstract. One can't in human affairs rule out any possibility. But one can't say more than that, because one would have to be confronted by an actual, concrete person, and be asked what one's advice would be in the case of that particular person.

Q: If, for example, you took advantage of being in a serene state and that was magnified by a drug such as LSD, if you could retain a degree of conscious control and use that state to enhance your ability to meditate, presumably the meditation would then be a weighty karma?

S: There's at least three ifs in that question! I wouldn't like to say. The drug-induced experience often seems to inhibit your volitional faculties, so that even though theoretically it might be possible to make the drug-induced experience the basis of a weighty karma, in practice I think it probably wouldn't be possible.
From a seminar on *Hedonism and the Spiritual Life* (1986, pp.9-14)

18. CONSULT YOUR OWN EXPERIENCE

You don't have to depend upon what Buddhaghosa says or what the Abhidharma says, or what I say. Consult your own experience and see what conclusions you come to.

Q: I seem to remember you saying that you thought that Buddhaghosa could have been wrong in his correlation of the *brahma-vihāra* practices with the four *dhyānas*. I think at the time you said that he, like other Theravāda commentators, saw things in too linear a way, and that, consciousness being multi-dimensional, it could well be that the practice of the four *brahma-vihāras* constituted a separate route to the *arūpāloka*.

Sangharakshita: That's true, I did say that. But I would like to suggest that you just compare whatever experience you have at least of the lower *dhyānas* with your experience of *mettā*. See if you can detect any common factors, and whether you do feel that *mettā* has a *dhyānic* element, or that there is an element of *mettā* in *dhyāna*. These are all matters of experience. You don't have to depend upon what Buddhaghosa says or what the Abhidharma says, or what I say. You can consult your own experience and see what conclusions you come to. And having consulted your own experience and come to certain conclusions, you can perhaps discuss the matter with other people and see if their experience has been similar. I think it is quite important to consult one's own experience when one can.

Q: The reason I asked was because I hardly ever practise the mindfulness of breathing, mostly the *mettā-bhāvanā* and the Avalokiteśvara *sādhana*, and I can't really relate to the *dhyānas* as you describe them.

S: I think there is a bit of misunderstanding here. In the traditional psychological analysis certain mental factors are mentioned; for instance, in the first *dhyāna* there is *vitarka* and *vicāra*, which are not present in the second *dhyāna*. Then there is mention of *sukha*, there is mention of *prīti*. Sometimes I think the impression is produced by this enumeration that that is all that is experienced in the *dhyānas*, in terms of psychological factors or mental events. That is certainly the impression one gets reading from certain Theravāda works on the subject. But one must remember that there are certain factors that are present in all states of consciousness, as well as some that are present in all skilful states of consciousness, including *dhyānic* states, these being pre-eminently skilful. Then of course you have those factors which are distinctive to the *dhyānas*. You've got to combine all these for a total picture, and it may be that in your experience of the *dhyānas* some of the more general factors or mental events present in the *dhyānas* are prominent. One mustn't think that the traditional psychological analysis of the *dhyānas* gives the whole picture; it doesn't by any means.

Q: I tend to have experiences of rapture and bliss without all that much concentration. Is that like the positive *nidānas*, which start off with joy, rapture, bliss and so on, and only at the seventh stage do you get *samādhi*.

S: Again, you mustn't take that literally. It is not that there is no *samādhi* at all present until you get to that particular point. There is a degree of *samādhi*, a degree of concentration, all the time. But it is intensifying all the time, and when you come to the link which is entitled *samādhi* it becomes very strong indeed. *Samādhi* in the sense of mental concentration is present all the way along. But when you experience intense *prīti*, the element of *samādhi* in the sense of mental one-pointedness is greatly reduced because *prīti* can be a very disturbing factor, and *samādhi* in the fuller sense is experienced only when the disturbing aspect of *prīti* dies down, and you are left with pure sukha, pure bliss, which can lead on to *samādhi* in a fuller sense, more directly and more easily.

Q: The two systems (the *dhyānas* and the positive *nidānas*) have a different emphasis, a different flavour, don't they?

S: That is true, yes. One must try to see from one's own experience what that is and what common factors there are, because both the *dhyānas* and the *brahma-vihāra*s are heightened states of consciousness, states of consciousness which one doesn't normally experience, or intensification of states which one does normally experience to a very limited extent.

From Q&A on The Bodhisattva Ideal (1986, pp.125-7)

19. HOW DOES ONE ENTER INTO THE ARŪPA-DHYĀNAS?

You have achieved the fourth *dhyana*, yes, very well, but it is not much of an attainment after all.

Q: In the *rūpā-dhyānas* there is a progressive unfoldment of one's being and a continuous process of a deepening of concentration. How does one enter into and pass through the *arūpā-dhyānas*? Is it by the continuation of this process of the deepening of concentration, or is a conceptual element involved?

Sangharakshita: There are several procedures, but I won't say much about them because for most people it is academic. The main point is that you enter upon the first of the four *arūpā-dhyānas* by distancing yourself from the last of the *rūpā-dhyānas*. You try to see it objectively, to as it were disengage yourself from it and look at it in an objective way. Then you expand that feeling of distance. That is all perhaps that one can say in a general way. The fourth *dhyāna*, if you are fully absorbed in it, is a transporting, overwhelming experience. You become, as it were, totally identified with it. It takes of possession of you, and you cling to it, even.

But if you want to enter upon the first of the *arūpā-dhyānas*, you must detach yourself from the fourth *dhyāna*; you must consider its faults. For instance, you tell yourself that it has arisen in dependence on causes and conditions, it is transitory, and it will pass away when those causes and conditions are removed, therefore one should not be attached to it. You have achieved it, yes, but it is not much of an attainment after all.

Obviously you can't afford to think in that sort of way until you have got there, but you start sitting loose to the experience and not allowing it to occupy the whole of your perspective. You start looking beyond it, you start, as it were expanding, and in that way you can enter upon the *dhyāna* of infinite space.

Q: Is there a discursive element there, or is it the bringing of awareness to one's own experience?

S: Well, obviously one must speak in terms of bringing awareness, but it might be difficult to disengage that awareness from the conceptual activity, which would mean that you would come down, so to speak, to the first *dhyāna* and perhaps reflect upon the inadequacies of the fourth *dhyāna* from that level, so that next time you got to the fourth *dhyāna* there would be less of a temptation to over-identify yourself with it. But perhaps it is best not to linger on the subject in view of the difficulty that most people experience getting into and staying in the first three *dhyānas*.

From Q&A on The Bodhisattva Ideal (1986, pp.127-8)

20. HOW DO YOU KNOW WHEN YOU'RE IN THE SECOND DHYĀNA?

If you start thinking 'What shall I do with this creative energy?', you are no longer in the second dhyana.

Q: Can I ask a question about my own experience of what I think might be the second *dhyāna*, just to check on what may be happening? What I generally interpret as a weak experience of it is when one reaches the stage where, having achieved concentration, say, in the mindfulness of breathing, you can simply maintain one-pointed attention on the object of concentration without any discursiveness. I have never experienced this kind of welling up of inspiration, as far as I am aware, but I have reached the level of pure concentration

Sangharakshita: Obviously there are degrees. Initially it can be experienced just as a welling up of happiness. That can become stronger and stronger, and then it can even feel like a creative energy coming from the depths. One has at that moment to be careful not to be disturbed by it, and not to start thinking about it, otherwise you lapse from the second *dhyāna*. If you start thinking 'What shall I do with this creative energy? Shall I write a poem, or should I just continue with the meditation?', you are no longer in the second *dhyāna*; perhaps you are back in the first, or even back in ordinary consciousness.

You can allow that process to continue without thinking about it, just observing it in a non-discursive way, and experiencing it. I think one would initially experience it in the form of increased happiness, as though happiness, independent of external conditions, is just bubbling up from within you.

Q: So is that pure attention without discursiveness merely an aspect of first *dhyāna*, would you say, rather than second? Or is it difficult to say?

S: If there is no discursiveness at all, then that is definitely second *dhyāna*. But if you don't have the experience of that energy, or that happiness, bubbling up, you are probably just at the beginning, so to speak, of the second *dhyāna*. You need to sustain that, go into it more deeply, experience it more fully, and then the experience which is suggested by the image for that *dhyāna* will start to occur.

Q: I suppose it's a matter of finding out for oneself, but when you reach that stage, how do you intensify it?

S: You intensify it by remaining in it. It naturally intensifies if you can remain concentrated and free from discursive thought. Its natural tendency, if it is prolonged, is to deepen. If you keep on rolling the snowball, it will automatically grow. You don't need to make any special effort to make it bigger, you just need to go on rolling it over the snow.
From Study Group Leaders' Q&A on the Noble Eightfold Path (1985, pp.145-6)

21. WHY BOTHER GETTING INTO THE HIGHER DHYĀNAS?

The neighbourhood concentration to which you, so to speak, come back after traversing the four *dhyanas* is not the neighbourhood concentration with which you started.

Q: Why should you bother getting into the higher *dhyānas* if you can get into a preliminary *dhyānic* state and then start *vipassanā*-type reflection?

Sangharakshita: Well, you can't. You are taking the process too literally. The neighbourhood concentration to which you, so to speak, come back after traversing the four *dhyānas* is not the neighbourhood concentration with which you started; it's a much fuller, easier, more natural, relaxed state. It's only technically the same state.

Let me give a comparison. Suppose you haven't eaten anything, then you have a good meal, and then you stop eating. Are you in the same state as before? You've returned to the state of not eating, but you've got a full stomach this time. In the case of the *dhyānas*, you've absorbed them in a way; your being has been suffused with them. Even though now you're not technically in the *dhyāna* state, the fact that you have had that experience is affecting your whole being and making it more possible for you to develop Insight.

Q: So you're returning to the same sort of mental functions, but your state of mind is not the same state of mind.

S: Yes, you could say that. You return to the same function but in a different state.
From a seminar on *A Survey of Buddhism*, chapter 1 (1982, p.144)

5 Working in meditation

One's first experience of meditation, like one's first love, retains in memory a virginal freshness too delicate and too delicious for words.

From *The Rainbow Road* (1997, p.202)

1 Preparing to meditate

1. A SPONTANEOUS EXPRESSION OF THE WAY YOU ARE

It's quite unfortunate that very often we have to fit meditation into life, as it were, instead of getting into it gradually and naturally, because we just feel like getting into it.

> *Having abandoned doubt he lives having passed beyond uncertainty; as one who is not questioning what things are good, he cleanses his mind of doubt.*[38]

He knows what things are good, he knows what things are skilful. In other words, he has a definite skilful purpose in life, and as a result of this he has no doubts. He has no doubt about what he is doing, he has no doubt about the value and benefits of meditation. If you've got all sorts of doubts – 'Should I be meditating or not? Is this going to do me any good? Maybe the spiritual life itself is just a waste of time; maybe it's all just a delusion' – you won't get into the *dhyāna* states. You have to be quite convinced that what you're doing is worthwhile. So there's a lot of preparation to be done: not only the more general preparation, but this more specific preparation of making sure that none of these five hindrances is present in the mind when you embark upon the meditation. Before you take up the mindfulness of breathing or the *mettā-bhāvanā*, you should check your mental state. Are you still angry with someone and dwelling upon that? Have you got a particular craving? Is your mind on what you're going to have for supper, or for breakfast?

Are you very disturbed and agitated? Or have you got doubts about the practice itself? You've got to deal with these things, and put them out of the way before you can really get on with the meditation. And of course tiredness – I suppose that comes under sloth and torpor – you have to be quite sure you're not feeling tired. (For more on the five hindrances, see pages 313-58.)

It's quite unfortunate that very often we have to fit meditation into life, as it were, instead of getting into it gradually and naturally, because we just feel like getting into it. It should be a natural state. In the sutta, here's this bhikkhu, living his life quietly. He's found a nice tree to sit under, he's gone to the village to collect some food, and he's come back and eaten it quietly and mindfully. He's digested the food and now he's feeling very relaxed and calm, so he's sitting under the tree and he just goes into a meditative state. We shouldn't think too much of meditation as an exercise that we do at certain times, even when we're not feeling like it. That isn't very natural: that isn't how it should be, ideally.

Ideally, a *dhyāna* state is something you slip into, almost, because conditions are right, and because you're ready, and that's the natural tendency of your mind. Maybe you've had your meal, and you're just sitting there in your chair. Everything's calm and quiet, you've no particular desires or cravings, you're not annoyed with anybody, not thinking about anything in particular. Then your mind should quite naturally tend to a *dhyāna*-like state. This is how it should be. We shouldn't think of meditation as a sort of artificial practice that we do. Perhaps it has to be like that for a while, but that's only because of our limitations and the bad state we've got ourselves into. We have to do the *mettā-bhāvanā* as a practice, but in a sense *mettā* should be our natural state of mind. If we are happy and healthy ourselves, why should we not wish well to others? We shouldn't need an exercise to help us do it. The fact that we need meditation as a specific practice means, in a way, that something has gone wrong. In an ideal way of life you'd find yourself meditating spontaneously on certain occasions, in certain circumstances. And eventually, ideally, this is what should happen. You should develop such a way of life or be in such a mental state that you can go into a meditative state whenever circumstances allow. When you find yourself alone in a room or even sitting quietly with someone else, and with nothing particularly to think about, in quite a positive emotional state, you should naturally enter a *dhyāna*-like state. One should think of meditation not as something that you do on a certain occasion, when the bell rings, with a lot of effort and struggle. No doubt that is the way it has to be for the present, but that's not the ideal, one should remember that.

The spiritual life in the end should not be just a discipline, or something you have to impose upon yourself, but a natural, spontaneous expression of the way you feel, the way you are. It's the same with vegetarianism. It's not that you've imposed upon yourself this rule or this discipline that 'thou shalt not eat meat,' or 'thou shalt not eat fish'. It's just the way you feel. You don't want to eat meat, you don't want to eat fish, just because of your general sensitivity to other forms of life. It's not that if the prohibition was removed or somebody wasn't looking, you'd immediately go and have a steak. And it's just the same with meditation. It's not that if that bell wasn't ringing you wouldn't go and meditate. You are prompted to do so by something within you. So though meditation classes and courses and all these things may be good and necessary for quite a few years, we mustn't forget that they aren't ends in themselves. Though you mustn't start telling yourself that prematurely.

From a seminar on the *Samaññaphala Sutta* (1982, pp.145-50)

2. VIRTUALLY MEDITATING ALREADY ...

Learning meditation solely from books isn't enough, unless one is exceptionally gifted. By its nature, meditation is a personal, individual thing, for which no amount of general guidance and instruction can be enough.

Preparations for meditation are essential. If we find ourselves dissatisfied with our progress in meditation – if the milestones are not exactly flashing by – it is probably because we have plunged straight in without doing the necessary preparation first. If on the other hand we are really well prepared, we are virtually meditating already, whether we know it or not.

First – and most important – is ethics. Of course, all Buddhists try to observe five fundamental ethical precepts, i.e. to abstain from taking life, from taking what is not given, from sexual misconduct, from false speech, and from intoxication. But precisely how does ethics relate to one's practice of meditation?

Modern Indian meditation teachers usually speak of the ethical preparation for concentration and meditation in terms of bringing under control – of moderating – three things: food, sex, and sleep. As regards food, they say that you should never overload the stomach. At the same time you shouldn't, they say, ever leave it completely empty, unless you are deliberately undergoing a fast. The way they explain it, a quarter of your stomach should be for food, a quarter for water, and half of it should be empty. It is also said that you should avoid certain kinds of food – especially hot, spicy food, which is supposed to stimulate the passions (and of which Indian people are inordinately fond). However, one can probably take this idea of certain foods having particular psychological effects with a pinch of salt. Suffice it to say that heavy food, and food that is conducive to flatulence, should certainly be avoided. A gathering of a whole roomful of people who have dined 'not wisely but too well' on hot curry can produce a volume of noise that is seriously disruptive of any attempt to meditate.

Moving on to the question of sex, it is said, of course, that celibacy is best, but this is simply not a realistic aim for everyone. So, instead, we can say that moderation at least – some degree of restraint – should be observed. Meditation calls for a great deal of nervous energy, particularly as you go into deep concentration, and this nervous energy is dissipated in sexual release. However, it is up to the individual to work out exactly where the most effective balance in this respect may be struck, according to their own particular circumstances, and based on their own observation and reflection.

The third thing to be restrained is indulgence in sleep. This is not often mentioned in connection with meditation, but – again according to Indian meditation teachers – what we should find when we meditate is that we need to sleep a little less than before. If we sleep well as a general rule we probably tend to take it for granted, but of course sleep is a wonderful and mysterious thing indeed, as poets throughout the ages have testified. There is, for example, a particularly beautiful and striking passage in Cervantes' *Don Quixote*, in which Sancho Panza sings the praises of sleep. However, it is only recently that we have begun to understand the real purpose of sleep. It is not, as was formerly thought, just to rest the body. The generally accepted view nowadays is that you sleep in order also to be able to dream, to sort out all the vast mass of perceptions and impressions of the day and file them away for future reference.

When you meditate deeply, you aren't aware of the body, and therefore you are no longer taking in impressions, no longer registering input. So you don't need to process so much data – there is much less sorting out and filing away to be done, and thus much less need to dream. In this way, deep meditation drastically reduces the number of hours you need for sleep.

This does not mean that one should necessarily sleep less in order to meditate more effectively. In fact, most people nowadays tend, if anything, to sleep rather less than they need to. It seems that since the widespread use of electric light at the beginning of the twentieth century, people sleep, on average, an hour less than they did before then. There is no need to deprive oneself of sleep – this will lead to alienation. But wallowing in bed after one has had enough sleep will obviously promote lethargy and mental lassitude.

So ethical preparation is, in the first place, control of food, of sex, and of sleep. On top of these, however, and equally important, is the need to curb aggressiveness. Not just overt physical aggression, but any rude, harsh, domineering speech or posture (one sees this especially in the way many parents behave towards their children) will impede the development of positive mental states. And a vegetarian diet should be adhered to – conditions permitting – as an expression of one's dedication to a harmless way of life.

In summary, ethical preparation for meditation consists in leading, as far as possible, a quiet life, a harmless life, and a simple life. What is required is a peaceful life without loud noise, hectic social activity, or violent physical exertion. All these things can leave one's whole system too 'tingling', 'raw', and altogether too grossly stimulated to transmit the refined impulses that are generated by meditation.

I should add, though, that while strenuous exercise is not to be recommended as preparation for meditation, some kind of gentle exercise or relaxation technique – like Hatha yoga or T'ai chi Ch'uan – together with careful attention to finding a meditation posture that enables one to stay relaxed, comfortable, and alert, is very beneficial. One need not feel obliged, by the way, to adopt the classical cross-legged meditation posture. Sitting astride meditation cushions, or sitting on a chair, does just as well. The important thing is to experiment until one finds a comfortable way of sitting. One of the advantages of attending a meditation class is that one can get some help with establishing an appropriate and supportive meditation posture.

The issue of work, of livelihood, is also an aspect of preparation for meditation. Working at a certain job for six, eight, even ten hours a day, five or six days of the week, year after year, inevitably has an enormous cumulative effect upon the mind. You are being psychologically conditioned all the while by your occupation. Choosing a means of livelihood that is peaceful and beneficial in one way or another is crucial, not only as preparation for meditation, but as a basis for one's whole development as a healthy human being.

Checking through all these factors might seem like more than enough preparation to deal with. But there is more. A most important part of the ethical preparation for meditation is to be mindful and self-possessed. One needs to be aware of the body and its movements, aware of emotions and emotional reactions, aware of thoughts, aware of what one is doing and why one is doing it. One needs constantly to cultivate calmness, collectedness, mindfulness, in everything that one does, whether speaking or remaining silent, working or resting, cooking or gardening or doing the accounts, walking or driving or sitting still. One must always remain watchful and aware. This is the best preparation for meditation. Maintaining a constant level of awareness in this way means that as soon as you sit down to meditate, as soon as you summon up an object of concentration, you slip into a meditative state without any difficulty at all.

There are just two further points of importance. Learning meditation solely from books isn't enough, unless one is exceptionally gifted. By its nature, meditation is a personal, individual thing, for which no amount of general guidance and instruction can be enough. Moreover, a personal teacher will bring to bear upon our difficulties a degree of objectivity that we are unlikely to be able to attain on our own. A teacher is needed at least until we have some advanced spiritual experience under our belt. Even then, there can arise all sorts of spiritual dangers that a teacher who knows us well can see us through.

Lastly, there is preparation by way of devotional exercises. These don't appeal to everybody, but for those who are devotionally – which can often mean emotionally – inclined, they may be very helpful indeed. They come in all sorts of different – and some very elaborate – forms, but at their simplest they involve making symbolic offerings to a *rūpā* or image of the Buddha before starting to meditate. Lighting a candle symbolizes the light of vision that we are about to try to light in our own hearts; flowers symbolize the impermanence of all worldly things; and finally incense, permeating the air all around us, represents the fragrance of the good, the beautifully-lived life, which influences the world around us wherever we go in subtle, imperceptible ways.

We have examined the subject of preparation for meditation in some detail for a very good reason. If you are prepared to pay attention to all these details, then there will be very little more to do. One might almost say that you won't then need to meditate at all; you will have only to remain still and close your eyes and you'll be there – concentrated.

From *What is the Dharma?* (1998, pp.184-8)

3. THE SECRET LIES IN THE PREPARATION

If you want to meditate, it's no good thinking you can just sit down and do it.

We are usually in far too much of a hurry. In our anxiety to get results quickly we often neglect the very conditions upon which the results depend, and so, very often, we don't succeed. But if we make sufficiently careful preparations, we can leave the results to look after themselves; indeed, we find that we succeed almost without noticing.

This very much applies to meditation. If you want to meditate, it's no good thinking you can just sit down and do it. In the East the tradition is that first of all you go into the room in which you are going to meditate and, very slowly and carefully, sweep the floor, tidy up, and if necessary dust the image of the Buddha on the shrine. You do it all slowly, gently, and mindfully. Then, in a meditative mood, you throw away the old flowers (in some Eastern countries you are meant to throw them into running water if possible, not on the dust heap) and cut fresh ones. You put them in a vase and arrange them thoughtfully, taking your time over it. Then you light a candle and a stick of incense. You look around to see that everything is in order – perhaps you need to open the window for a bit of fresh air, or shut the door to keep out disturbances. Then you arrange your seat – making sure it is placed square – and then you sit down. You adjust your clothing, and put your feet and hands into the proper posture. Even then, very often, you won't begin the meditation. First you'll recite the Refuges and Precepts, and chant a few invocations to the Buddhas and Bodhisattvas. Then – and only then – you start meditating.

Paying attention to the preparations in this way, one is much more likely to succeed, not just in meditation but in all activities. If one wants to write a book, or paint a picture, or cook a meal, the secret lies in the preparation.

From *The Bodhisattva Ideal* (1999, p.46)

4. THE WAY YOU LIVE HAS AN EFFECT ON YOUR MIND

The important thing is to make the connection between what you do during the meditation class and what you do during the rest of the day.

Sangharakshita: One has to accept that if people are engaged in very unskilful activities, meditation may bring them quite unpleasant experiences. To take an extreme example, a slaughterman really might get visions of slaughtered animals or himself cutting their throats. Such a person would be well advised to go slow with meditation and think very seriously about where they stand, ethically speaking, in connection with their means of livelihood.

Q: Suppose one worked as, say, a motorcycle messenger in London. With a hectic occupation like that, one might feel a strong need to learn something like meditation, but at the same time find it very difficult to meditate. Should one persist with meditation?

S: Well, you would need to recognize that the way you live, the way you behave during the day, has its effect on your mind, and if you are trying to do one thing when you meditate and a quite different and opposite thing the rest of the day, that can bring about conflict and tension. It is up to you to regulate either the amount of meditation you do or the amount of dashing about you do. It might be a completely new idea to you that your means of livelihood has an effect on your mind at all; you might even consider whether another occupation would suit you better. The important thing is to make the connection between what you do during the meditation class and what you do during the rest of the day.
From Study Group Leaders' Q&A on the Noble Eightfold Path
(1985, pp.120-1)

5. THE BENEFITS OF COLLECTIVE PRACTICE

The Westerner learning to meditate is quite likely to do so alone, buying a book on the subject and beginning the practice in the comfort of his or her own home, but this is not to be recommended.

In the *Satipaṭṭhāna Sutta* the Buddha launches straight into a description of how the bhikkhu should go about meditation practice. He is directed to go into the depths of the forest, or to the foot of a tree, or just to an empty place. Then, sitting down with his legs crossed, he is to keep his body erect and his mindfulness alert or 'established in front of him', and start to become aware of his breathing. Thus we learn straightaway that the right place, the right time, and the right posture are all important for successful meditation.

The right place, we gather, is a place of solitude. In the Buddha's time, of course, there was plenty of space in the depths of the forest for meditators to sit there for long periods without being disturbed, but I think the Buddha's instruction here means something more. We need to imagine what it would be like to take up this practice if you had always lived in the traditional Indian family, which was the core of brahminical society in the Buddha's day. An Indian village, with all its noise and bustle, was hardly conducive to the development of mental calm, and the psychological and moral pull of the family group would have been just as inimical to spiritual practice. Even today in India, if you live in a traditional extended family it can be very difficult to steer your life in a direction not dictated by your family. For anyone seeking an awakening to truth, simply going forth to the undisturbed solitude of the forest, abandoning anything to do with home and family life, at least for a while, was – and continues to be – a major step.

Finding solitude is just as much of a challenge for us in the West today, although for us 'solitude' might mean getting a respite from the world and worldly concerns rather than literally getting away from other people. Indeed, the companionship of other people following the same spiritual tradition as yourself can be a great source of encouragement, especially when you are just starting out. To meditate in isolation, you need to know what you are doing and be very determined. It is all too easy for discouraging doubts to arise about whether you are doing the practice properly, and in the absence of an experienced guide you might lose interest in meditation altogether. While the Buddha's instruction to seek out the foot of a tree certainly suggests finding a place where you are likely to be undisturbed for a while, it does not necessarily mean going off into the depths of the forest or isolating yourself from other meditators.

People didn't always meditate alone even in the Buddha's day. The Pāli suttas contain striking descriptions of the Buddha and his disciples sitting and meditating together, sometimes in very large numbers. We come upon such a scene at the beginning of the *Sāmaññaphala Sutta*.

THE PURPOSE AND PRACTICE OF BUDDHIST MEDITATION

On a full-moon night, King Ajātasattu decides to have his elephants saddled up (five hundred of them) and ride with his entourage deep into the forest in search of the Buddha. It is quite a long way, and the king (who has a guilty conscience) is beset by all sorts of fears as they journey through the darkness. But at last they come upon the Buddha, seated in meditation with twelve hundred and fifty monks, all of them perfectly concentrated and spread out before him like a vast, clear lake. The silence, says the sutta, fills the guilty king – he has murdered his own father to gain the throne – with a nameless dread, making the hairs on his body stand on end. But he is sufficiently moved to ask to become a lay disciple of the Buddha on the spot.

Since those early times, Buddhists throughout the tradition – especially in the Zen schools, which place a particular emphasis on meditation – have well understood the benefits of collective practice. The Westerner learning to meditate is quite likely to do so alone, buying a book on the subject and beginning the practice in the comfort of his or her own home, but this is not to be recommended. It is hard to tell from the printed page how much experience the author has, and in any case no book can cover every contingency. There is also the danger that you will end up just reading about Buddhist meditation and never getting round to doing any. It is certainly possible to learn the basic techniques from a book, but if you can, it is worth seeking out a meditation teacher and other meditators with whom to practise.

As for the Buddha's instruction that the bhikkhu should sit cross-legged, this posture is recommended because it spreads the weight of the body more broadly and evenly than any other sitting position, and thus gives stability and enables you to sit comfortably for a long time. However, while it would have come naturally to the people of the Buddha's time and culture to sit cross-legged on the floor, we might find it more difficult. If so, any posture can be adopted, whether on the floor or on a chair, as long as it is stable and comfortable. Incidentally, this is another reason to go along to a meditation class – to get some help with working out a suitable meditation posture.

From *Living with Awareness* (2003, pp.26-8)

6. SITTING DOWN IN A STATE FIT FOR MEDITATION

As long as you are paving the way, trying to create the conditions by means of which you will be able to meditate properly and have a good meditation, the fact that you can't do it properly straight off doesn't mean that you shouldn't do it at all.

> *The supreme Buddha praised pure meditation which gives instantaneous results. There is nothing equal to that meditation. This precious jewel is in the Dhamma. By this truth may there be peace!* [39]

Sangharakshita: How is one to take this statement? Do you find that when you meditate, you get results instantaneously?

Q: Perhaps the way to look at it is that if you are in a perfect state of mind when you sit down to meditate, you will become Enlightened instantaneously. The means of getting towards that state is more meditation beforehand.

S: Yes, right. If you sit down to meditate in a state fit for meditation, you will invariably be successful in your meditation. This underlines the importance of preparation – not only preparation for meditation in the form of meditation, but for instance making sure that you're properly rested before you start, that you've got enough time, that you've been able to unwind, making sure you're in an emotionally positive state, and so on. If you can sit down to meditate in that way, you can be reasonably certain that you'll have a successful meditation. But it also includes many other things. For instance, something might have happened the day before yesterday which upset you. Maybe you haven't resolved that, so the recollection of it and certain after-effects come into your mind while you're trying to meditate, and upset you. The conditions aren't perfect, so you don't have a perfect meditation. But to the extent that your preparation for meditation is perfect, to that extent your meditation will be perfect; to the extent that your meditation is perfect, your Enlightenment will be perfect. In that sense, the results of meditation are instantaneous. If all the obstructions within your mind are removed, you can depend upon the meditation to get you there.

Q: I suppose it also depends what you mean by a successful meditation.

S: It does not mean performing a sort of ritual. It doesn't mean that if you just sit there faithfully at eight o'clock every morning, you will get there in the end. Perhaps you will, but not by just sitting there at eight o'clock every morning, however regularly. Something has got to happen while you're sitting there, you've got to do something. So it is not just going through the motions of meditating regularly. It's quite easy to fall into that habit without realizing it. You can be having quite successful meditations, but not realize that it has become a routine. It's only successful if you are pushing on all the time.

Q: But isn't it worth sitting even if you know you're not properly prepared?

S: Oh yes. As long as you are paving the way, trying to create the conditions by means of which you will be able to meditate properly and have a good meditation, the fact that you can't do it properly straight off doesn't mean that you shouldn't do it at all, because it's only by doing it as best you can that you can gradually improve the way you do it. Even if you feel very tired, never mind, sit; even if your mind wanders, never mind, sit. Just try not to behave foolishly. One sees that on retreat sometimes. People know that they are going to be getting up for an early morning meditation, but they nonetheless insist on going to bed late after talking a lot. So, of course, they feel tired in the morning. It's not just a matter of dragging yourself into the shrine-room regardless of how you feel; it's a question of making sure you go to bed early enough, and get enough sleep so that you can be fresh and bright in the morning, in other words ensuring the whole complex of conditions upon which successful meditation depends. You can't neglect all the other conditions and expect force of will to carry you through at the last minute.

Q: Can you change the length of time you need to sleep in order to feel fresh the next day?

S: I think to begin with you should not interfere with your normal sleep requirements too much. You can't necessarily get more deeply into meditation just by cutting down your sleep. You will find that if you are meditating regularly and well, by which I mean you are experiencing some higher, more positive levels of consciousness, you will naturally need less sleep. But that doesn't mean that if you cut down your sleep, a better meditation will automatically follow.

From a seminar on the *Ratana Sutta* (1980, pp.23-4)

7. IS THERE A WRONG TIME TO MEDITATE?

One would have thought that as far as the practice of meditation is concerned, any time would be all right, but apparently, it isn't so.

*Knowing not the right time to
Practise, one's Yoga will stray.*[40]

Sangharakshita: One would have thought that as far as the practice of yoga was concerned (by yoga here is meant meditation), any time would be all right, but apparently it isn't so: there's a right time and a wrong time to practise meditation. Do you think that this is so? Could there be a wrong time to practise meditation?

Q: If you've said you'll do something for someone else and then you say, 'No, I want to meditate,' that would presumably be wrong.

S: Yes. Is there any other way in which you could practise at the wrong time?

Q: When you need a certain degree of intellectual clarity and conceptualization. Having just come out of deep *dhyāna* states, you can hardly speak sometimes.

S: Yes. Or, quite simply, immediately after a big, heavy meal, or when you may be unduly interrupted – that is the wrong time to practise.

Q: Or when it isn't quiet enough for you to practise ...

S: ... and you just become irritated. So that is quite straightforward, really. 'Knowing not the right time to practise, one's yoga will stray.'

From a seminar on 'Rechungpa's Departure',
Songs of Milarepa (1980, pp.80-1)

8. MAKE YOUR MEDITATION INDEPENDENT OF CONDITIONS

Don't allow your meditation, don't allow your spiritual life, to depend on any special set of circumstances.

> *Though the best temple is one's own body*
> *We need a place for cover and sleep;*
> *Without mercy, the wind and rain attack all.*
> *Because of this, we always need a temple.*[41]

Sangharakshita: Don't you think this is true? We need a place for cover and sleep, somewhere we can be protected from the elements. It's quite difficult to live without a house, without shelter, especially somewhere like Tibet (which is where Rechungpa, the speaker here, lives). You might just about manage in some parts of India, at certain times of the year. But even in the Buddha's day, even the Buddha himself and his disciples, though they were wandering from place to place for eight or nine months of the year, had to take shelter for three or four months of the year during the rainy season.

Q: It's certainly easier to meditate in some sort of shelter. I think it's very difficult to meditate in the open air.

S: It seems that the Buddha and his disciples normally did meditate in the open air, in the forest. It's strange that we should find that more difficult. I wonder why. I suppose it's because indoors you're sheltered from the wind and from draughts, as well as from insects – gnats and mosquitoes and ants. You may also be protected from noise. But it seems that in the Buddha's day, more often than not people did meditate out of doors.

Q: It may be what we're used to. If one is not used to living outdoors, it's distracting to hear breezes or birds. And it's a bit cooler outside here than it is in India.

S: Yes. Tibet of course is cooler still. So it does seem that we do need shelter. But we have to make sure that we don't demand more than we need. You need very little in the way of shelter really: just four walls and a roof that are weatherproof, and where you can be sufficiently comfortable and warm (or cool) to be able to get on with your meditation without being distracted.

Q: There were wandering Christian friars and hermits even in this country in the Middle Ages. They survived in very primitive conditions, when you come to think about it.

Q: Did you find that you could get on quite easily meditating outside in India?

S: I didn't find meditating out of doors particularly difficult. What did make things difficult at one stage was walking from place to place. I don't know whether that was because I was physically not in very good condition, or because it was exhausting, especially in that climate, but I did find that that made meditation very difficult. But I didn't find meditating in the open air difficult; in fact I rather liked it. It can be very conducive to meditation, especially when you're sitting at evening time on the banks of a broad, slow river, and it's very quiet, very still, and the sun is setting. You get quite a different feeling, quite a different experience, when you meditate in those conditions. I've never done it, but I'm sure it would be very different also to meditate out in the open air high up in the mountains, as Milarepa did.

Q: I know it's not quite the same, but I was once on a walking holiday on the South Downs, and meditated on the tops of the hills every day, and the broad expanse of countryside and the enormous amount of space did seem to make a difference.

S: Yes. I remember on some of the summer retreats I used to lead we had meditation in the open air sometimes. Sometimes we were troubled by some kind of gadfly, or even by ants, but we used to sit in a circle round a big tree. This does give you quite a different kind of experience. I think we should be aware that we meditate under rather special conditions, that is to say almost always indoors, and be careful not to associate with meditation a feeling that we get just because we are meditating indoors. What you may think of as an essential part of the meditation experience may just be due to the fact that you're meditating in a shrine-room. It might be a good idea to experiment gently and try meditating under different conditions, if you get an opportunity – if you're out hiking, say, or living in the country, and can sit in the open air without disturbance.

Q: Are you saying that the real aspects of meditation are what is in common between meditations in these different conditions?

S: You could say that. For instance, when you meditate you might experience a feeling of security, but it may not be because of the meditation, but because you're safe and secure inside a house. When you're meditating in the open air, depending on your temperament, you may feel very different; you may even feel threatened. That would be nothing to do with the meditation, but due to the fact that you are meditating in the open air, exposed and vulnerable instead of tucked away safely in your shrine-room. One should be quite clear what is due to the meditation itself and what is due to the circumstances under which you are meditating, and not associate your meditation too strictly or exclusively with any one set of circumstances. That may be necessary at first, but gradually you should acclimatize yourself to meditating under different conditions. Some people can't meditate unless they meditate in the shrine-room. Some people can meditate only in their own room. Others can meditate only at a particular time of day. To begin with these limitations have to be accepted – you have to start somewhere – but they shouldn't be accepted as permanently valid, and after a while you should try to get over them.

I had a friend in India who had a number of disciples, and he used to encourage them to meditate at that time of the day which they found most difficult, which was usually of course at midnight and in the early hours, just when they felt most sleepy. You shouldn't of course take up this sort of practice prematurely, but as time goes on you should try to make your meditation independent of conditions, even your own bodily conditions. Some people think that if they're a bit unwell, they can't meditate. Perhaps if you're a beginner it is not advisable to try to meditate when you're not well, but as you become more established in meditation you shouldn't give up meditation just because you're not feeling very well. You should be able to break through that. So in principle Milarepa is right. He's saying to Rechungpa: Don't allow your meditation, don't allow your spiritual life, to depend on any special set of circumstances: that you are well-fed, that you are healthy, that you are well, that you are not tired. Don't let your meditation depend on conditions of that sort.

In the end it mustn't depend on any circumstances, any conditions. By agreeing to stay in the valley, Milarepa recognizes that Rechungpa isn't yet able to follow his instructions to that extent, but nonetheless he has stated the principle involved without any compromise.

Q: Rechungpa keeps saying we always need a temple. He does seem to regard these conditions as permanently valid.

S: We don't always need a temple. We certainly need one at the beginning, but in the end you should be able to meditate anywhere, under almost any conditions. The Buddhists in our movement in India are very good in this respect. They're able to meditate under conditions that people in England would think were impossible. When I was in India I heard about one woman who was having to sleep at night in a room occupied by 22 other people, and she had her bed on a shelf up against the wall, but she still managed to meditate every day. Not many people in England could meditate under those conditions. Many members of the Sangha in India meditate at home in what we would regard as intolerably crowded conditions, but they meditate nonetheless, just sitting in a corner of the room while the rest of the family life is going on all around them. There's no question of their having a separate room in which to meditate, or meditating in the bedroom; there's no separate bedroom. People just bed down at night in the room or rooms where they're living during the day. So they just have to find a corner where they can sit, maybe turning their backs on the rest of the family, and there's people talking and cooking and getting on with their homework and so on while somebody is meditating in the corner. But they manage, and their standard of meditation is at least as good as that of people in England, if not better. It shows itself on retreats; they really do get deeply into their meditation. I remember how they sat on through a violent hailstorm when we were on retreat. Hailstones as big as marbles came bouncing in through the door amongst them, and there was thunder and flashes of lightning, but no one took any notice.

One should accustom oneself gradually to being less dependent on external conditions in every way, otherwise we become their slaves. We become quite precious: we can't meditate unless we've got a nice quiet shrine-room and a decent cushion, and unless people are not fidgeting.

From a seminar on Milarepa's *Story of the Yak Horn* (1980, pp.239-42)

9. 'DO NOT FORCE YOUR MIND OR BODY'

You have to stop forcing things, stop even doing things. That's the first step before you can start relaxing or even think of relaxing.

> *To begin with, pay urgent attention to impermanence,*
> *Then strongly turn your mind towards taking Refuge,*
> *And direct your prayers to the lamas (Teachers).*
> *These are the preliminaries without which no means exists.*

> *After that, disposing yourself physically to be calm,*
> *As in an empty house the raindrops slowly gather,*
> *Relax – do not force your mind or body.*[42]

Sangharakshita: It's a mysterious phrase: 'as in an empty house the raindrops slowly gather'. How do raindrops slowly gather in an empty house? And why an *empty* house particularly? I suppose one must bear in mind the Tibetan house. Do the raindrops come down the chimney or the smoke hole or whatever? They didn't have much in the way of windows in traditional Tibetan houses. But anyway, the meaning is clear, isn't it? – basically that you should relax, not forcing your mind or body. Why do you think this comes immediately after the preliminaries? First of all you relax physically, you sit comfortably, and then you relax mentally. Why is this mentioned?

Q: The feeling I get is that it's guarding against reliance on willed action. Once you've got things set up and you're ambitious for yourself, it's quite an easy trap to fall into.

S: It's a question of overall growth and development, not just conscious volition. But what is the difference, would you say, between making a real effort and forcing mind and body? How can you tell the difference? Should you not make any effort, just sit back and let it all happen?

Q: If you could sit back and let it all happen, nothing probably would happen.

S: That is possible. But can you really 'sit back'? You may think you can, but it's actually very difficult to sit back and let it all happen. Actually if you could *really* sit back it *would* all happen. But when you think you're sitting back, the chances are that you're as busy as anything. Sitting back from your ego, sitting back from your ambition, sitting back from forcing, is not as easy as it sounds. It's not even easy to relax. You can't *make* yourself relax. If you're not relaxed, how do you bring about the state of relaxation?

Q: Conscious effort in most cases.

S: But it can't really be a conscious effort. That's a contradiction in terms. It usually means stopping doing whatever you're doing, and that might have to be a conscious effort. If you can persist in that, after a while there won't be any urge to do those things that you stopped yourself from doing. You'll just be able to sit there content not to do them, and then you can begin to relax. So you have to stop forcing things, stop even doing things. That's the first step before you can start relaxing or even think of relaxing. You have to stop and let things die down, so to speak, though sometimes they won't, sometimes they keep surging up again.

Q: Most of us probably relax by getting into activities that are a bit more refined than our usual daily life.

S: You need an intermediate stage; you can't just suddenly stop. It's like when a train is hurtling along at 80 miles per hour. You can't just apply the brakes, you have to slow it down gradually.

Even when you go on retreat, sometimes you find it takes a day or two to unwind, to adjust your pace, especially if you've been working hard and going all out right up to the minute that you left. It might have been a real scramble and then you go on retreat and you're expected to be all calm and quiet and mindful. It sometimes takes a day or two to get into that sort of state. If it's a longer retreat it might even take a whole week.

Even when people go on solitary retreats very often they say that when it was time to end the retreat, say after three or four weeks, they felt it was just beginning. They'd just started settling into it, they'd just started relaxing. It isn't so easy. It's a very important Tantric teaching – relax, just relax, but it's so difficult. Clearly it isn't just letting things go, letting things slide in the ordinary mundane sense.

Q: It is rather interesting how people have a tendency to think that listening to music is very relaxing, whereas if music is really doing what it's trying to do, it surges you around enormously.

S: Well, it depends on what sort of music it is, of course.

Q: It's easier perhaps to relax if you have been working hard.

S: It seems that a lot of people have energies which need to be used, and if those unemployed energies are just whirling around, you can't relax immediately. It's a question of relaxing at ever deeper levels until in the end you relax at the level so to speak of the ego itself. The ego relaxes. It isn't concerned any longer to keep itself going and to fend off attacks and so on.

Q: Would you classify entering into the *dhyānic* states as relaxing?

S: Oh yes. As mundane relaxation at least, yes. They're so very much more refined than everyday states of mind.

Q: But how about all the energies arising?

S: *Prīti* – yes, that would be *dhyānic*, though maybe you'd experience it more in terms of relaxation when you came out from it. Perhaps we could say that there's relaxation when mental processes, thought activities, cease, and there's also relaxation when the *prīti* experience ceases, and also when the *sukha* experience ceases and there's only *upekkhā* left. These are progressive stages of relaxation, at higher and higher, more and more refined levels.

So relax. You ought to be able to relax while working, paradoxical as it may sound. It's possible to work in a relaxed way, though usually we have to get things done and arouse our energy by means of some sort of ego insistence. We don't work smoothly and gently and relaxedly, so we have to relax afterwards, which in a way is ridiculous. You shouldn't have to relax to counteract what you've been doing while working. You can work in a relaxed way and then just rest. Ideally you relax while working. There's no tension. Sometimes it does happen, doesn't it?

Q: Once a carpenter showed me how to saw wood properly. You don't get tired out because you're having to make a huge effort. It's not like that. You let the weight of the saw do it. He did it so smoothly, as if there was no effort involved.

S: A lot of life is like that, you could say. You just lean on it.

From a seminar on *Advice Given to the Three Fortunate Women* (1980, pp.16-21)

10. COLOURS FOR A MEDITATION SPACE

If one is prone to mental distraction, a cool colour is more suitable, having a calming, pacifying effect, but if one is of a dull and sluggish disposition, a warm colour which is more stimulating is advisable.

Q: When it comes to choosing colours for a meditation space, are particular colours suitable for particular people?

Sangharakshita: Colours are usually divided into hot and cold colours. Hot colours are red and orange and yellow, cold colours are blue and green. I think that if one is prone to mental distraction, a cool colour is more suitable, having a calming, pacifying effect. Perhaps white could be included, certainly blue and perhaps green even more so. But if one is of a dull and sluggish disposition, a warm colour which is more stimulating is advisable. It's also said that if you are prone to distraction, you should meditate in a darkened room, but if you are prone to dullness, then you should meditate in a bright well-lit room.
From a seminar on *The Forest Monks of Sri Lanka* (1985, p.291)

11. TAKE A DEEP BREATH

People used to come along straight from work, and very often, after a journey by bus or tube, they'd walk through a crowded street ... so more often than not they arrived in a rather crumpled state.

Q: Do you have any suggestions about how to prepare for meditation?

Sangharakshita: When I used to teach evening meditation classes, people used to come along straight from work, and very often, after a journey by bus or tube or both, they'd walk through a crowded street to get to the Buddhist centre. So more often than not they arrived in a rather crumpled state. I used to feel that one couldn't expect people to get straight into meditation; they needed something intermediate between their present state and the state of meditation. So I used to suggest from time to time, not as a regular practice but when I felt there were sufficient people present who needed it, that they should just relax and give themselves time to get into the meditation practice. I would sometimes ask them to sit there and take a few deep breaths, deliberately to breathe in very deeply and then breathe out, and experience themselves as doing that. And in connection with the *mettā-bhāvanā* I used to feel that people weren't very much in touch with their emotions, and it would help if first of all they got in touch with their bodies. So I used to ask them to be aware of their bodies, starting from the tips of their toes, then through the rest of the body, experiencing a feeling of the whole body, from the tips of the toes to the crown of the head. And then we used to do the *mettā-bhāvanā*.

From Q&A on the *Mitrata Omnibus* (1981/2, Part 2, Session 20, pp.1-2)

12. A STRAIGHT BACK

When you become deeply absorbed, you quite spontaneously straighten up.

Q: Why is it so important to have a straight back when you are sitting in meditation?

Sangharakshita: Well, the body does affect the mind. I don't know whether anyone has experienced deep concentration as a result of meditating, but you'll find that when you become deeply absorbed, you quite spontaneously straighten up. It's as though there's some force inside you just pulling you up gently but firmly, in a pleasant way. When you're concentrated you are straight. So to help induce that feeling of absorption, you adopt the posture which is the natural expression of that absorption, in the hope that the physical posture will act on the mind and help it to become more absorbed. It's as simple as that. So when you're sitting cross-legged on the floor or sitting in a chair (which you can do if you find sitting cross-legged difficult), you sit straight. But however straight you are, you will find that when you become deeply absorbed you become even straighter, not ramrod-stiff in a military sort of way, but straight in a relaxed, firm way.

From Q&A in Christchurch (1979, p.25)

13. CUSHION-FLUFFING

Buddhist centres need to pay very close attention to their cushions ...

I think quite a lot of people don't pay sufficient attention to their posture when they're sitting and meditating, and I've asked yoga teachers within the Order to correct people's postures whenever they see that they need correction. I would suggest that if you're a yoga teacher and you know what is a correct posture, you should not be shy about correcting people's postures or giving them advice or demonstrating. I also suggest that those whose postures are incorrect, whether they know it or not, take in good part, in fact with thankfulness, any advice that they may get from a yoga teacher. It's all to their benefit. They will be able to meditate better.

I've also been thinking that cushions need more attention. When I was in India I never used a cushion. In India meditation cushions are quite unknown. I'd not even seen one until I came to England, strange to say. They originate in Japan, and perhaps people in the West do need them because they normally sit on chairs, they're not accustomed to sitting cross-legged. But if we're going to use cushions, we should be careful to see that they are proper ones. A lumpy, saggy cushion is not a proper meditation cushion, and far too often cushions are allowed to get into a terrible state, so that people have to pile up three deflated-looking cushions one on top of the other to get a proper height. As I've understood it, not that I've been through the Zen tradition or anything like that, a cushion should be round and springy, but firm. When you sit on it, it shouldn't be so thinly stuffed that you can feel the floor through the cushion. You should almost – not exactly bounce on the cushion but you should be almost balanced on it, it should be springy, so that there is no hard pressure on the part of the body which is in contact with the cushion because that will cut off the circulation of blood. You should be quite finely balanced or poised on the cushion, which should feel a little springy beneath you – not like a hard lump.

So Buddhist centres need to pay very close attention to their cushions. They need to be re-stuffed from time to time, or at least the kapok needs pulling out and plumping up. In India they've got a special instrument for this, because they use similar stuff in pillows and mattresses. A man comes along with something that looks like a harp and he somehow fluffs the hard lumps of kapok with this. It makes a twang, twang sound. It's a very familiar sound around the villages. Perhaps someone who goes to India should learn this art, get one of these bow-like things and learn how to fluff the kapok. Then they could go round from centre to centre plumping all the cushions for a small fee. It would be a good means of right livelihood for somebody, and a pleasant occupation. You could sing or chant as you twanged your harp, as it were. By the time you'd got around all the centres, it would be time to start again because in the interval all the cushions would have gone hard and lumpy again. So your livelihood would be well provided for.

This is a serious point, because these hard lumpy unsatisfactory cushions don't help meditation at all. You might just as well be sitting on a folded towel like I used to do in India. Cushions should be firm and at the same time springy – cushions on which it is a pleasure to sit, not something through which you feel the floor, or all sorts of hard edges and uncomfortable lumps. That certainly doesn't encourage meditation.

From a Men's Convention (1985, p.14)

14. GETTING UP EARLY

I think we have to use our common sense about this.

Devoting ourselves to spiritual exercises instead of sleeping in the first and last parts of the night ...[43]

Sangharakshita: That's a hardship, isn't it? This refers to getting up early in the morning to meditate, and meditating in the evening before you go to bed. There's really not much to be said about that.

Q: Were there traditionally certain watches of the night?

S: Yes. I think it was different in India and Tibet, but I think it was from eight to twelve, then twelve till four, then four till eight; these are the three watches of the night. This envisages that you cut down on your sleep to quite an extent. I think we have to use our common sense about this. What it really means is, don't indulge in more sleep than you actually need. Certainly take whatever sleep is necessary for your physical and mental well-being, but don't stay lying in bed wallowing in the comfort and pleasure and luxury of it. This isn't very conducive to one's development as an individual. But don't try to cut down on sleep deliberately as a result of some preconceived idea. I think you'll find that as you meditate more, you will need less sleep, but it should happen naturally. But when you have woken up and you have had your full night's sleep, get up. There's no point in just lying there.

From a seminar on *The Jewel Ornament of Liberation,*
Patience and Strenuousness (1980, pp.48-9)

2 Ending the meditation

1. DON'T JUST THROW IT AWAY

If you've gained something in the meditation or puja, it's a pity to just dissipate it immediately afterwards, wasting the effort you've made.

Q: Recently we had a festival at the Buddhist centre and we had quite an elaborate puja, lots of offerings, lots of lights, lots of readings. I came out of the puja as if I was on another planet; it was really quite a strong experience. But everyone else came out and started chatting immediately, as if nothing had really happened.

Sangharakshita: Ah, yes. I've noticed this sort of thing time and time again, but I'm still surprised when it happens after meditation. Within half a minute people are chatting as though they haven't meditated. Sometimes I wonder whether they *were* meditating. They were sitting there; they were pretty still; they weren't moving. But what sort of state were they in? One knows from one's own experience that if you've been meditating for an hour, you can't walk straight out of the door and start chatting. You don't want to. But here people are, doing that very thing; it's a very common occurrence. So, sometimes I wonder what they've been doing while they've been sitting there. I've also wondered whether people have a negative streak in them which almost compels them to undo the good that they have done.

Q: It's like you're relieved to get out ...

S: Yes, a reaction sets in. Even though you've had a good meditation you at once want to go to the other extreme. The gravitational pull at once asserts itself. But I think one has to be very mindful of that possibility, so that one doesn't immediately dissipate the fruits of meditation or puja or whatever. One sees people doing that, and it's so sad. They just throw away immediately, instantly, whatever benefits they've gained. You can see it happen.

Q: I'm very much in favour of having a period of silence after meditation, or a puja.

S: You could do that. Announce that there will be a ten or fifteen minute silence. Tea can be served, and people can have ten or fifteen minutes of silence and then just slowly and mindfully start talking. Otherwise people pour out of the door and at once start chatting: 'Hello, did you see that film last week?' and: 'Oh yes, I bought a new coat'.

Q: I would suggest that if you were to do that, attendance at meditation classes would drop, because a lot of people come along almost for the tea-break, for the social occasion.

S: Well, that's fair enough. But let it come in due time. Presumably they have sat through the meditation in order to get to the socializing; well, let them wait a bit longer! One has to follow a middle course. One doesn't want to stifle people. But if you've gained something in the meditation or puja, it's a pity just to dissipate it immediately afterwards, wasting the effort you've made.

Q: But sometimes I've found when I've a good meditation that I've very much enjoyed, I feel like dancing around and whistling. I feel that that's quite healthy. I don't feel it's always appropriate to be silent. Do you see what I mean?

S: Yes. But we were especially referring to mindless chatter immediately after meditation and puja. Harmonious dance-like movements, or even a tuneful whistle, might be more acceptable!

From a seminar on the *Parabhava Sutta* (1982, pp.49-51)

2. YOU MUST BE ON YOUR GUARD

Just two minutes after a good meditation you can be nattering away about all sorts of stupid things as though you've not been meditating at all.

Q: Can you say something about ways of carrying over the feeling from your meditation practice into the day? Sometimes you can have a really positive feeling in your practice which helps set you up for the day but at other times, although when you walk out of the shrine room you can feel more alive and more aware, that seems to drain away very quickly.

Sangharakshita: I'm sure everybody experiences that. You just need to bear in mind the fact that it happens. As you go out of the shrine room door, you have to say to yourself, 'Be careful. There are hundreds of Māras around waiting to rob me of whatever I've gained.' Just be aware that the gains of meditation can be very easily dissipated, and be aware of your own reactive mind, which is what Māra essentially is, in a way. I've noticed so many times people coming out of the shrine room and proceeding straight to breakfast, and it's as though they've haven't been meditating. At once they start gabbling. It's not that anyone has asked them anything or that they have had to do anything. It's entirely them. They've started it. So once must be aware that the reactive side of one's own mind so easily and automatically swings into action again. Just two minutes after a good meditation you can be nattering away about all sorts of stupid things as though you've not been meditating at all. It's your fault, plain and simple. It's not the world that's disturbed you. It's just yourself.

So you must be on your guard against yourself, and then you will be able to deal more easily with distractions coming from outside, and things that objectively need doing, without straying too far from your concentrated state. Be careful of your reactions to what people say to you or what they ask you to do.

Q: Would it be a good idea after meditation to go outside for a quiet walk?

S: Yes, that's good; it's communing with nature, so to speak. Nature won't ask you any questions. Nature can be very calming, very restful, and at least no verbal communication is required.

Q: After every meditation I have a definite period of silence.

S: Well, that would be very helpful, no doubt. Sometimes that's the practice on retreats, isn't it? Sometimes it's good to carry on the silence until the end of breakfast. I think most people discover that when silence is being observed they conserve energy so they feel more alive, because they've expended less of their vitality than they usually do.
From a Men's Order/Mitra follow up event at Vinehall (1981, pp.42-4)

3. COMMUNICATION WITHOUT CHATTERING

After meditation perhaps it isn't easy to strike a middle point, to remain quiet and mindful but not to give the impression of being alienated or unfriendly or cut off.

Sangharakshita: For many people, it's as though the minute they are out of the shrine-room, they're not meditating any more. It's as though meditation is strictly a shrine-room activity, which is a pity. Not that one should make a point of not speaking after meditation, but at least one should retain one's mindfulness and not get carried away by an impulse to chatter immediately afterwards, an impulse which you shouldn't really be having if you've meditated properly.

Q: At the Buddhist centre, if you meditate and then you have a tea break, this can be a problem.

S: Well, you can organize the programme accordingly – or if you do enter into that situation, enter it quite willingly. Recognize that you're going to have to talk after meditating and accept it. Just try to talk mindfully and retain the meditative experience. You can say quite a lot and communicate without chattering. You can communicate to the other person that you are with them, you are listening, but you haven't moved too far from the meditative state. You don't have to go to the other extreme, though obviously that's quite difficult. You can easily get carried away, especially if everybody else is chattering. But to be sociable and friendly and communicative you don't necessarily have to be unmindful. This often happens around the breakfast table. Half a minute ago all these people were supposed to have been meditating; it seems so strange to see them chattering gaily away now. Though after meditation perhaps it isn't easy to strike a middle point, to remain quiet and mindful but not to give the impression of being alienated or unfriendly or cut off.

From a seminar on *The Jewel Ornament of Liberation,*
Ethics and Manners (year unknown, pp.44-5)

3 Identifying hindrances to meditation

1. THE FIVE MENTAL POISONS

Enlightenment is within us all, but it is shrouded in spiritual ignorance, as the vast azure vault of the sky may be obscured from horizon to horizon by dark clouds.

Enlightenment is within us all, but it is shrouded in spiritual ignorance or *avidyā*, as the vast azure vault of the sky may be obscured from horizon to horizon by dark clouds. This obscuring factor of *avidyā*, when it is analysed, is found to consist of the five mental poisons. The first poison is distractedness, inability to control wandering thoughts, mental confusion; and the meditation practice that acts as its antidote is the mindfulness of breathing. Then the second poison is anger, aversion, or hatred; and its antidote is the meditation practice called in Pāli the *metta-bhāvanā*, the cultivation of loving kindness. The third poison is craving or lust, and it is countered by the 'contemplation of decay'. Ignorance, in the sense of ignorance of our own conditionality, is the fourth poison, and it can be tackled by the contemplation of the twelve links of conditioned co-production. Finally, the fifth poison is conceit, pride, or ego-sense, whose antidote is the analysis of the six elements.

From *What is the Dharma?* (1998, p.188)

2. DESTROYING THE BANDITS' HIDEOUT

One has to find the centre of operations of the passions, which of course is the mind.

What are the passions, and how are they to be eradicated? The term covers all mental defilements – that is, all negative emotions, psychological conditionings, prejudices, and preconceptions. There are several traditional lists of these passions. First, there are the three unwholesome roots: craving, hatred, and ignorance, symbolized by the cock, the snake, and the pig depicted in the centre of the Tibetan Wheel of Life. In any depiction of the Wheel, with all its circles and subdivisions, right at the centre, right at the hub of our own lives, are these three creatures, each one biting the tail of the one in front. These are the driving forces of our existence. Another list of passions is the five *nīvaraṇas*, the five hindrances to meditation: desire for sense experience, ill will, restlessness and anxiety, sloth and torpor, and doubt and indecision.

Then there are the five poisons: distraction, anger, craving, conceit, and ignorance. The word poison is apposite. Negative emotions are literally poisonous, and when we indulge in them we literally poison our system. Sometimes when one is overpowered by a strong negative emotion, especially anger or hatred, one gets a stabbing pain in the stomach or the heart; this is the poison eating into one's vitals.

The best way to eradicate the passions is to attack them at source, like stopping the activities of a band of robbers by destroying their hideout, to use a traditional illustration. One has to find the centre of operations of the passions, which of course is the mind. That's where they are to be rooted out; and this is one of the effects of meditation. There are five basic meditation exercises in the Buddhist tradition which act as antidotes to the five poisons.

The first poison to be dealt with is distraction, the tendency of the mind to jump from one thing to another – having a butterfly mind, so that one can't settle on one thing steadily for any length of time. In T.S. Eliot's famous line, we are 'distracted from distraction by distraction'. The antidote to this mental state is the meditation practice called the mindfulness of breathing, which involves watching the breath to achieve a one-pointed concentration on the breathing process.

The second of the five poisons is anger, said to be the most un-Bodhisattva-like of all passions. You can give way to craving and desires, you can steal and lie, and in your heart of hearts you may still be a Bodhisattva. But if you lose your temper, bang goes all your Bodhisattvahood, and you have to start all over again. The reason is that anger is directly opposed to the spirit of compassion. In his *Śikṣā-Samuccaya* Śāntideva says – to paraphrase: 'Well, here you are, promising to deliver all beings from difficulties and be kind and compassionate to them, and then what do you do? You go and get angry with one of them! There can't be much substance to your Bodhisattva vow.'[44] The Bodhisattva is advised to avoid anger at all costs.

The antidote to anger is again quite simple: it's the *mettā-bhāvanā*, the development of universal loving-kindness. This meditation is one of four practices called the *brahma-vihāra*s, the sublime abodes, the other three being for the cultivation of compassion, sympathetic joy, and equanimity. The *mettā* practice was first taught by the Buddha, as recorded in the very beautiful *Mettā Sutta*. A fuller description of the practice is given by Buddhaghosa in his *Visuddhimagga (The Path of Purity)*.[45]

One starts the practice by developing a feeling of loving-kindness towards oneself, wishing that one may be well, happy, and free from suffering; then one extends that feeling to a close friend, then to a person one can visualize but doesn't know well – perhaps someone at work, or someone one sees every day at the bus-stop – and then to someone with whom one has difficulties. The fifth and last stage of the practice involves extending one's *mettā* equally to all four people (oneself, one's friend, the 'neutral person', and the 'enemy') and then allowing the feeling to radiate out to those in the surrounding area, then wider and wider, until one's *mettā* is flowing out to all beings, animals as well as human beings, wherever they may be in the world, or the universe.

The *mettā-bhāvanā* is a beautiful practice, though one which many people find extremely difficult. But if one perseveres, one can be confident that anger and hatred will gradually be dispelled through the deliberate, mindful development of love and good will towards all living beings.

Thirdly we come to craving. This is not just desire, but neurotic desire. Take food, for instance. We all have a desire for it – it is natural to have a healthy appetite – but that desire has become neurotic if we find ourselves trying to use food to satisfy some other need. As is all too obvious, craving is a big problem: it creates drug addiction, alcoholism, and a host of other problems. The vast advertising industry is geared to stimulating craving, trying to convince us, with or without our knowledge, that we must have this, that, or the other thing.

There are several practices designed to reduce craving; perhaps the number reflects the scale of the problem. Some of these antidotes, it must be said, are quite drastic. For instance, there's the contemplation of the ten stages of the decomposition of a corpse. This is still a popular practice in some Buddhist countries; it is said to be especially good as an antidote for neurotic sexual desire.[46] I won't describe the practice itself – that would make rather gruesome reading – but there is a milder version, which is simply to meditate alone, at night, in a cremation ground. But if even the occasional visit to the cremation ground is too much (of course our Western versions of these places – graveyards – are not usually so elemental), for a still milder form of the same practice one can simply meditate on the reality of death. One can reflect that death is inevitable; it comes to everybody in due course; no one can escape it. So, since it must come, why not make the best possible use of one's life? And – here we get to the main point of the reflection – why indulge in miserable cravings which don't bring any satisfaction or happiness in the long run?

One can also meditate upon impermanence. Everything is impermanent. From the solar system to one's own breath, from instant to instant everything is changing, flowing, transient. When one remembers this, one can view things as being like clouds passing through the sky. One can't hang on to anything very determinedly when one knows that sooner or later one will have to give it up.

Every day the newspapers are full of reports of fatal accidents, and this gives, as well as the occasion for compassion, an opportunity for reflection. Human life is liable to unexpected termination; one may not live to a ripe old age. As Pascal said, just a grain of dust is sufficient to destroy us if it gets into the wrong place. Life is very precarious. Such reflections can be sobering and fruitful; but they will be counter-productive if what they produce is a kind of neurotic timidity. One has to be sensitive to one's own nature in this regard. When it comes to counteracting craving, one should select whichever exercise is appropriate to one's needs. For many people the sight of a decomposing corpse would just give rise to feelings of disgust and revulsion. One might be physically sick but not affected spiritually at all. One has to be sufficiently mature spiritually to be able to absorb the lesson, to be impressed by the fact of impermanence, not merely shocked or disgusted. If one is sensitive enough, even the falling of a leaf will bring home the truth of impermanence. Perhaps each of us needs to experiment a little. Is a falling leaf enough, or keeping a skull in one's room (this is something Tibetan Buddhists often do), or does one need something stronger? Perhaps one might need to try another traditional antidote to craving, the 'contemplation of the loathsomeness of food'. I won't go into the details of this practice either; they are rather unpleasant, deliberately so.[47] Suffice it to say that it is a powerful antidote to food addiction.

The fourth poison is conceit – sometimes translated as pride, but conceit is a more effective translation. Conceit is said to be particularly associated with the human realm, as opposed to the other five realms of existence depicted on the Tibetan Wheel of Life.[48] The human realm is characterized by self-consciousness: and when one experiences oneself as separate from other people, one may feel not only separate but isolated; not only isolated but superior.

According to the Buddha, thinking in terms of one's status in relation to others *in any way* – whether one concludes that one is superior, inferior, or equal – is a form of conceit.[49] It is perhaps surprising at first that the Buddha should have said this, but a little reflection makes it clear that egalitarianism – insisting that everyone is equal – and self-conscious humility – insisting that others are superior to oneself – are both inverted forms of conceit. Someone may present themselves as a lover of equality when what they really want to do is bring everybody else down to their own level. This is a great weakness, and a great loss. If there is nobody above one, spiritually speaking, one has nobody to look up to or learn from, so it is going to be very difficult to make spiritual progress. Conversely, if one adopts a fixed position of inferiority, one denies one's own potential – and the negation of the possibility of spiritual development is a very serious thing. The traditional antidote to conceit is to meditate on the six elements: earth, water, fire, air, space, and consciousness (listed in increasing order of subtlety).[50]

The fifth poison is ignorance, by which is meant spiritual ignorance, unawareness of reality. In a sense this is the basic poison, the raw ingredient from which all the others are made. The traditional antidote for ignorance is meditation on the *nidānas*, the links, of conditioned co-production. This formulation gives us a way of reflecting on the truth of conditionality: that in dependence upon A, B arises It asks us to see that from our ignorance flows a whole chain of events; one could say that it's a reflection on the workings of the law of karma.

Buddhist tradition enumerates many lists of these links, one of the best known being the chain of twelve links depicted around the rim of the Tibetan Wheel of Life. This chain 'begins' – really a beginningless beginning – with ignorance, and ends with decay and death. As well as the twelve nidānas pertaining to conditioned existence depicted on the Wheel of Life, there are another twelve – the *nidānas* pertaining to, or at least leading to, unconditioned existence, Nirvāṇa. The twelve worldly *nidānas* represent the cyclical type of conditionality, the Wheel of Life, and the reactive mind, while the twelve spiritual *nidānas* represent the spiral type of conditionality, the stages of the path, and the creative mind.[51]

These five poisons and their antidotes give us just one way of considering the negative mental states we need to overcome, and the ways we can do this.

From *The Bodhisattva Ideal* (1999, pp.76-81, 84)

3. KEEP THE INITIATIVE

Everything changes – everything can change – and mental states are no exception.

> *And how, bhikkhus, does a bhikkhu abide contemplating mind-objects as mind-objects? Here a bhikkhu abides contemplating mind-objects as mind objects in terms of the five hindrances. And how does a bhikkhu abide contemplating mind-objects as mind-objects in terms of the five hindrances? Here, there being sensual desire in him, a bhikkhu understands: ' There is sensual desire in me'; or there being no sensual desire in him, he understands: 'There is no sensual desire in me'; and he also understands how there comes to be the arising of unarisen sensual desire, and how there comes to be the abandoning of arisen sensual desire, and how there comes to be the future non-arising of abandoned sensual desire.*
>
> *There being ill will in him ... There being sloth and torpor in him ... There being restlessness and remorse in him ... There being doubt in him, a bhikkhu understands: 'There is doubt in me'; or there being no doubt in him, he understands: 'There is no doubt in me'; and he understands how there comes to be the arising of unarisen doubt, and how there comes to be the abandoning of arisen doubt, and how there comes to be the future non-arising of abandoned doubt.*[52]

The nature of the mind is to go wherever it wants to go, but when we meditate, our task is to persuade it to move in the direction of skilful modes of mental and physical activity. In his commentary on the *Satipaṭṭhāna Sutta*, Buddhaghosa associates meditation with *sammā vāyāma*, perfect effort. This is described as being fourfold: the effort to prevent the arising of unskilful mental states; the effort to eliminate unskilful mental states that have arisen; the effort to cultivate positive mental states; and the effort to maintain positive mental states that have arisen. This is a good description of the aims of meditation: as a method of cultivation it enables one to develop blissful and radiant concentration, while as a process of prevention and elimination it banishes and stills distracting thoughts. The quicker we can respond to what is happening in our mind, feeding skilful impulses and starving unskilful ones, the better. But to do this, we have to become aware of the mental state in the first place; this is the function and practice of mindfulness.

A mental object – sensual desire, for example – does not arise in the abstract; it comes in a specific form – a desire for food, say. It is then up to you to recognize that that is what is going on in your mind: hence the *Satipaṭṭhāna Sutta*'s instruction that one should ascertain 'how there comes to be the arising of the unarisen sensual desire'. The usual generalized explanation for this is 'unwise attention': it is because you have thoughtlessly indulged in this sort of mental state in the past that it is able to arise now. Probably, though, by the time you have become aware of the distraction, you will have no idea where it has come from. It has apparently arisen out of nowhere. For example, you might be sitting trying to meditate when you become aware that for quite a while – you're not sure how long – you have been sitting there thinking about food. You might be able to brush this distraction aside, but it is still important to acknowledge that it hasn't popped up out of nowhere – it has a definite origin. Tracing the origins of your mental states helps you to discover more about their background, so that you can make adjustments to the way you live your life and specifically to the way you prepare for meditation.

The intention of dividing unskilful states into those characterized by sensuous desire, by ill will, by sloth and torpor, by restlessness, and by doubt – this is the list commonly called the five hindrances – is to give us the opportunity to transform them. The sutta says that the monk knows 'how there comes to be the abandoning of arisen sensual desire'. But how do you 'know'? If you are being plagued by a mild form of a hindrance, just becoming aware of it will usually be enough to dispel it.

Sometimes, however, you might need to change your external conditions to influence your mental state for the better. If you are sleepy in meditation, for example, you might need to check your posture, making sure that you are sitting upright so that energy can flow through your body without obstruction. You might also try finding a brightly lit place in which to meditate, or perhaps even sit in the open air. *Dhyāna* is a state of brightness and clarity in every sense, so light, even the light of a candle, will stimulate brighter states of consciousness. You could also freshen your face with cold water, or walk up and down for a while before returning to your meditation seat. If on the other hand you are experiencing distraction, worry, and restlessness, you will need to set up calming conditions, perhaps by making the lighting softer. There are all kinds of things you can do. However, even the most perfect conditions are of little use if you are in a state that seeks distraction. The mind works incredibly fast. The smallest external stimulus – the distant rattle of cups, the sound of conversation outside the meditation room – can trigger trains of association that draw the mind far away from the object of meditation in next to no time.

If awareness of a hindrance is not enough to shift it, you can bring to mind the various antidotes recommended by the Abhidhamma tradition for dealing with the hindrances as they arise. They are all described in Buddhaghosa's *Visuddhimagga*, and include the cultivation of the opposite quality, considering the consequences of allowing that mental state to continue and so on. The antidotes are useful as a sort of first aid measure during the meditation session itself. If your states of awareness are to be radically transformed, however, you will have to do more than that. The relatively small amount of time spent in meditation will not on its own outweigh the consequences of a life lived without a consistent level of mindfulness. Our experience in meditation is influenced – for better or worse – by our whole way of life. We experience the hindrances because this is our usual state in daily life. By the same token, the more we can simplify and unify the mind, whatever situation we are in, the closer our mental state will naturally be to meditative concentration.

In other words, we cannot rely solely on the first aid of the antidotes. A systematic course of treatment is what is required: a consistent practice of mindfulness outside meditation will do far more to overcome the hindrances than anything we do once we have started to meditate. Achieving concentration depends on establishing a way of life that is more harmonious, contented, energetic, confidence-inspiring, and other-regarding, and less restless, grasping, and doubtful – and this requires us to understand the way we are affected by things. In the sutta's words, we need to know how 'there comes to be the arising of unarisen sensual desire' – or the arising of the unarisen irritation, or whatever it is. We have to make a habit of watching out for the hindrances in daily life and setting up conditions in which they are unlikely to occur, or will occur only in a weakened form.

Once you get to know your habits of mind, you can avoid situations that tend to stimulate recurrent patterns of behaviour. All that is required is a little foresight. If you are going out for a run, you won't eat a large meal beforehand because you know that if you do, you will end up with a stomach ache. The hindrances are similarly linked to their causes. If you stay up late, for example, it is not realistic to look forward to a concentrated and alert meditation first thing in the morning. At the very least, you are likely to be setting yourself up for an extended battle with sloth and torpor – a battle that could have been avoided by planning ahead, organizing your time around the things that matter to you most in the long term.

When you do give way to the temptation of the moment, usually you know full well that you will regret later what you are doing now – sometimes you regret it even while you are doing it. (Perhaps this is an especially English trait, if we are to believe the Duc de Sully, who remarked that 'the English take their pleasures sadly'.) It is understandable that one might occasionally decide to sacrifice one's morning meditation for the sake of something one thinks is worth such a sacrifice. Our real failing when we indulge ourselves in this way is our unwillingness to take full responsibility for our actions, our failure to make a clear choice between long-term goals and short-term distractions, and be clear which we are choosing at a particular time.

Hindrances tend to arise when we react mechanically to situations – when we grab things without thinking, when we react to things, fidget, daydream, or dither without really being aware of what we are doing. If the television is in the room, we switch it on, and if it is on, we change channels rather than switch it off. Learning some self-discipline in matters like this will support your meditation practice. If you just let yourself follow semi-conscious impulses, this will undermine your intention to become more conscious, whereas if you can learn to pause and consider quietly whether an action is skilful or not, you will inhibit the tendency to give in automatically to your impulses and this will help you to stay focused when you are meditating.

Traditionally, virtuous conduct (*sīla*) is said to cast out craving and distraction, and it does this by inculcating a habit of self-control. This is the point of many of the practices of the orthodox bhikkhu, including that of not taking food after noon. If you do not allow craving for food uncontrolled expression, that hindrance is gradually weakened (it can be eliminated altogether only with the arising of Insight). If we do not observe such rules ourselves, we have to exercise extra vigilance instead; with a wider range of possible courses of action before us, we still have to be prepared to take responsibility for our mental states, acknowledging that certain avenues of thought and action lead to certain kinds of consequences.

The sutta's advice to 'set up mindfulness in front of you' was taken quite literally in the Buddha's day, and in some Buddhist countries the monks still follow the practice of walking looking straight ahead or with their eyes downcast as they go about their daily almsround. The *Satipaṭṭhāna Sutta* might well be the inspiration for this practice, whose aim is simply to prevent the mind from being led astray into unskilful thoughts. In the modern city there is obviously even more need for such a practice. Not that there is any kind of virtue in looking at the floor, and this practice would be too drastic for most of us. Perhaps more effective, and in a way more radical, is the cultivation of the mental attitude of *appamāda* or 'non-heedlessness' – that is, an overall vigilance that takes into account a broad range of conditions, both within and outside us, enabling us to be active and open to what is going on around us while still maintaining mindfulness.

It is a tremendous challenge to sustain this combination of openness and vigilance. In the media-free India of the Buddha's day, you would not have known about events in the neighbouring kingdoms until perhaps years after they had happened – much less about floods in China or earthquakes in Peru. On the whole life was very peaceful, because there were so few things to occupy the mind. We on the other hand have more information – and input generally – available to us than we can possibly keep up with, and we therefore need to develop some kind of filter. We cannot cut ourselves off from the society in which we live, but we can try to give such attention as we devote to issues of the day mainly to matters within our own sphere of influence. We should not surrender our initiative to the torrent of information coming at us, which is presented as hugely important today only to be replaced by something else tomorrow. As Thoreau says, 'To a philosopher all news, as it is called, is gossip, and they who edit and read it are old women over their tea.'[53] When we switch on the television or pick up a newspaper or log on to the Internet, we have to consider not only the value and interest of what we find there but also the cumulative effect of developing a habit. If we have regular recourse to these resources when we are bored, we get used to adopting an unduly passive attitude towards our sensory input. We drift from one thing to another, exercising less and less critical judgement and becoming less and less capable of dealing creatively with those times when we are at a loose end.

When it comes to the hindrances, it is essential to keep the initiative. This is largely a question of taking responsibility for the situations we find ourselves in. Unfortunately, we tend to shrug off responsibility by disguising as a practical necessity what is really our personal choice. We present our decisions as being dictated by circumstances or by other people, as though the whole matter were out of our hands. It is a useful way of diverting blame; it allows you to present yourself as the victim when you feel resentful about something, and to do what you really want to do while pretending you are only doing it because you have to. Even if we cannot help deceiving others in this way, we should not deceive ourselves. In reality there are very few occasions when we can truthfully say, 'I had no choice.' Every moment of awareness, indeed, presents us with an opportunity to choose what to do, or at least how to do it. It isn't 'the world' or 'life' that draws us away from the path, but our own motivation. Sooner or later we have to acknowledge that we are influenced not by external distractions in themselves but by our own tendency to become enmeshed in them. The fact that we succumb does not let us off; we are still making an active choice to succumb. If you are dissatisfied with your circumstances, you need to remind yourself that you are really dissatisfied with your own decision not to change them. You may then decide that you don't want to do anything to change things, but at least you will be able to stop feeling dissatisfied about the state of affairs. By refusing to be the victims of circumstances we begin to steer circumstances towards our goals.

The ability to be decisive and single-minded is rare enough but it is especially so with regard to any spiritual objective. The conditions of modern living seem almost to conspire against it, and most of us are only too willing to join the conspiracy. However, we can decide to change our attitude at any moment. We will no doubt forget our decisions as often as we make them, but there is no need to despair – changing habits takes time. Being ready to assume full responsibility for the decisions one makes, consciously or not, is perhaps the defining characteristic of the true individual: one's continuity of intention might have to take into account some inner conflict, but should not be undermined by it.

You do need to be vigilant, but there is no need to be too defensive. You don't have to hole yourself up like a rabbit in a burrow cowering from a fox. The best method of defence is attack: why not use the challenge and stimulation of ordinary life to cultivate even more positive states of mind than those you enjoyed on retreat? The whole point of spiritual practice is to be able to operate in difficult and challenging circumstances. Just be aware that the gains of meditation can easily be dissipated, and aware, above all, of the nature of your own reactive mind. If you live among spiritual friends you have a very good base upon which to take your stand.

This somewhat military-sounding approach is as traditional as anything in Buddhism. Our battle with the hindrances is personified in the tradition in the figure of Māra, the wily adversary who so often appears in the stories of the Pāli canon to tempt and taunt Buddhist practitioners as they strive for mindfulness and positivity. Māra is not to be underestimated: he is cunning and resourceful. That is the nature of the reactive mind – to get its own way by underhand means. But there is no need to assume that Māra will inevitably get the better of you. If you know what you are doing and keep one step ahead of what he is up to, if you are prepared to give him a good hammering, he is not going to have it all his own way. No doubt we should be wary of Māra, but we can remind ourselves that he is just as wary of us. We may even be able to give him a bit of a fright. He is called 'the lord of life and death' and is thus said to have a vested interest in keeping us in the world of distraction and delusion, since if we escape it, he loses his power. But that power is illusory. In the many encounters between Māra and the Buddha's followers recounted in the suttas, the punchline is always the same: 'Māra retreated, sad and discomfited.'

Whatever the distraction, it doesn't appear in the mind at random; it arises in dependence on definite causes and conditions. And – this is the important thing – you don't have to put up with it. The list of hindrances helps us to identify the many kinds of thoughts and feelings that interfere with the process of unifying and concentrating the mind, and by becoming familiar with the list we can become aware of the arising of our unconscious habits of mind before they have really taken hold. However subject one might be to the five hindrances, there is always this measure of hope. The essence of the matter is not complicated or intellectual. It is simply the fact that phenomena arise in dependence on causes and conditions – in other words, we are back to the plain fact of impermanence. Everything changes – everything can change – and mental states are no exception. Your state of mind is within your control, and to be convinced of that is more than half the battle.

From *Living with Awareness* (2003, pp.92, 94-102)

4. SAILING INTO THE DHYĀNAS

Most meditation exercises don't lead directly to higher states of consciousness; they simply help us remove the obstacles.

We all have to struggle and sweat, even curse under our breath sometimes, as we try to concentrate in meditation. We feel disappointed; we feel that it isn't worth the effort, that we are making fools of ourselves, that we might just as well be at the cinema or watching television. But although we have to strive and struggle, the effort isn't to get into the *dhyāna* state. All that effort has to go into removing the hindrances to meditation. If we could only do that, we would go sailing at least into the first *dhyāna*.

So most meditation exercises don't lead directly to higher states of consciousness; they simply help us remove the obstacles. Practising the mindfulness of breathing removes the obstacle of distraction, practising the *mettā-bhāvanā* helps remove the obstacle of ill will, and so on. If we remove the obstacles with the help of these methods, the higher states – at least the first of them – will naturally manifest themselves.

From *The Bodhisattva Ideal* (1999, pp.162-3)

5. KNOW THE ENEMY

It's very important that when you sit, you sit down with a real determination that you're going to do something with this half hour, or this hour. Something is really going to happen; this is a piece of work that you've got to get on with.

Sangharakshita: The first of the five hindrances is *kāmacchanda*. *Chanda* means 'urge' – it's a strong word – and *kāmacchanda* means something like 'urge in the direction of sense experience'. So one can see the relation of this particular hindrance to meditation quite clearly. If you are trying to get into a *dhyāna* state, which is on a higher level, a higher plane, than sense experience, if your mind is constantly turning in the direction of sense experience, you won't be able to get into a *dhyānic* state. Have you noticed that? If, for instance, you're hungry, you may keep on turning over and over in your mind the thought of food, mentally savouring it. So long as you are bringing to mind sense experiences that you had in the past and savouring them over again, or relishing them in the mind by anticipating them, you won't be able to get into *dhyāna*. To get into the *dhyāna* state, you have to turn away from all preoccupation with sense experience, whether through the eye, the ear, the nose, the tongue, or even the lower mind. In other words, there must be no preoccupation with sense objects. You must be able to forget about them completely. In fact, if you get deeply into meditation, or at least concentrated, absorbed, there's no consciousness of sense objects except in a very vague and distant way. You might hear a sound in the distance, but the mind doesn't turn towards it. It's that turning of the mind towards the sense object that gets in the way.

Q: If you try to maintain a *dhyānic* state even when you come out of meditation, how does that affect your sense perception?

S: It doesn't. You will see objects, but your mind will not be turning towards them, getting interested in them, latching onto them in the usual way. They will just be there. Notice how when you are thinking about something deeply, you may be sitting in the garden and seeing the trees and the flowers, but the mind is not turning towards them, the mind is not particularly interested. They're just there. You are preoccupied with something else, something quite different. In fact, when you have had a good meditation and you come out and walk about, you'll find that your mind doesn't turn towards anything for a while. It's quite content within itself. External things don't attract it even though you can see them, hear them, smell them, and even taste them when you start eating.

Q: You still experience them.

S: You still experience them.

Q: I've often wondered about that. I've got this feeling that as soon as you come out of meditation you ought to be in contact with the objects of sense perception.

S: Well, there's no question of 'ought to be' in contact. You *are* in contact by virtue of the fact that you perceive. You see the forms, you hear the sounds, but there's no inclination on the part of your mind towards them, it's not interested in them, it doesn't latch onto them. That only happens gradually as you get out of meditation, as it were.

But so long as you are actively preoccupied with sense objects you can't get into the *dhyāna* state, so for this reason *kāmacchanda* is said to be a hindrance to meditation. You have at least for the time being to turn aside from your preoccupation with those things. It's not a question of saying that that sort of preoccupation is bad or wicked. It just pertains to a particular plane. If you want to get onto another plane – the next highest plane as represented by a *dhyāna* state – then you have to cease to preoccupy yourself with the objects which belong to the lower plane.

Q: How does this relate to the fourth stage of the mindfulness of breathing? When you're concentrating on that point on the tip of your nose or wherever, you're experiencing that sensation. If you're experiencing that sensation, can you not enter a *dhyānic* state?

S: You're not fully in a *dhyānic* state so long as you experience that sensation.

Q: That's the jumping point.

S: Yes, that's the jumping point. You've brought all your sense experience to one fine point. So the thing to do then is forget about that point but retain the concentration on the point, if you see what I mean. After a while, you don't perceive the breath at all. The point vanishes. Of course you go on breathing, but you don't notice it. The breath has, as it were, disappeared, but you remain suspended in that state of concentration, your concentration doesn't disappear with it. You're left concentrated.

All right, what's the next of the hindrances after *kāmacchanda*?

Q: Anger and hatred.

S: The Pāli word here is *vyāpāda*, which means extreme anger and hatred and antagonism. It's quite obvious that as long as your mind is occupied by thoughts of anger and hatred you can't get into a *dhyāna* state. Maybe there's nothing so inimical to *dhyāna* as a feeling of anger and resentment and hatred. If just before you sit to meditate someone has annoyed or irritated you, and your mind continues to be preoccupied with that, you can't possibly get into a *dhyāna* state. You just can't get it off your mind. Your mind keeps running over it, 'He did this to me, he said this to me. He behaved in such and such a way or he was in such and such a way.' He doesn't even need to do or say anything, if he's someone you intensely dislike. But if you allow your mind to run in this way you won't get into a *dhyāna* state. This is pretty obvious, isn't it? So this is when the *mettā-bhāvanā* comes in useful. Sometimes you might have to do the *mettā-bhāvanā* just to counteract these sort of feelings so that you can get into the *dhyāna* states. Sometimes the mindfulness of breathing doesn't help you very much here because you keep being dragged away from your concentration by your strong feelings of anger and hatred, resentment and irritation.

Then after *vyāpāda* there's *thīna-middha*. The Buddha is described as *thinaṃ yassa panūditaṃ*, which Hare renders as 'void of all indolence'. *Thīna-middha* is usually translated as sloth and torpor. *Thīna* is said to be more mental, *middha* more physical. *Middha* or torpor is the state you get into after you've had a very heavy meal, maybe with a bit of alcohol, or on a very hot day, and the mental equivalent of that is sloth. Sloth and torpor covers drowsiness, sleepiness, indolence, lack of energy, lack of effort. The sort of state that is implied here is not very bright, not very wakeful, a bit dull, heavy, stagnant, torpid, like a boa constrictor after an enormous meal. You know quite well that when you get into that sort of state you can't meditate. So what causes such a state? It may be due to quite simple reasons. You may have had a heavy meal just before you were going to meditate, so naturally you feel a bit sluggish. Some people can break through that, others can't. But if you haven't eaten heavily, and it isn't a hot day, and you're not tired from working hard, what brings about sloth and torpor? Why is one indolent? Why doesn't one make an effort? Why isn't one buoyant and lively?

Q: The energy gets blocked.

S: In the case of sloth and torpor, it's not so much that the energy gets blocked, it's more that the energy doesn't move.

Q: There's no desire or will for the energy to move. It's more like laziness.

S: But what is laziness? It's easy to say that someone is lazy, but what is laziness?

Q: Someone who is lazy has got the energy available but won't apply it.

S: But why won't he?

Q: Lack of inspiration.

S: Lack of inspiration, lack of interest. It's more like that.

Q: Half-heartedness.

S: Half-heartedness. You feel this in connection with meditation when maybe it hasn't been going all that well and you begin to think that perhaps there's not much point in it all. You don't feel much zest, much interest. Then you get all sluggish and torpid and lazy.

One must be careful when one speaks of laziness to be sure that it really is laziness that one is talking about. For instance, you may be a very busy, active person, doing all sorts of things. Somebody else may seem not be doing anything much, and you may think that he is very lazy, but that is not necessarily so. He may be choosing not to do anything, certainly not the things that you are doing. He may just be thinking quietly; he's not necessarily being lazy. Genuine laziness seems to be a by-product of lack of interest, lack of enthusiasm, lack of inspiration, lack of zest. This is one of the great difficulties of the whole spiritual life, and it is why pleasure is important in the spiritual life, to keep you alive, interested in things, happy. Otherwise it becomes very difficult.

Q: There's also lack of confidence. Some people don't feel they can do something, so they do nothing.

S: Yes. In a way that's a lack of faith in the sense of *śraddhā*. Where there is faith there will be energy. So that's *thīna-middha*. The opposite is *uddhacca-kukkucca*, sometimes translated as hurry and flurry or worry and flurry. It's mental restlessness or instability and physical restlessness, excitability, flightiness. If you are very restless, very excited, then you can't meditate, so this is also a *nīvaraṇa*, a hindrance, an obstacle to meditation. You have to get this out of the way.

And then fifthly and lastly there's *vicikicchā*. This is usually translated as doubt, but it's a bit more than doubt: it's more like indecision, lack of commitment, lack of faith – it's when you don't have full confidence in what you are doing. How can you do something wholeheartedly if you don't have full confidence in what you are doing, or in yourself as doing it? If you start thinking, 'I don't know why I'm doing this. I don't know why I'm sitting here trying to meditate', you probably won't have a good meditation.

To put it all in positive terms, when you sit to meditate, first of all your mind must be firmly turned away from all the sense objects. You must be in a state of positive good will towards everybody, you must feel light and buoyant and fresh and energetic. At the same time you should be calm and peaceful and very confident with regard to what you are about to do, and about your spiritual life in general. If you can fulfil these conditions, you will find it *relatively* easy to get into a *dhyānic* state; in fact you will gradually *be* in a *dhyānic* state.

Q: That's the irony, isn't it? You've got to be like that to get like that, but we do it to get like that anyway.

S: Little by little, yes?

Q: I never thought of applying confidence in all of that to my practice.

S: It's confidence in whole-heartedness. It's very important that when you sit, you sit down with a real determination that you're going to do something with this half hour, or this hour. Something is really going to happen; this is a piece of work that you've got to get on with. Tackle it quite vigorously.

Q: And with no 'shoulds', presumably.

S: Yes, quite. You feel interested and enthusiastic. This is why Zen speaks in terms of 'beginner's mind'. The first time they try meditation or a particular method of meditation, most people are very interested, even if it's simply because it's a new thing, something they've not done before. The chances are that they will get on with it relatively well. One should bring that same interest to every session, because in fact every session is new, no two sessions are ever the same. So don't think that this is the same old meditation all over again: 'Here we are sitting in the same old place, same old cushions, same old people, same old practice.' Remind yourself that it's completely different, completely new.

From a seminar on the Great Chapter, *Sutta-Nipāta* (1976, pp.277-86)

6. DROWSINESS AND DISTRACTION

Ask yourself whether you really want to do what you are at present doing or trying to do. Ask yourself what is it that you do really want to do.

Neither drowsy nor distracted, I march ahead;
Following the Path of Light, I march straight on.
Though my practice may be poor, I have no regret.[54]

Sangharakshita: Why do you think drowsiness and distraction are especially mentioned?

Q: They are the two extremes of what can happen to energy; it can either be dull or scattered.

S: Yes. They are usually regarded as the two great hindrances to meditation. You can either become dull and drowsy and sluggish and torpid, or restless, distracted and so on. Rechungpa seems to incline to the second of these two hindrances.

When I climb the mountain of Practice, I see
The snares of drowsiness and distraction,
The perilous passage of constraint,
And the danger of misleading, wandering thoughts.
Pray, my Father Guru, Buddha's Nirmānakaya,
Pray escort and protect me
Until I reach Non-being's Plain.

Q: Could you say something about the 'snares of drowsiness and distraction'? I often find myself drowsy in meditation for no obvious reason.

S: This raises the question of when, or how, one becomes drowsy. Sometimes one becomes drowsy when one is just depleted of energy. That's the simplest explanation. Sometimes, however, one becomes drowsy because of unconscious conflict, a conflict between a wish to do something and a wish not to do it. Conflict can be a great drainer of energy.

Q: Could that occur where part of you wishes to do something, but due to social or some other kind of conditioning you are repressing it?

S: That could be, because that is still a kind of conflict. Energy is going into the desire to do that thing but perhaps equal energy is going into holding that desire back. If you are getting your normal food and sleep, and you are not over-working, but you still feel devoid of energy, drowsy, tired, and if there is no deeply-rooted disease, as occasionally is the case, you may well conclude that there is some psychological conflict going on.

Q: I frequently experience it as a sort of blockage. Then perhaps something diverting or genuinely engaging happens, and immediately releases what has previously been trapped. And yet this verse seems to imply that through the practice there is a way of unlocking that, and avoiding those snares.

S: Well, with regard to meditation it is said that if you are particularly prone to drowsiness, you should meditate in a brightly lit room, and if you are visualizing a Buddha figure, you should visualize one which is brightly coloured. You can even surround yourself with bright colours, meditate in the fresh air, or bathe your face in cold water before you start meditating. There are all kinds of things that one can do.

On the other hand if you are prone to distraction, meditate in a dim light, in a slightly darkened room, and don't have too many bright colours around. It isn't actually suggested that you should wash your face in warm water, but perhaps one could try that, and try to create a soft, warm atmosphere.

Q: That would seem to imply that the two states are rather separate, but I quite often experience them as linked. You can be quite drowsy and break out of it, but you only break through into distraction. You oscillate from one to the other.

S: That makes things rather difficult, doesn't it? I think what you have to do is to find something in which you are really interested and which engages your whole attention and all your energies. I think if you get very drowsy or very distracted, or both drowsy and distracted, in connection with meditation or any kind of spiritual practice, or the spiritual life itself, you need to delve pretty deeply into yourself and find out what is happening to your energy and whether there are any deep-seated conflicts. Ask yourself whether you really want to do what you are at present doing or trying to do. Ask yourself what is it that you do really want to do. Sometimes it is very important at least to establish contact with that and acknowledge it, even if you think that the thing that you want to do isn't very skilful. At least establish contact with it and feel it and acknowledge it, and then try and lead it in the right direction.

You might discover, for instance, that you don't really want to plaster walls (or whatever task you're 'meant' to be doing); you want to go and play, strange to say! Acknowledging whatever desires you have doesn't mean that you are necessarily going to indulge those desires, but at least you must acknowledge them rather than blocking them off and staying unconscious of them.

If you feel drowsy, it's sometimes a good idea just to go to sleep and then see how you feel when you wake up. Sometimes things may sort themselves out in your sleep. Things may come to the surface, you may become more aware of what is actually going on. You might catch your mind just as you wake up and see what it is you really want to do. Very often when you wake up there is a moment, at least, when you are not thinking. Have you experienced that? Before you start thinking at all, before discursive mental activity starts, you can be quite clearly conscious, quite aware, but no thoughts arise. The first discursive activity that arises is usually a sense of where you are, and the next is usually the thought of what you have got to do that day. At that point, watch your mind and try to see your spontaneous reaction. If you wake up and you are in a clear bright state of consciousness, and then you suddenly think, 'Oh, today I have to go to the dentist,' then just see what your reaction is. Or if you think, 'Today I have to knock that wall down,' what's your reaction? That will perhaps tell you quite a lot about what you really want to do or what you don't really want to do – assuming, of course, that you can experience this clear bright state of consciousness, at least momentarily, when you wake up, and that you can follow the discursive mental activity as it arises. But if you observe yourself carefully, you will notice that this is what happens. Even though the instant of non-discursive awareness may be just momentary, it is there. With practice you can even prolong it.

So when the thought of what you have to do that day occurs to you, try to see what your spontaneous reaction is. If it fills you with joy, that is very good. If it makes you feel depressed and wretched, well, that's not so good. Usually when we have that experience, we just cover it up and immediately think 'Ah well, I've got to get on with it. Of course, I like doing it really, this is just a momentary weakness.' But it may not really be so. It may be your quite deep-seated attitude to that particular task, and it may be that that attitude is underlying your conscious attitude all the time.

From a seminar on 'Rechungpa's Journey to Weu',
Songs of Milarepa (1980, pp.92-3)

7. THE SENSATION OF WAKING UP

Unless you are utterly exhausted, which is another matter, if you remain aware and mindful, and continue to make an effort, you can break through that barrier of tiredness and sleepiness.

Q: Quite often, especially shortly after having begun a practice, I am clearly beginning to become quite concentrated and it looks as if I'm heading for *dhyāna*; then I fall asleep!

Sangharakshita: Oh!

Q: It's quite an odd sensation. On the one hand I've got the experience of invigoration, and just as it's apparently about to burst into bloom, suddenly I find I'm overcome by drowsiness.

S: I vaguely remember very many years ago having experienced something like that, but not to that extent, so I find it rather difficult to say anything from my own experience, but my guess is that you're tired. You're tired, and it's taken you quite an effort to get into that concentrated state. You've got enough energy to get there but not enough to stay there, and therefore you fall asleep. I think that unless you are utterly exhausted, which is another matter, if you remain aware and mindful, and continue to make an effort, you can break through that barrier of tiredness and sleepiness.

Q: It just seems rather odd that it should be preceded by what appears to be a process of deepening concentration.

S: Well, if you are in the habit of concentrating and you know the ropes, as it were, you won't find it very difficult to come to that point of concentration, but then you've used up all your energy in getting there. There's no further energy to sustain you. So you are tired and you fall asleep. Of course, another more subtle possibility is that you are not willing to face the experience of deepening concentration, and therefore you fall asleep as an escape from that. But having heard a lot of people talk about their meditation experience, I would say that it's very often due to tiredness, that you don't have enough energy to sustain you at the point you've reached. Very often people are very tired – more tired than they should be, especially perhaps when they are supposed to be meditating.

Q: That sort of subtle suggestion seems to correlate with suddenly getting very concentrated when the bell goes to end the meditation. Suddenly the pressure's off, you don't have to do it any more, and away you go. It's when you've got to do it that there's lots of resistance to prevent you from doing it.

S: Where does this 'got to' come from?

Q: Ah, well, that's a good question.

S: Ah! It does seem important that you make sure that you are well rested, and aren't tired when you meditate.

Q: I think often tiredness is brought about by conflict.

S: That's also true.

Q: It seems to be quite a common experience that morning meditation is a pretty groggy sort of affair, not very clear or concentrated.

S: I wonder why that should be? Well, I have my own little theories. Quite a lot of people don't take sufficient care to get to bed by a reasonable time. They hang about in the kitchen chatting and having extra cups of tea or coffee and they don't get to bed until quite late, and therefore they are not properly rested by the time the bell goes for the morning meditation. I also think it's a mistake only to start scrambling into your trousers when you hear the bell go for meditation! I know people do this, and it can't be conducive to good meditation. You should get up twenty to thirty minutes beforehand, have a wash, preferably in cold water, and just stroll around and adjust to the new day. I don't know whether it's a good idea to rush for a cup of tea as soon as you wake up. Do you really need tea first thing in the morning? If so, why? Are you thirsty or what do you want?

Q: Stimulation.

S: Well, what stimulation do you need after a good night's sleep? You've got interesting things to do as soon as you get up.

Q: Could it be just habit?

S: It could be, I suppose, but then one must scrutinize all one's old habits and see whether they are still relevant. It's a bit of comfort, I think; you feel the need of a pleasant sensation, and I think that is very suspect, or rather tell-tale. I mean, the sensation of waking up should be pleasant enough!

From Q&A on the Noble Eightfold Path (Tuscany 1983, p.113-6)

8. AN UNWILLINGNESS TO MAKE UP ONE'S MIND

If you keep your options open indefinitely, you avoid having to do anything.

We need a strong sense of initiative, responsibility, and decisiveness if we are to counteract the hindrances. But the taking of this kind of initiative might itself be obstructed by one of the hindrances: doubt (Pāli: *vicikicchā*). This is not intellectual doubt, but an unwillingness to make up one's mind and clarify one's thinking. It is a deliberate muddying of the water to avoid facing up to the truth of a situation, a culpable refusal to take responsibility for one's view of things and for the things one does based upon that view. To give an example, when I lived in India, I would from time to time challenge some brahmin on the subject of 'untouchability', almost invariably to be fobbed off with mystical obfuscation. 'Truth is one, God is one,' he might say. 'Who, then, is touching whom? There is no toucher, no touched, only God.' As this smoke-screen settled over the whole issue, any discussion of the moral dimension of the caste system would successfully be avoided. It is one thing to experience doubt in the struggle towards the resolution of a genuine intellectual difficulty, but it is quite another to be doubtful in order to avoid any decision that might involve a definite course of action. In the case of the brahmin, whether he was conscious of it or not, his refusal to acknowledge the fact of untouchability meant that he could continue to benefit from an unjust system he would rather not question.

To take a less controversial example of doubt and indecision as moral muddle, someone might say, 'What do you mean, that was a selfish thing to do? Everyone is ultimately selfish.' Or again, you can always tell when someone doesn't want to do something but won't admit it. They turn the issue into a mass of imponderables: yes, a walk this afternoon sounds like a nice idea – but it is going to depend on the weather, and there might not be time, and do you think you should go for a walk when you haven't been very well?

If you keep your options open indefinitely, you avoid having to do anything. Doubt is a kind of camouflage: if you don't take up a clear position, no one can attack you – you are beyond criticism, or rather you haven't yet reached a point where you can be criticized. You might not be certain, but at least you can never be wrong, and this is a comfortable position – or non-position – to be in. Once you eliminate doubt, you have to act, you have to stand up for something – or if you don't act upon your conviction, you are obliged to admit to your own shortcomings. You have to say, 'Well, I'm just lazy,' or 'I'm afraid'; you know where you stand, you aren't pretending.

Doubt is essentially resistance to the positive, forward-looking spirit of the path. As soon as you are convinced that the Buddha was Enlightened, you have to take what he said seriously enough actually to do something about it. If, on the other hand, you give yourself the luxury of doubting whether the Buddha was really Enlightened at all, or at least postponing committing yourself to a view until you are 'really sure', you don't need to take his teaching so seriously and, best of all, you don't need to do anything about it. The ideal way to free yourself from doubt is thus to clarify your thinking, not necessarily in a bookish or abstract way, but simply by reflecting on what you know of the spiritual path.

From *Living with Awareness* (2003, pp.99-100)

9. HAVE FAITH THAT YOU REALLY CAN

If you eat food, you can just go through the process of eating and the stomach will look after the rest. But it's not like that with meditation.

Q: Do you think the importance of meditation as a stage of the spiritual path is undervalued in our movement?

Sangharakshita: I don't think it's undervalued in theory. Whether it's undervalued in practice is more difficult to say. I rather suspect though that the quality of practice is not what it might be. People may sit quite regularly. It's perhaps significant that a lot of people talk about 'sitting'. Perhaps they don't dare to speak about meditation! So yes, a lot of people do 'sit' regularly and faithfully, but the question is, what happens when you sit? I suspect that even in the case of those who sit, the quality of meditation isn't what it might be.

I think there are mainly two reasons for that: insufficient preparation and insufficient determination. By insufficient preparation I mean, perhaps you don't get up early enough so you have to rush to the shrine-room, or perhaps you haven't made sure that your stomach is neither too full nor too empty, or perhaps you haven't given yourself time after work just to settle down a bit. Maybe you haven't tidied the shrine or lit the candles slowly to get yourself into a devotional mood, or maybe you've just not had the right sort of day. Perhaps it's your fault, perhaps not. So that I think is the first reason why the quality of meditation is not what it might be: insufficient preparation.

And the second, I would say, is insufficient determination. That is to say, when you've completed all the preliminaries and you've got into the shrine room, you've sat down and you've adjusted your posture, you don't wholeheartedly put aside everything else, quite definitely – what you're going to do afterwards, what you were doing before – and really put all your energy in a very conscious way into what you're doing in complete determination that you're definitely going to concentrate, that you're definitely going to do your practice, and you're going to go all out to do it successfully for the whole of that period. I think people often don't have that determination.

In other words, one begins to treat it as a bit of a routine and actually to think more in terms of 'sitting' for an hour. Perhaps you don't believe you can get very far. I think you've got to have faith that you really can. I know that many people have had the experience that when they thought they were not going to have a particularly good meditation, actually they did. Maybe they thought they were much too tired, or much too busy, and that nothing much would happen that session, but actually it sometimes just happens that they have a particularly good meditation. You can never be sure.

So first of all there has to be adequate preparation and then that very definite determination. The fact that one has to mention these things means, I think, that meditation has become a bit of a routine. It is just something that you go through. If you eat food, you can just go through the process of eating and the stomach will look after the rest. But it's not like that with meditation, it's not that you just sit and your mind will automatically do the rest. It won't. You've got to make a definite, conscious, deliberate effort. You've got to put all your energy into it. You've got to go all out to meditate during that hour, otherwise you won't have a particularly successful meditation. This is not to say that you're to strain or to be wilful, but quite slowly, systematically, deliberately, you put all your energy and all your interest into that particular session, that particular practice.

From Q&A on a discussion on Channel 4 (1984, pp.8-9)

10. FLOATING THOUGHTS

Hindrances can be not only crude but very subtle too, and no doubt, as you get deeper into meditation, various mental impressions are uncovered.

Q: Is it possible for discursive thoughts to arise in meditation that have nothing to do with any of the hindrances?

Sangharakshita: Well, you could be reflecting on the Dharma itself. You could be reflecting on impermanence or death. That would be discursive mental activity from the standpoint of meditation, from the standpoint of *samatha*, but that is the way in which *vipassanā* arises or one of the ways in which *vipassanā* arises.

Q: I'm more thinking of a thought popping into one's mind, 'Oh, I must remember to do that' – a thought that is definitely irrelevant to the meditation but nothing to do with the hindrances.

S: Even though the discursive thought that floats in at that moment does not seem to be very obviously or crudely connected with one or other of the five hindrances, I would say that it's almost always subtly connected. For instance, you might think of an appointment that you have next week. Well, there is no craving, there is no hatred. Maybe there is no sloth and torpor, restlessness or anything like that. But that thought quietly floats in. Why? It suggests a slight anxiety that you might forget that appointment or you might not make it or it might not go quite right. There'd be that very slight subtle anxiety. So that would be a subtle form of a hindrance. Do you see what I mean?

Hindrances can be not only crude but very subtle too, and no doubt, as you get deeper into meditation, various mental impressions are uncovered. Everybody experiences this. You have got various things on your mind or in your mind, things you've got to do, things you've got to remember, things you've got to think about. As you get more deeply concentrated, these things are uncovered. Perhaps, to risk a generalization, one could say that they are always associated with some sort of subtle hindrance. For instance, you might suddenly think, 'I must remember that next week I've got to take my son to see the doctor.' Why would you have uncovered that particular thought? There is that subtle attachment to your son, that subtle worry about him, and this will be a hindrance to meditation in very subtle form. One couldn't, I think, claim that that discursive thought was hindrance-free, that it was a pure thought without effective content. The only possibility might be from thoughts arising in connection with disturbances coming from outside. If the wind started blowing and you had the thought 'It's going to be a windy night', you might argue that that thought was hindrance-free, but on the other hand, why should you worry whether or not it's going to be a windy night? Even that thought is tinged, even though very slightly. So I think that the most that could be said would be that discursive thoughts may arise which are not associated with any of the five hindrances in their cruder forms. I think the question of whether or not they are associated with quite subtle forms of hindrances – which are in some ways the more dangerous in the long run – has to be left open.

Q: So in the first *dhyāna*, all discursive thoughts would be connected with the Dharma in some way or other?

S: Yes – in the case of those discursive thoughts which after a spell of *samatha* you actively encourage so as to provide a basis for the development of Insight. Of course, the human mind and our spiritual experience being as they are, that is not to say that even those Dharma-connected discursive thoughts are completely hindrance-free. All that is said in the tradition is that you do not get fully into even the first *dhyāna* unless the five hindrances have subsided. Perhaps it should be made clear that the five hindrances are of various degrees of subtlety and grossness, and very subtle hindrances can persist even after that and can cling around your discursive thoughts with regard to the Dharma itself. You may be thinking about impermanence, you may be thinking about developing Insight quite genuinely, quite sincerely, but at the same time there may be that subtle thought that if I understand impermanence, if I develop Insight into impermanence, that will be a definite achievement on my part. Do you see what I mean? That hindrance may still be there in a very subtle form. So it isn't at all a cut-and-dried business. But certainly there is no experience of *dhyāna* unless the five hindrances in their cruder forms are eliminated from the conscious mind.

Q: So are you saying that in the first *dhyāna* there could be hindrances in subtle forms?

S: No, I'm not saying that. I'm saying in effect that it is very rarely that we experience *dhyāna* without any admixture of any hindrance, even in a subtle form.

Looking at the hindrances more comprehensively, if they are, as it were, coterminous and synonymous with ignorance and craving, they are not fully eliminated until you develop Insight. When one says that the hindrances are in abeyance in the *samatha* state, what does one mean by 'in abeyance'? In a sense they are still present otherwise they would not be able, so to speak, to come back. They are latent, but their latency is a degree of actual existence. Beware of literal-mindedness. The literal mind is not a spiritual mind; literal-mindedness is itself a hindrance.

From Q&A on a pre-ordination retreat, Padmaloka (1982, 30-2)

11. SUBTLE FETTERS

One might even say that ignorance is the only fetter and that all the others are different aspects of it.

As one gets deeper into meditation the variety of subtle mental impressions, hitherto overlooked, begin to stand out more clearly, and very subtle forms of the fetters become apparent: the fetter of restlessness, for example. It may be experienced in a subtle form as a mental sensation which troubles you even when your meditation is apparently going very well. You might be quite deeply absorbed and then, for no apparent reason, the idea might suddenly arise that you should end the meditation and get back to mundane consciousness, even if you have no need to do so. Or perhaps a breeze begins to blow outside and although your meditation is becoming more concentrated, the thought 'It's going to be a windy night' arises in your mind. There might be no craving present, no hatred, no sloth or torpor, but still a thought will just quietly float into the mind as a slight anxiety, a subtle failure of confidence, a wisp of self-concern. Restlessness rises from deep within the psyche. On the threshold of Enlightenment it is obviously not merely a psychological fidgeting. One might call it a sort of oscillation between the most subtle mundane experience and the Transcendental, a last flicker of attachment to the conditioned.

If it seems strange that this hindrance should recur so far up the spiral path, we can remind ourselves that these lists and categories are not to be taken too literally. Doubt, for instance, is listed as one of the first three fetters to be broken, and certainly a substantial degree of sceptical doubt, the wilful indecisiveness that stops us from entering on the Transcendental path, disappears at Stream-entry. But even when such doubt is out of the way, there is still the possibility of doubt arising with regard to that which, for the time being, lies beyond one's own experience. At any stage you can entertain doubt with regard to what a higher stage might be like and what you have to do to get there. You might even wonder whether there is a higher stage at all; you might think you have got as far as it is possible to go, a doubt which is clearly linked to the fetter of desire for continued existence in the realm of immaterial form. Thus, even though doubt is one of the first three fetters to be broken, you cannot abolish it conclusively until you have abolished ignorance, the very last fetter to be broken, according to the Pāli commentaries. In other words, only an Arhant or a Buddha is absolutely free of the fetter of doubt. Inasmuch as you do not have actual knowledge of the Transcendental, because it is beyond your present experience, you are to that extent ignorant, and where there is ignorance there must be at least a degree of doubt.

Indeed, one might even say that ignorance is the only fetter and that all the others are different aspects of it. All the fetters, gross and subtle, imply the continued presence of the conception of a separate self: the self-view eliminated when the first three fetters are broken is only a relatively gross form of that mental attitude, which recurs in subtler forms in the fetters that are broken at more advanced stages of development. Conceit, the idea of oneself as being in some way comparable to other people (whether as superior, inferior, or equal), is the most obvious example, but even this is not the subtlest self-view of all.

Dualistic consciousness is what splits our experience into 'me' and 'the world' – and this, according to the Buddhist analysis, is our fundamental mistake. Subject and object arise in dependence on each other – there is no continuity of an unchanging person. The 'ego', with its likes and dislikes, views and opinions, is a self-perpetuating illusion, arising in dependence on our previous actions, our ingrained habits of consciousness. But although in reality there is no separation between subject and object, we are unable to plunge into that realization because of the mind-made fetters that hold us back. Herein lies the importance of contemplating the six sense bases and their objects. When the internal sense base comes into contact with the external object, if you give very careful attention to what happens as a result, you will in the end come to see how the mind fabricates from that interaction a self and a world, unable to stay open to the ever-changing flux of things. Humankind cannot bear very much reality, said T.S. Eliot. But we can learn to bear it – indeed, it is the wellspring of freedom and joy – if we train ourselves to see it steadily and see it whole.

From *Living with Awareness* (2003, pp.132-4)

12. WHAT WOULD LIFE BE LIKE WITHOUT THE HINDRANCES?

Quite a lot of people would say, if you talked about getting rid of covetousness and ill will and all that, what would be left in life?

> *It is as if a man, having contracted a debt, should engage in work and be successful in it, then should discharge the debt and perhaps have a surplus with which to maintain a wife. It would seem to him: 'Formerly I contracted a debt, engaged in work which was successful; I was enabled to discharge the debt, and there was a surplus with which I could maintain a wife.' Because of this he would be joyful and happy.*
>
> *It is just as if a man were bound in prison and after some time should be freed, with safety, without cost, and with no loss whatever of his property. Because of this he would be joyful and happy.*
>
> *It is just as if a servant or slave, a man not his own master but dependent on others, and not able to go about as he liked, should, after a time, be freed from his servitude, become his own master, and be able to go about as it suited him. Because of this he would be joyful and happy.*
>
> *It is just as if a wealthy owner of property should start out on a famine-stricken and dangerous desert way, and should, after a time, cross over that desert and reach safety and with peace the outskirts of a village. It would seem to him: 'Formerly I, a man of wealth and property, entered on a famine-stricken and dangerous desert way; now I have reached peace and freedom from danger.' Because of that he would be joyful and happy.*
>
> *In just the same way, the bhikkhu in whom the Five Hindrances are not destroyed sees in himself the states as of debt, sickness, imprisonment, slavery, and the desert path. Similarly, the bhikkhu in whom the Five Hindrances are destroyed sees in himself the states of freedom from debt, of health, of deliverance from prison, of freedom from slavery, and of being on safe ground.*[55]

The Buddha is speaking here about how joyful you would feel to rid of the five hindrances, even temporarily, but people usually regard indulgence in these hindrances as the aim and object, the meaning and purpose of life. People want to satisfy their cravings and indulge their ill will, and be all agitated and worried; in a sense people like to be in this sort of state, and they don't want to give it up. But the person who is entering upon the *dhyānas* gets rid of these hindrances, at least temporarily, and then he feels liberated; he feels like someone who is freed from debt, or who recovers from illness, or who is released from prison or slavery, or someone who has found the right path after being on the wrong path. He experiences getting rid of the five hindrances as a tremendous liberation and he feels very happy on that account.

Quite a lot of people would say, if you talked about getting rid of covetousness and ill will and all that, what would be left in life? What enjoyment would there be? They don't think of these things as a burden or a hindrance; they think of them very often as constituting the meaning and purpose of life, and they wonder how anyone could possibly be happy without these things.

From a seminar on the *Samaññaphala Sutta* (1982, pp.151-3)

13. OUT OF GLADNESS IS BORN JOY

You're embarking on a whole series of positive mental states, each one more positive and creative than the preceding one.

To one who sees within himself the Five Hindrances destroyed is born gladness.[56]

Sangharakshita: When you see that in your mind there's no covetousness, there's nothing that you're craving for, you don't feel any ill will towards anyone, you just feel good will, you feel *mettā*, you feel *karuṇā*, when you're not agitated, you're not in a hurry, you're not disturbed, you're not dull and sleepy, and you've no doubts, on account of that, you feel really happy. You feel in a highly positive mood, and out of this positive mood, out of this gladness, is born joy. Then the body and the whole collection of mental states become calm, and with this calm one feels ease, and because of that ease one's mind becomes concentrated. It reminds one of the positive *nidānas*, doesn't it? You're embarking on a whole series of positive mental states, each one more positive and creative than the preceding one.

From a seminar on the *Samaññaphala Sutta* (1982, p.158)

4 Antidotes to the hindrances

1. CULTIVATING THE OPPOSITE

The cultivation of the opposite as a method is more successful when the object whose opposite you are trying to cultivate is something rather painful and disagreeable.

Q: We were discussing the methods of overcoming the hindrances, and when we were discussing the second method, the cultivation of the opposite, we were wondering whether in the case of *kāmacchanda*, the craving for sensuous experience, you cultivate the opposite by reflecting on the loathsomeness of things, as outlined in some meditation practices.

Sangharakshita: I think that would be getting away a bit from the cultivation of the opposite, because the opposite of the hindrance should be a positive quality, surely. The classic example is that of *mettā* in relation to hatred; you extirpate hatred by cultivating its opposite, which is *mettā*. So in relation to the other hindrances, the question arises: what is the opposite? One has to determine that before one can cultivate it, and the opposite has to be a positive quality, something skilful rather than unskilful.

Take craving, for sensuous experience, *kāmacchanda*. Why is it a hindrance? A hindrance is something that prevents you from entering the *dhyāna* state, so any preoccupation with, or any strong desire for, sensuous experience is a hindrance, because that desire directs you to the *kāmaloka*, whereas your meditation practice is intended to direct you to the *rūpāloka*.

So what would be a positive counterpart of *kāmacchanda*? It would be more like desire, *chanda*, for experience on the *rūpāloka* level. Cultivating the opposite in this case would surely consist not in contemplating the loathsomeness of a corpse or something like that but in cultivating a positive and active appreciation of refined forms of beauty, for instance through the arts, through literature, poetry, painting, sculpture. That would be more of the nature of a positive counterpart.

You could even say that the positive counterpart of *kāmacchanda* is aesthetic appreciation, if you wanted a real, positive counterpart, a positive quality that you could cultivate, as distinct from exercises to get rid of something. So the opposite you would need to cultivate in order to get rid of or subdue *kāmacchanda* would be the cultivation of a more refined aesthetic appreciation of beauty.

But do you think that is actually possible? Does it work like that? Do you find that? After all, presumably you have all experienced *kāmacchanda* and you have all experienced some measure of aesthetic appreciation. Does it actually work like that? Does aesthetic rapture drive out naughty thoughts?

Q: It's very hard to appreciate something aesthetically when there is desire or craving there, I find. It's very hard to see something higher, because the object of your craving is much more tangible.

S: Of course, it doesn't help when the work of art itself is concerned with the presentation of some of those very sensuous objects that you are trying to get away from. But nonetheless I suggest that a more refined, a more intense aesthetic appreciation could be considered as the positive counterpart of *kāmacchanda*, and therefore to be cultivated as the remedy or antidote. I am not satisfied that it is an opposite in the full sense, but I think it comes somewhat near it.

Q: The opposite would probably be generosity, wouldn't it, *dāna*?

S: Well, that is usually considered the opposite or positive counterpart of greed, but yes, perhaps *kāmacchanda* is a form of greed. But the question arises more, say, in the context of meditation. Here you are, trying to concentrate your mind, trying to get into a *dhyāna* state, at least the first *dhyāna*, and then there swims into your mind from somewhere or other this thought, this feeling, of *kāmacchanda*. If you adopt the method of cultivating the opposite in order to eradicate it, what particular quality, analogous to *mettā* in the case of hatred, are you to try to cultivate? You could conjure up a vision of some beautiful work of art, or a beautiful natural scene. Perhaps that would work. This is also where the visualization practices are very helpful, because they represent a more ideal, a more ethereal form of beauty which gives you a certain emotional satisfaction, and therefore enables you to detach yourself from grosser forms of satisfaction.

The cultivation of the opposite as a method is more successful when the object whose opposite you are trying to cultivate is something rather painful and disagreeable, whereas the opposite is something pleasant. In the case of anger and hatred, this is not a very happy state to be in; it is rather unpleasant, it is disagreeable; in extreme cases it can be painful. So it isn't so difficult, perhaps, to wish to cultivate the opposite, the positive counterpart of that, *mettā*, which is pleasant and agreeable.

But in the case of *kāmacchanda*, it isn't quite like that, because *kāmacchanda* itself is pleasurable, perhaps intensely so, and so it's not easy to detach yourself from it. You certainly can't detach yourself from it easily by thinking of something disagreeable, even though that may be a genuine opposite. You've got to think of something even more pleasurable, even more enjoyable, even more inspiring and rapture-inducing, and perhaps a more refined aesthetic appreciation, a more intense enjoyment of works of art, can be helpful in this connection. It seems as though you can detach yourself from something that you find very pleasurable only by discovering something even more pleasurable, if one is to do it in a natural way as distinct from imposing a certain discipline on yourself. This is why I have some reservations about the *asubha bhāvanā*, though I'm sure it does work in extreme cases.

Q: This is the contemplation of ...

S: Impurity, the contemplation of the ugly, the repulsive, especially the ten stages of decomposition of a corpse (see pages 499-510). One might even say the *asubha bhāvanā* practice really consists not in seeing something as ugly, but seeing something else as more beautiful. One can perhaps break down one's attachment to physical bodies in that way, but it isn't enough just to detach from them. Perhaps in a lot of ways it's better to think in terms of cultivating this positive, more refined, more pleasurable counterpart. It's not quite a counterpart, but does shift one's energies just a little bit higher. And eventually a lot of those feelings can be absorbed in the visualization practice, inasmuch as the object of one's concentration, a Buddha or a Bodhisattva, is aesthetically very appealing.

From a seminar on the Noble Eightfold Path (1982, pp.383-7)

2. WHY ON EARTH AM I DOING THIS?

You kick the cat, you snap at your friend, you have a thoroughly bad meditation – and all for what? When you really reflect upon it, you realize the absurdity of it.

Q: In connection with the methods for eradicating unskilful mental states, we found a list of five in the Pāli canon – a slightly different list from the five you usually mention. There were four of the methods you list: consider the consequences, cultivate the opposite, just let the hindrance pass, and forcibly suppress it. You also say if all that fails, the only thing left to do is Go for Refuge to the Buddha.

Sangharakshita: The last one isn't a method attached to the previous four. I have attached it myself, because it is sometimes said, especially in the Tibetan tradition, that this is a way of overcoming hindrances generally – that you just Go for Refuge when all else fails. But there is no such list of five in Buddhist texts as far as I know, though that list of four does occur. But you said you had found a fifth?

Q: Yes. The fifth one is just saying to yourself, 'Why am I feeling negative?' – if you are feeling negative – 'Why don't I just feel positive?' and then just begin feeling positive. I've got the text here.

> *Monks, if when the monk has brought about forgetfulness of, and lack of attention to, those thoughts, there still arise even unskilled thoughts associated with desire, associated with aversion, associated with confusion, that monk should attend to the thought-function and form of those thoughts. While he is attending to the thought-function and form of those thoughts, those that are evil unskilled thoughts associated with desire*

and associated with aversion and associated with confusion, these are got rid of, these come to an end. By getting rid of these, the monk subjectively steadies, calms, is one-pointed, concentrated. Monks, even as it might occur to a man who is walking quickly, 'Now, why do I walk quickly? Suppose I were to walk slowly.' It might occur to him as he was walking slowly, "Now, why do I walk slowly? Suppose I were to stand.' It might occur to him as he was standing, 'Now, why do I stand? Suppose I were to sit down.' It might occur to him as he was sitting down, 'Now, why do I sit down? Suppose I were to lie down.' Even so, monks, the man, having abandoned the very hardest posture, might take to the easiest posture itself.[57]

S: This text refers to the three unskilful roots, desire, aversion and confusion, rather than the five hindrances, but what do you make of this fifth method of dealing with obstacles to meditation? It's certainly a useful way of thinking. People have told me sometimes – especially when they get involved in a relationship, which one might say is a form of organized *kāmacchanda* – that one day they wake up and think, 'Why on earth am I doing this? Why on earth am I involved in this? What am I really doing?' It is this sort of thing the Buddha is thinking of as a practice. Or suppose you get very angry, and then you start coming to your senses and you ask yourself: 'Why on earth am I becoming angry? What good is it doing me? Am I really enjoying it? Is it the sort of thing I really want to get into?' Unfortunately, you don't usually start asking yourself these sorts of questions until the anger has abated somewhat. While the anger is still in full force, it is very difficult to reflect in this way. But if you can think 'Why on earth am I behaving like this? Why on earth am I feeling like this?' – it can very often help. So it can be regarded as an additional, fifth method.

Q: You don't include it in your teaching about overcoming the hindrances?

S: No, because this fifth method is very rarely given. The four that I do give is a standard list, but here the Buddha seems to give an extra method. It certainly is useful.

Q: Isn't it rather similar to the first method, reflecting on the consequences of such thoughts?

S: In a way it is, but in a way not, because one is not asking 'What will be the consequences of this mental state?' but 'What are the causes of this mental state?' Not only that; you are seeing it as simply incompatible with the things you really want. To quote again the instance of the relationship, you might think, 'What am I doing? I was looking for happiness, I was looking for companionship, I was looking for pleasure, bliss, paradise on earth, and what have I got? It's more like hell on earth.' It's the same when you are carried away with anger, or when you get into a state of depression. You could ask yourself, 'Why am I in this state? What reason is there for being in such a state? Here I am, a healthy human being; I've got my whole life before me, I've got my friends, I've got the Dharma, and here I am feeling miserable and depressed. Why on earth have I allowed myself to get into this state? How utterly ridiculous!' This is the way of reflecting that the Buddha gives here. You start realizing the utter absurdity of being in the state you are in.

If you ask why, presumably you see that there is no real reason. You've got every reason not to be in a state like that, despite whatever reasons you may feel you have to be in that state. If you are in a state of utter depression, well, why? Perhaps you got up and you discovered there weren't any cornflakes. That upset you, and you've been in a bad mood for the rest of the day. You can't meditate, you are grumpy with other people. You kick the cat, you snap at your friend, you have a thoroughly bad meditation – and all for what? When you really reflect upon it, you realize the absurdity of it. It does help, because you see that you have put yourself in a ridiculous position, you are in fact being ridiculous feeling the way that you do, and seeing it you can snap out of it.

But there is another point in this passage which we have overlooked. The Buddha represents the monk as reflecting on one thing after another, the subsequent one being easier, more pleasant, more agreeable, than the preceding one. This suggests that when you indulge in negative states, in unskilful mental states, you are giving yourself a hard time. Why give yourself a hard time? Why not give yourself an easy time? Why not allow yourself to experience skilful, positive mental states?

Q: I think it comes down to a lack of self-responsibility. I can see that in the past I almost got myself into a negative state in the hope that Mummy or Daddy would come along and make it better. It seems like you have to make the transition between that sort of existence and taking responsibility for your own states of mind.

S: Yes, you have to accept responsibility, ultimately, for your own mental states. Sometimes you hear people say, 'He made me angry.' But he didn't. He may have provoked you, but he didn't actually make you angry; if you became angry, that is your responsibility. Sometimes you find people, for one wretched reason or another, hanging on to their negativity, clutching their unskilful mental state. You try to talk them out of it, but they don't want to be talked out of it, they want to hang on to it. They insist on being negative. They hang on to it, apparently, till they feel it has really sunk in and that you really realize how miserable they are. If they think that you are taking it a bit too lightly, they go off, all sad and miserable, to convince you that they are sad and miserable, so that you will feel sorry for them. These are just some of the games that people play.

From a seminar on the Noble Eightfold Path (1982, pp.388-92)

3. STAND UP TO MĀRA

Mara doesn't bother to attack those whom he has already enslaved. He doesn't bother to attack his faithful servants! It is when you try to get away that you feel what can be called the gravitational pull.

Sangharakshita: Sometimes it seems as though there is some sort of force, almost of a personal nature, frustrating one's efforts. This is what in the Buddhist tradition is called Māra.[58]

Q: Given the kinds of occasion when Māra tends to appear, could we draw the conclusion that we are most likely to come under his attack or influence at the point when we are going to leave the *kāmaloka* or make a powerful spiritual effort?

S: Yes, Māra doesn't bother to attack those whom he has already enslaved. He doesn't bother to attack his faithful servants! It is when you try to get away that you feel what can be called the gravitational pull.

Q: Can you suggest what we should do if we believe we are under attack from Māra?

S: Well, you can argue with him. I had an experience of that sort myself once. It happened the first time I meditated seriously, which was in

Delhi shortly after I arrived in India. I was only 19 then, and this was the first time, believe it or not, that I had sat down to meditate in a formal manner. Until then, I had only been concerned with studying Buddhism and reading about it and writing about it. So I was sitting and meditating, and suddenly a head appeared in front of me, which I can only describe as the head of Māra. I can see this head in my mind's eye even now. It was quite an old man, with a yellowy-brown complexion, and a white stubble on his chin and on his head. His expression was that of someone who had led a wicked life; it was stamped on his face. And as I was sitting there meditating, I saw this head, sort of floating in mid-air in front of me, and he said: 'You're wasting your time. All this meditation, it's a sheer waste of time. You won't get anything out of it.' So – I think perhaps I was slightly argumentative! – I said 'No! You're wrong. I know you're wrong, because I'm getting something out of it here and now. That is my experience.' When I said that, he disappeared. This is what I mean when I say you must argue with Māra. You must stand up to him; and if he speaks to you, don't be afraid to answer back.

There was a sequel to this, because years later I met him again, as it were, but in a human form. The strange thing was – I won't go into details, but I met this person, and I knew at once it was the same face. It had the same features, and it was that same Māra. So one can have these experiences. I don't think one could say in my case that it was my unconscious doubts about the usefulness of meditation speaking; I'm not aware that I had any unconscious doubts (though of course if they are unconscious you won't be aware of them). I regard it as an encounter with something or someone who was in a sense actually there, not just reducible to my own mental states. I just mention it as an example of what you should do; you should stand up to Māra. Or you could recite a mantra; I didn't think of that then. I don't think I knew much about mantras at that time.

Q: How is one to deal with it when somebody tells you, 'Meditation is a waste of time'? Some people even say that meditation is associated with madness.

S: Well, it's true that if people meditate in the wrong sort of way – do a lot of *prāṇāyāma* or something of that sort – it may affect them mentally, but that is not to say that meditation as such is going to have that effect. To say about meditation in general that it induces madness is nonsense. If anything, it is those who don't meditate who are mad, not those who do.

Q: In *Dhyāna for Beginners* there is a whole section devoted to getting to grips with Māra; and it is said that there are periods of the day when Māra causes distractions in meditation.

S: I'm not sure about that, but there are parallel traditions in other parts of the world. I don't remember any such teaching in the Pāli canon, but the Sufis have a teaching that there are different kinds of spirit for the different times of day, and in the Christian tradition there is what they call the noonday demon. Have you heard about that? It was a demon that was especially supposed to afflict monks in the desert at the time of noon. According to Indian or Vedic tradition, the early part of the afternoon is a period of lowered vitality. They say that during the morning your vitality is building up, and then during the afternoon it's tailing off. I think it's true to say that the early afternoon is that period when you are at your lowest ebb. It is not a good time for meditation. Because it's a period of lowered vitality, you may then be more susceptible to a sort of invasion from your own unconscious mind; you may have semi-daydreams and you may perhaps be more open to the attacks of Māra at that time. But, with regard to this Tendai tradition of specific Māras for particular hours of the day, I am not sure whether that is a Buddhist tradition or something taken from Chinese tradition. It may be that at particular hours of the day you are more exposed to one type of temptation than another. I haven't looked into it sufficiently to be able to say. But I do know about the noonday demon, and I do know from what I have observed on retreats that the period between 2 and 4 o'clock is a time of definitely lowered energy. So it is perhaps good to study one's natural rhythms in this respect. You may notice that there are certain times of day when your energies are definitely aroused and when you can do certain things more easily and happily, and other times of day when your energies are at a low ebb, and when you shouldn't perhaps try to do certain things, if you can help it – without, of course, being too precious about it.

From Q&A on Nanamoli's *Life of the Buddha*,
(Tuscany 1986, pp.32-5)

4. THE VAJRAYANA APPROACH TO THE HINDRANCES

When you visualize a wrathful form, you feel some sympathy with that wrath, with that anger, as it were. It draws it out of you.

Q: Is the Vajrayāna approach to dealing with defilements and negative mental states, i.e. that of transforming them into the five wisdoms, similar to Going for Refuge with your hindrance, and cultivating its opposite, e.g. developing love to counteract hate?

Sangharakshita: In a way it is, although the Pāli scriptures don't use the term transformation. But, yes, I would say it has the same effect. You are replacing, say, hatred by *mettā*, so you could be said to be transforming the hatred into *mettā*. The energy which was formerly expressed in a negative manner is now expressed in a more positive manner.

Q: Are there particular Vajrayāna practices for the transformation of that energy?

S: Well, in a way, all the Vajrayanic meditations are intended to do that, especially when they have a ritual side. In the Mahāyāna, on which the Vajrayāna is based to a great extent, you have meditations on the sort of teaching that is contained in the *Heart Sūtra*, where *rūpā* is *śūnyatā*, *śūnyatā* is *rūpā*. That is the philosophical basis of the possibility of transformation, because if *rūpā* can be *śūnyatā*, *kleśa* can be *bodhi*. But in the Vajrayāna you face the *kleśas* more directly, for instance by visualizing the wrathful form of a Bodhisattva. In a sense anger is brought out into the open, integrated into the figure of the Bodhisattva. It ceases to be anger in the mundane sense, ceases to be a *kleśa*; but the energy of anger is there.

Q: Can you only make use of this when you have been practising for a while?

S: Yes, whatever the Tibetans may say, I think you need to do a lot of preliminary work. Otherwise it's just words. You say 'Oh, these *kleśas* are *bodhi*, so there's no need to control them, no need to eradicate them.'

Q: So you have to learn to control them to some extent first?

S: Yes. Otherwise you cannot develop the Insight which enables you to see their fundamental voidness, which is the basis of the transformation.

Q: What about visualizing the wrathful form, in terms of putting the energy of that anger into seeing the wrathful form?

S: If you visualize a wrathful form, the wrath in the form doesn't represent a *kleśa*. But when you visualize a wrathful form, you feel some sympathy with that wrath, with that anger, as it were. It draws it out of you. You in a way enjoy it, but you do that with a clear conscience because the wrath, the anger, is there in a highly sublimated form. To the extent that you visualize it, it is in a way a part of you, an aspect of your psyche. So that raw anger in you is being refined and integrated into what you visualize. You can do the same thing verbally. If you talk about something with other people, you bring it out into the open, and in that way you integrate it. If you admit your anger, for example, to the extent that you are able to talk about it, to bring it out into the open, to recognize it, it ceases to be anger, it ceases to be a *kleśa*.

From a seminar on Canto 39 of *The Life and Liberation of Padmasambhava, 'Princess Mandarava abandons the world to follow the Dharma'* (women's pre-ordination course 1987, p.32)

5. VERY DIFFICULT TO RESIST

Sometimes the thing that forces itself on our attention is something to which at another time we would be very glad to pay attention.

Distraction could be described as something that forces itself on our attention when we do not really want to pay attention to it. Of course, we experience distraction almost every time we try to meditate. We may be trying to concentrate on the process of our breathing, but the noise of the traffic outside intrudes and it seems that we just can't help listening to it. Sometimes the thing that forces itself on our attention is something to which at another time we would be very glad to pay attention. It may be something of which we are very fond or even something by which we are fascinated, something that appeals to our most basic interests and desires. I hardly need spell out the kinds of thing this might be. The distraction then becomes very difficult to resist.

From *What is the Sangha?* (2004, pp.190-1)

6. IF ALL ELSE FAILS

It is not just a question of accepting your failure in the psychological sense; it is taking your failure with you when you Go for Refuge, which is quite a different thing.

Q: We are advised that after trying to overcome a particular hindrance with one of the four antidotes, if all the antidotes fail we should Go for Refuge to the Buddha, together with our failure, and just let it rest there. What does this mean?

Sangharakshita: It means that even when all these methods fail, you are still not beaten, not in principle, because the mere fact that you have made all those four efforts, even though you have failed, means that you still are striving, you still have an ideal, you still Go for Refuge, you are still committed. So it is as though you are saying to yourself: 'I have tried very hard, but I have had no success whatever. But nonetheless, despite my failure, I am committed. I do Go for Refuge.' You don't say that the failure doesn't matter; but you don't give up, even when you are totally beaten, or at least when you have totally failed in that respect.

Q: I wondered if it was in a sense another method of overcoming that hindrance by invoking faith.

S: It may well have that effect. But in any case it is good to remind oneself that, even though you have failed, perhaps completely for the time being, in principle you are still committed, you still Go for Refuge, you live to fight another day.

Q: In discussing this before, you have said that if you are working within the context of the psychological, there is nothing you can do; but in the context of the spiritual, you can do this.

S: Right, yes.

Q: Is there no psychological equivalent?

S: How can there be? Going for Refuge is Going for Refuge to the Transcendental, essentially, and psychology in the ordinary sense does not recognize that dimension. So the possibility of as it were throwing oneself upon the Transcendental does not exist for psychology in that sense.

Q: Is it not just accepting yourself?

S: No, it is more than that. You *commit* yourself. It is not just a question of accepting your failure in the psychological sense; it is taking your failure with you when you Go for Refuge, which is quite a different thing.

Q: So if you are working on the psychological plane, at that point you are stuck?

S: Yes – or at least you may feel that you are stuck. Nobody is ultimately stuck, because you can still start looking beyond psychology. Maybe that would be the significance of that experience: to make it clear that psychology is not enough and you have got to look elsewhere.

From Study Group Leaders' Q&A on the Noble Eightfold Path
(1985, pp.134-5)

5 Keeping a meditation diary

1. FRESH HOPE

If you don't write it down, the chances are that you will forget it, however important it seems at the time and however strongly you feel you couldn't possibly forget it.

Q: Do you recommend keeping a meditation notebook?

Sangharakshita: Yes indeed. Just taking a note of what happens is very useful if you can keep it up. Then you can trace the ups and downs of your progress from week to week and month to month. You can look back and say, 'That's odd, I seem to have all my good meditations round the full moon day', or 'I seem to have a good week, then a bad week, a good week, then a bad week' or 'I don't seem to have done the *mettā-bhāvanā* for a month'. You notice things like that.

Q: And you think one can use knowledge like that in a constructive way?

S: Yes. For instance, you may have had a very good meditation, and then you can completely forget about it. Some months later, when you've struck a bad patch, you might start thinking 'I can't get on with meditation, maybe I'm not cut out it. I never have any good experiences, I never get anywhere', but then you look through your notebook: 'Oh, so many months ago I had a really good meditation,' and the notebook brings it back to you. 'It is possible, I did manage it before.' You might have completely forgotten it, especially in the sort of mood that you are in at the moment. So your notebook creates fresh hope. Not just with meditation, but with study, or listening to lectures or even discussion, write down something that strikes you as important. If you don't write it down, the chances are that you will forget it, however important it seems at the time and however strongly you feel you couldn't possibly forget it. Very few people have such a retentive memory that they can remember everything without external aids. Speaking personally, I wish that I had written down much more in my earlier days. I've got quite a good memory and I remember quite a lot, but a lot of things I have quite forgotten.

Q: Very often, just a few words ...

S: You don't have to make long elaborate notes. Just a few words are often quite enough. That's all you need.
From a seminar on Nāgārjuna's *Precious Garland* (1976, pp.442-3)

2. MEDITATION IS A SERIOUS BUSINESS

If you find yourself worrying more because you are keeping a meditation diary, just don't keep one.

Q: Have you any views on the value of keeping a meditation diary or journal?

Sangharakshita: I did keep a meditation diary for a number of years, and I think it can be useful, in two or three different ways. First of all, it enables one to check one's regularity of practice. If you look back you can see how regularly you have meditated: how many days a week, whether once or twice a day, whether there were any serious gaps. I also noticed that if I made even a brief note of experiences that I had had, this could be quite encouraging later on. Also, perhaps it has the function of confirming your feeling that meditation is a serious business, that it is something to keep watch over. You need to keep a constant check on what is happening, without being too precious about it. If you plant a seed, you mustn't pull the plant up every few days to see how it's getting on and whether the roots are sprouting. In the same way, you shouldn't worry about your meditation; just get on with it regularly. Your meditation diary shouldn't be a source of worry. If you find yourself worrying more because you are keeping a meditation diary, just don't keep one.

Another reason is that you can see the ups and downs of your practice. You might see that for a whole month your meditation followed a particular pattern, or that there was a particular difficulty recurring and that then it faded away. In that way you can come to know yourself better, and understand what sort of effect meditation is having on you.

So I think it can be a useful thing to do. I think also that one should keep one's diary strictly for one's own private information. It's probably not a good idea to show it to other people, unless it's a spiritual friend whose advice you are seeking.

From a seminar on the Noble Eightfold Path (1982, pp.164-5)

3. FIRST OF ALL, GET A GOOD BIG NOTEBOOK!

Odds and ends of distractions you need not preserve for posterity! Once you've overcome the distractions it's best maybe to forget all about them.

Q: Could you give some practical ideas for keeping a meditation diary?

Sangharakshita: I would have thought it was really quite simple but perhaps it isn't. Practical ideas? Well, first of all, get a good big notebook! And write it up every day – I think this is quite important. Even if nothing much happens, just mention that nothing much happened. You should give the time that you sat to meditate, maybe sometimes where; the length of time for which you sat, and how the meditation proceeded – whether you had good concentration or not, whether you felt in a positive mental state or not, whether you felt buoyed up, whether you had any ecstatic experience, whether you experienced *prīti*, whether you were subject to distractions, and if so, what sort of distractions. You could note whether you had any visions or any particular sensations, or whether any flash of Insight occurred to you or any deeper understanding of things. This is the sort of information that you should record.

You have perhaps already found that even if you have a quite striking and important experience in meditation, if you don't write it down, as with a dream, you can forget about it very quickly. So one of the reasons for keeping a meditation diary is so that after two or three months you can look back over it and recall positive experiences which you would otherwise perhaps have forgotten. Especially if you have had experiences in the nature of insights, you can reflect further upon them and make them more of an integral part of your whole conscious attitude. Also, if you look back over your meditation diary you can sometimes see a pattern emerging. You can see ups and downs. You might even notice that around the time of the full moon you don't have particularly good meditations or you have very good meditations. You can observe patterns of that sort.

I think it is quite a good idea to keep a meditation diary, especially on retreat. As with other diaries, in that way you record a lot of information, some of it useful, that otherwise you would very likely forget. Once the meditation diaries have served their purpose you can burn them, as I did mine. There's no point in hanging on to them unless there are very special insights which you want to preserve, in which case you could copy them out separately in another book. You might even hear words or phrases in the course of your meditation, giving you teachings. You might like to write all those down in a special notebook so they're always with you for reflection. Odds and ends of distractions you need not preserve for posterity! Once you've overcome the distractions it's best maybe to forget all about them.

I think it's good if you can keep up writing in the diary regularly. I remember that when I was keeping one I wrote it up immediately after each session, or at least shortly after. Once I'd had time to emerge from the meditation, I at once wrote down an account, as full as I could, of how the meditation session had gone. If you leave it till later on in the day, other things will have happened, the clarity of the impression will have been blurred and you'll definitely forget things. You won't be able to remember whether you were distracted by hatred first and lust afterwards or lust first and hatred afterwards! You'll get it all mixed up, and your diary won't be a faithful record. So write it all down as soon as you can after the session.

It's an exercise in mindfulness, one might say. If you're more mindful of your meditation experience, that can only be good for you, and good for the Buddhist community as a whole.

From Part 2 of a seminar on the Past and Future of the Order (1985, pp.19-20)

6 Dangers and difficulties in meditation

1. THE GRAVITATIONAL PULL

We have to learn just to let go. This is the most difficult thing in the world.

The Buddha described the path to Enlightenment in terms of three stages: ethics or morality (the Pāli word is *śīla*), meditation and wisdom. Meditation as the second stage of the Threefold Path consists of what one can call 'concentration' and 'meditation proper'; it doesn't include contemplation, which, though it is usually practised within the context of meditation, really belongs to the third stage of the path, the stage of wisdom. Meditation is thus the intermediate stage of the spiritual path, in which there operate both gravitational forces: the force of the conditioned and the force of the Unconditioned. This, one could say, accounts for two things.

One thing it accounts for is the ease with which we sometimes fall from the heights of meditation right down into the depths of worldliness. Most people who practise meditation have had this experience at some time or other. We enjoy what seems to be a really beautiful meditation. We may begin to think that we're really getting somewhere. We may even think we've really made it at last, spiritually speaking. After all that effort, we've really got up there, we're amongst all these beautiful experiences, floating around us like so many pink and blue clouds. We think, 'This is wonderful, this is going to stay with me all my life, for ever and ever. Here I am, floating on these clouds, timelessly. I'm never going to have any more problems, any more worries. At last I've got there.'

But what happens? Within a matter of minutes – not hours, not days, not weeks, but minutes – we are overwhelmed by what can only be described as highly unskilful mental states. Not only that: we find ourselves even acting in accordance with those highly unskilful mental states, within minutes of floating up there blissfully on those beautiful clouds. In this way we oscillate between the heights and the depths. Sometimes we are right up there with the gods, as it were, thinking, 'I'd like to devote my whole life to meditation,' and the next minute we are right down in the depths.

It is only natural when this happens to start wondering whether meditation is really worth while. One could be forgiven for thinking, 'I make all this effort, spread my wings, and soar up there for a while ... then my wings seem to give way somehow, and crash! I find myself back on the earth, maybe with a few damaged feathers. Is it worth it? If I could get up there and stay there, it would be worth it perhaps; but to get up there only to sink down again is so disappointing.' We begin to wonder whether such a thing as spiritual progress is possible at all. Are we just fooling ourselves? Are we doomed to ricochet in this way between the heights and the depths for ever?

Not necessarily. All this trouble is due to the gravitational pull of the conditioned – from which we can become free in the third stage of the path. But until then, we are liable to fall at any time, from any height, regardless of the length of time we spend meditating. We might have stayed up there for a couple of hours, even a whole week. It doesn't make any difference – we come tumbling down just as easily.

In India there are lots of stories about this sort of thing, usually stories about Indian rishis. We are told that thousands of years ago Rishi So-and-so went off to the Himalayas, and he spent thousands of years meditating – meditating in caves, meditating in deep forests, meditating in hermitages, meditating on snowy peaks, oblivious to everything. There are all sorts of wonderful stories about how one rishi's beard grew miles and miles long and went flowing over the whole countryside, and how another rishi was so indifferent to what was going on around him that he just went on meditating even when a colony of ants came and built a great anthill over him.

But of course, eventually any rishi has to end his meditation – or at least he decides to end it – and then what happens? It's the same story every time. As soon as the rishi comes out of his meditation, as he comes down from the mountain or emerges from the forest, he encounters a nymph, a heavenly maiden, and within a matter of minutes, despite those thousands of years of meditation, he succumbs to her temptations and he's back where he started.

What do these stories mean? They all mean the same thing. They mean that meditation is not enough, so far as the spiritual life is concerned. It can only take you so far. But though it's not enough, at the same time it's indispensable. It is the basis for the development of wisdom, just as skilful action is the basis for the development of meditation. If morality is the launch pad of the rocket, meditation, we may say, is the first-stage rocket, from which the second-stage rocket is fired when the first-stage rocket has reached a certain height. This second-stage rocket, of course, is wisdom.

So meditation is indispensable because it is only from meditation that one can reach wisdom. One must reach a certain level of meditation experience and sustain oneself at that level, if one can, for a certain length of time at least, and then try to develop wisdom. Once wisdom has been developed, there is no longer any danger, you're no longer at the mercy of the gravitational pull of the conditioned.

This, then, is one thing accounted for by the fact that at the stage of meditation both gravitational forces operate. The other thing accounted for by this fact is that if we've been meditating fairly successfully for some time, we sometimes feel as though we are about to slide down into fathomless depths, or be carried away by a great stream flowing strongly and powerfully within us and beyond us. At such times usually what we're experiencing, however obscurely, and without necessarily knowing it, is the gravitational pull of the Unconditioned. But what usually happens? When we start feeling this pull, when we start feeling ourselves going, slipping, sliding, being carried away, we usually resist. We usually pull back. This is because we feel afraid. Oh yes, we say we want Enlightenment, we want Nirvāṇa, but when it really comes to the point, we don't want to be carried away. We don't want to lose ourselves.

This calls to mind a story about an old woman in Japan, a devout Buddhist. She used to go along to the temple of Amitābha, the Buddha of Infinite Light, who presides over the Pure Land into which – according to Japanese Buddhism – you are reborn after death, if you recite his mantra. She would go along to this temple and she would worship there every morning, bowing down many times and crying, 'Oh Lord, oh Amitābha, oh Buddha of Infinite Light and Eternal Life, please take me away from this wretched, sorrowful, wicked world. Let me die tonight and be reborn into your Pure Land. That's where I want to go, so that I can be in your presence night and day, and hear your teaching and gain Nirvāṇa.' In this way, tearfully and with great sincerity, she used to pray every morning and sometimes in the evening too.

A certain monk in that temple overheard her praying and weeping, and he thought, 'All right, we shall see.' The Buddha image in the temple, like many images in Japan, was an enormous one, about thirty feet high. So when the old woman came next, the monk hid behind the image. As she sobbed, 'Lord, please take me now, let me be reborn in the Pure Land. Take me.' The monk called out from behind the image in a great booming voice, 'I shall take you *now*.' At this the old woman leapt up with a shriek of terror and rushed out of the temple. And as she rushed out she called over her shoulder to the image, 'Won't the Buddha let me have my little joke?'

We say that we want to gain Enlightenment, and we say, with complete sincerity, that this is why we meditate. But as soon as we start feeling that pull, feeling that we're going to be carried away, that we're going to lose ourselves, we draw back. Just like the old woman, we are afraid. We don't want to lose ourselves. But this is in fact just what we must learn to do, whether in meditation or in any other aspect of the spiritual life. We have to learn just to let go. This is the most difficult thing in the world: just to let go. We have to give up if you like – not in the ordinary, everyday sense of the expression, but in a more spiritual sense. To use more religious terminology, we just have to surrender to the Unconditioned.

From *What is the Dharma?* (1998, pp.95-8)

2. COPING WITH FEAR IN MEDITATION

I think if you possibly can – I won't say handle it because sometimes it is beyond handling, but if you can possibly endure it and live through it, do so.

Q: People who are doing a lot of meditation sometimes experience states of madness akin to paranoia and fear. When one is in this state, what is the best counteractive measure to take?

Sangharakshita: First of all, I'm not so sure that people who are doing a lot of meditation experience states of madness. If you are doing a lot of meditation you are in a *dhyāna* state, and that is not a state of madness. I think what you mean is, when you are *trying* to meditate, *tryin*g to concentrate. Then, yes, you may sometimes experience states of – I'm not sure about madness but certainly paranoia and fear. So, what one is to do? If you possibly can, you should sweat it out, because it is quite an important experience, and one that a lot of people have. Sometimes, though, it is so terrible and so overwhelming that you can't do that. I think if you possibly can – I won't say handle it because sometimes it is beyond handling, but if you can possibly endure it and live through it, do so. But if you feel that you might even go mad, the best thing you can do is to get into contact with your spiritual friends. I don't necessarily mean deep spiritual contact – you won't be capable of that, probably, for a while, after having that sort of experience – but just into contact, even physical contact, just holding them or letting them hold you, or talking to them. Maybe tell them about your experience, maybe not, but just get into contact with them. If you can avoid it, don't just seek comfort and warmth but engage in spiritual communication to the extent that you can. But this can be a very terrible experience, and when it is full-blown, there is nothing you can do about it. You can't even struggle with it. It is quite overwhelming. It takes you over and you just have to live through it. There is nothing else you can do, except just get back into contact with your spiritual friends.

Q: Is it an integrating process, sweating it out?

S: I think it is, in the long run. If you have done some amount of meditation and reached some spiritual maturity, it certainly can be part of the process of integration. If you contact that experience prematurely, that way madness does lie. But if you have done some meditation, then you have got a basis on which you can encounter the shock, so to speak, and you can live through it. People who, as it were, go mad are people who have that sort of experience without any spiritual preparation, so that it has a disintegrating effect on them. They have not been able to integrate it. Well, in a way you can't integrate it, because you are quite changed by this experience. The old self is modified to an extreme degree. You just don't see things in the same way afterwards, perhaps. So you certainly don't integrate it in the ordinary way, it's much too devastating an experience. Most people, I think, go through it to some degree – some much more than others for one reason or another. I won't say that it is inevitable, but it seems very common. I think that the more preparation you've done in the way of meditating and developing emotional positivity, the more you can cushion the shock, the impact of that experience, and the more 'easily', if that is the right expression, you can live through it.

Q: What is reaching the limits of one's integration? What's happening?

S: I suppose one could say that you come to a point where you realize, you see, that what you have always thought of as you, yourself, is just not there. It modifies your sense of your own ego identity. That's why it's so devastating.

Q: Does the experience of these states of madness indicate that something is wrong with the way that we are practising?

S: Sometimes it does. There are some schools of meditation where you are precipitated into an experience of this sort before you are really ready for it, and that can result in a breakdown. Some of the more extreme forms of so-called *vipassanā* meditation catapult people into experiences for which they are not prepared. If you are doing your mindfulness, *mettā-bhāvanā* and visualization practice, it is very unlikely that you will be catapulted into anything for which you are not ready. But nonetheless you may still have, depending on your psychological and spiritual history, a more or less extreme experience, perhaps not of paranoia but at least of a considerable measure of fear that you may find very difficult, or even impossible to handle. You may just have to 'submit' to it, as it were. If you survive, well, you have survived, that's the main thing.

Q: Do you think it is an inevitable process?

S: I don't like to say that anything is inevitable, but lots of people do seem to go through it, at least to some degree. With some people it is no more than a rather unpleasant half hour, whereas with others it may be a totally devastating day and night.

From a discussion on a Women's Order Convention (1985, pp.118–20)

3. EXTREME MEDITATION EXPERIENCES

Very often experiences aren't what they seem to be.

Q: In the text, a monk is described as having a meditation experience like a great noise and the cave roof falling in.[59] Have you any guidelines on how to deal with extreme meditation experiences of this type in oneself and in others?

Sangharakshita: It is difficult to say just from this text, but I would have thought that the person referred to here needed reassurance that he was on the right path. Judging just from my impression of the text, and obviously that isn't very much to go by, he wasn't doing things forcibly. I think he could well have continued in that way of practice and deepened that experience. The experience described seemed to me, as I read it, quite definitely like the collapse of his present personality. It may not have been a real Insight experience, but at least it was the collapse of whatever personality he was at that time identifying himself with.

Q: If you found yourself having that sort of experience, if it seemed to you that the roof was falling in, but actually your personality was falling apart, how would you work out what was going on?

S: If you are in contact with someone who is more experienced than yourself, provided that they have had that sort of experience themselves, or that they intuitively know what is happening, they can perhaps advise you. But very often experiences aren't what they seem to be. You might have the experience for instance that you have no head, or that you have a body and no head, or a head and no body – you can have all sorts of experiences. Very often it's best to persist with the experience and reflect on what it means.

Q: I suppose there's no reason to expect an Insight experience necessarily to be subjectively benign. It could be terrifying.

S: Well yes, it can affect your conditioned personality in almost any way.

Q: So the fact that a meditation experience is frightening or shocking or alarming isn't necessarily a sign that something is terribly wrong.

S: No, but on the other hand you should be sufficiently prepared so that the shock is not too devastating; otherwise you are tempted to give up. This is where a basis of emotional positivity and even devotion comes in.

Q: What should you do if one of these experiences comes up?

S: Well, you play it by ear. How can one generalize? Someone may be able to advise you from their own experience or from their intuition, or they may not be able to advise you at all, in which case they would be best just to suggest that you do whatever you think best, or go and consult someone with more experience.

Q: And if it happened to you on solitary retreat?

S: It depends on the nature of the experience. Some experiences are just psychological – fears and horrors coming up from past experiences, your early childhood. Sometimes you know this and you can grapple with them on that basis, or let them just pass over you. But sometimes you may have stirred up more than you can cope with. You might even have to leave your solitary retreat. That suggests that you have not built up a sufficient basis of positivity, and that you were perhaps forcing things – by which I mean precipitating an experience before you have a sufficient basis of positivity within yourself to be able to support it and as it were live with it, and live through it.

From a seminar on *The Forest Monks of Sri Lanka* (1985, pp.282-3)

4. IS MEDITATION DANGEROUS?

In the whole time I've been taking meditation classes, I've never known anybody who was the worse for practising meditation, even in the case of those who overdid it a bit.

Sangharakshita: When I arrived on the Buddhist scene in London in 1964 there were constant dire warnings being given at the London Buddhist Society against the danger of practising meditation. I remember Christmas Humphreys himself telling me, 'Oh, I never encourage people to meditate for longer than five minutes. That's the most that they can stand.' There was quite a lot of talk in those days about meditation being dangerous, and how you could easily go off your head if you meditated too much (i.e. more than five minutes a day). The whole thing may have arisen because of a rather extreme form of '*vipassanā*' meditation that was fashionable at that time. At least 11 or 12 people who had practised it turned up at the Hampstead Buddhist Vihāra after my arrival, and I found they were very badly affected mentally. Three more people were in mental hospitals. The latter must have been in a pretty bad state even before encountering '*vipassanā*' meditation and should never have been put on to that sort of practice in the first place. All this had created quite an atmosphere in Buddhist circles in London, and the Buddhist Society tended to discourage meditation quite strongly. Meditation was 'dangerous' – a word that one often heard.

Q: What are the dangers of meditation?

S: Really, none at all. I don't think there are really even any wrong methods. The main danger, or the main difficulty, is trying to do too much too soon and thinking of meditation as a sort of achievement, as something from which you must automatically get such and such a result, if you work at it. This egoistic, grasping attitude is the greatest danger, because it builds up tension, but I don't really see any serious danger apart from that, except in the extreme case of a person whose latent schizophrenia could perhaps come out as a result of practising meditation.

I must say that, in the whole time I've been taking meditation classes, I've never known anybody who was the worse for practising meditation, even in the case of those who overdid it a bit. But I certainly know there were a few, especially in the earlier days – people who had rather rigid personality structures, and were somewhat emotionally repressed – who tried to do more and more hours of forcible concentration and landed up with severe headaches. That's the kind of attitude I was referring to: straining, and making an egoistic effort. Otherwise, I don't see any danger except, perhaps, if you have a prolonged experience of meditation on retreat and then let yourself go back into the hurly-burly too quickly. That can have a rather unpleasant effect, even quite a bad effect, but it isn't the meditation itself that is responsible, it's your own lack of caution in making the transition to a different kind of life. Really there are no dangers in meditation at all.

Q: Would those remarks apply also to the cautions that are sometimes directed to so-called Tantric meditation? Even the Dalai Lama has said that unless one does these things under the right circumstances, with full facilities, they can be dangerous.

S: I wouldn't agree with that as a blanket statement. To the best of my knowledge, the only dangerous practice – and it does occur in some branches of the Tantra – is breath control, or *prāṇāyāma* in the strict sense. There, certainly, one needs a teacher and the right sort of environment. Apart from that I don't think there is anything that is actually dangerous, though there are many things that you could do wrongly and thus ineffectively. The only danger lies in a general misunderstanding of the Tantra that would be detrimental to your whole spiritual life, as when people think of Tantra in terms of sex, and think that getting into the Tantra means getting into a more and more active and variegated sexual life and dignifying that with the name of Tantra because they need some an excuse, at least in their own minds. But that's just part of the general danger of slipping back. There's no specific danger in the form of madness or anything like that. Tantric Buddhism is often misunderstood. There are four great divisions of the Tantra, and three of them don't even make use of sexual symbolism, never mind sexual practices.
From a seminar on *The Endlessly Fascinating Cry* (1977, pp.182-4)

5. THE PROTEST OF HASTILY DEPARTING NOTIONS

Certain wrong views or attitudes are departing, and as they depart, they make their little protest. But there is nothing to worry about.

In assimilation of the inner practice with veins and breath
and bindu,
The obstructions and the hesitations that manifest themselves
Do not mean the teaching's faulty;
They are the protest of hastily departing notions.[60]

Sangharakshita: The sort of experience that Milarepa is referring to here is a very general one, though here it's described in specifically Tantric terms. The 'veins and breath and *bindu*' have a technical sense here. It's not really veins, it's more like nerves, *nadi*, the currents of nervous energy within not just the body but the whole psycho-physical being. Essentially Milarepa is saying that when one is concerned with inner practice in connection with the assimilation of the nerves, the basic psycho-physical energy and sexual energy. In other words when one is trying to transmute and sublimate that energy, obstructions and hesitations may manifest themselves, but that does not mean the teaching is faulty. 'They are the protest of hastily departing notions.' In other words, on account of the sublimation or redirecting of energy that is taking place within you, there are all sorts of little symptoms. These symptoms might seem at first to mean that something is going wrong – maybe the teaching is wrong, or maybe you're not practising it properly – but really they're just reactions of your conditioned being that show that something is happening, in fact that things are going alright. Milarepa refers to these reactions humorously as 'the protest of hastily departing notions'. Certain wrong views or attitudes are departing, and as they depart, they make their little protest. But there is nothing to worry about. That is all that is happening.

Q: Is this something that can go on over quite a long period of time?

S: Oh yes – one would imagine right up to the last moment, as it were, so long as there is a conditioned being to react at all, though presumably the reactions would be on ever higher and more subtle levels. There can of course be physical symptoms. A quite well known one is diarrhoea. This is well known in meditation centres.

Q: I thought it was the food!

S: Well, apparently not.

Q: So if you experience unpleasant sensations in the course of meditation that's really nothing to worry about.

S: Broadly speaking, it's nothing to worry about. Nausea is a quite common symptom. But it is possible on occasions that one is practising wrongly and is therefore experiencing physical symptoms; especially if one is over-tense, one may experience headaches or tensions in different parts of the body. That means that one is practising wrongly, and one should adopt a more relaxed attitude.

Q: Would it be worth practising just sitting if you are experiencing that sort of tension?

S: It certainly wouldn't do any harm, but to practise just sitting if you are in a tense state isn't very easy. You might just start feeling bored. You need to be really relaxed to practise just sitting.

Q: What would you do then in a situation like that? I seem to get it more with visualization – sometimes if I'm trying to do things mentally without much feeling, I get very tense.

S: I think that headaches that come when one meditates can't be dispelled by a few words of advice about relaxing. It may be a question of a complete change in one's basic attitudes, one's whole way of life. If you are quite stiff and rigid, it may not be appropriate for you to be meditating yet. Maybe you even need some therapy first, to help you let go a bit and establish contact with your emotions. One has to go back and start right from the beginning, strengthen the psychological foundation, especially the positive emotions.

Q: Do you think it's helpful to do the *mettā-bhāvanā*?

S: Oh yes. But people who are really seriously alienated from their emotions are often quite suspicious of the *mettā-bhāvanā* and find it quite difficult or impossible to do, or else they believe that they're full of *mettā* and don't need it. They will tell you – if you suggest they ought to practise *mettā-bhāvanā* – that they experience *mettā* all the time. They have the idea of *mettā* – they know what the definition of it is and they agree with it – so they think that they have it, because they don't know the difference between a thought and an emotion. They really are extreme examples of alienated awareness.

Q: For milder cases, do you think the *mettā-bhāvanā* is effective?

S: Well, people have to get in touch with their emotions, and if they're alienated because they've got unrecognized negative emotions, it seems almost standard procedure that they have to get into contact with these negative emotions first and experience them and from the negative go on to the positive. I suspect that if you're blocked and alienated because you're refusing to recognize and experience negative emotions you can't go directly to the cultivation of positive emotions. I think you have to go through the experience of the negative emotions first – or at the very least acknowledge them.

Q: Is there any connection between these physical irritations we get and the psychic centres? I met someone who described what he got in his head as a sort of vortex of energy which was turning round and round.

S: I think it's quite suspicious if you start having experiences in the head without having them lower down first. You can experience a sort of dry, electric energy in the forehead, but that is not really a spiritual experience. It does sound a bit alienating. But people do have experiences in the psychic centres, as it were. They can feel bubbly or tickling sensations up their spine or near the heart or in the stomach and so on. This is all a sign of energy loosening up. If people are psychically sensitive they may have visions associated with these sensations. These are not of any great significance but in a sense they show that there's something happening, something being churned up, something loosened. If you're having such experiences, you should just carry on with whatever practice you are doing.
From a seminar on Milarepa's *Song of a Yogi's Joy* (1978, pp.83-6)

7 Discipline in meditation

1. TO DO IT AND WANT TO DO IT

One should be quite careful not to fall into the attitude that you shouldn't do anything unless you really want to do it because that would be a sort of hypocrisy.

> *Those who outwardly profess but do not practise religion may be mistaken for true devotees.*[61]

Sangharakshita: You can see where people who 'outwardly profess' go wrong. They are simply conforming for reasons which have got nothing to do with the actual following of the spiritual path.

Q: But can it sometimes be a good thing to do the right things for the wrong reasons? Is there a hope that the wrong reasons will transform themselves into the right reasons?

S: You can do things as a discipline. You're not fooling yourself. You know quite well that your motives are mixed, there's a lot of conflict. But at the same time you are convinced that if you can go through the motions sufficiently – and it isn't simply going through the motions, you're doing it because in the end you want to do more than just go through the motions – that will work, in many cases. If you don't feel like meditating, but you go and sit there anyway, very often after a while you *do* feel like meditating. A little block seems just to dissolve. So then you meditate. But if you never go and sit, of course you're unlikely to have that experience.

I think therefore that one should be quite careful not to fall into the attitude which I've sometimes heard people expressing that you shouldn't do anything unless you really want to do it because that would be a sort of hypocrisy. It wouldn't be hypocrisy if you were consciously meditating as a discipline, so that in the end you could both do it and want to do it. You've got to have both, in the end – to do it and want to do it – so it doesn't matter, in a way, which you start with. You can want to do it and then do it, or you can do it and then want to do it, because in the end you've got to have both.

It's a bit of a *micchā-diṭṭhi* (a wrong view) to say that because you want to be sincere you're not going to do something until you really want to do it. This assumes that you're a completely integrated person, and that you should only do something in a completely integrated way, which just isn't possible. You have to do things in a disintegrated way in the sense that part of you does whatever it is, and the rest of you catches up later, just as you may understand something long before you can practise it yourself. Does that mean that you should refuse to understand it, because you can't immediately put into practice what you understand? No. This is just the usual course of events. Sometimes we understand what to do and then develop a corresponding feeling which prompts us to act, and sometimes we do something because we understand that it is the right thing to do, and our feeling catches up later on.

So one shouldn't say 'I'm not going to get up and meditate in the morning because I don't feel like it, and I want to be completely honest and act in accordance with my feelings.' It would be better to say, 'I can't be fully involved all at once, because that would assume a very high degree of integration in myself. So I'm going to involve myself as much as I can. At least I'll be physically there; that will be a good start. And then I hope that sooner or later I will be emotionally and mentally there as well.'

Q: In meditation that's one of the most valuable things, I think – just to discover just how seldom you're emotionally and mentally there when you do it. If you're not doing anything else, at least you're sitting looking at yourself not being there!

S: Yes, right. You can at least say to yourself, 'Well, how extraordinary this is! I'm supposed to be thinking in terms of my spiritual development, I'm supposed to want to evolve, I'm supposed to want to grow. And of course I'm convinced that meditation is the quick and easy way to grow. But the strange thing is I don't want to meditate. I can't even concentrate. I can't even drag myself into the shrine-room very easily. I don't even want to get up in the morning. Isn't it astonishing, how paradoxical, how contradictory human nature is!' At least you can reflect in that way. 'Here I am, convinced that meditation is the royal road to Enlightenment, and I want to be Enlightened, but I don't want to meditate; why is this?'

There's this tremendous gap between understanding and emotion, for want of a better term. But we have to involve ourselves at some point and gain a foothold, and then gradually pull the rest of ourselves up on to that same level, as it were.

From the fourth seminar on *Precepts of the Gurus* (1980, pp.36-7)

2. NO NEED TO MEDITATE WITH CLENCHED TEETH

At all costs you need to associate meditation with feelings of interest and joy.

If you're just learning to meditate, perhaps starting to meditate on your own at home rather than with others in a class, and you're finding meditation difficult or not very agreeable, cut down the length of the session. Cut it down to ten minutes. It's important that you learn to enjoy it, because if you enjoy it and it isn't a strain or a struggle, the time will come when spontaneously you will sit longer and again longer. So, provided you keep up regularity and really try to meditate in the time you have, don't be afraid of just having a short meditation session rather than trying to sit for a whole hour and getting so fed up with it that you start dreading the approach of the meditation. It is much better to have a short sit and enjoy it than a long one that you don't enjoy because your knees are aching, your mind is wandering and you are tired. I think it is very important from the very beginning to associate the idea of meditation with the idea of enjoyment.

Even if you sit just for fifteen or twenty minutes and you really enjoy it, that is much better than sweating it out for an hour and a half, and developing almost a disgust for meditation because it is so unpleasant. I have often advised people who were having difficulty with their meditation and were going off it to shorten the period of meditation. Just sit for twenty minutes, and make sure that you enjoy it, because even if it is difficult and painful, the fact that it is only twenty minutes means you won't mind it so much and you will go more readily the next time. I think you have to be very careful that you don't develop an aversion to meditation by prolonging it in an unwise way and insisting on sitting on when your knees are aching and all the rest of it. In principle, it is far better to have a short meditation and enjoy it than a longer one just for the sake of a longer one. It isn't a longer meditation, it is just a longer period of forcing yourself to sit. For the average beginner, if you can keep up twenty minutes even, in the morning or evening, and enjoy it, that is quite enough. You will increase the period quite spontaneously sooner or later. You may not even realize that you have lengthened it. You may just look at the clock one day and realize that you've been sitting for forty minutes. That shows that you are making progress, because you are getting into it naturally.

But I think it's dangerous only to meditate if you feel like it. At least sit for a short time, even if it's only for ten minutes. Perhaps you could develop a practice of having a number of short sits during the day, which you enjoy and look forward to. Even if you aren't feeling like it, you'll think, 'Never mind, it's only ten minutes.' But if you're not feeling like it and think, 'Oh good heavens, I've got to sit for an hour', you will start to associate meditation with feelings of boredom and dread. That isn't good. At all costs you need to associate meditation with feelings of interest and joy. I am not in favour of the clenched teeth approach.

From a seminar on *The Forest Monks of Sri Lanka* (1985, pp.288-9) and a seminar on *The Jewel Ornament of Liberation*, 'Patience and Strenuousness (1980, pp.392-3)

3. REALLY ENJOY IT

Push yourself a bit over little humps and difficulties, don't pamper yourself, but meditation shouldn't become nothing but a grim driving of oneself.

Q: In relation to meditation, I know it's desirable to have a regular daily practice but of course you have good periods and bad periods. Should you push your meditation through the bad periods?

Sangharakshita: It depends on what sort of person you are. If you're one of these lazy easy-going people who gets up late in the morning, you need a bit more discipline, so you may need to force yourself a little bit to sit, or to try to concentrate a bit more. If on the other hand you are one of these over-conscientious dutiful people, you needn't bother so much. One general piece of advice would be that it's very important that you enjoy meditation. If you find that you've stopped enjoying meditation and you start dreading it and not looking forward to it, that is the time to consider your approach very carefully. It's best to cut down your period of meditation to a very short period which you faithfully observe and you enjoy, and only lengthen it as your enjoyment of it increases. It's quite dangerous to get into a situation where you don't enjoy your meditation. It's very important that you should enjoy and look forward to it, whether or not it's very regular, and whether it's for a longer period or a shorter period.

So if necessary don't be so ambitious, cut your meditation period down, but faithfully observe that as far as you can. Really enjoy it – that's the most important thing. It's better to have a short period that you enjoy rather than a long period, which won't be meditation anyway, that you don't enjoy. If you enjoy your meditation it'll start prolonging itself spontaneously sooner or later because you'll want to go on meditating. Sure, push yourself a bit over little humps and difficulties, don't pamper yourself, but meditation shouldn't become nothing but a grim driving of oneself. It should never become that.

Q: Wouldn't you say that the more you enjoy your meditation, the less of a challenge it is?

S: No, I'd say it's the other way around. The challenge is to go on to something further and not get stuck in the enjoyment, because enjoyment is not the last word in meditation, though it's an important part of it.

From Q&A in Christchurch (1979, pp.19-20)

4. THE PROBLEM WITH THE WORD 'MEDITATION'

I haven't met anybody yet who meditates in an over-disciplined, over-structured way, I have to say, whereas I've encountered scores of the other kind!

Q: Is there a danger of becoming too disciplined in meditation?

Sangharakshita: I haven't met anybody yet who meditates in an over-disciplined, over-structured way, I have to say, whereas I've encountered scores of the other kind! But if you are meditating, even supposing you are over-structuring it, you are meditating, and the meditation eventually contains its own antidote. You will not be able to go on structuring in that rigid way if you get on sufficiently with your meditation. The meditation itself will start loosening you up, so there's no real practical danger.

Q: Perhaps the problem is with the word 'meditation'. I've met Catholic priests who thought they had been meditating for years and years, but had no method of meditation to support that. They used the word meditation to refer to a half-hour session before the morning mass, but there was no kind of instruction at all. People were completely at sea. The session began with a few prayers but no one gave any guidance, and it seemed quite clear that no one was actually meditating.

S: When I use the word 'meditation' to refer to people practising meditation, especially within a group, I mean that they are practising according to proper instruction, that there is someone keeping an eye on them who will know whether they are really meditating or not. If there are these safeguards and they really are meditating i.e. entering into higher states of consciousness from time to time, any over-structuring in their way of life including their regular pattern of meditating will be looked after by the loosening effect of the meditation experience itself. So for anyone functioning within the framework of the Buddhist community there's no problem at all. We don't have to worry about that. Let them be as over-structured as they like. If they meditate effectively, the problem will be resolved almost automatically before long. In any case, hardly anybody tends to over-structure, it's much more the other way around. People need structure – in a positive way. Maybe in other circles over-structuring is a danger, but it certainly isn't for us. Under-structuring is the danger, a vague jellyfish-like drift.

From a seminar on *The Three Jewels* chapters 10, 13 and 15 (Aryatara 1977, pp.32-3)

5. REGULARITY IS VERY IMPORTANT

If you possibly can, see that your lifestyle permits you to sit and meditate at the same time every day.

Q: Given the amount of work most of us are involved in, could we meditate in a more systematic and effective way?

Sangharakshita: I think this is very much connected with the question of mindfulness. If you manage to keep up your mindfulness in the affairs of everyday life, when the time comes for you to sit and meditate you will be able to meditate more effectively. But if you are immersed in things and don't give a thought to meditation and don't even try to be mindful and then suddenly the bell rings and you drop everything, rush into the shrine room and sit down to meditate, you are not going to be able to meditate very well. You've got to keep up a thread of connection and if possible you've got to slow down a bit before the bell rings for meditation, as well as being mindful and aware during the whole of the day.

I think regularity is very important. In my own earlier days I certainly found this. If you keep up a regular practice – when I say regular I don't just mean every day, but the same time every day – when the time comes you will find yourself getting into that mood, that mental state, and you'll find it easier to meditate. So if you possibly can, see that your lifestyle permits you to sit and meditate at the same time every day. I think this is quite important for those who are as it were stationary. If your work obliges you to move around, then the situation is more difficult; you have to meditate when you can. But very often even when you're moving around you can plan your day in such a way that you can stick to the same regular meditation time. You usually manage to stick to the same mealtimes even when you're travelling around; why not the same meditation time?

From a seminar on the Past and Future of the Order (1985, p.19)

6. HOW MUCH MEDITATION IS GOOD FOR YOU?

Rather than thinking in terms of an hour or two hours one should ask oneself, 'Am I in contact with a different level of consciousness every time, or nearly every time I meditate?'

Q: How much meditation a day is good for you?

Sangharakshita: Well, as much as possible!

Q: Sixteen hours a day?

S: I think you need to do enough so that every time you meditate you can reach a really concentrated state. Of course, different people have different amounts of time available, and some people have their own particular difficulties with meditation, but I think that if you feel that your meditation is becoming just a routine and that you aren't having at least some inkling of an experience of higher consciousness, if you're not experiencing real concentration and emotional positivity whenever you meditate, you need to increase the amount of meditation you do each day. I wouldn't like to speak definitely in terms of so many hours – individuals vary so much, and people's conditions vary so much. One could say that one hour in the morning and one hour in the evening is a minimum. It would be very good if everybody could do that at least, but even that may not be possible in some cases. But rather than thinking in terms of an hour or two hours one should ask oneself, 'Am I in contact with a different level of consciousness every time, or nearly every time I meditate?' If you're not, you probably need to do a bit more or to do it more carefully, more mindfully – with a bit more preparation, less hurriedly and so on.

Q: Is this different level of consciousness a self-evident thing?

S: Oh yes, I think you'll recognize it as a state that you don't generally experience during the day when you're going about your various activities. You are more calm and more collected, more concentrated. There is a minimum of mental activity. You feel emotionally positive, clear, buoyant. It's a very recognizable state. And you should be in this state each time you meditate. You should end the *mettā-bhāvanā* feeling positive and exhilarated, with your emotional positivity radiating out towards everybody that you've been recollecting. It's not all that difficult really. It just requires fairly steady practice and reasonable general positivity. It's certainly not beyond the capacities of the average person; it's even possible for someone who is not really into spiritual life, in the sense of not explicitly recognizing a Transcendental factor in existence. Even if you look at it as a sort of mental or emotional hygiene, you can still do the *mettā-bhāvanā*. A non-Buddhist can do it. After all, it's just about your emotional attitude towards other living beings, including yourself. You could say that it's in a sense psychological, a very necessary foundation for anything in the way of spiritual life. And no one objects to being happy, presumably. You don't have to be a Buddhist to want to be happy.

Q: Do you think it's more difficult to take up meditation when you're older than when you're younger?

S: It's very difficult to generalize. Some young people get into it easily and quickly, and some old people do likewise. It seems to depend on factors other than age. Younger people can have turbulent energy which gets in the way, but older people can have more worries and responsibilities that get in the way.
From a Men's Order/Mitra event at Vinehall (1981, pp.41-2)

7. A TRACE OF JOY

I'm sure everybody has had the experience of sometimes going into the shrine-room for a meditation when you've just not wanted to meditate at all.

Sangharakshita: Why, when you don't feel like it, when you don't want to at all, do you get up in the morning and trot or stumble into the shrineroom and sit there and meditate? What is it that makes you do it? It isn't fear, surely.

Q: It's because you're committed. There's a sufficiently large part of you …

S: Yes. If even you're not yet a completely integrated person, quite a big part of you wants to do that, even though there's another part, a smaller part, hopefully, that doesn't want to do it. But could you say there was a joy sustained through all that, or at least a trace of joy?

Q: Sometimes you lose touch with the joy and then it seems like a hardship, and then you get back in touch with the joy.

S: Yes. It's like when you're driving a car and it gathers a certain momentum. If the engine cuts out, the car doesn't stop all at once. Momentum keeps it going forward, even though the engine is no longer running. You can keep moving, especially if you're going downhill, but you've got to get the engine started again before the car stops. It's rather like that. Even though you don't have any faith or any feeling of commitment at the present moment, or even any joy, the momentum from those feelings in the past is enough to keep you going, at least for a while. I'm sure everybody has had the experience of sometimes going into the shrine-room for a meditation when you've just not wanted to meditate at all. You may even have thought, 'It's just a waste of time, I'm not going to be able to meditate', but you've gone to the shrine-room anyway, and perhaps you had a good meditation, which made you glad that you stuck it out and did meditate, even though you didn't feel like it to begin with.

Q: When that's happened I've felt good in being able to overcome myself enough go into the shrine-room and sit down.

S: Yes. It shows that the resistance, the difficulty, is only superficial. There is a deeper level which you can contact if you can just resist your own resistance on that superficial level. The fact that you can have a good meditation even though you didn't want to meditate shows that. So it's important sometimes to give yourself a bit of a push, not just to succumb to what may well be a temporary lazy feeling of not wanting to meditate or not wanting to get up early in the morning or not wanting to communicate, whatever it may be.

Q: My experience is that when meditation is what I need most, that's sometimes when it's hardest to do it. When I know that what I need is to go and do the mindfulness of breathing, that's the last thing I want to do.

S: Well, you know the old proverb: 'If you can't, you must; if you can, you need not!'

Q: It seems very subtle, that resisting sloth gives you a joy and a resistance which gives you the push to enjoy what you thought you didn't want to do.

S: Sometimes when people haven't been on retreat for a long time and resist going, if they do go, afterwards they say that they'd not been on retreat for so long that they'd forgotten how good it was – and it's because they'd forgotten how good it was that they'd resisted going on retreat. It can be a bit like that with meditation: you can get out of touch with it, you forget how good it is, and so it presents itself to you in the light of some dull, routine chore, not a pleasure that you're free to engage in every evening but something that's got to be done, a sort of hardship. From that point of view, regularity of practice is important, to keep you in touch with the joy of it.

Q: I suppose it's the gravitational pull that makes it so difficult.

S: Yes there's that too, because one is not an integrated person; one is not a true individual. You say you are committed but actually it's only a very small part of you, the leading part perhaps but it still has to deal with all the resistance from the other parts of your being.

From a seminar on *The Jewel Ornament of Liberation*, 'Patience and Strenuousness (1980, pp.222-7)

8 Talking about meditation

1. 'WHAT DO YOU THINK I EXPERIENCED THIS MORNING?'

Meditation is an inner experience, and if you talk about it too much, you externalize it, and to that extent you almost lose touch with it.

Q: Why do you say that you're not keen on people talking about their meditation experience?

Sangharakshita: For several reasons. First of all, meditation is an inner experience, and if you talk about it too much, you externalize it, and to that extent you almost lose touch with it. You can even get into arguments with people about experiences. Sometimes you can become a bit competitive. That means that a slightly negative association clings to meditation or to the meditative experience. One must to be very careful about talking about these things because if you talk with people, there is always the possibility of disagreement. If you disagree over such things, quite negative emotions come to be associated with them, and that doesn't help you.

So, be very careful about who you talk about these things with and in what sort of situation. Don't announce at breakfast, 'Oh, what do you think I experienced this morning?', in a light sort of way. Take it quite seriously.

From Q&A on a discussion on Channel 4 (1984, p.10)

2. BECOMING AWARE OF THE DETAILS OF ONE'S PRACTICE

You should be quite sure that you are remaining aware, not getting carried away, and if you have any extraordinary experiences, not to be bragging about them.

Q: You've said that it's not a good thing to talk about one's meditation, but generally I have found that talking helps people to become more aware of the details of their practice. Would you still stand by what you said?

Sangharakshita: Well, I certainly think that talking lightly or in a casual way about meditation, just a little chat over lunch or something like that, is not a good idea. It might be that a serious exchange on the subject of meditation is helpful, especially in the case of the beginner who isn't sure what he or she is doing or should be doing next. But if one has got well into one's practice, talking about it can be a distraction. So I think one should be quite careful about that.

Q: I was thinking of talking to friends, somebody you know quite closely who has quite a deep interest in meditation.

S: Yes, no doubt the nature of the personal relationship has to be taken into consideration. It can result in a deepening of your communication. But I think one should still be mindful about how one talks about one's meditation experiences. You should be quite sure that you are remaining aware, not getting carried away, and if you have any extraordinary experiences, not to be bragging about them. Perhaps I am to some extent conditioned by my Indian background, because there people often talk very freely about their experiences in a way that clearly isn't very desirable.

Q: My observation is that people's experience of their own practice can be very vague and unformed.

S: Perhaps we are not talking so much about meditation as about efforts to meditate.

Q: Yes.

S: So it's not that someone has a meditation experience about which they can talk. When you question them about their meditation experience, they themselves may start realizing that actually they don't have much in the way of meditative experience, and that can spur them on to intensify and clarify their practice. That isn't quite the same thing as talking about meditation. It is more like, as I said, talking about one's efforts to meditate.

Q: But that seems to be the state of most people's practice.

S: Well, if that is the case, clearly talking about one's failure to meditate very deeply can be very helpful. It can perhaps help to arouse interest in the practice and give a greater sense of direction and greater clarity. Some people might for instance be genuinely under the impression that if you do a bit of wool-gathering during meditation it doesn't really matter very much. They might not realize that this can be stopped, if one makes a sufficiently determined effort.

Q: And to talk about it to someone else is quite often to admit it to oneself.

S: Sometimes I get letters from people saying things like: 'At last I am able to count from one to ten, three times in succession, without any wandering thoughts. It's the first time I have been able to do this for years.' A few people are aware in this sort of way, but in other cases, perhaps it is quite helpful to talk about one's efforts to practise with someone who can help one realize what is happening.
From a seminar on *The Forest Monks of Sri Lanka* (1985, pp.297-8)

9 Reflections on effort in meditation

1. THAT LAST DELICATE, SUBTLE EFFORT

When you sit for meditation, your effort should not be a great struggle against all the impediments that have accumulated in your mind.

Q: You've said that the *dhyānas* unfold quite naturally and effortlessly if we live ethically wholesome lives. Is that to suggest that more effort is required for preparation and indirect methods of development than for sitting meditation practices?

Sangharakshita: Yes. When you sit for meditation, your effort should not be a very forcible effort, a great struggle against all the impediments that have accumulated in your mind. With the help of the indirect methods and the proper preparation, you should have got your mind into such a state that you just need a little touch, that last, delicate, subtle effort, to enter into higher states of consciousness.

Q: But I thought you'd also said that meditation is the major manifestation of effort in the spiritual life?

S: Well, it is the practice of meditation that carries you further into the *dhyānas*. No amount of preparation in the ordinary external sense would carry you all the way into the fourth *dhyāna*. It might carry you into the first, but I doubt if it would carry you any further; a definite meditative effort would need to be made. But inasmuch as you had set up all the conditions beforehand, you could make that effort in a much more relaxed way. You would not be having to fight off a whole lot of hindrances which were the product simply of external circumstances.

From study group leaders' Q&A
on the Noble Eightfold Path (1985, p.148)

2. A STRONG DETERMINATION

It is a good practice to apply clear comprehension of purpose to whatever it is one is doing.

Q: I'm curious about the way the mind drifts away from the object of meditation, and then one regains mindfulness and returns to the object. Is it possible to say what is happening when one passes between these two states?

Sangharakshita: It should be possible to look at one's own experience and see for oneself. It might well differ from one person to another. These are sometimes quite complex processes.

Q: Although I can see in a general way what circumstances make me more likely to drift away, in a specific sense I find it completely unaccountable, both as to why I drift away and also how I manage to come back again.

S: There are several reasons of a general nature. In the first instance, a lot depends on the intensity of your initial sense of purpose. You may sit down without a very strong intention to meditate. It may have become a habitual thing; you just sit down and in a semi-mechanical, or maybe 90% mechanical, way, start meditating, but without a strong, clear, definite, even intense intention of meditating. So the very slight momentum, the very slight sense of purpose, with which you originally started is very quickly lost. Then again, regardless of the degree of intensity with which you formulate that purpose when you start meditating, there is the question of the degree of variance between that purpose on that occasion and the overall purpose, so to speak, of your whole life. If there is too great a variance between them, the overall purpose of your life, or rather overall purposes, because they may not be fully integrated, will start tugging away at that relatively minor purpose that you have set up for yourself for that period of meditation. And there is also the question of tiredness, because when you are tired your lower nature always takes over. This is one reason why you must not allow yourself to get really tired. It is very difficult to sustain anything new or creative, or to build up any new pattern, when you are tired.

If there is a combination of all three of these, obviously it is going to be very difficult to sustain your comprehension of purpose; even with one of them it is going to be quite difficult. So there are three things to which you need to pay attention. First, you have to be sure that the purpose that you set yourself when you sit to meditate is not too greatly at variance with the overall trend of your being. For instance, you should not sit down with the intention of meditating uninterruptedly for the next ten hours or even the next hour, if that is too much at variance with your present state of being and your overall intentions. Secondly, you should sit down with a very strong resolution, a very clearly formulated purpose of exactly what you are going to do, and a strong determination to do it. And thirdly, make sure that you are fully rested and not tired.

If you make sure of these three things, it would be very surprising if you were not able to maintain your clear comprehension of purpose. There probably are other factors, too, but these three are the most important. I am taking it for granted that you are free from external disturbance; that you have not just had a heavy meal (because that will tend to bring about drowsiness); that you do not have any great worries on your mind; that you are in a reasonably good state of health; and that you are not hungry. If you meditate regularly, it is very important to make sure that you sit to meditate with very clear, conscious comprehension of purpose, and a definite resolution to meditate, and meditate well, with all your energy.

Q: Are there any verses that could be chanted or recited before meditation that would be directly related to meditation itself?

S: One can, for instance, recite verses expressive of the shortness of human life, the rarity of the opportunity of a human birth, the difficulty of making contact with the teachings, to remind oneself as it were of the urgency of the situation. That would no doubt help.

Q: The Root Verses of the *Tibetan Book of the Dead* are very good for that, aren't they?

S: Yes, one could certainly use the Root Verses. In the Zen tradition they emphasize that you should meditate as though your life depended on it, as though someone was standing over you with a sword, ready to cut your head off if your mind started wandering.

Q: I suppose Zen monks got to a point where they did really feel like that.

S: Yes, I am sure they did, and perhaps still do.

Q: Do you think that's a healthy thing?

S: It depends on the circumstances. We must not forget that when the Buddha sat down beneath the Bodhi tree, according to legend, before his Enlightenment, he said: 'Flesh and blood may dry up, and my veins may wither, but I will not move from this spot until I have gained Enlightenment.' That utterance is typical of the sort of determination that is required.

If you do a daily meditation practice, the chances are that it will become a routine, and you will lose that strong, even intense, clear comprehension of purpose in relation to your meditation practice; so one has to beware of that. It is a good practice to apply clear comprehension of purpose to whatever it is one is doing. One will function much more effectively and happily, and get more done. That does not mean being goal-oriented in an obsessive, neurotic way; one must be determined but, strange as it may sound, in a relaxed way. Though perhaps on second thoughts, on certain occasions at least, it doesn't matter if you are keyed up and almost tense. One doesn't want to rule that out altogether. But you should start off in a relaxed way, and let your determination gather momentum as you get more and more deeply into the practice.

Q: Are you talking specifically of meditation now?

S: Not necessarily. Whatever you're doing, determination and intense comprehension of purpose should not be confused with hurrying or trying to rush things or being impatient or greedy for results, or anything of that sort.

From study group leaders' Q&A
on the Noble Eightfold Path (1985, pp.163-5)

3. WITH MINDFULNESS, STRIVE

If you mean to attain Stream-entry in this lifetime, everything of which you become conscious is significant.

The Buddha's last words, we are told, were *appamādena sampādetha* – with mindfulness, strive. *Appamāda* is a kind of zeal that never lets a single opportunity go by, a keenness to get on with the things that really matter in the knowledge that there is no time to waste. If you mean to attain Stream-entry in this lifetime, everything of which you become conscious is significant and you cannot afford to let it slip past. Conditions change continuously and as they change, any of the fetters, or a combination of fetters, is likely to get a grip on us. We have to strive constantly to be aware of whether our responses to input through the six senses, including the mind, are conducive to freedom or to bondage, whether our efforts (or lack of them) are making the fetters stronger or weaker, and whether or not our states of consciousness are conducive to our ultimate liberation. If you go for a walk, you have to be aware of the thousands of impressions that come crowding in on you, and know just what effect they are having on you. And you have to keep this up from instant to instant, minute to minute, hour to hour, all day and every day throughout the weeks, months, and years. There can be no holiday, no time out from mindfulness. You have to be ever-vigilant. And you must be vigilant not because any authority tells you that you must, but because the price of slackening off – an endless succession of rebirths in the six realms of existence – is simply not worth paying.

From *Living with Awareness* (2003, p.134)

4. THE DEGREE OF EFFORT NEEDED

You can practise anything if you make sufficient effort.

Q: I believe that in the *Visuddhimagga*, Buddhaghosa says that the mindfulness of breathing and the meditation on death are the only two meditation practices suitable for everyone, and that the other *kammaṭṭhānas* have to be applied to specific types of personality.

Sangharakshita: Well, that is Buddhaghosa's classification. We don't know where he gets it from, presumably from the commentarial tradition. I don't know that it has any basis in the Pāli canon, because I don't think the classification into temperaments has any basis in the Pāli canon. Perhaps we might say that those two methods are more generally suited to everyone, but that doesn't mean that there aren't other methods that can be practised by people of quite a number of different temperaments. I think we have to beware of rigidity.

You can practise anything if you make sufficient effort, regardless of temperament; it is just a question of the degree of effort that is needed. If you were of a hate type, you might say that the *mettā-bhāvanā* wasn't suited to you, but that's what you need, even though it's very difficult for you to practise it, and maybe someone of a greedy temperament will find it much easier. So what does one mean by saying that a person of a particular temperament can or cannot practise a particular method? It is almost meaningless. Inasmuch as everybody has some trace of all the poisons, every practice is suitable, but perhaps in different degrees. There is no one who is completely free from hatred, and therefore no one who doesn't need the *mettā-bhāvanā*, or to whom the *mettā-bhāvanā* is not suited. Is anybody really free from anger, or potential anger? They may be of a greedy temperament, but if you cross them enough times, they will become angry and resentful. It might be useful to look at this distribution of methods among the different temperaments with a critical eye, but I think it isn't to be taken too literally or rigidly.

From a seminar on *The Forest Monks of Sri Lanka* (1985, pp.281-2)

5. GROWING NATURALLY

The gaining of a higher meditative experience isn't by means of the very forcible application of a technique backed up by an egoistic will, but by a process of natural growth and development.

> *In the Mahāsaccaka Sutta, one of the great autobiographical discourses of the Pāli canon, the Buddha describes to the Jain ascetic Saccaka, whom he addresses by his clan name, the course of fearful asceticism to which he had subjected himself prior to the attainment of Enlightenment. After relating how the attempt had failed he continued: 'This, Aggivessana, occurred to me: "I know that while my father, the Sakyan, was ploughing, and I was sitting in the cool shade of the rose-apple tree, aloof from pleasures of the senses, aloof from unskilled*

states of mind, entering on the first meditation, which is accompanied by initial thought and discursive thought, is born of aloofness, and is rapturous and joyful, and while abiding therein, I thought: "Now could this be a way to awakening?" Then, following on my mindfulness, Aggivessana, there was the consciousness: This is itself the Way to awakening.' [62]

Sangharakshita: Earlier on the Buddha represents himself as traversing even higher *dhyānas* when he was under his teachers in his very early days, but he didn't manage to achieve the goal. But on this occasion, just before his Enlightenment, having failed to achieve the goal, despite practising under those teachers, despite achieving higher states of consciousness, he found the way just recollecting an early experience of his when he was a boy which had occurred spontaneously.

Now, what is the significance of this incident? In effect, that in those early days, he hadn't succeeded because he was trying to force himself. He had taken the practice as a sort of exercise and had decided that by sheer will power he was going to get there by doing the exercise. He did get quite a long way, but it was as it were only with part of himself. He pushed himself forward, but he wasn't really ready, so he sank back. He was on what I've sometimes referred to as the path of irregular steps.

What he had to do was to grow naturally, and this is what happened when he did finally gain Enlightenment. He sat at the foot of the Bodhi tree and he just recollected that experience of spontaneous bliss which happened when he was a boy, and thought, 'Is this the way?' When he asked himself that, I think he was referring not to the stage of meditation he had reached, but more to the manner and the method. Letting things grow naturally, encouraging and coaxing them, not forcing them by sheer effort of will – allowing the previous stage to develop, and on the basis of that moving into the next, not trying to push ahead more rapidly than was natural.

This incident shows that the gaining of a higher meditative experience isn't by means of the forcible application of a technique backed up by an egoistic will, but by a process of natural growth. Not that effort isn't needed – but it's a wise, gentle, smooth, regular effort, not a violent thrust of the will. This is very important in connection with meditation, because people often think of it in terms of an efficacious technique. You might think that if you have an intensive weekend and do forty hours, you'll get there forty times as quickly – but not at all. Certainly sometimes you need an intensive practice, but even that should be mindful. It mustn't have the thrust of the will in a narrow, negative sense. It will be a movement forwards of the whole being, or at least the greater part of the being should be following not too far behind the more advanced part.

The nature of this process is exemplified by the positive *nidānas*, as they're called. When one stage is fully developed, the next stage arises almost spontaneously. If you go through all these *nidānas* faithfully and fully, you will find yourself in higher states of consciousness almost without knowing it, almost without effort, so that as soon as you sit to meditate you are in such a positive frame of mind already that the concentration, say on the breath, will just put the finishing touch and there you are, in *samādhi*. But it's no use being in a totally different state all day and all week, turbulent, confused, craving, fearful, angry, and then sitting and thinking that by forcibly applying a technique and practising a method, you're going to get there. You may, but even if you do, you're just straining yourself and creating tension, because you're trying to create such a different state of mind from the one you've been in all day or all week. It's much better to go very smoothly and slowly, look after your mental state all day and nurse it, as it were, then when you sit to meditate, just develop your mental state in a natural, smooth way.

Q: It sounds marvellous, but if you're working all day it's very difficult.

S: Yes, sure.
From a seminar on *The Three Jewels* (Aryatara 1977, pp.84-6)

6. THE MIND ALMOST WANTS TO BE DISTRACTED

It's not as though Mara comes along with a big powerful temptation, offering you three beautiful lovers or a whole kingdom.

> *Since the tranquillity of Sunyata is the foundation,*
> *by forcefully turning your mind to Emptiness*
> *you chase misconceptions. In the thoughts which arise,*
> *understanding will come without doing anything.*
> *Again and yet again work on whatever estranges you from meditation!*
> *Lay bare whatsoever arises, good and bad thoughts alike!*
> *The child who knows his way carries along the path every harmless thing he happens upon and nothing that harms him.*[63]

Sangharakshita: 'Again and yet again work on whatever estranges you from meditation!' What do you think this means? What place does it occupy in the overall scheme of spiritual development?

Q: Is it the fetters?

S: Perhaps. But it's interesting that it comes after some experience apparently of *śūnyatā*, though clearly not a complete experience. You've had some glimpse, some experience even of *śūnyatā*, but the tendency is to become estranged from that. This is something that often happens. You have a higher, better, even a peak experience, whether on retreat or back home or at work, but the tendency is to become estranged from it. It doesn't last. Even if you've got the opportunity to continue with it, strangely, you don't take advantage of that opportunity.

There's a strange side of the mind that almost wants to be distracted. Even though it is enjoying that higher experience so much, any little foolish distraction is sufficient. It's not as though Māra comes along with a big powerful temptation, offering you three beautiful lovers or a whole kingdom; no, it's some silly little thing like a fly buzzing in the window to which you will direct your whole attention rather than that experience of *śūnyatā*. You become estranged from your experience because of the deep-seated almost primordial tendencies in yourself and it's these that have to be worked upon. It's a bit like the eightfold path, the path of vision and the path of transformation; these tendencies still have to be worked upon for a long time even after this realization of *śūnyatā*.

Hence the text that follows the reference to *śūnyatā*: 'Again and yet again work on whatever estranges you from meditation!' This means not so much meditation in the narrow sense but meditation as the means, the precondition, for this higher experience. Don't waste it, don't throw it away. Preserve it, cherish it. Set up the conditions that will enable it to continue. Don't allow yourself to be estranged from it. Take the tranquillity of *śūnyatā* as the foundation, the basis, and on that foundation bring about a transformation of your whole being, your whole existence, your whole life. This is made clear by what follows: 'Lay bare whatever arises, good and bad thoughts alike!' Negative emotions can't just be dismissed or ignored. You have to confront them, and this is where the Vajrayanic aspect comes in. The energy that is locked up in those negative emotions is your raw material. You can't alienate yourself from that. You'll have to deal with that, you'll have to come to terms with it, sooner or later.

From *Advice Given to the Three Fortunate Women* (1980 pp.24-5)

6 Insight and its relationship with *dhyāna*

1 Insight

1. TANGIBLE REALITIES

Insight meditation is designed to help you to experience the truths of the Buddha's teachings not just as religious or philosophical ideas but as tangible realities.

In the Buddhist tradition meditation practices are generally classified as being of two kinds: *samatha*, 'calming', and *vipassanā*, 'insight'. Through *samatha* meditation one develops mindfulness of the body and an ardent, energetic one-pointedness of mind, building up an intensity and subtlety of concentration on the basis of which a deeper, more far-reaching understanding can be developed. At this point you broaden the scope of your concentration by introducing some method of Insight meditation, designed to help you to experience the truths of the Buddha's teachings not just as religious or philosophical ideas but as tangible realities. The distinction between these two kinds of meditation is not as clear-cut as it is sometimes thought to be – the mindfulness of breathing, for example, is far more than a simple concentration technique.

From *Living with Awareness* (2003, p.8)

2. 'WITH MIND THUS COMPOSED ...'

You can't develop Insight with the same mind with which you carry on your work, or talk to your friends, or read books and newspapers.

With mind thus composed, cleansed, free from defilements, pliant and fit for work, remaining unperturbed he directs and bends it to the purpose of perfect Insight. In this way, he comes to know: This is my body, possessing material qualities, formed of the four elements, produced by father and mother, an accumulation of rice and fluid, a thing by its very nature impermanent, fragile, perishable, and subject to total destruction; and this is my consciousness, bound up with and dependent on it.[64]

This paragraph represents an extremely important point: the point of transition from *samādhi* to *prajñā*, from *samatha* to *vipassanā*. It represents the point at which Insight arises, or begins to arise. It's quite important to see or to realize that Insight can be developed only by a mind of a certain kind. With your ordinary, everyday mind you can't develop Insight. Your mind needs to be trained, or it needs to go through certain experiences first, represented mainly by the whole range of *samatha*-type experiences, especially the *dhyānas*.

In other words, the mind has to be prepared before Insight can arise. This is the important point. You can't develop Insight with the same mind with which you carry on your work, or talk to your friends, or read books and newspapers, or plan your day. In a sense it's the same mind but in a sense it isn't, because it's that much more highly developed and refined. Hence terms like 'composed, cleansed, free from defilements, pliant and fit for work'. It's as though the mind, by passing through the whole *samatha* experience, passing through the *dhyānas*, is cleansed and purified, and refined and made more pliable, and therefore able to develop Insight.

With that kind of mind you start seeing everything more clearly. And the first thing you see is your own body, because there you are, sitting, and you just realize the true nature of the body. You see that it's impermanent, and this is the point of this passage. This is not something to be taken negatively, it's quite a positive experience. You see that the body is impermanent, and you see that your usual, everyday consciousness is bound up with that body. You see how it is conditioned. So this is the beginning of Insight. You don't regard the body as a self, you don't regard it as unchanging. You see that the body is also a process – a process that has a beginning and an end. So you are less attached to it.

From a seminar on the *Samaññaphala Sutta* (1982, pp.164-5)

3. A DIRECT INTUITIVE PERCEPTION

Ultimately, Insight is something that transcends the intellectual workings of the mind.

Seeing conditioned existence, seeing life, as invariably subject to suffering, to impermanence, to emptiness of self, is called *vipaśyana* (Sanskrit) or *vipassanā* (Pāli), which translates into English as 'insight'.

Insight is not just intellectual understanding. It can be developed only on the basis of a controlled, purified, elevated, concentrated, integrated mind – in other words, through meditative practice. Insight is a direct intuitive perception that takes place in the depths of meditation when the ordinary mental processes have fallen into abeyance. A preliminary intellectual understanding of these three characteristics is certainly helpful, but ultimately, Insight is something that transcends the intellectual workings of the mind.

So in meditation, through Insight, you see that without exception everything you experience through the five senses and through the mind – everything you can feel and touch and smell and taste and see and think about – is conditioned, is subject to suffering, is impermanent, is empty of self. When you see things in this way then you experience what is technically called revulsion or disgust, and you turn away from the conditioned. It is important to note that this is a spiritual experience, not just a psychological reaction; you turn away not because you are personally repelled by things as such, but because you see that the conditioned is not, on its own terms, worth having. When that turning away from the conditioned to the Unconditioned takes place decisively, it is said that you enter the 'stream' leading to Nirvāṇa.

From *What is the Dharma?* (1998, pp.65-6)

4. WATCHING A LEAF FALL

In all Buddhist traditions, ordinary people with no cultural or intellectual gifts have gained Insight.

One could gain Insight into the truth of impermanence just by watching a leaf fall. In fact, people have done so. But what would the actual process be? How does one move from that experience to the universal truth of impermanence? It is probably not enough just to see one leaf fall. One must see another leaf fall, and another, and thus come to realize that all leaves fall. One doesn't just see the leaf fall; one's mind goes through certain conceptual processes.

One can develop Insight through visualizing an image of a Buddha or Bodhisattva, but one has to recognize the image for what it is. Insight arises through such a practice not because the image visualized is an image of the Transcendental, but because one sees it as both real and unreal. In the course of the practice the image comes intensely and vividly to life while at the same time one reflects that it has arisen in dependence on causes and conditions, and is thus not completely real. Reflecting in this way, one sees that neither the concept 'real' nor the concept 'unreal' is sufficient to exhaust the true 'reality' of the situation. 'Reality' transcends real and unreal, existence and non-existence. Thus the truth is realized with the help of certain conceptual formulations which on their intellectual level reflect the Transcendental reality they express. This is the traditional procedure. One doesn't go directly from perception to Insight; there is always the intermediate conceptual stage.

However, meditation is in itself a process of clarifying the mind. In fact, one can't separate meditation and clear thinking. In all Buddhist traditions, ordinary people with no cultural or intellectual gifts have gained Insight. In most cases they have done so having, through meditation, got rid of all mental one-sidedness, all biases, prejudices, preconceptions, and psychological and even cultural conditioning. Their minds can thus function freely and spontaneously.

Meditation includes not only *samatha-bhāvanā*, the development of calm, but *vipassanā-bhāvanā*, the development of Insight. By means of *samatha-bhāvanā*, by means of the experience of the *dhyānas*, one purifies one's intelligence so that it can recognize the conceptual formulations presented by tradition, or make its own conceptual formulations which then act as a springboard for the development of Insight.

Meditation – here I am using the term to signify a combination of *samatha* and *vipassanā* – is a union of purified emotion and clarified intelligence. In Buddhist terms it is *cinta-maya-prajñā* – 'the wisdom that comes from reflection' – combined with the emotional positivity of the *dhyānas* and the four *brahma-vihāra*s. This combination, intensified and raised to a higher level, is what brings about the arising of Insight. Hence Insight is as much an emotional as an intellectual experience. One could say that Buddhism is synonymous with these two things:

emotional positivity and intellectual clarity. At their highest level they are compassion and wisdom; and at that level the two, though distinguishable, are inseparable.

From *The Bodhisattva Ideal* (1999, pp.148-50)

5. THE AIM OF ALL BUDDHIST PRACTICE IS ULTIMATELY INSIGHT

You have to look actively for Insight into the true nature of things, but without looking for it in any particular direction or in any particular way. It is a sort of active receptivity.

> *In this way he abides contemplating the body as a body internally, or he abides contemplating the body as a body externally, or he abides contemplating the body as a body both internally and externally. Or else he abides contemplating in the body its arising factors, or he abides contemplating in the body its vanishing factors, or he abides contemplating in the body both its arising and vanishing factors. Or else mindfulness that "there is a body" is simply established in him to the extent necessary for bare knowledge and mindfulness. And he abides independent, not clinging to anything in the world. That is how a bhikkhu abides contemplating the body as a body.*[65]

The way Buddhist meditation practices are described can make it seem as though some of them are designed to develop concentration (*samatha*) while others are meant to develop Insight (*vipassanā*). In fact, though, all these practices are part of a single system of mental development leading towards higher states of awareness. The aim of all Buddhist practice is ultimately Transcendental Insight, and there is thus no need to draw too clear a line between *samatha* and *vipassanā* meditation. The process is essentially the same: you start by becoming aware of the aspects of existence most immediately apparent to you – your own body and its functions – and then you narrow the field of concentration in order to cultivate the *dhyānas*. This preparatory stage can take the form of the mindfulness of breathing, or the *mettā-bhāvanā* (the development of loving-kindness), or even a practice traditionally thought of as '*vipassanā*' – the six element practice, for instance. Whatever the method, you have to develop concentration as a first step if the reflective aspect of the practice is to be effective. Having narrowed the field of your attention to deepen your experience, you expand that field to increase the breadth of your vision, placing your experience of concentration, intensely absorbed as it is, within the broader perspective of *vipassanā*. Without these two aspects – the harmonization of consciousness and the cultivation of Insight – no system of meditation is complete.

How the effort to develop Insight within meditation is made is quite difficult to explain. You have to look actively for Insight into the true nature of things, but without looking for it in any particular direction or in any particular way. It is a sort of active receptivity: you are actively holding yourself open to Insight. These two aspects of the practice – receptivity to something outside yourself, so to speak, and an active searching – are equally important. The quest for Insight demands exertion – not intellectual exertion, but a meditative, intuitive searching: not trying to think your way to reality but trying to see it directly.

This is not to say that Insight will necessarily arise directly as a result of Insight practice. Sometimes it happens that you are trying too hard, or not in quite the right way. When you release that effort, the momentum of your practice may continue to build up and Insight may suddenly strike you out of the blue when you are doing something ordinary like peeling potatoes. There is no situation, whether positive or negative, pleasant or painful, in which Insight may not arise. All that is needed is mindfulness.

From *Living with Awareness* (2003, pp.33, 35-6)

6. SEEING THROUGH CONDITIONED EXISTENCE

It's like a flash of lightning on a dark night which shows everything, and then there's darkness again; but you've had that glimpse.

Sangharakshita: Sometimes you get the expression '*samatha* meditation'. Do you know what that is all about?

Q: It's the mindfulness of breathing, basically.

S: Yes, that's a *samatha* method, but what is *samatha* meditation?

Q: Concentration.

S: In what sense?

Q: In the sense of the mind being fixed on an object, whatever the object may be.

S: Has anybody else got any views?

Q: I thought *samatha* meditation was the whole practice of quietening the body and mind, as opposed to *vipassanā* which I've understood as a bit higher than that.

S: Yes, there is some truth in that. Strictly speaking, the basic, central meaning of *samatha* is meditation practice pertaining to the four *dhyānas*. Any meditation practice that aims at no more than the achievement of the four *dhyānas* is a *samatha*-type practice, i.e. one that does not aim, at least for the time being, at developing Insight or wisdom. Unfortunately in modern times the two types of meditation have become much too sharply differentiated, with the result that one has *samatha* without *vipassanā* and *vipassanā* without *samatha*, whereas really the *vipassanā* should grow quite naturally out of the *samatha*. You even get *vipassanā* or 'Insight meditation' teachers who don't bother about *samatha* at all. At worst, they just give you what are in fact psychological exercises, and a lot of strain and tension develops, and they then tell you that you have developed Insight into the truth of suffering!

 The classical Buddhist method – whether in the Theravāda or the Mahāyāna – is to have quite an extensive experience of *samatha* and then gently go on to *vipassanā*. *Samatha* meditation is what I call simply meditation. *Vipassanā* I usually now call contemplation. Or sometimes, if I use three terms, I say concentration for the preliminary stage, the stage of getting started, meditation for the middle stage when you are actually getting some *dhyānic* experience, and contemplation when Insight starts to arise. What we teach in our meditation classes – our mindfulness of breathing and our *mettā-bhāvanā* – is *samatha* meditation, though it's not *samatha* as sharply distinguished from *vipassanā*. Sometimes *vipassanā* may arise quite spontaneously without your knowing it in the sense of being able to describe it correctly in the traditional Buddhist terms.

Q: Could you say a bit more about the development of Insight? I'm very hazy about it.

S: In terms of very basic Buddhism – which ought to extend right into the Mahāyāna – Insight means the understanding of the unsatisfactoriness, impermanence and selfless (or un-ensouled) nature of conditioned existence. It means seeing through conditioned existence as it really is – not just as a mental idea, but as an actual living experience. This is Insight or *vipassanā*. For instance, if you see that everything is impermanent – if you really see that you are going to die – and if this is not just a little idea that means nothing to you but something that you really see, something that you feel and experience to such an extent that you cannot but act upon it, that is *vipassanā*. As I have already indicated, *vipassanā* has three major forms. When you see that everything mundane is unsatisfactory – that, try as you might, you are never going to lead a completely satisfactory worldly life – when you really see this and are utterly convinced of it, and behave in accordance with it, this is Insight into *dukkha*. The same with impermanence and with regard to no separate self-nature – which is much more difficult and abstruse and leads on into the Mahāyāna *śūnyatā* or voidness. When Insight is developed in any of these ways, there you are, in the Transcendental dimension.

Q: Is Insight sudden or gradual, or can it be both?

S: It depends on temperament. It can dawn on you gradually, as it were, or you can have a sudden terrifying flash which may or may not be repeated but which is in any case quite a shattering experience. It's like a flash of lightning on a dark night which shows everything, and then there's darkness again; but you've had that glimpse. *Prajñā* or wisdom is the same sort of thing, only it's daylight, as it were, and you just see steadily and clearly all the time, or most of the time.

Q: I wouldn't claim to have had specific moments of Insight, but at the same time, my entire attitude towards living and what life is has definitely altered in a very subtle way since I started meditating. I wonder if this is a kind of gradual process of Insight?

S: In a way, yes. Insight can be very diluted and general, rather than concentrated in these short, sharp, powerful flashes. It depends partly on the method of practice as well as on the surroundings and so on – maybe even on karma. But if one practises much meditation, there will be a definite subtle reorientation, which is not Transcendental, but which predisposes one to, and as it were softens the impact of, the Insight. If your life is rather uneven, and sometimes you're rather spiritual and sometimes not at all spiritual, then the impact of whatever flash of Insight you do get might be almost unpleasant, because there is a lot in your life which is completely out of tune with that. However, if you are more meditative, if you're leading an ethical life – practising right livelihood and observing the precepts – and if you are filled with devotion, then when the Insight 'hits' you it's a softer impact and it's spread through the whole being, and absorbed easily. In a sense you don't notice it very much, but if you look at yourself you certainly see that changes have occurred. The Insight was there, but it was present in this diluted, gentle sort of way, because that's the way in which you happen to be developing it. Other people might have a rather terrifying 'Road to Damascus' type of experience which is quite catastrophic.

It's important to get very clearly in your mind what *samatha* traditionally means and also what *vipassanā* means. But in teaching meditation I usually prefer simply to use the English words and speak in terms of concentration, meditation and contemplation – concentration and meditation covering *samatha* and contemplation covering *vipassanā* (Insight) and *prajñā* (wisdom). Probably that is the most straightforward usage. If we can avoid using Sanskrit and Pāli words it's better, and I think we can here.

From a seminar on *The Endlessly Fascinating Cry* (1977, pp.176-8)

7. A DIFFERENT SORT OF MENTAL ACTIVITY

This is the classic pattern: the concentration, the immersion in the thought-free state, and then the return to deliberate conceptual activity, and on the basis of that the development of Insight.

Sangharakshita: *Samatha* is usually translated as 'calm', and *vipassanā* means 'insight' or 'clarity'. *Samatha* refers to the experience of the *dhyāna* states, because it's the pacification of all unskilful mental states and, in the long run, of thought processes. One has a state of mind – though it's more than a state of mind, you could say it's a state of being – in which all the energies are concentrated, they all flow together, they're all refined. You're in a state of emotional positivity and awareness. This is what is meant by *samatha*.

But *vipassanā* is Insight into existence itself, or you could say Reality itself. It's not just an experience of conditioned existence in a highly refined state; it's an understanding or realization of or Insight into its true nature. This comes as a result of a certain kind of mental activity, which becomes the basis or the support of your Insight. But no mental activity is possible beyond the first *dhyāna*, so what does that mean?

Q: It means you've got to get to quite a concentrated state and then just let yourself come back ...

S: Yes, right. Inasmuch as *vipassanā* has for its basis a certain kind of conceptual activity, and inasmuch as that conceptual activity is incompatible with any of the *dhyāna* states beyond the first, after experiencing those higher *dhyāna* states you have to allow yourself to come back into the first *dhyāna* state, and deliberately start up that skilful conceptual activity which can function as the basis for the development of *vipassanā*.

So what then is the function of that *samatha* experience beyond the first *dhyāna*? Its function is the transformation of the conditioned being, to become more and more positive and refined, and therefore more and more amenable to the transforming influence of Insight. What happens is, when you're meditating, you get very deeply concentrated. First of all there's a certain amount of mental activity, but after a while there's no mental activity, and for a while you stay in that state. Maybe you get more and more deeply into it. That only lasts for a while; there's a sort of gravitational pull that brings you back. But once you've been through those higher *dhyāna* states, there's a certain effect on your whole being. It's more rested, as it were; it's as though you've had a really good sleep – in a sense, though of course you're fully aware and fully conscious. You're refreshed, your emotions and your energies are all straightened out, you're very calm, you're very aware.

And then, in the midst of that, you can start up mental activity in a completely deliberate, free way, a very positive way, and you can generate certain reflections about the nature of existence which then become the basis for Insight. You actually see the import of the thoughts which you are then having. But you have only those thoughts, because as the result of your immersion in the *samatha* experience, you are so concentrated, so balanced, that you have only the thoughts that you want to have. For instance, you might take up a certain line of thought about *śūnyatā*, based on your study of the texts – that *śūnyatā* is like this, that it's like that. But since you are now in a highly balanced, positive, skilful, aware state of mind, when you start up these mental activities, there can develop an actual Insight. And that Insight will have a further transforming effect on your whole being. In fact, if the Insight is sufficiently intense and powerful, it will have a permanently modifying effect on your whole being.

So this is the classic pattern: the concentration, the immersion in the thought-free state, and then the return to deliberate conceptual activity, and on the basis of that the development of Insight.

Q: Is it possible to experience *vipassanā* without a strong basis of *samatha*?

S: This is a question that has been much discussed, though I suspect not so much by people who actually meditate. There is a movement in some parts of the Theravāda world today which maintains that there is such a thing as 'dry' *vipassanā*, that is, *vipassanā* that arises on a purely conceptual basis, that conceptual basis not having the support of a prior *samatha* experience. Some teachers, though, disagree about this. Some of those who uphold the possibility of dry *vipassanā* maintain that the *samādhi* experience that precedes it, which they admit must be there to some extent, is instantaneous. But the broader, or even the older, tradition does not uphold that, in my view, because the essence of the matter is that the *samatha* experience so pervades your being that it is straightened out, it's made more positive and more refined, and this is the work of much more than an instant.

It would be highly unusual to have one great big *samatha* experience and then on the basis of that, one great big *vipassanā* experience, and that's that. Usually you're working away on both of them, and *samatha* alternates with *vipassanā*. This is the traditional method. Not necessarily in the same session or the same sitting, but over a period of time, in order to strengthen your *vipassanā*, your Insight, you repeatedly plunge yourself into the *samatha* experience, and on the basis of that, you can strengthen whatever *vipassanā* you were able to develop before. Then, having developed some *vipassanā*, it becomes easier to attain an experience of *samatha*, because the distractions that would otherwise prevent you from enjoying the *samatha* experience begin to be cut off or at least to be weakened. The stronger your *samatha*, the stronger your *vipassanā*; and the stronger your *vipassanā*, the stronger your *samatha*. The aim is in the end to get them both coinciding, as it were, at their peak. You've got the fullest possible experience of *samatha*, and on the basis of that you put the finishing touches to your experience of *vipassanā*; in that way the *vipassanā* experience itself also becomes complete. And then, of course, you can enjoy *samatha* experiences at will. It's not so necessary to enjoy them as it was before, but it's pleasant and you might as well have a pleasant experience as not. But the *vipassanā* experience is inseparable from a certain amount of *samatha* by its very nature. As some of the unskilful mental states have been permanently cut off, in a sense you're in a meditative state all the time, though you may not be actually sitting cross-legged with your eyes closed.

This whole idea of dry *vipassanā* seems to me highly suspect. I really doubt whether such a thing is possible. I think that what has happened is that some people have confused the recollection with the ordinary wandering mind of certain doctrinal categories with the deliberate construction of the conceptual basis for *vipassanā* after a period of immersion in the *samatha* experience. Thinking about the Dharma prior to *samatha* experience is rather different, in fact very different, to thinking about the Dharma after you have immersed yourself in the *samatha* experience. It's that immersion that makes all the difference. But there are in the East many scholarly monks who know their texts very well, but who don't meditate, and they seem in some cases to have confused *vipassanā* with simply the recollection of the things that they have learned and the turning of those things over in the mind and understanding them intellectually. I think this is what has happened.

Q: Can you have an intellectual understanding without an emotional aspect?

S: Oh yes. There can be understanding with no emotional correlate, with no support from positive emotional states. It can be then quite alienated. You really sense this when you read some articles on Buddhism. Some of them are almost as if they were written by machines, they're so scholarly and dry. It's as though Buddhism means nothing to the authors personally. They might just as well have written a statistical study or a treatise about earthworms or the degrees of stress in metals. There's no more feeling to it than that.

But, to give some sort of idea of this sort of thing in ordinary experience, you might find one day that you're quite naturally, quite spontaneously, in a very 'deep' mood. You might feel quite calm. Perhaps it's the evening, and you feel naturally very calm and still, and it's as though your thoughts, except you don't have any thoughts particularly, are just going deeper and deeper. It's as though you yourself are becoming deeper and deeper. You might start thinking about something that interests you, not in a hasty, compulsive way, but calmly and quietly going into it. And then you think, 'Ah yes! I understand that now. That's what it was all about.' The *samatha-vipassanā* experience, on a very much higher level, is rather like that. There's that period of calm and depth preceding the actual Insight or understanding, in a way preparing the ground for it or leading into it.

From the fourth seminar on *Precepts of the Gurus* (1980, pp.17-9, 23-5)

8. THOUGHT PROCESSES ARE OF THREE KINDS

One mustn't think that in the Enlightened person there's no mental activity. The Buddha clearly was mentally active, otherwise how did he think, how did he speak? But it's a different sort of mental activity.

Cessation of thought processes may be mistaken for the quiescence of infinite mind, which is the true goal.[66]

The cessation of thought processes which comes about as you pass from the first to the second *dhyāna*, and which is a characteristic of all the *dhyānas* other than the first, cannot or must not be mistaken for what this text calls the 'quiescence of the infinite mind', which presumably, as it's said to be the true goal, is Reality itself. There is a possibility of misunderstanding here. One mustn't think that in the Enlightened person there's no mental activity. The Buddha clearly was mentally active, otherwise how did he think, how did he speak? But it's a different sort of mental activity. Mental activity is made use of as an instrument, so to speak. It is not compulsive. When there's no need for it, it just stops. One can't imagine that when everybody had gone home and the bhikkhus had all gone to bed or gone off to meditate, the Buddha's mind was still ticking over as a result of what he'd been saying. Unless he chose to follow up some particular line of thought, mental activity ceased, and he just enjoyed a state free from mental activity in a completely natural manner.

So it is not to say that mental activity is excluded from the experience of Enlightenment, but when there is no need for mental activity, it ceases. At the same time, it is not the ordinary mind that is using thought. The ordinary mind is used by thought; in fact it *is* thought. But in the Enlightened mind, thought arises out of your potentiality for thought in response to certain needs. You've no interest in thinking, you don't particularly want to think, but when occasion arises you can do so.

In other words, thought processes are of three different kinds. There are the thought processes that we usually experience, that is to say rather distracted, broken, fragmentary, confused thought processes connected with sense experience, mental experience, memories, dreams, desires. These thought processes persist in a subtle form even into the first *dhyāna*, at least with reference to the concentration practice itself, but disappear by the time we reach the second *dhyāna* – or rather, their disappearance constitutes entry into the second *dhyāna*. These thought processes are very rapid, very confused. So this is what we mean by thought processes in the first sense.

Then there are thought processes which we deliberately develop after emerging from the experience of the higher *dhyānas*. These are completely directed and under our own control, and they function as a basis for the development of non-conceptual Insight. In this state, owing to our experience of the higher *dhyāna* states, we are so concentrated, so emotionally positive, that we've no need to think; there's no question of all that confused mental activity that we had before. We can choose to think, we can choose what to think about, and we choose to think about Reality, we choose to think about the Truth, we choose to try to understand certain things and to that end follow a certain line of thought in a very meditative, reflective way, getting deeper and deeper into it. In this way, we use thought processes as a support for the development of Insight. So this is thought processes in the second sense.

And then, Insight having been developed, or even Enlightenment itself gained, the thought processes can become a means of communication of the Insight or the Enlightenment experience to other people who have not had that experience.

So there's in the first place thought processes as hindrances or distractions; secondly, thought processes as a support for the development of Insight; and, thirdly, thought processes which are related to conceptual expression of Insight or Enlightenment. If you're thinking, 'What am I going to do tomorrow, and will I have enough money?', those are thought processes of the first type. Even if you're thinking, 'My meditation's going quite well now', that's still a thought process of the first type. But if, having deeply meditated and being free from thoughts arising, you think, 'What does *śūnyatā* really mean?', that is a thought process of the second kind. And if, as a Buddha, you speak with regard to your experience using thoughts and words, that is a thought process of the third kind.

One mustn't think of infinite mind as quiescent in a literal way. There's no compulsive, confused mental activity, nor even any thought processes of a supportive kind; but it's not as though there is no mental activity at all. One can see from all this that meditation is far from being a matter of just making the mind a blank. In fact, you can't do that; you can't become like a stone.

Q: It's a lot more dynamic.

S: It's more dynamic, and it's also more truly calm. There's also the point that you can't really have much of a concept of the true goal. You shouldn't be too positive about what it's going to be like when you get there; that would be appropriation. Sometimes you can be taken unawares. When you're meditating, a quite unforeseen experience might arise, an experience which you might not only have not expected but which might be actually contrary to your idea of what was to be expected.

From the fourth seminar on *Precepts of the Gurus* (1980, pp.19-21)

9. A CALM AND GENTLE AURA

It is a breaking through, yes, because there's a definite obstruction and resistance but you don't break through forcibly. You break through gently ...

> *During the time of insight which is surrounded by a calm and gentle aura openness and appearance are inseparable.*[67]

Sangharakshita: Insight corresponds to *vipassanā*, as distinct from *samatha*. *Samatha* literally means 'calm', and refers to the experience of concentration, the experience of the four *dhyāna* states or states of higher consciousness, whereas *vipassanā* or Insight refers to Insight into the true nature of existence, in this context especially Insight into *śūnyatā*. The traditional procedure is that first of all by means of one or another concentration technique, you develop *samatha*, especially the four *dhyāna* states and then on the basis of that concentrated, purified and elevated mind you develop Insight. You make the *samatha* experience your basis for the arising of Insight – or, in more Mahāyāna terms, wisdom.

The text describes the time of insight as being surrounded by a calm and gentle aura. What do you think is meant by that? What is this aura? The translation is quite literal and accurate, presumably. It's not simply the aura of the *dhyāna* state; it's as though the insight itself has an aura. Insight has a permanent transformative effect on the whole of one's conditioned being, and this permanently transformed mundane or conditioned being surrounds the Insight like an aura. Insight arises in connection with your psycho-physical personality but inasmuch as that personality now 'houses' Insight, it becomes a sort of aura of the Insight. It isn't simply that the aura of *dhyāna* surrounds the insight. The insight suffuses or permeates the *dhyāna* state itself. 'Calm and gentle' also suggests that Insight isn't violent. The word *vipassanā* may suggest a piercing or a penetrating, but don't take that literally.

Q: Then why in other contexts do we talk in terms of breaking through like Vajrapani?

S: Again, you mustn't take it literally. Or rather, take it literally by all means, but in the right way. Don't think of it as forcible in the literal sense. It isn't a literal using of power. It is a breaking through, yes, because there's a definite obstruction and resistance but you don't break through forcibly. You break through gently – at least in a manner of speaking – but from another point of view neither violence nor gentleness has any meaning at that level. It's a different mode of operation. When a beam of light passes through glass, does it break through violently? No, it goes straight through. A stone might break through violently, but not a beam of light. It's rather like that. In a sense the beam of light is more powerful than the stone but it goes through the pane of glass gently. It doesn't crash through like a stone.

From a seminar on *Advice Given to the Three Fortunate Women*
(1980, pp.27-9)

10. INTELLECTUAL UNDERSTANDING AND INSIGHT

If the Insight is sufficiently powerful, sufficiently penetrating, then it has a transforming effect upon your whole being, and you will never lose that.

What makes the difference between a purely intellectual understanding and the direct penetration which is of the nature of *vipassanā*? Basically, Insight involves a unification of all the energies, especially the emotional energies and most of all the positive emotional energies. This is what makes the difference and this is why you practise meditation before you try to develop Insight. When we try to penetrate into things intellectually, usually the mind is quite scattered. There are all sorts of pulls from various levels and aspects of the being. So meditation, from this point of view, is a gradual unification of all the energies of the unconscious as well as of the conscious mind, bringing them all together, heightening them, making them more and more positive, more and more powerful, gathering all those energies into a single channel, and then putting that energy behind your efforts to understand, to penetrate, to see. This is what makes the difference. Without meditation to back it up, intellectual understanding remains just intellectual understanding. It doesn't develop into Insight or *vipassanā*.

This is why the usual procedure is that you spend a period practising what is called *samatha*, 'calming down' – though this is a rather misleading term in a way. It's only a calming down of unskilful mental states; it's a raising up of all the skilful states, an actualizing of all the positive potentialities of the mind. Then, when you are feeling emotionally very positive – when you are experiencing strong *mettā* or strong *karuṇā* or strong *muditā* – so that your mind is in a very powerful, buoyant, malleable condition, you direct that mind to understanding and seeing.

What you get then is a quite different sort of experience, not just an intellectual understanding but an actual experience, an actual vision or Insight. You can just look or just try to see with that concentrated mind, or, to help yourself, you can recall some of the teachings or doctrines of Buddhism which are intellectual or conceptual supports for the development of Insight. You can for instance take a very simple one like 'all conditioned things are impermanent'. You certainly understand it – you have an intellectual understanding of it which is quite thorough, quite comprehensive – but when you call to mind the truth that all things are impermanent with a concentrated mind, with all your energies behind the understanding, then the understanding is transformed into an Insight, which is an experience, and if the Insight is sufficiently powerful, sufficiently penetrating, then it has a transforming effect upon your whole being, and you will never lose that. Intellectual understanding, by contrast, is very easily lost and in any case doesn't have that sort of powerful, transforming effect.

So this is the difference that meditation, in the sense of the heightening and the concentrating and the making more positive of one's energies, makes. It enables you to make the transition from intellectual understanding to what we may call a spiritual Insight or spiritual vision. If you haven't got any idea about meditation, if you don't understand its function, then it'll be impossible for you to understand the difference between intellectual understanding and spiritual Insight. Spiritual Insight would appear to you just as another kind or another degree of intellectual penetration.

Traditionally meditation is usually divided into two kinds or two levels. There's *samatha*, which literally means calm, and consists in the experience of the *dhyāna* states, the states of superconsciousness, where one's energies become progressively more unified, where one becomes emotionally more positive and buoyant, and *vipassanā*, in which you use that heightened and intensified positive consciousness to launch yourself into reality itself in such a way that you develop a spiritual Insight. In the Theravāda tradition and in the older Buddhist tradition generally, these two were kept separate. They were two distinct kinds of practice – the *mettā-bhāvanā*, for instance, being considered to be a *samatha* practice, and the six element practice a *vipassanā* practice. In the Mahāyāna, and especially in the Vajrayāna, the two tend to be much more unified, so that if you do a visualization practice in the full manner, you usually get some experience of both *samatha* and *vipassanā*.

But unless you understand how the experience of a higher level of consciousness puts much more impetus behind your understanding, so that it becomes transformed into Insight, you'll never understand the difference between intellectual understanding and spiritual Insight. For example, in Trevor Ling's account of the Buddha's life, he speaks of the 'intellectual penetration into the nature of the human situation which the Buddha then achieved'. Well of course it was very much more than that. Just intellectual penetration would never have been sufficient to transform Siddhartha from an ordinary human being into an Enlightened human being or a Buddha. It's very important to understand this; it's a crucial point.

In the *dhyāna* states, the hindrances are temporarily suspended, but once you come out of the *dhyāna* state, you are again susceptible to them. But once you've seen through them, as it were, once you've seen into the real nature of things, through the spiritual Insight of *vipassanā*, then, depending upon the strength of the *vipassanā*, the hindrances are permanently destroyed. The fetters are permanently broken, and then you attain Stream-entry, and after that you can't ever fall back. You may not make any further progress in this life, but you'll never fall back, you'll never regress. If you have only experienced *samatha*, you may go right back to the beginning; you can commit any crime or indulge in any kind of unskilful action. But once you've become a Stream-entrant, once you've passed as it were the Point of No Return, you may not make any further progress in this life, but what progress you have made can never be undone. That is a permanent achievement, something on which you can build thereafter.

From a seminar on Trevor Ling's *The Buddha* (1976, pp.223-5)

11. A TOTAL EXPERIENCE

You don't really approach the Transcendental either from the intellectual angle or from the emotional angle.

The terminology of Insight is cognitive, but it could just as well be emotive, so you don't really approach the Transcendental either from the intellectual angle or from the emotional angle. When you experience the Transcendental, you don't experience it just with your intellect or just with your emotions. It's a total experience. It affects all of you. But then in accordance with your temperament, your cultural background and so on you may express it in predominantly cognitive or predominantly emotional terms. It's not that the Insight experience itself has either an intellectual or an emotional basis. It isn't a one-sided thing.

From a seminar on *A Survey of Buddhism*, chapter 1 (1982, pp.182-3)

12. CERTAIN CHANGES ARE GOING TO TAKE PLACE

Sometimes you need time to absorb whatever experience you may gain as a result of the *vipassana* practice, and you don't want to have to turn your attention to practical matters while that process is going on.

Sangharakshita: There's not much point in trying to develop *vipassanā* via a *vipassanā*-type practice unless there is a quite solid foundation of *samatha* to begin with. Also, usually one needs to be comparatively secluded, because if you are really going to develop *vipassanā*, that means that certain changes are going to take place in you, certain bits and pieces of your ego, as it were, are going to be permanently dismantled or at least chipped away at, and that can be quite a devastating experience. While you are going through that, you shouldn't have to be attending to other things. I would suggest that unless you are very firmly established in *samatha* practice and are quite a stable sort of person, you should confine *vipassanā*-type practice to retreat situations, when you can be quite sure you can devote the necessary time and attention to that, and any possible repercussions.

Sometimes you need time to absorb whatever experience you may gain as a result of the *vipassanā* practice, and you don't want to have to turn your attention to practical matters while that process is going on. You should be relatively free or even, if possible, completely free, at such a time. It usually means cutting off contact with other people and external activities.

From a seminar on Trevor Ling's *The Buddha* (1976, p.226)

13. WON'T INSIGHT ARISE NATURALLY?

The artistic vision comes quite close to Insight in the Buddhistic sense.

Sangharakshita: Insight is the vision of the whole person, not just of one part, or one level: not just a vision of the rational mind. When you are completely unified and all your energies are flowing together, you're much more of a total person, and not just on the same level you were before, but a much higher level. And what that total person sees is of the nature of Insight. This is sometimes where the artistic vision comes quite close to Insight in the Buddhistic sense. The artist is, at least to some extent, someone who is much more unified, and on a much higher level than the ordinary person. When I say 'artist' I don't only mean the visual artist, of course, I mean the poet or the composer and so on too.

Q: If one continues with the practices, continues raising one's level of consciousness, doesn't it follow naturally that one will develop Insight?

S: Not necessarily. *Samatha* meditation is the unification of all the energies of one's being with the accompanying positive emotions and spontaneity, at higher and higher levels. And then arises the possibility of developing *vipassanā*, but that doesn't come, as it were, automatically. According to the Buddha's teaching, you have to make a conscious and deliberate effort to develop it. But if you make that conscious and deliberate effort on the basis of *samatha* experience, then you are almost bound to succeed, depending upon the strength of the *samatha* experience and the solidity, as it were, of that base.
From a seminar on Trevor Ling's *The Buddha* (1976, pp.227-8)

14. WHEN CAN ONE STOP MEDITATING?

If you can be sure that you have got some definite Insight, you don't need to sit and develop *samatha*.

Q: So far as I understand, you yourself do not meditate in the sense of practising a formal sitting meditation on a daily or even regular basis. Is this true? If so, when did you stop, why did you stop, and on what grounds did you feel confident in taking that step?

Sangharakshita: This goes back to some of the things I've said about *samatha* and *vipassanā*. If you develop any degree of genuine *vipassanā*, you cannot lose that. The question then is simply of developing that Insight. If you can be sure that you have got some definite Insight, you don't need to sit and develop *samatha*, unless you feel that your Insight is very weak, in which case you have to develop *samatha* in order to put more concentrated energy behind that *vipassanā*. For some years now I have felt that I was quite easily able to go on deepening my Insight without recourse to a deeper experience of *samatha*, so this is what I now do. One can go back to *samatha* from time to time if circumstances require, but it has ceased to be necessary as a support for the further deepening of *vipassanā*.

Q: Does that mean that the *vipassanā* for you is deepening in a way of itself?

S: No, I wouldn't say that, but I can work on it without having been in that more deeply concentrated state which is represented by *samatha*. For instance, if I wake up in the night, I can work on it, I don't need to sit up. Or if I am sitting in my chair I can work on it; sometimes I do this in the early morning. I haven't said very much about this for obvious reasons! I don't want to discourage those who need to meditate from meditating.

Q: When you talk about working on your *vipassanā*, presumably you don't mean discursive thought about Insights that arise in you?

S: Discursive thought can certainly be a basis for the development and deepening of *vipassanā*. You can deepen it by extending a particular Insight to a wider range of objects, or have a deeper Insight into the same thing. For instance, you could take up the topic of impermanence or death; you can go on deepening and broadening your realization of that all the time. In a way there is no limit. But that's the only excuse for giving up *samatha* meditation – that you can get on with your *vipassanā* without needing a deep experience of *samatha* to support it.
From a seminar on *The Forest Monks of Sri Lanka* (1985, pp.298-9)

15. HOW MUCH CONCENTRATION IS ENOUGH?

If you are developing real Insight, your reflection on say impermanence really grips you. That's quite a different sort of experience from a little gentle discursive mental activity.

Q: How would one judge when one had consolidated *samatha* sufficiently in order then to go on to more *vipassanā*-type practice?

Sangharakshita: Well, if you hadn't consolidated your concentration sufficiently, you would find that your so-called *vipassanā* would become a purely discursive experience, and you would eventually find your mind wandering, because your concentration wasn't sufficiently strong to sustain directed reflection, directed discursiveness, if I can use that expression. As your discursive reflection goes deeper and deeper, because it is supported by a quite strong *samatha*, you start feeling that you are understanding something, you are seeing something, in a way that you didn't see it before. That's quite a different thing from becoming more and more mentally active and in a way more and more scattered, which is what happens if the basis of concentration is inadequate.

If you are developing real Insight, your reflection on say impermanence really grips you. That's quite a different sort of experience from a little gentle discursive mental activity which gradually gets and more dispersed, so that after a few minutes you find yourself thinking about something totally different. If that happens, then you know that your basis of concentration is not nearly strong enough.

Q: So would you leave off attempting to develop Insight until, perhaps in a few years time, your practice was strong enough?

S: You might, or you could go back to the *samatha* and try to develop that, and then go back to the *vipassanā* when you feel that you have developed enough *samatha* to be able to do that. But if you did that a number of times and every time your mind wandered and became distracted, you could conclude that you need to do a lot more work on developing *samatha*, and put aside any attempt to develop *vipassanā* for a few months, or a year or two, and concentrate on developing *samatha*.
From a seminar on *The Forest Monks of Sri Lanka* (1985, p.274)

16. JUST SITTING QUIETLY

You don't necessarily have to be sitting cross-legged in the shrine-room, officially meditating, as it were.

Q: Would it be true to say that Transcendental experience would come in very short bursts?

Sangharakshita: It seems that this is what usually happens. You don't suddenly find yourself completely Enlightened. You get little glimpses at first. You may not even be sure whether they are real glimpses, or whether they are particularly refined mental experiences and theoretical understandings. It may be quite difficult at first to see where the one ends and the other begins, especially if the one is the vehicle or the support of the other.

But it can happen that while you're quietly thinking and reflecting, and developing a theoretical understanding of the truth of impermanence, if you are very quiet and clear, if the mind is very balanced, then on the basis of that you may get an actual Insight – not dramatically, but calmly, quietly, gently. So the turning over in one's mind of the fact of impermanence is certainly quite useful, especially if you do it in the context of meditation. After a period of meditation, when the mind is very calm, you can deliberately start up mental activity, exclusively on this topic. That mental activity, because it takes place within the context of, or on the basis of, the purified consciousness, can then much more easily act as support for Insight into the truth of impermanence or whatever you might be contemplating. This is the classic Buddhist method of *samatha* and *vipassanā*.

A preceding practice of *samatha*, mental calm, experience of the *dhyānas*, is assumed here. But even when you're not formally meditating, even when you're just sitting quietly, maybe with a cup of tea, just feeling very peaceful and reflective, and turning things over in your mind, you can be very calm and concentrated, and on that basis, if you reflect and consider in the right way, Insight can be developed. You don't necessarily have to be sitting cross-legged in the shrine-room, officially meditating, as it were. It may be that insights are developed more frequently in the shrine-room than elsewhere, but they are not limited to meditation. There are examples of monks having their illuminations while sitting on the toilet-seat, or chopping vegetables in the kitchen. On such occasions you may be quite calm and collected. Say you're just chopping vegetables in the kitchen. It's a nice day, the kitchen is quiet and peaceful, the sun is shining, maybe you've had a good meditation, your mind is quite fresh, bright and clear, and you're chopping away, and you just think, 'Well, in a sense everything has to be chopped up. Father Time is chopping into our life, it's all impermanent.' You can have an insight just like that. It can come quite unexpectedly. Maybe it's all the more likely to come because you are not looking for it. It's something that naturally arises out of your experience, it isn't artificial. And that is very often how it does come. Even if you just see a leaf falling when you're in the right sort of mood, it may mean much more to you than lengthy discourses on the impermanence of all conditioned things. You really do see that, yes, that leaf is falling, it's had its day and we're all like that. You see it very clearly, and it means something to you, and continues to mean something to you. You are permanently changed, not in a highly dramatic way, but your attitude towards life is subtly modified, which means that that experience was an experience of Insight. You need not consciously reflect, 'Ah! the truth of impermanence'. No! You just see that the leaf falls. And then it's a feeling that's with you all the time. One can't quite say that you're not conscious of it; you are, but not in an artificial kind of way. You don't have to say it aloud to yourself; you know it without that.

Q: Is it more than just a memory?

S: Yes, it's not just a memory, though you may have a memory of an insight when the insight is not actually present. But one can also say that the memory of an insight is to some extent an insight itself. How could you remember it unless you had some sort of contact with it? Even the memory of an insight is of the nature of Insight. Maybe not so powerfully as the original insight itself; but the time must come when all sorts of situations have these subtle associations for you. They don't exactly remind you of the truth of impermanence or any other truth, in a very 'conscious' way, but that subtle reminder is there, and you just see things, but in a natural way. When you're aware that the sun is shining, you don't say to yourself, 'Oh, yes, the sun is shining'. You're just aware of it shining. In the same way you're just aware that things are impermanent, and your whole attitude, your behaviour and your relations with people are modified accordingly.

Q: This question may seem naive, but is there not the danger, if you're just realizing, say, the truth of impermanence on the intellectual level, if you start thinking that everything is impermanent so nothing really matters, that you might start getting very dry and unfeeling towards people?

S: It's true that if you reflect on impermanence theoretically, so to say, you may end up rather dry in your approach. But the Buddhist tradition is that you cultivate *samatha*, one component of which is an immensely positive emotional state. So you take up the serious reflection on the truth, say, of impermanence, only when you are in that very emotionally positive state. Then you don't see it as something dry that detaches you from people in a negative way. You see it as something very inspiring, you see in it the possibility of change and transformation.

I think that somebody who wasn't practising meditation and wasn't seriously involved in spiritual life wouldn't bother to think about impermanence theoretically. If the thought did occur to him he'd probably dismiss it straight away. So I think it is probably the sort of difficulty that isn't very likely to arise. There are people who have a cynical feeling that nothing is worthwhile, but I think that comes not so much from deliberate reflection on impermanence, as from their negative emotional state. And meditation, of course, could change that negative emotional state.

From a seminar on 'Conditions of Stability in the Order' (1979, pp.61-3)

2 The relationship between Insight and *dhyāna*

1. DHYĀNA IS ESSENTIALLY A SKILFUL MENTAL STATE

Dhyana is not an end in itself, though it may be very satisfying. It's essentially a means to the development of Insight.

Q: If Insight is the main goal that you are aiming for, you don't really have any need to dwell in states higher than the first *dhyāna*, do you?

Sangharakshita: Well, yes and no. Even though you, so to speak, come down to the first *dhyāna* to develop Insight via reflection and discursive thought, if you have some experience of the higher *dhyānas*, your energies are much more behind that discursive thought, because they are much more unified.

One isn't trying to get into those higher states for their own sake, but to achieve a basis for the development of Insight. In order to develop Insight one needs very steady, concentrated, sustained thinking, and most people are not capable of that. Their minds are not sufficiently concentrated, there's not enough energy, not enough power behind their thinking. But if one has some experience of the *dhyānas*, if one's energies are much more collected, much more together, if one is much more concentrated, then it is possible to develop Insight by reflection, by discursive mental activity. So *dhyāna* is not an end in itself, though it may be very satisfying. It's essentially a means to the development of Insight.

Q: Speaking of the higher *dhyānas* in terms of god-realms and lasting a long while, that would imply that if you really wanted to get into higher states of consciousness in meditation, you would have to go away and devote quite some time to developing those states. When you sit to meditate every morning, you probably couldn't expect to zoom up into the higher *dhyānas*.

S: No, but one point that is made very strongly in the Buddhist tradition is that rebirth in these higher realms, these heavens, where *dhyānic* experience is natural, is, or can be, the result purely of ethical activity. Clearly it can be the result of meditation, but it can also be brought about just by ethical activity, ethical life, inasmuch as in order to act ethically you must be in a skilful mental state, and that skilful mental state is of the essence of *dhyāna*. Do you see what I mean? You mustn't think of meditation in a narrow sense, or even *dhyāna* in a narrow sense. Dhyana is essentially a skilful mental state. We call a skilful mental state a *dhyāna* when it is sufficiently prolonged, uninterrupted and intense. Meditation is just the gathering or re-collection of all those skilful mental thoughts which are normally present anyway, as the basis of our activity – that activity being, of course, ethical activity, or *śīla*.

It's as though for *śīla* to be possible, a meditative state must be present, in the sense of concentrated, prolonged and sustained skilful mental states. The point I'm making is that traditionally rebirth in the *brahmalokas*, for instance, is not regarded simply as the result of meditation, though of course it can be that, but also the result of an ethical life.
From a seminar on *The Buddha's Law Among the Birds* (1982, pp.44-5)

2. REALLY PUTTING MEDITATION INTO PRACTICE

The word Insight may sound intellectual but actually it isn't any nearer to what we know as intellect than to what we know as emotion.

> *Is not Nhamdog dissolving in the Dharmakāya*
> *Called spontaneous practice – a yogi's glory*
> *Confirming meditation principles?* [68]

Sangharakshita: This Tibetan term *Nhamdog* refers to the ceaseless flow of thoughts. I think – this is my guess – it must be the equivalent of the

Sanskrit term *cittadhārā*, which means almost a waterfall of thoughts, the constant flow or stream of thoughts. It also suggests distraction and mental disturbance because when you try to meditate and to be one-pointed it's this that disturbs you.

And what is the *Dharmakāya*? It is the highest spiritual reality, Transcendental reality, as actually realized and in that sense as having become the 'body' in inverted commas of the person realizing it. If you realize something you incorporate that, you assimilate it, you embody it, so in that sense it is your body. The *Dharmakāya* is the highest reality as realized by you and therefore has become your body. It's not abstract. That's why one speaks of the *Dharmakāya* of the Buddha, but not the *śūnyatā* of the Buddha, because *śūnyatā* is an abstract term, so to speak. Of course it's only a Buddha who has a *Dharmakāya* or the *Dharmakāya*.

Milarepa spoke in the previous verse of clearing up misunderstandings, but here he is speaking of this stream of thoughts dissolving because after all, the misunderstandings are part of this stream of thoughts, part of this mental disturbance, and the deeper you go, the more you develop your understanding, the more all these misunderstandings are cleared up, and the stream of thoughts simply dissolves. But what does it dissolve into? There are two kinds of dissolving, though Milarepa doesn't mention this: a temporary dissolving and a permanent dissolving. The temporary dissolving is when the stream of thoughts dissolves into the second *dhyāna* and onwards (because up to and including the first *dhyāna* there's mental activity). You can have a temporary quiescence, a temporary dissolving of thoughts in the second, third and fourth *dhyānas*, but they come back to trouble you again when you emerge from the *dhyānas*, so to speak. They only dissolve entirely when Insight is developed and this is of course what Milarepa refers to as the dissolving of the *Nhamdog* into the *Dharmakāya*, which is Transcendental. In other words one can think of the whole of the spiritual life and spiritual experience as a constant steady dissolving – permanent dissolving – of all one's misunderstandings, all one's wandering thoughts, all one's mental disturbances, the whole stream of thoughts in the fullest sense, into the *Dharmakāya*, as it were spontaneously.

Milarepa says this is called spontaneous practice. I wonder why? Perhaps it's because it's something that happens naturally when your spiritual practice reaches a certain momentum.

Q: I suppose it's something you can't 'do'.

S: Yes. If you're doing it in a sense it's still over-self-conscious so there are still thoughts. 'This also is a yogi's glory, confirming meditation principles.' In other words, this is really what meditation is all about. This is really putting meditation into practice. Meditation isn't just experiencing a blissful mental state for a while. It's really the permanent dissolution of the whole stream of thoughts into the *Dharmakāya*, which means of course that the *Dharmakāya* is more and more 'realized'. It's as though the energy that was in those thoughts all goes to increase or to enhance one's realization, one's experience of the *Dharmakāya*. It's not that the energy in those thoughts is lost and you're left in a kind of blank state.

Q: But if in the process of sitting you haven't reached the point of Insight, isn't there a measure of alienation?

S: If you have an experience of the *dhyānas*, even short of Insight, your thinking will be less alienated because through the *dhyānas* you're in contact with rarefied quite intense feeling. I think one could say there will come a sort of intermediate stage. If you have had some experience of the *dhyānas* but haven't yet developed Insight, nonetheless your thinking will become, as it were, more real, more genuinely intellectual, and from that you will develop actual Insight.

Q: Are you saying that you can't gain Insight with the alienated intellect, because it's alienated?

S: Yes. And the alienated intellect is, as it were, softened and harmonized through the *dhyāna* experience. This is in a way the significance and value of *dhyāna* experience. The *dhyāna* experience, as it were, comes between the alienated intellect on the one hand and the Insight on the other. There are people who have a relatively less alienated intellect because they are in contact with their feelings, but if you experience the *dhyānas*, you come into contact with very powerful rarefied feelings which have a strong influence on the intellect, so that the intellect becomes much more integrated and much more able to develop into Insight. But certainly there's no question of the alienated intellect directly developing into Insight. This just is not possible. The mediating factor is the powerful emotions generated in the *dhyānas*, which may arise when you're technically meditating or outside meditation. The

general principle is that unless your alienated intellect is transformed by being brought into contact with very strong emotion so that the two are fused, there is no possibility of developing Insight. Insight is no nearer to intellect than it is to emotion. The word Insight may sound intellectual but actually it isn't any nearer to what we know as intellect than to what we know as emotion. Even ordinary creative thinking requires intellect and emotion to be brought together to some extent, and Insight requires intellect to be brought together with very highly developed emotions which are usually experienced only in connection with the *dhyānas*. Only on the basis of that sort of intellect or intellect-cum-emotion, can Insight or even the higher imagination be developed.
From a seminar on Milarepa's 'Heartfelt Advice to Rechungpa' (1980, pp.18-20)

3. THE BODHISATTVA WAY OF LIFE

This to-ing and fro-ing between contemplation of the Dharma and becoming absorbed in a *dhyana* state is quite an important aspect of the spiritual path.

Sangharakshita: Your contemplation of a particular aspect of the Dharma, or your reflection on it, can become so intense that it becomes deeply concentrated; and then, as a result of that concentration, you just stop thinking about the Dharma for the time being. You are just concentrated. You could even say you are absorbed in that aspect of the Dharma without mental activity. This to-ing and fro-ing between contemplation of the Dharma and becoming absorbed in a *dhyāna* state is quite an important aspect of the spiritual path. You become absorbed in *dhyāna* without mental activity for a while; then you emerge, so to speak, from that, you allow mental activity to start up again, and you turn your attention to a certain aspect of the Dharma and try to understand that. But then, as perhaps you find your mind is wandering just a little, you allow the mental activity to calm down; again you immerse yourself in that higher *dhyāna* where there is no mental activity. You can alternate in this way, deepening your experience of the *dhyāna* state on the one hand, and deepening your understanding of the Dharma on the other, almost indefinitely.

Q: Presumably that alternation could occur within the context of a single meditation period or over a longer period, even a period of years.

Do you think, in the latter case, it would be fair to say that the principle you have outlined is one of the one of the foundations of the Bodhisattva way of life?

S: Not only the Bodhisattva way of life. The same principle applies to the path of the Arhant. The only difference is that in the case of the path of the Arhant, the conception of Insight is possibly more limited, inasmuch as it extends, technically speaking, only to *pudgala-nairatmya* and not to *dharma-nairatmya*. But the principle is the same: alternating between immersion in the *dhyāna* state free from mental activity, and immersion in mental activity with regard to the Dharma. Inasmuch as you emerge from the higher meditative state with a very concentrated mind, you are able to understand the Dharma better. And inasmuch as you have understood the Dharma better, you are able to plunge still more deeply into a meditative state. So you alternate between the two whether within a shorter time or a longer time. You can alternate between the two within the context of a single session of seated practice, or over a period of some years, devoting, say, a year or two just to *samatha*, and then a year or two to intensive study of the Dharma. Probably the latter would not be advisable; most people need both within a much smaller time span. But one does help the other.

From a seminar on the *Jewel Ornament of Liberation*
(Tuscany 1985, pp.271-2)

4. THE CLASSICAL APPROACH

You don't allow that mental activity just to take any direction it pleases but encourage it to assume the form of a conceptual understanding of the teaching.

Q: After coming out of the *dhyānic* states, do you have to sort of push forward to develop Insight, or is it enough to be in a receptive mood and see things as they really are?

Sangharakshita: It seems that both things can happen, but the classical Buddhist method is that as you emerge, so to speak, from the *dhyāna* experience – you don't actually emerge from it but it fades into the background – and mental activity starts up again, you don't allow that mental activity just to take any direction it pleases but encourage it to assume the form of a conceptual understanding of the teaching. In other words, you turn over in your mind what has been said about the truth or reality in conceptual terms, but because that has the backing of your *dhyāna* experience it can be transformed into an actual Insight into whatever it is that those concepts are merely symbols of.

For instance, you may know the words of the teaching that everything is suffering, but it's just words, you've just got intellectual understanding. But suppose you come down from the *dhyāna* experience, you're very concentrated, all your energies are together, and then you repeat the conceptual formulation over to yourself. You are using concepts but in that concentrated state, with the background of the *dhyāna* experience, you start not just thinking about it in a conceptual way but really penetrating into and understanding it, seeing the truth of it. That can develop into Insight.

Q: That's traditional?

S: Yes, that's the classical approach.

From a seminar on Milarepa's
'Heartfelt Advice to Rechungpa' (1980, p.22)

5. INSIGHT IS THE FUNDAMENTAL THING

There are Insight-type reflections to be applied to the *dhyanas* themselves.

Q: Can you function in the world while in the fourth *dhyāna*?

S: If by functioning you mean walking about and talking with other people, no. That is not possible. You may not even be conscious of the physical body in that state. What you have to do, on the basis of your experience of the *dhyānas*, is to develop Insight. Insight does not come and go; Insight is permanent. So with that Insight, you can move about in the world.

Q: Once you've got the Insight, does that mean that you can retain the fourth *dhyāna* state?

S: No! You don't need to. What is important is that you develop Insight. If you have Insight, you can move about in the world without being affected by the world. But *dhyānic* experience is dependent upon favourable conditions.

Q: So what kind of state are you in, when you have got Insight? Are you not in a *dhyānic* state?

S: Well, you are in a state of – to use a strange expression – 'partial enlightenment'. *Vipassanā* permanently destroys unskilful mental states, whereas the *dhyānas* only temporarily suspend them. That is the difference. The *vipassanā* Insight cuts at the roots of greed, hatred and ignorance, but in the *dhyāna* states, you have only temporarily removed yourself from them. When you are again in contact with very powerful stimuli, those unskilful states can return. So therefore, one uses the *dhyānas* as a basis for developing Insight. Insight remains permanent and affects your character, regardless of the experiences that befall you. If you have Insight, you may still experience pain, but you will not react to that experience with anger or hatred or impatience. So to that extent you will remain in a higher state of consciousness. You experience the pain or suffering, but you're not disturbed by it. Not that you don't feel it – you do feel it, but it doesn't affect you. It's quite peripheral, because you are so strongly centred; it can't throw you off balance.

Q: Does it operate through the recollection of the *dhyāna* state in any sense, or is it totally unconnected?

S: It's totally unconnected. You can escape from pain by withdrawing into a *dhyāna* state, where you are not conscious of the physical body, but when you return to consciousness of the physical body again, you will experience the pain and your mind may be overwhelmed by that, and give rise to unskilful mental states. But if you have Insight, then the experience of the pain and suffering will not give rise to unskilful mental states, even though you are not in a *dhyāna* state – even though you are in the ordinary consciousness and experiencing pain and suffering. You can have Insight and yet be subject to suffering, and it doesn't matter then.

Q: Why not? Why doesn't it matter?

S: Because the experience of suffering will not give rise to unskilful mental states, and that is all you are really concerned with. If the Insight is sufficiently developed, you become incapable of unskilful mental states. The root has been entirely destroyed. Coming back to the original question, it's not possible to move about in the world in a high *dhyānic* state. The two things are quite incompatible. But you can move about in the world with Insight. So if you want to be able to move about in the world without succumbing to its various temptations and stimuli, you need to develop Insight. Just *dhyāna* states are not enough, because they will help you and protect you only so long as you are living under those conditions which enable you to develop the *dhyānas*.

Q: So we're kind of vulnerable ...

S: Yes, indeed.

Q: Doesn't having Insight make it easier to get into the *dhyānic* states?

S: Oh yes, because what prevents you going into *dhyānic* states is basically – according to general Buddhist tradition – the five hindrances: craving and aversion. The more Insight you have, the less craving and aversion you have, the more they have been permanently destroyed. So when you have the opportunity, when you're not having to concern yourself with practical matters or talk to other people, when you are just quiet and by yourself, you can very easily go into the *dhyāna* states. In fact, someone who is Enlightened, if they don't have anything to do or anyone to talk to, will spontaneously go into a *dhyāna* state. There's nothing to prevent them.

Even in a quite ordinary way, if you've nothing to do and no one to see and you are in a calm peaceful state of mind, as soon as you are left to yourself, as it were, you just enjoy that calm, peaceful state of mind. So Insight is the fundamental thing. *Dhyāna* states are secondary. But if one has developed Insight, the *dhyāna* states will come naturally when conditions permit, almost without your making an effort.

Q: You've said that a serious ideal for every Buddhist would be to become a Stream-entrant. Is a Stream-entrant just someone who has had an experience of Insight?

S: Well, a Stream-entrant is one who has had an experience of Insight sufficiently strong to break the first three fetters.

Q: So you could have an experience of Insight and not break the first three fetters?

S: Yes. You have to build up your experience of Insight depending on the strength of the meditation behind the Insight.

Q: Is it true that once you've developed Insight, you never lose it again?

S: You never lose it again. It's not like the *dhyānas*, in that sense.

Q: Even if you're reborn?

S: Even if you are reborn, yes. If you die a Stream-entrant, you will be reborn a Stream-entrant.

Q: What are the chances of gaining Insight in the *dhyānas*?

S: The question is, what enables one to have Insight? In what way does Insight differ from ordinary intellectual understanding? The main difference, in fact the only difference, is that Insight has the whole of one's being behind it, all the energies of one's being. That suggests that those energies have been unified, they have all been brought together, and that sort of unification takes place only in connection with meditation. In fact, meditation, in the sense of *samatha*, is the bringing together of all the energies of the complete unification of the mundane consciousness, so that when you start reflecting upon something – say, upon impermanence – you understand it, in a manner of speaking, with your whole being. And because you understand it with your whole being, your whole being is permanently transformed. That is what is meant by saying that Insight cannot be lost.

Q: You would think that it would be a matter of course, for someone who could get into the *dhyānas* to gain Insight.

S: No, it wouldn't be a matter of course. For instance, they might not know that there was such a stage to be developed. But within the Buddhist tradition, of course, this is very well known indeed. It is said that, having experienced the *dhyānas* even up to the fourth *dhyāna*, you then apply your mind to the development of Insight, by reflecting upon such topics as impermanence or no-self or *śūnyatā*, or reflecting on the Buddha, which provides a base, an object, for the development of Insight. In order to do that, you have to come down a bit. You come down to the first *dhyāna*, where mental activity is possible. But the mental activity that you take up in that way is of a quite different nature from that which is not preceded by an experience of the *dhyānas*. It's not scattered, it's not undirected.

Q: Is it necessary to go right through the four *dhyānas* and then back?

S: It isn't necessary, but that is the best way. Usually in a complete practice of meditation, you alternate between trying to develop *vipassanā* – Insight – and experiencing the *dhyānas*. You experience the *dhyānas*, say, for a while – or at least you have a good meditation – and then you reflect, say, on impermanence, or on no-self or on the *nidānas*, and you try to develop Insight. After a while, the mind may become a bit tired, or you may feel that your reflection is becoming just intellectual, or that as the *dhyāna* experience fades away, your attention is becoming scattered. So you then go back to the practice of *samatha*; then having established the *samatha* again, you go back to the *vipassanā*. This is the usual procedure.

Q: Would someone who is in a higher *dhyānic* state resist 'coming back'?

S: Yes. You might not want to start up the mental activity which becomes a basis for the development of Insight, because the *dhyāna* experiences are very pleasurable, and you can become attached to them. A teacher like Milarepa would point out to someone like Rechungpa, 'Don't linger in the *dhyānas*. If you have achieved the *dhyāna* experience, and gone quite far, it's time you started developing Insight' – even though you have to come down a little in the *dhyānic* scale in order to do that.

Q: Would you say that greed types find it harder to gain Insight?!

S: It does seem like that, yes. A greed type is more inclined to linger over or become attached to any pleasurable experience, including that of the *dhyānas*. Of course, the difficulty with the hate type is that they might not be able to get into the *dhyānas* at all! Their minds may be too disturbed by hate.

Q: What about the deluded type?

S: Well, they sometimes behave like the greed type and sometimes like the hate type – that's why they're deluded, they're not fixed. In some ways they have the best of both worlds, and in some ways the worst of both worlds. They find it difficult to get into the *dhyānas* and once they get into them, they find it difficult to get out!

There are Insight-type reflections to be applied to the *dhyānas* themselves. One starts reflecting: 'These *dhyānas* are not the ultimate attainment; they arise in dependence on conditions. They cease when those conditions are no longer there. Therefore, they are mundane. They are conditioned. This is not the experience that I am after. I am concerned with Enlightenment. And in order to achieve Enlightenment, I have to develop Insight.' In that way one makes the transition from the *dhyānas* to Insight – by reflecting upon the *dhyānas* themselves and their limitations.

Q: So presumably there must be something else there, even in the high *dhyānic* states, to kind of ...

S: To start you up again, you could say that. On the other hand you may need some external help in the sense of the teacher reminding you or the tradition reminding you. It may be that before entering into the *dhyānic* state, you understood very clearly that *dhyāna* states are not the be-all and the end-all of spiritual life. So after you've been in *dhyāna* for a while, the thought may occur to you, based on your previous reading and study and understanding, 'Perhaps I should now be developing Insight.' From the point of view of the *dhyāna* experience, there is a sort of interruption, a positive distraction – if one can use that expression.

From a seminar on Milarepa's *Story of the Yak Horn* (1980, pp.162-6)

6. IS DHYĀNA A DETOUR?

Haven't you said somewhere that one could gain Insight without having gone through the *dhyanas*? I've always clung hopefully to that piece of information.

Q: Apparently, the Vipassana school of Buddhism sometimes says that *dhyāna* is a detour when you're trying to develop Insight, and so they don't encourage the development of it at all, and even advise people positively to suppress the development of *dhyāna*, Is that the same *dhyāna* experience that you talk about or do they mean something else, a kind of trance?

Sangharakshita: Judging by the articles that I have read, and a lot of the discussion that has gone on, they do seem to mean *dhyāna* or *samatha* in the traditional Buddhist sense. With people of a more 'scientific' bent, meditation without *dhyāna* has great attractions because *dhyāna* represents the sort of emotional element that they instinctively avoid. And there's always the danger that without *dhyāna* to back up your understanding you can mistake a purely conceptual understanding for actual Insight, which does seem to happen.

I think that to try to eliminate *samatha* is to misunderstand and misrepresent the Buddha's teaching. Some people are in too much of a hurry to rush on to so-called *vipassanā*. They need to lay a much stronger foundation; otherwise you get a half-baked pseudo-*vipassanā* which is of no spiritual value at all. Some later *vipassanā* teachers recognize this. There are some, like Goenka, who even teach the *mettā-bhāvanā*; that's a departure from the strict *vipassanā* meditation orthodoxy, perhaps in response to their experience with people learning to meditate.

Q: Some *vipassanā* teachers seem to think that visualization or imagination is a sidetrack as well.

S: Well, in a sense it is, but can you attain real Insight without going through that? That is the real point. I think you can't.

Q: Haven't you said somewhere that one could gain Insight without having gone through the *dhyānas*? I've always clung hopefully to that piece of information.

S: You can develop a very rudimentary Insight but you can't sustain it. You need that basis in *dhyānic* experience to be able to sustain it and incorporate it into your overall experience.

From Q&A with women study group leaders
on the Higher Evolution (year uncertain, pp.51-2)

7. INSIGHT AND STREAM-ENTRY

The *dhyana* state is not just a state of concentration, much less still forcible concentration. It's the bringing together of all the psycho-physical energies into a sort of equilibrium.

Q: What is the relationship between the initial flash of Insight and Stream-entry?

Sangharakshita: It is the universal Buddhist teaching in virtually all traditions that *vipassanā* or Insight or, if you like, wisdom, develops only in dependence upon a degree of concentration or *dhyāna*, and usually it is said that there needs to be quite a build-up of *dhyāna* before there can be any hope even of a momentary flash of Insight. The *dhyāna* state is not just a state of concentration, much less still forcible concentration. It's the bringing together of all the psycho-physical energies into a sort of equilibrium. In that equilibrium, especially in the higher *dhyānas*, there's no mental activity but there's a sort of direct seeing, or at least the possibility of direct seeing, and when that seeing actually takes place, that is *vipassanā*, or Insight. And at first this is usually just momentary. The tradition is that one builds up *dhyāna* as a basis for the Insight.

In some traditions, in some teachings, *dhyāna* and *vipassanā* are alternated. That is to say, you build up the *dhyāna*, then you work on developing Insight. Having worked on Insight, you build up the *dhyāna* again; having built up the *dhyāna* again, you work on Insight again, and so on. You might ask, 'Well, how does one develop Insight?' Sometimes it comes spontaneously, when you just turn the mind to something. You don't have to think about that object; in other words, your Insight is not conceptually mediated. You turn your concentrated mind to a particular object and then you 'see through' that object. That seeing through the object is what we call Insight. Insight, certainly in the Pāli texts and many Mahāyāna texts, tends to be described in conceptual terms which are expressive of the original Insight. In the context of *dhyāna* you can call to mind the traditional conceptual formulations of Insight and bear them in mind, and in this way you encourage the development of the Insight expressed in those conceptual formulations.

Do you see what I mean? You're not just recollecting conceptual formulations; you're using them as a basis for the development of actual Insight. Sometimes, of course, people mistake the one for the other. So some traditions teach that at a certain point you have just to drop the conceptual formulations, just stop thinking about them, and allow the Insight to arise spontaneously.

This is the general method. But then the question arises: 'If Stream-entry takes place in consequence of breaking the first three fetters, if those three fetters are broken by Insight, how strong does the Insight need to be to break the fetters?' And the answer is: it needs to be strong enough to break the fetters! That is the criterion, and you only know if the fetters are broken by your ordinary everyday life experience, behaviour, and so on. There's no other way of knowing.

From Q&A on the *Mitrata Omnibus* (1981/2, Part 2, Session 2, pp.22-3)

8. YOU CAN'T WORRY YOUR WAY TO INSIGHT

It can happen that the Insight is so intangible, so elusive, so subtle, that without a bridge in the form of conceptual formulations, it's as though you just haven't had the experience.

Sangharakshita: There were some early Buddhist schools which maintained that the Buddha was always in *samādhi*, but the majority of schools did not agree with that, because there must be mental activity if one is to communicate, and mental activity is inconsistent with the *dhyānas* from the second *dhyāna* upwards. So when the Buddha was speaking he could not have been in the second, third or fourth *dhyāna*; but his Insight remained undiminished.

When you have Insight you don't cease to experience objects of the senses, as you may do in deep *dhyāna* but your attitude towards them will be different, your understanding of them will be different. The senses will continue to experience the sense objects, the eye will continue to see visual forms, the ear will continue to hear sounds and so on when you're not in the *dhyānic* state, but your Insight will not be affected, nor will you do in relation to those objects anything which is inconsistent with that Insight experience.

Q: You've said that one way of achieving Insight is to turn your mind to a formula while experiencing the first *dhyāna*, but that's not necessarily the only way to do it. Does that mean to say you can achieve Insight through the other *dhyānas*?

S: The classical procedure is to immerse yourself in the *dhyānas*, and having done so, let us say, for a few hours, you then come down to the first *dhyāna* and start up mental activity, recalling the conceptual formulations of Insight. For instance you might reflect, from the Theravāda point of view, that all *dhammas* are *anattā*. Or you might reflect, from the Mahāyāna point of view, that all *dharmas* are *śūnyatā*, or all *dharmas* are pure from the beginning. You can actively think about the formulation, but that would mean you were less in the first *dhyāna* than you imagined, because it is subtle mental activity, not gross mental activity, that is present there. You don't think or worry about those formulas; you just hold them in the mind, or even repeat them, and allow the corresponding Insight to arise. One can't put it more clearly than that. You're not going to worry your way to Insight. You're providing the Insight with a basis, because for the Insight to be comprehensible, for it in a way to be thinkable, it requires a basis, and that basis is provided by the conceptual formulation.

It's much the same in the visualization practice. Say you visualize the figure of Mañjuśrī. If you see Mañjuśrī quite clearly as a visualized form – you see the colour, the attributes, etc., just like a picture you see with your eyes closed – this corresponds to *dhyāna* experience. But then you can start reflecting on what Mañjuśrī embodies or represents. This corresponds to the calling to mind of the conceptual formulations. Thus, corresponding to the visualized form of Mañjuśrī you can have a spiritual experience which will be an Insight. In other words, to paraphrase very much, you will experience not just the visualized Mañjuśrī but the 'spiritual' Mañjuśrī or even the presence of Mañjuśrī. In Tantric tradition the first is called the *samayasattva* and the second is called the *jñānasattva*, and the first provides the basis for the second. Sometimes you have to 'get rid of' the *samayasattva* so as to give the *jñānasattva* a chance to arise. The experience of the *jñānasattva* in that context corresponds to the experience of *vipassanā* in the previous context.

Q: When you get a story of a Zen monk walking along and the bottom drops out of his bucket and he has an Insight experience, is there some sort of subtle element of reflection on the experience?

S: It need not be a reflection, it can be just a seeing. The mind is so clear due to the *dhyāna*, so unobscured and so free from perturbation, that when it just looks at something it sees a certain truth or a certain aspect of the truth. You could say that if your mind is entirely clear and pure, when you see a bucket, you see a bucket. Normally you don't see the bucket. When the bottom drops out, well, you really see the bottom dropping out of the bucket. It means much more than it usually would. Usually you don't see the bottom of the bucket dropping out at all. You think you do perhaps, but you don't. But because you're in that highly concentrated aware awake state you really see what is happening. That actual seeing of what is happening is the Insight experience. Zen tends not to proceed by way of reviewing conceptual formulations, though it does to some extent. That's shown by the fact that Zen practitioners recite the *Heart Sūtra* so much. That's a reviewing. You could say that the *Heart Sūtra* is a sort of extended conceptual formulization.

Q: Can you 'see' in the third and fourth *dhyānas*?

S: If your mind is in the third or fourth *dhyāna* you can see, but if by 'seeing' you mean *vipassanā* and if *vipassanā* necessarily involves an element of translation into conceptual terms before you can even think or speak about it, then of course, it isn't possible to develop *vipassanā* directly from those higher *dhyānas*.

Q: But why does it have to have the translation into conceptual terms?

S: Because the experience has to be assimilated by the total being, and it's assimilated via – to use that term – the intellect. Otherwise it is ungraspable; you can't assimilate it. It's like a dream. You know, sometimes you wake up, and you know that you have dreamt, you can almost catch it but not quite. It escapes you, so you're not able to assimilate it into your conscious attitude. It is a bit like that. It can happen that the Insight is so intangible, so elusive, so subtle, that without a bridge in the form of conceptual formulations, it's as though you just haven't had the experience. You can't recall it, it's gone, just like a dream that vanishes as you wake.

Q: So it doesn't change you?

S: It doesn't change you.
From Q&A on the *Mitrata Omnibus* (1981/2, Part 2, Session 2, pp.30-4)

9. IT ALL SEEMS SO SELF-OBSESSED ...

Q: So meditation doesn't automatically lead to Insight? S: Well, nothing is automatic.

Q: I must say I always have difficulty with all these *dhyānic* states. I don't mean in terms of experiencing them, which is difficult enough, but it all seems so self-obsessed to me – all this talk about feelings and perceptions of this and that ... Is that just a basic misunderstanding? It all seems so self-experiential in a way, nothing to do with anything.

Sangharakshita: Well, it *is* self-experiential. You could say it's clearing the decks for action, because what prevents you very often from being more effective in the world? It's unskilful mental states. The only way to get rid of those permanently is by the development of Insight, and Insight arises on the basis of positive mundane states of consciousness, i.e. meditation.

Q: Can't you develop Insight in any other way?

S: One cannot confine Insight to any particular context. But according to Buddhist tradition the easiest way, the best way, is in connection with meditation, which as you know concentrates and refines all one's energies, and prepares a proper basis for the development of Insight. That's all.

Q: So meditation doesn't automatically lead to Insight?

S: Well, nothing is automatic.

From a seminar on 'The Stages of the Path',
The Three Jewels (1977, pp.85-6)

10. A GLIMMERING OF INSIGHT

You can get so far away from your previous skilful experience. That's one of the reasons why you need to take advantage of opportunities to develop at least a glimmering of Insight which will remain as it were constant.

Sangharakshita: We all know from our own experience that you can be in a very friendly, kindly mood and then two minutes later, you can be in a real rage, forgetting all about your former friendly feelings. It's the same in the case of *dhyāna*; you can get right away from it into almost a quite demonic sort of state. One of the things I often hear from people who have not been on retreat for a long time and then go on retreat is 'I'd forgotten how good it was'. They are so alienated from the memory of the experience, even though it was so good at the time and might have included many meditations, that they don't even remember that it was so good, never mind being able to really feel it in recollection. You can get so far away from your previous skilful experience. That's one of the reasons why you need to take advantage of opportunities to develop at least a glimmering of Insight which will remain as it were constant.

From Q&A with men study group leaders
on the Higher Evolution (year uncertain, p.101)

11. THE ARŪPĀ-DHYĀNAS AND INSIGHT

I suspect that in the course of hundreds of years, especially in some forms of Buddhism, the labels have got a bit mixed up ...

Q: I believe the four formless *dhyānas* are described as refinements or aspects of the fourth *dhyāna*. Do any of them have a specific relationship with developing Insight?

Sangharakshita: This is quite a big question. To answer this it properly one would really have to call into question the whole of the later traditional interpretation of *dhyānas*, *rūpā-dhyānas* and *arūpā-dhyānas*, and perhaps it would be a bit premature to do that at the moment. I will just say this: I think that the later traditional view of the *dhyānas* is probably mistaken in thinking of the *arūpā-dhyānas* in purely mundane terms. They could be looked at as being at least, to use what may seem a paradoxical expression, quasi-Transcendental.

For instance, the second of the *arūpā-dhyānas* is 'infinite consciousness'. But what is meant by that? Does not the Buddha himself in at least two or three passages of the Pāli canon seem to speak of ultimate Reality in terms of infinite consciousness and of a completely pure radiant consciousness? Does not the Yogācāra seem to speak of Reality in terms of absolute mind? So could one not take the view that infinite consciousness could be regarded as a way of speaking about absolute

Reality itself, rather than as representing an entirely mundane higher spiritual attainment? Certainly I think the whole question of *arūpa* and *rūpa-dhyānas*, and their relationship as represented in Buddhist tradition, has to be radically re-thought: not just re-thought in the ordinary sense but experienced, because one is really dealing with labels for experiences here. It's a question of attaching the appropriate labels to the appropriate experiences.

I suspect that in the course of hundreds of years, especially in some forms of Buddhism, the labels have got a bit mixed up, in the sense that certain experiences have perhaps been slightly wrongly labelled, and there's something now to be sorted out. When one reads the Buddhist scriptures, one should read them very critically, though at the same time with faith, and try all the time to relate what one reads, and what one thinks about, to one's own spiritual experience. If you do that, the texts may take on a rather different meaning than the one they seem to have at first.

From Q&A on the Bodhisattva Ideal (1984, p.238)

12. A KEY TO SUCCESSFUL MEDITATION

Why is it that so few seem to set their sights firmly on deepening their meditation practice leading towards the arising of Insight?

Q: Many people who have learned to meditate in our Buddhist centres have heard *dhyānic* states described in glowing terms and have had some experience of higher states of mind through their own meditation practice. Why is it that so few seem to set their sights firmly on deepening their meditation practice leading towards the arising of Insight?

Sangharakshita: I think there is quite a wide range of experience in this respect. Some people seem to experience *dhyānic* states relatively easily and naturally, while others have extreme difficulty in experiencing them at all. To a great extent, no doubt, it depends upon one's way of life, the conditions under which one lives and works, and sometimes a modification of one's environment is needed. But I can't really say why more people don't have a more positive *dhyāna*-type experience, apart from the fact that probably they are trying to do, perhaps even having to do, too many other things.

I was going to say that you can't just slip in a bit of meditation, a bit of *dhyāna*, in between other things, but actually you can if you are sufficiently experienced or sufficiently determined. I wonder whether it may be due to a lack of confidence that one can attain such states. But I think most people have experienced them at least a few times, so at least they know what is possible.

Q: Could you say more about lack of confidence in relation to attaining *dhyānic* states?

S: Well, I think it's an aspect of lack of confidence in general. A lot of people seem not to have much confidence in their own ability. They don't have faith that they could learn a foreign language, or learn to be an effective speaker, or improve their English, and in the same way they don't have faith that they could attain *dhyāna* states: not that they would necessarily have any particular difficulty attaining *dhyāna* states, but they don't have much confidence in their ability to achieve very much at all. The development of self-confidence and self-belief is a key to successful meditation, as to all these other activities.

From Q&A on the Bodhisattva Ideal (1986, pp.121-2)

13. THE VITAL POINT OF MIND

The words that make up the Dharma are meant to direct our attention to a certain kind of experience, to hint at a certain kind of reality.

> *It is most hard to find a man*
> *Who can merge both Dhyana and "Insight";*
> *It is most hard to find a man who knows*
> *How to work on the vital point of mind.*[69]

Sangharakshita: If one thinks in terms of growth and development, then one has to think in terms of a growth and development from which one does not fall back. You don't want to have this week a spiritual development which you lose next week. But so long as your experience is confined to *dhyāna* or *samādhi* this is in fact what happens. The only thing that can fix the development, the only thing that can make it permanent, is Insight.

Q: Is study very important to the development of Insight? Sometimes I've got the impression that you just need to do a lot of *samatha* meditation and wait ...

S: Well, *samatha* meditation provides the basis. But then you need material for reflection so that Insight may develop, and you can derive that material from study. That doesn't mean that you've got to go over in your mind everything that you've gone through in a study group. You can select certain topics that particularly appeal to you and turn those over in your mind, reflect on those after you have had a degree of *samatha*-type experience. It may be just a sentence or two that you turn over in your mind. You take it like a sort of koan, almost like a mantra.

Q: Is it possible to have what might be called flashes of Insight, or are they something else?

S: Insight usually comes to begin with in flashes. One can perhaps compare it to the recollection of dreams. Sometimes when you wake up you just catch the tail end of a dream, you see it for an instant and then it's gone, and even though you rack your brains you can't recall it. Insight is like that. Samuel Taylor Coleridge once said that seeing Edmund Kean acting was like reading Shakespeare by flashes of lightning. Flashes of Insight are rather like that. A flash of Insight lights up the whole of existence, but before you can grasp it, it's gone, and you're left wondering 'What was it? What did I see?'

But it's too big for the mind to grasp. The flash of Insight is no longer there, so the illumination is no longer there just as the dream is no longer there. You just get the tail end of it, just a vague recollection. It was about a mountain, say, and you can't remember anything more than that, or you just get a feeling left over from the dream. But just for an instant you see the whole dream and then the unconscious mind closes, and you don't see anything more. The flash of Insight is like that. Just for a fraction of a second the whole of reality is revealed to you, your mind sort of cracks and opens up and then, in the blink of an eye, it closes again, and you can't remember anything, perhaps because what you've seen is so big that the mind can't contain it. You've got no time to translate it into conceptual terms; in a sense you've got no time even to experience it.

With practice the flashes become more and more frequent, and maybe each flash lasts longer and you begin to get some idea of this vast landscape of reality, to recognize certain leading features. It is very much like seeing an unfamiliar landscape at night lit up by occasional flashes of lightning. You see that there's a tree here, a mountain there, and that's about all you manage to pick out, otherwise it's pitch dark. You don't really see anything until the day starts dawning, and that, to continue with the comparison, is when you start becoming Enlightened. Until then it's just these flashes of Insight, just for an instant, lighting up everything, but not long enough for you to do more than pick out one or two features and perhaps remember them.

Q: In what way would Stream-entry fit into that analogy?

S: Stream-entry is measured by the breaking of fetters, which is an entirely different analogy. So how do you translate one analogy into the terms of the other? Perhaps, just to speak off the cuff, it's as though you were walking forward through this darkened landscape, and Stream-entry is when there have been enough flashes for you to see where the major ditches are and to avoid them.

Q: It's the beginning of some coherence. Up to that point the flashes are completely discrete but with Stream-entry there's …

S: Yes, a certain continuity.

Q: What is likely to cause the flashes in the first place, assuming you're not doing serious meditation or other spiritual practices?

S: But you are. It very rarely happens that Insight develops to any degree unless you have a basis of spiritual practice, and especially a basis of *samatha*. They don't really just happen like lightning flashes happen in reality, so to speak.

Q: I was just thinking of reports of people having overwhelming visionary experiences.

S: Yes, people do, but that may not be a *vipassanā* experience.

Q: So that's something distinct.

S: Yes. That's not to say that formal meditation is necessary. After all, what does meditation mean? It's essentially a concentration of all one's energies, an integration of all the energies of one's being. That may not necessarily happen when you're technically sitting and meditating. You could be sitting quietly under a tree not actually thinking about meditating but it might so happen that you became very concentrated, your energies became unified or harmonious, you might start to turn over certain things in your mind and you might in that way develop Insight. I would say that Insight is developed more often than not in connection with actual formal meditation but it is certainly not confined to that sort of situation. It's important to understand what meditation essentially is. It's essentially this unified and heightened consciousness.

You know yourself that if you're reading a difficult book, say a book about philosophy, sometimes you grasp what you're reading quite well and other times not at all. When you're in a very concentrated state and there's no distraction, you concentrate easily on what you're reading; but sometimes that just doesn't happen – you don't understand what you're reading so well, you seem to be not so much in tune with it. The relationship between *samatha* and *vipassanā* is a bit like that. When your energies are concentrated, then when you take up some topic of reflection you can understand it much better, much more deeply, understanding it with your being, not just with your intelligence. Since you have understood it with your being, it transforms that being – there is a permanent modification as a result of your Insight. If that Insight is sufficiently strong, then, in the traditional terms, certain fetters are broken. You see through certain things for good.

Sometimes there's just a series of small flashes that don't amount to much individually, but over the months or the years they bring about change, though you may see that only in retrospect. But if you have a really brilliant and blinding flash, that may bring about a quite dramatic change quite suddenly, and you will know it at the time.

What do you think is this vital point of mind? This verse would seem to suggest that merging both *dhyāna* and Insight is in fact the vital point of mind. That's a guess – the text isn't really clear – but I think it's quite reasonable to guess that it means that the vital point of mind is blending these two, harmonizing these two.

Q: Does it mean that Insight wouldn't be likely to arise in a *dhyānic* state?

S: The traditional teaching is that one experiences the *dhyānas* first, and then develops *vipassanā* by taking up a traditional doctrinal topic and reflecting on it with one's absorption-imbued mind. But reflection means discursive mental activity. Discursive mental activity is found only in the first of the four *dhyānas*, therefore it is said that having experienced the four *rūpā-dhyānas*, having practised absorption to this extent, you, so to speak, return to the first *dhyāna*, you start up discursive mental activity again and this discursive mental activity takes the form of directed reflection on one or another of the doctrinal categories or teachings of the Dharma, which form a basis for sparking off the development of Insight. In doing this, one is essentially connecting with the Buddha's own Insight into reality. Having had the experience of Enlightenment, he sought to communicate or to express or to hint at this experience through words; the words that make up the Dharma are thus meant to direct our attention to a certain kind of experience, to hint at a certain kind of reality. So there is a connection between those words and the reality to which they point. They are the best words that the Buddha could find to express his experience.

Having suffused the mind with the absorptions, having come down so to speak to the first *dhyāna*, having got discursive mental activity going, one takes up one of these teachings in which the Buddha gave expression to some aspect of his realization of the Truth, and with one's mind now more sensitive and more integrated and also more powerful, one tries to make the leap from the conceptual formulation to the experience of which it was originally the expression. The doctrinal formulation is the bridge between the two. Do you see what I mean? It's just like when you read a poem – by reading the poem you re-capture the experience or the feeling that the poet had when he wrote it, but to do that you have to be quite receptive. You have to be receptive to a still greater degree when you turn over in your mind the words in which the Buddha expressed his experience of Enlightenment or Reality, so that you may get from the words to the experience which the words try to communicate and have that experience for yourself. You can develop that degree of receptivity, and that degree of energy and unification of being, only through *samatha*. So you practise *samatha* first and then with that *samatha*-suffused mind or consciousness you take up the reflection on those combinations of words which express or indicate the Buddha's realization. This is the classical procedure.

Q: Couldn't the couplet just have said, 'It is most hard to find a man who can develop Insight?' Why is it necessary to talk of merging the *dhyānas* and Insight?

S: Perhaps Milarepa wants to warn against trying to develop what some schools call 'dry Insight' – that is, Insight developed without going through the *dhyānas*. The central tradition of Buddhism maintains that this is not possible. There have arisen schools which maintain that you can develop *vipassanā*, Insight, without going through the *dhyānas*, but that sort of *vipassanā* would seem to be just an intellectual understanding. Some traditions of modern so-called *vipassanā* practice simply put you through certain '*vipassanā* exercises' and don't encourage the practice of *samatha* – in fact, discourage it or even dismiss it as very inferior elementary stuff. Among these *vipassanā* teachers, some have now admitted the value of some element of *samatha*, but others still won't admit it at all. They get you just sitting and going through the categories of the Abhidharma and this is supposed to constitute an Insight experience. It is quite important to understand the difference between *samatha* and *vipassanā*, how they are related and how the whole system works.

Q: What would be the Mahāyāna approach to developing Insight?

S: It is, in theory, exactly the same. In the case of the Theravāda tradition, Insight is usually developed by reflecting on the three *lakṣaṇas*, that is to say, *dukkha*, *anattā* and *anitya*, and through these finding one's way into or through the three *vimokṣa-dvaras*, the three doors of liberation. But in the case of the Mahāyāna it is usually some kind of *śūnyatā* meditation, on the different kinds or degrees of *śūnyatā*. In the case of the Yogachara it is reflection on the truth of the One Mind.

From a seminar on 'Rechungpa's Journey to Weu',
Songs of Milarepa (1980, pp.138-9)

14. MAKE YOUR MIND PLIABLE

Millions of people experience the fact of suffering without having any Insight into the truth of suffering – that is quite another matter. And you can have Insight into the truth of suffering without any painful experience, on the basis of a blissful meditative experience.

Sangharakshita: A lot of so-called *vipassanā* meditation appears to consist in a discursive reviewing of very complex doctrinal schemes and categories with minimal concentration, so that actually no Insight is generated. This is my basic quarrel with the way in which *vipassanā* meditation, so called, is often taught.

Q: Do you think it would be better to take up a *vipassanā* practice which encouraged more concentration?

S: Well, in a way no *vipassanā* practice encourages concentration. In a sense it's inimical to concentration, because you don't develop Insight without at least minimal mental activity. If you want to develop a higher degree of concentration, that's different from thinking in terms of developing Insight. But it is important, I feel, that before trying to develop Insight, you soak yourself in the *dhyāna* states to the greatest extent that you possibly can. This will make your mind pliable, so that Insight may be more easily developed. In many cases, people who try to practise *vipassanā* remain satisfied with a minimum of concentration, usually with neighbourhood concentration, and try to develop Insight with the help of that. I don't say that that is impossible, but I think it is very much more difficult. For the average practitioner it is safer to develop concentration, *samatha*, to a point as far beyond neighbourhood concentration, as you can, which has an integrating effect on the whole psycho-physical organism, and then 'return' to a state of mental activity, and try to develop Insight from that state with the help of the various doctrinal categories. This is the standard Buddhist, especially Theravāda procedure, and it would seem to go back to the days of the Buddha himself.

So looking at the way that *vipassanā* meditation is usually taught, apart from the fact that sometimes people are forced beyond what they should really do, the main defect is insufficient attention to *samatha*. The *vipassanā* exercises themselves are not wrong, provided that they are not allowed to become too elaborate, but people tend to have insufficient experience of *samatha* before undertaking these exercises.

Q: It does seem that such methods can lead to harmful effects, even the development of some kind of alienated awareness. Could you say something about that?

S: In some *vipassanā* meditation centres the hours of sleep are artificially reduced, and the *satipaṭṭhāna* is practised in such a way as to produce an alienating effect. For example, the mindfulness of walking is sometimes practised by chopping up the continuity of one's bodily movements into discrete disconnected bits, and trying to be aware of each section of movement, as it were, separately. That can have a very unpleasant effect, leading to alienation. Also, people sometimes haven't got much experience of *samatha* and are not much in touch with their emotions, because there is usually nothing in the way of devotional practice in *vipassanā* centres, though some of them recommend the *mettā-bhāvanā*. Another factor is that inasmuch as one is occupied discursively with sometimes very elaborate doctrinal categories, one is mentally very active.

So you've got all these different factors. You are out of touch with your emotions, sleep, food and speech are reduced, almost to a minimum sometimes, and you are mentally intensely active. These factors, it seems to me, are mainly responsible for producing a state of alienation. One might also say that the kind of person who is attracted to *vipassanā* may be someone with a rather rational, not to say rationalistic attitude to Buddhism and the spiritual life, and they may be alienated to a considerable degree before they even start practising *vipassanā* meditation.

I have no quarrel with *vipassanā* meditation in principle, and certainly no quarrel with *satipaṭṭhāna* in principle, but I believe that, especially in the West where people tend to be out of touch with their emotions, the meditative effort needs to be supported by such things as puja and other devotional practices, and the *satipaṭṭhāna* needs to be supported or balanced by the *mettā-bhāvanā*. I also think that before embarking on *vipassanā* one should have a somewhat deeper experience of *samatha* than teachers of *vipassanā* usually consider necessary. It is also important to distinguish carefully between mere discursive preoccupation with elaborate doctrinal categories and use of those categories, whether elaborate or simple, on the basis of a deeper experience of *samatha* in such a way as to produce Insight.

There have been cases where people practising *satipaṭṭhāna* or *vipassanā* meditation have had all sorts of strange experiences, and I have known such people to be told that that was an experience of Insight. For instance, sometimes they suffer intense physical pain, and then they are told that that means that they are developing Insight into the truth of *dukkha*, which shows that they are on the right path. And so they persist and as the pain gets worse, they think that their Insight is developing, so they push themselves on. This is really a terrible thing to happen. It is not understood sometimes that experience of *dukkha* is to be distinguished from Insight into the truth of *dukkha*. That is a very important distinction, and it is not always made. Millions of people experience the fact of suffering without having any insight into the truth of suffering – that is quite another matter. And you can have insight into the truth of suffering without any painful experience, on the basis of a blissful meditative experience.

From a seminar on *The Forest Monks of Sri Lanka* (1985, pp.268-70)

15. 'DRY' INSIGHT

The Question arises, what is the minimum degree of *samatha* that has to be experienced?

Sangharakshita: If you go through the Pāli canon, the general impression that you are left with from many passages is that first you practise *śīla*, then you practise *samādhi* and you go through all the *dhyānas,* and then you develop Insight. This is the standard picture. The only difference is that some people might get further into the *dhyānas* before developing Insight than others. So the question arises, what is the minimum degree of *samatha* that has to be experienced? The followers or advocates of *sukkha vipassanā* (usually translated as 'dry insight' – note that the Pāli term is *sukkha*, dry, not *sukha*, which means bliss) believe that this minimum level is *upacāra-samādhi*, which can be translated as 'neighbourhood concentration'.

However, although there is no explicit statement in the Pāli canon to the effect that you need to develop a higher degree of concentration than that, that is certainly the impression given, inasmuch as in hundreds of passages, the Buddha describes the bhikkhu practising the *śīlas* and then going through all four *dhyānas* (or sometimes eight *dhyānas*) and then taking up the practice of Insight. Of course one can't be dogmatic, but it would certainly seem that even supposing you could develop 'dry Insight' on the basis of neighbourhood concentration, that would be a relatively rare attainment, so that it would be safer, so to speak, to attempt a deeper experience of the *dhyānas* before taking up the development of Insight.

I'm not saying that nobody could possibly develop Insight merely on the basis of an experience of *upacāra-samādhi*, but it seems highly unlikely. The general trend of the Buddha's teaching is to encourage an extensive experience of *samādhi* before taking up the development of Insight.

When it comes down to methods, techniques and practice in the field of meditation, it must be said that the Mahāyāna, and perhaps even the Vajrayāna, still rely very heavily on the Theravāda. If one goes at all closely into so-called Mahāyāna and Vajrayāna meditation, one realizes that there isn't very much that is distinctive. In the case of both the Vajrayāna and the Mahāyāna, therefore, the great danger is an inadequate base in the earlier traditions. For many Vajrayanists on a more popular level, and perhaps for Mahayanists too, the repetition of the mantra is the principal means of developing concentration, and concentration certainly can be developed in that way. Visualization is perhaps the principal method of developing both *samatha* and *vipassanā*, if one reflects on the real nature of what has been visualized – that is to say, that it is produced and it is made to cease and therefore it is impermanent, and so on and so forth. But one can't sustain the concentration to do this effectively unless one is grounded in the more Theravāda-type practices.

From a seminar on *The Forest Monks of Sri Lanka* (1985, pp.272-3)

16. IS VIPASSANĀ MORE DIFFICULT THAN SAMATHA MEDITATION?

If you are starting from scratch, clearly it's difficult enough to develop samatha, but it is probably impossible to develop vipassana.

Q: Is *vipassanā* is more difficult than *samatha* meditation?

Sangharakshita: I suppose one must say that it is, because *vipassanā* represents a breakthrough into the Transcendental, whereas *samatha* represents only a refinement of the mundane. That is, in principle. But someone might have had to struggle for years to achieve *dhyāna* experience, but once they have done so, they might achieve *vipassanā* experience more quickly. Does that mean it is easier to develop *vipassanā* than *samatha*?

If you are starting from scratch, it's difficult enough to develop *samatha*, but it is probably impossible to develop *vipassanā*. But once

you have developed *samatha*, the development of *vipassanā* becomes much easier, though still very difficult.
From a seminar on *The Forest Monks of Sri Lanka* (1985, p.281)

17. INSIGHT EXPERIENCES CANNOT BE LOST

One has to be very aware of the extent to which one's mind can be influenced by one's surroundings.

Sangharakshita: Usually when you are meditating what you experience is *samatha*, *dhyāna* states, not *vipassanā* – that comes along later, on the basis of your experience of the *samatha*. In terms of ordinary life it makes a big difference whether you have experienced *samatha* only or *samatha* and *vipassanā*. I would say that if you have experienced only *samatha*, your meditative experience can be very quickly and easily disrupted by contact with the world. Even someone with quite prolonged experience of *dhyāna* states can generate very unskilful states of mind even within a matter of days after a retreat.

I would say that you can only safely expose yourself to what would otherwise be deleterious conditions if you have developed some degree of Insight. Anyone who has tried to meditate knows how difficult it is to experience *dhyāna* states even under favourable conditions – and *dhyāna* states do depend very much on conditions, they depend on your regularly sitting and meditating. You may not always be able to do that when you are out and about in the world. You may find that you have been talking to people for a long time or that you need to sleep or get some food. Before you know where you are, you haven't meditated, i.e. you have not experienced *dhyāna* states for some days. Then you find that, not having experienced *dhyāna* states for some days, you start experiencing quite unskilful mental states, which are the antithesis of *dhyāna*. And before you know where you are, within a week or two you are far away from your meditation.

But if you have developed Insight to any degree, that Insight, by its very nature, is not something that can be lost. Even in the absence of further *samatha* experience, the *vipassanā* experience is still there, the Insight is still there. It has become a permanent part of your being, so to speak, and you cannot really fall back.

It's almost as though you shouldn't expose yourself to the full impact of the world without any external supports in the form of your hermitage, your regular meditation programme, your spiritual community, unless you are practically a Stream-entrant. It does seem that the world is a very dangerous place. Unless you have developed Insight, you should flit quickly from one Buddhist centre to another, from one spiritual community to another. You cannot afford to spend too long on the road in between. It's as though the spiritual community, in whatsoever form, is like a lifeboat. One can't afford to swim too far away from it. One has to be very aware of the extent to which one's mind can be influenced by one's surroundings.

From a seminar on 'Rechungpa's Journey to Weu', *Songs of Milarepa* (1980, p.36)

18. IT'S NOT ENOUGH TO MEDITATE; WE DO HAVE TO STUDY

It's not quite so cut and dried as one might think ...

Q: Would you say that most of us need to engage our rational intellectual thinking faculty in order to really penetrate the Dharma. I mean, it's not enough just to meditate, we do have to study.

Sangharakshita: No, it's not enough just to meditate. One has to develop Insight, and Insight for most people seems to be mediated by conceptual symbols. But let me give you an example. There is this question of Insight into impermanence. Now, this can be mediated by conceptual symbols; that is to say, you can develop Insight by reflecting after meditation on a formula such as 'all conditioned things are impermanent'. Here conceptual symbols, as I've called them, are brought into play; you can develop Insight by reflecting on that formula and thereby developing Insight into the truth, the reality, which that particular formula represents in the form of those conceptual symbols. On the other hand, you can be meditating, and you may just see a leaf fall, and just seeing that leaf fall may mean the same thing in symbolic terms. It may not give rise to a train of thought. As you see the leaf fall, somehow you see everything fall, but you don't think about it in a conceptual way. Do you see what I mean?

You could say that the faith follower would be more likely to see things in that way, not conceptually mediated, but mediated by some sort of image, whether a natural image, something seen in the world of nature, or an archetypal image, whether imagined by oneself or mediated through a work of art.

Q: Somewhere I heard that in order for Insight to arise you had to go through the four *dhyānas* and then make a conscious decision to return to the first *dhyāna*, where there is some mental activity going on, in order to allow the Insight to arise. Is that so?

S: This is the standard procedure, but it's not quite so cut and dried as one might think. What is very often said is that you have to alternate between *dhyāna* and what one might call directed thinking, purposive thinking. The *dhyāna* keeps the mind, keeps the consciousness, keeps the energies together, gives them a more powerful thrust. When you start this purposive thinking, then of course you have more of a basis for the development of Insight, but there is the danger that your thoughts may start wandering, so again you have to immerse yourself in *dhyāna*. If you are practising quite intensely, say on a solitary retreat, you can spend half an hour or an hour or whatever seems an appropriate period meditating, getting as deeply into meditation as you can, then you 'emerge' from your meditation. In a sense you come down to a lower level, but in another sense you don't. You allow a train of reflection related to the Dharma, related to truth or reality, to start up. You try to penetrate, to understand things deeply with your concentrated mind, with all your energies. But if you find that your train of reflections is beginning to lead you astray, if you get a bit distracted, you again plunge yourself into the meditation, into the *dhyāna* states if you can. When you have spent some time there, again you 'emerge'; again you allow the train of reflection to start up; again you start trying to penetrate that topic – impermanence or *anattā*, or *śūnyatā*, or whatever it may be.

Q: This is while you meditate, not in between meditations?

S: You can do it in between, though you may then lose much of your concentration. Monks in the East often do this reflection and developing of Insight, while walking up and down. But you get the basic pattern?

Q: What would somebody who is more of a faith follower do?

S: Well they could visualize the Buddha or a bodhisattva, reflect deeply upon that figure's particular attributes, and be as it were carried away by that.
From a seminar on the *Mahāparinibbāna Suttanta* (1982, pp.30-1)

7 *Vipassanā* practices

1 Impermanence

1. KEEPING ONE'S AWARENESS FRESH AND ALIVE

Reflection on the five *khandhas* shows that one's experience and indeed one's self is complex and fluid, never for an instant to be thought of in terms of fixed identity.

From the very beginning the Buddha urged his followers to recognize the impermanent and conditioned nature of existence. But it is very difficult to acknowledge this fully; powerful measures are needed to help one break through one's resistance to the hard reality behind this simple idea. One way is to seize the opportunity of those times when the fact of impermanence is painfully impressed upon us by circumstances. But even such sharp reminders are dulled by the passage of time. One has to find a way of keeping one's awareness fresh and alive. Clearly just saying to oneself that all things are impermanent – even repeating it over and over again – is not going to do that. But one can take it further by breaking one's experience of things down into its constituent parts and considering that each and every part is not fixed but ever-changing. Thus the apparent solidity of things is revealed as illusory, and even the very idea of personal existence, the notion of a 'self' or 'soul' which is somehow impervious to change, is challenged. Reflection on the five *khandhas* shows that one's experience and indeed one's self is complex and fluid, never for an instant to be thought of in terms of fixed identity. It is no doubt because of the power of these reflections to change one's perception of existence that the *khandhas* are one of the most frequently cited classifications in the whole of Buddhist literature, both in the texts of the Pāli canon and in centrally important Mahāyāna scriptures such as the *Heart Sūtra*.

The term *khandha* (Sanskrit *skandha*) is often translated simply as 'heap', and according to the Buddhist analysis, everything in existence can be understood to be composed of a collection of these 'heaps', inextricably mixed together. The word heap, though, suggestive as it is of something concrete and substantial, does not capture the ever-changing nature of the five *khandhas*: form (*rūpa*), feeling (*vedanā*), recognition (*samjñā*), volition or formations (*sankhārā*) and consciousness (*viññāna*). In the normal course of things we experience the *khandhas* all together – as one big heap, one might say. But for the purposes of this practice – which is meant to help us break the chain that seems to hold them together and thus prevents us from seeing that our experience is composite – we are given the challenge of contemplating them as separate items in a systematic way. They have already been considered as objects of mindfulness – mindfulness of the body, mindfulness of feelings, and so on: now you reflect on their very nature.

From *Living with Awareness* (2003, pp.104-105)

2. NO BIG SECRET

Impermanence is what enables us to turn our whole lives towards the ideal of Enlightenment.

The contemplation of decay or impurity, which counteracts lust or craving or attachment, is not a practice that many people care to take up, though it is popular in some quarters in the East. There are three different forms of it. The first, and the most radical, is to go to a charnel ground and sit there among the corpses and charred remains. It may sound a drastic course of action, but it has to be so, in order to counteract the fierce power of craving. You look closely at what death does to the human body and you think, 'This is what will happen to me one day.'

There is no special teaching here, nothing esoteric or difficult to understand. There is no big secret in this practice. You simply recognize that one day your own body will be swollen and stinking with putrefaction like this one, your own head will be hanging off, and your own arm lying there on its own, like that one, or that you too will be a heap of ashes in somebody's urn (cherished somewhere, we hope).

These are all clear models of our own end, so why not admit it? Why not face the fact? And why not change the direction of our life to take account of this fact? It is in order to bring out such a vein of self-questioning that monks in the East make their way – often quite lightheartedly – to the charnel ground and sit looking at one corpse after another: this one quite fresh, recently alive; that one a bit swollen; and that one over there – well, rather a mess. They go on until they get to a skeleton, and then a heap of bones, and finally a handful of dust. And all the time a single thought is being turned over in the mind: 'One day, I too shall be like this.' It is a very salutary practice which certainly succeeds in cutting down attachment to the body, to the objects of the senses, the pleasures of the flesh.

If this practice seems too drastic, or even just rather impractical, there is another way of doing it. Rather than literally going to the cremation ground, you can go there in your imagination and simply visualize the various stages of the decomposition of a corpse. Or even more simply, you can just remind yourself, you can just reflect on the fact, that one day you must die, one day your consciousness must be separated from this physical organism. One day you will no longer see, you will no longer hear, you will no longer taste, or feel. Your senses will not function because your body will not be there. You will be a consciousness on its own – you don't know where – spinning, perhaps bewildered, in a sort of void; you just don't know.

If even this sort of train of reflection seems a bit too harsh and raw, a bit too close to the bone, we can reflect on impermanence in general. Every season that passes carries its own intimations of impermanence. The sweetness of spring is all the more intense, all the more poignant, for its brevity, for no sooner are the blossoms on the trees in full bloom than they start to fade. And of course in autumn we can contemplate the decay and end of all things as we see the leaves turning yellow and falling, and our gardens dying back into the earth. This kind of gentle, melancholic contemplation, so often evoked in English poetry, particularly the odes of John Keats, and in the poetic tradition of Japan – this too can have a positive effect in freeing us to some extent from our unrealistic perception of the solidity and permanence of things.

But really there is no need to approach even the most drastic of these practices in a mournful or depressed spirit, because they are all about freeing ourselves from a delusion that just brings suffering in its wake. It should be exhilarating – if you take up this practice at the right time – to remind yourself that one day you will be free of the body.

I did the cremation ground practice myself once when I was a young monk in India. I went along to a cremation ground at night and sat there on the banks of the river Ganges. There was a great stretch of silver sand, and at intervals funeral pyres had been lit and bodies had been burned, and there was a skull here and a bone there and a heap of ashes somewhere else... But it was very beautiful, all silvered over by a tropical moon, with the Ganges flowing gently by. The mood the whole scene evoked was not only one of serious contemplation, but also one of freedom and even exhilaration.

The body is essentially a part of the natural world. We have quite literally borrowed our bodies from the universe, and after death they will crumble away into a few handfuls of dust. It is essential to recollect this, and keep recollecting it, if we are ever to come to terms with this unpalatable but inescapable aspect of our existence. The practice of the contemplation of a corpse is traditionally said to overcome fear, and it is said that the Buddha himself used it for this purpose. If you can stay alone in a graveyard full of corpses at night, you are unlikely ever to be afraid of anything again, because all fear, basically, is fear of losing the body, losing the self. If you can look death – your own death – in the eye, if you can absorb the full reality of it and go beyond it, then you'll never be afraid of anything again.

However, the more challenging forms of this practice are not for beginners. Even in the Buddha's day, we are told, some monks who practised it without proper preparation and supervision became so depressed by contemplating the impurity and decay of the human body that they committed suicide.[70] So normally one is advised to practise the mindfulness of breathing first, then the *mettā-bhāvanā*, and go on to contemplate corpses only on the basis of a strong experience of *mettā*. But all of us can at least recall the impermanence of all things around us, and remember that one day we too will grow old and sicken, that we too must die, even as the flowers fade from the field and the birds of the air perish, to rot and return to the ground.

In the secularized culture of the modern West, for many people the body's physical decease signals an end to everything, which is perhaps why an encounter with death sometimes raises fears of nightmarish proportions. Not wanting to die, unable to face the fact that everything we hold dear will one day just be snuffed out, we hide the realities of death away from view. In many parts of the East, people – at least those with a more traditional outlook – tend to accept the idea of death far more readily, due to their confidence that bodily death is not the end. For them, ancestral spirits and realms of rebirth remain very much a reality. The emphasis is not on what might happen after death – they know they will be reborn – but on what kind of rebirth they can expect to have.

In western societies these days comparatively few people have even seen a dead body. At an English funeral, the only suggestion that a corpse is involved is usually the sight of a shiny black car containing a coffin discreetly covered with flowers – hardly a basis for reflecting on death in the way the *Satipaṭṭhāna Sutta* suggests. Even if we go down to the local cemetery, it will be nothing like a charnel ground of the Buddha's day; all those gravestones in neat rows cannot bring the fact of physical decomposition before the mind's eye.

If one were serious about doing this practice, one would therefore need to seek out opportunities to see corpses in the process of dissolution. Some kinds of work – that of hospital porter or care home worker, for example – do of course involve very close contact with the realities of death. One could also conceivably arrange to visit a crematorium and ask to see a body being cremated. Of course, it is important to be aware that such experiences can be disturbing. In its full form the contemplation of the stages of the decomposition of a corpse is a practice for the spiritually mature; you have to know what you are letting yourself in for.

But most of us, sooner or later, will have to face a version of this practice with the death of someone close to us. Bereavement, dreadfully painful though it often is, provides a special opportunity to come to terms with our own impermanence. It is definitely not a good idea to do this meditation practice in relation to the body of someone you were close to. You might be able to contemplate the body of a stranger with equanimity, but the sight of a friend or relative literally deteriorating before your eyes can be terribly upsetting. In any case, when somebody close to you dies, the shock alone is enough to concentrate the mind. Death is an existential situation, and you don't have to sit down and meditate on impermanence at a time like that – you just need to maintain a clear awareness of what is happening in and around you, observe your reactions and responses, and try to understand why you think and feel the way you do. One thing you will almost certainly feel is fear. By its very nature, death threatens one's whole being. The instinct for survival is so strong that when death comes close, it is a terrifying experience, because one identifies so completely with the body.

We cannot afford to forget the fact that human life is essentially an unstable, fragile thing. Without a real sense of that impermanence, we cannot free ourselves from the idea that there are at least some things that we can depend upon never to change. Reflecting upon bodily death reminds us that everything is changing – our families, our homes, our country, even ourselves. There is nothing we can hang on to, nothing we can keep. Perhaps this is what we are really afraid of. Awareness of impermanence can be terrifying at first – it seems to deprive you of everything. But if you become fully convinced, both intellectually and emotionally, that the body will come to an end one day, and if you have sufficient positivity to make real changes to your priorities in life as a result, surely this is the way to the arising of Transcendental Insight.

Reflecting on impermanence is so important because through it we begin to break down the tendency to over-identify with the body, and thus the delusion of a fixed self is weakened. This is the heart of the matter. An experience of bereavement, for all its pain, is a precious opportunity to grow. If everything changes, indeed must do so, then you can change too. You can develop and grow; you need not be confined to what you are at present, or have been in the past. Impermanence is what makes the path possible, for without it there could be no transformation or creativity. You would be stuck with your old self for ever, with no hope of release. Think how terrible that would be! You might be able to put up with it for quite a while, but eventually life would become truly unbearable. Yet, paradoxically, here we are, clinging to this fixed view of self for all we are worth.

Impermanence is what enables us to turn our whole lives towards the ideal of Enlightenment. To speak of death is not necessarily to lapse into pessimism – it is just being realistic. Old age, grief, lamentation, and death are after all just facts. But life can still be positive, even though it sometimes involves having to face things we find unpleasant. If we are to grow, we will need to face those things, acknowledge them, and go beyond them. The overall process is positive, and the Buddhist vision expresses that positivity without seeing everything through a rosy mist or refusing to face unpleasant facts.

The recollection of death should therefore be as familiar to the Buddhist as it is strange to the person who hasn't given any thought to the fact that they will one day die. If you have never reflected on impermanence in any serious way, you will be in a difficult position when the time of your own death draws near. You won't suddenly be able to intensify your mindfulness if you haven't already developed sufficient momentum in your practice of it. This is when you will need to call your spiritual friends around you, to give you help and moral support. But although they will be able to help you to some extent, the best and wisest thing is to keep up your spiritual practice as an integral part of your life when you are free from sickness and danger. Do not leave it too late. One does not wish to be morbid, but we are reminded sometimes that we never know when we are going to be run over by the proverbial bus. The best policy is to concentrate your energies and pour them wholeheartedly not just into your practice of meditation or study, but into the whole of your spiritual life.

From *What is the Dharma?* (1998, pp.192-4) and *Living with Awareness* (2003, pp.68-72)

3. ONE MUST REMEMBER THE PRINCIPLE OF THE THING

You don't want to reflect on impermanence in such a manner that you are afraid to set foot outside the door in case you are going to be knocked over by the proverbial bus.

Q: I was wondering how relevant the decomposition of the corpse meditation is for the present time: not so much with regard to needing positivity or a strong stomach but more due to the lack of opportunities. I was wondering if there was a substitute, something more satisfactory, possibly using the image of a cremation. I saw one in the film called 'Tibetan Trilogy' and it seemed that it might be easier to relate to in a meditation, and you end up with ash which will blow away.

Sangharakshita: I think it depends to some extent on the strength of the particular *kleśa* which you are trying to get rid of. It may require very drastic treatment. But for most people the sight of a decomposing corpse would just give rise to feelings of disgust and revulsion on a purely psychological, not to say inorganic level. You might be literally sick and it might not affect you spiritually at all. One must remember the principle of the thing, because if you are sufficiently sensitive, the falling of a withered leaf will have the same sort of effect, will impress you in the same kind of way. So you have to try to ascertain what it is that you need. Is a falling leaf sufficient, or if you keep a skull in your room is that sufficient, or do you need something stronger? But yes, perhaps it would be quite helpful to see a film of a cremation, or a series of pictures of a cremation in progress, the physical details of which wouldn't be enough to revolt you in a purely negative, even unskilful way, but which would definitely impress on you the fact of impermanence.

Sometimes when one sees bits and pieces of corpses it is merely unpleasant, it doesn't have any spiritual significance. For instance, if you are out driving and you notice that rabbits and pheasants have been run over it doesn't inspire you with thoughts of impermanence; it is just unpleasant, or maybe you feel sorry for those animals. Sometimes one sees reports in the papers or hears on the radio of motor accidents with many people killed, and one can then reflect that human life is liable to these accidents. One may not necessarily live out the full span of one's human existence. As Pascal said, I think, just a grain of dust is sufficient to destroy us if it gets into the wrong place. Life is very precarious. On the other hand you don't want to reflect on that in such a manner that you are afraid to set foot outside the door in case you are going to be knocked over by the proverbial bus. I think you have to be sufficiently mature spiritually to be able to absorb the lesson, to be impressed by the fact of impermanence without being merely shocked or disgusted.

From Q&A on The Bodhisattva Ideal (1986, pp.71-2)

4. ESTIMATE HOW MUCH YOU CAN TAKE

Meditation on the ten impurities is just a quiet, almost gentle, seeing of the facts as they really are. It's not a question of curdling your blood.

The Ten Impurities, the ten aspects of a decomposing corpse ... seems to be a favourite of Śantideva.[71]

I wouldn't say that the subject of the ten impurities was a special favourite of Śantideva's. He doesn't go into it in all that much detail. If you want to read a really thoroughgoing account, read the one in the *Visuddhimagga* of Buddhaghosa. He really does go to town on this, and seems to put much more zest and enthusiasm into his description of this exercise than into his descriptions of some of the others. It's a very lengthy description. Śantideva's is only a few verses. One should also realize that it's a matter of degree. You must estimate how much you can take, as it were. For many people, sitting in a cemetery would be quite a negative experience. It would really put them off, or frighten them. If one reflects on death and impermanence without going to the cemetery – of course in Indian cemeteries you've got half-burned or decayed bodies all around – then that's quite enough. Or you can keep a small piece of bone in your meditation corner, or even a skull – just to give yourself a taste of the impurity meditation, and to act as a *memento mori* reminding you that one day you will come to this yourself, like everybody else. But one shouldn't aim to horrify oneself with this sort of practice; that just produces the opposite effect and may even drive one into a reckless and despairing hedonism. Meditation on the ten impurities is just a quiet, almost gentle, seeing of the facts as they really are. It's not a question of curdling your blood. The facts of life are horrible enough, even when looked at in this more objective way.

From a seminar on *The Endlessly Fascinating Cry* (1977, pp.202-3)

2 The six element practice

The Six Elements Speak

*I am Earth.
I am rock, metal, and soil.
I am that which exists in you
As bone, muscle, and flesh,
But now I must go,
Leaving you light.
Now we must part.
Goodbye.*

*I am Water.
I am ocean, lake, rivers and streams,
The rain that falls from clouds
And the dew on the petals of flowers.
I am that which exists in you
As blood, urine, sweat, saliva and tears,
But now I must go,
Leaving you dry.
Now we must part.
Goodbye.*

*I am Fire.
I come from the Sun, travelling through space
To sleep in wood, flint, and steel.
I am that which exists in you*

As bodily heat, the warmth of an embrace,
But now I must go,
Leaving you cold.
Now we must part.
Goodbye.

I am Air.
I am wind, breeze, and hurricane.
I am that which exists in you
As the breath in your nostrils, in your lungs,
The breath that gently comes, that gently goes,
But now I must go,
For the last time,
Leaving you empty.
Now we must part.
Goodbye.

I am Space.
I contain all,
From a grain of dust to a galaxy.
I am that which exists in you
As the space limited by the earth, water, fire, and air
That make up your physical being,
But now they have all gone
And I must go too,
Leaving you unlimited.
Now we must part.
Goodbye.

I am Consciousness.
Indefinable and indescribable.
I am that which exists in you
As sight, hearing, smell, taste, touch and thought,
But now I must go
From the space no longer limited by your physical being
Leaving nothing of 'you'.
There is no one from whom to part,
So no goodbye.

THE PURPOSE AND PRACTICE OF BUDDHIST MEDITATION

Earth dissolves into Water,
Water dissolves into Fire,
Fire dissolves into Air,
Air dissolves into Space,
Space dissolves into Consciousness,
Consciousness dissolves into - ?
HUM

(Summer 2002)

1. NOTHING REALLY BELONGS TO US

The six element practice is a direct negation of one's usual grasping, ego-based tendency.

The analysis of the six elements is the antidote to conceit or pride or ego-sense: i.e. the antidote to the feeling that I am I, this is me, this is mine. In this method of practice we try to realize that nothing really belongs to us, that we are, in fact, spiritually (though not empirically) just nothing. We attempt to see for ourselves that what we think of as 'I' is ultimately (though not relatively) an illusion; it doesn't exist in absolute reality (even though clearly it does exist at its own level).

Before starting, we develop a degree of meditative concentration, and establish a healthy emotional basis for the practice to follow with perhaps a preliminary session of the *mettā-bhāvanā*. Then we contemplate the six elements in an ascending order of subtlety: earth, water, fire, air, ether or space, and consciousness.

So first of all, earth – the earth upon which we're standing or sitting, and the earth in the form of trees and houses and flowers and people, and our own physical body. In the first stage of the practice we consider this element of earth: 'My own physical body is made up of certain solid elements – bone, flesh, and so on – but where did these elements come from? Yes, they came from food – but where did the food come from? Basically, the food from which my body is substantially made came in the first place from the earth. I have incorporated a portion of the earth into my physical body. It doesn't belong to me. I have just borrowed it – or rather, it is temporarily appearing in this form of myself. To claim that it is mine is, in a sense, theft, because it does not belong to me at all. One day I have to give it back. This piece of earth that is my body is not me, not mine. All the time it is returning to the earth.' When we see this clearly enough we relinquish hold on the solid element in our physical body. In this way the sense of 'I' starts to lose its firm outlines.

Then we take the element of water, and we consider: 'so much of this world is water: great oceans and rivers, streams and lakes and rain. So much of my body, too, is water: blood, bile, spittle, and so on. This liquid element in me – where have I got it from? What I assume to be mine I have only taken on loan from the world's store of water. I will have to give it back one day. This too is not me, not mine.' In this way the 'I' dissolves further.

Now we come to a still subtler element: fire. In this stage we consider the one single source of light and heat for the whole solar system – the sun. We reflect that whatever warmth there is in our own physical body, whatever degree of temperature we can feel within us, all of it derives ultimately from the sun. When we die, when the body lies cold and still and rigid, all the warmth that we think of as our own will have gone from it. All the heat will have been given back, not to the sun of course, but to the universe. And as we do this the passion of being 'I' cools a little more.

Then, air: we reflect on the breath of life, on the fact that our life is dependent upon air. But when we breathe in, that breath in our lungs is not ours; it belongs to the atmosphere around us. It will sustain us for a while, but eventually the air we make use of so freely will no longer be available to us. When the last breath passes from the body we will give up our claim on the oxygen in the air, but in fact it was never ours to begin with. So we cease to identify ourselves with the air we are, even now, taking in; we cease to think, even tacitly: 'This is *my* breath.' And thus the 'I' gradually begins to evaporate.

The next element is called in Sanskrit *ākāśa*, a term translated either as 'space' or as 'ether'. It isn't space in the scientific sense, but rather the 'living space' within which everything lives and moves and has its being. We reflect that our physical body – made up of earth, water, fire, and air – occupies a certain space, and that when those constituent elements have gone their separate ways again, that space will be empty of the body that formerly occupied it. This empty space will merge back into universal space. In the end we see that there is literally no room for the sense of 'I'.

At this point we should, at least in principle, be dissociated altogether from the physical body. So sixthly we come to the element of consciousness. As we are at present, our consciousness is associated with the physical body through the five physical senses and through the mind. But when we die we are no longer conscious of the body; consciousness is no longer bound up with the material elements, or with physical existence at all. Then consciousness dissolves, or *re*solves itself, into a higher and wider consciousness, a consciousness that is not identified with the physical body.

In the meditation, you think: 'At present part of my consciousness depends upon the eye, part upon the ear, and so on. But when there's no eye, no ear, no physical body, where will that consciousness be? When my present individuality as I experience it ceases to exist, where will the consciousness associated with that individuality be?' Reflecting in this way, you attempt to withdraw from the different levels of consciousness associated with the physical body, and thus to realize higher and higher levels of consciousness.

This shift arises quite naturally out of the previous stages of the practice. You have already envisaged the four elements that make up your physical body as occupying a certain space, and when those elements are no longer present, that space is no longer delineated. Associated with one's physical body is a certain consciousness. When the physical body and the space it was occupying are no longer there, the consciousness can no longer be associated with that physical body, or with that space. If there is no demarcated space for consciousness to be associated with, it cannot associate itself with an undemarcated space, i.e. an infinite space, either. It can only proceed infinitely outwards, not finding any line of demarcation or any material body with which to identify. In this way meditation practices like this one culminate, ultimately, in a kind of spiritual death, in which individual consciousness dies into universal consciousness, and in a sense realizes its everlasting identity with it. As the Tibetans say, the son-light returns to and merges into the mother-light.

The classic opportunity for the transition to an experience of universal consciousness is the time of death. But unless one has already had some experience of this kind in meditation, one is unlikely to be able to sustain it for more than an instant after death – if indeed it happens at all; for it isn't an automatic part of the death process.

In fact, dead or alive, it is almost impossible for us to imagine what this experience might be like. One way to approach it when doing the six element meditation practice is to take universal consciousness as a poetic image. Many people find the traditional image of the dewdrop slipping into the shining sea very helpful.[72] More prosaically, one can think of all limitations to consciousness being removed, so that it becomes infinite in all directions. The essential thing is to have the experience of an infinite expansion of consciousness. One shouldn't take this image of the smaller consciousness merging into the greater too literally; the metaphor of a dewdrop slipping into the sea, shining or otherwise, is just a metaphor. The infinite expansion of consciousness is so difficult to describe because if one were to experience it fully, one would become Enlightened; infinite consciousness is the Enlightened state. Furthermore, as the Mādhyamikas would be careful to add, this infinite consciousness is an *empty* consciousness; that is, it is not an entity or a thing.

The physical universe isn't excluded from this infinite consciousness, but it doesn't constitute a barrier to it. It's as though one's consciousness goes through it. It is not that something literally isn't there that was there before, but it is no longer seen as an obstacle; it becomes transparent, as it were. The six element practice, leading as it does to this perception of reality, is a direct negation of one's usual grasping, ego-based tendency. It helps one to dissolve the idea of one's own individuality, in the narrow sense of the word, and thus destroys the poison of conceit.

From *What is the Dharma?* (1998, pp.196-7)
and *The Bodhisattva Ideal* (1999, pp.82-4)

2. A VERY EFFECTIVE PRACTICE

It is a very effective practice – which is why there will very often be a certain amount of resistance to it.

Q: I have some difficulty with the six element practice. For one thing, after we get rid of the earth element, the other elements are no longer contained, so conceptually it's difficult. And then sometimes I just come up against something and I don't want to continue the practice.

Sangharakshita: Perhaps one shouldn't try to understand it in too rational a way. One first of all relinquishes the earth element, and then the water element, and then the fire element, and the air element, but most people have a bit of difficulty when it comes to space. Because the first four elements are gross elements, it's relatively easy to imagine oneself giving those up, divesting oneself of those, but when you come to space it isn't quite so easy. But the point is that the four gross elements do occupy space, and when they are no longer there, there is no longer any space that they occupy. When they occupy space, of course, they don't just occupy it in a general way, they occupy it in a very specific way. They occupy a certain area of space, they demarcate a certain area of space. That area of space is you-shaped, it has the shape of your physical body, like (as it were) making a mould in several pieces. The mould encloses a certain area of space which corresponds to the configuration of the face of the person whose face is being moulded. But when you open the pieces, what's left?

Similarly, it's as though the space that was formerly demarcated by those four gross elements is no longer demarcated. There is no longer (as it were) a line of demarcation between that part of space which is occupied by the four elements in that particular way, like the taking apart of the pieces of the mould. You could say, in a manner of speaking, that the smaller space is merged in the larger space, the enclosed space is merged in the unenclosed space.

Indian philosophy has a simile for this: the simile of the pot, which is a bit like the idea of the mould. The pot encloses a certain area of space; this they call the pot space. Then outside the pot there is an area of space which is not enclosed. If you break the pot, the space which formerly was enclosed by the pot is no longer enclosed; it so to speak merges back into the space which is not enclosed. So in this way the space element enclosed by the pot is given back to space at large. In the same way, after you've given back the four elements within you to the four elements without, the space which those four elements had demarcated is also given back.

Then, to take it just a step further, your consciousness was associated with your physical body, made up of four elements. So what happens to that consciousness when those four elements are given back, and when even the space which they occupied is given back? The consciousness has nothing to hold onto. It has no more reason to associate itself with that particular part of space than with any other part. So one can speak here in terms of the limited consciousness merging with the greater consciousness, though it is probably better not to do so for philosophical reasons, but simply to think in terms of a letting go. When even the space formerly occupied by the physical body has been given back into the larger space, there is nothing for the consciousness to identify with. At this point one imagines 'oneself' just letting go, no longer attaching the consciousness to that particular physical body, which is no longer there, and even the space it formerly occupied is no longer there.

It is a very effective practice – which is why there will very often be a certain amount of resistance to it. If you experience resistance, you're probably doing it properly. If you're not experiencing any resistance, probably you're just going through the stages mentally, but without really experiencing them or realizing them, or even imagining them very deeply.

Q: How much time should we spend on this practice? How much importance do you attach to it?

S: Well, it depends how much time you've got. I think it's probably not a practice that you should do outside the retreat situation, because it can shake you up quite a bit. But if you're away on retreat, especially on solitary retreat, it's quite good to include a session in your daily meditation programme. If, say, you do a session of mindfulness, a session of *mettā-bhāvanā*, and two sessions of your visualization practice, as a fifth session you can have a session of this practice.

Q: Is there any reason for the particular order of the elements? Well, it seems obvious that you start with the earth element and then water, and then fire …

S: You're going from the more gross to the more refined, and that means that concentration gradually becomes more intense. If you start off with a gross object it is more easy to do the practice than if you start off with a quite subtle object, because concentration gathers momentum as you go along.

Q: But maybe if you start with air, which is the air you breathe, that is what keeps the whole system together. If you give that up, you don't breathe any more. That means everything breaks up and it's almost like giving up everything gross in a way. It almost seems more logical to start with that because that seems to be the thread that holds you together.

S: Yes. That's more logical, but then one might say it's more psychological, and psychologically it's probably better to start with something which is grosser, which you experience more tangibly.

Q: Some people seem to get into difficulties taking the practice logically and literally. For instance, they may think that if you give away the earth element, you really give it away, so when you get to the air element you can't breathe because you haven't got any lungs to breathe with.

S: That is a bit literal-minded, yes. You shouldn't be even thinking about the earth element once you've given it away.
From a seminar on *The Ten Pillars of Buddhism* (1984, pp.291-3)

3. SOURCES OF THE PRACTICE

The six element practice one could see as clearing the way to the experience of *śunyata* as symbolized by the blue sky.

Q: I've been looking for sources which give descriptions of the six element practice, and the ones I've found so far are in the Pāli canon. In these descriptions the sixth stage seems to rely on reflective thinking, for example on *vedanā* and its impermanence. This seems to be very different from how we do the sixth stage, in terms of expanding consciousness or letting go into universal consciousness. Why have you preferred this latter approach, and is there a text or a source for this?

Sangharakshita: I received the six element practice as we do it in the Order from Yogi Chen. I can't say why I preferred it to the account we find in the Pāli canon. Of course there is a passage in the Pāli canon where the Buddha speaks of giving up the earth element in one's own personality, and giving up the water element and so on, but as far as I remember he speaks only in terms of giving up four elements. But in the Order we follow the tradition of the Mahāyāna, specifically Yogācāra, tradition as I received it from Yogi Chen.

Q: When I looked up the sources, I found a sutta in the *Majjhima Nikāya* called the *Exposition of Elements*[73] which gives quite a long description of the first five elements, so that's form and space, then it says something like 'Thus is one's mind made clear and bright'. Then you apply that clear and bright mind to what seems to be a description of mindfulness of feelings, whether pleasant or unpleasant, and you reflect on their impermanence. The sense of the practice was like what we call dwelling in the gap. Could we do it that way?

S: I'm just thinking. One gives up the earth element in one's own personality, the water element, fire element, air element, so one gives up the material, physical body – this is the way we practise. And that material, physical body occupied a certain space, so when you give up that physical body, or you let it go, the space it occupied is no longer demarcated from the rest of space, so you experience so to speak the infinity of space. So what experiences it? Consciousness. And inasmuch as your consciousness is no longer tied to the physical body, or to the space occupied by that body, your consciousness is freed from limitations. So you experience, one could say, in the language of the text you quoted, a clear, bright consciousness. From the Yogācāra point of view, that clear, bright consciousness is non-dual and that is what you, so to speak, experience. But I'm not quite sure what would be meant by using that to examine *vedanā*. That sounds like coming down to another level of experience.

Q: It could be that having gone some way to gain that pure, clearer consciousness, you just take that further by looking at what is in your immediate experience, because that seems to be what's described.

S: Yes, but then the question arises, why should one need to do that at that level? If you have genuinely reached that level, and it's not just a mental reviewing or reflection, then why should you need as it were to go down to the level of *vedanā*?

Q: If you have a glimpse of that clearer but not fully non-dual consciousness, perhaps the mindfulness of *vedanā* could take it further?

S: Could be. One would just have to try it and see. As we move towards ordination and then keep up our practice afterwards, it's one of our major – I won't say *vipassanā* [Pāli] but *vipaśyanā* [Sanskrit] practices, one of our major Insight practices, and it has a very definite cutting edge. It is very effective, and one can have a very definite experience as a result of doing it, so we should keep it up as much as we can.

Perhaps I'll add a sort of footnote here. In some traditions, in the Buddhist movement in the West as well as in the East, there's quite a lot of talk about *vipassanā*, meaning a certain kind of *vipassanā*. Sometimes the suggestion seems to be that that is the one and only way of practising *vipassanā*. But this is certainly not correct. There are a number of different ways of practising, and the six element practice is one of them. So these days I prefer to use the term *vipaśyanā*, the Sanskrit term for insight or clear vision, just to make it clear that insight practice is not confined to what some people call *vipassanā*. There are so many ways of practising *vipaśyanā* in that broader sense.

Q: In the system of meditation the six element practice usually comes before the *sādhana* practice.

S: Yes.

Q: I think we often see it in that context. So do you think it needs to be used in that way, with another practice, or can it stand on its own?

S: You can practise the six element practice on its own, so to speak, but you can also practise it as a sort of introduction to *sādhana* in the sense of a visualization practice because the six element practice one could see as clearing the way to the experience of *śūnyatā* as symbolized by the blue sky with which most *sādhana* practices begin. So yes, one can certainly connect the two in that way.

From Theris' Q&A, Tiratanaloka (2002, pp.8-9)

4. DIFFERENT FORMS OF ELEMENT PRACTICE

I've borrowed it, and one day I will have to give it back.

The antidote to the mental poison of conceit is the six element practice. In the various forms of the practice we also introduce the element of visualization, which is very important. As a *vipaśyanā* method, the six element practice doesn't necessarily include visualization. But the form in which we do the practice in this particular sequence is that we reflect, taking the elements one by one. First of all, there is the element earth. It's present in my own physical body but it does not belong to it. I've borrowed it from the element earth which is outside in the universe as a whole, and one day I will have to give it back, so it is not really part of me. I should not be attached to it. I should be prepared to let it go. I shouldn't identify myself with it. In this way, conceit in the sense of the identification of oneself with what in fact is not oneself is resolved, is in fact broken up rather forcibly. So in this way the contemplation of the six elements – earth, water, fire, air, ether or space and consciousness – is the antidote to conceit in this sense.

So now, a word about the other forms of five or six element practice. There are two other forms, one of which is simply a concentration exercise: the visualization of the five elements making up the *stūpa*. As a concentration exercise, it corresponds to the mindfulness of breathing, but it differs a bit, at least for some people, in that it's more interesting. There are forms, there are colours – the yellow square, the white disc and so on – which perhaps draw the mind more. This is a *samatha* method inasmuch as no element of *vipaśyanā* is involved. But it's a very useful preliminary exercise before one takes up the visualization of a Buddha or Bodhisattva form.

Then there's also the five element practice, which is just a psychological exercise, though it does verge on mindfulness in the sense of the integration of energies. This particular version does not appear in the tradition; it is my own contribution, in the form of a lowly psychological exercise. In this exercise, first of all you become conscious of whatever energy is blocked in you. (If your energy feels free, of course, let it stay that way. Don't even pretend to be blocked!) Think of whatever energy is not free within you as the element earth: something heavy and solid, as our energies are sometimes – coagulated, stuck, solid, frozen, petrified, at least to some extent. Then the next stage is water, which here represents energy which is beginning to move, but at first can only move from side to side. This is oscillating energy. When you're tightly bound and beginning to get free, a little slack gradually develops and you can move within that, you can wriggle from side to side within your bonds. Or it's as though you're in prison, in a very narrow cell; you can pace up and down, so at least you're not tightly bound any more. The third stage is that of fire. The energy starts ascending, being sublimated, becoming more refined and escaping upwards. And the fourth element, air, represents energy expanding in all directions. You feel very free, you can move in any direction. Space, the fifth element, is the objective possibility of that freedom. If you wanted to imagine a fifth stage you could think not only of being free to move in any direction; you can move in all directions simultaneously, to fill the whole of space. This particular way of experiencing the elements is intended just as a sort of loosening up exercise.

So that is the distinction between the different kinds of method: a four or five element practice which is just a loosening-up exercise; a five element practice which is a concentration exercise, in a way looking back to the mindfulness of breathing and looking forward to the fully fledged visualization of Buddhas and Bodhisattvas; and a six element practice as a *vipaśyanā* exercise to break up the feeling of conceit or personal identity in a narrow sense.

From a seminar on *Dhyana for Beginners* (1976, pp.87-94)

5. INFINITE CONSCIOUSNESS

You can think of your consciousness extending as far as the other side of the universe, if you can imagine such a thing.

Sangharakshita: In the sixth stage of the six element practice, you reflect that your consciousness can proceed infinitely outwards, not finding any line of demarcation, not finding any sort of material body with which it is identified. To help this process you can think of your consciousness extending as far as the other side of the universe, if you can imagine such a thing. After all, your consciousness does extend as far as that, it's not limited. The essential thing is to have the sense of the indefinite or infinite expansion of your consciousness. It is not that a drop literally slips into the sea, shining or otherwise, because of course the sea is horizontal, whereas here there is expansion in all directions, you're not limited in that horizontal direction. So don't take this image of the smaller consciousness merging into the greater too literally – maybe drop that image altogether, thinking simply in terms of barriers in the sense of lines of demarcation being removed.

Q: You've described that as unenlightened consciousness merging with Enlightened consciousness. Is that universal consciousness Enlightened?

S: Well, when one speaks of unenlightened consciousness merging with Enlightened, clearly there's no actual merging. It's that the line of demarcation between the two has been removed.

Q: So if you were to do that practice, try to have that experience, then you would become Enlightened?

S: I wouldn't make a literal distinction between consciousness and Enlightenment. I would say that the infinite consciousness is the Enlightened state, though of course one must also bear in mind that that infinite consciousness, as the Mādhyamikas would be careful to add, is an empty consciousness. It's not an entity, it's not a thing.

Q: In the last stage of that practice, with the removal of barriers, trying to imagine yourself into the experience, would you imagine your experience as encompassing all kinds of dimensions of experience including the physical universe?

S: Well, the physical universe wouldn't be excluded, but it wouldn't constitute a barrier. It's as though your consciousness would go through it, rather like the mutual intersection of the beams of coloured light that the *Avataṁsaka Sūtra* talks about. It is not that literally something isn't there that was there before, but it is no longer seen as an obstacle or as a barrier, it becomes as it were transparent, so that you can go right through it. Difference is not negated, but it is seen as not constituting any hindrance.

Q: We usually do the *stūpa* visualization as a sort of warm-up practice for visualization, but I was wondering if one could do the *stūpa* visualization as a sort of six element practice, if one includes the sky as consciousness, and thereby make the practice an Insight practice.

S: How would it be an Insight practice? The six element practice is an Insight practice by virtue of the fact that a certain kind of understanding is developed. You understand that the earth, the element of which your body is composed, doesn't belong to you, you have to give it back. That is a direct negation of one's usual grasping ego-based tendency. But if you simply visualize the element earth, simply visualize that yellow cube, there's no element of understanding in that simple visualization.

Q: Could you do the visualization, and as a sort of *stuti* repeat a phrase like 'There is in me the element earth. I must give that back.'

S: You could. I don't know that that was a traditional practice, but there's no reason why one shouldn't practise in that way. One could only try it and see whether one found it helpful. The concentration on the visualized yellow cube would help one to develop concentration, so that one could then reflect undistractedly that the element earth, which is in my physical body, does not belong to me. Personally, I've always found the repetition of those words sufficient. The words are like a sort of mantra, and repeating them does concentrate the mind. But if that is difficult for you, and if you find visualization easy, there's no reason why you shouldn't also visualize the element about which you are reflecting. If you were able to do it, it would be in some ways a fuller and richer practice. Some people of course might find it too much, might find it quite enough to repeat the words reflecting in that particular way.

From Q&A on the Bodhisattva Ideal (Tuscany 1984 pp.121-2)

6. THE SIX ELEMENT PRACTICE AND THE BLUE SKY

If you're a beginner – and you remain a beginner for several years – you have to be quite careful how you try to combine something like the six element practice with a working day.

Q: Thinking about visualizing the blue sky at the start of visualization practices, what I can't understand is, if we are thinking of this blue sky as representing *śūnyatā*, and blending in with form, *rūpā*, how can I imagine that? I have an experience of form, sure, but I don't have any experience of *śūnyatā*. So how can I possibly imagine a form as being *śūnyatā*?

Sangharakshita: This is where doing the practice in regular steps comes in. At the beginning of most practices you have this mantra, *sarva dharma śūnyatā* or *sarva dharma suddha*: all dharmas are pure by nature, *svabhāva*, and I also am pure by nature. In other words, all things are *śūnyatā*. This represents the stage of the realization of *śūnyatā*, and it is supposed to embody the whole of the Perfection of Wisdom. So one is really supposed to be deeply engaged with that before going on to the visualization, if you do it thoroughly and properly.

Q: So how do you develop that stage?

S: The six element practice will help. The Tibetans themselves very often just repeat that mantra, then pass onto the visualization, but that's not really enough.

Q: You're supposed to stop and reflect?

S: Yes. Not necessarily at that time, but that mantra should call to mind all the experience you've had in previous reflections. It recapitulates your previous experience of that whole dimension. This is why we do the six element practice before ordination – because in connection with the ordination you get the visualization practice, and the six element practice helps lay the foundation, connecting with the mantra, in the case of those practices which have the *śūnyatā* mantra, the *sarva suddha, sarvadharmah svabhāva suddho 'ham* – *suddha* here meaning *śūnyatā*.

Q: But most of us have probably only done a few sessions of the six element practice before taking up a visualization.

S: Well, if one wanted to criticise, one could say that all these things should be done much more than they are. The stronger the foundation you lay, the better. You could even say that most people haven't perfected their *śīla*, their ethical behaviour. If you're going to be strict about the path of regular steps you should give much more attention to that – and to mindfulness too.

Q: Would that be a good basis for a solitary retreat? – mindfulness, *mettā*, six element practice?

S: I've suggested that Order members do all of these five practices in the course of the day: mindfulness, *mettā*, six element practice then recollection of death or, in some cases, the contemplation of the chain of the *nidānas*, and then the visualization practice.

Q: I suppose in a daily practice one could do, say, *mettā* and six element practice or some *śūnyatā* practice, and then in the evening do a visualization practice.

S: If you're a beginner – and you remain a beginner for several years – you have to be quite careful how you try to combine something like

the six element practice with a working day. It could result in a bit of disorientation. People normally do it more when they're away on retreat. In order to be able to do the six element practice one needs to have built up a reasonable amount of emotional positivity.
From a seminar on *The Buddha's Law Among the Birds* (1982, pp.260-1, 266)

7. HOW BUDDHISM SEES THE ELEMENTS

In practical terms the difference between the elements as conceived in Buddhist philosophy and a more materialist theory has important consequences.

> *Again, bhikkhus, a bhikkhu reviews this same body, however it is placed, however disposed, as consisting of elements thus: "In this body there are the earth element, the water element, the fire element, and the air element." Just as though a skilled butcher or his apprentice had killed a cow and was seated at the crossroads with it cut up into pieces; so too, a bhikkhu reviews this same body ... as consisting of the elements thus: "In this body there are the earth element, the water element, the fire element, and the air element."*[74]

Here we are being called upon to divide the human body mentally into what pertains to each of the four elements, just as the butcher physically divides the carcass of the cow into the various joints of meat. Clearly, the same analytical quality is being applied to the body as in the previous section, but the emphasis here is on one's own body, and we are looking not for the impurity of the body but for the four great primary elements: earth, water, fire, and air.

There is often no direct equivalent for a Pāli term in English, and superficial resemblances between Pāli terms and their English translations can hide deeper and more subtle differences of meaning. This is certainly the case with the word 'element': while it is the only translation available to us, its associations and shades of meaning are quite at odds with the basic concepts by which traditional Buddhist thinking is shaped. To state the difference very briefly, Buddhist thought understands the elements in terms of the changing processes that constitute our world, rather than as basic substances from which the world is made up. In the *Satipaṭṭhāna Sutta* the word translated as 'element' is *dhātu*, but an alternative term frequently used is *mahābhūta*. *Mahā* means 'great', and *bhūta* comes from the word *bhavati*, which literally means 'become'; so the derivation of the word *mahābhūta* reflects the underpinning analysis: that the elements are not fixed but in a constant process of coming into being. In the *Visuddhimagga* also, Buddhaghosa is careful to define the elements not as substances in their own right, but as tendencies: a tendency towards solidity for *paṭhavī* (earth), motility or undulating movement for *āpo* (water), expansiveness for *vāyo* (air) and radiation for *tejo* (fire). The elements, in other words, are to be thought of as different qualities of physical form.

Rūpa is the Pāli term for the physical aspect of our existence, the mental aspect being covered by the term *nāma*; the two terms usually appear together in the compound *nāma-rūpa*, which covers the whole of our psychophysical being, both mind and body. According to the analysis of the Abhidhamma, the four material elements are the first four items on a whole list of subdivisions of *rūpa*. *Rūpa* is usually translated into English as 'matter', but here also there is potential for confusion, because *rūpa* is not matter in the sense of something that exists independently of human consciousness; here Buddhism parts company with Western science. In Buddhist philosophy there is no conception of a split or opposition between mind and matter; 'matter' is said to arise in dependence on human consciousness, and there can be no consciousness without some kind of form. Form (to use another possible English translation of *rūpa*) is not just an idea. It has a reality. In our contact with things, there is always a factor that is not under our control. When your body comes up against a solid object, you certainly know about it – and whatever it is that you come up against can be termed *rūpa*. *Rūpa* is – in the words of Dr Guenther in *Philosophy and Psychology in the Abhidhamma* – 'the objective content of the perceptual situation'. This may seem a dry and academic way of describing experience, but it does explain quite accurately what is meant by the term. A perceptual situation, an experience, comprises two basic components: first, the object of consciousness, and second, what you as the perceiver bring to the situation. When you see a flower, the recognition 'this is a flower' comes from you, not from the flower. Similarly, all the characteristics of the flower – its colour, its fragrance, a sense of its beauty, and so on – arise in you as perceptions. But not everything in this perceptual situation arises from or in you. There is the flower itself, the external object or stimulus to which the act of perception refers. And this – whatever it is – is *rūpa*.

I say 'whatever it is' because in a sense it can only be a mystery. We can only know it through our senses, never 'objectively'.

What distinguishes physical form from other aspects of our experience, such as ideas or emotions, is that it is knowable to us through the five physical senses, principally touch and sight, rather than through the mind alone. As we move about in the world and *rūpa* impinges on our consciousness, the senses first of all register bare sensations without interpreting them. But if we are to function, we need to be able to discriminate between these various sensations and work out what they might mean, so the mind rapidly sets about organizing that contact with the objects of the senses into the subdivisions of *rūpa*.

If *rūpa* is the objective component of perception, the four primary elements, the *mahābhūtas*, are ways of classifying what kind of form that objective component appears to take. There is solidity, or the quality of resistance to our touch; there is fluidity and cohesiveness; there is the quality of heat or cold; and there is the quality of lightness and expansiveness. Each of these primary qualities can be further classified, but for our present purposes it will be enough to focus upon this fourfold designation of *rūpa*. The important point is that earth, water, fire, and air are not properties of the objects of which we are conscious, but ways of understanding consciousness itself.

The Pāli commentaries say that a *mahābhūta* is a great feat such as that performed by a magician when he makes you perceive clay as gold or water as fire. In just the same way we perceive *rūpa*, the objective content of the perceptual situation, as if it were literally earth, water, or fire. But this is an illusion born of our limited understanding. We cannot say categorically what is there, but only what appears to us to be there. What earth or water are in themselves, if in fact they are anything at all, we cannot know. Earth and water are just names we assign to particular kinds of sensation. We have no option but to connect up our sensations to form ideas of things that we suppose to be 'out there' in the world beyond our selves, but if we are not careful, that quality of resistance or fluidity takes on a life of its own and we turn what is essentially an experience or a mode of experiencing into a supposedly concrete thing. We make sense of experience through language – this is how we learn to cope with it – but the problem with language is that it almost compels us to treat ever-changing processes as entities. We need to be on our guard against this, especially when we are engaged in conceptual thinking. *Rūpa*, for instance, is a conceptual term which does not refer to any 'thing' we can directly experience. We only experience the things for which *rūpa* is the general term – that is to say, the four elements. But can we even say that we experience the elements directly? We do not experience a thing called earth, but only a sensation of resistance; not water, but only wetness. And we do not experience wetness or solidity as they are in themselves; we only experience them as they seem to us to be. As the *Perfection of Wisdom* sūtras tell us, forms are like dreams, illusions, the reflection of the moon in water. All things are like ghosts: when they appear, we know that we see them, but what they are in reality, we do not know. This is brought out by another meaning of the term *mahābhūta*: 'great ghost'.

As far as the *Satipaṭṭhāna Sutta* is concerned, the aim of the first part of the practice is to be aware of the four elements as qualities extending through and beyond one's own body. The very fabric of your body is in perpetual change; you are the nexus of all kinds of interactions which are going on as the body powers away, continually renewing itself by taking in foodstuffs, water, and heat, and continually expelling them again. This analysis does not conceive of a finite number of inanimate elements combining and recombining according to fixed physical laws. There is only the awareness of one's body as it impinges upon consciousness according to these various modes of contact. Unlike the elements of science, these great elements are alive. We ourselves are composed of them and it is our own living consciousness that contemplates their incessant flux across the field of the body in the meditation practice called the six element practice.

In practical terms the difference between the elements as conceived in Buddhist philosophy and a more materialist theory has important consequences. It requires us to bring a responsive awareness to what we perceive, because we are active participants in consciousness, not merely receivers of messages from a fixed external universe. This is tremendously significant, calling into question the whole distinction between a living 'me' and a non-living 'not me'. In our modern techno-scientific culture we are able to do all kinds of things with and to the natural world, but as a result we have lost our affinity with it. Alienated from nature, no longer experiencing it as a living presence, we sorely need to recapture the sense that to be human is to be part of nature.

This feeling, of course, came naturally to people in the early days of Buddhism. The Buddha and his disciples lived in the midst of nature, wandering on foot for eight or nine months of the year from one village to another through the jungles of northern India. Their days and nights were spent in forests, in parks, on mountains, or by rivers; out in the elements, sleeping under the stars. Theirs was a world populated not only by human beings and animals, but by gods and spirits of the hills and streams, trees and flowers. The sense of the physical environment experienced as a living presence is a significant theme in all the oldest texts of the Buddhist tradition. For all its factual content, the Pāli canon also reminds us that the supernatural world was a reality for the early Buddhists; and one might say that it was the continuous presence of nature that made it so.

All the episodes of major significance in the Buddha's life history unfolded in close contact with a natural world which actively responded to his presence. He was born in the open air, we are told, while his mother supported herself by holding a bough laden with flowers. He gained Enlightenment beneath the bodhi tree, seated on a carpet of fresh grass. And in the end he passed away between twin *sāl* trees which sprinkled his body in homage with blossoms out of season. This sense of nature as a vibrant and animated presence is often the part of the Pāli canon that is edited out of selected translations into English; the editors tend to leave intact the outline of the Buddha's teaching but include little of the world in which it is set. If some mythic strands are left, the modern reader is likely to skip over the accounts of nāgas, yakṣas, and other supernatural beings to concentrate on the 'real' stuff, the doctrine. But the gods and goddesses, and all the various kinds of non-human beings, are not there simply as ornamentation. Their presence is itself part of the teaching. They provide glimpses of an ancient mode of human consciousness fully integrated into a universe of value, meaning, and purpose. To miss them is to miss the poetry, and the heart of the Buddha's message.

If we are really to understand the contemplation of the four elements in the *Satipaṭṭhāna Sutta*, therefore, we need to find ways of deepening our understanding of what this elemental imagery meant to the early Buddhists, how they knew those mythic figures and lived in relation to them. To help us do this, we can return to the term *mahābhūta*, whose meaning hints at the living, inherently ungraspable quality of the elements. *Mahābhūta*, 'great ghost', means something that has somehow arisen, or has been conjured up – a mysterious, other-worldly apparition. To think of the four elements as 'great ghosts' suggests that we are dealing not with concepts or inanimate matter, but with living forces.

The universe is alive, magically so, and the haunting appearance within it of the four great elements makes that experience inherently mysterious and inaccessible to definitive knowledge. Rather than trying to pin down reality with technical and scientific thinking, the Buddhist conception of the four elements helps to bring about a fusion of objective and subjective knowledge, enabling us, like Shakespeare's King Lear, to 'take upon's the mystery of things'.

This does not mean that the Buddhist conception of the elements is vague or imprecise, nor that the rational faculty is no longer necessary. Concepts are vital – but they do not exhaust the whole of life's mystery. To understand the four elements as psychophysical states rather than as material substances or states of matter undermines the conventional idea of what the body is. It reminds us that the division between inner and outer worlds is a product of dualistic thinking. Rather than any division between a thing called matter and a thing called mind, or a thing called body and a thing called consciousness, there is a continuity running all the way through, a continuity of our awareness patterned in different ways. If we can really understand this, those inner and outer worlds become interfused in a deeper, more meaningful vision of what it is to be alive.

All this runs counter to the way we in the West have been conditioned to experience the body and the world of which it is a part. But it must surely be better – or at the very least more fun – to be an animist and feel that the whole world is animated by spirits, rather than gazing out at a world of non-living matter which occasionally and haphazardly comes to life, and in which even our own life is ultimately reducible to inanimate matter. All the same, it is not easy for us to develop a genuine feeling that the material elements are really living entities. Conversely, it is all too easy to generate a false and sentimental notion that 'the hills are alive' by projecting all kinds of imaginary properties on to the world. We cannot generate a belief in, say, naiads and dryads by force of will; nor can we deny what we know scientifically about the way the universe operates. We have somehow to hunt for a real feeling for the life of things, even from our sophisticated viewpoint. It starts with intuitive knowledge, not a set of beliefs.

There is a hierarchy: rocks are not as alive as plants, and plants are not as alive as human beings. We have to draw the line somewhere – it would be hard to regard, say, stainless steel as a living substance; each of us will have a point at which we stop acknowledging and respecting the life of another being or 'thing' and start simply using it for our own convenience. For some unfortunate people this line is drawn even at certain other human beings – of course this is also unfortunate for the people with whom they come into contact. At the other end of the spectrum, the Tibetans used to refuse to engage in mining for minerals: they would pan for gold but not, as the Chinese are now doing in Tibet, disturb the earth and the dragons that they believe guard the gold it conceals.

I would go so far as to say that a universe conceived of as dead cannot be a universe in which one stands any chance of attaining Enlightenment. (Whether you stand any chance in a living universe is of course up to you.) It may be difficult for us to get back to the view of the world that came naturally to our ancestors, but poets have persisted in seeing the universe as alive: surely no poet could have a totally Newtonian outlook, the kind of attitude that Blake termed 'single vision' and 'Newton's sleep'. Milton, for example, traces the origin of mining to Hell itself: in *Paradise Lost* the devils start excavating minerals in order to manufacture artillery to use against heaven. One could even interpret the whole romantic movement as expressing a great protest against the Newtonian picture of nature and a reassertion of essentially pagan values.

To get a more vivid sense of the elements, you could think of them in terms of the colours and shapes of the Buddhist *stūpa*, which is said to symbolize the elements. Or you could let your imagination go even further and think of the elements as gods or goddesses (traditionally, earth and water are goddesses and fire and air are gods), building up connections with them that will gradually deepen and enrich your feeling for them, so that you experience them more and more vibrantly, with more and more emotional colour. You could also make use of the mythological system of elements connected with western alchemy, though it offers not single personifications so much as multiple denizens of each element: gnomes in the earth, undines in the water, salamanders in the fire, and sylphs in the air. Suggesting that one should summon up such beings through the imagination is not to say that they are imaginary. Local spirits do not represent a primitive attempt to explain things in a pseudo-scientific way: when people speak of dryads in the trees, they are trying to express their actual experience of these 'things' as living presences.

The elements that we experience as earth, water, fire, and air are represented at the highest, Transcendental level by the four female Buddhas of the Vajrayāna mandala of the five archetypal Buddhas (the fifth, central figure representing the element of space) just as different characteristics of wisdom are represented by the male Buddhas. The female Buddhas inseparably united with their male consorts thus represent the highest conceivable sublimation of one's experience of the four great elements. In other words, there is a continuity of experience running all the way through our everyday classifications and categories to Enlightenment itself. Mind and matter, body and spirit, are not separate things but patterns we can recognize in what is really an unbroken continuity of experience.

From *Living with Awareness* (2003, pp.56-63)

3 The *chöd* practice

1. EGOISM IS NOT AN ENTITY, BUT AN ATTITUDE

Its meaning is to be found only in the doing of it.

Chöd is a Tibetan word which means 'cutting', and it corresponds to the Sanskrit *chedana*. This same word is part of the title of the *Vajracchedikā Sūtra*, known in the West as the *Diamond Sūtra*, the teaching of the Transcendental wisdom that cuts like the diamond. However, whereas the *Diamond Sūtra* is meant to cut off ignorance at the root, the *chöd* practice is concerned simply with the cutting off of ego or, to be more precise, with the cutting off of attachment to the ego or self, especially attachment to the physical body, with which we so firmly identify ourselves much of the time.

Before we look at what happens in the *chöd* practice, we should pause to consider briefly what is meant by ego. In one of his songs, the Tibetan yogi Milarepa refers to what the translator calls 'the demon of egotism', but we have to be rather careful with this language. There is much talk of the ego in spiritual circles: people say things like, 'Oh well, I mustn't let my ego get in the way,' or, 'I suppose my ego just caught me napping,' as though the ego were a mischievous entity, like a disruptive sprite. Such expressions reflect and reinforce a subtle confusion of the point at issue, suggesting as they do that the ego is not you, when that is exactly what it is. It *is* you. It is you adopting a particular attitude, being rigid, or unreceptive, or stubborn. Egoism is not an entity, but an attitude. One may say for example that generosity counteracts egoism, but not that it gets rid of your ego (or the demon of egoism). The obvious problem of using language that seems to postulate a separate ego identity is that it can allow you to abdicate responsibility for your own selfishness: 'It isn't me, it's my ego.' The ego is like the 'it' in the phrase 'it's raining'; the psychological or spiritual reality is simply that one behaves egoistically. It is this egoistic attitude that the *chöd* practice is designed to cut off.

The *chöd* practice was originated by Padampa Sangye and Machig Labdrön. To do the practice, the Tantric yogi leaves the town, leaves his friends and companions, and goes far away, to a wild and solitary place, preferably to one that is haunted, such as a cremation ground. He takes with him various articles that he will need in the ritual part of the practice, including the skin of a beast of prey, complete with claws, a tent, a staff surmounted by a trident, a trumpet made of a human thigh bone, and a large double-sided drum.

This yogi settles himself in that solitary spot, perhaps with corpses and bones round about, seeing the occasional glimpse of glowing eyes in the dark from the quick stare of the resident jackals, or even having a sense of non-human beings around as well. In this eerie setting, he starts upon various preliminaries to the *chöd* practice, and offers up a prayer to the great Tantric guru Padmasambhava. He then turns his attention to his physical body, beginning to identify it with the corpses lying around him in various stages of decomposition. Next, he tries to experience his mind, his true mind, as being separate from his body, visualizing it as the 'knowledge *ḍākinī*' or 'awareness *ḍākinī*'. She is completely naked except for a few ornaments of bone, though this *ḍākinī* is usually black in colour. She has a wrathful expression and three eyes, the third eye being the eye of wisdom. She holds a kind of chopper in one hand and a skull-cup in the other. Identifying yourself with this knowledge-*ḍākinī*, you see your physical body lying there dead, a fat, luscious-looking corpse, while your true mind stands beside it, independent from it, imagined as the knowledge or awareness *ḍākinī*.

This terrible *ḍākinī* proceeds to wield her chopper. Suddenly, she chops off the head from your own dead body. Your severed head rapidly becomes a skull, which the *ḍākinī* turns upside down and places on top of three smaller skulls, thus creating a sort of three-legged cauldron. She then cuts your corpse into bits and throws them into the skull cauldron as an offering to the deities. This done, certain mantras are pronounced – that is, you, the yogi, pronounce them – and as you do so the pieces of flesh and bone in the skull cauldron are transformed into *amṛta*, the nectar of immortality.

Next you invite the Three Jewels, and the guardian deities together with spirits of various kinds to come and partake of the feast of nectar. You tell them that you are sacrificing your physical body because it is the root of duality, making you distinguish between subject and object. Your mood is happy and triumphant, even heroic, as you call upon a disparate array of spiritual beings, high and low, to come and enjoy the nectar in whatever form they please, peaceful or wrathful. As a Tantric yogi you must actually experience all this. It isn't just an idea, or a fantasy to read about in a well-lit room. It is something you actually go through, on your own in some solitary spot, by conjuring up all this terrifying imagery. Its meaning is to be found only in the doing of it.

Chöd practitioners are usually wandering yogis; whenever they find a suitable spot, especially a cremation ground, they stay there for a few days to perform the *chöd* practice. Over time, if you do this practice consistently, you come to feel as though your body is a corpse already, and your attachment to it starts to wane. You see more and more clearly that only the mind, in the sense of a pure and radiant reality, exists – whether or not it is realized in its *ḍākinī* form.

From *Creative Symbols of Tantric Buddhism* (2004, pp.150-3)

4 The unpleasantness of the body

1. RESTORING A BALANCE

The message is that we have to go beyond the superficial appearance of the body, just as we have to go beyond the literal meaning of the words of the sutta, any sutta.

> *Again, bhikkhus, a bhikkhu reviews this same body up from the soles of the feet and down from the top of the hair, bounded by skin, as full of many kinds of impurity thus: "In this body there are head-hairs, body-hairs, nails, teeth, skin, flesh, sinews, bones, bone-marrow, kidneys, heart, liver, diaphragm, spleen, lungs, large intestines, small intestines, contents of the stomach, faeces, bile, phlegm, pus, blood, sweat, fat, tears, grease, spittle, snot, oil of the joints, and urine." Just as though there were a bag with an opening at both ends full of many sorts of grain, such as hill rice, red rice, beans, peas, millet, and white rice, and a man with good eyes were to open it and review it thus: "This is hill rice, this is red rice, these are beans, these are peas, this is millet, this is white rice"; so too, a bhikkhu reviews this same body ... as full of many kinds of impurity thus: "In this body there are head-hairs ... and urine."*[75]

We do not normally think of our bodies as intrinsically unpleasant. We might spend a while in front of the bathroom mirror each morning preparing our body for public view, but we generally feel that these preparations are enough to render us inoffensive in the eyes of our fellow human beings. After all, when we look at the bodies of other people, and even when we come into physical contact with them, it is often quite a pleasant experience. But, of course, we don't see the whole picture. When we see or touch the body, we are aware of its surface – but what about all those internal processes, the organs, the fat, the blood and bones? These are not the features that usually spring to mind when we think of bodies, especially not our own, and yet they are as necessary to the body's make-up as anything we can see.

This section of the *Satipaṭṭhāna Sutta* is designed to give us a more complete perception of the body, a more balanced response to it, and therefore a deeper awareness and understanding of its nature. You are meant to start the meditation by mentally comparing the body to a bag in which various kinds of grain are mixed together, the body's outer skin being imagined as the container of all the thirty-one kinds of bodily substance. Thus far, unpleasantness does not enter into the picture – the analogy is meant simply to enable us to view the body's constituents with the attitude that we would bring to the neutral task of sorting out a bag of mixed grains. This will lessen both our personal identification with the body and our resistance to taking notice of its unpleasant aspects. For, of course, the recollection of the body's 'foulness' is not an abstract, conceptual affair, and the sutta drives this home by relentlessly listing the contents of this 'bag'. When we start to consider them in isolation – the hair, nails, and teeth, organs such as kidney, heart, and liver, and various kinds of pus, grease, blood, sweat, and so on – we are likely to feel a sense of revulsion. And this is the object of the practice: not only to become aware of the body's contents but actively to cultivate a sense that it is revolting.

Why then should we want to cultivate revulsion towards the human body? Is it any more objective to view the body as foul than to view it as fair? Would it not be more positive to cultivate a sense of the beauty of the human form? In fact, the Buddha's intention here is not to tell us what an objective view of the human body would be like, but to restore a balance in our response to it, to enable us to experience it more as it really is. It is because we have a fundamental bias towards wanting to see the body as beautiful that we must acknowledge that it is repulsive as well – although in itself it cannot be said to be either one or the other. It is a case of bending the bamboo the other way, to use a traditional metaphor, or looking at the other side of the picture. We will consider later the extent to which this practice might be appropriate for us; first, let us try to grasp its original purpose.

The things we are enjoined to perceive as impure or unlovely are exactly those aspects of life about which we delude ourselves most compulsively. The body is impermanent – sooner or later it will break down and die, and thus it cannot make us permanently happy, however much time, effort, and money we spend on keeping it healthy and beautiful. It is simply not worth expending energy on pampering the body, adorning it and trying to make it attractive; it will not repay the attention we lavish upon it. The only reason for looking after it is so that it can function as the basis for the cultivation of truer, deeper beauty – the beauty of higher states of consciousness. If we are too attached to the attractive physical aspects of our own body and the bodies of other people, we can all too easily fail to see that deeper beauty.

The main target in cultivating revulsion of the body is of course the huge power over our lives of sexual desire. Followers of the Theravādin tradition commonly recite the list of bodily constituents like a sort of mantra as an antidote to this, the strongest form of attraction of all. In the grip of sexual attraction we can scarcely help relating to other people just as bodies, or even as objects. The more we look to others to gratify our own desires, seeing them as members of a particular sex, the less we can relate to them as individuals. The point of cultivating revulsion towards the physical body of someone whom we find attractive is in fact to give room to the imagination so that we can see that person as an emergent individual rather than just as someone who arouses our sexual interest.

So the aim is not to see ourselves or other people as loathsome. The practice is a corrective meant to help us see through our infatuation with the surface of human existence and learn to adopt a more objective view, so that we can relate more truly and deeply to life's essential purpose. By drawing our attention to those aspects of the body we normally experience as repulsive, and away from those aspects that are attractive to us, the practice encourages us to reflect on what bodies are really like, to see the skull beneath the skin, as Eliot says.

Love is blind, as the saying goes: we simply overlook someone's less attractive features if we are strongly drawn to them. Of course, it is not just someone's body to which we are attracted; we are also drawn to the character inside the body, so to speak – indeed, one may be attracted to all sorts of aspects of a person to which a relationship with their body may give access. These features often – in a way quite rightly – make us oblivious to a person's physical defects. However, there is a difference between freely choosing to look at a person's best qualities and being 'captivated' by them. What the sutta is concerned with here is freedom from sexual craving.

We say that we are 'captivated' or 'charmed' or 'bewitched' by someone when in truth we are in thrall to our own craving. We might think that it is their sparkling eyes or shining hair that attracts us, but it is really what that feature has come to represent in our own mind. If the features of our beloved are less than perfect, our desire will override our direct experience of what is actually there – after all, very few people are perfect to look at. Our capacity to be selective in the way we perceive the loved one shows that what we think of as attractive in someone's appearance is a function of our craving rather than anything intrinsic to that person.

The method offered by the sutta is to reflect on an organ or some recognizable bodily tissue in isolation from the rest, to prevent it from being subsumed in the general perception of the body as a whole as being essentially attractive. A lover is thrilled at the idea of taking his beloved in his arms, but the romance inevitably palls if he starts to think of that alluring figure as a bundle of physiological processes. The technique is to keep focusing on the parts of the body separately – all the traditional thirty-one items. One cannot deny that the thirty-one substances are present in the body, nor that the idea of handling them separately would dampen one's enthusiasm for handling the body as a whole. Thinking of the snot or spittle of one's beloved is hardly calculated to inflame the passions. By reversing our normal view of the body, the recollection of the foulness of the body helps us to look unblinkingly at what exactly we are attracted to. It can be helpful, when you are losing sleep and mindfulness and self-respect over some very attractive person, to ask yourself, 'What really is this thing that I am so obsessed with getting intimately involved with? Let's see, there's head-hairs, body-hairs, nails, teeth, skin, flesh, sinews, bones, bone-marrow, kidneys ...'

In the *Therīgāthā*, the verses of the early Buddhist sisters, there is a tale that illustrates in a shocking manner how the list of body parts prescribed for recitation in the *Satipaṭṭhāna Sutta* differs from the infatuated lover's recital of beautiful qualities – 'Her hair! Her eyes! Her lips! ...' The story concerns Subhā, a female wanderer of exceptional physical beauty. One day, while walking alone in the forest, Subhā is accosted by 'a certain libertine of Rājagaha' who bars her way and tries to 'solicit ... her to sensual pleasures' in contravention of her monastic vows. '"Tis thine eyes,' murmurs the youth (in Mrs Rhys David's Edwardian translation) 'the sight of which feedeth the depth of my passion.' Subhā, however, is no ordinary woman. She has, so the verse tells us, strengthened her resolve towards Enlightenment under former Buddhas in previous lifetimes, and having received the precepts from Śākyamuni himself, has at last established herself as a 'non-returner' (a very high level of spiritual attainment). This is unfortunate for the young man in our story, whose passion continues to grow despite all Subhā's efforts to help him see sense. She repeatedly points out that the body is an aggregation of foul substances and that no ultimately real self or beauty can be found in it. 'What is this eye but a little ball lodged in the fork of a hollow tree?' she asks. But the youth will not take no for an answer, and drives Subhā to a drastic and dramatic gesture. She gouges out one of her own eyes and offers it to him, to do with as he wishes. The youth, as one might expect, is horrified: his passion withers on the spot and he implores her forgiveness.[76]

Subhā's story shows how craving turns objective truth on its head. *Subha* means 'shining', 'beautiful', and also 'auspicious'. But Subhā is not beautiful because of her good looks. Her beauty is not physical but spiritual, even Transcendental. When she plucks out her eye, it does nothing to blind her spiritual vision or diminish her loveliness. It is the libertine who, with two good eyes, remains truly blind in the spiritual sense. The concern of the sutta is not to denigrate what seems to us beautiful but to expose the lack of spiritual vision exemplified by the young man, and thus to encourage us to look beyond mundane beauty.

The story is meant to jolt us out of our usual distorted way of seeing things, which is summarized in the Buddha's teaching of the four *viparyāsas* or 'topsy-turvy views'. Firstly, we see things that are impermanent as though they were permanent. Secondly, we see things that are intrinsically painful as if they were pleasant. Thirdly, we see things that are insubstantial as if they had some ultimately real essence, and especially we imagine that we ourselves have some kind of fixed self. And fourthly, we see things that are crude and unremarkable as if they were beautiful. It is especially this last *viparyāsa* that the practice of *asubha bhāvanā* is designed to put right.

From the upside-down perspective of worldly consciousness, the physical body is the centre of all our activity and interest. We work to feed the body and give it shelter, we clothe it and decorate it, we might even fall in love with other bodies and, in time, bring new bodies into being. According to Buddhism, however, we are determined not by the physical body but by consciousness. Our concern should therefore be less with the quality of what we look at and more with the quality with which we look. By transforming our level of awareness, we can transform not only what we are but also the world we live in. The polarity, if it can really be described as such, is not between the pleasant and the unpleasant, but between the relatively crude and the relatively subtle. Through concentrated meditation, one's interests and desires come to be more and more absorbed in refined states of being and are led upwards towards forms that are purer and more intrinsically beautiful than anything to be found on the gross material plane.

Without direct experience, a tremendous leap of the imagination is required to trust in the possibility of such refined states. Usually, not daring to make the leap, we stay firmly attached to 'the devil we know', the physical body and the material world it inhabits. This, essentially, is the problem faced by Nanda, who was another of the Buddha's disciples, as well as being his cousin. According to a story from the *Udāna* of the Pāli canon, Nanda wants to pursue the spiritual life, but he is held back from committing himself fully by his lack of experience of higher modes of consciousness. Instead, he finds himself longing for his former lover, a beautiful Śākyan girl. He cannot develop faith in the Dharma when the greatest pleasure he knows is the love of a beautiful woman: he can't imagine anything more satisfying than that. The Buddha knows that Nanda will have to broaden his spiritual perspective if he is to commit himself to the spiritual path. By means of his magical powers, he therefore transports Nanda to the Heaven of the Thirty-Three, a 'deva realm' coterminous with highly absorbed states of meditative concentration. There, Nanda at last encounters a beauty deeper and lovelier than he has ever imagined, enjoying the company of celestial nymphs whose 'dovefooted' beauty far outshines the crude, merely physical beauty of his earthly lover. This is enough to make his confidence in the Dharma unshakeable: he can see for himself that higher states of consciousness exist. From this point onwards he is able to make swift progress on the path, because material objects of desire no longer attract him.[77]

From the perspective of heightened consciousness, the apparent beauty of the mundane world appears grotesque. This is Subhā's teaching to the libertine from Rājagaha: it is not her eye plucked from its socket that is grotesque, but his lust for her 'beautiful eyes'. Her objectivity is not so much about what is beautiful as about what is true. Unable to see how cramped and gloomy, how mediocre, our experience really is, we presume that all we have ever known is all there is to know and form our judgements accordingly.

The traditional teaching as delivered to celibate monks can sometimes give the impression that the repulsiveness of the body is the reality of it and that its attractiveness is purely illusory. But, of course, a sense of the repulsiveness of the body does not constitute a dispassionate view. I am reminded of a doctor friend of mine who once read the passage of Buddhaghosa's *Visuddhimagga* in which the process of digestion is described as part of the meditation known as the 'contemplation of the loathsomeness of food'. Buddhaghosa goes through the whole process with what one can only call gusto, lingering almost lovingly over the way in which great lumps of coarse, heavy matter are tossed into the mouth and from there descend to the stomach, where all sorts of unspeakable things happen to them. It is another example of 'bending the bamboo the other way', of course, but my friend was quite indignant about it. 'It is clear,' he said, 'that Buddhaghosa has not understood the delicate, complex, and miraculous phenomenon which is the human digestive process.' Clearly, attractiveness and repulsiveness are both subjective judgements; my friend's admiration of the digestive system was in its way just as valid as the repulsion advocated by Buddhaghosa.

The approach of the Theravādin monk might be to say, 'You may think this woman is attractive, but she is really just a bag of impurities', but to take this attitude literally is to make the classic mistake of confusing method with doctrine. It is on some occasions recommended that one should dwell on a certain aspect of something not because it is the absolute, objective truth of the matter, but because to see it that way is beneficial to one's spiritual development. The methodological approach consists in fastening your attention upon one aspect of something – while for the time being ignoring other aspects – for a specific practical purpose. The fundamental Buddhist teaching of *dukkha*, for example, the idea that existence is characterized essentially by suffering, is to be understood as methodological truth rather than 'objective' truth. Obviously there is more to life than suffering, but it is essential to the development of awareness and faith that we keep the truth of *dukkha* in mind. Likewise, one might choose to reflect on a particular aspect of bodily existence for a particular purpose. The emphasis of Tibetan Buddhism on the preciousness of the human body is an encouragement to make the most of the unique opportunity we have to practise the Dharma – an opportunity that is indeed precious. But it is simply a method of practice, just as much as the Theravādin exhortation to reflect on the body's foulness; in reality, the body is no more precious than it is foul. Neither approach is intended to push home a point about what bodies actually are – they are techniques, not statements of metaphysical truth.

However, perhaps we need to question whether 'bending the bamboo the other way' by contemplating the foulness of the body is likely to have the desired effect in our own case. Most western Buddhists have considerable work to do to establish the basis of healthy positivity necessary for any sort of spiritual life, and this might be made still more difficult if we were to dwell upon ugliness. Viewing each other as bags of manifold impurities is hardly the best way to start developing compassion and empathy and appreciation, particularly at the start of our spiritual career. Better, perhaps, to banish thoughts of all that pus and phlegm and bile, and with them the limited, literal perspective of attraction and repulsion, of mundane beauty versus ugliness, to apprehend an altogether higher beauty, a beauty that is not reliant on physical conditions at all. Lama Govinda made this the theme of a short story called 'Look deeper!' The narrator is walking along a road with a Theravādin bhikkhu when a young village girl passes them by. 'What a beautiful girl!' says the narrator, whereupon the monk, as might be expected, replies, 'Look deeper. It's only a bag of bones.' At this point the Bodhisattva Avalokiteśvara manifests before them and in turn tells the monk to look deeper still – to look deeper than the bag of bones and see the living, suffering human being, with all her potential for spiritual development.

The message is that we have to go beyond the superficial appearance of the body, just as we have to go beyond the literal meaning of the words of the sutta, any sutta. Bodies as we encounter them are never simply bodies. The most truly beautiful aspect of any human being is the fact that he or she is, potentially at least, a spiritual being. Even though that spiritual potential is sometimes well hidden, we cannot afford to reduce anyone to a bag of impurities if we want to appreciate that beauty. The beauty we experience through the senses is not the highest beauty available to us, and when we have some experience of this higher beauty, we are at last able to shake off the hold that worldly desire has on us. We can begin to transform our habitual attachment to what we think we see and, by extension, to what we think we are.

From *Living with Awareness* (2003, pp.47-55)

2. A VERY POSITIVE KIND OF DETACHMENT

There's nothing morbid or melancholy about these practices – not when they are done in the right way, and by the type of person to whom they are suited.

> *The physical body is only a loathsome thing of many loathsome parts ...*[78]

This type of reflection is especially recommended to those in whom craving and desire for sense experience is present, and who are very much attached to the physical body. In strict objective terms, the physical body is neither loathsome nor attractive. It's made up of parts which are bits and pieces of 'matter' and which, in themselves, are neither loathsome nor anything else. They are whatever they are – just chemicals and so on. But the monk, or the practitioner, reflects on the body as loathsome to counteract his purely one-sided attachment and craving, which is due to seeing the body only as desirable. He tries to see the other side of the picture – tries to get things more in perspective.

> *The attitude of the* Bodhicaryāvatāra *and the* Śikṣāsamuccaya *is on the side of melancholy common sense.*[79]

I don't quite agree with Matics' expression 'melancholy common sense'. The experience which results from these practices is certainly not one of melancholy – a very ego-centred emotion – but very much one of exhilaration, zest, and enthusiasm for getting on with the spiritual life, as well as a very positive kind of detachment. It's certainly not a dull and depressing experience. If you think that it's likely to be that, then that type of practice isn't for you. You should feel exhilarated after visiting the cemetery, not depressed. If it makes you depressed, don't do it. Depression isn't very helpful. In Tibetan Buddhism, especially, they engage in these practices in a very positive spirit, and make use of human skins and human skulls with a kind of glee. They're not at all depressed, or sorrowful, or melancholy, because they really do rise above the ego. They really do get a much loftier perspective on things – really do see the whole chain of birth and death, and feel themselves a bit detached from that, and rising above it and getting on to the spiritual path that leads beyond rebirth. Thus it's all very positive and very inspiring. There's

nothing morbid or melancholy about these practices – not when they are done in the right way, and by the type of person to whom they are suited.
From a seminar on *The Endlessly Fascinating Cry* (1977, pp.203-4)

3. SURELY CONTEMPLATING 'LOATHSOMENESS' CAN ONLY BE OFF-PUTTING?

One mustn't look at this question of *asubha-bhavana* in a moralistic way; it's more like refining your appreciation of the arts.

Sangharakshita: *Subha* means 'pure' and also 'beautiful, so *asubha* can be translated as 'impure' or 'the unlovely' or the 'unbeautiful'. This is connected with the way we see things. If you are attached to something, you see it as pleasant and desirable, even as beautiful, but if you are not attached to it, you may not see it in that way. Very often we see as pleasant and desirable, or as beautiful, something which is not really very good for us, but we see it as pleasant and even beautiful because of our desire. So we have to reverse the usual way in which we see things. This is especially applied in Buddhism to the relations between the sexes, and this is why one is asked as an extreme antidote to one's extreme craving, say, for physical bodies, to reflect on what those bodies are really like, or will be like in a few years' time. Here the so-called 'corpse' meditation comes in. You start off by bringing to mind the body – the sort of body that maybe you're usually quite attracted to – but you think, well, when it's dead what's it going to be like? And you just go through the ten stages of the decomposition of a corpse – I won't go through all the stages – ending up with just a handful of dust that blows in all directions, and you think, 'Is this really what I'm drawn to? Is this really what I'm attracted to?' And it gives you food for thought.

If you are in a mood of intense sexual desire, you're likely to see almost any person who takes your fancy as attractive, but once the desire has passed, you may take a second look and wonder, 'What was I thinking?' You see something or someone as beautiful and pure because of your subjective desire, so to curb that desire, or at least limit it, you cultivate this other way of seeing: you try to see the object of your desire as impure and unbeautiful, especially by the way of the ten 'corpse' meditations.

But surely to think in terms of contemplating 'loathsomeness' can only be off-putting to the newcomer to Buddhism. How is one to explain it? One can put it more positively. One can speak of a higher, more spiritual beauty – the beauty of the forms encountered in meditation, when you visualize forms and figures more beautiful than anything you can see in ordinary life, and you can thus lead your interest and your desire in that direction. Or you can try to refine your desire through the enjoyment of the fine arts. One can say that there are degrees of beauty, and that these are very often linked up with one's own state of mind; the more refined your state of mind, the more refined the objects which you find beautiful, and to which you are attracted. If you are in a rather crude state of mind, you can be attracted to almost anybody, but as you get a bit more refined, you get a bit more choosy – you place more importance on certain features, or certain expressions. Then perhaps you think in terms of somebody's nature or temperament, or intellectual characteristics, without paying too much attention to the physical side of things, and then maybe you start thinking of purely ideal qualities, existing on the meditative level, but not necessarily associated with any particular human being, and you're more and more drawn to those. In that way, your desires become more and more refined and drawn more and more upwards. Similarly, in cultural terms, when you are young and crude and vigorous you may like rock-and-roll, but as you get more emotionally refined, perhaps you start liking Mozart or Beethoven. One mustn't look at this question of *asubha bhāvanā* in a moralistic way; it's more like refining your appreciation of the arts.

Q: Is that what Plato's *Symposium*'s about? – progressive refinement from physical love through to *sophia*, love of wisdom.

S: Yes, that's right. But it must be genuine, not a purely mental thing. Some people go through the stages mentally, but in all practical senses they're just where they always were. And again it mustn't lead to a cynical depreciation of beauty. The Buddha was once misrepresented as teaching that when you reach a certain stage of spiritual development you see the whole world as ugly. But the Buddha said, 'No, I didn't teach any such thing. I said that when you reach that stage of development, then you know what beauty really is.'[80] There is a subtle difference.

Q: You meet people every so often who have this natural inclination to look on the world as ugly, so they nip off to the forest and do tons of 'impurity' meditations and then walk around like skeletons, with big staring eyes, and when they look at you, you can see them thinking 'Bones, bones, bones'.

S: Well, it's one side of the picture, but what you mustn't think is that seeing someone as bones is seeing the truth, and seeing them as flesh and blood is not seeing the truth. In a little book I was once given on Buddhism, there's an X-ray picture of a human being, and then there's an ordinary photograph, and then there's a picture produced by thermal photography which comes out in different colour patches, green and red. All of these give you a picture of the 'same' human being or human body, but which is the true picture? You can't say that one is true and the others are false. What they tell you is that there are different ways of looking at the same thing, and you shouldn't identify any one way of looking at things, including your own, as the only true way. When it's suggested that you see people as skeletons, that is only to show you that when you see a flesh-and-blood human being walking about that's only seeing things from one point of view. Seeing them as skeletons helps to correct that one-sidedness. But if you think that seeing them walking about as flesh-and-blood human beings is a false perception, but seeing them as skeletons is a true perception, you've only changed the absolutization of one relative and limited point of view for the absolutization of another relative and limited point of view, instead of using the one to help you appreciate the relativity of the other.

When you try to see things you usually find pleasing as displeasing, you're not asserting that in ultimate metaphysical reality they are displeasing rather than pleasing; you are looking at another side of the matter in order to counteract your naturally, or normally, one-sided attitude – ideally not just to develop a different point of view, though that may be useful, but to reach a higher, and more developed point of view. A skeleton, as such, is not more 'real' than flesh and blood. But it's useful sometimes to remind oneself that there is a skeleton behind the flesh and blood, a 'skull beneath the skin'. That gives you a more balanced picture.

From a seminar on 'Conditions of Stability in the Order' (1979, pp.71-3)

5 The *nidāna* chain

1. THE TRUTH OF CONDITIONALITY

From our ignorance flows a whole chain of events …

Ignorance, by which is meant spiritual ignorance, unawareness of reality, is in a sense the basic poison, the raw ingredient from which all the others are made. The traditional antidote for ignorance is meditation on the *nidānas*, the links, of conditioned coproduction. This formulation gives us a way of reflecting on the truth of conditionality: that in dependence upon A, B arises. It asks us to see that from our ignorance flows a whole chain of events; one could say that it's a reflection on the workings of the law of karma.

Buddhist tradition enumerates many lists of these links, one of the best known being the chain of twelve links depicted around the rim of the Tibetan Wheel of Life. This chain 'begins' – really a beginningless beginning – with ignorance, and ends with decay and death. As well as the twelve *nidānas* pertaining to conditioned existence depicted on the Wheel of Life, there are another twelve – the *nidānas* pertaining to, or at least leading to, unconditioned existence, Nirvāṇa. The twelve 'worldly' *nidānas* represent the cyclical type of conditionality, the Wheel of Life, and the reactive mind, while the twelve spiritual [positive] *nidānas* represent the spiral type of conditionality, the stages of the path, and the creative mind.

From *The Bodhisattva Ideal* (1999, p.84)

2. HOW WE MAKE OURSELVES WHAT WE ARE

Much of the time we are really no more free, no more spontaneous, no more alive, than a well-programmed computer.

In this meditation practice one consciously reflects on a chain of links – or *nidānas* – illustrating the principle of conditioned coproduction in terms of human existence, by means of the images that depict it in the outermost circle of the Tibetan Wheel of Life, as follows:

1) Ignorance, *avidyā*: represented by a blind man with a stick; 2) volitions or karma formations, *saṁskāras*: a potter with a wheel and pots; 3) consciousness, *vijñāna*: a monkey climbing a flowering tree (we climb up into the branches of this world and reach out for its flowers and fruit); 4) mind and body, *nāma-rūpa* (i.e. name and form): a boat with four passengers, one of whom, representing consciousness, is steering; 5) the six sense-organs, *ṣaḍāyatana*: a house with five windows and a door; 6) sense-contact, *sparśa*: a man and woman embracing; 7) feeling, *vedanā*: a man with an arrow in his eye; 8) craving, *tṛṣṇā*: a woman offering a drink to a seated man; 9) grasping, *upādāna*: a man or woman gathering fruit from a tree; 10) becoming or coming-to-be, development, *bhāva*: a man and a woman copulating; 11) birth, *jāti*: a woman giving birth; 12) old age and death, *jarā-maraṇa*: a corpse being carried to the cremation ground.

Here is the whole process of birth, life, death, and rebirth according to the principle of conditioned coproduction. As a result of our ignorance, and of the volitions based upon our ignorance in previous lives, we are precipitated again into this world with a consciousness endowed with a psychophysical organism, and thus six senses, which come into contact with the external universe and give rise to feelings – pleasant, painful, and neutral. We develop craving for the pleasant feelings, and thus condition ourselves in such a way that inevitably we have to be born again and die again.

These twelve links are distributed over three lives, but at the same time they are also all contained in one life – even in one moment. They illustrate – whether spread over three lives or a day or an hour or a minute – the whole way in which we condition ourselves; how we make ourselves what we are by our own reactions to what we experience.

When we look at the Wheel of Life we are looking in a mirror. In all its circles and all its details, we find ourselves. When I contemplate anger, in the image of a snake at the centre of the Wheel of Life, it is not anger in general I am concerned with. When I contemplate greed, in the likeness of a cock, I am not considering the universal psychological phenomenon of greed. When I contemplate ignorance, in the form of a pig, I am not studying some category of Buddhist thought. It is me there, just me: the anger, the greed, and the ignorance – they're all mine.

Seeing, next, a circle of people either going from a lower to a higher state or slipping from a higher to a lower state, I recognize myself in them. I am never standing apart from that wheel: at any one time I am going either one way or the other, up or down.

Looking beyond these figures I may imagine that at last I am examining a representation of six different and separate realms of existence – which in a sense they are. The human realm is clearly my own, where people are communicating, learning, creating. But when I look at the realm of the gods I find there my own moments and dreams of bliss and joy, and in the realm of the titans, my own ambition and competitiveness. Grazing and snuffling with the animals is my own lack of vision, my own consumerism, my own dullness. In the realm of the hungry ghosts is my own desolate yearning for some solid satisfaction from the objects of my craving. And in hell are my own nightmares, my own moments of burning anger and cool malice, my own brief seasons of hatred and revenge.

Finally, in contemplating the twelve *nidānas* of the outermost circle we get a picture of how the whole process goes on, the mechanism of the whole thing. We see ourselves as a piece of clockwork, as indeed we are most of the time. Much of the time we are really no more free, no more spontaneous, no more alive, than a well-programmed computer. Because we are unaware, we are conditioned and therefore fettered. So in this practice we become aware of our conditionality, the mechanical, programmed nature of our lives, our tendency to react, our self-imprisonment, our lack of spontaneity or creativity – our own death, our spiritual death. Almost everything we do is just tightening our bonds, chaining us more securely to the Wheel of Life. The contemplation of the twelve *nidānas* provides a traditional support for this kind of awareness.[81]

From *What is the Dharma?* (1998, pp.194-6)

3. YOU CAN'T FIND ANY ABSOLUTE FIRST BEGINNING

It isn't that ignorance represents anything like an ultimate first cause of things.

Q: Does ignorance arise in the same way as the other *nidānas* in strict causal relationship with the preceding *nidāna*? The relationship in this case does not seem so clear cut as that between other pairs of *nidānas*, for example, six sense spheres and contact.

Sangharakshita: There is, or there used to be, a common misunderstanding on this point. Usually it's said that *avidyā* or ignorance is the first of the twelve *nidānas*, and because they're enumerated in this particular order, beginning with ignorance and ending with birth, old age, disease and death, it used to be thought, when Buddhism first came to be studied, that ignorance represented some sort of primordial first cause, that first there was ignorance and it was out of ignorance, as it were, that everything came, so that everything was caused by this great primeval cosmic ignorance. But that is not the Buddhist point of view at all. *Avidyā* may be enumerated first in the series of twelve *nidānas* but it's not to be conceived of as coming absolutely first, before all the others. Under some circumstances it does, and under other circumstances it doesn't.

The *nidāna* chain can be subdivided into those *nidānas* which represent the karma process or cause process, and those *nidānas* which represent the effect process. If you look closely at the chain of the *nidānas*, you'll find you've got a cause process of the past life, a result process or effect process of the present life, a cause process of the present life, and an effect process of the future life. So you've got in sequence, cause process, result process, cause process, result process; and this goes on and on, ignorance being included as part of the cause process looked at from one particular point of view. In a sense, of course, ignorance is present all the time. It's just that it's more noticeable, one might say, at some times than others.

But ignorance in the sense of privation of the realization of reality underlies all the *nidānas*. One mustn't think of it just coming first and then ceasing to exist. No; it goes on repeating itself all the time. But one has got this sequence of action process, result process, action process, result process, and this goes back and back and back. You can't find any absolute first beginning. So it isn't that ignorance represents anything like an ultimate first cause of things. One has to try to see it as an essential part of the whole process, either as actually operative or, so to speak, lying in abeyance and waiting to become operative when circumstances permit.

From Q&A on a Mitra Retreat (1985, p.3)

6 Śūnyatā meditations

1. A SPRINGBOARD FOR THE EXPERIENCE OF INSIGHT

That Insight, as it is deepened, will have a transforming effect on your whole personality, your whole being.

> *Since I have disposed of Samsara and Nirvāṇa*
> *And have nor hope nor fear in my mind,*
> *I shall ne'er regress in my meditation.*[82]

Sangharakshita: Why do you think that Milarepa is making this point that he will never regress in his meditation? Surely it is aimed at his disciple Rechungpa, who, if he hasn't regressed already, is certainly about to regress in his meditation because he is haring off to India in pursuit of logic and science. He hasn't been keeping up his meditation very well and perhaps won't be able to do so in India. So Milarepa is explaining that he himself will never regress in his meditation, and he also explains why. But how does one 'dispose of Samsara and Nirvāṇa'? What is meant by the words Samsara and Nirvāṇa?

Q: They're words or concepts which Milarepa has presumably transcended, whereas Rechungpa is still very much caught up with words and ideas, intellectual concepts.

S: But is it easy to dispose of those concepts? Is it easy even to think of disposing of those concepts? To dispose of the concepts of saṁsāra and Nirvāṇa means in a sense to go beyond the whole framework of Buddhism itself, certainly beyond the framework of the Theravāda For the Theravāda, saṁsāra and Nirvāṇa are ultimate concepts. The whole spiritual life is based upon them, on the idea that you get off the wheel of life, which represents saṁsāra, and you go up the spiral path, and realize Nirvāṇa. Your whole spiritual life is based upon those antithetical concepts of saṁsāra and Nirvāṇa, on a movement away from the conditioned in the direction of the unconditioned. The whole idea of development is from a lower to a higher state. Do you see what I mean? If you think in terms of spiritual growth and development at all, you think in effect in terms of saṁsāra and Nirvāṇa, a state which you get away from, and a state that you move in the direction of. If you dispose of saṁsāra and Nirvāṇa you dispose of the whole basis of the spiritual life itself. So is that an easy thing to do? How does one do that, or in what sense does one do that?

Q: It sounds rather like that Zen thing where you're breaking up the Buddha to obtain an ultimate realization.

S: Yes. The Mahāyāna would take the view that in the ultimate analysis saṁsāra and Nirvāṇa are concepts which are to be transcended if you are to reach the very end of the path, though of course if you dispose of the concepts of saṁsāra and Nirvāṇa you dispose also of the concept of the path – the path that as it were links saṁsāra and Nirvāṇa. So to dispose of saṁsāra and Nirvāṇa is something that for the vast majority of people, even those on the spiritual path, is quite unthinkable. It's cutting the ground from under their own feet. But nonetheless Milarepa is saying that that is what one has to do, if one does not wish to regress in one's meditation, and that suggests that he has a very deep conception of meditation. Meditation isn't just keeping the mind concentrated. He seems to use the word meditation for the whole spiritual life, for the whole process of raising the level of consciousness, the whole process of following the path. It's as though he's saying you won't really reach the end of the path until you get rid of the concept of path altogether. Probably it's quite impossible for most people really to realize that the path is only a concept, that saṁsāra and Nirvāṇa are only concepts. They can imagine themselves doing that, they can have a theoretical understanding of that, but can they really dispose of the concepts of saṁsāra and Nirvāṇa, can they really dispose of the path?

Q: Don't they just dispose of the thought that you can attain anything?

S: Well, do they even do that? Their experience is that they are striving, that they are making an effort, that they are experiencing, that they are attaining. Do they really, in actual fact, dispose of the concept of the self?

Q: Isn't it a process that happens over a period of time? You accept that they're operational concepts, not ultimate realities in themselves, and you start on that premise, and then through your meditation, you come more and more to realize in fact what you'd only understood theoretically?

S: You could even go so far as to say that the idea that such terms as saṁsāra and Nirvāṇa are only operational concepts is itself only an operational concept. Do you see what I mean? The idea that they're only operational concepts isn't real for you to begin with. That doesn't enable you to dispose of them in Milarepa's terms, it only enables you to have a theoretical idea of the fact that saṁsāra and Nirvāṇa are only operational concepts. So we shouldn't think it's all that easy. It's very easy to read the passage and to agree with it and say that saṁsāra and Nirvāṇa are only concepts, and the path is only a concept, and the self is only a concept, but you don't actually experience them as just concepts, which would mean really to go beyond them, we only have a concept of their being concepts. We don't have an actual experience or realization of them being concepts, and that is quite a different matter.

Milarepa's teaching is addressed to Rechungpa, but taking it more broadly it's addressed to people of a very high level of spiritual development indeed. If you reach that point of disposing of all such concepts, you won't regress in your meditation because you've even gone beyond the idea of progress. Regression is a concept which has significance only in relation to the counter concept of progress. But if you reach the level that Milarepa is talking about there's no question of progress. Well, what is progress? It's going from saṁsāra to Nirvāṇa, so if you've disposed of the concepts of saṁsāra and Nirvāṇa, what will you go from to what? There's nothing to go from and nothing to go to. There's no path, there's no person travelling the path, so the possibility of regression, even the possibility of meditation, is no longer there. So he is pointing out to Rechungpa a very profound state of realization indeed. He is saying that it isn't enough just not to regress in the sense of sticking at your meditation and making progress or experiencing yourself as making progress and believing that you're moving from a real saṁsāra to a real Nirvāṇa. You've got to transcend all these concepts altogether. Rechungpa is a very long way from doing that.

So Milarepa is pointing out to him a very high level of spiritual experience indeed. One can't even call it a level because to speak of a higher level presupposes a lower level, and that as it were presupposes a path, which is exactly what Milarepa is denying. He denies the concept of path when he disposes of the concepts of saṁsāra and Nirvāṇa. He's got no hope and no fear of Nirvāṇa or saṁsāra because he's disposed of those concepts, and therefore he doesn't regress. It's not that he doesn't regress in the sense that he's always making progress. He has gone beyond the concept of regression and therefore the concept of progress. In other words, he's gone beyond concepts altogether. But that isn't easy to do. We need what one might call a provisional framework made up of operational concepts to provide the basis of our spiritual life, and though those concepts are merely operational, we only have a theoretical idea of the fact that they are operational concepts. We cannot but take them for real. We cannot but think that there's a real saṁsāra and a real Nirvāṇa and a real path and a real person who's travelling that path.

Q: Do people mistake that spiritual experience for having no thought?

S: Well, what does 'having no thought' mean? Very often one means someone goes through the day with no directed thought, but only woolly wandering thoughts. Alternatively, somebody who is meditating may not experience discursive mental activity for the time being, but when he comes out of that meditative state he starts thinking again and using concepts in the ordinary way, so there is only a temporary suspension of the use of concepts. If someone did actually go through the day without thinking, he'd probably be in a sort of catatonic state, and that certainly isn't a state of transcending or disposing of concepts.

Q: If the aim is to transcend the concepts of saṁsāra and Nirvāṇa, isn't one of the traditional ways of doing that the practice of the four *śūnyatās*? And how is that practice done? Do you do it by, say, taking the reflection of the first *śūnyatā*, that saṁsāra is empty of Nirvāṇa, and turning it over in your mind every day for a period of time, just doing that regularly maybe for years? Then at a certain point you might start turning over in your mind the second *śūnyatā*, that Nirvāṇa is empty of *saṁsāra*. Do you think that this is a useful practice?

Sangharakshita: Oh yes. You would be practising *vipassanā* in the Mahāyāna way, because this is how Insight is developed according to the classical procedure. You practise meditation in the sense of *samatha*, the mind is calmed down, the energies are all united, and then you take up a particular consideration or reflection. In the Theravāda context it's the impermanence, the transitoriness, the painfulness, and insubstantiality of all phenomena. From a Mahāyāna point of view, among the formulations you can take up is the contemplation of the four *śūnyatā*s. Because your discursive mental activity has been brought under control and you're reflecting in a directed, purposeful way, you develop an understanding of those teachings and they serve as a bridge or springboard for the experience of Insight. They are means of transition from an intellectual understanding to an intuitive understanding. The Buddha originally had a certain spiritual experience, and wanted to communicate the means of realizing that, so he spoke in terms of impermanence and painfulness and so on, and in terms of the four *śūnyatā*s. Those concepts can be used as keys to unlock the experience that the Buddha had, provided that they are contemplated by a mind which has previously been suffused by the experience of meditation in the sense of *samatha*. This is the classical procedure.

If you think about them with your ordinary wandering mind, you won't penetrate very deeply into them, because usually your mind is disturbed and your energies are scattered. You need the preliminary practice of *samatha* to make your mind one-pointed, so that with that one-pointed mind you can take up any aspect of the Buddha's teaching, but especially these formulations which give some clue to the nature of the Transcendental, and contemplate them in such a way as to develop real Insight. That Insight, as it is deepened, will have a transforming effect on your whole personality, your whole being.

Inasmuch as one could say that the Mahāyāna goes deeper into the nature of reality, into the nature of the Buddha's experience, than does the Theravāda, instead of the three characteristics of conditioned existence to contemplate, you have the four *śūnyatā*s, or even the eighteen *śūnyatā*s or the thirty-two *śūnyatā*s, though the four really summarize all the others.

From a seminar on 'Rechungpa's Third Journey to India' (1980, pp.79-83)

2. HOW DO YOU MEDITATE ON ŚŪNYATĀ?

The six element practice is a sort of *sunyata* practice, or at least a very good lead into it.

Q: How do you meditate on *śūnyatā*?

Sangharakshita: You can meditate on *śūnyatā* very systematically. You can reflect for instance on the four degrees of *śūnyatā*: the emptiness of the conditioned, the emptiness of the unconditioned, the emptiness of the distinction between the two, and the emptiness of the very concept of emptiness. Or you can reflect on the eight 'nos' of Nāgārjuna: no arising, no destruction and so on, no existence, no non-existence.

Q: Is it enough to recite and reflect upon the *Heart Sūtra*?

S: Yes, that would certainly be a way of meditating on *śūnyatā*. Also, the six element practice is a sort of *śūnyatā* practice, or at least a very good lead into it.

From a seminar on *The Precious Garland* (1976, p.707)

3. JUST A MODE OF LOOKING AT THINGS

You see openness and appearance as inseparable, as really being one and the same thing, or as not-two, and that is Insight.

During the time of insight which is surrounded by a calm and gentle aura openness and appearance are inseparable.[83]

Openness seems to be a synonym here for emptiness. Some modern translators of Tibetan texts translate *śūnyatā* as openness, I think following Guenther, who sometimes calls it 'the open dimension of being'. In the phrase 'openness and appearance are inseparable', 'appearance' translates *rūpā*. So this statement is referring to *śūnyatā* and *rūpā* being inseparable, which of course is mentioned in the *Heart Sūtra*.

'During the time of insight', therefore, you see the inseparability – if you like, the non-duality – of *śūnyatā* and *rūpā* as outlined in the *Heart Sūtra*. This suggests an insight into a higher level of *śūnyatā*, the *mahā-*

śūnyatā, in which you see that the unconditioned is empty because it is empty of the conditioned, and the conditioned is empty because it is empty of the unconditioned. Both are empty, and when you see this, you see openness and appearance as inseparable, as really being one and the same thing, or as not-two, and that is Insight. That is wisdom. You don't think any more in terms of dichotomies or polar opposites. That is just a mode of looking at things which we derive from our practical experience; we need to break things up into pairs and opposites and dichotomies for practical purposes.

From a seminar on *Advice Given to the Three Fortunate Women* (1980, p.29)

4. EXPLORING ŚŪNYATĀ

The conditioned framework of the Insight drops away, and you are left with the Insight going further and further.

One starts developing *vipassanā* by, so to speak, coming down to the first *dhyāna* where mental activity is possible and starting up mental activity with regards to the nature of existence, perhaps using the traditional Buddhist formulas: reflecting on impermanence or on insubstantiality, *anātman* (Sanskrit; Pāli *anattā*). In this way Insight develops.

Among the characteristics of the conditioned – that it is *dukkha*, *anitya*, and *anātman* – one can take up one particular characteristic and dwell on that. That then becomes one's gateway or door into the corresponding aspect of the unconditioned. If you are dwelling, say, upon the selfless, the *anātman* nature of the conditioned, sooner or later you pass beyond, as it were, the framework of the conditioned. The Insight remains but the conditioned framework of the Insight drops away, and you are left with the Insight going further and further and going, so to speak, into the unconditioned through the gateway of the reflection or development of Insight into that particular aspect of the conditioned. So you go from *anātman* to *śūnyatā* and you go deeper and deeper into that. That is, of course what the Mahāyāna did. They were especially interested in exploring *śūnyatā*, levels of *śūnyatā*, types of *śūnyatā*, to the extent that the other gateways – *appaṇihita* and *animitta* – were rather lost sight of. It could be that the teaching of the three gateways, the *vimokṣas*, lost some of its significance, because of this heavy emphasis on *śūnyatā*.

From a pre-ordination retreat at Padmaloka (1982, pp.77-8)

8 Visualizations and recitations

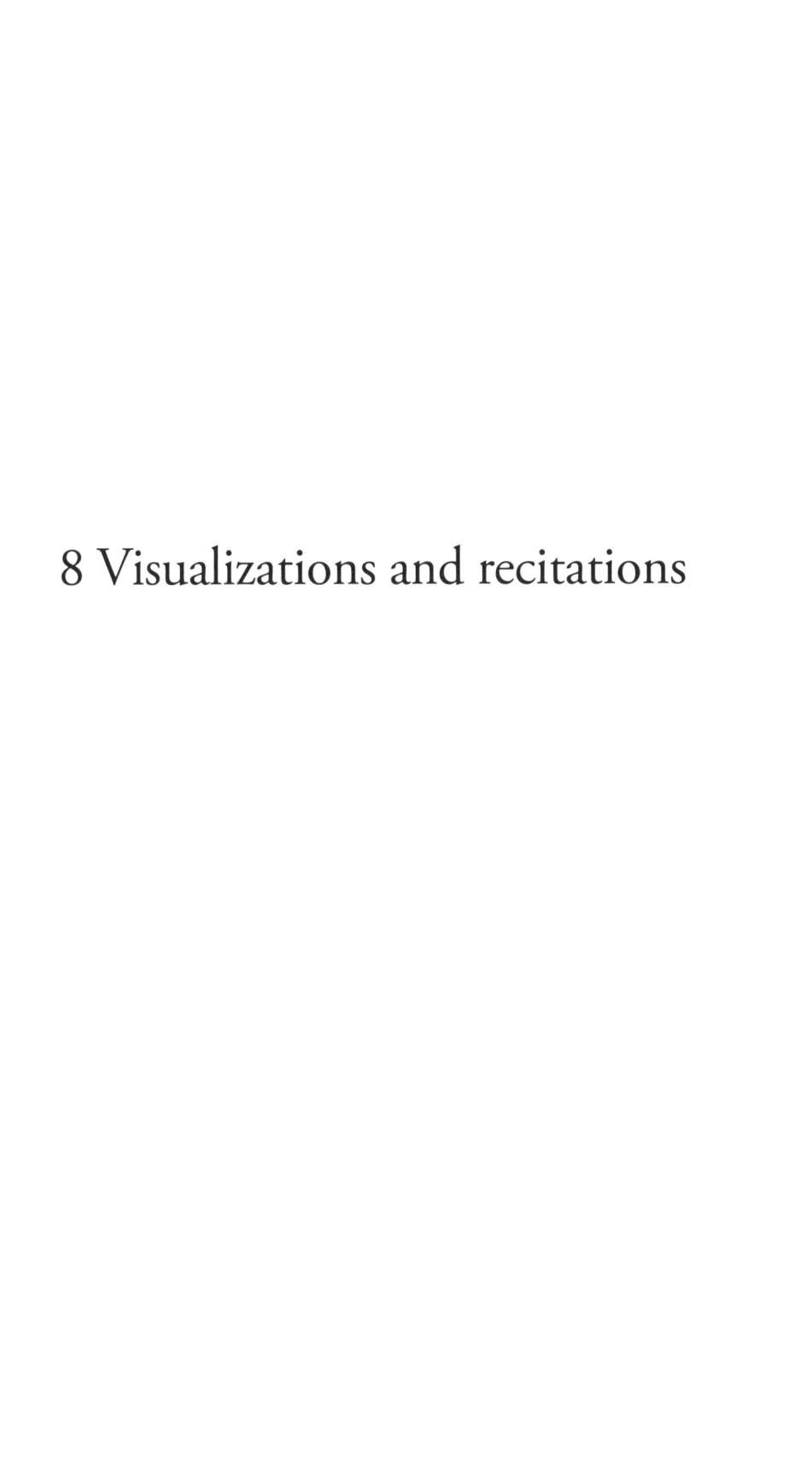

1 The foundation yogas

1. INTRODUCING THE FOUR FOUNDATION YOGAS

In a sense, the Tantra is a short and easy path. It's short if one practises it long enough, and it's easy if one practises it hard enough!

The four foundation yogas, the four *mūla yogas*, constitute the basis of the whole spiritual life of Tibet. You may know all about the Dalai Lama and you may know a certain amount of Mahāyāna philosophy and so on, but if you don't know about these practices, and essentially they are practices, if you haven't caught the feel of them, then really you know nothing about Tibetan Buddhism at all, spiritually speaking. These four *mūla yogas* underpin the whole vast superstructure of Tibetan religious and spiritual life.

Mūla is a Sanskrit word which literally means root, and also means a foundation. You can speak of either root yogas or foundation yogas because the two terms, the two interpretations, are very closely connected, just as the roots of a tree are the foundation of the whole tree. If the roots are weak, the tree may topple over. And in the same way, if the *mūla yogas* are weak, then the tree, the edifice of the spiritual life which one tries to erect upon that foundation is weak and may also topple over.

In Tibetan Buddhism, the four foundation yogas are preparatory to the practice of the whole system of Vajrayāna meditation and religious observance. They are the gateway to the practice of the Tantra. It is emphasized in Tibetan Buddhism, that there is no success on the Tantric path if the four foundation yogas are neglected. They come first. You must practise them before you can think of embarking on the practice of the Vajrayāna.

In the West some people have got into the habit of thinking that the Tantra, the Vajrayāna, is a short and easy path. We're always looking for short-cuts, and as soon as you mention the Tantra, people's ears prick up, and you can almost feel them thinking, 'Here's a nice easy way which circumvents all that meditation and all that asceticism and all that study.' Well, there's a certain amount of truth in this. In a sense, the Tantra is a short and easy path. It's short if one practises it long enough, and it's easy if one practises it hard enough!

The Tibetans themselves often spend years upon years working on these foundation yogas. Some Tibetan monks go into retreat for a period of three months, three weeks, three days, three hours and three minutes. This is the tradition. So, you might wonder, what do they do? There they are, shut up in their little hermitage, with just a glimmering of light coming through a small slit and their meal pushed through once a day, and they're all alone there in semi-darkness. What do they do? It's easy enough to say they meditate, but just imagine it. Just think of yourself sitting down in a darkened room and meditating, indefinitely. You wouldn't get very far. You wouldn't know what to do. After an hour you might be pacing up and down your cell and wondering what to do next. But when the Tibetans go into this sort of retreat, they really do get on with it. And one of the groups of practices they get on with is this group of the four foundation yogas. I have known Tibetan monks who have said after years of seclusion in this way, it's remarkable how quickly the time goes. The days, the weeks, the months just slip by because they're fully occupied with the practices, which they find very interesting, and the more they go on with them, the more deeply they go into them, the more fascinating they find them.

This is the Tibetan way. The Tibetans are prepared to devote a great deal of time. They're prepared to be patient. They're prepared to practise hard and to practise long. But in the West unfortunately we tend to be a little less patient, and we do tend to expect from our spiritual practices rather quick results. Thus it is perhaps that quite a lot of people tend to neglect the preliminaries of spiritual life, of meditation and so on. But the preliminaries, if these are mastered, are half the battle. If you prepare for meditation properly in the full sense then you are already meditating, or at least almost meditating.

Only too often we tend to think of the means and the end as being sharply separated, and sometimes we try to have the end without bothering about the means, but this isn't really possible. I remember on one occasion Mahatma Gandhi remarked that the end is the extreme of the means. If you really want the end, devote yourself wholeheartedly to the means and forget all about the end. In this way you will gain the end, sometimes before you've noticed that you've gained it. So if you peg away at the preliminaries you will find yourself, in due course, deep in the heart of the essentials. But if you try to neglect the preliminaries and leap ahead, then you may not find yourself anywhere at all.

Mūla means root or foundation. What does *yoga* mean? Here we must be rather careful, because the meaning of this word has been rather debased in the West. Nowadays if you mention the word 'yoga' to people, they'll take it to mean anything from standing on your head to practising an Eastern variety of black magic. Even in India the word *yoga* is rather ambiguous. Literally the word means simply 'that which unites' or 'that which joins', and it's etymologically linked to the English word 'yoke'. In popular Hinduism the word yoga means approximately that which unites one with truth or reality or God, in other words, any way of spiritual life which brings about a union between oneself and the object of one's worship or one's quest.

But in the context of the Buddhist Tantra, the word has a rather different meaning. In Buddhism, yoga refers especially to the union of wisdom, *prajñā*, awareness of reality, and compassion, or universal loving-kindness. It also means, in some more specifically Tantric contexts still, the union of the experience of the void, *śūnyatā*, which is the general Mahāyāna word for ultimate reality, and bliss, especially great bliss, or *mahāsukha*. In this connection, the Tantric tradition usually employs the term *yuga-nāda*, which is very well translated as two-in-one-ness, the two-in-one-ness of wisdom and compassion, the two-in-one-ness of the voidness and supreme bliss. This two-in-one-ness, this state of non-duality of unity in difference and difference in unity, is the highest goal of the whole system of Tantric practice. Summing up, we may say that the foundation yogas, are so called because they initiate the process of integrating one part of our nature with another, culminating in the state of perfect integration of wisdom and compassion, *śūnyatā* and bliss, at the highest level, which is Enlightenment or Buddhahood.

I have referred to the four foundation yogas of the Tibetan Buddhist Tantra. Tantra means the Vajrayāna, the third of the three stages of development of Buddhism in India. First of all there's what is sometimes called the Hīnayāna, the Little Vehicle or the Little Way, of emancipation. This of course is the unfairly belittling term given to that phase of

Buddhism by adherents of a later stage; it is fairer and more accurate to call it the stage of early Buddhism, and it can generally be characterized as the ethico-psychological phase or stage in the development of Indian Buddhism. This lasted about five hundred years. Secondly, the Mahāyāna, or the Great Vehicle, or the Great Way to emancipation, is generally characterized as the metaphysical/devotional phase in the development of Indian Buddhism, and this also lasted about five hundred years. And thirdly and lastly we have the Vajrayāna, which means the Diamond or the Adamantine Vehicle or Way to emancipation. This is characterized as the phase or the stage of esoteric meditation and symbolic ritual. Tibetan Buddhism is a direct continuation, a direct descendant, of Indian Buddhism, on the soil of Tibet, and Tibetan Buddhism is a synthesis of all three yanas. The monastic discipline of Tibetan Buddhism, as well as its general Buddhist teaching, and the Abhidharma, all come from early Buddhism, especially in its Sarvastivada form. The *śūnyatā* philosophy, the teaching of the voidness which underlies all forms of Tibetan Buddhism, and the Bodhisattva Ideal, which is the spiritual ideal of all forms of Tibetan Buddhism, come from the Indian Mahāyāna. And the spiritual practices, the rites, the ceremonies, the meditations, the symbolism, of Tibetan Buddhism, all come from the Vajrayāna.

The four foundation yogas constitute the introduction, the entrance, to the Vajrayāna. So at this point a question arises. Tibetan spiritual practice, as distinct from doctrinal study and institutional life, is mainly, if not exclusively, Tantric. Does this mean that the spiritual practices of the Hinayana and the Mahāyāna are ignored in Tibetan Buddhism, inasmuch as Tibetan Buddhism starts with the four foundation yogas and then goes on to the Vajrayāna? It may seem like it, but it isn't really so, because the most important of these practices are incorporated into the *mūla yogas* themselves.

The first foundation yoga is the Going for Refuge and prostration practice, the second is the development of the *bodhicitta*, or Will to Enlightenment, the third is the meditation and mantra recitation of Vajrasattva and the fourth is the offering of the mandala. These four foundation yogas are essentially the same in all four schools of Tibetan Buddhism, but here I will follow mainly the Nyingma tradition, because my own personal connection happens to be more with the Nyingma version of these four *mūla yogas*. It won't be possible to give a complete description of these practices because they're much too complex, even though by Vajrayāna standards they're rather simple practices.

Going for Refuge to the Buddha, the Dharma and the Sangha is a very common practice in all schools of Buddhism, all over the Buddhist world, but it is not always taken very seriously. I know that in India for instance, when there are public meetings, with various political figures on the platform and a mainly non-Buddhist audience, some people still insist on giving the Refuges and getting everybody to recite them even though it has no significance. But this is really an abuse of the tradition. In the Tantric Buddhism of Tibet, on the contrary, the Refuges are taken very seriously, and treated as an important spiritual practice in their own right.

As practised as the first of the *mūla yogas*, the Going for Refuge and prostration practice has three main elements: visualization, recitation and prostration. These three elements correspond to body, speech and mind. In Buddhism there's a constant reference to the distinction between body, speech and mind. Just as the Christian tradition speaks of body, soul and spirit, in the same way the whole Buddhist tradition speaks of body, speech and mind. These three are taken as exhausting the whole content of human personality. They are our three principal aspects, our three principal modes of functioning: the physical, the communicative, and the mental or spiritual. So in any complete spiritual practice, all three must be provided for. This is why in the Going for Refuge and prostration practice there are these three elements: visualization, which is something done by the mind, a sort of meditation; recitation, which is a kind of speech, and prostration, which is done by the body. In this way the whole being, the whole personality, is involved. This is one of the basic points of the Tantra: that it isn't enough to do something mentally, you've got to do it verbally and physically as well.

The mental element of the practice is the visualization of what is known as the Refuge Tree. So what does a Refuge Tree look like? I'll try to describe it, and I'm going to ask you not to follow my words so much as to try to build up the picture within your own mind. First of all, visualize an enormous lotus flower, in fact a whole lotus plant. It has to be enormously big, as big as a great oak. There's one great thick central stem to this lotus, and there are four branches rising out of the central stem in the directions of the four cardinal points, north, south, east and west. The central stem and each of the four branches terminate in a gigantic lotus blossom, so that there are five flowers in all.

When you've got that firmly in your mind, when you can see it quite clearly, then you direct your attention to the central lotus. At the calyx of the flower, you should see rows upon rows, layers upon layers of petals, folded back, and then right in the centre, sitting on the calyx of that central lotus, you visualize the founder of the tradition of Tantric practice to which you belong. For the Nyingmapas this is Padmasambhava, for the Kagyupas it's Milarepa, for the Gelugpas it's Tsongkhapa and so on. But one visualizes this figure, the founder of one's own particular tradition of Tantric practice, firmly seated right in the middle of the calyx of that central lotus. You don't just visualize; you think of that central figure seated there as being the embodiment of all the Buddhas, all spiritual perfections, all wisdom, all compassion, all peace, all perfection, all concentrated in that figure, which is the supreme embodiment of one's highest spiritual ideal in all possible aspects. So this is the next stage.

Then you notice that the lotus has many tiers of petals, sort of folding back, more like a chrysanthemum than a lotus. And then, underneath the figure of Padmasambhava or Milarepa, as the case may be, you visualize your other lamas or your other gurus, including your own personal guru, and then above him but still below the central figure, other gurus or masters from whom you have received instruction. And then lower down still, but still in line with that central lotus, you visualize what are known as the four orders of Tantric deities: Buddhas, Bodhisattvas, peaceful and wrathful – the deities of the four classes of Tantra. And then lastly underneath them you visualize the *ḍākinīs* and the *dharmapālas*.

You might be wondering what all this is about. It's pretty obvious why one might visualize the founder of the lineage of Tantric spiritual practice, whether Padmasambhava or Milarepa, but why these others? Why the lamas? Why the four orders of Tantric deities? Why the *ḍākinīs* and *dharmapālas*? Well, these represent the Tantric or Vajrayanic, that is to say, the esoteric aspect of the Three Refuges. In the Tantra there are three exoteric Refuges, three esoteric Refuges and there are also three secret Refuges and three suchness Refuges. Here, I will go only so far as the three esoteric Refuges. (The three exoteric Refuges are of course the Buddha, the Dharma and the Sangha.) The three esoteric counterparts of these are first of all the guru, who is the esoteric counterpart of the Buddha; then the deities of the path, which are archetypal embodiments or symbols of spiritual experiences which are the esoteric aspects of the Dharma; and then the *ḍākas* and *ḍākinīs* and *dharmapālas*, which represent the persons or even the spiritual forces in the company of which, or with the help of which, one practises and follows the Path, and they represent the esoteric aspect of the Sangha.

So in line with that central lotus you've got the symbols of the esoteric aspects of the three Refuges. Sitting on the calyx of the central lotus flower you've got the founder of the whole line of Tantric practice and underneath him (in order) the symbol of the esoteric aspect of the Buddha Refuge, the symbols of the esoteric aspect of the Dharma Refuge, and the symbols of the esoteric aspect of the Sangha Refuge. So in this way you've got the esoteric three Refuges lined up vertically underneath that central figure on the calyx of the central lotus blossom.

On the lotus blossom in front, the southern one as it were, is Śākyamuni, the historical Buddha, with the Buddha of the past, Dipankara, to the left, and the Buddha of the future, Maitreya, on the right. Then on the lotus to the left of oneself, there are the Bodhisattvas, usually the eight or ten principal Bodhisattvas, representing the Sangha, the spiritual community, in the purely Mahayanistic sense, including Avalokiteśvara and Mañjuśrī. Then on the lotus to the north behind the central lotus, one sees a heap of sacred books, representing the Dharma, the sacred scriptures. And on the lotus to the right, the eastern lotus, one sees an assemblage of Arhants, those who have gained Enlightenment or liberation for themselves alone. They constitute the Sangha, the spiritual community, in the Hinayana sense, and they include the great Arhant disciples of the Buddha, like Sāriputta, Moggallāna and so on.

The whole tree, with all its figures, has to be visualized, if possible, quite clearly and quite vividly before one begins. To do the practice you sit as for meditation and build up this mental picture in your mind. Tibetans are familiar with the appearance of the Refuge Tree from thangkas, painted scrolls; it's a quite popular subject. It isn't easy to get hold of copies, though, because so many figures are involved and they have to be so tiny, that it's an enormous amount of work for the artist, and very few artists are ready to undertake just one single thangka of this kind, which may keep them busy for months and months.

So this is the mental element in the practice of Going for Refuge and prostration. One has the feeling of and feeling for all these great spiritual figures, all these symbols and archetypal forms, which together make up the content of that Refuge Tree. The verbal element in the practice consists in the repetition aloud of a formula expressive of one's Going for Refuge to the founder of the whole tradition as the embodiment of all the Refuges. In other words, if one follows the Nyingma tradition, if the central figure of the Refuge Tree is Padmasambhava, then one's formula expresses one's taking refuge in Padmasambhava as the embodiment of the Buddha Refuge, Dharma Refuge and Sangha Refuge. This formula naturally varies a little so far as the words are concerned, from one tradition to another.

And finally there's the physical element in the practice, represented by the full-length prostration. As I've said, the body occupies an important place in the Vajrayāna. In some forms of Buddhism one finds that the body is depreciated, as in some forms of early Christianity. Sometimes the body is referred to as an animated corpse, or a bucket of filth that you're carrying around with you, and picturesque expressions of that kind. But not in the Vajrayāna. In the Vajrayāna it's a sin to speak in dispraise of the body and the senses generally, because the human body is the vehicle for emancipation. The human body can become a Buddha body, so therefore it's very important, it's very precious, it's very prized. It's not to be looked down upon or despised.

The Tantra thus has a very definite, very positive idea that your spiritual practice is meaningless if it doesn't involve the body, if the body doesn't participate. It mustn't be just a mental thing, not even a mental plus verbal thing, but a mental plus verbal plus physical thing. Tibetan spiritual life therefore tends to be very strenuous. Not for the Tibetan sitting down in a cosy corner and reading a book about the spiritual life. He doesn't look at it like that. I remember often hearing from the lips of my Tibetan friends a little proverb: 'Without difficulty, no religion'. If it's easy, then it isn't a religious practice. If it's difficult it probably is. If it's very difficult, it's probably quite a good practice. But they don't take it easy, and their spiritual life involves a great deal of physical exertion. This is partly on account of the very atmosphere, the temperature of Tibet – if you've got snow outside your monastery you need something strenuous to keep you warm – but this is only part of the explanation. They feel that if the body is not involved in doing something of a spiritual nature, then you're not really seriously practising. This is why you find Tibetans doing things like prostrating themselves all the way from Lhasa to Bodh Gaya, a distance of some five or six hundred miles. We'd think this perfectly crazy, but the Tibetans don't; they take it very seriously indeed, and they respect people who do this sort of thing very highly.

In this Going for Refuge and prostration practice, therefore, you don't just visualize and repeat this formula of Going for Refuge; you also prostrate. You fling yourself down full length in front of the visualized Refuge Tree with all its lamas and deities and so on. There are various forms of prostration, but the Tibetans always go the whole hog. You fling yourself right down on your hands and knees, and flat on your face, with your arms shooting out in front of you. They do it rather dramatically, not to say powerfully and impressively.

All these three, the visualization, the repetition of the formula and the prostration, have to be done simultaneously. To get the hang of it, you can practise separately, but when you do it properly, you do all together. You keep the mental picture in your mind, you repeat the formula and you fling yourself down. In this way mind, speech and body are all co-operating, all practising, all being influenced, all participating. And this has a certain effect. It's very difficult, in fact it's impossible, to describe the effect; it's known only to those who have had some experience of this sort of practice. Perhaps I should mention that according to tradition you have to do this whole thing one hundred thousand times. They say that if you're doing it full time it'll take you about three months. If you're just able to do a few hundred prostrations a day, which isn't really very much, though it takes maybe a couple of hours, then of course it'll take you several years. But the idea is to do as many as you possibly can. And believe me, when you've done these, even a few, the effect is quite tangible and sometimes even quite remarkable.

In case this all sounds very difficult I should mention that the Tibetans themselves do follow the tradition of taking up other Vajrayāna practices before they've finished their preliminary practices. You can be adding to your total of prostrations – you might have got up to 10,456, say – but you can at the same time be doing the meditation on Tārā, on Mañjuśrī, or even something more advanced than that, while continuing and trying to complete your preliminary practices. This is perhaps a concession to the corruptions of modern times, but the Tibetans themselves all do it.

One may say about the Going for Refuge and prostration practice in conclusion that it represents the Hinayana component in the four foundation yogas. The whole of the Hinayana in a way can be summed up in the Going for Refuge to Buddha, Dharma and Sangha, and the Going for Refuge and prostration practice as the first of the *mūla yogas* represents their force within a specifically Vajrayanic or Tantric context.

Secondly we come to the development of the *bodhicitta*, or the Will to Enlightenment. One develops this first of all by developing compassion for all living beings. This is an aspiration which reverberates throughout the whole of Buddhism, but the Tibetans give it their own particular twist, their own particular colouring. They say that one should regard all living beings as being just like one's own parents, one's own mother and father. Like most other Buddhists, they believe very strongly in rebirth and reincarnation, and they believe that if you look far back enough, everybody you know, everybody you meet, has at some time or other, in some previous life or other, been your mother or your father. The Tibetans attach a great deal of importance to this; for them it is a very vivid and very real thing. In our case, even if we happen to be Buddhists, sometimes the idea of rebirth and reincarnation, though we accept it intellectually perhaps, with more or less reservation, doesn't really get into our bones. But in the case of the Tibetans it is in their bones and their blood. If they are serious-minded, if they practise any kind of Tantric exercise, they can actually feel that the people that they meet were once closely related to them at one time in the remote past, and therefore they feel that they should be kind to them, they should love them, they should be affectionate towards them, and treat them decently.

The Tantric tradition emphasizes that inasmuch as one has this love and compassion for all living beings, one should develop the resolve to help them, to deliver them from suffering. It's only if you feel for others as though they were your own parents that you'll feel the urge really to help them in difficulties, they say, and they give a powerful illustration for this. They say, suppose one day you're going through the bazaar, and there are people selling vegetables and pots and pans and all sorts of other things all around you, and there's a noise and a crying of goods of various kinds. As you go through the market you notice that in one corner there's some disturbance going on, some sort of a row. This often happens in bazaars, and no one takes too much notice, not until people start killing one another. But for some reason or other you stop and look, and you see that there's quite a crowd, and there seems to be someone in the middle who's getting the worst of it. Just out of curiosity you decide to go and have a look. You draw nearer and you see that there's a great crowd of people beating and thrashing someone in the middle, who's down on the floor. You think, 'Well, it's not too good, but it's none of my business', but out of curiosity you go a little nearer, and then you see that it's a woman that all these big, hefty men are beating; in fact it's an old woman that's being beaten.

And as you get nearer until you're right in the throng, you see that the old woman is your own mother. You didn't know she was going to the bazaar, but there she is, and she's being beaten. At once you feel tremendous compassion welling up in your heart, because the person who is suffering is near and dear to you.

The Tibetan spiritual masters say that if you can see in each suffering human being your own mother or your own father, or someone near and dear to you, then love and compassion will well up in your heart; otherwise not. They emphasize this so much because we can see so much suffering all around us. We read in the newspaper that seventy people were killed in an accident, or twenty-five people were killed in a fire, or several hundred were killed yesterday in an uprising. But we may just turn over to the next page in the newspaper and look at the sports results. We don't think anything of it because no one near and dear to us is involved. This is why we are so, in a sense, callous. But the Tibetan tradition says one shouldn't look like that. One should try to see, try to feel, all living beings as intimately related with oneself. They make use of this idea of karma and rebirth to encourage us to feel and try to act as though, as in fact is the case, all the people with whom we are at present in contact are in fact our own reincarnated mothers, fathers and so on of previous existences. When one sees all the suffering beings around one in this way, then out of compassion one develops a tremendous urge to help them, and to lead them on the right path, to lead them to Buddhahood, to lead them to Enlightenment, and therefore one makes a vow, a resolution, that one will gain Enlightenment through the practice of the Vajrayāna, so that one may function as a spiritual teacher in the world.

This foundation yoga consists mainly in the repetition of a formula expressive of one's determination to gain Enlightenment, not just for the sake of one's own personal emancipation, but for the welfare and benefit for the whole world of sentient beings. This is the famous Bodhisattva Vow. And this too is to be repeated and recited one hundred thousand times. The Vajrayāna is very fond of repetition. They do this ten thousand times, do that a hundred thousand times, do that a million times, over and over and over again. The reason for this is that there's a tremendous need to penetrate, to break through, into the unconscious mind. Usually we just repeat something once and we think we've understood it and we put it aside. That's that. I vow to gain Enlightenment for the benefit of all sentient beings. What could be easier than that? That's the Bodhisattva Vow, you've repeated it, you've recited it, you've taken it. But there's not even a scratch on the surface of the mind. So the Vajrayāna says, go on repeating it. Say it a thousand times, ten thousand times, a hundred thousand times, a million times, and maybe when you've done it maybe a hundred or two hundred thousand times, the meaning will begin to soak down below the level of the conscious mind into the unconscious mind and start influencing you there where it really matters. So you do a hundred thousand repetitions of the Bodhisattva Vow at the time of the actual practice.

In between two sessions of practice of the foundation yogas, one should reflect in a certain way. One should reflect that with every outgoing breath that one breathes, one's good qualities, such as they are, fall upon others like moonlight and confer happiness upon them. In other words, one should feel that one's effect, one influence, upon others is beneficent and positive, just like that of the moonlight. This is obviously reminiscent of Indian tradition, because in India after the heat of the day, the moonlight is cool and soft and beautiful, and people appreciate it very much. Your influence on others should be like that. You should fall like moonlight upon others, and your whole influence should be soft and gentle and beneficent. Those who practise the *mūla yogas* have to ask themselves whether they have that effect upon others. Would your best friend compare you with moonlight? You have to ask yourself that question. And then with every ingoing breath you should feel that the sins, the weaknesses, the imperfections of all beings are entering your body and are being absorbed into the Will to Enlightenment itself. Also, if you have time, you should practise the *brahma-vihāras*, the four sublime abodes, that is to say, love, compassion, sympathetic joy and equanimity, which are incidentally common practices in both the Hinayana and the Mahāyāna. The development of the *bodhicitta*, the Will to Enlightenment, and the repetition of the Bodhisattva Vow represents the Mahāyāna, the Great Vehicle or Great Way component in the four foundation yogas.

The third foundation yoga is the meditation and mantra recitation of Vajrasattva. This *mūla yoga* may be considered the most important of the four. The Going for Refuge and prostration practice represents a Hinayanic component within the four *mūla yogas*, the development of the *bodhicitta* represents a more Mahayanic component, but the meditation and mantra recitation of Vajrasattva represents the purely Tantric element in the group of practices, and it is undertaken for what the tradition calls 'purification of sins'.

When I lived in Kalimpong, I knew a French woman who became a Buddhist nun but had been brought up Catholic. She said that as a Catholic she heard a lot about sin, but it wasn't until she started doing the Vajrayāna practice that she really heard about purification from sin. The Vajrayāna attaches great importance to this. Its conception of sin isn't quite that of Christianity, but it does recognize in a very realistic way that our minds are encumbered by all sorts of murk, all sorts of dark and rather dirty things that we'd rather forget about. But if we are to get anywhere with our spiritual practice we have to drag them all out into the light of day, into the light of the Buddha, and dissolve them, or at least recognize that they're there and see them clearly, and face up to them, before they can be purified. Purification is possible, but the condition is that we recognize the need for purification. And that's where the Vajrasattva practice comes in.

'Vajrasattva' is usually translated as the Diamond or Adamantine Being. Vajra is the diamond or the thunderbolt, sattva is being. Iconographically Vajrasattva is a Buddha in the form of a Bodhisattva; sometimes he is called the sixth Buddha, which means the esoteric Buddha, the hidden Buddha if you like. The Tantric tradition speaks of a sixth Buddha much as we might speak of a sixth dimension, something very mysterious which is almost a contradiction in terms, a sort of 'x' quantity which you don't really apprehend. To understand why Vajrasattva is spoken of as the sixth Buddha, not as the tenth or the eleventh, we have to refer to the scheme of the five Buddhas. The five Buddhas are the Transcendental counterparts, in Buddha form, of the five aggregates, the five constituents of conditioned existence. They're the five archetypal Buddhas if you like, the five ideal Buddhas. There's a red one, a yellow one, a green one, a blue one and a white one, and when they are depicted in the mandala, the circle of symbolic forms, you get one archetypal Buddha in the centre, and one at each of the four cardinal points, the central Buddha being a synthesis of the other four, just as white light is a sort of synthesis of all the colours of the rainbow. Vajrasattva is the esoteric aspect of the central or the fifth Buddha. You can only represent or depict him in the mandala by imagining him as being behind the central Buddha, in a different dimension as it were. So he's the sixth Buddha not in the sense of being added to the five, but as it were standing outside the plane on which the five-Buddha differentiation is made.

It's one of the fundamental principles of the Tantra and of Tibetan Buddhism generally that all the Buddhas and Bodhisattvas, *ḍākas, ḍākinīs, dharmapālas* and so on are to be found within one's own mind. Not within the ordinary individual, so-called subjective mind; to find them within one's mind one has to go deeper than that. So Vajrasattva also is to be found within the depths of one's own mind. He is to be found at a point beyond space, beyond time. He represents or symbolizes the primeval, original purity of one's own mind, beyond space and beyond time, its Transcendental purity, its absolute purity. In other words, Vajrasattva symbolizes the truth that whatever you might have done on the phenomenal plane, whatever sins you might have committed, however low you might have sunk in the scale of being and consciousness, your basic mind, your true nature if you like to use that expression, remains pure, untouched, unsullied. In the depths of your being, whatever you might have done or not done, you are pure.

Obviously this sort of teaching can be misunderstood. It's a deeply metaphysical truth, not just a psychological teaching. But in Tibet, at least in the old days, misunderstanding was unlikely. The purpose of the whole Vajrasattva yoga is to re-integrate us with our own innate purity, to purify us of our sins by the realization, the recognition, that underneath the sins there is an immaculate purity of our own mind which has never been touched and never been tainted. In other words, you purify yourself from your sins, which you acknowledge as your sins on their own level, by realizing that in the depths of your being you have never sinned, that you are primevally pure. This is the essence of this practice.

So how is it done? First you visualize Vajrasattva. You visualize him immediately above your head, a brilliant white figure, the colour of freshly fallen snow, youthful – the texts say sixteen years of age, which is supposed to be the ideal age so far as beauty is concerned – and with a smiling expression. And then you visualize the *bīja*, the seed syllable, Hum, blue in colour, at the centre of the heart of this visualized Vajrasattva figure and surrounded by the syllables of the hundred-syllabled mantra. This requires a little explanation. The circle of the hundred syllables of the Vajrasattva mantra stand upright around the central *bīja*. They're not as it were laid down flat, as on a clock face. It's rather as though you put the clock face horizontal, and then you stood all the figures up in their places.

Then, from these syllables, you visualize a stream of what is described as milk-like nectar which descends from them into your body through the crown of your head and goes right through your body and washes out all your sins. You have to visualize and feel this. With a little practice you can actually feel a cool sensation coming, descending into the top of your head and then flowing down through your whole body and even filling your body. You have to feel that eventually your body becomes like a crystal vase filled with curds. This is a traditional comparison. You feel so clean, so pure, so purified. Or it's also said you feel like clear, void light.

After you've visualized the Vajrasattva figure, the mantras and the flow of this milk-like nectar through your whole system, you feel completely purified, transparent like glass or crystal or even like emptiness and pure light. Like all these visualization exercises, it has a corresponding psychological effect. And having done the visualization you then recite the hundred-syllable mantra one hundred thousand times – not at one sitting, of course, you can do it two or three times or ten times or a hundred times at one sitting, and then add up the total day by day or week by week. The Vajrasattva mantra, which is a very famous mantra, expresses the idea of re-integration with one's own original nature. At the end of the practice there are several other visualization exercises, but I don't propose to go into them here. At the end of the practices the visualized Vajrasattva is dissolved back into the blue sky, the void, into *śūnyatā*, the usual procedure at the end of a visualization exercise.

The fourth and last foundation yoga is the offering of the mandala. The mandala is not the same here as the circle of symbolic forms such as the Mandala of the Five Buddhas. Here a mandala means a symbolical representation of the entire universe according to ancient Indian cosmological traditions. The ancient Indians had their own views about the nature of the physical universe, and the mandala is a symbolical representation of the universe according to these traditions. The practice consists in offering this mandala, offering this symbolical representation of the whole physical cosmos, to the Three Jewels, the Buddha, the Dharma, the Sangha, in their exoteric as well as in their esoteric aspects. These three, the Buddha, the Dharma and the Sangha, are visualized more or less as in the Going for Refuge and prostration practice, except that here there is no tree.

First of all you perform the sevenfold puja. In this context it's not the ordinary Mahāyāna sevenfold puja, but a special esoteric Tantric version of it. Then you build up and offer the mandala. The mandala, the symbolical representation of the universe, is made up of thirty-seven parts, and you construct it on a circular copper base by heaping rice and then putting rings of copper or silver around it until you have built up a sort of conical or pyramid-like structure with different tiers and different heaps of rice placed to represent different elements in the physical universe, and you bear these in mind and repeat their names as you build up the model. It's all too complicated to describe in detail. But there are several ways of making the offering. The usual way is that when you have built up the mandala, you lift it up in your hands and recite various mantras and verses expressive of offering up of the entire universe to the Buddha, the Dharma and the Sangha. And the whole thing of course has to be done one hundred thousand times.

What does the practice mean? The one who is doing the four *mūla yogas* wishes to gain Enlightenment, Buddhahood, for the sake of all living beings. In other words, he or she wishes to become a Buddha. For this purpose an enormous accumulation of what is technically called merit or *puṇya* is necessary. It's axiomatic for Buddhism in all its forms that merit is gained by *dāna*, by giving, by generosity. This is the basic, the cardinal Buddhist virtue, to give. One of the most wonderful features of life in Buddhist countries is that everybody is so generous, they so readily share with you whatever they've got. If you visit someone, at once you must be offered at least tea, if possible a whole meal, or some little gift, and if you go to see someone you must take something along with you, not go empty-handed.

If it's meritorious to offer a cup of tea or a little money, if it's meritorious to give one's time or one's energy, or to offer a monastery or a temple, how much meritorious would it be to offer the whole universe, to offer absolutely everything? Think how much merit you would gain from that! Buddhism teaches, especially in the Mahāyāna form, that it's the intention that counts. The sincere mental offering is the real offering. In all the religions of the world there are versions of the story of the widow's mite. It's not what you give, it's the will to give that counts. So this is the way in which merit is accumulated. Mentally, with sincerity, with devotion, you offer up the whole universe, a symbolical representation of the whole material world, in all its levels, all its aspects, all its features, with all its treasures, and you try to develop the genuine feeling that if everything was yours, you'd offer it all to the Buddha, you'd offer it all to the Dharma, you'd offer it all to the Sangha. And in this way you accumulate spiritual merits.

Of course it is very important that this shouldn't become a formula or a formality. You must genuinely feel that in offering the mandala you are offering up absolutely everything, that even if you became the richest person in the world, you'd devote it all to the Buddha, the Dharma and the Sangha, or even if you became master of the whole universe, you would be able to think of nothing better to do with it than offering it to the Buddha. Some Buddhist kings in the past in a very grandiose way actually offered their whole kingdom to the Buddha. Sometimes they took it back the next day, but that's neither here nor there! You get the idea. The will to give, to surrender, to offer up – this is what the offering of the mandala really symbolizes.

So these are the four foundation yogas. They are usually regarded as preparatory to the practice of the Vajrayāna as a whole, the practice of Tantric Buddhism, but it is also said that any one of them, if thoroughly, deeply and sincerely and continuously practised, will bring one very near to Enlightenment, especially the third *mūla yoga*, the meditation and mantra recitation of Vajrasattva. Perhaps it isn't necessary to say anything more. Perhaps all that remains is for us to practise.

From 'The Four Foundation Yogas' in a lecture series on Tibetan Buddhism; an edited version appears in *Tibetan Buddhism* (1996), pp.90-102

2. THE FOUNDATION YOGAS AND THE SYSTEM OF MEDITATION

It's very difficult to say it comes here or it comes there. It depends on the degree or extent to which you practise it.

Q: How do the prostrations and foundation yogas fit into the system of meditation?

Sangharakshita: The prostrations are one of the four foundation or *mūla yogas*: the Going for Refuge and prostration practice, the generation of the *bodhicitta*, the offering of the mandala and the visualization of Vajrasattva with the recitation of his mantra. How they fit into the system of meditation depends how you do them. Let's take for instance the Going for Refuge and prostration practice. You could do it in a purely external fashion, as 'prostration therapy', to coin an unfortunate phrase. That wouldn't be meditation in any form except maybe the most elementary concentration, if you got round to doing the visualization part of the practice, so it wouldn't fit into the system at all. But if you succeeded in having a good *samatha*-type practice, it would fit into the system of meditation within the second stage, the second level, that of emotional positivity, because great faith and devotion would be inspired. If you went further than that – because you also get a little of the *śūnyatā*-type practice in this *mūla yoga* – you could even enter upon the third stage of meditation. And then of course you conjure up, as it were, the figure of Padmasambhava or the Buddha (depending on which form of the practice you're doing) to prostrate before, so that would bring you into the fourth stage, the stage of spiritual rebirth. So where the Going for Refuge and prostration practice came within the system of meditation would depend on the spirit in which you practised it, and how far you were able to take it, but it could accompany you, as it were, all the way through your practice of meditation.

It's slightly different for the other *mūla yogas*. For instance, the generation of the *bodhicitta* is clearly a sort of Transcendental experience. One could say that it comes between the second and the third stages of meditation. The Vajrasattva practice can accompany you all the way, again depending on how you do it, whether it's just a concentration exercise or whether it's a real *samatha*-type of experience, done with great faith and devotion, whether it leads you into the experience of *śūnyatā* and whether the visualization of Vajrasattva himself represents for you the stage of spiritual rebirth. So it's very difficult to say it comes here or it comes there. It depends on the degree or extent to which you practise it.

From the Western Buddhist Order convention (1978, p.19)

3. DON'T SKIMP THE BASICS

The *metta-bhavana* is a very good foundation for visualization, because when you're happy and in a positive mood you feel creative.

> *I, and all else that moves, until Enlightenment,*
> *Take the Guru and the Triple Gem as Refuge,*
> *In order to gain perfect Buddhahood for others' sake.*
> *Whereby, may sentient beings possess happiness with its causes;*
> *Be parted from all grief with its causes;*
> *Not become parted from the happiness wherein no grief is;*
> *And dwell in the condition of equanimity.*[84]

These lines represent the Going for Refuge and the development of the four *brahma-vihāras* as the foundation of the *bodhicitta*, but usually in Tibetan Buddhism, certainly nowadays, these lines are just recited.

My teacher Mr Chen used to say that the Tibetans, many of them, had strayed away from the real Buddhist tradition and instead of actually Going for Refuge and practising the *brahma-vihāras* would simply recite these verses, neglecting the preliminaries which according to him were essential, neglecting the Hinayana and the Mahāyāna in their haste to get on to the Vajrayāna, the Tantra.

So it isn't enough just to recite these verses. We have actually to Go for Refuge with all that that implies. We need to do the Going for Refuge practice, the prostration practice, and the *brahma-vihāras*. The *mettā-bhāvanā* is a very good foundation for visualization, because when you're happy and in a positive mood you feel creative. We shouldn't just gabble our way through these things. We should stop and practise them. They are summaries of practice, not substitutes for practice.

From a seminar on the *Mañjughoṣa Stuti Sadhana* (1977, pp.24-5)

4. THE RELEVANCE OF THE FOUNDATION YOGAS

It's not a question simply of intensifying this or that aspect of the total experience, but of intensifying the total experience itself.

Q: The *bodhicitta* practice which some Order members do seems to correspond roughly to Vasubandhu's four factors. Given the importance of the *bodhicitta*, do you think that the *bodhicitta* practice should be more regularly and widely performed?

Sangharakshita: I think the question is more than that. One might ask, given that the breakthrough from the mundane to the Transcendental is so important, should not the Going for Refuge be intensified? Should not the arising of the *bodhicitta* be intensified? Should not the turning about in the deepest seat of consciousness be intensified? Should not the Going Forth be intensified? And of course the answer is that they should all be intensified. In a sense it doesn't matter which one you start on, and from which you work your way around gradually to the others, but at least you should start by intensifying one of them, with a view to intensifying all the others in turn. Maybe you start off by intensifying your Going Forth, or perhaps you decide to intensify your practice of the *bodhicitta*, so you devote more time to that particular practice. But it's not a question simply of intensifying this or that aspect of the total experience, but of intensifying the total experience itself, via a more intense practice of this or that aspect of it, and eventually all the aspects. So perhaps a general all-round intensification is in order.

Q: I was wondering about the relevance of the foundation yogas generally.

S: Well, they're relevant not for our Buddhist movement collectively, but for individuals. If individuals find that they help, then they're relevant. If individuals don't, then they're not relevant. Quite a few individuals do find at least some of them helpful. But obviously you must make the effort to try to find out, by actually practising, whether they are helpful or not, and whether they are relevant or not.

From Q&A on the Bodhisattva Ideal (1984, pp.73-4)

5. OFFERING THE MANDALA

When you offer the mandala, you offer the whole of material existence to the Buddhas and Bodhisattvas.

The offering of the mandala is one of the foundation yogas of the Tantra. In this context the term mandala has a slightly unusual meaning, referring to the universe, the cosmos, as represented in traditional Buddhist cosmology. Thus the offering of the mandala means the offering of the whole universe. When you offer the mandala, you offer the whole of material existence to the Buddhas and Bodhisattvas.

The suggestion behind this particular form of external offering is that your gratitude to the Buddha, to the Three Jewels, is intense to the point of being overwhelming. You feel so grateful for what you have received that in response you would like to give everything you have and experience, everything you could possibly own or enjoy or imagine. If you owned the whole world, you would want to give even that. You could think of nothing better to do with it than offer it to the Buddha. Although you can't do this literally, you can offer it symbolically. In this, as in the spiritual life as a whole, it is the heartfelt intention and the attitude that count.

The mandala represents not just the physical universe, but a system of intersecting planes or dimensions of being and consciousness, only one of which is identical with our own physical universe. It is usually said to consist of thirty-seven parts, but this is simply to give an idea of its most prominent aspects, and is not meant to be a comprehensive survey. Perhaps the number thirty-seven was chosen to correspond with the thirty-seven practices leading to Enlightenment, the *bodhipaksya-dhammas* – but sometimes only twenty-five parts are enumerated, and one list from Tibetan sources puts the number at thirty-nine.

The mandala has a foundation, called the 'diamond ground' which represents the ultimate reality that is the basis of the whole of phenomenal existence. Then there is a wall of iron, which marks the outermost limit or (thinking three-dimensionally) the outermost shell of this universe. Within the wall there are seven concentric circles of golden mountains, alternating with seven concentric circles of ocean. In this context are found, according to the list of thirty-seven, the constituent parts of the mandala. The first part is Mount Meru, the king of mountains, the axis of this whole system, which rises up from the innermost circle of ocean. Meru is popularly identified with a certain peak in the western Himalayas, but in reality it is not to be identified with any earthly mountain at all. Below Mount Meru are the lower worlds of suffering, the purgatories and hells, and above it are the worlds of the gods. Upon Mount Meru itself are four realms, the topmost of which is inhabited by the asuras or Titans, who are perpetually attacking the gods. (This world-picture shares many features with that other symbol of conditioned existence, the Tibetan Wheel of Life.)

Parts 2-5 are the four islands or continents situated in the outermost circle of ocean, immediately inside the iron wall. The eastern continent is white in colour and shaped like a crescent moon; its inhabitants have crescent-shaped faces, and are tranquil and virtuous. The southern continent is blue, and shaped, we are told, like the shoulder blade of a sheep – and the faces of its inhabitants are apparently this same shape. This continent – in which riches abound and both good and evil exist – is said to correspond roughly to our own world. The western continent is round like the sun and red in colour, with red-faced denizens who are powerful in constitution and greatly addicted to the flesh of cattle. The northern continent is square and green; its inhabitants have square faces like the faces of horses, and they get all they need from the trees that grow on their continent.

Parts 6-13 are the eight subsidiary continents. There are two of these to each of the main continents, and they are of the same shape as their parent continent. The fourteenth part of the mandala is the mountain of jewels, and the fifteenth is the wish-fulfilling tree, which the Titans are constantly trying to wrest from the gods. The sixteenth part is the wish-fulfilling cow, the cow of plenty; the seventeenth is the crops that grow without the necessity of cultivation. Parts 18-24 are the seven jewels of the universal monarch, the word jewel here meaning 'the best of its kind'. This is a well-known list: the wish-fulfilling jewel, the precious wheel, the precious queen, the precious minister, the precious elephant, the precious horse, and the precious general. The twenty-fifth part is the wish-fulfilling jar, a kind of Aladdin's lamp, sometimes considered to be identical with the vase of initiation. Parts 26-33 are the eight offering goddesses, who live in their own heaven worlds, adjacent to the paradise of Indra. Parts 34 and 35 are the sun and the moon – not just in the literal sense, but more as they appear at the top of the Tantric *stūpa* – as symbols of the complementary influences in the universe. The thirty-sixth part is the ceremonial umbrella, the umbrella of victory and sovereignty, which crowns the whole mandala, and the thirty-seventh part is a banner of victory, which flies from the top of the umbrella. Between them, these thirty-seven parts of the mandala represent the whole multi-dimensional universe.

According to a Nyingma tradition, the mandala is offered thus: First you visualize the cosmic refuge tree. You see in your mind's eye the glorious figure of the great Tantric guru Padmasambhava surrounded by the exoteric and esoteric refuges. Above him you see the gurus of the spiritual lineage up to the Buddha Amitābha and the *adibuddha* Samantabhadra, below him are gurus, *yidams*, *ḍākinīs*, *dharmapālas*, and so on, in front of him the Buddhas of the three periods of time (past, present, and future), behind him the sacred books, and on either side the two wings of the Sangha. You visualize all this in the sky before you, and as you do so, you recite a special esoteric version of the sevenfold puja, of which the following is a rendering into English that I made many years ago with the help of one of my Tibetan teachers, Dhardo Rimpoche:

> *To that Trikāya which is the true nature of all Dharmas,*
>   *non-dual,*
> *limitless, profound and vast, I make obeisance.*
> *I worship the unmade, the unlimited, and the eternal.*
> *I make confession of the sin of not knowing that my own mind*
>   *is the Buddha,*
> *Rejoicing in the natural state, the self-aware.*

I request the Buddha to revolve the ungraspable, omnipresent and all-accomplished Dharmacakra.
I pray that the mundane and the transcendental may be established in oneness.
Whatever obeisance and worship I have performed, I transmute into the voidness.
May all beings attain both voidness and great bliss.

This should be repeated many times and as you recite it you should feel that all living beings are repeating it with you. After that, you actually offer up the mandala. First you visualize it in your heart – the diamond ground, the iron wall, the golden mountains, the circles of ocean, Mount Meru, and so on, adorned with all the other items – and then you offer it in worship to the Buddhas, Bodhisattvas, gurus, and ḍākinīs of the cosmic refuge tree.

To visualize all this in detail is very difficult, even with a lot of practice. But there is another way of doing the practice which is commonly resorted to in Tantric circles. This is literally to construct a simplified three-dimensional model of the universe. You take a round metal base, like a deep tray turned upside down, to represent the diamond ground of existence, and you usually begin by symbolically cleaning it a few times. Then you recite a mantra, *om vajra bhūmi āḥ hūm* (meaning 'diamond ground'). As you do this, you try to realize, to feel, that this is the underlying reality of the whole phenomenal world. On this base you place a large metal circle or ring about one inch high, to represent the wall of iron enclosing the universe. You fill this ring with rice, and place on the rice a second ring, smaller than the first, to represent Mount Meru. After filling the second ring with rice, you place upon it a third ring, smaller still, to represent the higher heavenly realm. Around this stepped pyramid structure you then deposit a few grains of rice to represent each of the other parts of the mandala. Finally you crown the whole edifice with a jewel mounted on a silver *dharmacakra*. Having constructed the mandala, you are now ready to offer it up. The act of offering consists simply in lifting up the mandala you have created in the direction of the shrine and the figure of the Buddha or guru upon it, or actually placing it on the offering table. The whole procedure, from beginning to end, is to be repeated 100,000 times. It is important to remember that, although it involves physical actions, this practice is really an act of the imagination, and of the emotions. Furthermore, all these apparently solid phenomena, represented by rice and metal, are not as solid as they seem; the very 'ground' on which they are based is insubstantial, being represented in some descriptions of Buddhist cosmology by nothing more than two winds blowing across each other.

If you don't have time for this, there is a still more simplified form of offering the mandala. To do this, you just fill the palms of your hands with rice and make a certain ritual gesture or mudrā, to symbolize the mandala. To make this mudrā you place the backs of your two ring-fingers together, so that they are sticking up into the air, to represent Mount Meru. Then you cross your middle fingers and grasp their tips with your forefingers, and cross your little fingers and grasp their tips with your thumbs. You have thus made four corners, to symbolize the four continents. Holding your hands together in this way, you recite this verse:

> *The ground is purified with scented water and strewn with flowers.*
> *It is adorned with the king of mountains, the four continents, the sun and the moon.*
> *Thinking of it as the Buddha realm, I offer it to the Buddha.*
> *By virtue thereof may all human beings attain to the realm of bliss.*
> From *Creative Symbols of Tantric Buddhism* (2004, pp.143-9)

6. PRELIMINARY PRACTICES

They represent attitudes that you should be cultivating all the time, crystallized into those particular exercises.

Q: The *Torch of Certainty* gives four preliminary meditations to the four foundation yogas: the meditation on the precious human body, on the shortcomings of saṁsāra, on impermanence, and on karma and its result. Would you recommend doing these before starting the foundation yogas?

Sangharakshita: These are four standard meditations, and yes, they are certainly useful and it would be useful to do them before doing the foundation yogas. That is the general tradition. But one could say that those four practices are not just exercises that you do either on their own account or before other practices. They represent attitudes that you should be cultivating all the time, crystallized into those particular exercises. For instance, you ought to be mindful of the fact of impermanence all the time, not just on certain occasions when you do a particular exercise.

From a seminar on the Jewel Ornament of Liberation
(Tuscany 1985, p.63)

7. TOTAL WITHDRAWAL, TOTAL ENGAGEMENT

One experiences a sort of conflict – if one's nature is big enough to embrace the possibilities of such a conflict.

The *bodhicitta* is said to arise as a result of a coalescence between two trends of experience which are generally considered to be contradictory. (In ordinary experience they are in fact contradictory, in the sense that you can't pursue both of them simultaneously.) We may describe these as the trend of withdrawal and the trend of involvement.

Reflection on the Faults of Conditioned Existence
The first trend represents the movement of total withdrawal from mundane things, which is renunciation in the extreme sense. One withdraws from the world: from worldly activities, worldly thoughts, worldly associations. This movement of withdrawal is said to be aided by a particular practice, which is called 'reflection on the faults of conditioned existence'. You reflect that conditioned existence, life within the round of existence, is not only not very satisfactory, it is profoundly unsatisfactory. It entails all sorts of experiences of an unpleasant nature: things one wants but can't get, people one likes whom one is separated from, things one doesn't want to do which one has to do. There is the whole wretched business of earning a living. There is attending to the physical body – feeding it, doctoring it when it gets sick. There is looking after one's family – husband, wife, children, relations. You feel that all this is too much and you have to get away from it all, out of it all. You desire to escape from the round of existence into Nirvāṇa, into a state where you don't have all these things. You wish to get away from all the fluctuations and vicissitudes of this mundane life into the peace and rest of the Eternal.

Reflection on the Sufferings of Sentient Beings
The second trend, the trend of involvement, represents concern for living beings. One thinks, 'Yes, I would like to get out. That would be all right for *me*. But what about other people? What would happen to *them*? There are some who can't stand it even as well as I can. If I abandon them, how will *they* get out?' This trend is aided by 'reflection on the sufferings of sentient beings'. In the trend of withdrawal, you reflect on the faults of conditioned existence only so far as they affect you, but here you reflect on them as they affect other living beings. You reflect, therefore, on the sufferings of living beings.

You just have to look around at the people you know – all your friends and acquaintances – and reflect on all the troubles they have. There may be someone who has lost their job and doesn't know what to do. Another person's marriage has broken up. Someone else has perhaps had a nervous breakdown. Someone has been bereaved, may have lost their husband or wife or their child. If you reflect, you realize that there is not a single person you know who is not suffering in some way. Even if they are happy (in the quite ordinary sense), there are still things that they have to bear: separation, illness, the weakness and tiredness of old age, and finally death, which they certainly don't want.

If you cast your gaze wider, you can reflect on how much suffering there is in so many parts of the world. There are wars. There are catastrophes of various kinds, such as floods or famines. People sometimes die in very horrible ways – you need only think about World War II and of people dying in concentration camps. You can cast your eye further still and think of animals, how they suffer, not only through the actions of other animals but at the hands of man. You can thus see that the whole world of living beings is involved in suffering – so much of it! When one reflects on the sufferings of sentient beings in this way, one thinks, 'How can I think simply in terms of getting out of it all? How can I think of getting away myself to some private Nirvāṇa which may be very satisfactory to me personally, but which doesn't help them?'

One thus experiences a sort of conflict – if one's nature is big enough to embrace the possibilities of such a conflict. On the one hand, one wants to get out; on the other, one wants to stay here. The trend of withdrawal is there; the trend of involvement is there. To choose *either* alternative is easy: it is easy either to withdraw into spiritual individualism or to remain involved in a worldly way. Many people do in fact take the easy solution, some choosing to get out, others choosing to remain in.

Some get out into spiritual individualism, private spiritual experience. Others remain in the world, but in a purely secular sense, without much of a spiritual outlook.

Recollection of the Buddha
The point of what I am trying to explain here is that though contradictory, *both* of these trends – the trend of withdrawal and also the trend of involvement – must be developed in the spiritual life. We might say that the trend of withdrawal embodies the Wisdom aspect of the spiritual life, *prajñā*, and the trend of involvement embodies the Compassion aspect, *karuna*. Both of these are to be developed. That joint development is helped by what is known as 'recollection of the Buddha'. One constantly bears in mind the ideal of unsurpassed, Perfect Enlightenment, Enlightenment for the benefit of all sentient beings, as exemplified most perfectly by Gautama the Buddha himself, the human and historical teacher.

What one has to do is not allow the tension between these two trends to relax. If one does that, then in a sense one is lost. Even though they are contradictory, one has to pursue both simultaneously. One has to get out and stay in, see the faults of conditioned existence while at the same time feeling the sufferings of sentient beings, develop both Wisdom and Compassion.

As one pursues both of these trends simultaneously, the tension builds up and up (it is, of course, not a psychological tension but a spiritual tension). It is built up until a point is reached when one can't go any further. When one reaches that point, something happens. What happens is difficult to describe, but we may provisionally describe it as an explosion. This means that as the result of the tension which has been generated by following these two contradictory trends simultaneously, there occurs a breakthrough into a higher dimension of spiritual consciousness, where the two trends – of withdrawal and involvement – are no longer two, not because they have been artificially amalgamated into one but because the plane on which their duality existed, or on which it was possible for them to be two things, has been transcended.

When one breaks through one has the experience of being simultaneously withdrawn and involved, 'out' of it and 'in' it at the same time. Now Wisdom and Compassion have become non-dual (one can say 'one' if one likes, but it is not an arithmetical 'one'). When the explosion occurs, when for the first time one is both withdrawn and involved, having both Wisdom and Compassion not as two things 'side by side' but as 'one' thing, then one may say that the *bodhicitta* has arisen.

From *A Guide to the Buddhist Path* (1996, pp.186-7)

8. THE ARISING OF THE BODHICITTA

The Buddhas all started off with the same ignorance and weaknesses as we do.

According to Vasubandhu's method, the arising of the *bodhicitta* depends upon four factors.[85] The first of these is the recollection of the Buddhas. One thinks of the Buddhas of the past – Śākyamuni, the Buddha of our own historical era, and his great predecessors in remote aeons of legend, Dipankara, Kondañña, and so on.[86] Then, in the words of the *sūtras*, one reflects:

> *All the Buddhas in the ten quarters, of the past, of the future, and of the present, when they first started on their way to enlightenment, were not quite free from passions and sins any more than we are at present; but they finally succeeded in attaining the highest enlightenment and became the noblest beings.*
>
> *All the Buddhas, by strength of their inflexible spiritual energy, were capable of attaining perfect enlightenment. If enlightenment is attainable at all, why should we not attain it?*
>
> *All the Buddhas, erecting high the torch of wisdom through the darkness of ignorance and keeping awake an excellent heart, submitted themselves to penance and mortification, and finally emancipated themselves from the bondage of the triple world. Following their steps, we, too, could emancipate ourselves.*
>
> *All the Buddhas, the noblest type of mankind, successfully crossed the great ocean of birth and death and of passions and sins; why, then, we, being creatures of intelligence, could also cross the sea of transmigration.*
>
> *All the Buddhas manifesting great spiritual power sacrificed the possessions, body, and life, for the attainment of omniscience* (sarvajñā); *and we, too, could follow their noble examples.*[87]

In other words, the Buddhas all started off with the same ignorance and weaknesses as we do. If they could overcome them, so can we, if we make the effort. Apart from the obvious benefits of this practice for the development of faith and confidence, it has a very positive effect simply in that if one is thinking of the Buddha, one is mentally occupied with something positive and thus turning the current of one's thoughts away from unskilful actions. Occupying one's mind with thoughts of the Buddha, one is very unlikely to have an unskilful thought or commit an unskilful action. Instead, one will experience positive, skilful emotions: faith, joy, serenity, peace.

The second of Vasubandhu's factors is 'seeing the faults of conditioned existence'. 'Conditioned existence' refers to phenomenal existence of every kind: physical, mental, even spiritual – whatever arises in dependence upon causes and conditions. And the first 'fault' to be seen is that all conditioned existence is impermanent. It may be an idea or an empire, it may arise and disappear in an infinitesimal fraction of a second or over billions of years, but whatever arises must, sooner or later, cease. And – because everything conditioned is transitory – conditioned existence can never be truly satisfactory; this is the second fault to be reflected upon. Sooner or later the wrench of separation comes, and in its wake comes suffering. And thirdly, everything is, in a sense, unreal, insubstantial. This is a subtler 'fault' to find with conditioned existence. It is not that things do not exist – clearly they do. But nothing exists independent of its constituents, all of which are impermanent and liable to change. This book, for example – take away the typeface and the pages, the cover and the spine, and where is the book? It has no inherent existence; there is nothing 'underneath', nothing substantial about it. And all things are like this, including ourselves. There is no 'I' apart from my constituent parts, my *skandhas*. This is the famous *anātman* doctrine.[88]

So one sees that conditioned existence as a whole has these faults: it is impermanent, it is riddled with unsatisfactoriness, and it isn't ultimately real. One further reflects – one knows in one's heart of hearts – that nothing conditioned can fully satisfy the deepest longings of the human heart. We long for something permanent, something beyond the flux of time, something blissful, something permanently satisfying, something of which we never become weary, something which is fully and entirely real and true. But such a thing is nowhere to be found in mundane experience. Reflecting in this way, seeing the faults of conditioned existence, one pierces through the conditioned to the Unconditioned beyond.

The third factor is 'observing the sufferings of sentient beings'. And what a lot of sufferings there are. One has only to open a newspaper to encounter a whole host of them: people hanged, shot, burned to death – people dying in all sorts of painful ways, from disease, famine, flood, or fire. At this very moment, people are suffering in all sorts of agonizing ways, and one doesn't need much imagination to realize this. There are volcanic eruptions, earthquakes, and plane crashes, to say nothing of war – sudden death in so many fearful and horrifying forms. And, of course, there are many deaths on the roads: we have become almost inured to this phenomenon, but it is still truly horrible if we consider the reality behind the statistics.

Even apart from such horrors, simply getting on in the world, making ends meet, leading a happy human existence, is sometimes a tremendous struggle. We strive to do the decent thing, to be upright and honest, to lift our heads above the waves; but then a great wave comes along and overwhelms us again. Down we go, then up we come again; and so it goes on. This is human life.

Then there's the suffering of animals: all those animals that are trapped for their fur, or slaughtered for human consumption, or pursued for 'sport'. If one looks at it objectively one sees that in many ways life is a painful and miserable thing: 'nasty, brutish, and short'. This is only one side of the picture, but it is a side which we very often ignore, and which we need to bear in mind.

Worse still, in a way, are the sufferings we bring upon ourselves through our own mental states. It is not just that we are afraid of growing old or dying; we do absolutely nothing about our predicament. Full of anxiety, most people have no spiritual orientation to their lives, no real clarity. The *bodhicitta* starts arising when one sees what a mess we are all in. One can't begin to see that until one is a little way out of the mess oneself, but then one does begin to appreciate what a miserable time people have of it.

The great danger is that, having freed oneself to some extent, one may start looking down on others and pitying them. This sort of elitism – 'Oh you poor people! Have you never heard of Buddhism?' – does no good at all. At the same time, though, one can see that most people *do* need a spiritual path, and one wants to help – not just to alleviate or palliate, but help in a far more radical fashion, helping people to see that there is some spiritual dimension, some higher purpose, to life.

Tennyson speaks of having a 'painless sympathy with pain',[89] and it is this sort of sympathy that Bodhisattvas feel. They are keenly conscious of the suffering of others, but they don't suffer themselves as others do. If one were literally to experience the sufferings of others, it would be completely incapacitating: it would be too much. If one gets too personally caught up in someone else's predicament, one can end up simply joining them in their suffering. One needs a basis within one's own experience which is so positive that even though one is fully aware of other people's suffering and one is doing what one can to alleviate it, one is not overwhelmed by that suffering.

The last of Vasubandhu's four factors is the 'contemplation of the virtues of the Tathāgatas' – the Tathāgatas being the Buddhas, the Enlightened Ones, and virtues here meaning not just ethical virtues but spiritual qualities of all kinds. In the Pāli scriptures there are many instances of people being tremendously inspired by encountering the Buddha. They haven't heard a word about Buddhism; they are simply inspired by the presence, the aura even, of the Buddha himself.

We ourselves can have this kind of encounter in a sense when we do puja. Puja is essentially just thinking about the Buddha: not thinking in a cold, intellectual way, but keeping the ideal of Buddhahood in the forefront of one's consciousness. When one does a puja, the Buddha is there in front of one, either in the form of the image on the shrine, or vividly present in one's own mind through visualization and imagination. Through puja and the whole devotional approach – making offerings, arranging flowers, and so on – one becomes more open and sensitive to the ideal of the Buddha, and this in turn paves the way for the breaking through of that highest spiritual dimension which is the *bodhicitta*. One doesn't stop doing devotional practices when the *bodhicitta* has arisen. According to the Mahāyāna sūtras, no one makes more offerings than the Bodhisattvas; they are always doing pujas, praising the Buddhas and so on. Some Bodhisattvas, we are told, have a vow that they will worship all the Buddhas in the universe. They spend all their time – millions and millions of years – going from one part of the universe to another, worshipping all the Buddhas that exist. This is typical Mahāyāna hyperbole, but it does bring home the importance of acts of devotion.

Another way of contemplating the virtues of Enlightened beings is to read accounts of their lives, whether the life of the Buddha himself or, say, that of Milarepa, the Enlightened yogi from the Tibetan Buddhist tradition. One can also contemplate the spiritual qualities of the Buddhas by means of visualization exercises, as developed particularly in Tibetan Buddhism, by conjuring up a vivid mental picture, a sort of archetypal vision, of a Buddha or a Bodhisattva. What one does in these practices – to summarize very briefly – is to see this visualized form more and more brightly, more and more vividly, more and more gloriously, and then gradually feel oneself merging with it, one's heart merging with the heart of the Buddha or Bodhisattva, the heart of Enlightenment. In this way one contemplates, one assimilates, one becomes one with, the virtues of the Tathāgatas.

Even without going into the traditional details too closely, it isn't difficult to understand how the *bodhicitta* might arise in dependence on these four factors. Through recollecting the Buddhas we become convinced that Enlightenment is possible. They have gained Enlightenment; why shouldn't we gain it too? Through this kind of reflection, energy and vigour is stirred up. Then, through seeing the faults of conditioned existence – seeing that it is impermanent, basically unsatisfactory, and not ultimately real – we become detached from the world. The trend, the stream, of our existence begins to flow in the direction of the Unconditioned. Next, through observing the sufferings of sentient beings – whether in imagination or in actual fact – compassion arises. We don't think only of our own liberation; we want to help others too. Then, by contemplating the virtues of the Tathāgatas – their purity, their peacefulness, their wisdom, their love – we gradually become assimilated to them and approach the goal of Enlightenment. As these four – energy, detachment, compassion, and 'becoming one', as it were, with the Buddhas – start to coalesce within our hearts, the *bodhicitta* arises; the awakening of the heart is achieved; a Bodhisattva is born.

From *The Bodhisattva Ideal* (1999, pp.53-7)

9. THE PURIFICATION OF THE MIND

If you aren't able to incorporate all the *mūla yogas*, at least do this one.

Q: Am I right in thinking that you recommend that Order members should practise all the *mūla yogas* at some time in their lives?

Sangharakshita: In the course of their Order life, yes. Of course I leave it up to the individual Order members as regards at which stage you incorporate them, depending on the time you have, but they're all good to do, especially I would say the Vajrasattva practice, which is a practice of purification. Dudjom Rimpoche said, speaking within a specifically Vajrayāna context, that if you can't do anything else, do the Vajrasattva practice. It includes the practice of all the other Buddhas and Bodhisattvas, and it's a practice of purification – and clearly purification is needed.

It's very interesting that in the course of a little book I had read to me recently, *Counsels from my Heart*, Dudjom Rimpoche twice quotes a verse with which we're familiar from the Pāli scriptures, from the *Dhammapada*: *sabbapāpassa akaraṇaṃ*, that is to say, the ceasing to do evil, the doing of good, and the purification of one's mind, that is the teaching of all the Buddhas. Dudjom Rimpoche connects the Vajrasattva practice with that third line, the purification of the mind, saying that this is the essential point of the whole Vajrayāna. So this is a quite effective, concrete and imaginative way of purifying the mind and getting that experience of purification, of washing away all your faults and weaknesses, your sins of omission and commission, your failure to keep precepts and so on. If you aren't able to incorporate all the *mūla yogas*, at least do this one. At least, Dudjom Rimpoche says, recite the Vajrasattva mantra twenty times a day. That's not much, is it? Maybe you could do it at the end of whatever other practice you do. It's a mantra which does have a very great significance. Unlike many other mantras, it has a conceptual meaning, something that you can reflect upon.

Of course there's the Going for Refuge practice and the *bodhicitta* practice, but those are represented by other elements in one's spiritual life anyway – one is Going for Refuge all the time and inasmuch as you recognize that altruistic dimension to the spiritual life, you are doing the *bodhicitta* practice. And of course there's the Offering of the Mandala – but one practises *dāna*, one practises worship to the extent that one can, so that element presumably is always in one's spiritual life as a Buddhist anyway. And of course there's the Guru Yoga. Dilgo Khyentse says that if you just do the Guru Yoga that's enough, you don't need any other practice. You think of your teachers, you think of your spiritual friends, your *kalyāna mitras*, you're grateful to them. That's a permanent element in one's spiritual life too.

Q: Why do you think people find visualization difficult?

S: I suppose lack of imagination. Some people aren't able to build up mental pictures very easily. It seems connected with that. Perhaps they don't have much of a poetic streak. Maybe they're really rather prosaic souls. Not to say that they're less spiritually developed, of course, but they prefer something almost a bit drier, a bit more scientific. They don't like all this flowery imagery, these lotus thrones and moon mats and mandaravas and so on. Some people love that sort of thing! I personally rather like it.

Q: So temperamentally, for some people, although there is a reflective element in visualization, they find it easier to just contemplate the *lakṣaṇas*, without the symbolic imagery?

S: Yes – while some people seem to respond more strongly to symbols.
From Theris' Q&A, Tiratanaloka (2002, pp.10-11)

2 Visualization exercises: *kasiṇa* and stūpa visualizations

1. A DISC OF LIGHT

Later on in the Buddhist tradition this method led to the visualization of figures of Buddhas and Bodhisattvas.

Sangharakshita: Dr Conze mentions a meditation which involves 'staring at coloured circles', but the phrase doesn't do the practice justice. This is the *kasiṇa* meditation. There are ten *kasiṇas* mentioned in Buddhist tradition, and you practise the meditation like this: You make a coloured disc, a red disc, say, on the wall – in ancient times they did it with red clay – at about the height of your nose when you're sitting cross-legged. You make it about ten or twelve inches in diameter, and you take your seat about six or seven feet from that disc of colour. Another method, if you're living in the forest, is to gather flowers of a particular colour and make a disc on the ground in front of you, and then you sit and look at that. When you look at colours, what happens?

Q: There's an emotional response.

S: Yes. What else?

Q: It depends on the colour to some extent, doesn't it?

S: The emotional response depends on the colour; but what else generally happens when you look at colour, certainly if you look at it for some time?

Q: It blurs ...

S: No, I wasn't thinking of that. I was thinking of the potential psychological effect. What can happen is that you become mentally less active. A colour is sensuous, and when you're preoccupied with it, you tend to think less. If you look at a colour you can become absorbed in looking at it, and feel quite happy and satisfied, and to the extent that you're feeling happy and satisfied and absorbed, you don't think. You continue to be aware and awake, but you're not mentally active. Do you see what I mean? So you look at this disc of colour – you don't stare at it, as Conze suggests, you just look at it – and you allow your whole attention to be absorbed by that disc of colour.

The colour you choose should relate to your temperament. If you're a person who is very dull and sluggish, you set up a disc of red, bright red; if you're a person who is very mentally active, a green or blue one would be better; and so on. So you allow your whole attention to be absorbed by this disc of colour. You try to cut out all thoughts, so that you're completely focused on the disc. You're not thinking about it, you're just aware of it, and sort of sinking into it, and experiencing it. In other words, you concentrate on that disc of colour. I've avoided the word 'concentration' up till now, because that might suggest forcibly fixing your attention and really staring at the disc, but it isn't like that. It's more like allowing your attention to be absorbed. So this is the first stage of the practice. You're totally absorbed by that disc of colour.

Then, when you've done that to your satisfaction, you close your eyes, just sitting there as you are, and you mentally reproduce that disc of colour. You try to see it as clearly in your mind as you were seeing it before physically. If you find that difficult, if you find the mental image is slipping, you can open your eyes and look at that disc, refresh your memory, then close your eyes again. You carry on like this for as long as you think suitable until – and this may take you a number of different sessions, even weeks and months – you can see the disc of colour mentally as clearly as you see it with your physical eyes. That's the second stage.

The third stage is when you are able to see the mental disc of colour very clearly, and that becomes your object of concentration. When you've concentrated on this for a considerable length of time, you will have an experience in connection with that disc of colour. For example, you may have the experience of a disc of light emerging from that coloured disc.

When that disc of light emerges, a much more intense concentration develops, and this can carry you even into the *dhyāna* levels.

So you've got three levels or stages of practice: concentrating on the coloured disc painted on the wall; concentrating on the mental image of the coloured disc; and then concentrating on the disc of light that emerges from that mental image. This is called *kasiṇa* practice or *kasiṇa* exercise. *Kasiṇa* means 'a device', the device here being the disc of colour. You can also do it with a bowl of water. Sometimes monks used their begging bowls: filled them with water, and put them in front of them. Then you wouldn't get a disc – it would be more like a sort of ellipse, wouldn't it? But that also can be used as an object of concentration.

You can see how later on in the Buddhist tradition this method led to the visualization of figures of Buddhas and Bodhisattvas. This is the more abstract geometrical method; the devotional element doesn't come into it. You can see how it links up with the *stūpa* visualization too. But this is a very ancient and primitive form of practice. There are ten *kasiṇas* described in Buddhaghosa's *Visuddhimagga* (*The Path of Purification*). It's very rarely practised nowadays. I've only met a very few monks who ever practised it.

From a seminar on Edward Conze's *Buddhism* (1976, pp.64-7)

2. A STEPPING-STONE TO THE VISUALIZATION PRACTICES

It is not only an exercise in one-pointedness of mind, because colour has all sorts of emotional associations.

Q: Could the use of *kasiṇa* meditations, particularly using brighter colours, be helpful for people who are alienated from their feelings, to the extent that they can't get a toehold in the *mettā* practice?

Sangharakshita: It could be. I have sometimes spoken of it as a stepping stone to the visualization practices, because it is a much simpler matter to visualize a simple disc of colour. In fact one does that to some extent in *sādhana* practices when one visualizes first of all the blue expanse of the sky and then in the midst of that a lotus flower, then on the lotus flower the white moon mat. The *kasiṇa* in a way is an even more simple form of that same kind of practice. It is not only an exercise in one-pointedness of mind, because colour has all sorts of emotional associations. So it is particularly good perhaps for people who find it difficult to contact their emotions, and who perhaps are not ready for or inclined to a relatively elaborate visualization practice involving a Buddha or Bodhisattva.

One of the early methods of forming the *kasiṇa*, especially for the monk in the jungle who didn't necessarily have his paint box handy, was to gather flowers and mass them on the ground in a clean spot without any leaves – orange flowers or red flowers or white flowers, whatever one was able to gather. Then you'd concentrate on that disc of pure colour. The colour of flowers is of course rather different from modern chemical dyes. I would suggest that if you do practise the *kasiṇa* exercise you should be very careful not to make your *kasiṇa* disc of harsh glaring colours such as you get with some modern pigments, but try to get a very rich, glowing and natural colour. I think the emotional associations of that type of colour would be more positive.

Years ago in Kalimpong a friend of mine drew my attention to the very great difference with regard to colour and general aesthetic and emotional effect between the older kind of Tibetan rugs that were produced with dyes made entirely from minerals or vegetables and the modern rugs made with coal tar or aniline dyes. The contrast was dreadful and my friend thought that by using these aniline dyes we had ruined our colour sense. I think probably there was a lot to be said for this. I certainly noticed the difference and I have been sensitive to it ever since. You have only got to place two of these rugs side by side. One is rich and glowing and in a sense slightly subdued; the other is harsh and glaring and sometimes the colours clash. In nature colours never clash, however bright they are.

Q: Is there any evidence that the *kasiṇa* exercises were used in the Buddha's day?

S: It would seems that they were. It does seem to be a very ancient technique, one of the handful of practices that almost certainly go back to the days of the Buddha himself. It hasn't been a particularly popular practice down the ages; it seems to have been superseded by other practices. I've often thought that perhaps it should be revived, though I have never practised it myself to any extent. I have experimented with it to get the hang of it, nothing more than that.

Q: What do you think of colour therapy? I don't know much about it, but it seems that colour therapists stress that a particular colour will have a certain effect.

S: I think it's inevitable, given the fact that colours are highly emotive, one might say. I have had from time to time an idea which I would like one day to put into practice. I have thought that if for instance one was doing the Vajrasattva practice, reciting the mantra and doing the visualization, it would be really good if for the period of that practice, you were to live in an entirely white room and wear white clothes. Perhaps you could have your shrine white, with white candles and white bowls. I'm sure it would have a very pronounced effect. In the same way if you were doing the Tārā practice, you could have a room decorated entirely in green and perhaps wear a green robe. I think we should experiment a little with these things and be perhaps more adventurous than we have been so far. Perhaps we could even have a beautiful country retreat centre with rooms decorated in different colours so that people could move from one to another in accordance with the practice that they were doing.

From a seminar on *The Forest Monks of Sri Lanka* (1985, pp.291-2)

3. HOW CAN FOCUSING ON A SENSE-OBJECT LEAD BEYOND THE SENSES?

You may start with a material object in the kamaloka, but that doesn't mean that you are bound to the kamaloka.

Q: If one chooses a visual object as an object of concentration, e.g. a flower, presumably one's level of consciousness is limited thereby to the *kāmaloka*. If so, how is it that the breath being used as an object of concentration can lead to levels of consciousness beyond the *kāmaloka*?

Sangharakshita: Good question. The key word here is 'lead', because one thing leads to another – not directly, but it may lead to something which leads on to something else. But if you choose a visual object as an object of concentration, it doesn't necessarily limit your level of consciousness to the *kāmaloka*. There is a traditional practice called the *kasiṇa* practice, in which you concentrate on a coloured disc, red or yellow or blue or white, and with the help of this disc, you can pass up through all the *dhyānas*.

What you do is this. You first of all practise concentrating on that visual object, with your open physical eyes. You just look, until all your thoughts are absorbed in that. The colour as it were absorbs all your wandering thoughts and you're completely concentrated; that's the first stage.

Then you close your eyes and reproduce that coloured disc mentally as an eidetic image, just like you do in any other visualization. If you lose it from time to time, you open your eyes and go back to the original physical object. That's the second stage, and it corresponds to neighbourhood concentration.

Then, when you've practised with this mentally visualized disc for a while, you have what's called a photic experience, an experience of light of one kind or another. You may find that a bright disc like a full moon emerges from the red disc, or that the disc starts flashing or twinkling, or you may have some other kind of experience; it may be an intensely blissful emotional experience. That gives you your link to the next stage, from which you can go to the first *dhyāna*, and then to the second. In this way, starting with the visual object, the disc, you ascend through all the *dhyānas* and move from the *kāmaloka* to the *rūpāloka*, and then to the *arūpāloka* even.

It's the same with the breath. First of all you concentrate on the grosser breath then in the successive stages it becomes subtler and subtler until you're left just with this fine point, the sensation in the nostrils. When you've come to that point, when you're very, very concentrated, you can begin to approach the first *dhyāna*. So even though you started with the material object, the breath, by degrees you go more and more subtly, higher and higher, until you enter the *dhyānas*, and from one *dhyāna* you can go on to the next.

So you may start with a material object in the *kāmaloka*, but that doesn't mean that you are bound to the *kāmaloka*. You can go step by step. You can start with the gross physical object and then go to the subtle counterpart and then to something still more subtle until you rise up into the *dhyānas*.

From the Western Buddhist Order convention (1978, pp.8-9)

4 STŪPA VISUALIZATION: THE RELEASE OF PSYCHO-SPIRITUAL ENERGY

The central problem of the spiritual life is the conservation and unification of our energies.

The central problem of the spiritual life is the conservation and unification of our energies. Most of the time our energies are not available for the spiritual life: they are blocked, repressed, or draining away. Therefore we often find it difficult to get deeply into meditation. The *stūpa* visualization practice is intended to release, stimulate, and purify psycho-spiritual energy.

When one takes up a practice of this kind, one may at first see only an undifferentiated patch of colour; in time the colour will assume a certain definite form. To see the colour, and more than this, to 'feel' the colour, is of the utmost importance. It is the colour that gives one the feel, the inner feeling, of the particular aspect visualized, i.e. earth, water, fire, air, or space. This inner feeling is something that is very subtle and indefinable. One experiences the colour as a colour and as more than a colour, as a symbol. The colour becomes a vehicle for the experience of a spiritual quality, a spiritual state, which the colour symbolizes. Through the form and colour symbol one can experience the spiritual principle which the symbol embodies.

Visualization of the stūpa

1. Visualize an infinite, clear blue sky.

2. Appearing within the clear blue sky visualize a yellow cube, symbol of the element earth.

3. Above the yellow cube visualize a white sphere, symbol of the element water.

4. Above the white sphere visualize a red cone, symbol of the element fire.

5. Above the red cone visualize a pale green hemisphere, symbol of the element air.

6. Above the pale green hemisphere visualize an iridescent, rainbow-scintillating flaming drop, symbol of the element space.

7. The flaming drop is slowly dissolved into the pale green hemisphere.

8. The pale green hemisphere is slowly dissolved into the red cone.

9. The red cone is slowly dissolved into the white sphere.

10. The white sphere is slowly dissolved into the yellow cube.

11. The yellow cube is slowly dissolved into the blue sky.

12. Finally one allows the blue sky to fade away, thus bringing the practice to a close.

From *A Guide to the Buddhist Path* (1996, p.172)

3 The visualization of Buddhas and Bodhisattvas

One night I found myself as it were out of the body and in the presence of Amitābha, the Buddha of Infinite Light, who presides over the western quarter of the universe. The colour of the Buddha was a deep, rich, luminous red, like that of rubies, though at the same time soft and glowing, like the light of the setting sun. While his left hand rested on his lap, the fingers of his right hand held up by the stalk a single red lotus in full bloom and he sat, in the usual cross-legged posture, on an enormous red lotus that floated on the surface of the sea. To the left, immediately beneath the raised right arm of the Buddha, was the red hemisphere of the setting sun, its reflection glittering golden across the waters. How long the experience lasted I do not know, for I seemed to be out of time as well as out of the body, but I saw the Buddha as clearly as I had ever seen anything under the ordinary circumstances of my life, indeed far more clearly and vividly. The rich red colour of Amitābha himself, as well as of the two lotuses, and the setting sun, made a particularly deep impression on me. It was more wonderful, more appealing, than any earthly red: it was like red light, but so soft and, at the same time, so vivid, as to be altogether without parallel.

From *The Rainbow Road* (1997, p.338)

1. A TANTRIC VISUALIZATION PRACTICE: GREEN TĀRĀ

The lotus opened its petals and in its centre was sitting a beautiful green goddess.

Tibetan Buddhist meditation is mainly Tantric; that is, it belongs not so much to the Theravāda or even the Mahāyāna, but to the Vajrayāna, which is that phase in the development of Buddhism in India which specializes, as it were, in esoteric meditation and symbolical ritual. Tibetan Buddhism is triyana, that is to say it is a Buddhism of the three yanas or three ways. It is often spoken of as Mahāyāna Buddhism, and this isn't altogether wrong, but it isn't at the same time altogether correct. Tibetan Buddhism isn't even a form of Mahāyāna Buddhism; it's Theravāda plus Mahāyāna plus Vajrayāna Buddhism. It's a very rich thing. From the Theravāda it draws its Vinaya or code of monastic discipline, as well as its Abhidharma, its psychological analysis and general philosophical statements. From the Mahāyāna it derives its spiritual ideal, which is the Bodhisattva Ideal, as well as its underlying metaphysics, which is that of the voidness or *śūnyatā*. And from the Vajrayāna, from Tantric Buddhism, it derives its esoteric meditation and its symbolic ritual. So Tibetan Buddhist meditation is Tantric.

But what exactly is Tantric meditation, and how does it differ from other kinds? There are many possible answers, but the simplest is to say that Tantric meditation is that kind of meditation which is practised by the *sādhaka*, by the practitioner, after initiation by a guru. And by initiation I mean Tantric initiation. In a sense, when any kind of meditation practice is explained to you, that is an initiation, but it isn't a *Tantric* initiation. And what do I mean by a Tantric initiation? In Sanskrit the term for a Tantric initiation is *abhiṣeka*, and the Tibetan word for this is *wongkur*. This Tantric initiation usually, though not always, involves the giving of a mantra – a sort of sacred phrase to repeat over and over again. *Abhiṣeka* means literally a sprinkling, and it's so called because in the course of the Tantric initiation, the person to be initiated is sprinkled ceremonially, ritually, with water. But this doesn't tell us very much about the inner meaning, the essence, of the initiation; it's just one particular ritual aspect of it. The Tibetan word *wongkur* gives us a much better clue to its real meaning. It means transmission of power, and this is what initiation really involves. The sprinkling with water represents the transference of power, spiritual power, spiritual energy, from the guru to the disciple, so the Tibetans, following the inner meaning of the term rather than the literal meaning, render *abhiṣeka* as transmission of power. *Wong* is power; it's also sovereignty, energy, vigour, spiritual potency, and *kur* means transmission or giving or bestowal. Thus, the Tantric initiation is essentially a transmission of spiritual power from the guru to the disciple, symbolized by the sprinkling and embodied in the mantra which is given at the time of initiation.

The term *wongkur* literally means a giving of power, but we can also think of it in terms of an activation of power. What the guru does is not literally to give some of his power to the disciple, so much as to activate by his own spiritual presence and energy the latent spiritual energies of the disciple. At the same time it must be said that in the course of the Tantric initiation, many people do experience an actual transmission of power. They don't just feel something being activated within them, they actually feel something passing into them from the guru. Even though one may explain it as an activation of the disciple's own powers by the guru, it is often experienced quite literally as a transmission of power. If you have any experience of spiritual healing, you may be able to understand the sort of thing that is meant; not that Tantric initiation is akin to spiritual healing, but just as in spiritual healing a health-giving, positive force passes from the healer to the patient, in the same way in the Tantric initiation, on a much higher level, a charge of spiritual energy passes from the guru to the disciple.

Sometimes people ask whether Tantric meditation can be practised without a guru, but from my description it should be evident that this is a contradiction in terms. If one practises a so-called Tantric meditation without having received the appropriate initiation by the guru, it becomes a Mahāyāna-type meditation. In the same way, if what is technically a Mahāyāna-type meditation is practised with a Tantric initiation by a guru, it becomes a Tantric-type practice. In other words, you cannot categorize specific meditation exercises as either Tantric or non-Tantric. If you practise them after having been initiated in the Tantric sense by a guru, they are Tantric meditations, but if you practise them on your own, even though the book may label them Tantric, they're not Tantric at all, they're Mahāyāna at best. There are quite a number of meditation exercises which are never practised without Tantric initiation, and one can speak of these as being Tantric meditations proper. But one must bear in mind that the Tantric nature of these meditations is dependent not upon what you do in the course of the meditation, but upon the fact that you've been initiated into it by the guru.

Tibetan Buddhists, you might be interested to know, never have lectures on meditation; not because they're not interested in meditation, but because they are too busy practising it. It's only here in the West that we tend to have lectures on meditation. In Tibetan circles there's lots of practice and comparatively little talking; here, I'm afraid, only too often there's lots of talking and very little practice. There's no harm in our having a sound knowledge of the theory before we practise, or even while we are practising; but sooner or later we do have to get on with the practical side of things.

There are many ways of practising, many types, many methods. When I first came into contact with Tibetan Buddhism, and especially with Tantric meditation, I was bewildered by the profusion of material, and it took me several years even to start to get it all sorted out. Having a rather methodical and tidy mind, I wasn't quite happy with all these great heaps of unorganized material lying as it were all over the place, but it was very difficult to reduce them to any sort of order.

Here I propose to give a concrete example of a meditation belonging to the outer Tantra. Obviously I can't describe the inner Tantra; that's rather difficult, in fact in a way it's impossible, because it's one of the conditions of initiation into the inner Tantra that you don't speak about the practices to anybody who hasn't received the same initiation. But the outer Tantra is more open and accessible, and its practices are usually followed by lay people in Tibet and by ordinary monks – monks who are just getting on with their own practices and who are not teachers.

There are a number of good reasons for choosing to describe the meditation on Green Tārā as an example of a Tibetan Buddhist visualization practice. In the first place, Tārā, or Dolma, is one of the most popular of all the Buddhas and Bodhisattvas of Tibet. The Sanskrit name means 'the one who ferries across' – in the sense of the one who saves – and the name is in the feminine gender, so it's translated usually as 'the Saviouress'. Tārā is a female Buddha or Bodhisattva. In the Mahāyāna, Buddhas and Bodhisattvas, for some strange reason, are always male, but in the Vajrayāna there are just as many female Buddhas and female Bodhisattvas as there are male ones; and Tārā is the most prominent of these female Buddhas or Bodhisattvas.

All these Buddhas and Bodhisattvas represent some aspect or other of Enlightenment or Buddhahood, whether wisdom or love or peace or power, and Tārā is the embodiment of the compassion aspect. She is described as the spiritual daughter of Avalokiteśvara, the Bodhisattva of Compassion. In the Mahāyāna and the Tantra there are three main Bodhisattvas: Mañjuśrī, representing wisdom; Vajrapani, representing power or energy; and Avalokiteśvara, or Chenrezig as the Tibetans call him, representing compassion. So where does Tārā come in? We can understand this through a traditional legend which embodies a great spiritual truth. It is said that once upon a time Avalokiteśvara, the great Bodhisattva of compassion, was surveying the whole mass of humanity, and he saw that all over the world people were involved in many troubles, many difficulties, so much suffering. Some were engaged in protracted lawsuits, others were being devoured by wild beasts, others were lying sick on their beds, others were suffering bereavement, others were being slaughtered by robbers and highwaymen, others were dying painful natural deaths. When he saw this great mass of human suffering and misery, it is said that Avalokiteśvara, out of compassion, could not help shedding tears. He shed so many that a lake formed on the ground, and in the midst of this lake a beautiful white lotus appeared. The lotus opened its petals and in its centre was sitting a beautiful green goddess. This was the Bodhisattva Tārā. So the legend says that Tārā was born out of the tears of Avalokiteśvara, the Bodhisattva of compassion. If Avalokiteśvara is compassion, Tārā is the essence of compassion. It may well be that Tārā is given a feminine form because traditionally women are said to be more tender-hearted than men, and therefore the quintessence of compassion is given the beautiful feminine form of Tārā the Saviouress. In Tibet she has many forms, but there are two principal ones: a White Tārā and a Green Tārā. They're both very popular all over Tibet, Mongolia and the whole of the Himalayan region, but perhaps we may say that the Green Tārā – in Sanskrit she's called Khadiravani Tārā – is the more popular of the two.

There are many ways of meditating on the Green Tārā, but I'll describe the standard one. The procedure that I'm going to describe can be applied also to meditation on other Buddhas and other Bodhisattvas. It includes various standard practices which you encounter in all Tantric meditation exercises – visualization, mantra recitation, and so on. In this meditation there are ten successive stages of practice, the first of which is the Going for Refuge. When you take up any Tantric meditation practice, you start off by Going for Refuge; it represents a brief recapitulation of the Theravāda within the Vajrayāna context. The Three

Refuges are refuge in the Buddha, refuge in the Dharma and refuge in the Sangha; in other words, refuge in the Enlightened teacher, in the teaching of the way leading to Enlightenment, and in the community of disciples treading the way leading to Enlightenment. But in this context the Refuges are given a Tantric colouring, in the form of an extra refuge. In the Tantra there's not only refuge in the Buddha, the Dharma, and the Sangha; first of all you take refuge in the guru, because the Tantrics say that it's only through the guru that you really come to know the Buddha, the Dharma, and the Sangha.

When you practise Tantric meditation, the Refuges are also given a Tantric colouring according to the type of practice that you are doing. In the context of the Tārā meditation practice, when you go for refuge, you consider that Tārā herself is the Buddha; she is the Buddha for you in the context of this practice. And then what is meant by the Dharma here? The Dharma is the great compassion of Tārā; in other words, it is the compassion aspect of the Dharma with which you are particularly concerned in this practice, so you take refuge in the compassion of Tārā as the Dharma. And then what about the Sangha? You take refuge in the Sangha in the sense of the 21 forms of Tārā. And what about the guru refuge? If you look at painted scrolls of Green Tārā, you'll notice that in her hair there's a tiny image, which you could easily miss, of Amitābha, the Buddha of Infinite Light, because she belongs, as it were, to his family. He is the Buddha of whom Avalokiteśvara is the Bodhisattva, and she is the spiritual daughter of Avalokiteśvara; so she belongs to the Amitābha family, as it were. So you go for refuge to Amitābha as the guru, to Tārā herself as the Buddha, to her compassion as the Dharma, and to her 21 forms as the Sangha. This is going for refuge in the context of this practice. If you were practising, say, the Mañjuśrī meditation, it would be different. You would go for refuge to Vairocana as the guru, Mañjuśrī himself as the Buddha, his wisdom as the Dharma, and his eight forms as the Sangha. And it would be the same process for whichever of the Buddhas and Bodhisattvas was the focus of your meditation practice. So this is the first stage of practice, the Going for Refuge.

The second stage is the development of the four *brahma-vihāras*, the four sublime abodes, the four sublime states of mind: love, in the sense of universal friendliness; *karuṇā*, compassion for all who suffer; *muditā*, sympathetic joy, rejoicing in the happiness of all other beings who are happy; and *upekṣā*, peace and equanimity of mind. These four *brahma-vihāras* are also found in the Mahāyāna, and in early Buddhism; but there's a difference between the *brahma-vihāras* as found in the Mahāyāna and as found in the Theravāda. In the Theravāda the *brahma-vihāras* are what is known as a *samatha* practice; their purpose is to calm the mind down. But in the Mahāyāna they are not only *samatha* practices but *vipassanā* practices, practices for developing Insight, because when you develop love and compassion and so on towards all living beings in the Mahāyāna context, you realize at the same time that all living beings are void or *śūnyatā*, and this is the *vipassanā* aspect.

So this stage of the practice of the Tārā meditation in a way recapitulates these Mahāyāna practices, just as the Going for Refuge recapitulates the Theravāda in a Tantric form. Having taken the Refuges, you develop these four *brahma-vihāras* of love, compassion, joy and equanimity, and at the same time you realize that the beings towards whom you direct these emotions of love and so on are themselves void.

But what is meant by 'void' (the Sanskrit word is *śūnyatā*)? We come to this in the third stage of the meditation: meditation on the voidness itself, *śūnyatā*. It too is carried over from the Mahāyāna, and it is an extremely important stage, for it is said that without some experience of *śūnyatā*, there is no real practice of the Vajrayāna. In the Vajrayāna there are many visualizations and many rituals, but I remember that my good friend Mr Chen in Kalimpong used to remark that without the *śūnyatā* meditation, the Vajrayāna was nothing but vulgar magic. Unless you have some taste of the *śūnyatā* experience, there's no real Vajrayāna. You may be going on doing this and thinking that, but it isn't the Vajrayāna, it's something quite different, just on the psychological level. You have to go through the *śūnyatā* experience, through the Mahāyāna, in a way. There are many ways of meditating on *śūnyatā*; it is the main concern of Mahāyāna meditation proper. In the Green Tārā meditation it is represented by the visualization of the blue sky.

Next we come to visualization of the *bīja* mantra, visualization of the seed syllable of Tārā. In the background, as it were, there is the blue sky of the void, *śūnyatā*, the Absolute if you like; the Unconditioned, and in the midst of this we visualize the *bīja* or the seed syllable. In the Tantric system, every deity has a seed syllable of his or her own, and this is regarded as constituting the heart or the essence of that particular deity. Just as in a seed the whole tree or the whole blossom is contained, in the same way in this *bīja* is contained potentially the deity, the Buddha or the Bodhisattva himself or herself. This *bīja*, this seed syllable, is always one single syllable, and the *bīja* of the Green Tārā is the syllable *tam*.

This is visualized in the midst of the void, green in colour, in the form of a Tibetan or Sanskrit letter, and it is visualized standing upright on a horizontal moon disc, which itself rests on a white lotus. So first of all you've got the white lotus, on top of that a moon disc, and on top of that you have standing erect the green-coloured *bīja* of the Bodhisattva or Buddha Tārā, and you visualize light radiating from this in all directions.

Then you come to the visualization of Green Tārā herself; this is the central stage in the whole practice. She appears out of the seed syllable – she sort of grows out of it or springs out of it – and she is of course green in colour. She wears a crown ornamented with the five Buddhas representing the five wisdoms. Her right hand rests on her right knee, palm upwards, representing generosity or giving, and her left hand is held near her left breast, and holds a blue lotus with three blossoms. One of her legs is folded underneath her in the meditation posture, and the other hangs loose as though ready to step out or to step down, to show that she is always immersed in meditation and the experience of the Absolute, while at the same time she is ready to enter into the world and help people out of compassion. And of course she has a beautiful smiling expression. Sometimes it is said that the Green Tārā embodies the three natures of the virgin, the mother, and the queen. She is spoken of as virgin to represent her complete purity and Transcendental nature, as mother to represent the love and compassion aspect, and as queen to represent the aspect of spiritual sovereignty and as it were dominion.

When the Tārā image is visualized it is important that it should be seen or visualized in a particular way. There are different kinds or levels of visualization. For instance, if you see something in a dream, or by way of a hallucination, that's a visualization, but it's not the same as the sort of visualized image created in meditation at this level. This has to be very fine, very delicate, diaphanous; it's said to be like a rainbow. Visualized forms or figures which you see in meditation mustn't be solid and opaque; they must be as though cut out of the colours of the rainbow, or like reflections seen in a mirror – evanescent, subtle, delicate.

Visualization plays a very important part in Tibetan Buddhist meditation. Generally speaking, the aim of the visualization exercise is to enable you to project from the depths of your own mind higher aspects of yourself of which you are not as yet aware. But what does this mean? You may feel that to speak in terms of projecting from the depths a higher aspect is a mixture of metaphors, and that we ought to get straight whether it's up or down, deeper or higher; but really it's both. So how is this? Let's try to make it clear with the help of a comparison. Suppose you're standing on the edge of a lake looking down into the water. You will see first of all your feet and then your knees, and going down and down you'll see your head; so your head appears below your feet, even though the head is in actual fact the highest part of the body. It's like that when as it were you look down into the unconscious: what is in fact higher in you, but unrealized, appears as deeper. The visualized image, whether it is Tārā or any other, acts as a focal point for corresponding qualities which are undeveloped in the unconscious. Tārā represents compassion, so she becomes a focal point on the level of the conscious or even superconscious mind of the unrealized capacity for compassion existing deep within yourself. By means of that projected, visualized image, these undeveloped feelings of compassion deep within you, which at the same time represent the higher part of your nature, are brought to the threshold of your consciousness and can be integrated into your conscious, aware being at ever higher levels. In other words, through the Tārā practice, we become more compassionate.

The next stage is the visualization and repetition of the Tārā mantra. Here we begin by visualizing in the heart of the visualized image of Tārā her seed syllable, *tam*, and around that we see the ten letters of the Tārā mantra. These ten letters stand up around that central seed syllable vertically, rather like the stones of Stonehenge, and you visualize them revolving in an anti-clockwise direction. (In the case of a male deity, the rotation is clockwise; in the case of a female deity, it's anti-clockwise.) These moving letters are the most difficult things to visualize of all. It's comparatively easy to visualize something stationary, but to visualize a mantra in motion is very difficult. But this is what one has to do at this stage: to visualize the seed syllable in the heart of the goddess and the letters of her mantra revolving in an anti-clockwise direction and emitting light. It is said that if you're mentally very restless and your mind is full of thoughts, the letters of the mantra should go round very slowly; but if you're sluggish and sleepy, you should visualize the letters of the mantra going round very briskly indeed. As you visualize them going round, whether slowly or fast, you repeat the mantra to yourself, and you repeat it at least 108 times – the longer the better. In between periods of meditation, you can go on reciting the mantra as long as you like.

In the next stage, you resolve the Tārā figure back into the voidness. Do you remember how you experienced the voidness, or you even visualized the voidness, then you superimposed upon that voidness the figure of Tārā, then you visualized the seed syllable and the mantra? Well, now you've got to resolve it all back into the voidness from which it came. There are many ways of doing this. One way is to resolve Tārā back into the lotus on which she sits. You sort of collapse her into the lotus. Then you collapse the lotus into the moon on which it stands; you collapse the moon into the mantra; you collapse the mantra into the seed syllable, and the seed syllable you allow to disappear into the voidness. This stage is very significant, because it represents the fact or the truth that all these forms, whether they're Buddhas or Bodhisattvas, Tārā or Mañjuśrī or whichever form they take, emerge from the void, from our own minds – not just our ordinary everyday minds but the depths or, if you like, the heights of our 'own' minds, from universal consciousness. In other traditions different gods and goddesses, saints and sages, saviours and so on are visualized, but usually it is considered that there is something that actually appears. But not in the Buddhist Tantra. Here it is recognized that all these forms, all these images, are the products ultimately of one's own mind or one's own consciousness, of Absolute Mind itself. One experiences this in practice by dissolving, by resolving, this Tārā figure back into the void from which she came.

The next stage is the stage of the double meditation of Tārā and the voidness. Here, the figure of Tārā appears instantaneously; there's no building up. It just comes. The comparison is with a fish leaping from the water. Just as the fish appears as a silvery flash against the background of water, so Tārā just emerges against the voidness. In this stage one visualizes the form of Tārā, and one sees or experiences the voidness at the same time. The two are not contradictory, but interpenetrate. Until this stage of the practice, when the void was there, Tārā wasn't, and when Tārā was there, the void wasn't. But here you get them both together, just as in the *Heart Sūtra* there's the identity of *rūpa* and *śūnyatā*. The *Heart Sūtra* says 'What is *rūpa*? It is *śūnyatā*. What is *śūnyatā*? It is *rūpa*.' There's no difference between them. 'What is form? That is void. What is void? That is form.' No difference. So Tārā here represents form, *rūpa* (*rūpa* also means body) and the void, of course, is the Void itself.

So in this stage we realize the truth of the *Heart Sūtra*'s teaching. Through practical experience we realize the truth that the noumenal and the phenomenal, the absolute and the relative, are not different; they are one. Also in this stage we identify ourselves with Tārā, and we identify also with all other beings that we see. Likewise, whatever we hear we are supposed to identify with the mantra. If anyone says anything, we feel, or to experience, that this is Tārā herself speaking, this is the mantra of Tārā resounding. In this way, identifying ourselves with Tārā and all sentient beings, we become ourselves embodiments of compassion.

Tenthly and lastly there is the stage of dedication of merits, which is the conclusion to all Buddhist spiritual practices. You say that whatever merits I may have gained from this practice, from this meditation, I share them with all living beings. There's nothing that I want to keep back for myself.

So this is the meditation of the Green Tārā. I've gone through these stages of practice very briefly, but I hope that I've been able to give you some idea of the nature of each of them. To hear about them, of course, is one thing, to practise them is quite another. If one really wants to understand or to have any idea of what they are like, what they represent, what it's like to experience them, one just has to practise them oneself. There's no other way.

This sort of pattern, this sequence of stages, can be applied to other deities: Mañjuśrī, Amitābha and so on. In this description, incidentally, I've left out the entire ritual part; I've confined myself to the meditation side. Even so, the whole practice is simple by Tibetan standards. But it must be admitted that many ordinary practitioners, especially lay people, simplify it even further. To begin with, they just keep in their room, or in their shrine or their meditation room if they have one, an image of Tārā, and/or a painted scroll of Tārā, to give them an idea of what they should try to see. They will lay out seven water bowls and fill them with water, usually repeating a mantra, and they will light a lamp and some incense. And then every morning, as soon as they get up, they come into the shrine and look at the picture, and perhaps bow to it; and they change the water in the seven bowls, and light the lamp and the incense. This usually suffices for the ritual part of the practice. Then they sit down cross-legged on a rug and recite various hymns, as we would call them, praising Tārā and her great compassion. Usually in these hymns the goddess is described limb by limb, almost, and ornament by ornament, to build up the picture in the mind. They go on reciting and chanting for quite a while, and then they recite verses expressive of their Going for Refuge to Buddha, Dharma and Sangha in the Tantric way, and then verses indicative of their practice of the four *brahma-vihāras* and taking of the Bodhisattva Vow.

Then, just sitting there, and perhaps looking at the picture or trying to see the image of Tārā in their minds, they go on repeating the mantra of Tārā for half an hour or whatever length of time they can spare. And they conclude by bowing down and dedicating and sharing their merits. This is the way in which the ordinary person will practise this sort of visualization meditation. But if you've got two or three hours to spare before you go to the office, you can go through the whole practice. I remember that one of my own teachers, after I'd had the initiation and the practice had been explained, gave me two versions: a short version, to be done every day, and a lengthy version – there were 20 pages of it – to be done when I had two or three days to spare.

The simple sort of practice is very common among Tibetans, both monks and lay people. What usually happens is that as they get older and they've got fewer responsibilities in the world, they'll devote more and more time to it. Eventually they may end up spending the greater part of the day in this way – not just with one particular practice, but with a sequence of different practices. When I lived in Kalimpong and I used to go and see my Tibetan friends – among Tibetans the proper hour for calling on friends is about 9.30 or 10 in the morning, because then you can stay the whole day – very often I would arrive, and the servant or the disciple would say, 'Please wait a few minutes; he hasn't quite finished his meditation.' This happened very often; they'd start at about six and finish at about nine. Even government officials or busy abbots in charge of monasteries, or quite ordinary people, traders and suchlike, would spend two to three hours chanting mantras before starting the day's work, and at intervals during the day you could hear them reciting their mantras. One of my pleasantest memories of Kalimpong is of going for an evening stroll in the direction of the bazaar. As the shades of evening were falling I'd pass so many elderly Tibetans, men and women, walking along turning a prayer wheel in one hand and telling their beads with the other, and murmuring a mantra. Lots of writers who have described Tibet have spoken about mechanical practices and rites and so on, but believe me, there was nothing mechanical in this sort of practice. You could tell from the way the people were walking, the way they were absorbed, that they were really concentrating on what they were doing. In this way, even comparatively advanced practices of Tantric Buddhist meditation become an integral part of daily life. There are many other practices, but perhaps this brief description of the Tārā meditation practice has sufficed to give an idea of Tibetan Buddhist meditation. Even from the little I've been able to convey, I think it should be clear that in this country we still have much to learn about these things.

From 'Tantric Initiation' in a lecture series on Tibetan Buddhism given in 1966; an edited version appears in *Tibetan Buddhism* (1996), pp.105-115

2. AN EMBODIMENT OF REALITY ITSELF

When you are contemplating the visualized image, you are not just concentrating on a pretty picture; you are contemplating an embodiment of reality itself.

Q: Are visualization practices a combination of concentration and Insight practices?

S: Yes, in their full form they are, or they should be, a combination of *samatha* and *vipassanā*. If, for instance, you close your eyes and visualize a yellow square, this is just a concentration exercise. But you can then make the yellow square appear or disappear, and because you are able to do that, you know that the yellow square is impermanent, it arises in dependence upon causes and conditions. If I make the effort it appears; if I cease making the effort it disappears. Then you can go on to reflect that everything is like that, whether it is a yellow square or a blue one, whether it is a tree or a house or anything. In that way it becomes a means of developing *vipassanā* or Insight. Since you have been concentrating on the yellow square, hopefully your energies are very much together, so your reflection on the impermanent nature of things in general will not just be intellectual; you will actually start seeing things in that way. So even a simple visualization exercise can contain elements of *samatha* and *vipassanā*.

The standard form of visualization practice is of course the visualization of a Buddha or Bodhisattva and this definitely embodies elements of both *samatha* and *vipassanā*, to use those terms, though they aren't used in the Tantra at all. First of all, to visualize the form at all, just as a form, requires a great effort of concentration, so concentration, *samatha*, is there. But it isn't just a form, like a geometric form; it's the form of a Buddha or a Bodhisattva, and that embodies, so to speak, the unconditioned, embodies reality, because the Buddha or the Bodhisattva is regarded as having realized ultimate reality. So when you are contemplating the visualized image, you are not just concentrating on a pretty picture; you are contemplating an embodiment of reality itself. You are occupied with it, so to speak, in that way, you reflect upon it in that way, and you are drawn to it in that way. So it becomes a means of developing *vipassanā*, a means of developing *prajñā*. You could say that here you are concerned with the *subha* (beautiful) aspect of reality.

From Q&A on a pre-ordination retreat, Padmaloka (1982, pp.77-8)

3. THE ULTIMATE DEPTHS OF ONE'S BEING

To see the colour, and even to feel it, is very important in this type of practice, because it is the colour that gives you the inner feeling of that particular Buddha or Bodhisattva, so subtle a feeling that it cannot be put into words.

The experience of oneself in the ultimate depths of one's being is to be achieved, according to the Tantra and all other Buddhist traditions, with the help of meditation. There are very many methods of meditation, and the Tantra has certain methods of its own (in some cases developed from Mahāyāna techniques). One of the best known of these is visualization. It is considered that we can only conceive of the Enlightened mind, ineffable and absolute as it is, in terms of a variety of aspects. It may be approached under the aspect of love, of compassion, of beauty, of primordial purity, of complete peace, of wisdom, or of spiritual power and sovereignty; and each of these aspects of the Buddha mind can be – in a sense, *is* – personified in the form of a particular Buddha or Bodhisattva. Love, for instance, is personified as Kurukullā, compassion as Avalokiteśvara, wisdom as Mañjuśrī, and purity as Vajrasattva.

This superabundance of divine forms appears on the horizon of Tantric Buddhism, and you select for yourself – or your guru selects for you – a form that corresponds to some quality you especially need to develop, or towards which you are especially drawn – love, wisdom, energy, or whatever it may be. After all, Bodhisattvas are within us potentially, just as the Enlightenment experience is within us potentially. When we repeat the mantras of Bodhisattvas, we are therefore in a way calling up our own inner forces, trying to get in touch with them. When we repeat the mantra of Mañjughoṣa we are invoking our own innate undeveloped wisdom, and when we repeat the mantra of Avalokiteśvara we are trying to make contact with our own innate compassion.

The selection made, you learn to visualize that figure in meditation. You practise until you can see it in your mind's eye: the shape, insignia, dress, and – perhaps more than any other aspect – the colour. Sometimes when you start visualizing you just see an undifferentiated patch of colour before it gradually assumes, with practice, the definite form of the Buddha or Bodhisattva. But to see the colour, and even to feel it, is very important in this type of practice, because it is the colour that gives you the inner feeling of that particular Buddha or Bodhisattva, so subtle a feeling that it cannot be put into words. In the course of time, however, if you are meditating on, say, a red Buddha, or a green Bodhisattva, or a white *ḍākinī*, you will experience something rather strange. For example, if you have been doing the visualization practice of Green Tārā, you eventually experience what might be described as the spiritual equivalent of greenness. Or, to put it the other way round, the colour green is the equivalent in terms of colour of the spiritual experience known in its personified form as Tārā – the very quintessence of tenderness and compassion. When you start to experience greenness as more than a colour, as a symbol, to that extent you experience Tārā. As a symbol, the colour becomes a vehicle for the experience of the spiritual state that it symbolizes. If this idea seems mysterious, it should be reiterated that such symbolism can be understood only from one's own practice and experience.

From *Creative Symbols of Tantric Buddhism* (2004, pp.168-9)

4. THE WHOLE TEACHING DISTILLED INTO A SINGLE FIGURE

Becoming absorbed in the yidam, you thereby absorb the spiritual qualities and principles and experiences which the yidam represents, which the yidam *is*.

Yidam is a Tibetan word which literally means 'oath-bound'. It is sometimes translated as 'guarantor', that is, one who guarantees that the disciple will eventually gain Enlightenment, and it is equivalent to, though not an actual translation of, the Sanskrit term *devatā*, which means 'chosen or selected divinity'. The *yidam* is thus that special aspect of the Dharma, that special aspect of reality, through which the disciple approaches the Enlightenment experience. The *yidam* is not an abstract concept or an idea but a figure – a figure of a Buddha or Bodhisattva, embodying a particular aspect or attribute of Enlightenment. Your *yidam* could be Amitābha, the red Buddha of infinite light and eternal life; or Mañjughoṣa, the golden Bodhisattva of Wisdom with the flaming sword; or Tārā, the saviouress, usually white or green in colour, carrying lotus flowers; or Vajrasattva, the embodiment of the innate purity of one's own mind. Whichever figure it is, as a disciple of the Tantra, the whole of the Dharma is contained, embodied, in your *yidam*, and you direct all your attention to that. You don't bother too much about scriptures, studies, teachings, doctrines. The centre of your attention, spiritually speaking, is occupied by the figure of the *yidam*, and you devote yourself to becoming familiar with that figure.

You first make the acquaintance of the *yidam* in the course of Tantric initiation. In effect, in giving you the initiation of, say, Tārā, the guru is introducing you to her, saying to her, 'Tārā, this is So-and-so,' and to you, 'This is Tārā. Now I've introduced you to her, you know each other and there is a connection between you.' Once you have made the acquaintance of a *yidam* in this way, your practice is to keep the *yidam* at the centre of your attention. One way of doing this is to visualize the figure in meditation. With your inner eye you see the *yidam* before you, and you contemplate and become absorbed in that figure, and chant the *yidam*'s mantra. Becoming absorbed in the *yidam*, you thereby absorb the spiritual qualities and principles and experiences which the *yidam* represents, which the *yidam* is. Eventually, you are absorbed into the *yidam*, or the *yidam* is absorbed into you, so that the two of you become one. If you have been focusing on Mañjughoṣa, for example, you absorb the wisdom that Mañjughoṣa represents, while if your *yidam* is Tārā you develop the purity, the tenderness, the compassion, which is Tārā, and if you have Vajrapāni as your *yidam*, you acquire the energy, strength, courage, even spiritual ferocity he stands for. For you, your *yidam* is the whole Dharma, the whole teaching, distilled into a single figure with which you become spiritually intimate, and into whom, or into which, you are incorporated.

Your *yidam* is your *iṣṭa devatā*, the chosen divinity. But who or what does the choosing? The important point here is that you do not choose a *yidam* with your conscious mind. Your *yidam* is chosen by your nature, your needs, your spiritual requirements, or even weaknesses to be corrected. So you can't be trusted – that is, your conscious mind can't be trusted – to make the choice. Usually, therefore, your guru does it for you, saying, 'This is what you need. This is the divinity chosen not by what you think or what you want, but what you are.' The guru, of course, knows what you are better than you know it yourself. If your guru doesn't choose your *yidam* for you, the Tibetan tradition says that it is better to leave it to chance than to make the choice yourself. Chance is more likely to be right.

In the end it doesn't really matter which Buddha or Bodhisattva is chosen, or whether or not you make the choice yourself. In the course of ordaining people and passing on these practices in that context, I have found that it is comparatively rare for there to be a strong affinity between a particular person and a particular visualized form. People do have their preferences, and sometimes the preference is for quite a superficial reason – but that doesn't matter, because as you do the meditation, your relationship with the figure will deepen. The important thing is that the choice is made, that you make a start and get on with the practice – with the guidance of the person who has given it to you.

From *Creative Symbols of Tantric Buddhism* (2004, pp.86-8)

5. DELICATE, TENDER, SUBTLE

You feel that you are absorbing wisdom, that wisdom is flowing from Manjughosa into your own heart, your own being. You feel that your ignorance is being dispelled, that you are being transformed, transmuted ...

Sādhana practice, the visualization of a Buddha or Bodhisattva, with accompanying mantra recitation, involves a convergence of colour and sound, but in a much more subtle way than can be achieved in the collective, external setting of ritual. To give an idea of it, here is a résumé of a Mañjughoṣa *sādhana*, the visualization of Mañjughoṣa, the sweet-voiced one, the Bodhisattva of Wisdom.

The practice begins, as all such exercises do, when you see before you with your inner spiritual vision a vast blue sky – blue sky in all directions. You see it, concentrate on it, become absorbed in it. Then, in the midst of the blue sky, you see rainbow tinted clouds massing and drifting together. Framed by the clouds, you see a pale blue lotus throne with beautiful unfolding petals, on which is spread what is known as a moon mat. It looks like an oval because you are seeing it from the side, but it is round, white and softly brilliant, just like the moon. On this moon mat is seated cross-legged the figure of Mañjughoṣa. He appears in the form of a beautiful sixteen-year-old youth – sixteen being the ideal age as far as beauty is concerned, according to the Indian tradition. He is a deep rich yellow colour, not opaque like paint on a wall, but luminous, transparent, diaphanous, like a reflection in a mirror, or a section of rainbow – delicate, tender, subtle.

The figure is clad in the silks and jewels of a Bodhisattva, and the long black tresses of his hair spread across his shoulders, while on his head he wears a garland of five pale blue lotus blossoms. His face wears a smiling and compassionate expression. This figure of Mañjughoṣa, the sweet-voiced one, sitting there on that moon mat, on that pale blue lotus throne, beautiful yellow in colour, is the embodiment of Transcendental wisdom, the lord of speech, the patron of the arts and sciences. His right arm is uplifted, and in his right hand he flourishes above his head the flaming sword of knowledge with which he cuts the bonds of karma and ignorance. In his left hand he holds the book of the Perfection of Wisdom, pressing it to his heart. The whole figure is surrounded by a shining aura of blue and green and golden light.

At the heart of the Bodhisattva you see a letter, a seed syllable, *dhīh*, which represents the essence of wisdom. It is fiery orange-golden in colour, and from it comes a ray of amber light, which falls on the top of your head and from there passes down into your heart. Along that ray, from the heart of Mañjughoṣa into your heart, the letters of the mantra descend: *om a ra pa ca na dhīh, om a ra pa ca na dhīh*. Having received the mantra into your heart, you go on reciting it, and as you do so, you feel that you are absorbing wisdom, that wisdom is flowing from Mañjughoṣa into your own heart, your own being. You feel that your ignorance is being dispelled, that you are being transformed, transmuted, into the image of Mañjughoṣa. As you feel the presence of Mañjughoṣa, you become more and more like that presence: you assimilate it, or it assimilates you. It's as though you and Mañjughoṣa are coming closer and closer together, even merging, or at least touching, as though you are in the process of becoming wisdom itself. When that happens, or when that begins to happen, you are realizing the wisdom aspect of the Enlightened mind, and through it, entering into the Enlightened mind itself. And at that point you are really beginning to understand, to some extent at least, the Tantric symbolism of colours and mantric sound.

From *Creative Symbols of Tantric Buddhism* (2004, pp.174-6)

6. THAT WHICH YOU'RE TRYING TO BECOME

One of the ways of putting yourself into contact with your own 'higher being' is by visualizing it 'out there'.

In visualization, you try to experience yourself as that which you're trying to become. You try to have an experience of your own as it were higher being, higher personality, to use expressions which aren't really very Buddhistic. It's a creative process. If you're painting a picture, the picture is out there, objective, but there is a connection between that picture and your mental state. In a way, the picture is you. Whatever you create – a picture or a poem – is you, you objectified, as it were, so creating it, producing it, you can see yourself more clearly. It's just the same with the visualized form. The mere fact that you create it, that you produce it 'out there', means that you bring out something which is within you. You experience it and realize it more vividly than you did before. So one of the ways of putting yourself into contact with your own 'higher being' is by visualizing it 'out there'. In that way it becomes more real to you; you experience it more concretely, more vividly.

From a seminar on *The Precious Garland* (1976, p.700)

7. TWO ASPECTS OF VISUALIZATION

If you reflect, 'This form was created by my own efforts; it is impermanent; all things are impermanent like this', and if you really see that, that is *vipassanā*.

There are two aspects of visualization: the simple visualization, which is a *samatha* type of meditation, and reflection on it, which is more of the *vipassanā* type. When you conjure up the visualized form of a Buddha or Bodhisattva, and see it clearly, with a steady consciousness, and enjoy what you see – when you're in a highly concentrated and blissful state – this is *samatha*. But if you start up mental activity and reflect, 'This form was created by my own efforts; it is impermanent; all things are impermanent like this', and if you really see that, that is *vipassanā*. Thus there is a connection between one aspect of the visualization and the *vipassanā* type of meditation. But simple visualization is a *samatha*-type practice, it belongs to the realm of *dhyāna*. Of course people sometimes quite spontaneously start up their own reflections, thus developing a degree of *vipassanā*. You can't make an absolutely sharp distinction between *samatha* and *vipassanā*; the one shades off into the other.

From a seminar on *The Endlessly Fascinating Cry* (1977, p.255)

8. THE RELATIONSHIP BETWEEN METTĀ AND VISUALIZATION

It isn't a question of just producing almost coldly, by virtue of sheer concentration, an eidetic image of a Bodhisattva. That is not the visualization practice.

Q: Could you say a bit about the relationship between the feeling of *mettā* and the visualization? Would it be possible to do an effective visualization without having developed quite a lot of *mettā* in the first place?

Sangharakshita: Inasmuch as *mettā* or the *brahma-vihāras* generally represent a high degree of positive, even spiritualized emotion, and inasmuch as that emotion, in the form of devotion, is an essential element of the visualization practice, which is not just a visualization practice, to that extent you really need a considerable experience of the *brahma-vihāras* even, not just the *mettā-bhāvanā*, before embarking on a visualization practice. It isn't just a concentration exercise. In some of the Pāli texts there is a linkage of the experience of *subha*, the beautiful, with the *brahma-vihāras*, and that would seem to be quite appropriate as an intermediate stage in between the *brahma-vihāras* and the visualization, because if you see everything in terms of *mettā*, everything will seem more and more beautiful to you.

If you're in a very good mood, if you're full of *mettā*, the whole world looks more beautiful. You can dwell upon this element of beauty, *subha*, which is pure beauty, you could say, a sort of ideal beauty, and then you can imagine this ideal beauty as being condensed into an actual form. Then of course you get your link with a Bodhisattva figure, the Bodhisattva being extremely beautiful. It's that which holds and fascinates you, initially, or it's a very large part of it. And then you can start developing a definite feeling towards that figure. It isn't a question of just producing almost coldly, by virtue of sheer concentration, an eidetic image of a Bodhisattva. That is not the visualization practice. So yes, you do need a very strong foundation of *mettā-bhāvanā*, and of the *brahma-vihāras* generally, in order to be able to practise the visualization properly.

Q: If somebody is ordained, and they are given a visualization practice, but they feel that they haven't developed their *mettā* adequately, what are they to do? Is it better for them to leave aside the visualization practice altogether and concentrate on *mettā*?

S: I would say that if you find the visualization difficult because of a lack of positive emotion, work on both. Do the *mettā-bhāvanā* and then do the visualization. Build up the one from the other, gradually.
From Q&A on the *Mitrata Omnibus* (1981/2, Part 2, Session 20, pp.18-9)

9. CAN VISUALIZATION CURE ILLNESS?

The more positive the mental state, the more beneficial the effect of that state will be upon the body.

Q: I've heard it said that doing a Bodhisattva or Buddha visualization practice, particularly that of Vajrasattva, can cure deep-rooted and even potentially fatal physical illness. Do you have any thoughts on this, assuming the visualization is done with concentration and devotion?

Sangharakshita: I certainly don't doubt that mind can influence body, and that meditation practices of all kinds, including visualization practices, can have a very positive and healthy effect on the physical body. Whether they can cure physical illness I wouldn't like to say, but I certainly wouldn't like to say that meditation in whatsoever form could *not* cure, if that is the right word, even potentially fatal illnesses. But can even a skilled and qualified doctor be absolutely sure that a certain illness is going to be fatal? I think sometimes that's very difficult to say. So therefore one doesn't know whether the illness has been cured by the meditation practice or whether it wasn't going to be fatal anyway.

As a general rule, I would say that the more positive the mental state, the more beneficial the effect of that state will be upon the body. But you may be carrying over illnesses which are the result of karmas created in past lives and which you can't perhaps do very much about in this life. You may have become so ill that even the vigorous practice of meditation, though it might have cured you if the disease hadn't been so bad, won't be able to arrest it, because it's too far advanced. But I don't want to generalize. To what extent the curing of disease might be possible or not possible I think it's impossible to say. I don't think we have any evidence or statistics to go on as yet. Perhaps it's safest to stick to the general principle that a positive mental state, a mental state imbued with the *brahma-vihāras*, is bound to have positive effects on one's physical state.

From discussion on a Men's Order Convention (1985, p.16)

10. VISUALIZATION AND DHYĀNA

Perhaps I can make it clearer by referring to that well-known phenomenon, falling in love ...

Q: For some time I have felt slightly puzzled about the relationship between visualization practice, the *sādhana*, and entry into the *dhyānas*. It would seem that if one undertakes a visualization or *sādhana* practice, which involves a high degree of mental activity in the form of the recitation of verses, in a way one is inhibiting oneself from going further into the *dhyānas*, where no mental activity is required. Similarly, if one feels that one is in a state of *dhyāna* in which there is no mental activity, one is reluctant to take up the *sādhana* practice. I see a tension between the two.

Sangharakshita: In a way there is, but not really. Visualization practice is not in itself inimical to the *dhyānas*, because you can use a visualization practice in two ways: either as a *samatha* practice or as a *vipassanā* practice, or both. For instance, if you succeed in visualizing a particular Bodhisattva and simply seeing, without mental activity, that can be a *dhyānic* experience. You're not thinking, 'How beautiful it is,' or 'I wish I could be like that one day,' or 'This means such-and-such.' If you can stay simply contemplating that visualized form, without any such mental activity, that will certainly be tantamount to a *dhyānic* experience, because there is nothing in a subtle visual experience which is incompatible with *dhyāna*. So that is looking at the visualization practice from the *samatha* point of view. But if you start up a train of reflection, such as: 'This visualized form arose in dependence on certain conditions, therefore it is not ultimately real, therefore it is *śūnyatā*', or if you start reflecting on the meaning of different aspects of that visualized figure, the meaning of the colour, or the meaning, say in the case of Mañjuśrī, of the sword and the book, that represents mental activity. That is incompatible with the higher *dhyānas*; that is a *vipassanā*-type experience.

Q: But there seems to be a conflict between reflecting on a visualized form and reciting the verses in an automatic, habitual way.

S: The recitation of the verses will carry you so far, but by the time you have come to the end of the appropriate number of recitations you should have succeeded in visualizing the figure, and then you just see the figure without the recitation. You can then either just continue contemplating it, that is to say, doing a *samatha*-type practice, or start reflecting on the meaning of its various attributes, that is to say, doing a *vipassanā*-type practice, or you can alternate between the two.

Perhaps I can make it clearer by referring to that well-known phenomenon, falling in love. If you refresh your memory, you may recall the experience of being so entranced with someone that you are quite happy just gazing at their face, or their photograph, without any mental activity. That corresponds to the *samatha* type of practice with regard to the visualized image of the Bodhisattva. But then again, with regard to that same person, instead of simply looking at them without any mental activity, you can start having thoughts about them; you can even start asking them questions. That corresponds to practising with the visualized form of the Buddha or Bodhisattva in a *vipassanā*-type way.

Q: If you're absorbed in a visualized form, is it OK at that point to drop the verse and mantra recitations associated with the practice?

S: Most practices lay down a particular number of times that you are to recite, and I think you'll find that you usually won't reach that degree of steadiness of the image before you have completed that number of recitations. In fact, it may well be the other way round: you may need to do more recitations. I don't think there will be a practical problem here.

Q: What about the experience of *dhyāna* and recitation of the mantra? Do you think it is possible to be reciting the mantra and at the same time also experiencing a *dhyānic* state?

S: No, I think this will not happen. I think, as you get into a *dhyānic* state proper as distinct from the experience of *upacāra-samādhi*, you will tend to want to stop the mantra recitation. You will start experiencing it as a distraction, an encumbrance almost, because your mind will be wanting just to concentrate, just to become absorbed; and it is quite appropriate then to do that. But then, after a while you may find that your mind is restless, it can't settle down in that state of absorption; you get wandering thoughts. Then, come back to the mantra recitation and carry on with that until you feel like being concentrated again.

From a seminar on the *Jewel Ornament of Liberation* (Tuscany 1985, pp.272-4)

11. A DEEPLY SPIRITUAL MEANING

If you just hold the reflex image of the Buddha picture there and look at it almost like any other picture, you might just as well have visualized a picture of an advertisement for beer.

Thought forms, being the revelry of Reality, are not to be avoided.[90]

Sangharakshita: One could translate or paraphrase that to say that visions of Buddhas and Bodhisattvas, peaceful and wrathful, being the revelry of Reality, are not to be avoided. But in what sense are they the revelry of Reality? What does that phrase, 'the revelry of Reality', suggest?

Q: It's almost as though Reality is an active thing, which can create its own thought forms rather like ideas are created by the mind.

S: Yes, right, yes. It's as though the precept is saying, 'Don't have a purely conceptual notion of Reality.' Reality is not just an empty concept, not just something abstract. It is concrete, it is living. There is a sort of creative play, and the thought forms, the visions, the images, of Buddhas and Bodhisattvas, are that revelry, that play. They give content to Reality. Reality is not just abstract.

It's a bit like the Tibetan tradition of the Buddha families. Originally there was just one historical Śākyamuni Buddha, so you've got Reality as it were in the form of, or embodied in, a single Enlightened human being. Then the Buddhas of the different Buddha families and their Bodhisattvas, present so many different aspects of that one original single Buddha figure, to bring out more and more fully, more and more richly, the inherent content of that Enlightenment experience. Having just one Buddha is like having a perfect sphere of polished crystal, or a diamond shaped like a perfect sphere. But to bring out the lustre of the precious stone, you'd cut facets, to catch the light and produce all sorts of colours. It's as though you take this perfect sphere of the one Buddha and you cut first five facets and then each of those facets is cut to give you many many more, and in this way the whole thing becomes a faceted jewel which reflects all sorts of rainbow colours and because of that you're able to appreciate the beauty and the value of the jewel much more than if it was just a plain polished sphere.

This revelry in the form of the thought forms is like that. It brings out the content of Reality, or at least it enables you to experience and appreciate it more than if Reality was just conceived of as something blank and abstract and inert. Do you see what I mean?

Q: Would it not be more accurate to say that the thought forms are Reality itself?

S: You could say that.

Q: Because it seems to imply that there's a reality which manifests itself through different sort of beings.

S: One could say there is something which remains unmanifest. It's not that Reality is simply the sum total of these manifestations. But there is a limitation of language. One says 'revelry of Reality' – well, language compels you to distinguish in that sort of way.

Q: Presumably for ordinary folk, the thought forms wouldn't take the form of visions of Buddhas and Bodhisattvas, would they? Would you say that the revelry of Reality necessarily involves seeing visions of Buddhas and Bodhisattvas?

S: It would seem like that, though it is also said that the Enlightened person sees all phenomena as the revelry of Reality, sees everything as the *Dharmakāya*. Again one has to be a little bit careful about what one might call rather naive pantheism. It is more expressing your experience or vision in that sort of way rather than making a philosophical statement in a logical manner. The important thing is the general idea that although you are using abstract thought to think about Reality, you shouldn't identify Reality simply with a highly generalized concept or think of Reality too much in that sort of way. You have to bring into consideration the aesthetic aspect of Reality, in a manner of speaking.

Q: Is it doing more than calling them just images or symbols?

S: We tend to devalue the word 'symbol'. A symbol is not just a mark or sign, it is much more than that. A symbol, a real symbol, doesn't symbolize anything – it *is* something. It doesn't simply point to something beyond itself. The artist creates thought-forms. They're not just arbitrary creations; they reflect Reality. In a way they *are* Reality. In *Prometheus Unbound* Shelley says: 'And from these create he can' – 'these' meaning the natural objects which he perceives – 'forms more real than living man'. It's as though the artist recreates nature and produces forms which are even more real than the natural reality, so to speak, of nature herself. He has raised the forms of nature to a higher degree of Reality. It's as though the artist takes the forms presented by nature and simplifies them, strips away the inessential, so that through that image, reality is manifested more clearly than it is in that particular form as it occurs in nature.

Q: Would you say that the visions in meditation are more real because they're more obviously a manifestation of consciousness rather than sensual objects?

S: One could say that. On the other hand it occurs to me that one must make a distinction between purely eidetic images, images that you produce as part of a concentration exercise, and images, especially those of Buddhas and Bodhisattvas, which have for you a profoundly emotive and deeply spiritual meaning. There's quite a difference between visualizing a yellow disc and visualizing the image of the Buddha. Visualizing the Buddha isn't like visualizing a coloured picture towards which you've got no feeling and which doesn't particularly mean anything to you. If you visualized the figure of the Buddha without its having any meaning for you, it would not be a thought-form in this sense. If you were to experience the Buddha figure as a thought-form, you would be profoundly stirred by it, it would have tremendous spiritual significance, whereas someone who was just good at visualizing could reproduce a picture of the Buddha mentally, an eidetic image, but it would not be a thought-form. It's the strongly emotional flavour and the spiritually significant content which makes it a thought-form in this sense.

Q: Thought-forms have a life of their own.

S: They have a life of their own. This is one of the reasons why I'm not too keen on people just doing visualizations of Buddhas as a concentration exercise. One should stick to abstract visualizations if one just wants to improve one's technical concentration. One shouldn't use Buddha figures to do that, because that might blunt one's feelings towards the Buddha. Do you see what I am getting at? If you just hold the reflex image of the Buddha picture there and look at it almost like any other picture, you might just as well have visualized a picture of an advertisement for beer. It would serve just as well as a means of concentration, and you might even have more feeling towards it!

From the second seminar on *Precepts of the Gurus* (1979, pp.327-9)

12. VISUALIZATION AND EMPTINESS

The form emerges from the void for an instant and goes back into it, like a fish leaping from the sea and flashing for an instant ...

Sangharakshita: In some of the visualization practices, you get a sequence of practices. For instance, suppose you're visualizing a particular Buddha or Bodhisattva; you're visualizing that particular *rūpā* – *rūpā* in the sense of 'form', not in the sense of a physical image. So that image is there, and you're concentrating on it. Then suppose after a while you dissolve that image. What you have left is, as it were, *śūnyatā* – not the real, ultimate *śūnyatā*, but *śūnyatā* in the sense that it is devoid of that image; that image is no longer there. So for a while you meditate upon that. So you've got these two stages. You've got the stage of meditating upon the Buddha or Bodhisattva, on the form, and then you've got the stage where you're meditating on *śūnyatā*, understood as the absence of that particular form.

So the question arises: Can you logically have the form and the absence of form at the same time, in the same sense, in the same place? No, you can't. You're either doing the one practice or the other. You can either meditate on the form, or you can meditate on the void. When you're meditating on the form, you're not meditating on the void. When you're meditating on the void, you're not meditating on the form. So there are these two levels of practice, and you have to alternate them. Meditate on the form of the Buddha or Bodhisattva, then meditate on the absence of that form, on the void, then on the form, then on the void. But what do you do after that? What's the third stage?

Q: They come together.

S: But how can they come together?

Q: They just do!

S: Well, that'll do! The third stage is: you have to meditate on them both together. And you're given a bit of help. You're given the analogy that the form emerges from the void for an instant and goes back into it, like a fish leaping from the sea and flashing for an instant, then diving back.[91] This is to give you a glimpse, an intuition of both at the same time, even though they're contradictory. That is the real experience of *śūnyatā*, the *śūnyatā* which is beyond the antithesis of fullness and emptiness.

In the visualization-type practice, this is what one does. This is how visualization becomes a means of approach to the Absolute, to *śūnyatā* in the real sense. First you learn to visualize the form of the Buddha or Bodhisattva to whom you're particularly devoted. Then you dissolve him or her back into the void, and you meditate only on the void, and then you go back to the form. You alternate them for quite a while, then you try to bring them together, even though logically they can't be brought together, because one is the absence of the other. And that brings you to that third point, as it were.

But this is another way. There's an analogy with the koan practice of Zen. In that too you go beyond the rational mind, you go beyond logical thought. Or, when your mind is concentrated, you can just reflect on the *Diamond Sūtra* teachings. It's like the old story of going to see the Zen Master. He asks you 'What are you carrying?' and you say 'I'm not carrying anything.' And he says, 'Well, drop it then!' Do you see the connection? You think that carrying something and dropping it are two contradictory things, because how can you drop something unless you're carrying it? But the Master doesn't see things like that, apparently. According to his way of thinking, you can drop something even though you're not carrying anything. But you then have to say or do something to show that you've also gone beyond that duality. If you can't, well, you're just thrown out! You haven't passed the test. You're just slung out on your ear to go back to the meditation hall and try again. And if you were to say: 'Well, that's a logical contradiction', you'd get hit over the head with a long bamboo pole!

From a seminar on Edward Conze's *Buddhism* (1976, pp.116-7)

13. THERE'S NO POINT IN PUTTING OFF ENLIGHTENMENT

If you find on any occasion that you have developed a very strong basis in the form of *samatha*, there is no reason why you should restrain yourself from developing *vipassana* on the spot.

Q: Would I be right in thinking that trying to develop Insight on the basis of the visualization practice is particularly effective in part because a visualization is a very beautiful, attractive thing to concentrate on and therefore you have a lot of emotional attachment to it?

Sangharakshita: Yes, right. Your emotional energies are much more fully engaged and therefore you are much more integrated and much more concentrated. In dependence upon that sort of visualization practice an Insight or *prajñā* experience or realization is much more likely to arise. You are naturally gripped by the visualization experience, if you do it at all successfully. Since your emotions are engaged, they are not likely to be led astray by other things, so that you can remain concentrated and develop a measure of insight. I think this is one of the great benefits of visualization-type practices, if one is able to do them, that they do engage one emotionally and therefore contribute to a much higher degree of integration and therefore of concentration. I believe one can produce very much the same effect just with the simple recitation of the mantra, if you find visualization difficult. Just recitation of the mantra by itself will very often produce virtually the same effect, have the same effect of integrating all your emotional energies, and providing a solid basis in concentration for reflection on the meaning of the mantra.

Q: In those practices where there is no explicit *vipassanā* element, do you think it is ever necessary to introduce an element of contemplation, or will *prajñā* naturally arise from the visualization?

S: I think you would need to have very strong *saṁskāras* to be able to produce Insight as it were spontaneously, but in all the practices there are elements of insight, though they may need to be drawn out. For instance, what does the mantra mean? Each repetition has a particular meaning which leads into a kind of Insight experience. And if you visualize yourself as the figure, you are as it were void, you are empty, and that is quite clearly an Insight-type experience, isn't it? Perhaps the *vipassanā* content isn't stated conceptually but it is certainly represented symbolically. So perhaps one needs to make it more explicit in conceptual terms to oneself.

Q: Is it perhaps useful to develop a flexible attitude towards *samatha*, so that when one feels that one has had quite a strong *samatha* experience, one could direct one's mind to contemplation in the *vipassanā* sense, instead of having a rigid way of thinking that I have to develop *samatha*, and then after so many years I start *vipassanā*?

S: Yes. If you find on any occasion that you have developed a very strong basis in the form of *samatha*, there is no reason why you should restrain yourself from developing *vipassanā* on the spot. It might be your opportunity, you might have a real breakthrough then. So there is no need to stick to a rigid schedule. Take advantage of any opportunity that you get, being careful to distinguish that from just a sort of restlessness that is getting tired of the meditative state. But there is no point in putting off Enlightenment.
From a seminar on *The Forest Monks of Sri Lanka* (1985, pp.274-5)

14. LIGHT THROUGH A STAINED GLASS WINDOW

Reality is not something that cancels out the whole world, but something in the light of which you see the whole world in another way.

> *The things of this samsaric world are all illusion,*
>   *like a dream.*
> *Where'er one looks, where is their substance?*
> *Palaces built of earth and stone and wood,*
> *Wealthy men endowed with food and dress and finery,*
> *Legions of retainers who throng round the mighty, –*
> *These are like castles in the air, like rainbows in the sky.*
> *And how deluded those who think of this as truth!*
> *When uncles – nephews – brothers – sisters gather*
>   *as kindred do,*
> *When couples and children gather as families do,*
> *When friends and neighbours gather in good fellowship, –*
> *These are like meetings of dream friends, like travellers*

> *sharing food with strangers.*
> *And how deluded those who think of this as truth!*
> *This phantom body grown in uterine water from a*
> *union of seed and blood, –*
> *Our habitual passions springing from the bad deeds of*
> *our past,*
> *Our thoughts provoked by divers apparitions, –*
> *All are like flowers in autumn, clouds across the sky.*
> *How deluded, O assembled birds, if you have thought of*
> *them as permanent.*
> *The splendid plumage of the peacock with its many hues,*
> *Our melodious words in which notes high and low*
> *are mingled,*
> *The link of causes and effects which now have brought us*
> *here together, –*
> *They are like the sound of echoes, the sport of a game*
> *of illusion.*
> *Meditate on this illusion, do not seize on them as truth!*
> *Mists on a lake, clouds across a southern sky,*
> *Spray blown by wind above the sea,*
> *Lush fruits ripened by the summer sun, –*
> *In permanence they cannot last; in a trice they separate*
> *and fall away.*
> *Meditate on their illusion, do not think of them*
> *as permanent!* [92]

Q: Could you say that from the Transcendental point of view, all the mundane, all saṁsāra, is illusion?

Sangharakshita: From the Transcendental point of view one wouldn't think in terms of illusion, one wouldn't need to. From the point of view of the Transcendental you'd see conditioned existence as it is; you wouldn't have to think in terms of illusion. One speaks in terms of illusion to draw people's attention to what the conditioned is really like. It's their false perception which is illusory, which constitutes the illusion. If you don't have a false perception, there's no point in speaking in terms of illusion. So from the point of view of the Transcendental, there's no illusion, it sees the conditioned as conditioned. That's the end of the matter. It has no false perception to understand as being illusory.

Q: In a visualization practice, I understand that the clear blue sky is supposed to resemble a sort of refinement, or something closer to reality. So on the one hand you've got seemingly real, solid entities which are impermanent, and on the other hand you've got something which points to this vast kind of nothingness, a big void or something. How does all that relate to the concept of illusion? I'm a bit puzzled about illusion ...

S: Well, in the first place the clear blue sky relates to or symbolizes *śūnyatā*. But it's a sort of one-sided *śūnyatā*, because one is thinking of the blue sky of *śūnyatā* as the unconditioned as distinct from the conditioned. But reality in a deeper sense transcends the distinction between conditioned and unconditioned, between the relative and the absolute. So the blue sky stands for *śūnyatā*, for reality, for the unconditioned, as it were provisionally. So long as your outlook is dualistic, you cannot but distinguish the unconditioned from the conditioned, Nirvāṇa from saṃsāra. Now, what you visualize stands for the conditioned, for *rūpā*, for form. In fact, what you visualize has a form. So to begin with, you see the form as one thing and you see the sky as the other; you see *rūpā* as one thing and you see *śūnyatā* as another, but that is still dualistic. What you have to try to see, what you have to try to experience, is *śūnyatā* as *rūpā* and *rūpā* as *śūnyatā*; that is to say, the sky not obstructing the form, the form not obstructing the sky.

It's also said that you have to try to see the forms that you visualize as rainbow-like. If you see them as solid objects, you can't see them as non-differentiated from *śūnyatā*, so you try to see them as transparent, diaphanous, or illusory in a positive sense. Illusory here means, in a paradoxical way, real; because they're not really solid, they really are diaphanous, they really are transparent, they really are letting you see *śūnyatā* through them. In other words, it's as though the stage at which you see *śūnyatā* and *rūpā* as two separate things and try to join them together is provisional; you have to blend them, you have to unite them, so that you experience the two things at the same time, even though on the logical level they are contradictory. This is what the *Heart Sūtra* says: *rūpā* is *śūnyatā* and *śūnyatā* is *rūpā*. In the course of the visualization you try to actually experience that.

Q: The fact that the form appears out of the blue sky and dissolves back into it does help a bit.

S: Yes, although this is still, as it were, on a dualistic level. When it is said that the form appears out of the blue sky or that *rūpā* appears out of *śūnyatā*, it doesn't mean that the one is really different from the other. It's as though you see the blue sky, then you see the form, you see *śūnyatā*, then you see *rūpā*. If you see the one you must see the other, because they're not separate, they're not two.

Q: What I can't understand is, if we are trying to think of this blue sky as representing *śūnyatā*, and sort of blending it with form, *rūpā*, I have experience of form, but I don't have experience of *śūnyatā*, so how can I imagine a form as being *śūnyatā*?

S: Ah. This is where doing the practice in regular steps comes in. At the beginning of most visualization practices you have the mantra *sarva suddha, sarvadharma svabhāva suddho 'ham – suddha* here meaning *śūnyatā*. All dharmas are pure by nature, *svabhāva*, and I also am pure by nature. In other words, all things are *śūnyatā*. This is supposed to embody the whole of the Perfection of Wisdom. So you are really supposed to be well versed in that before going on to the visualization, if you do it thoroughly.

Q: So how do you develop that stage?

S: Well, the six element practice will help. The Tibetans very often just repeat that mantra, then pass onto the visualization; but that's not really enough.

Q: You're supposed to really reflect ...

S: Yes – not necessarily at the time you're doing the practice, but that mantra should call to mind all the reflection you've previously done. It recapitulates your previous experience of that whole dimension.

Q: Would that mantra hold true for all the visualizations?

S: Yes. In the case of some of them, it occurs in the text of the practice, but it is to be understood in all of them. It's represented by the blue sky – the blue sky is it in visual terms. This is why we do the six element practice before taking on a visualization practice. It helps lay the foundation.

Q: So it's on that basis that you should do the visualization practice.

S: Yes. When you're visualizing the form, it's not a material form you're visualizing. That's why the standard description is that it's like a rainbow, or a reflection seen in a mirror, or an illusion, a magical city. It's not something solid, not something seen in dualistic terms. You see it, as it were, from the standpoint of reality, from the standpoint of *śūnyatā*. It's as though *śūnyatā* doesn't cancel out *rūpā*, the unconditioned doesn't cancel out the conditioned, but it makes it, as it were, transparent; so that the conditioned becomes an aspect of the unconditioned, you could say. *Rūpā* becomes *śūnyatā*. Do you see what I mean? You try to see these visualized forms in this way; in a way you see the *sambhogakaya* and the *Dharmakaya* together. And then, starting from that practice, you try to see everything around you in those terms. It's not that you don't see anything any more, but you see it in a different kind of way. Things become purified, brighter, or more transparent. Reality is not something that cancels out the whole world, but something in the light of which you see the whole world in another way.

Q: So when you do a practice like that, you begin to see things more as they really are. It's not as if it's sort of fabricated. And that's the way you should begin to see things outside your practice as well.

S: Yes.

Q: So after having done the practice in that way, you would come back to a situation like sitting down with people, and your experience would be different ... and that's what meant by illusion?

S: Illusion is, in a way, used quite ambiguously. It can be used in a negative sense, but it can also be used in a positive sense. It's not very easy to explain this, but it's as though when you no longer perceive things in an illusory way, you no longer see them as illusions, or they are no longer illusions, they've become, as it were, more real. But they're not real in the sense in which one thought of reality before.

    The analogy of the stained glass window may help to illustrate this. It isn't completely adequate as an illustration, but one can say something like this; suppose you're inside an old building, and there's a stained glass window, but it's all covered with grime and dirt. You gradually clean it, and once you've cleaned it, what comes through is not just pure white light, but the light of all the colours of the window, and the picture they make. In the same way, when you get rid of illusion, it's not just a sort of bare, featureless reality that you see, separate from the world. Yes, that light is there, but it lights up the world, the world corresponding to the stained glass window with all its beautiful colours.

Q: So the stained glass window represents the reality of the conditioned, whereas the light is the reality of the unconditioned.

S: Yes, you could say that. And you bring the two together ultimately.

Q: You kind of fuse together the form and *śūnyatā*. Because without the light shining through the window, we wouldn't see it at all.

S: Yes. And without the window there wouldn't be the beautiful colours, there'd only be the white light. The white light is there, but the colours are also there.

Q: Is it the dirt on the window that stops the light from coming through, that stops you from seeing the light?

S: Well, to pursue the analogy, the dirt on the window not only prevents you from seeing the light, it prevents you from seeing the colours. It's as though the light represents the unconditioned and the colours represent the conditioned seen in its reality – not of course solid, opaque colours, but transparent, diaphanous colours. Do you get the idea?

Q: So the conditioned means that you can't see the light?

S: It's not the conditioned itself that stands in the way, it's more the way you see the conditioned that stands in the way; just as it's not the stained glass window that prevents you from seeing the light and the colours, it's the dirt on the stained glass window. In other words, when you get rid of illusion or when you get rid of delusion, you're not just left with the unconditioned as opposed to the conditioned. You haven't sort of wiped out the conditioned entirely so that you're left only with the unconditioned. That would be a dualistic way of thinking. You also wipe out the distinction between conditioned and unconditioned so that you see the conditioned as the unconditioned, the unconditioned as the conditioned, just as you see the light coming through the stained glass window and the colours of the stained glass window at the same time. Your experience of the visualized form should give you a foretaste of that. This is why it is said at the conclusion of some practices that afterwards one sees all beings as Tārā or Avalokiteśvara and one hears all sounds as mantras. But this is quite a big thing, one needs to go step by step.

Some people who do visualization practices – especially in Tibet – don't bother about all this, they just visualize. They develop feelings of devotion and concentration, and that, as it were, is enough. But you can't really say that this is the full practice.

Q: So you can't just think in terms of doing the visualizations to alter your psychological and emotional states.

S: Well, you can, but that is limiting it very much indeed.

Q: It's almost like you have to alter your psychological state first, say with the *mettā* and devotion and so forth, and even *śūnyatā* practice.

S: This is why I laid down the system of practice I did. First of all there's the mindfulness of breathing, which helps with awareness and integration; and then there's the *mettā-bhāvanā*, which creates emotional positivity; and then from that you can come onto the six element practice, which sort of breaks down your crude egocentricity. And after that there's the visualization practice, where you get onto a different level altogether.
From a seminar on *The Buddha's Law Among the Birds* (1982, pp.260-5)

15. CHOOSE METTĀ

After all, you can be mindful all the rest of the time!

Q: Do you think that it's more important for people to keep up their visualization practice or find time for *mettā* and mindfulness?

Sangharakshita: If you have to choose, then definitely do the visualization, quite definitely. And if you have to choose between either mindfulness or *mettā* plus visualization, choose *mettā*. After all, you can be mindful all the rest of the time! *Mettā* is more difficult than mindfulness, but it seems to be a better foundation for visualization practice. It's in a way more creative.

From a seminar on the *Mañjughoṣa Stuti Sadhana* (1977, p.59)

16. YOU'RE JUST SUPPOSED TO DO IT!

Think in terms more of doing your practice, and experiencing it for yourself rather than talking about it too freely.

It is important to be careful not to talk about your visualization practice too much. I think probably it's best only to talk about it with other people who have the same practice, and even then not to talk in a conversational or chatty way but only in a serious way, comparing notes about your experiences, and perhaps sorting out difficulties, clarifying things for one another. The Vajrayāna tradition is quite emphatic about this. I myself was specifically told in connection with certain Vajrayāna initiations that you do not discuss the practice with anybody who has not received that same practice from the same teacher. This is quite a strict rule, and in Tibetan Buddhist circles certainly practices of this sort are not made the subject of general conversation. So, while I don't exclude the possibility that those who have the same practice might like to get together and talk it over, one should nonetheless be very careful not to talk about it too much or in the wrong sort of way, or with people who have no personal experience. Rather than talk about it, you're just supposed to do it!

In the West generally the tendency to grab at spiritual practices before you're really ready for them is very strong. One shouldn't encourage that. Think in terms more of doing your practice, and experiencing it for yourself rather than talking about it too freely. In India it is very strongly believed that if you talk too much about your spiritual practice, especially your meditation practice, any benefit that you have gained from it is likely to leak away. You've externalized it, or even vulgarized it, cheapened it, and this isn't desirable. So one needs to pay some attention to this, as well as to actually keeping up one's practice.

Q&A on the *Mitrata Omnibus*
(Part 2, concluding remarks 1981/2, pp.16-7)

17. 'WESTERN' VISUALIZATIONS?

We can start off with the traditional forms as they come to us from the Eastern tradition but as they change, if they change, well, let it be so.

Q: As an Order we do prostrations and visualization practices but for most of us our visual content is grounded in a Western tradition. Does this mean that the Buddhas and bodhisattvas that we visualize will have the same dress in our *sādhana* but Western facial features?

Sangharakshita: I think the only thing one can do here is start off with tradition exactly as it is given and allow it to change quite naturally – and it will change. It has changed in the past. If you look at the Buddhas of Japan and China, Central Asia, they're quite different in many respects from the Buddhas of India, Sri Lanka, Nepal. They've got different facial features, and even sometimes a different style of dress. This will happen in our case too. There will be a Western version of a Bodhisattva, a Western version of a Buddha. We're moving in that direction already but we don't want to do it too rashly, or too much on an intellectual, theoretical basis. We should let it just evolve naturally. We can start off with the traditional forms as they come to us from the Eastern tradition but as they change, if they change, well, let it be so. That's a quite natural and normal thing. But I think we shouldn't try to change anything in a deliberate way.

From the Western Buddhist Order convention (1978, p.10)

18. THE RELATIONSHIP BETWEEN VISUALIZATION PRACTICES

In the long run, all these different practices are united.

Q: If one has two visualization practices, what should the relationship between them be?

Sangharakshita: Well, suppose you want to do the Tārā practice and also the Amitābha practice, and suppose the Tārā practice is your basic practice, that is to say, the practice you received at the time of your private ordination. How do you go from the Tārā practice to the Amitābha practice? Like this. You do the Tārā practice, whether it's an in front production practice or a self production practice, and then you think that you yourself are Tārā, and as Tārā you do the Amitābha practice. In this way you bring the two practices together. If you have a third practice, say you also want to do the Mañjughoṣa visualization, then again you visualize yourself as Tārā and think and feel yourself as Tārā doing the Mañjughoṣa practice.

The relationship between them is pretty much as you wish, in the sense that it's up to you, in consultation with whoever gives you the practice, whether you add in, say a Mañjughoṣa practice to your existing Tārā practice or a Vajrasattva practice to your existing Padmasambhava practice and so on. You can build up a small repertoire of visualization practices to which you have recourse on different occasions, perhaps doing them at different times during the day when you're on solitary retreat, or doing one in the morning, one in the evening, in the course of your daily life. Though you start off with one practice, and though you should make that your main practice and get thoroughly into that before taking up any second or third practice, you can certainly have this small repertoire of visualization practices. You don't have to stay with one. In any case, in the long run, all these different practices are united inasmuch as all the Buddhas and bodhisattvas are united. Eventually they all form one great and glorious mandala which is, of course, the mandala of the five Buddhas with their respective bodhisattvas, *ḍākas*, *ḍākinīs*, *dharmapālas*, and so on.

More often than not all one's different visualization deities, to use that term, are from the same Buddha family. You know that the five Buddhas, as it were, preside over five different Buddha families. Amitābha, for example, presides over the Lotus family, the Padma family, which is quite large and one might say distinguished. There's Avalokiteśvara, Tārā, especially the White Tārā, Padmasambhava, and so many others. Amitayus belongs to it, because Amitayus is a form of Amitābha. So very often all one's different practices are taken from the same family. But again there is a sort of complementarity between families. If you feel you need to balance an element of the Padma family with an element of the Vajra family, you might feel that in addition, say, to doing the Tārā practice, you'd like to do the Akṣobhya practice, to even yourself up a bit.

From the Western Buddhist Order convention (1978, p.12)

19. DIFFICULTY IN VISUALIZING

Once you have visualized the blue sky, there's the lotus seat to visualize – you can spend quite a lot of time on that ...

Q: Many Order members seem to find difficulty in visualizing in the sense of evoking an eidetic image. While you have said that what is important is the feeling evoked by the meditation rather than the creation of a mental image, do you think it might be useful to think in terms of a more structured training in visualization, beginning with *kasiṇas* and gradually elaborating?

Sangharakshita: I think this may well be so. In a way we already have a graduated training, because when we do a visualization practice we start off with the blue sky, which is just a single expanse of colour. If you find that difficult, and of course everybody does to begin with, you could start off with just say a blue disc and if you find even that difficult, yes, you could start off with a blue *kasiṇa*. You could paint a blue disc on a sheet of paper and put it up on the wall and sit in front of it, focusing your attention on it in the traditional way, first concentrating on the disc of material colour and then closing your eyes and trying to reproduce that, and then, as it fades, opening your eyes and having another look. In that way you'd get a mental picture, for want of a better term, of that blue disc. When that was reasonably stable, you could try to expand it into a blue sky. And once you have visualized the blue sky, there's the lotus seat to visualize – you can spend quite a lot of time on that – and then the moon mat.

So it already is a graduated practice, but perhaps we could make it even more graduated, and perhaps even have meditation retreats designed to help us build up our visualization, whatever it might be, from the very beginning, spending a lot of time on each successive stage, just to build up the visualization more and more clearly and successfully. That might well be useful, especially for people who find it particularly difficult to visualize.

From the Men's Order Convention (1985, p.13)

20. THIS IS WHAT I WANT TO BE LIKE

Enlightenment as a word is a bit abstract. You need that word to be embodied in a person, a Buddha or Bodhisattva with whom you can establish a connection.

Q: Do you think it is important that all Order members receive a *sādhana* at ordination in terms at least of being introduced to a Bodhisattva or Buddha through the repetition of a mantra, and continue to maintain some sort of connection with that figure or other *yidams* through their Order lives?

Sangharakshita: I'd say yes, but I know a lot of people have difficulty with visualization and this needs to be addressed. Broadly speaking, when one is ordained, when one commits oneself to the Three Jewels, one is committing oneself ultimately to the achievement of Enlightenment, and Enlightenment, *sambodhi*, was first realized (at least in our world era) by the Buddha. Apart from the historical Buddha Śākyamuni, there are other Buddhas and Bodhisattvas representing or symbolizing different aspects of that Enlightenment experience. So when you are ordained you try to think or try to see what aspect of Enlightenment it is that you are particularly drawn to. Enlightenment as a word is a bit abstract. You need that word to be embodied in a person, a Buddha or Bodhisattva with whom you can establish a connection, so that you can think, this is what I want to be like in the long run. I want to be like Śākyamuni, or like Mañjughoṣa, or like Tārā. This is what the choosing of the *yidam* at the time of the private ordination represents. And of course the connected mantra is the sound syllable embodiment of that *yidam*, and you repeat it to keep in contact.

But some people, as I've said, have difficulty visualizing. So for them we've more recently decided there's the possibility of taking up some other practice, or being given even some other practice at the time of their private ordination which will enable them to bridge the gap between their aspiration to gain Enlightenment and the achievement of that. But they will still have a *yidam*, representing a particular aspect of their ultimate goal, and also a mantra which they can repeat on occasion or incorporate in their practice as they wish. So there has more recently been this development in order to help those Order members, whether new or old, who find visualization difficult.

It's as though one continues to have a *sādhana* practice of a simplified kind but within that there is another practice. It can be a practice, say, of formless meditation which enables one to bridge that gap between one's aspiration to Enlightenment and the realization of that.

Q: Could you give an example of what sort of practice that might be?

S: Well, some people are drawn to a simplified form of *dzogchen*. I say simplified because I don't mean the full-blown Tibetan tradition, but – what shall I say, it's not very easy to put into words – well, something similar to the Pāli tradition, the reflection on the three *lakṣaṇas* and their corresponding *samādhi*s, that would be another way of practising. Or doing the fully-fledged *satipaṭṭhāna* practice, in the four or the sixteen stages.

Q: In the Order there seems to be a growing interest in other forms of Insight meditation – the use of the mindfulness of breathing as a route to Insight, the six element practice, reflections on impermanence, etc. Is it a matter of temperament which type of Insight meditation we choose to apply ourselves to or are some types more conducive to the maturing and developing of our Insight into reality? Is one route to reality enough, or do we need to approach it through a variety of different meditative routes?

S: In principle one route is enough. People can get a bit distracted if they chop and change, and try this route and then that route. Every route gets you there in the end. I'm just recollecting a story I read somewhere recently, I think it was from a Chinese Mahāyāna source. There were two friends who were both monks. One of them went off, and practised for 30 years, practising various forms of meditation under thirty different teachers. But his friend just stayed in the monastery and practised one method of meditation under one teacher. At the end of the thirty years, the first monk came back and he was talking with the one who'd stayed in the monastery all those years. So he said rather proudly to his friend, 'Aha, you see I've practised thirty different meditation methods under thirty different teachers. You've only practised one!' So the monk who'd stayed in the monastery said 'Yes, I've been practising one meditation for thirty years, but I've practised meditation for thirty years. You in effect have only practised it for one year!' Because in the course of one year you can't go all that deep with any method.

So it's better to stick to one method, one route, one road, and get deeper and deeper into that. Of course, that's not to say that in the course of your *sādhana* practice, using the word *sādhana* in the broader sense, you may not incorporate different elements into one method or stream of practice, but you stick with that over the years, or at least you stick with certain basic elements of that over the years.

It's very easy to think that the grass is greener on the other side of the fence, and people can be very easily distracted. People talk about exploring different methods of meditation, but have they explored our system of meditation yet? And if they haven't, what's the point in trying to explore other ways of practising? You've got enough to get on with already. Even if you just practise *mettā* – I say *just* practise, but it's an enormous thing – just practise the mindfulness of breathing and the *mettā-bhāvanā*, they'll carry you a long, long way.

Q: I think you are sometimes used as an example, because you had many teachers and practices …

S: So I did, so I did, but I did lots of other things. I was a monk for so many years. If you're going to take seriously this following in my footsteps, be a monk or a nun, go the whole hog. Don't just pick out those aspects of my life that happen to suit you. I don't think this is a very good thing to do. I lived in the Himalayas for fourteen years. Do you want to do that? I went on lecture tours in India for many, many years. Do you want to do that? Why select my having had so many teachers, as a justification for going here and going there. I hadn't started the Western Buddhist Order [now Triratna] then. I wasn't lucky enough to have that kind of Order to join. You've got a path to follow in a way I didn't. So don't try to rationalize things you want to do by referring to what I might have done or not have done. For many years I didn't eat after twelve o'clock. Do you want to follow that one?

From Theris' Q&A (2002, pp.8-9)

21. AN IMPORTANT DISTINCTION

You've as it were taken a bit of your own mind, like a bit of elastic, and stretched it out and formed it into Manjusri or Tara or whatever 'out there' .

Q: Is there a difference between the responses that a Bodhisattva form evokes, both actually and potentially, and the Bodhisattva him/herself?

Sangharakshita: This introduces the very important distinction between what is called the *samayasattva* and what is called the *jñānasattva* in Tantric tradition. Suppose you start visualizing, and with practice you see quite clearly and steadily an image or form of a particular Bodhisattva. Once you're quite experienced, you see it clearly and steadily, and you're able to concentrate on it whenever you wish. This is what is called the *samayasattva*. *Samaya* is a very difficult term. It's usually translated as 'conventional', and *sattva* is 'being', so the *samayasattva* is the 'conventional being'. This can be explained in two ways. It's Mañjuśrī, or Tārā, or whatever, visualized by you according to convention, according to tradition. Also it's the conventionally or relatively real form; it's the conditioned form. It's a product, in a way, a construction of your own mind. You've as it were taken a bit of your own mind, like a bit of elastic, and stretched it out and formed it into Mañjuśrī or Tārā or whatever 'out there' – do you see what I mean? This is what is called the *samayasattva*. Then you meditate and reflect upon this. But what happens next is that, inasmuch as this has come down from tradition, inasmuch as behind this form as originally described by some yogi, by some teacher, there is an actual Transcendental experience, there is an analogy between this conventional form that you visualize and some aspect of Reality. Because of that correspondence or affinity, that built-up form, that *samayasattva*, becomes the vehicle for the manifestation and experience of an aspect of the Transcendental. This corresponding aspect of the Transcendental is called the *jñānasattva*, the 'knowledge-being' – knowledge in the sense of the Five Knowledges of which the Five Jinas are an embodiment. So you see the idea. First you build up the *samayasattva* and then make it sufficiently vivid and intense and concentrate on it sufficiently, until it becomes a vehicle for the manifestation of something which is Transcendental. That is the *jñānasattva*, which is in a way neither subject nor object, neither subjective nor objective. It goes beyond that, it bridges the two.

So – to come back to the question – the Bodhisattva form corresponds to the *samayasattva*, and the Bodhisattva himself or herself is the *jñānasattva*. But there is a difference. The *samayasattva*, the conventional visualized form, is produced by *samatha*-type meditation, as it were, whereas the *jñānasattva* is *vipassanā*-type. That is the difference.

If you just see the *samayasattva*, you'll be uplifted, you'll have a beautiful, devotional feeling, but you can completely lose that and sink away from it. But if you sustain it to the point where it becomes a vehicle for the manifestation of the *jñānasattva*, then that corresponds to a flash of Insight which has a permanent modifying effect on your whole being. That is the difference.

So here we see this distinction between *samatha* and *vipassanā* sustained even at the level of the Tantra, within its particular context. This distinction runs through all forms of Buddhism and all kinds of meditative practice, including that of the Vajrayāna.

From the 2nd Western Buddhist Order convention (1975, pp.267-8)

22. don't force it

If you are experiencing the sound of the passing traffic, or something really excruciating and awful, it isn't much good to try to convince yourself, 'No, it isn't really awful, it's really the sound of the Tara mantra'.

Q: I've heard of a Tibetan practice where – say your main visualization practice was Tārā, for instance – the idea would be that you should reflect that every sound you hear is the Tārā mantra, that everything you see is the colour of Tārā, and that everyone you meet is Tārā.

Sangharakshita: I think the important thing is not to be too self-conscious about it. Let it come naturally. For instance, suppose you're doing the Tārā practice, and you visualize this beautiful turquoise-green colour, and you've seen it vividly many a time in your meditation. If you happen to see a green tree of the same colour, you will naturally think, 'Oh, that's just like the colour of Tārā.' That's all right. But if you have got this idea that you've got to connect everything with Tārā, you might think, 'Oh, yes, the sound of the motor car passing by is just like the sound of the mantra', though actually you hear something quite unpleasant. You might feel you have to connect it forcibly, as it were – but this isn't what you're meant to do. It should be a natural thing.

Q: So basically, it's something you see or experience, just because you are permeated with it.

S: Yes! You can coax along the recollection if you like; but if you are experiencing the sound of the passing traffic, or something really excruciating and awful, it isn't much good to try to convince yourself, 'No, it isn't really awful, it's really the sound of the Tārā mantra'. This becomes a purely mental exercise which I think is not what is meant. It's supposed to be more of the nature of an actual realization which comes spontaneously as a result of your spiritual practice. You are so much imbued with the feeling and the spirit of Tārā, that you can't help being reminded of it wherever you look; whatever you see sparks off something connected with that. It's like when you're in a state of mind which is full of *mettā* because you practise the *mettā-bhāvanā*; when you look around, people seem so much nicer than they usually do, so much more pleasant, so much more attractive, because you are in that state of mind. But it's not much good when you're not in a *mettā*-ful state of mind looking around at people and seeing them as a miserable unhealthy, unpleasant, unfriendly lot but telling yourself, 'Oh no, I really must love them, and they're really lovely people', when you don't really see it, and you don't really believe it. You mustn't artificially or forcibly try to make connections in that way.

From a seminar on 'Conditions of Stability in the Order' (1979, p.63)

23. FALLING IN LOVE WITH A BODHISATTVA

You could even say you were in love with everybody, or everything. That is rather different from a little lukewarm metta, thinly spread over everything, like workhouse jam.

Q: Can one fall in love with the Bodhisattva visualized in meditation, and if this is possible, is it desirable?

Sangharakshita: I think it is possible. I would say it was desirable, but very difficult, because there has to be a definite emotional connection established, and that is not easy, because the figure of the Bodhisattva represents or embodies quite a high spiritual level. Sometimes we are reliant, at least to begin with, on pictorial representations, on *thangkas* and so on, and very often they are not especially inspiring or attractive, so it's not easy to latch on to them emotionally. You very rarely find a thangka that you can latch on to in that way, one that is deeply attractive. You can recognize it in theory or in principle, but that emotional response is very often not there, whereas you do respond powerfully to certain figures in Western art, because the art is very fine, or because culturally you are in sympathy with it.

Our emotions are much more under our control than we usually think. Well, maybe 'control' isn't quite the right word. You can mould or shape your feelings to a much greater extent than you usually think. You are not just the victim of your feelings; they are raw material which you can use. So I think one must be very careful to guide and direct one's positive feelings, rather than try to check them or even suppress them, because you are afraid that they may lead you in an unskilful direction. If you do that, you impoverish your life emotionally.

Q: If you did fall in love with the Bodhisattva you visualized, where would that experience fit in with an actual experience of the Bodhisattva?

S: Well, to begin with, you would fall in love with the *samayasattva*, but that would mean that you would be able to concentrate on that particular Bodhisattva in the *samayasattva* form quite intensely, and eventually have a quite vivid subjective experience, and that would lead to the experience of the Bodhisattva in the *jñānasattva* form. You might have the problem, on a certain level, of detaching yourself from the *samayasattva* Bodhisattva form, but no doubt you would deal with that when you came to it. This is what one finds happening in the case of certain mystics, especially in the Sufi tradition, and with some Christian mystics too. They manage to fall in love, as it were, with whatever happens to be the object of their devotion, whether a particular saint or spiritual guide on a higher plane, or whatever. In the case of Muhammad, there is a record of a strange spiritual experience that he had in relation to a very beautiful youth. It is as though he fell in love with him just for a short period, and had quite a profound spiritual experience. Plato describes something similar in the *Symposium*.

There are two extremes one must avoid. One is letting one's emotions go wherever they want to go, even in an unskilful direction; and the other is suppressing one's emotions, including one's positive emotions. We usually oscillate between the two, indulging our emotions to such an extent that they become unskilful, or suppressing them. I think you have to be careful that you don't do that, otherwise you are in a situation where in your daily life you are just indulging your emotions in a somewhat unskilful way, but when you go away on retreat, you are sitting on them. What is needed is a middle way: a powerful development of your emotions in a positive way, so that you are in a state of being in love, though there is no one in particular that you are in love with. You could even say you were in love with everybody, or everything. That is rather different from a little lukewarm *mettā*, thinly spread over everything, like workhouse jam. Do you see what I mean?

From a seminar on the *Jewel Ornament of Liberation*
(Tuscany 1985, pp.164-5)

24. THE YIDAM AND SEXUAL DESIRE

According to some teachers, all one's feelings, one's emotions, including one's sexual feelings, should or could be put on to one's spiritual ideal. One might add that perhaps they are safer there than anywhere else.

Q: Once one has got a relationship with one's *yidam*, can the relationship be sexual as well?

Sangharakshita: It obviously can't be fully sexual, because the *yidam* doesn't exist on the physical plane, so it can only in any case be a question of sexual feeling or sexual desire. According to some teachers, all one's feelings, one's emotions, including one's sexual feelings, should or could be put on to one's spiritual ideal. One might add that perhaps they are safer there than anywhere else. According to some spiritual teachers, it is not even just not a bad thing but even positively a good thing to allow even one's sexual feelings to flow in that direction, because one is after all trying to put all one's energies, all one's emotions, all one's feelings, on to that ideal; to gather them up, as it were, and place them there. So certainly this is an approach which is sanctioned by tradition.

I don't think it matters whether the *yidam* has a masculine form or a feminine form from this point of view. The important thing is that the feelings, the emotions, including the sexual ones, get raised and hopefully eventually sublimated. I think one has to be quite sure that that is what is actually happening: that you are not merely sort of thinking it; that you haven't, in D.H. Lawrence's phrase, merely got sex in the head.

From a seminar on the *Jewel Ornament of Liberation*
(Tuscany 1985, pp.208-9)

25. THE RIGHT ONE

I am sure that you could get on reasonably well with any visualization practice that you took up as your first practice.

Q: I have heard it said that when choosing a *sādhana* it would be better to leave it to chance than choose the *sādhana* yourself, that ideally a guru should choose the *sādhana*, or failing that, a feather falling on a mandala, and that only as a last resort should one choose a *sādhana* for oneself. Could you comment on the apparent contradiction between this method of choosing a *sādhana*, and the way people choose a *sādhana* for themselves in our own Order, with who knows what motives?

Sangharakshita: I think I have said myself, jokingly, that the Tibetans think that almost the worst method is choosing your *yidam* yourself. But the idea that one method is more suited to someone than another can be a little overdone. The main thing is to get started. I am sure that you could get on reasonably well with any visualization that you took up as your first practice. In our Order, the practice of people saying what they would like to choose arose because I think it's important that some emotional connection is established from the very beginning, even if it is perhaps on slightly the wrong basis; that will get corrected as people do the practice.

Quite often people say that they have a practice in mind, but if I feel that they ought to do another one, they are happy to do the practice I suggest. I hardly ever feel that someone is choosing a particular practice in a grabby or individualistic way; in fact I don't think I've ever felt that. People usually make it clear that their own choice is quite tentative. Even if they've got a definite feeling for a particular *sādhana*, they often say that they would be happy for me to suggest another one. So I don't feel that there is such a difference with the tradition as perhaps might appear.

The main thing is to make a start. Quite a few Order Members take up a second practice, which they add to the first, after perhaps coming to understand themselves and their needs better. Not that the first one was a mistake – not by any means – but as a result of practising the first *sādhana* they understand themselves more clearly and see that now the time has come, maybe after a few years, to take up a second practice which will have a complementary or supplementing effect.

Q: When somebody asks you to choose a *sādhana* for them, on what basis do you choose?

S: I suppose it's intuition. I don't try to work it out. I don't think 'This particular person is a bit intellectual, so maybe they had better take up Tārā' – no, it is definitely on a more intuitive basis than that. Sometimes, especially if someone doesn't make any suggestion of their own, I get an instant, intuitive and quite strong sense of what they should take up. It's difficult to explain it rationally. It is as though it is sparked off between us, because of their openness and because I am concentrating on what is right for them, or helpful for them. The answer just comes between us like that, and they always feel, or at least this has always been my experience so far, 'Yes, that was the right one'.

From a seminar on *The Forest Monks of Sri Lanka* (1985, pp.289-90)

26. WHY VISUALIZE AN ENLIGHTENED BEING?

If you think in terms of a Buddha or Bodhisattva, you are thinking in terms of a person, not an abstract principle or idea.

Q: When we Go for Refuge within the Western [now Triratna] Buddhist Order, the Insight practice we receive takes the form of a visualization of a Buddha or Bodhisattva. Given that there are many other *vipassanā* meditations, is there a reason for this emphasis on visualizing an Enlightened being? Why not the contemplation of the twelve *nidānas*, for example?

Sangharakshita: Well, one can certainly do these other *vipassanā*-type practices, but there is a reason why the visualization of a Buddha or Bodhisattva – perhaps especially a Bodhisattva – is connected with ordination, and that is that the Buddha or Bodhisattva is not just a being outside yourself. That's what it seems like at present, but in reality that Buddha or Bodhisattva represents what you yourself can become. On a deeper level, a very much deeper level (and I usually use this sort of language only with caution) they are yourself, outside time, outside space.

If you think in terms of a Buddha or Bodhisattva, you are thinking in terms of a person, not an abstract principle or idea. You are not thinking of 'impermanence' or 'reality' or the 'Absolute'; it's an Enlightened being, because that's what you aspire to become, or what you basically are: an

Enlightened being. All the different insights and *vipassanā*s are aspects of the wisdom and understanding of that being, who is essentially you.

Q: Why did you say 'especially a Bodhisattva' rather than a Buddha?

S: I think it's easier for us to identify with the Bodhisattva. It's as though the Buddha is the sun, and the Bodhisattvas are the rays of that sun; and those rays as it were connect up with us. It's easier for us to go, I think, to the Bodhisattva figure rather than to the Buddha directly. But just as if we follow the ray we go back to the sun, if we follow the Bodhisattva we arrive at the Buddha. Also, from another point of view, there are male and female Bodhisattvas, but we don't have male and female Buddhas in the historical sense. So if one finds it difficult to identify with a being of the opposite gender, well, there are both male and female Bodhisattvas. I don't know whether that is actually a problem for anybody, but if it is easier for, say, a woman to think of herself as Tārā than as Avalokiteśvara, there is Tārā, there is that option.

Q: I have heard some women say that they've had a reluctance to connect with Tārā, and realized it was because of almost a reluctance to believe that they as a woman could gain Enlightenment.

S: Well, they've got the Buddha's word for it. But there's also the evidence of the Theris. Perhaps their stories should be more widely known, because they are historical characters. That does make a difference, at least for some people. They are not, as it were, mythic beings. Of course, quite a number of male Order members do the Tārā practice. They seem not to have any difficulty in making that connection; in fact, in some cases they are very strongly drawn to that particular figure.

Q: Are you very often surprised by people's choice of Bodhisattva or Buddha form, or is it quite predictable?

S: I won't say it's predictable; sometimes rather unpredictable. I do notice that very often people think in quite psychological terms. For instance, if they feel that they are lacking in energy, they tend to go for Padmasambhava. That's understandable, because one needs to make the connection, but Padmasambhava doesn't really represent energy in a one-sided psychological sense. But the important thing is to make the connection. If you make the connection in that way, fair enough. In doing the Padmasambhava practice, you'll gradually get more and more deeply into it, and transcend your original, more psychological standpoint.

From a women's ordination retreat (1988, pp.22-3)

27. WHY BOTHER VISUALIZING AT ALL?

Doing the visualization practice allows you to put yourself in contact with what you yourself are, on a much deeper level of your being.

Q: I must confess I don't generally tend to do my visualization practice, and at the moment I don't feel particularly bothered about this. How important do you consider visualization to be?

Sangharakshita: It depends what one understands by visualization. When you visualize a Buddha or a Bodhisattva, you aren't simply doing a visualization exercise, as you might visualize a ball or a spade. The visualized form represents an embodiment, from a particular aspect or a particular angle, of the spiritual ideal itself, and it is that that you are trying to get in contact with, in a very direct and tangible way. I think it is the experience of all those who have done a proper *sādhana* for any length of time that one does get a quite different experience from that produced by doing the mindfulness of breathing and the *mettā-bhāvanā*, effective though they are. Doing the visualization practice allows you to get in contact with what you yourself are, on a much deeper level of your being. So the significance goes considerably beyond that of the mindfulness and the *mettā*, without depreciating or undervaluing those practices in any way.

From a seminar on the *Jewel Ornament of Liberation*
(Tuscany 1985, p.275)

28. MAKING A START

You've got this source of knowledge, this source of understanding, within you, and you should use it, perhaps more than you do.

Q: In the course of my reading, I came across the five 'Dhyani Bodhisattvas'. They seem to be a quite significant group. Is there any reason why you haven't included them among the material you have presented?

Sangharakshita: Not really. Sometimes I have been concerned not to bring in too many unfamiliar names. But as people become more and more familiar with the names of different Buddhas and Bodhisattvas, there is no reason why these five should not be brought in

Q: But I know absolutely nothing about some of them – say, the Bodhisattva Ratnapani. How could I bring him into my practice?

S: Well, I don't know anything about Ratnapani either! I don't know anybody who does. I know the name, and what it means, but I have not come across any description or *sādhana*. The Mahāyāna texts mention thousands of names of Buddhas and Bodhisattvas, so it is not surprising that there are some we don't know much about. But one can always make a start. If you want to know about Ratnapani, I suppose the best thing to do, if you can't find any material in books, is to meditate on him. Say to yourself: 'Ratnapani ... that means 'Jewel in the Hand'; that must have some significance. He is associated with the Buddha Ratnasambhava, so what would he probably look like?' As far as I recollect, in Buddhist iconography he is shown like any other Bodhisattva, but in his hand he is holding a jewel. So that is your starting point: a Bodhisattva who has a jewel in his hand; and presumably, because he is associated with Ratnasambhava, he is golden in colour. What more do you need? That is how all the visualizations started. People didn't originally get them from books, they got them from their meditations, and then they wrote down descriptions of their visions.

I think people generally underestimate what they can learn from meditation. You don't have always to ask me, you don't have to look it up in books, not even in the dictionary. You can just reflect on it, meditate on it, and try to understand, try to see it in your meditation itself. You've got this source of knowledge, this source of understanding, within you, and you should use it, perhaps more than you do. You don't necessarily have to have a gift for visualization, as some people seem to have. Just reflect: what could Ratnapani mean, what could he look like? There are some visualizations we can trace back to a certain lama or teacher. We know they didn't go back to the Buddha. So, if there is not in existence, let's say a tradition of Ratnapani, there is no reason why you should not start one. Obviously you won't be able to do it just yet; it may take many years of practice.

From a seminar on the *Jewel Ornament of Liberation*
(Tuscany 1985, p.130)

4 Mantras

1. WHAT COMPASSION WOULD SOUND LIKE

A mantra is essentially an inner sound, an inner vibration, even an inner feeling.

Mantra used to be translated as 'magic words', which is as unhelpful as the old translation of mandala as 'magic circle', and sometimes even now mantra is, again rather less than usefully, rendered as 'spell'. The traditional etymology of mantra is 'that which protects the mind', and it is undoubtedly true that reciting a mantra has this effect, but so does every other spiritual practice, so this doesn't get us very far either. The most important thing to understand about a mantra is that it is a sound symbol, just as the figure of a Buddha or Bodhisattva is a form and colour symbol. It is a sound symbol, that is to say, of a particular aspect of the Enlightened mind. Just as the figure of Avalokiteśvara is what compassion would look like if we could see it, the mantra associated with Avalokiteśvara is what compassion would sound like if we could hear it.

Some people explain the efficacy of mantras in terms of physical vibrations: after making certain measurements, technicians have pronounced that if you recite such-and-such a mantra you produce such-and-such a density of sonic vibrations, and that the mantra that produces the highest density is the most spiritually efficacious. Such crude and materialistic calculations have rightly been ridiculed by Lama Govinda, who pointed out that if the efficacy of mantras were a matter of physically measurable sonic vibrations, all you would need to do in order to derive benefit from them would be to get a recording of mantras being chanted and play it over and over again.

But although mantric sound can be external in the sense of being produced by the voice, its significance does not lie in the actual physical sound. A mantra is essentially an inner sound, an inner vibration, even an inner feeling. Not that the external sound has no significance at all – there is certainly a place for reciting mantras aloud – but the recitation is only a means to the subtle internal experience of the mantra. The relation between the two is rather like that between a painting of a Buddha or Bodhisattva and the same figure as visualized in meditation. In both cases the gross leads to the experience of the subtle, or acts as a catalyst for it.

The recitation of mantras occupies an extremely important place in the Tantra, so much so that an early term for Tantric practice, predating 'Vajrayāna', was *mantranaya*, the 'path of mantras' (generally referred to nowadays as Mantrayāna). *Mantranaya* was paired with *pāramitānaya*, the 'path of perfections', and together the two paths were considered to constitute the Mahāyāna. Spiritual progress was said to be more rapid in the *mantranaya* than in the *pāramitānaya* – but it is not obvious why this should be so, given that the practice of the perfections is itself said to represent a complete scheme of ethical and spiritual development. One reason for this is that the practice of the perfections, at least in its early stages, is aimed at the conscious mind, while the *mantranaya*, by contrast, is directed more to the unconscious depths. It is aimed at contacting the spiritual forces latent within us, the forces that are ultimately the various aspects of the Enlightened mind and are personified, or crystallized, in the form of Buddhas and Bodhisattvas. These forces can be contacted, according to the Tantra, through the joint practice of visualization and invocation: visualization of form and colour, and invocation with mantric sound.

It is possible to get very technical about mantras and to classify them in a variety of ways, but I propose to attempt a definition by means of a short, simple description. First of all, a mantra is a string of syllables from the Sanskrit alphabet, sometimes, but not always, including Sanskrit words.

Secondly, mantras are not susceptible to conceptual analysis, and it is therefore traditional not to translate them, even though it is in some cases possible to give them a literal rendering. In a sense they are meaningless; that's the point of them, in a way. Take, for instance, the Tārā mantra. It consists of just a series of modulations of the vocative form of the name Tārā. There is no analyzable meaning; you are just juggling with the sound of the name. Some mantras do contain meaningful words; for instance, in the famous mantra *om mani padme hum*, *mani* means 'jewel' and *padme* means 'lotus', so that while you can't translate the initial *om* or the concluding *hum*, *mani padme* has often been translated as 'the jewel in the lotus' – though as Donald Lopez makes clear in *Prisoners of Shangri-la*, the translation should really be 'Jewel-Lotus (One)'. Either 'the jewel in the lotus' or 'Jewel-Lotus One' is perfectly plausible philosophically, with all sorts of ramifications in Buddhist thought and practice, but to say that the mantra *means* that doesn't give the real – much less the total – meaning of the mantra; it gives just a facet of it, and not even the most important one. Mantras cannot be logically analysed; they don't have a meaning in the ordinary conceptual sense. Even when they do contain words with an assignable meaning, these only suggest the spirit of the mantra and the general direction in which its meaning may be found.

Thirdly and most importantly, a mantra is the sound symbol of a particular Buddha or Bodhisattva. When that divinity becomes or manifests as a sound, which according to the Tantra he or she can and does, that sound is the mantra. Just as the visualized image is the equivalent of the Buddha or Bodhisattva in terms of form and colour, so the mantra is the equivalent in terms of sound. The mantra is therefore, in a sense, the name of the divinity. It may or may not include the name usually used to refer to the divinity – that doesn't matter. When we call people by name they come, and when we invoke a Buddha or Bodhisattva with a mantra, the divinity appears, or manifests, or becomes – in a sense – present.

Fourthly, the mantra is given at the time of initiation, otherwise it is not really a mantra. In fact, traditional initiation can consist wholly in the giving of a mantra. Usually one repeats the mantra three times, by which means energy is transmitted. Of course, it is possible to learn a mantra through hearing it chanted in a puja, and start reciting it yourself. You will get some benefit from this, but what you are reciting is not really a mantra. Mantra includes as part of its meaning that you are empowered to use it by the guru. The usual method is to receive it from a living human teacher, though it is possible to be given a mantra in a dream or in meditation by a guru figure or even by a Buddha or Bodhisattva. If you get the mantra in any other way, it may be a good religious practice, but it isn't Tantric recitation.

Fifthly and lastly, a mantra has to be repeated. Having received it, you must repeat it with the energy with which it was transmitted to you; otherwise, the energy is eventually lost. Sometimes it is said that if you neglect to repeat the mantra for three years, its original energy is entirely lost, and reinitiation is required. But if you repeat the mantra regularly the energy increases and eventually repetition becomes spontaneous, continuing without conscious effort.

From *Creative Symbols of Tantric Buddhism* (2004, pp.169-72)

2. WHICH IS MORE IMPORTANT, VISUALIZATION OR MANTRA?

It is very rarely that we have an experience without vocalizing it to ourselves.

Q: I'm interested in the idea that one could be quite absorbed in the mantra. It's tempting to think of the visualized form as being the main attraction and the mantra as being a bit of a sideline, I think because of the powerful attraction of colour. Do you think it's a matter of temperament?

Sangharakshita: I think to some extent it is, and also different people's capacity or incapacity to visualize. It is as though for some people sound is more meaningful, for others colour is more meaningful, and for others perhaps both are equally meaningful. If you aren't able to visualize very well you tend to be thrown back a bit on to the mantra recitation, but if you can visualize very successfully, you naturally tend to neglect the mantra recitation. It may be best if you can do both successfully, but I think it doesn't matter all that much if you are neglecting one, for one reason or other, provided you are very intensively into the other, whether the mantra recitation or the visualization.

Q: Would it be helpful to enter into any sort of discursive or semi-discursive activity while you were visualizing, to help you to see?

S: Well yes, I think one could do that. It's as though you embroider the figure you are visualizing with your reflections. You don't lose sight of that figure, you keep it steadily in view, but at the periphery of your mind you are engaging in these discursive reflections which deepen the experience of the visualization, giving it another dimension, the dimension hopefully of Insight.

Q: I understood you to say once that it was not possible to develop Insight without engaging the rational mind in some way conceptually. But when you visualize yourself as a Bodhisattva, you have said that that would be a non-conceptual recognition of the void nature of your own being. Would that not constitute Insight?

S: I think it could, but I think at the same time that there is an almost subconscious conceptualization going on, a subtle discursiveness. If you have this experience of yourself 'as' a Bodhisattva, in whatever way the practice describes it, I think very subtly you vocalize that to yourself as you experience it, and that either assists or even perhaps constitutes the Insight element. I think that it is very rarely that we have an experience without vocalizing it to ourselves.

Q: Are you saying that it is not possible to have any sort of experience without some kind of subtle vocalizing?

S: It would seem like that, though I won't be too positive about it, because one doesn't want to limit the possibilities. But in the case of this vivid visualization, I think there is an almost sub-vocal conceptualization in the sense that you are saying to yourself in conceptual terms what is happening, so there is a very faint conceptual commentary on your own experience going on. When you are very concentrated, this can be tantamount almost to *vipassanā*, a very refined *vipassanā*-type element. Perhaps you should watch your own experience very closely and see what actually happens. If you are visualizing yourself in a certain way, look at your own mind and see whether you are in a very subtle way *thinking* the visualization as well as *seeing* it. If so, that would point, however subtly, to the possibility of a *vipassanā* experience. It might be very difficult to suspend that subtle activity. It might be possible to have a state in which you visualize in that way without that subtle mental commentary, in which case *vipassanā* could not be developed, but I won't be sure about that. Perhaps it depends upon the degree of subtlety of the conceptual commentary. Perhaps it can be so subtle so that you can hardly tell whether it is there or not.

Q: Is this sub-vocalization *vipassanā*, or would it be more true to say that it is a support to *vipassanā*?

S: It is a support which could become *vipassanā*. One might even say that in self-conscious beings, that kind of visualization is inseparable from a subtle commentary. It might be so. I can't make any definite statement. I suggest you look at your own experience and see what is happening. Looking at it another way, can you see a leaf falling from the tree without thinking that the leaf is falling from the tree? Do you merely *see* that it is falling, or do you not at the same time, inseparably perhaps, *think* that it is falling? Is it possible to distinguish the two? If it isn't, then to visualize yourself, say as Tārā, is tantamount to a reflection which could be the support of an Insight experience.

From a seminar on *The Forest Monks of Sri Lanka* (1985, pp.276-8)

3. ATTEND TO THE SOUND

You can be so absorbed in the sound of the mantra that it will seem to be going on spontaneously.

Q: Is it true that one can go further into *dhyāna*, as it were, through contemplating a visualized image than through contemplating a mantra?

Sangharakshita: Not necessarily. It depends on the individual, because someone may not be able to visualize as well as he can recite. But if you recite the mantra and if you are moved by that, or if you visualize the image, the form and you are stirred by that, the fact that you are emotionally moved will mean that more of your energies are involved, so you are in a better state for concentration in the sense of absorption in *dhyāna*. The fact that you have visualized the form of a Buddha or Bodhisattva will make you more able to enter *dhyāna*, if you wish to do so; and the fact that you have had some experience of *dhyāna* will enable you to visualize more clearly and vividly if you wish to do that. Similarly, inasmuch as your interest has been aroused and you are concentrated, you will be in a more fit state to enter into *dhyāna*. And having become absorbed, you will be better equipped, should you wish to do so, to develop Insight. So one helps the other, in a way, even though they are not, in a sense, strictly compatible.

Q: How far into *dhyāna* can one go while visualizing a *yidam* or while reciting a mantra? At what point does that practice have to drop away?

S: Well, you can visualize, in the sense of seeing an image before you, up even to the fourth *dhyāna*; but by that time, you will have lost your external bodily consciousness and will visualize in a vivid dream, as it were, and will only be conscious of that particular figure. Similarly with the mantra: you can be so absorbed in the sound that it will seem to be going on spontaneously, though you may not be conscious of your surroundings, and that will amount to fourth *dhyāna*. There won't be any mental activity, in the ordinary sense, at such times.

Q: That is clear. Previously I thought you'd said that even if the mantra was sounding and you were listening to it, at best that would only be what you called a quasi-*dhyānic* state, and I couldn't see why one shouldn't be able to go into *dhyāna*.

S: I think you are likely to go less deep with the mantra than with the visualized form, inasmuch as the mantra usually has an analyzable meaning; so there is the possibility of your being mentally occupied with that meaning. But it is possible to stop thinking about the meaning and attend merely to the sound of the words, just as you might see before you a few words in a script that you didn't understand; you would be concentrating on those forms, but no meaning would be attached to them. With practice you can even do that with written words to which you do attach a meaning. You can look at a piece of writing without any mental activity, so that you merely see the form of the letters. That can happen with the sound of the mantra: you merely attend to the sound, and it does not add up to a meaning with which you are mentally occupied. That is rather more difficult, however, than visualizing a form or a figure.

Q: But if the mantra has no analyzable meaning, surely there is no difference between hearing the sound and visualizing the image?

S: No, except that even if the mantra doesn't have on the surface an analyzable meaning, you will have attached some meaning to it in the course of your earlier practice. But if it doesn't have an analyzable meaning, obviously it is much easier just to listen internally to the sound of the mantra, without any discursive mental activity arising from it.

From a seminar on the *Jewel Ornament of Liberation*
(Tuscany 1985, pp.298-9)

9 Indirect methods, retreats and taking meditation further

1 Indirect methods

1. IS MEDITATION THE ONLY WAY?

It is not enough just to try to tackle the mind directly, through meditation. It is also necessary to tackle it indirectly in all sorts of other ways.

Q: Some Buddhists I have encountered have seen the spiritual life just in terms of meditation. Is that valid, do you think?

Sangharakshita: In a way, if spiritual life is the development of consciousness to higher levels, yes, meditation is the most direct way of doing that, but it doesn't mean that that is the only way. There are so many indirect methods which are supportive of the direct method. In my view, it is not enough just to try to tackle the mind directly, through meditation. It is also necessary to tackle it indirectly in all sorts of other ways, through for instance Yoga or T'ai Chi, or even through study. People who just concentrate on meditation, changing the mind directly, often neglect the external world, the whole of the physical side of life, so that they become alienated.

Spiritual life is *bhāvanā*, it's development, which is the term which is used for meditation, so meditation is development *par excellence*, one might say, but in practice it needs to be supported quite strongly by indirect methods of development, except perhaps in the case of very exceptional people. I wouldn't like to exclude completely the possibility of someone being engaged in full-time meditation and nothing else and 'breaking through', so to speak, without the support of any indirect method, but I think it is quite rare. Even asceticism is an indirect method, isn't it? *Śīla* (ethical conduct) is also an indirect method, and I don't think any Buddhist would say that you could develop a meditative life independently of *śīla*.

From a seminar on *The Forest Monks of Sri Lanka* (1985, p.272)

2. WRITING INSTEAD OF MEDITATING?

One has to ask oneself what meditation is.

Q: When I started writing my book, I found that once my inspiration took off, my meditation became very difficult, not so much for the negative reason that I was full of worry, but rather because I couldn't stop my ideas flowing, and I was frankly reluctant not to follow them through. When you are acting and living in a very integrated, very concentrated way, do you think there is an argument for even forsaking meditation? I wanted to keep meditating, but I really did find it a tremendous conflict.

Sangharakshita: I think one has to look even more closely at the question, and ask oneself what meditation is. I would say that if you are writing in that sort of way, and especially if your writing is about the Dharma, that is, up to a point, tantamount to meditation. You are certainly not in a *dhyāna* state, but you could well be in a state of *upachara samādhi*, that is, neighbourhood concentration, which is compatible with intense mental activity, and indeed compatible with Insight. It is not impossible that in the course of that intensive literary work, connected with the Dharma, you could develop Insight, at least to a minor extent. So one might say that there was something to be said for allowing oneself to continue in that way, for even a period of months without doing very much in the way of meditation, because you are in a very concentrated, skilfully concentrated, mental state. The ideas that are passing through your mind, your mental activities, are all connected with the Dharma, and presumably you are in a quite blissful and even ecstatic state at times. When that phase is over, perhaps one should think in terms of balancing it by a period of meditation proper. But if you are engaged in creative work, I don't think you can switch that off.

Q: But aren't writing and meditation quite a good combination?

S: Yes, if your inspiration is not flowing so urgently, but more gently, as it were, I think the two are very compatible, but if inspiration is flowing in full flood, I don't think you would want to stop it, and perhaps you shouldn't stop it, even in order to engage in a related activity.
From a seminar on *The Forest Monks of Sri Lanka* (1985, pp.42, 43)

3. INSIGHT IN DAILY LIFE

We need to try to develop vipassana, Insight, and thereby gain Stream-entry, both in the specifically meditative situation and in the more workaday situation.

Q: Assuming that one's activity in the world is a reflection of one's Going for Refuge, and that one maintains a daily meditation practice, do you think it is necessary to spend a prolonged period devoted to meditation at some point in order to reach Stream-entry?

Sangharakshita: I suppose it depends what you mean by 'prolonged'. I certainly think that solitary retreats should be part of one's personal programme. At least have a short one every year, not so much from the point of view of meditation as just to enable you to be free from external pressures and influences and to get to know yourself and achieve a certain measure of inner clarity. Strictly speaking, meditation in the sense of *samatha* is not necessary to reach Stream-entry, because it is on *vipassanā*, on Insight, that Stream-entry depends. In practice you need to have got up a good head of steam, as it were, as regards *samatha* before you are in a position to develop *vipassanā*; and it's usually only on some kind of meditation retreat that you can develop sufficient *samatha* to be able to develop *vipassanā* based on that. But the development of *vipassanā* in ordinary workaday situations is by no means ruled out, as the Zen tradition shows. So yes, a prolonged period – say, a month or so – every now and then devoted to meditation is certainly necessary for spiritual health, but one ought to be at the same time making an effort to develop Insight in one's ordinary life.

Supposing you are at work, and someone else is working with you, and they are not working properly. If you feel anger rising within you, there's an opportunity. You can ask yourself: 'Who is getting angry? Why should I be angry? What's the reason for that?' You may think: 'The other person has made me angry.' But is that the situation? Do you have to be angry? Does it not depend on your own volition, your own mental attitude? And who is it that is getting angry, anyway? Who is making who angry? What is this 'I' that is becoming angry? In this way you can develop Insight in that particular situation, sometimes all the more strongly because there is a charge of emotional energy there, which can be turned and utilized.

Or perhaps you experience a great disappointment. You might have been looking forward to something very much, maybe a visit to the theatre. Maybe you have not been to the theatre for months, or even years, and suddenly the friend who promised to take you doesn't turn up, or you fall ill, and you can't go. You experience that keen disappointment, but then you can say to yourself: 'Why am I feeling disappointed? It is because of my strong desire, my craving even, for that kind of experience. If I am not going to the theatre, why should I make that an occasion of suffering for myself?' Just see the way your mind is working: how you have looked forward to it, you've built up hopes and expectations, and then they are dashed; you feel disappointed, upset, annoyed, angry with circumstances. It's all unnecessary; you could be just as happy staying at home, even just as happy lying in bed and being ill. It depends on your mental attitude. So in that situation, too, you can develop *vipassanā*, you can develop Insight. You can develop it not only in connection with meditation, but in connection with all these other life experiences. Mothers have many such experiences, because children give one opportunities of not just knuckling under but practising patience in a very positive way. Sometimes I'm sure you feel the child's will, even the baby's will, up against yours, and there is the tendency to pit your will against theirs, have your way. But you have to ask yourself: 'What is this will that has come up so strongly and is opposing the child's will? Am I really functioning for the benefit of the child? Am I really aware, or am I not just instinctively reacting, and pitting my will against that of another person?'

We get all these opportunities for developing Insight within our ordinary everyday life. That doesn't mean that we should neglect meditation, because indirectly meditation will strengthen our concentration, and provide a stronger basis for *vipassanā* in the long run. But we need to operate in both these ways, and try to develop *vipassanā*, Insight, and thereby gain Stream-entry, both in the specifically meditative situation and in the more workaday situation. Sometimes we can have a terrible flash of insight into ourselves and the workings of our own mind, even the nature of conditioned existence, in the midst of all sorts of worldly circumstances.

From a women's pre-ordination retreat (1988, pp.9-10)

4. I'M AFRAID THAT WHEN THE BIG MOMENT COMES I WILL MISS IT

The time to watch out is when things are going well ...

Q: Could you say something about the importance or otherwise of some experience of the *dhyānas*?

Sangharakshita: Well, the normal procedure is for Insight to arise on the basis of *dhyāna* experience, though the traditional practice is that after experiencing higher *dhyānas* you go down to the first one where there is *vitarka-vicāra* and start up reflection. But sometimes that isn't dramatic enough. I think sometimes the more existential situation is more likely to provide suitable conditions for the arising of Insight. It is easy to have a nice pleasant gentle *dhyānic* experience, not anything very intense.

Q: Could one console oneself with the thought that a certain amount of horizontal integration arises from the activities one engages in, and that a certain level of positivity, an increasing level of positivity, would do in the absence of tingling up the back of your neck?

S: Yes, it would do. But looking at it from a completely different point of view, one mustn't associate the arising of Insight just with the experience of *dhyāna*. Sometimes Insight can arise in very painful and difficult situations, when you might feel you are going a bit crazy.

Q: I'm clear about that. My understanding had been, though, that one might need a lot of *dhyāna* under one's belt, so to speak, to make the most of the intense situations that do arise. This has bothered me slightly over the years. Because I don't have hours and hours of second *dhyāna* experience tucked away, I'm afraid that when that big moment comes I will miss it. Am I being a bit literalistic?

S: The important factor is concentration. When one has this flash of Insight, if that does arise, one has a sufficient degree of concentration to be able to dwell upon it quite one-pointedly and absorb it. That concentration may or may not be accompanied by other *dhyāna* factors.

Q: If we've been working in Right Livelihood for years and not had much experience of *dhyāna*, but have become fairly positive and reasonably integrated, might we be concentrated enough to be able to absorb that sort of insight?

S: Well, if you are fairly well integrated, you are in a slightly *dhyānic* state. This is what *dhyāna* is all about, from a certain point of view.

Q: So perhaps we are thinking of *dhyāna* too much in terms of its being strictly within meditation, sitting down on a cushion. We could recast it in terms of being integrated and concentrated outside the meditation situation.

S: Sometimes people have Insight experiences reading the scriptures, or just hearing them – perhaps hearing them even more so, because you are not making the effort to read, you are just receptive, you just take in the words. That is especially the case if the words are chanted and you understand them. So yes, though the standard approach to Insight is through *samatha*, the *dhyānas*, it is certainly not the only approach, though on the whole it is the one most cultivated and developed within the Buddhist tradition. But the Zen tradition at least shows that there are alternative ways.

Q: The Pāli canon does too. It describes people just meeting the Buddha and experiencing Insight. They don't think 'Now I've got to go and meditate'.

S: That's true; those incidents show that Insight can arise on the basis of strong devotion.

Q: Could you gain Insight by reflecting on a strong positive emotion?

S: You could try, but it is not quite the same thing, it hasn't got the same existential edge, in a way unfortunately. When you suffer you are really up against your ego. People ask 'Why do I suffer?' but who asks 'Why am I happy?' Suffering makes you think and reflect, but if anything happiness usually makes you forgetful. The time to watch out is when things are going well. That is when you are likely to make mistakes. You can see it happening. People get over-confident, and therefore careless, therefore they make mistakes. In a way, success is more dangerous than failure. That is when Māra starts taking a real interest.

From a seminar on Right Livelihood (1993, pp.84-6)

5. CAN YOU ENTER DHYĀNA THROUGH READING A NOVEL?

It does seem that quite a degree of spiritual experience, including Insight experience, is compatible with sense experience.

Q: Can one enter the first *dhyāna* through reading a novel or poetry?

Sangharakshita: It depends on the novel, it depends on the poem. It may be one that arouses skilful mental states or unskilful ones. I would say that it certainly is possible to enter a *dhyānic*-type state, possibly amounting to the first *dhyāna*. Of course there is *vitarka-vicāra*, initial and sustained mental activity, while you are reading. I would say that is more likely to occur if you are reading a scripture, a Buddhist text, which inspires in you a deeply concentrated mood, with strong positive emotions. I wouldn't rule out the possibility of your approaching that sort of state while reading a poem or even a novel; but it would depend very much on the kind of mental states that your reading of it gave rise to. If you were simply concentrated and absorbed in the poem or the novel, that wouldn't be enough; it would depend also on the nature of what you were absorbed in. If it was a pornographic novel, you might be absorbed, but not in a skilful way.

I certainly wouldn't rule out someone attaining a state not very far short of the first *dhyāna* through study, certainly through Dharma study and possibly in other ways, too. One can become very absorbed, the experience can be very intense. I don't know with what degree of intensity people do experience poetry, but one can experience it very intensely indeed. If you read a Buddhist text written in poetic form, clearly some kinds of poetry could lift you to that sort of level. But does it even have to be ostensibly Buddhist? You could raise that point too. There are poems by non-Buddhist poets which dwell, say, on impermanence in a highly positive and skilful way. One isn't necessarily concerned even with any cognitive content, because *dhyāna* as such is not concerned with Insight, but only with concentration and very intense positive emotion; and, certainly, through the reading of literature, whether Buddhist or otherwise, you can have that experience. Perhaps you need to learn to make use of literature or poetry in that way. I think that if you did, you could very probably – certainly with the help of *Buddhist* literature – lift yourself to a state amounting to that of the first *dhyāna*. One can only try; one can only experiment. No need to take it from me one way or the other. Just see whether in your case it happens or doesn't happen.

Q: What about the idea of *dhyāna* involving a shift from sense experience to mental experience?

S: It does involve a shift, but tradition says that it is only in the fourth *dhyāna* that experience of the five physical senses is entirely in abeyance. Short of the fourth *dhyāna*, you do continue to be aware of the external world, although your attention is greatly withdrawn.

Q: Say, for instance, reading Keats' 'Ode to a Nightingale' induces *dhyāna* in you. The poem seems to be almost an enhancement of sense experience. How does this tie up with *dhyāna*?

S: I wouldn't say that Keats' experience of the nightingale, assuming he did literally hear a nightingale, which I believe was the case, was just a sense experience. The fact that he wrote a poem about the nightingale meant, I would have thought, that the nightingale was much more than a nightingale; that it became, for want of a better term, a symbol. And it was because he apprehended the nightingale in that way that his experience of the nightingale was extremely intense – so intense that it produced the poem.

Q: But there was an element of sense experience.

S: Oh, yes, that provided the starting point. It may be that there was an actual nightingale there, and he heard its song, but that had all sorts of other associations for him, and on that account he had a very intense experience. It is not just an ornithological experience, so to speak.

Q: What about art, for instance Turner's landscape painting? That seems a very intense positive emotional response to sense experience.

S: Well, what is it that makes Turner Turner? What is it that makes a painting of a landscape by Turner different from a colour photograph? Clearly, there is something that Turner sees in the landscape which he manages to communicate. There is colour; there is a certain way of looking at the landscape, not perhaps in a very obvious way; a certain way of seeing it so that it is *made* to mean something, almost. Perhaps one sees this most of all in some of the Zen landscapes, where the artist has succeeded in communicating his vision. One could even say he sees the blade of grass or the bamboo as it really is, or at least in greater depth, in a way that a lesser artist does not see. He succeeds in communicating something of that.

Q: But is there a withdrawal from sense experience in a case of that kind?

S: This raises the question, what does one mean by withdrawal? The sense object is there, and you mirror it. You could say there is no unskilful mental state arising in connection with it. It is a pure sense experience. Nonetheless, there is sense experience there, and that provides the starting point, the medium of communication for the artist. If you were to go deeper than that, if, say, you were to get into the fourth *dhyāna*, you would no longer experience that particular sense object. In a sense, you would have gone beyond art. But it does seem that quite a degree of spiritual experience, including Insight experience, is compatible with sense experience. There is nothing wrong with sense experience; it is the unskilful mental states that arise in connection with it that as it were contaminate the sense experience. The sense experience itself – the fact that the eye sees a visual object, or the ear hears an auditory object – is not in the least unskilful or unspiritual. That is pure *mano-niyama*; it is karmically and ethically quite neutral. The senses are quite innocent in themselves. They are merely perceptive mechanisms. So sense experience is incompatible only with a very high level of *dhyāna* experience; it is not incompatible with a lower level of *dhyāna* experience, and it is not incompatible with Insight. When you have Insight, you don't cease to see things and hear things; you carry on seeing and hearing, in a sense, exactly as before, but you see or hear them in a different way, or with a different attitude.

Q: Does this correspond with the *kasiṇa* meditation practice?

S: In a sense, yes, because in the case of a *kasiṇa* you've got a disc of colour or a disc of light and you just allow yourself to become absorbed in that. So you have a pure sense experience without any reaction, without any unskilful mental state arising in connection with it. You are able to become absorbed in it because colour is of that nature; it draws the attention. There is nothing to think about. You just experience, you just perceive the colour. So in that way you can become very absorbed, very concentrated, and from the *kasiṇa* you can progress to *dhyāna* experience.

From a seminar on the Jewel Ornament of Liberation
(Tuscany 1985, pp.262-4)

6. AN UNINTERRUPTED FLOW

Meditation is essentially the uninterrupted, continuous production of skilful mental states. So if, while active, you are producing skilful mental states, then in that sense you are meditating.

If you do not renounce activity, do not say you are a great meditator.[93]

Q: This is something that has worried me quite a lot. How, practically speaking, if one is doing a lot of meditation, does one cope with the need for physical activity?

Sangharakshita: Mm. Some people say you should just walk up and down your cell. But if you are the sort of person who really needs a lot of physical activity, maybe you are not cut out for meditation, maybe that isn't your way. Here, obviously, it is the full-time meditator that Atīśa has in mind.

Meditation is essentially the uninterrupted, continuous production of skilful mental states. So if, while active, you are producing skilful mental states, then in that sense you are meditating. Here Atīśa is referring to the specialized practice of meditation in the sense of sitting and meditating and producing the uninterrupted flow of skilful mental states in that sitting posture, but we mustn't limit meditation in the true sense to that, even though it is most easy of access for most people, at least for a while, from that posture or in that manner.

Q: So if someone of such a temperament did a solitary retreat, would you advise them not to do so much meditation, or to engage in physical activity deliberately?

S: One would have to enquire into the nature of this need for activity. Some people are just neurotically restless, but others do definitely seem to remain in a healthier state, both physically and mentally, if there is a certain amount of physical activity. They need scope for physical activity of a kind which will help the generation of skilful mental states, or at least not lead to the generation of unskilful mental states.

Q: Could you give an example of that?

S: Well, even walking might be an example. You can walk and say a mantra to yourself. In the Pāli scriptures we often find the Buddha described as walking up and down and meditating. Or you could just engage in physical activity but try to be very aware.

Q: Perhaps we ought to have another word that means this skilful state of mind, or some other word specifically for sitting meditation.

S: Mm. The purpose of meditation is to produce this uninterrupted flow of skilful mental states, and some people do produce that flow when not technically sitting and meditating. The ideal is to be in that state all the time. It is a normal, healthy and human state – maybe not up to the point of the *dhyānas*, but certainly bordering upon that.

Q: Presumably a healthy person would know how to change his or her mode of living in order to keep that going.

S: Yes, they would instinctively or intuitively correct any imbalance.

Q: When somebody says that in their day to day activity they are in a continual skilful mental state and so it's not necessary for them to meditate, but then they also say that they get restless when they try to meditate, do you think they are just kidding themselves?

S: Very likely. At least they should be able to sit calmly, at least for a short period. If they aren't used to sitting cross-legged, it may be difficult for them to do that and therefore they may get a bit restless physically, even though mentally they may be in quite a skilful state. But I would be a bit suspicious of someone who can't meditate but who claims to be in a skilful mental state all the time. It suggests that they are just keeping themselves busy, and become restless when there isn't something to do. If they were in a skilful state of mind all the time, when there was nothing to do, they would be able to sit down and enjoy their skilful mental state. This is all that you are really doing when you sit and meditate, if you are a healthy person. You are just enjoying your naturally skilful state.

Q: And you wouldn't get bored.

S: You wouldn't get bored. You do find with some people that they can work very hard but when there is nothing to do they can sit and do nothing quite happily. But some people get restless and irritable when there is nothing to do.

Q: Isn't the sitting part of the practice to enable you to practise intensifying your skilful mental state, so that you do need to do that for quite a long while?

S: Yes, you certainly do at the beginning. One of my own teachers, Jagdish Kashyap, was quite remarkable in this respect. He was capable of working really hard for twenty-four hours without stopping, without any difficulty, but he was also capable of lying on his bed not doing anything for twenty-four hours, equally happily. He never got restless if there was nothing to do.

In a way it's like the way an animal lives, but on a higher level. You should be able to enjoy work and really get really into it, but when there is nothing to be done and you have no inner creative prompting to do something, do nothing completely happily, with a clear conscience. Don't think, 'I really ought to be doing something', don't make something to do when there isn't anything to do.

You might, when you are sitting and doing nothing, suddenly be confronted by a situation where action was required, and then spontaneously you would leap into action. But you would be equally happy, equally in a skilful state, whether active or doing nothing. Your sitting and meditating should be an intensification under specially helpful circumstances of your naturally skilful state.

Q: Is this the significance of the depiction of Avalokiteśvara with his leg down, ready to step out into the world? His mind is in the same state whether he is sitting or ...

S: Yes, one could say that – in his case of course on a much higher level.

Q: But from the Bodhisattva Ideal point of view, isn't there always something to be done?

S: Ah yes, but in the case of the Bodhisattva, sitting and doing nothing and engaging in activities have become one and the same thing. On a lower level they are different things, though even so, they should be things that we can engage in at different times with equal ease and satisfaction. But for the Bodhisattva they have become one, he's functioning and he's completely calm, and his calmness is not incompatible with his activity. He doesn't need to rest; he is always resting and he is always active.

Q: But not doing something when it has to be done and just saying 'I don't feel like it' is quite different.

S: Yes, that's quite different. That is a sort of laziness, a sort of indifference to the situation.

Q: But if you really don't feel like doing something, should you do it?

S: It's a question of taking all the relevant factors into consideration.

Q: I think you can say 'I don't want to do it' and somehow that gives you the energy to go and do it, even though you don't want to.

S: This is why I sometimes say that if you are not sure what you ought to be doing, just stop and don't do anything for a while, until a desire emerges. When it occurs to you, 'Well, I'd like to do that', then go and do it. But if you are uncertain, if there are a lot of things you could be doing but you are not sure whether you should or whether you want to, then just stop. Do nothing until a definite urge to do a certain thing arises.

Q: It's very hard just to stop, but then once you *have* stopped, instead of all these pieces of you saying go here and go there, go everywhere, you can allow another part of yourself to be integrated, so there is more of yourself available to do whatever you do.

S: And sooner or later, whatever really has to be done will be done.

Q: It is often very difficult though, to sit with all these conflicting things pulling you this way and that.

S: Well, run away!

Q: It's not that easy.

S: This is one of the things I like about retreats, speaking personally. I have only two or three things to do, whereas usually there are two or three hundred.

Q: What's your personal 'plan of attack' when you have a lot of different things to do and you don't know which one to start with?

S: I follow my own advice, I just stop. I don't do anything, take a holiday. Especially if there is a lot of work, just take a holiday. That's the best time! Then a definite feeling will arise, 'I'll do this' or 'I'll do that.' Of course, I'm simplifying to some extent. Life isn't all that straightforward. Sometimes one is not even confronted by this sort of choice. You may have got yourself into a situation which you don't feel like facing up to but which you can't avoid. There may be very strong reasons why you should face up to it, though you don't feel at all happy about it. You can't opt out – sometimes that happens. But then you must learn the lesson and be careful next time not to put yourself into situations which are likely to develop in that sort of way.
From a seminar on *The Door of Liberation* (year unknown, pp.272-6)

7. PHYSICAL LABOUR AND MEDITATION

Some people have suggested that Buddhism is particularly suitable for introverts because of its emphasis on meditation, but this is to fail to take account of the balance of qualities called for by this teaching of the five spiritual faculties.

Although the *dhyānas* are intensely positive and beneficial attainments, they can be taken to extremes if they are practised on their own, without reference to anything or anyone else, without being balanced by energy and vigour. You can end up with inertness or passivity, even laziness or drowsiness. You find this particularly in the case of people who sit naturally and comfortably in meditation posture, and are happy to sit there, more or less undisturbed by gross mental activity, but not putting any effort into really deepening their awareness.

So *samādhi* must be balanced by *vīrya*, especially work that benefits other people, and especially physical labour. In the Zen monasteries of Japan, as in the pre-communist Ch'an monasteries of China, you get your full share of both meditation and work. However many hours of meditation you do, you will be expected to do almost an equal number of hours of hard physical work – and this means being down on your knees scrubbing floors or up to your elbows scouring pans, not deliberating over the arrangement of a couple of flowers or taking a delicate paintbrush to a porcelain bowl.

A friend of mine, Peggy Kennett, who became a Zen teacher in Japan after many years of difficulties (being foreign and female), once wrote to me describing the daily programme in her small monastery, where she had three or four disciples. They began at four in the morning with hard physical work until nine, and then had a simple meal, after which they got down to four or five hours of meditation, and finally they had another light meal in the afternoon. That was their life, she said: physical labour and meditation.

If they had been spending all their time in meditation you can be quite sure – in the case of the comparative novices, anyway – that they would have become just lazy. On the other hand, if they had been spending all their time in physical labour they would eventually have become – unless exceptionally gifted – more or less brutalized: just hewers of wood and drawers of water. So both must be there, at least to some extent: so much meditation, so much physical effort – a balance between the two.

Most people are naturally inclined either towards activity or towards meditation, depending on their psychology – on whether they are extrovert or introvert. Some people have suggested that Buddhism is particularly suitable for introverts because of its emphasis on meditation, but this is to fail to take account of the balance of qualities called for by this teaching of the five spiritual faculties.

Besides, once an individual has made some definite spiritual progress, they are beyond this sort of classification. You can say neither that they are introvert, nor that they are extrovert. It is important to balance a natural introversion, which may express itself in an affinity for meditation, with outward-looking activity and healthy work (or vice versa) – certainly in the earlier stages of one's spiritual career.

From *What is the Dharma?* (1998, pp.154-5)

8. WOULDN'T IT BE BETTER TO OPEN A SOUP KITCHEN?

If you do what you have to do with a positive mental attitude and keep it up, if there is an uninterrupted flow of skilful mental states alongside that activity, you are meditating.

Sangharakshita: People sometimes say things like 'Meditation doesn't matter. What is important is to serve people, to open a soup kitchen. Why bother about meditation?'

Q: Meditation in action.

S: Yes, if you can do it. Meditation is a flow of skilful thoughts, skilful mental states, not necessarily associated with the sitting posture of a concentration exercise.

Q: Skilful mental states?

S: That is to say, those that are not connected with *lobha*, *dveṣa* and *moha* i.e. craving, anger and ignorance but which are associated with contentment, with love and with understanding, with wisdom. This is what meditation really is. So, though you must be very honest about what is really happening in your mind, you can be going from door to door, with a collection box but actually be meditating in the sense that you are sustaining a flow of skilful mental states. It isn't that at the same time you are trying to say 'Om Mani Padme Hum', or trying to keep your mind on your breathing process. In a way that isn't necessary. If you do what you have to do with a positive mental attitude and keep it up, if there is an uninterrupted flow of skilful mental states alongside that activity, you are meditating. This is what *samādhi* really is. Of course, it is difficult, and you learn how to do it when you are sitting and meditating. But you eventually have to learn how to carry it over into everyday life.

From a seminar on 'The Stability of Societies' (year unknown, pp.15-6)

9. MEDITATION AND ACTIVITY: TWO SIDES OF THE SAME COIN

Although the effects of our meditation experiences will carry over into our everyday life, it will be a long time before we can meditate when we are stuck in traffic, or when we are washing the dishes, quite as effectively as we can on our meditation cushion.

The Bodhisattva's practice of meditation does not exclude external activity. We ourselves probably find that in order to meditate we have to find a quiet place, sit still, close our eyes, and practise some form of mental discipline. But the Bodhisattva should be able, as the scriptures repeatedly stress, to be immersed in *dhyāna* while at the same time carrying on with various activities. Not that the Bodhisattva suffers from a sort of split personality. What appear to us to be two contradictory things are one thing in the case of the Bodhisattva. Activity is the external aspect of meditation, and meditation is the inner dimension of activity; they are two sides of the same coin.

This will eventually be our aim too, but probably for a long time to come meditation will exclude external activity and vice versa. Although the effects of our meditation experiences will carry over into our everyday life, it will be a long time before we can meditate when we are stuck in traffic, or when we are washing the dishes, quite as effectively as we can on our meditation cushion.

From *The Bodhisattva Ideal* (1999, p.163)

10. A VERY DYNAMIC STATE

Even when we consider that we are in a skilful mental state, it isn't usually very skilful at all, is it?

If you describe meditation as the development of positive mental states, people could understand that to mean simply that you feel reasonably well-disposed towards other people, and your mind is moderately calm and quiet, but actually it means, or can mean, very much more than that. When you experience a *dhyāna* state, you are in a state of consolidated, heightened and intensified skilfulness. Even when we consider that we are in a skilful mental state, it isn't usually very skilful at all, is it? We're just mildly full of *mettā*, or our minds are not too restless, or we're moderately concentrated, or reasonably happy. But being in a skilful mental state is very very much more than that. All your energies are liberated, you experience very intense *mettā*, *karuṇā*, *muditā*, or *upekṣā*, and the experience is, as it were, consolidated. There are no gaps in it, no breaks or flaws, and your emotional positivity is at a very high pitch of intensity. Instead of just the odd skilful thought floating through your mind every few minutes, there's an uninterrupted succession, a whole stream of hundreds and thousands of skilful thoughts every instant, virtually. This is what is really meant by meditation in the sense of *samatha*.

We don't usually think of meditation in those terms, do we? But this is what it really is. In the state of meditation the mind is in a very active and powerful and dynamic state but absolutely positive, at least for the time being, a stream, an uninterrupted succession of positive mental states. Inasmuch as they're all positive, there's no conflict between them. That means that they're unified. It means the stream is flowing in one direction. There's no conflict of energies. *Mettā* doesn't conflict with *karuṇā*, does it? Nor does *muditā* conflict with *upekṣā*, and so on. So meditation isn't just meant to produce a gentle goodwill or a vague sense of uplift.

One has to try to convey a sense of exhilaration, emotional positivity, freedom, buoyancy, expansion, liveliness, joy. This is more of what the word 'meditation' covers. Otherwise, for most people, meditation means a dreamy state in which you drift along, not thinking of anything in particular, and 'spiritual' means something vaguely uplifting or even something somehow connected with spooks and ghosts. So we really have to use words carefully, and, more than that, make quite sure we are conveying to people what they really mean.

From a seminar on Trevor Ling's *The Buddha* (1976, pp.226-7)

11. MEDITATION IN A BUSY LIFE

It is very easy to think 'I'm too busy to meditate,' but if you make a definite resolve to start the day off with a period of meditation, you can stick to that almost regardless of circumstances.

Q: Presumably someone who is leading a very busy life will be at a disadvantage when it comes to their meditation.

Sangharakshita: I think there is no doubt about that, unless you have really trained yourself. It is possible, but you have to be very strict with yourself. It is very easy to think, 'I'm too busy to meditate,' but if you make a definite resolve to start the day with a period of meditation, you can stick to that almost regardless of circumstances. The danger is that people think that they have not got the time, when in fact that is not the case. It might very occasionally happen that you have to sacrifice that particular time, but I think that is rare if you organise your life well.

I don't think that it is impossible to combine a daily period of meditation with a very active life, provided that you go about it in the right way. For one thing, during the activity itself you must remain aware and alert and mindful. If you allow yourself to lose your mindfulness while engaged in activities, of course it will be difficult to meditate. But whatever you do, whether you are strolling around the garden or engaged in business negotiations, you must maintain awareness. It's necessary in all situations outside the situation of meditation itself.

Obviously you can't do more than a certain amount of meditation, and even if you do manage to have a good meditation every day and carry on with your normal duties, you will still need to go away from time to time and have a solitary retreat, or a week or a fortnight of nothing but meditation. If you aren't getting on very well with your meditation due to your duties and responsibilities, you will need to go on retreat all the more, and it's short-sighted not to make provision for that. It's counter-productive in the long run, because if your sources of inspiration dry up, what can you do, even in connection with your Dharma-related activities? They'll become merely activities and cease to have much relation to the Dharma.

Q: Do you have any general advice for those who are so busy with Dharma-related activities that their meditations are detrimentally affected?

S: If your meditations are detrimentally affected, either you must cut down on your Dharma-related activities or increase your meditation, or both. Or you must change your attitude to the way in which you work, or even your attitude to your meditation, or you must get away more often. Perhaps all these things. You need to review the whole situation quite carefully from all these different points of view. Possibly even – this is another possibility – you could change your type of meditation, depending on what you were doing before, your temperament and so on.

From a seminar on *The Forest Monks of Sri Lanka* (1985, pp.40-1)

12. ARE THERE PLACES THAT MEDITATION DOESN'T REACH?

Meditation would resolve things if you could get deeply enough into it, but very often people don't go deep enough for long enough.

Q: In my observation, many people have some real, authentic meditation experience, built up over years of practice, but it is set about by quite deeply rooted reactive patterns of behaviour which seem at odds with the meditation experience. Year after year these patterns seem to go untouched and unchanged. Are there areas – our communication with other people, for instance – that meditation doesn't affect and that therefore need to be tackled in other ways?

Sangharakshita: I think meditation would resolve things if you could get deeply enough into it, but very often people don't go deep enough for long enough. Sometimes one's problems may need to be tackled on their own level, as it were, bearing in mind that human beings are basically spiritual beings. Perhaps one's spiritual friends are the best people to do that, by pointing out to you things you can't see yourself; and perhaps in extreme cases you may even need some professional help.

Q: Do you think our spiritual friends do enough pointing out of our basic patterns?

S: Probably not. To be able to point out these patterns you have to know someone very well, you need a strong positive feeling for them, and they have to trust you. This implies a considerable degree of friendship. If one doesn't function in this way as a friend, that may be because one isn't sufficiently a friend. I think people could do a lot more for one another in this way.

From a seminar on the *White Lotus Sūtra* (1986, p.120)

13. MEDITATION VERSUS PSYCHOTHERAPY

Jung said once that of all the patients that had come to see him there wasn't one whose problem was not at bottom a religious one.

To consider the topic of meditation versus psychotherapy, we are obviously going to have to consider three things: the nature of meditation, the nature of psychotherapy, and the relation between the two. To speak of meditation versus psychotherapy suggests that whatever the relationship between them it is one of antagonism, so we will need to investigate the extent of this antagonism. We shall be considering all of this against the background of the Higher Evolution of the individual – that is to say the individual's development from simple consciousness to self-consciousness and from self-consciousness to what we have come to call Transcendental consciousness – and we will need to take into account some of the problems that it seems necessarily arise in the course of this development that I choose to call the Higher Evolution of the individual. We shall also be considering these topics against a background, unfortunately a rather dark background, of mental suffering, mental disorder, and mental disease.

First of all, what is meditation? It comprises three things. In the first place there is concentration, what is called in the eastern tradition 'fixing the mind on one point'. It may be a point inside us, it may be a point outside us, it may be a point located in or on the surface of our own body, or it may be a point situated outside, as it were, in space. But whether the point is inside or outside wherever it is situated, we almost invariably find that to concentrate the mind, to bring all the forces of the mind to bear on that one point, is extremely difficult, so much so that we are hardly ever concentrated in that sort of way. When we try to account for the fact that we are unable to keep our minds fixed on any one point for any length of time, whether it is the one point of the breath, or of the print we are reading, or the picture that we are looking at, we usually explain it by saying that there are too many distractions, too many other things luring away our minds insidiously, so that we are unable to keep up that one-pointedness of the mind. But when distractions arise or when we say a distraction arises, what does this mean? It means that our energies are not unified, they are not all pulling in the same direction. One part of us, as it were, wants us to concentrate, is trying to concentrate, wants to meditate, is trying to meditate, but there are quite big parts that don't want to meditate at all. So one's energies are divided. Some are pulling in one direction, others are pulling in another, and we are not able to concentrate on any one point. We are subject to distractions because not all our energies are available for the activity of concentration.

Real concentration, concentration in the full sense, concentration without even the possibility of distraction, thus means unification of all the energies of the psyche, bringing them all together into one focus of energy, bringing them all to bear on that one point. But we don't usually think of concentration in those terms. We usually think of it as a more or less forcible fixation of the conscious mind on the point concerned. We make up our minds, our conscious minds, that we are going to concentrate, that we are going to force the mind onto that point. But that isn't good enough. Distractions still arise, because all of our energies are not available. If we want to concentrate, we have to unify our psychic energies. It isn't a question of forcible fixation of consciousness, it is a question of unification of energies, even unification of interests. It is not just exerting willpower. If you grit your teeth and try hard enough, you will be able to concentrate for some time, but not for very long. Some distraction, sooner or later, is bound to come along.

Concentration, therefore, is much more a question of understanding that we do have a multiplicity of interests, that some of these interests are in conflict, that these sometimes conflicting interests share our psychic energy among them, and that it is for this reason that we are unable to concentrate for long upon any one thing. We like to think that we are as it were ourselves, that there is, as it were, just one of us. But this is not in fact so. We are not just one self but a whole series, a whole succession of selves, one popping up after another.

To put it in a slightly different manner, we can say that we are a bundle, a rather untidy bundle, even a heap of selves, of which only one is operative at any given time. We are not one unified completely integrated continuously operative self as we tend to assume – or rather, one of our selves tends to assume. The general problem is that of the integration of selves and fragments of selves; in other words, of the achievement of true selfhood, or true individuality. But in the context of meditation, the problem is that of unification, of integration of energies – in other words, achievement of true concentration. These two things, the achievement of true selfhood and the achievement of true concentration, are obviously quite closely related. We might even go so far as to say that they are different aspects of one and the same process. The levels of concentration it is possible to attain are in Buddhism traditionally known as the four *dhyānas*.

I have sometimes referred to the second of the three things comprising meditation as 'meditation proper', but in this context I'll call it the stage of intensification and expansion. With the attainment of concentration, with the unification of all one's energies, true individuality, at least on the ordinary empirical human level, has been achieved, but that is not the end, that is not enough. That individual must now grow, must now develop, and according to the Buddha's teaching, that individual grows and develops by passing through successively higher spheres or states, if you like, of existence. In as much as these are somewhat remote from the experience of most people, I'm just going to mention the names which Buddhism gives to these spheres, or these states.

The first is called the sphere of infinite space, or infinite extension; if you like, the sphere of the cosmos, the universe. The second is called the sphere of infinite consciousness, the consciousness that has no limit, that goes beyond all limits. The third is called the sphere of neither perception nor non-perception, in other words, where subject-object distinction begins to be transcended, and the fourth is called the sphere of nothingness, or nothing in particular, the sphere of one thing not being discriminated as a separate object from any other thing.

These four spheres, these four states, represent not only a growth, not only a development, not only an intensification, not only an expansion, of individuality, but also, paradoxically, a transcendence of individuality. It's rather as Sir Edwin Arnold puts it in *The Light of Asia*, when he says 'Foregoing self, the Universe grows "I"'.[94] The more you give up yourself, as it were, the more perfectly yourself do you become. Meditation in this sense marks the transition from the psychological to the metaphysical, or from the psychological to the Transcendental, and this brings us to the third and last of the three things comprising meditation.

I have sometimes called it contemplation. It is traditionally known in Buddhism as Insight or wisdom, or as the perfection of wisdom. And it consists simply in seeing existence, or seeing things exactly as they are. This is the simplest, but most difficult of all things to do: to see things just as they are, without addition, without subtraction, without falsification, without projection. It means seeing them free from all subjective conditionings whatsoever, free from all merely personal bias.

So this in brief is the meaning of meditation. It means in the first place the unification, and the integration, even the harmonization, of all one's psychic energies. This unification, this integration, leads to the achievement of true individuality, true selfhood, through the achievement of true concentration. And this experience of selfhood, of individuality, becomes more and more intense, and more and more positive; as it becomes more intense, it begins to expand; and the more it expands, the more it transcends itself. The more it transcends itself and its own limitations, the more it sees existence as it is; and the more it sees existence as it is the closer it is to reality. This, in a nutshell, is the whole process of meditation.

So, to take our second topic, what is psychotherapy? Psychotherapy is briefly defined as 'the treatment of disorders by psychological methods'. That's clear, but it's very general, not very detailed, so let's turn for a little help to Karl Jaspers. In his *General Psychopathology*, Jaspers defines psychotherapy as: 'The name given to all those methods of treatment that affect both psyche and body, by measures which proceed via the psyche. The co-operation of the patient is always required. Psychotherapy has application to those who suffer from the many types of personality disorder, psychopathies, also the mildly psychotic patients, to all people who feel ill, and suffer from their psychic states, and almost without exception to physical illnesses, which so often are overlaid with neurotic symptoms, and with which the personality must inwardly come to terms'. So this is Jasper's somewhat more comprehensive, even philosophical, definition of psychotherapy. He goes on to describe the various methods of influencing the psyche, which psychotherapy has at its disposal, classifying them as: methods of suggestion; cathartic methods; methods involving practice and training; methods of re-education; and finally, methods that address themselves to personality.

One of the best known and most fruitful kinds of psychotherapy is that known as psychoanalysis. Psychoanalysis began round about the turn of the twentieth century, with the discoveries of Freud, and according to Jaspers, it is one of the cathartic methods. Catharsis means simply 'purging', and in a psychological context it refers to the liberation, to the purging as it were, of repressed emotion. Of course, the great question is: How did the emotion come to be repressed? It was repressed, according to Freud because, putting it very generally, it was unacceptable to the conscious self. The conscious self didn't want it, didn't like it, as it were. Being unacceptable to the conscious self, incompatible with its attitudes, its beliefs, and so on, it was thrust out of consciousness. In other words, it became unconscious. This thrusting out of consciousness of the emotion which is not acceptable to the conscious self is itself not a conscious, but an unconscious, an automatic process,

This emotion which has been cast out from the heaven of consciousness may be repressed, it may be unconscious, but it is still alive, still active. According to Freud, and here he agrees very much with Buddhist psychological teaching, mental life is dynamic on every level. Being active, the repressed emotion can go on producing effects, even on the level of the conscious self, the conscious mind. But the conscious mind does not know what is producing these effects. It only knows that something seems to be going wrong, something seems to be working against it, counteracting its wishes and desires, its intentions and ideas. The repressed emotions themselves of course remain all this time unconscious.

All this means that there's a split – not only a split, but a conflict. In the first place there is a split between the conscious self and the unconscious self, or between the conscious mind and the unconscious mind, or between consciousness and the unconscious. And in the second place there is a conflict between the desires and intentions of the conscious self, and the desires and the intentions of the unconscious self, or between emotions which have been repressed and emotions which have not been repressed. Freud speaks of a conflict between what he calls the Pleasure Principle, which dominates the unconscious mind, and what he calls the Reality Principle, which directs the conscious mind. Putting it more simply, we can say that the conflict is between what we would like to do and what we are obliged to do on account of the circumstances in which we find ourselves. This conflict, which can go very deep and be very intense, finds expression in various ways. It finds expression in dreams, which are very often just simple wish-fulfilment, and in what Freud called 'the psychopathology of everyday life' – for example in the little slips of the tongue which express the opposite of one's conscious ideas and intentions. It expresses itself also in the symptoms of the various kinds of mental disorder.

The method of treatment employed in psychoanalysis is what is known as continuous free association. It sounds very simple. The patient just goes on talking about, well, anything that comes into his or her head. Eventually, after talking for quite a long time – it may be days, or weeks, or even months – he or she eventually approaches the ideas or incidents associated with the repressed emotion. When that stage is reached, then, with the encouragement of the analyst, he or she recalls the ideas or incidents, experiences the repressed emotion, discharges the energy it contains, and comes to some sort of terms with it. In this way the catharsis takes place. What was unconscious has become conscious. This process may take not just weeks or months, but years. And of course according to Freud the repressed emotion is usually, perhaps invariably, associated with sex.

Psychotherapy is a fairly recent development, and psychoanalysis is a more recent development still, but they already play an important part in the lives of very many people, especially in the West. Some well-to-do people have a psychotherapist as a matter of course, just as they have a doctor and a solicitor. In some circles, the psychotherapist has replaced the priest. The priest hasn't got very much to do these days. Sometimes, even the priest goes to the psychotherapist, and more rarely, the psychotherapist goes to the priest, at least for some discussion.

It is clear that psychotherapy has come into existence for a reason. It didn't just drop down out of the clouds. It came into existence because more and more people are becoming mentally ill – in Jaspers' phrase, 'feeling ill, and suffering from their psychic state'. This sort of thing is a characteristic feature of modern life, of modern society. I recently happened to read in a newspaper a tiny little item – apparently no one considered it very important – to the effect that in the course of the preceding year not less than five thousand young people had committed suicide. Now obviously they didn't commit suicide because they were happy. They were suffering from their psychic state, so badly that death was preferable to life on those terms. Five thousand is quite a large number, but the number of those who suffer in a lesser degree, or less acutely, than the five thousand young people who committed suicide is even greater. Perhaps it runs into hundreds of thousands, even into millions. Freud said that everybody is neurotic to some extent, and the Buddha went even further, saying that all worldly people, that is to say all who are not Enlightened, are mad.

Where are all these people to go for help? There are of course the priests – they were first in the field. So far as the West is concerned, you can go to the whole range, from Billy Graham to the Archbishop of Canterbury. And then you've got all kinds of psychotherapists and many schools of psychoanalysts. You've got the Freudians, and the Jungians, the Adlerians, the Neo-Freudians, and the Kleinians, and the Reichians, and the Frommians and so on. And more recently, at least in many of the larger metropolitan centres in the West, various oriental meditation teachers have appeared, from the Maharishi downwards, or upwards, as the case may be! You pay your money and you take your choice. But which shall it be? Shall it be the local vicar, or Ronald Laing? Shall it be electric shock treatment or Zen? Shall it be meditation or psychotherapy?

This is the sort of question that confronts any person who suffers from his or her psychic state. It is also a question which may confront, at least at times, anyone who is devoted to the spiritual life and has been making some progress. And with this question, we come to the third and last of our topics: the nature of the relation between meditation and psychotherapy, and the nature of any antagonism between them. Now let me say at once, to reassure those who don't like conflict, that this antagonism is only partial, and it arises much less out of the intrinsic natures of meditation and psychotherapy than out of their respective contexts. Meditation and psychotherapy have in fact a great deal in common.

Meditation in the narrower sense of the term, including simply integration of the psychic energies, and intensification and expansion of selfhood, can even be included in psychotherapy. We saw that according to Jaspers, psychotherapy has at its disposal various means of influencing the psyche, and these means he classifies into five groups. The third group is that of methods involving 'practice and training', and here Jaspers specifically includes 'breathing exercises'. One might say that other methods of concentrating the mind could equally well be included. Again, referring back to Jaspers, psychotherapy has application to all people who 'feel ill, and suffer from their psychic state', and Buddhism traditionally begins with the fact of suffering, not because it is pessimistic, but because it is concerned with experience, with actual life, with real problems.

Suffering is in fact the first of the Four Noble Truths, which are the general framework of Buddhist teaching. The first truth is that suffering exists; the second truth, that the cause of suffering is craving; the third truth is that of the cessation of suffering, which involves the cessation of craving, and the fourth truth is the way leading to the cessation of suffering, through the cessation of craving, by following what is called 'The Noble Eightfold Path'. It is significant that the formula of the Four Noble Truths is said by many scholars to be based on an ancient Indian medical formula: a formula of disease, its cause, health, and a way to the cessation of disease and restoration of health.

Suffering in Buddhism is also the first of what we call the twelve positive *nidānas*. That is to say, the experience of suffering is the first stage of the spiral path leading ultimately to Enlightenment. Buddhism says in effect that the higher life, the Higher Evolution of humanity, starts with the experience of suffering, or if you like, with the realization of suffering.

In the therapeutic situation, there is on the one hand the therapist, on the other the patient; or, in psychoanalysis, the analyst and the analysand. In much the same way, traditionally, in the case of meditation, there is the master, and there is the disciple. In both cases, the relationship is not just formal, not just a matter of giving teaching or advice, but existential; not static but dynamic. Moreover, people practising meditation in the narrower sense and those undergoing therapy or analysis, often experience the same curative symptoms. They may for instance, experience intense anxiety, anger, fear, sexual desire, sweating, nausea, palpitations and so on. The fact that there are these common symptoms, at least sometimes, would seem to indicate that a similar kind of process is going on in meditation in this narrower sense, and in psychotherapy or psychoanalysis.

From these observations, which are just illustrative, it seems clear that the antagonism between meditation and psychotherapy is only partial, because they have indeed quite a lot in common. At the same time, it must be recognized that there is an antagonism, or at least a vitally important difference. The difference is this. So far as Buddhism is concerned, meditation forms part of a complete and coherent system of spiritual self-development. It is one stage in a path leading from a state of ignorance to Enlightenment, from simple consciousness to absolute consciousness. Moreover this system, or this path, represents the direct practical application to human existence of a whole philosophy of existence, a total view of reality. This philosophy, this view, is not the product of rational thought; rather, it is the expression in conceptual terms of the nature of existence, or the nature of reality, or the state of things as they are, as revealed to the enlightened mind, or the absolute consciousness of a Buddha.

Psychotherapy is not part of a complete and coherent scheme of spiritual self-development. It has no philosophy of existence, no total view of reality. What it does have is a number of methods, and a number of theories associated with those methods. The methods appear to work, at least sometimes and with some people, and some of the theories appear to be true. But they do not between them add up to anything coherent and complete, either practically or theoretically, either philosophically or therapeutically. They do not add up to anything within the framework of which one can live out one's entire life, pursue the whole path of spiritual self-development. They do not constitute a framework that would have to be abandoned only when no framework of any kind was any longer needed – in other words when the full human potential had been realized or Enlightenment attained.

Therefore, if anybody who suffered from their psychic state was to come to me and ask whether he should take up meditation or go for psychotherapy, I would reply 'take up meditation'. In other words, I would advise taking up the practice which is part of a complete scheme of spiritual self-development, associated with a philosophy of existence. This is not to say that at the moment a particular method of meditation will necessarily help that particular person more than a particular method of psychotherapy. It is only to say that as a human being, capable of evolving, in the long run you stand to gain more from and through meditation than from psychotherapy.

This leads us to a few objections, counter-objections and qualification. It may be pointed out that some psychotherapists are interested in meditation, even practise meditation, have indeed incorporated meditation among their methods of treatment. So it may be said that there is no need to go to a meditation teacher. You can just go to the psychotherapist. In any case, the psychotherapist is a much more modern and scientific type of person. He speaks a language that we can all understand. There is no mystification. There are not even any mantras.

It is true that some psychotherapists do utilize traditional oriental meditation methods to some extent, but they utilize them only as psychological exercises, and this deprives them of at least half their value and significance, because the full value of these methods depends upon their being pursued within the total context to which they traditionally belong. We can verify this for ourselves in our own experience. Suppose, for example, we are practising the 'mindfulness of breathing' exercise. Suppose we practise it on our own in an ordinary room, just for the sake of calming our minds, enabling us to get through the day and work, whatever our work may be, more effectively. We will certainly derive benefit, even a lot of benefit, from practising the exercise in this way. But suppose then we practise the same method in a group. Suppose we sit with a number of other people, not just anywhere but in a shrine, a place which is especially dedicated to the purpose of meditation. Suppose that in the shrine there is a sort of altar, and suppose that on the altar there is an image, a figure of the Buddha, reminding us of what we are aiming at, what we are trying to achieve, what we are trying to realize. And suppose that also on the altar there are flowers, suppose candles have been lit, and suppose before getting down to the practise of the mindfulness of breathing exercise we do some chanting, maybe in a language we don't even understand. And suppose when we come to do the exercise itself we do it not just to concentrate the mind, but also to develop positive emotion, to develop Insight, to gain a glimpse of reality, in other words so that we can evolve, so that we can grow, so that eventually we can become enlightened, so that eventually we can become like the Buddha, can become Buddhas ourselves. If we practise in this way, with these associations, in this traditional context, then the overall effect of that same exercise is very different. In a sense it is the same practice, the same method, but in that wider and richer context it possesses a far greater significance, and consequently we get far more out of it.

The same principle applies in other ways. Psychotherapy is said to be applicable to all those who feel ill and suffer from their psychic state. But what is illness? How do we know when we are ill? We can't answer this question without first determining what health is. Illness is illness only in relation to health. Furthermore, we can't determine what health is in the case of a human being without understanding what a human being is, without understanding the nature of human existence, the nature of life itself, the nature of the whole evolutionary process. And this sort of understanding psychotherapy does not have, does not even profess to have. It doesn't have it because it has no philosophy of existence. Indeed, we can press matters even further. People suffer from their psychic state, and some at least, perhaps quite a large number, suffer because their lives as human beings, their lives here and now in society –with their friends, with their families, at work and so on – seem to have no significance, no meaning, no overall purpose, no real goal towards which they can aim. In other words, what they are suffering from is really the lack of a philosophy of existence, a philosophy of life. To put it in the crudest possible traditional terms, they are suffering from lack of religion.

Jung said once that of all the patients that had come to see him there wasn't one whose problem was not at bottom a religious one. What we need is not so much therapy, not so much a cure, as a philosophy of existence in which we can believe, which we can accept as truth, a philosophy that will give significance to our life, within the general framework of which we can live and grow and develop. Psychotherapy as such doesn't give this. But does this mean that psychotherapy is useless? Does it mean that no one should ever go to a psychotherapist or a psychoanalyst? Are all the analysts' couches to be left vacant? Not only that, what of the various methods of treatment discovered by psychotherapy? Many of these methods are extremely useful. Are they to be discarded altogether? Or is it suggested that they should be appropriated by the teacher of meditation?

I am not proposing that all the psychotherapists should at once be put out of work. In any case, there aren't enough meditation teachers to take their place. But I do think that teachers of traditional types of meditation should know more about modern methods of psychotherapy: not only know about them but be able to use them, not in a haphazard fashion but understanding exactly what part they can play within the total context of the Higher Evolution.

But it is time to rise above any antagonism between meditation and psychotherapy, even above any agreement. It is time to make a constructive suggestion: an appeal for synthesis. We have been concerned with meditation versus psychotherapy against a background of mental suffering and against the background of the Higher Evolution of the individual. But there is a wider background still: the background of the Higher Evolution of humanity.

What I have come to call the Higher Evolution represents a complete restatement in contemporary terms of the essentials of the Buddha's teachings. Indeed, we may even claim that in principle it represents a restatement of all that is essential, all that is truly significant, in human culture and religion. But this restatement is theoretical. What we need is a practical counterpart to the theoretical restatement – and this practical counterpart is what I call the 'dynamics of the Higher Evolution'. Ideally, the dynamics of the Higher Evolution should include whatever traditional methods of concentration, meditation and so on are still valid and useful. (Some, I am convinced, are no longer useful, no longer valid, at least in the West.) It will also utilize modern therapeutic techniques. In other words what we really need is a synthesis, a synthesis that will be both theoretical and practical, both philosophy and religion. The world very badly needs such a synthesis, and to this end I feel that both meditation and psychotherapy must co-operate.

Such co-operation has already started in a small way, theoretically. Jung's interest in Eastern religions is well known; Fromm was familiar with Zen; and all the activities even of the movement I founded can be seen as such a contribution. I am convinced that such a synthesis will constitute the philosophy and the religion, and possibly the art and the science, of the future, and that it is on the foundation of such a synthesis that humanity must start building.

From *Meditation versus Psychotherapy* (1970, unpublished lecture)

2 Going on solitary retreat

In June the rainy season began. The grey clouds came rolling up from the plains, first of all infiltrating the valley of the Teesta in loose, detached masses, then moving in across the hills in a solid wall of rain that at times blotted out the entire landscape. For days on end Mount Kanchenjunga could not be seen. Instead, even when the sky cleared, there was only thick white cloud piled up against the horizon. Though the rain fell heavily enough at times, the rainy season was much less severe in the hills than in the plains. In between the downpours the sun was hot and bright, and the sky intensely blue, though the thick white cloud hardly ever moved aside to reveal the snows of Mount Kanchenjunga sparkling through the rain-washed air. It was my fourth year in India. Already I had learned to love the rainy season. I loved the heavy drumming sound of the rain on the roof. I loved the sense of green things thirstily drinking up the rain and growing as they did so. Above all, I loved the way in which the rain insulated one from the rest of the world, weaving around one a silver-grey cocoon of silence within which one could sit, hour after hour, and quietly muse. No wonder the Buddha had advised his monks not to wander about during the rainy season but to remain in one place, whether in a mountain cave, a woodland shrine, or a shed at the bottom of somebody's garden! No wonder the rainy season had come to be regarded, in the course of centuries, as a time of spiritual retreat – a time of more intensive study of the scriptures and more intensive practice of meditation!

From *Facing Mount Kanchenjunga* (1991, p.42)

1. CAN YOU GET BY ON YOUR OWN?

A solitary retreat shows you the extent to which you are dependent on the company of other people for your positivity and your sense of who you are.

While it is good to learn to be vigilant and aware within the jumble of impressions and opinions that is modern life, we do need some respite from the bombardment. Even within the most positive and inspiring spiritual community, it is easy to start functioning as a group member rather than as a true individual, becoming dependent on other members of the community in one way or another and to that extent using them, albeit not consciously. This is why it is important to get away on your own from time to time – on solitary retreat, if you can. When you are on your own you can take stock of things and assess your relationship with other people. Can you get by on your own? Can your spiritual practice survive without the support of other people? What happens when you are setting your own programme? A solitary retreat shows you the extent to which you are dependent on the company of other people for your positivity and your sense of who you are, including your attitudes and views. If you can demonstrate to yourself that you can function at least for a while without support, you will be able to interact much more positively with other people.

Setting up the conditions for a solitary retreat is simple. You seek out a place to stay in a quiet and preferably remote part of the country, take a supply of food, and spend your time meditating, reflecting, and studying your reactions to being on your own. Community or family life needs such a counterbalance of self-reliance to make it work. On solitary retreat you can meditate or read or do whatever you want whenever you want, without reference to anyone else. You can let your energies flow freely, not just in the predetermined channels of habit or circumstance. A solitary retreat doesn't have to be long – a month is fine, or a week, or a weekend if that's all you can manage.

Even if you find that blissful meditations elude you, there is still much to be gained from a solitary retreat. As well as giving you the chance to experience what it might be like to be truly self-sufficient, both physically and mentally, it also gives you time and space to think creatively about the situation to which you will be returning and in particular to consider what distractions are most likely to arise. For one person the major distraction might be work: they might work so much that there is not enough time left for meditation, study, or contact with spiritual friends. For another person it might be the excitement of city life, while someone else might end up slumped in front of the television. All these things can be insistent and seductive in their appeal. If you don't plan your strategy in advance, they will catch you unawares and rob you of a week's hard-won mindfulness in a day. But if you are realistic about your weaknesses and go back into the world with a positive attitude, this need not happen.

From *Living with Awareness* (2003, pp.100-1)

2. CONSULT YOUR OWN EXPERIENCE

If you are a healthy human being, you will want to get away from time to time; it will be an actual need, in a quite healthy objective sense, for you to get away and to be really on your own.

Q: Maybe we don't send people away enough to consult their own experience, in the way that in one of the stories about Milarepa, he sent away the young shepherd to find out the colour and shape of his mind.[95]

Sangharakshita: Well, there are difficulties. In Tibet there are lots of mountains and solitary places to which young shepherds could go – not that we get many young shepherds coming along to our meditation classes anyway! Maybe it is significant that Milarepa's disciple is a young shepherd. After all, how would he be spending his time? Grazing his sheep in the uplands somewhere, with not a soul for miles and miles. So even as a shepherd he would have plenty of time for thought and reflection. But in the modern West it is not easy to go off and reflect on things for months together. If you get the chance, perhaps you need to keep things simple: just reflect, and maybe keep a notebook. Don't read, not even your favourite Shelley or D.H. Lawrence, or Virginia Woolf or Barbara Cartland! Just take yourself and perhaps a notebook.

Q: Perhaps at some point people will be able to go away for a number of years on solitary retreat.

S: I think it wouldn't be a bad idea in some cases, but they have got to be capable of doing it well. It is not just whiling away your time, it's not like going to a Greek island and sunbathing. I think you would have to go away as a relatively mature person, having read a lot, even thought a lot, known a lot, and just spend time reflecting on what you know and trying to deepen your experience: not just your experience of meditation in the technical sense but your whole experience of life, your whole experience of yourself.

I have begun to wonder what sort of understanding people have got of the nature of the solitary retreat. I think at least some people have got rather strange ideas about it. One person told me that during his solitary retreat he was watching TV, and he seemed to think that quite normal. He was watching it every day. And somebody else wrote to me, and she seemed to think it was quite normal on your solitary retreat to receive mail from all your friends back home, even though you were only away for a couple of weeks, and to visit various people in the neighbourhood and have tea with them, and even outings with them, all on your solitary retreat! All this was related to me in a completely naive, open way, as if to suggest that that's all part of a solitary retreat; you were just away somewhere different. So has the understanding of the nature of a solitary retreat changed? Am I out of touch? I can understand people going away on holiday for a quiet couple of weeks. I am not saying it is wrong to go away to a quiet place, do a bit of reading, see a few people; if that is what you need, fair enough. But my understanding of a solitary retreat is that you are literally solitary, not seeing anybody else at all and concentrating only on meditation and perhaps a bit of Dharma study, not just ordinary reading, and the rest of the time just doing nothing, being mindful. That is what is really meant by 'solitary retreat'.

Choose a place, if possible, where there aren't any local people; not on the edge of a village, but somewhere out on the moors, where no one can see you, no one knows that you are there. If someone is, say, supplying you with milk, make it clear that you are there to be on your own. Otherwise well-meaning people, not understanding, may want to cheer you up and give you a bit of company. It may not occur to them that you have come there because you want to be on your own. Perhaps people find it very difficult to imagine that anyone should actually want to be alone; and they may feel like having a chat, anyway, so along they come, and say, 'I hope I'm not disturbing you' ...

Q: Do you think that there is a place for the traditional three-year retreat?

S: Yes. Perhaps one need not think so rigidly in terms of three years, three months, three weeks, three days and three hours; but yes, a long, genuinely solitary retreat, devoted almost exclusively to meditation and Dharma study, would be a good idea – at least for those who have prepared well for such a retreat.

Q: Could you say something about the role of the solitary retreat in the whole range of practice?

S: I think you need to be alone sometimes. It is quite essential for every human being, ideally, to be alone for some part of every day. It can be difficult to arrange, but I think you certainly need to go away and experience yourself independently of your interaction with other people. Usually, we know and experience ourselves only to the extent that we are interacting with other people. We can't separate out what is just us, what is ours. I think we need to be able to do that; we need to be able to breathe, almost, sometimes. Especially if you live in a city, it is very difficult to get away from other people and from their influence on you in one way or another. So first of all, you need to get away and experience yourself by yourself. I think you need to do that before you can start deepening your experience of yourself very much. This is essential to the leading of a balanced human life, not to speak of spiritual life. If you are a healthy human being, you will want to get away from time to time; it will be an actual need, in a quite healthy objective sense, for you to get away and to be really on your own. If you can't do this, or don't want to do it, I think you need to ask yourself why not.

Q: Could you say something about preparation for a solitary retreat?

S: As far as possible, go off without having anything on your mind that is going to trouble you while you are away. Certainly don't take work away with you to do, or even things to think about of a practical organizational nature. Once you are on retreat, you should not have to think about anything that you have left behind at all; just put it completely out of your mind. You must be able to do that to get the full benefit from the solitary retreat. You mustn't go away with any worries or any backlog of work that you have to think about, much less still things you have to do. And ideally you should not arrive for the solitary retreat straight from work; well, that holds true for any retreat. You should arrive sufficiently rested, though in the case of a solitary retreat it may be a little difficult, because you may have had a long journey to get there. But certainly you shouldn't arrive worn out from weeks and weeks of overwork. That is not the best way of starting a solitary retreat. You should plan in advance: take the things that you will need, or make arrangements for supplies to be delivered, so that during the solitary retreat itself you don't have to think about these things. It's all just common sense, really.

From a seminar on the *Jewel Ornament of Liberation*
(Tuscany 1985, pp.131-6)

3. IT'S NOT WHAT YOU DO, IT'S THE WAY THAT YOU DO IT

Try to take the self you experience on solitary retreat back with you into the world, and into your relations and communications with other people.

> *Once having experienced spiritual illumination, commune with it in solitude, relinquishing the worldly activities of the multitude.*[96]

Sangharakshita: This precept introduces the question of the solitary retreat. What do you think the attitude of most people is to solitary retreats? They are quite popular nowadays, it seems, but why? What do you think people's motives are? What do you think they get out of them?

Q: I think some people go to learn more about themselves, just to get in touch with some aspect of their conditioning, to see it more clearly, see how they react when they don't have their everyday life around them.

S: Do you think you can see your reactions more clearly when away from other people?

Q: No, not all reactions. Not reactions to other people.

S: Right, yes. So what is it that emerges more clearly in solitude than it does when you are with other people?

Q: You are in a natural, non-reactive state. I think that most of us, when we are in contact with other people, are to some extent reacting, and that creates a tension and an anxiety, which removes us from our more confident and more natural and assured sense of well-being.

S: But don't you think it would be a rather odd state of affairs in which we lost our confidence when we were with other people, but we felt confident when we were on our own? That doesn't sound very positive.

Q: You lose self-consciousness, to some extent.

S: Yes, that is true, but that could be both positive and negative. No, what I was thinking of was the projective type of relationship or reaction. When you're on your own, you have an opportunity of studying your mental state, and you realize that it is something that belongs to or pertains to you. It is not something that is to do with other people; certainly not the people with whom you are at present in contact. For instance, suppose you are on solitary retreat and you feel really angry – not with any particular person, you just feel angry, but you feel that you want to direct that anger towards somebody. Then perhaps you realize that this is your normal state. Usually you get angry with somebody and say that he makes you angry, it's his fault; if only he wasn't around, you wouldn't become angry. But then you find, to your surprise and dismay, perhaps, that on solitary retreat you feel just the same; in fact you'd rather like there to be somebody around so that you could get angry with them. So then you recognize that it isn't that other people are making you angry – the anger is inherent within you. This you can certainly learn on solitary retreat, and you might find it difficult to learn it if you were actually in contact with other people. And it's similar with other emotions.

Q: Don't you think that perhaps the best time to go on solitary retreat is after a retreat with others, where you've got into a positive state of mind? I think we tend to think of going away on solitary retreats as like running away from a situation, having a bit of space for oneself. That may have its uses, but ideally one would go away when one was in a very healthy, clear state.

S: I think it's better not to go away on solitary retreat when you feel very tired or dispirited. Sometimes you need a holiday or change of scene rather than a solitary retreat. You should go away for a solitary retreat when you feel really good. Then you can make positive use of your retreat. Certainly don't go when you are exhausted. If you're going on solitary retreat for a month, it's no good spending the first two weeks recovering and getting back your health and strength. That shouldn't be the main function of the retreat. You should be in reasonably good condition when you go on solitary retreat, so that you can take full advantage of it.

When you're in contact with people, however positively, much of the time you are expending energy in talking. If you're on solitary retreat the mere fact that you're not talking means you're conserving energy. As you conserve more and more energy, it builds up and leads to a sort of joy which perhaps normally you don't experience, and you experience yourself then in a rather different way: not only full of energy but joyful, clear, aware, bright. In that way you intensify the experience of yourself. So perhaps it isn't such a good thing to think of going on solitary retreat in order to get away from it all, and get away from other people – that sounds a bit negative. It's better to think of going in order to have that more intensified experience of yourself. Then you can go back and interact with other people in a more intense, more genuine way: being more truly and more fully yourself. Try to take the self you experience on solitary retreat back with you into the world, and into your relations and communications with other people.

Q: How long do you think a solitary retreat needs to be to have the desired effect?

S: It depends on the person. For some people a few hours or a day or two might be sufficient. Others might need a month, or longer. One can't really generalize. But it would be good if people could give themselves a long enough period to experience something of that sort, and go back after the solitary retreat not just rested and refreshed but inspired.

I think it's a question of calling things by their right names. If you are just going away for a quiet couple of weeks' holiday, say so. Don't say 'I'm going away on solitary retreat'. It's as though you feel a need to make it official, so you can give yourself a legitimate excuse to go away. Who could possibly object to your going away on solitary retreat? After all, you're going to be meditating most of the time, and reading good books. But subconsciously you may not really be wanting to do that; you may just want a holiday. You call it a solitary retreat to make it sound acceptable; but you know quite well that you're going to do your meditation in the morning and, yes, probably in the evening too, because you'd do that anyway; but you're not going to be doing very much in between. You know, or at least you half-know, that you're just going to potter around and maybe wash a shirt in the morning and do a bit of cooking, and maybe stroll along to the shops, or go for a little walk, and have a nice early night and read in bed. That's not really a solitary retreat, is it? If you need that, fine; there's no reason why you shouldn't have it. But I detect a tendency to use this term solitary retreat rather too loosely; because clearly it's a highly respectable activity!

If you need a holiday, fair enough. Just make your needs known quite openly and honestly. But what happens is, I suspect, that people feel guilty about enjoying themselves, so they don't feel quite happy about announcing 'I want to go away on holiday'. Perhaps they think they wouldn't be allowed to, or that they might be told rather sternly, 'There are no holidays in the spiritual life.' But there is certainly room for a solitary retreat, no one could object to that; so that's the way they put it. They're not consciously practising any deception; they just don't allow themselves to think too clearly about it. But they certainly don't have a definite intention of having a real solitary retreat and really getting in contact with themselves and experiencing inner clarity and luminosity. They just want a bit of a change and a rest and an easy time. Being on their own is the price that they have to pay for that, as it were. But they think that, so long as they are on their own, that counts as a solitary retreat, regardless of what they do during those two or three or four weeks.

Q: Does a solitary retreat need a particular format, or a daily programme?

S: It may. I suggest that you start off the solitary retreat with a definite format, unless you feel a need just to rest for a day or two. I suggest, for instance, six sessions of meditation during the day. If, after a week or two, you feel that you can sustain the necessary level of mindfulness and emotional positivity and devotion without that regular format, don't hesitate to drop it. But the main difference between the solitary retreat proper and the other forms of going away by yourself is that on the solitary retreat, whether spontaneously or with the help of a definite programme, you are primarily concerned with experiencing yourself with a higher degree of intensity and clarity and emotional positivity than you usually do, and the whole retreat is geared to that.

Q: So it's not just what you do but the way that you do it. You could have a solitary retreat where you didn't do a lot of meditation but you were getting in touch with yourself quite deeply.

S: Yes. And on the other hand, you might have a very regular programme and follow it faithfully, but in a dull, uninspired way out of a sense of duty. Then you might remain on a very dull, pedestrian level even though you'd been faithfully doing all these things. One has to see what is actually happening. Sometimes you have to give yourself a few days to feel your way into things. One can't lay down any hard and fast rules, but just say that the main function of the solitary retreat is to enable you to experience yourself in that more intensified manner.

Q: Do you think that the surroundings are very important – for example, whether the countryside is beautiful?

S: I wouldn't say it's all that important. I think different people attach different degrees of importance to it.

From the third seminar on *Precepts of the Gurus* (1979, pp.117-23)

4. IS GOING ON SOLITARY RETREAT ESCAPISM?

We don't realize the extent to which we pander to our own unskilful reactions or unskilful mental states.

Sangharakshita: I think usually we don't realize the extent to which we pander to our own unskilful reactions or unskilful mental states. In small subtle ways they are being pandered to all the time, and this is why we keep in a reasonably good mood. But when we go away on solitary retreat, there is very much less of that sort of thing. You can see it with regard to things like food, and members of the opposite sex. When you are away on solitary retreat, so many of these things are removed. You are just left with the bare unskilful reaction carried over from your contacts with those things in the past, and you've no other work to do except to deal with those. So the situation is much more acute than everyday life.

Q: Does that not presuppose a need for a certain degree of emotional positivity and integration before going on a solitary retreat? Otherwise the trauma of the situation might be too much. You might be confronted with all these desires and be unable to deal with them.

S: I think most people who decide to go away on a solitary retreat will already have experienced some degree of integration, otherwise they wouldn't even think of going away on solitary retreat. But if you haven't been away on solitary retreat before, don't go for long. I usually suggest just a week, to begin with, and if that goes well consider later on going away for two or three weeks and possibly even a month after that. Don't plunge straight into a long solitary retreat if you haven't done one before.

It is a very good thing to experience the strength of one's own unskilful reactions. One can do that much more easily and much more successfully in the course of a solitary retreat. Do you see the way in which we usually feed our unskilful tendencies? It may not be anything big or dramatic, it's lots of little things. For instance, just to take a very ordinary one, say contact with members of the opposite sex. Maybe you don't have a relationship, let's say. But there are attractive people around you all the time, you're in constant contact with them, you see them, you talk to them, you hear their voices on the radio, see their pictures everywhere, so that unskilful tendency within you, to the extent that it is unskilful, is being constantly nourished in all these little ways which keep you satisfied to some extent. When you go away on solitary retreat, that's all cut off. You might hear just the voice of a milkmaid or a shepherd in the distance, and that's all. Maybe not even that. That sort of situation enables you to study your own mind and your own mental reactions, skilful and unskilful, in much greater detail, much more thoroughly, and to do something about them.

Q: You could say then that it's really the hero that runs away.

S: Yes. If you wanted to turn the tables on people, you could say, 'Are you telling me that going on retreat is escapism? It's you that's running away. How can you spend a whole evening watching telly and then talk to other people about escapism? Who are the escapists?' Maybe one should be assertive rather than apologetic. They've just got their sense of direction all wrong. You're running to confront the enemy. It's they who are running away.

To come back to this question of the satisfaction of unskilful mental states, I've given one rather prominent example, but don't let that mislead you; the same sort of thing is happening in lots of other ways. We remain in what we think is a reasonably skilful, happy, good-tempered frame of mind, not because we have any real positivity in the sense of really skilful mental states within us – states of *mettā, karuṇā, muditā* and *upekkhā*, for instance – but just because we are getting all these little satisfactions most of the time. Take those away, and it's a very different story. Going away on solitary retreat helps us to realize that it's the good regular meals, the friendly gregarious contact with other people, the constant titillation of the senses in various ways, that keeps us happy much of the time, not our spiritual ideals. Someone might have the reputation of being good-natured, friendly, not losing his temper, always being pleasant; but it may not be because of any really positive inner experiences, it's just because of his inner state of general sense-satisfaction. That is a quite different thing. Persevering in solitude enables us to appreciate this fact.

Q: Do you mean that one should deliberately deprive oneself of sense-satisfaction?

S: As an experiment, yes. This is what you do in respect of certain sense satisfactions when you go away on solitary retreat. After all, what is the essence of experiment? It is to control the situation. Scientific experiments are done in the laboratory because you can control the situation, you can determine what factors are to be there and what are not to be there, so that you can work out what is causing what. It's just the same when you go on solitary retreat: you eliminate quite a large number of factors, so you can just deal with a limited number of factors and find out how they work, what is causing what. If it's other people who are making you angry all the time, well, once they're not there. You shouldn't be angry at all. If you're still angry, you will realize that it isn't due to other people; the source of the anger is in your own mind. So one can look upon the solitary retreat situation as a sort of psychological cum spiritual laboratory. You go away to carry out various experiments so that you can get a better working knowledge of your mind and your mental reactions.

Most people notice in the course of a solitary retreat that they go through various phases, and it's quite interesting to follow these and try to understand what is happening and why. There might be an initial phase of boredom, and then a phase of feeling very refreshed, and then maybe a phase of wanting to sleep a lot. Then you might have a phase of having very good meditations, and then a phase of feeling violent emotions, and then maybe another phase of restlessness, and after that a phase of good positive states and good meditations. In this way one can trace one's own successive experiences.

From the third seminar on *Precepts of the Gurus* (1979, pp.205-8)

5. SLEEPINESS IN SOLITUDE

Sometimes you go to sleep on solitary retreat not out of real drowsiness, but to escape the retreat situation.

> *Should there be great drowsiness, persevere in thine efforts to invigorate the intellect (or to control the mind).*[97]

Sangharakshita: It's very often said that there are two great enemies, two great distractions as regards meditation, especially when you go away into solitude. The first is drowsiness, and the second is not just distraction but mental restlessness and disturbance and over-abundance of thoughts, hectic, feverish mental activity. But this precept is concerned with drowsiness. So what is drowsiness, especially 'great drowsiness'? It's an inclination to sleep, but why should you get sleepy? Has anyone had this experience on solitary retreats?

Q: Yes, very much, for the first few days. You feel dragged down into an almost subterranean state. It's really difficult just to remain awake.

S: But why? What is happening? To what extent is it positive, to what extent is it not so positive?

Q: It seems to be positive in the sense that you are trying to contact some deeper source of energy. What seemed to be happening was that my consciousness would be sort of sucked out into the environment. That's what it felt like. It was an effort to remain clear and bright, and have sufficient energy to keep myself as a separate identity.

S: It's almost as though, in that case, there was no individuality, apart from the purely reactive individuality that one has built up in the course of one's dealings with other people. When the stimulation of contact with them is no longer there, there is nothing to sustain that false identity, that false personality. You feel tired because the task of keeping it in existence is entirely on your side, and it becomes an impossible job; and you feel less and less bright.

Q: Is that the same sort of drowsiness as some people experience – I experience it myself – at certain times of day, the afternoon, for instance?

S: This is said to be due to purely physiological, metabolic reasons. Practitioners of Ayurvedic medicine say that in the early part of the day, up to midday, the energies within the body are ascending, and then you feel bright and lively. But they start descending in the middle of the afternoon, and then you feel drowsy and not very energetic. Whether this is an explanation or just a description in other terms, it is difficult to say. But it does seem to have physiological reasons.

Coming back to this drowsiness in connection with meditation, especially on solitary retreat, I think what happens with some people is that they contact a level of tiredness that they have not until then allowed themselves to be conscious of. Actually they had been quite tired before they left to go on retreat, but they were working hard and had things to do, so they ignored their tiredness and just went on working. When they get away on to solitary retreat and when that need to work is no longer there, they can afford to allow themselves to feel tired. This is quite a common experience when people have been very busy right up to the time of going on solitary retreat. Sometime they work extra hard because they've got things to get finished before they can go. If that's your situation, I think the drowsiness that you might experience for the first two or three days is a quite natural and healthy reaction. It means you've got to give yourself a bit of time to recuperate, even physically. Maybe you've got to allow yourself for a few days to have extra sleep. You might find that for the first two or three days you just sleep for ten hours every night. You might be rather surprised: 'Well, here I am away on solitary retreat and I'm sleeping so long. Even when I was working I didn't need so much sleep.' Actually you did, but you were forcing yourself to take less sleep than you needed. But now your natural bodily and mental needs are reasserting themselves.

If this occurs, if you have been working very hard and you have really needed a bit more sleep than you've been getting, don't try to deal with this sort of drowsiness as though it's some kind of unskilful reaction.

You just need time and a few good nights' rest and you'll be all right, you won't feel drowsy in that way.

But there is another kind of drowsiness which comes from a reluctance of the whole being, especially the unskilful tendencies within you, to make any real effort. They just resist. It's almost as though there's a conflict going on within you. Part of you wants to do something, part of you doesn't. Part of you wants to grow, part of you doesn't. One of the greatest sources of drainage of energy is internal conflict, because the energy is going into the conflict, so the energy is divided: one energy is cancelling out the other. Your energy is used up in that way, and so you feel drowsy. That is sometimes what is happening. If something is going on that you're not very happy with, and there's a lot of unconscious resistance on your part, you solve the problem by just going to sleep, by refusing to face it. Sometimes you go to sleep on solitary retreat not out of real drowsiness, but to escape the retreat situation, because you are unwilling to face up to the fact that here you are with your own self, with your own reactive mind, and you've got to do something about it. The time has come! You find it very difficult to face up to that situation, so you escape from it by just going off to sleep.

From the third seminar on *Precepts of the Gurus* (1979, pp.209-11)

6. BEING SURE YOU ARE REALLY AN INDIVIDUAL

Going away on your own, on solitary retreat, is just as important as assembling together regularly and in large numbers.

Going off into the forest is one of the ways that individual members of the spiritual community can ensure that the spiritual community as a whole never becomes a group. This is very, very important. Going away on your own, on solitary retreat, is just as important as assembling together regularly and in large numbers. If you can go away, whether it is to the forest or into a cave, or – more likely – into a cottage or a caravan somewhere, and stay on your own happily and productively for a whole month, if not longer, then you can be sure that you are really an individual, at least up to a point, and are functioning as an individual, and therefore treating the spiritual community as a spiritual community: not making it into a substitute for the group. You can only know this for sure if you can go away and be on your own, all on your own, happily, for at least a month from time to time. That's your guarantee, that's your safeguard. It's in that way that you can know that you are an individual, that you've not unconsciously turned your spiritual community into a group.

From a seminar on 'Conditions of Stability in the Order' (1979, pp.61-3)

7. DO YOU NEED SOLITUDE TO PRACTISE DHYĀNA?

If you shut yourself up in your room for an hour by yourself you've 'gone away' to some extent, and to that extent you can meditate, but if you want to get really deeply into it, you have to go away in a much more radical fashion.

Q: Is it the case that you can't practise *dhyāna* unless you go away – on retreat, say?

Sangharakshita: Well, put it this way: there are degrees of going away and there are degrees of practising *dhyāna*. To the extent that you go away, to that extent you'll be free to meditate. If you shut yourself up in your room for an hour by yourself you've 'gone away' to some extent, and to that extent you can meditate, but if you want to get really deeply into it, which might mean hours of practice a day, then you have to go away in a much more radical fashion. That might mean going into solitary retreat for a month. The principle is that to the extent that you want to practise *dhyāna*, to that extent you have to go away – that is, if you are a beginner. If you are advanced and you can maintain a positive, *dhyānic* state of consciousness in the midst of your ordinary everyday activities, that's fine. You just mustn't fool yourself about that. The beginner needs to go away in order to practise *dhyāna*, whether you go away into your room for an hour, or into the forest for a weekend, or into solitary retreat for a month, or into a hermitage for two or three years.

From a seminar on *Dhyana for Beginners* (1976, p.1)

8. THE WHOLE ART OF LIFE

When you go away on solitary retreat, that is an opportunity of getting into things for as long as you naturally feel like it.

Sangharakshita: I think one of the most satisfying features of retreats is that on retreat, you are doing one thing at a time. Interruptions are really the bane of life! One of my little aphorisms is, 'The whole art of life is to be able to do one thing at a time'. If you are free to do one thing at a time, you are really fortunate. But you do have that experience on retreat. When you go away on solitary retreat, that is an opportunity of getting into things for as long as you naturally feel like it, without being interrupted or even interrupting yourself with the next item on your programme. It's almost a luxury to be able to carry on doing something – something skilful – for as long as you want to do it. Some people look on it as a luxury to be able to carry on meditating for as long as they feel like meditating, not having to stop because it's breakfast time, and after breakfast you have to start work.

Q: This is where the balance comes in, surely, between patience and strenuousness, because you've also got to develop tolerance at times when you will be interrupted.

S: Yes, indeed. Well, it depends on your general life situation, doesn't it? But if there are too many interruptions, your energy gets, so to speak, discouraged. It won't flow into things because it knows it's not going to be allowed to flow into them for very long; it's going to be checked and switched onto something else.

> From a seminar on *The Jewel Ornament of Liberation*,
> 'Patience and Strenuousness' (1980, p.298)

9. IN A WAY QUITE SIMPLE

As soon as you get on solitary retreat, something should come bubbling up, some creative energy, some inspiration.

Q: We know that it is not possible in ordinary life to course in the second *dhyāna* outside the meditation session, because of the absence from it of discursive mental activity. But do you think it possible that one could course in the second *dhyāna* for the greater part of a solitary retreat, both in and out of actual sitting practice?

Sangharakshita: I think you could, at least mildly, leaving aside the time that you spent sleeping.

Q: Should it be possible for most practitioners to reach a stage of practice whereby they could contact almost at will those deeper creative energies represented by the subterranean spring – short, that is, of attaining Stream-entry?

S: I think so; but – and this is quite a big but – it depends upon very definite conditions. The conditions are mainly that you must be sufficiently quiet and undistracted and undisturbed for it to be possible for those deeper, more creative energies to start bubbling up. So long as your mind is concentrated on, or diverted or distracted or disturbed by, a dozen, even a hundred, other things, it just is not possible. You have to isolate yourself. You have to remove yourself from all possible sources of distraction and disturbance, and just wait. Another condition would be that you sorted out all your problems, as it were. Otherwise, if you remove yourself to the conditions of a solitary retreat, what will start coming up will be things from the past, memories of painful experiences and so on. So the assumption is that those are all out of the way: that you are clear and free of all those, or relatively so. You can see the sense of that, obviously. Also, you should not be forcibly cutting yourself off from all those diversions and distractions; you should be quite happy to be on your own. There is no hankering after the things that you left behind; you are quite content.

Under those conditions, it should be possible for you to contact your deeper creative energies. As soon as you get on solitary retreat, something should come bubbling up, some creative energy, some inspiration. It need not be to write a poem or paint a picture; it may be simply to get more deeply into your meditation. But something of that nature should come bubbling up, even if you are just left alone for a while and people are not bothering you and you have got an hour to spare. At least a little ripple of happiness should come up, or a little spark of creative energy.

Q: So ideally, we should be able to get to a level where we can do that, without getting away for three or four weeks, but just finding a free hour?
S: It would be good, certainly.

Q: Do you think we are a long way from that?

S: I really don't know. I have been very much encouraged in the past by seeing what happens to people, very often with no previous contact with Buddhism, when they just get on retreat for a day or two. After two or three days they are in a quite different mental state. They are much happier, brighter, more cheerful, more relaxed. So you can change quite quickly when conditions are changed. Not that that is the whole trick, because after two or three weeks you could start getting bored, or you could start craving for the previous distractions. We know that quite well. Nonetheless, that does suggest that external conditions are very important. You should be potentially creative all the time, and if you are not actually creating in some way, it should be just because you are mentally or perhaps physically occupied with other things. When you are not occupied, you should not relax into a state of boredom and frustration, but just enjoy your own company, as it were, and feel the creative energies beginning to bubble up, regardless of the particular form that they may eventually take. It seems in a way quite simple, doesn't it?

From Study Group Leaders' Q&A on the Noble Eightfold Path
(1985, pp.143-5)

3 Progress in meditation

1. CAN YOU TELL IF MEDITATION IS CHANGING YOU?

'I've been expecting a hell of a lot more than this.'

Q: Is it possible to get a sense of someone's objective progress in meditation? If they don't seem to be changing much, might you suspect that they are not meditating, or not meditating effectively?

Sangharakshita: If you say to someone, 'You've been meditating for a year now but you're not in the least bit more emotionally positive than you were when you started', that is a very direct criticism. It's almost an attack, or could be taken as an attack on him as a person, and he of course will usually resist that. So it's not so much that there are not objective criteria, but that psychologically, or shall I say pastorally speaking, it is difficult to apply them.

If someone had been learning judo for a year and had not managed to do a certain move, they would probably be feeling a bit of a fool. But if someone has been doing the *mettā-bhāvanā* for a year but hasn't yet managed to feel more *mettā*-ful, you wouldn't think that he was a fool. You would be more likely to think, 'Well, maybe there isn't anything in it. He likes people a lot. Who says he hasn't developed *mettā*?' You'd be likely to develop that sort of attitude to your own practice too. 'After all, I don't hate anybody', you might think. I have heard this statement quite a number of times: 'I don't need to develop *mettā*, I've got it already.' But the judo practitioner can't get away with saying, 'I've no need to show you, I know that I know how to do it.' He's got to come out there on the floor and do it.

Q: Progress in terms of being seems a lot slower. It's much harder to see.

S: Yes, that's true. It's especially hard to see for those people who are in regular contact with the meditator. Someone who sees them after a few months, or a year or two, is likely to see a much greater change.

Q: Someone the other day said that he had been doing the *mettā-bhāvanā* for eight years and he was wondering whether it had had any effect. He said, 'I've been expecting a hell of a lot more than this.'

S: If he really had been doing it for eight years, almost regardless of the temperament he started off with, he would certainly have been changed to some extent.

Q: But looking back on yourself over eight years, it would be very difficult to see a change, I would imagine.

S: No, I wouldn't say that, especially not if you are young. I would say that in a six or seven year period, even a three or four year period, you could look back and see a great change in yourself. As you get older the rate of change perhaps becomes slower. But I am sure that some very young people can look back and see a tremendous change as having taken place within the course of the last year – not just external changes but changes within themselves. Don't you notice this?

Q: The first thing that I see is a change in attitude, taking the spiritual life a bit more seriously.

S: Well, that is the beginning of a change of being, isn't it? That's the change in, as it were, the vision aspect as distinct from the transformation aspect, after which the transformation is only a matter of time.

Q: In my experience, you find the foundation of your own individuality, as it were, and having established that, somehow, it's a more subtle kind of change which is taking place. It's less obvious externally, I think.

S: Yes, especially if the change involves any change in your whole way of life, as when people leave home and go and live in a community. You can only do that once, as it were; you can't leave home every week. When you do the external things for the first time, the change is very big and very evident, but after you have done all those rather dramatic things, the changes cannot but be more subtle and less perceptible.
From a seminar on *The Tibetan Book of the Dead* (1979, pp.128-30)

2. 'MORE ADVANCED PRACTICES'

It's not just a question of going forward, as it were, but also of rounding out one's experience.

Q: As an Order member with a full-time job and family life, I have just one hour per day for meditation. There are the basic practices, the mindfulness of breathing and the *mettā-bhāvanā*, but I've also got a visualization practice. Should I make sure I do the mindfulness and *mettā* as a priority above my visualization practice?

Sangharakshita: It sounds as though you're assuming that one practice is more advanced than another, but I'm not sure that's a valid assumption. What does one mean by advanced? One could say more difficult – but more difficult for whom? One has to be a little careful even in speaking about more advanced practices. Surely the advanced practice is the practice which, for you at least, works. There are people practising allegedly advanced Tantric teachings but these practices don't seem to make any difference to the practitioners' actual behaviour, so in what sense are those practices more advanced than something like the *mettā-bhāvanā* or the mindfulness of breathing? I would say – well, first of all I'm not querying whether you really only an hour in the day which you can devote to meditation, I won't question that! – but if you are confronted by a choice between, let's say, the mindfulness of breathing, the *mettā-bhāvanā*, your visualization practice or even, for good measure, the six element practice, you should ask himself which practice is the one that benefits you most at present, and devote your hour to that. Then, when you go away on retreat, devote time to those practices for which you don't have time in the course of the daily round.

Q: Would you say that the visualization practice would be more advanced than say the *mettā* or the mindfulness to the extent that it presupposes a certain level of commitment, and that it would be inappropriate to practise the visualization practice without that degree of commitment?

S: Yes. If one wanted to speak in terms of a more advanced practice, one might say that the more advanced practice was that which included a greater number of elements. The visualization practice isn't an entirely different practice; it still has a lot in common with mindfulness or *mettā*. Visualization practice is not an alternative to weak mindfulness and weak *mettā*, but when your mindfulness and *mettā* are strong, you take them with you into your visualization practice, and you can't really do the visualization practice without them. The more advanced practice is, in a way, the more complex one which includes as elements within its greater complexity, practices which you've already done separately.

Sometimes we perhaps tend to think of higher meditative experience in too cut and dried and linear a fashion, progressing from this state to that state. In practice it's sometimes very difficult to keep track of one's progress. One doesn't know whether one is going up or down or round and round, because often one explores different dimensions, different facets. Perhaps one should reflect that one isn't just going up and up, as it were, along a path up the side of a mountain, but that also the different petals of a lotus are expanding from a common centre. It's not just a question of going forward, but also of rounding out one's experience.

From Q&A on the Noble Eightfold Path (Tuscany 1983, pp.9-10)

3. PRESS ON

Make sure you make some progress every day, but don't bother too much exactly where you are.

Q: I find it quite difficult to use words or concepts to describe experiences in meditation.

Sangharakshita: Using them in what context?

Q: Well, talking about it or reading about it – but I suppose it works in that way. One gradually gets a feeling for it. You know, as I am now it's a complete blank. I just don't understand it at all.

S: One has to wait until one's experience catches up and then you say, 'Ah yes, that's what that doctrine's talking about!' or 'That's what that illustration means!' When I first mentioned the illustration to the second *dhyāna* (the subterranean spring bubbling up inside the lake) I could see little smiles appearing on the faces of several people. 'Oh, it's that!' they seemed to say. They recognized it and could link up their own experience with what the scripture said. This is what happens. And it all becomes much more meaningful then. Your experience in a way becomes clearer, at least rationally speaking. You know a bit more definitely where you stand, and also, when you read the text it means much more to you, because you can now see it in the light of your own experience.

Q: I've felt very reluctant to go very deeply into these teachings because, I think now, of a reluctance to find out where I really am. I've been involved in such a competitive kind of education that I'm just not interested in that kind of learning.

S: There's a saying of Oliver Cromwell to Cardinal de Retz, a saying that is quoted by Nietzsche, 'A man never flies so high as when he doesn't know where he's going.' There's a great deal of truth in this from a Buddhist point of view, because your sense of direction – when there's still somewhere further to go – is determined by your lower mind, and if you abandon all that, well, you don't know where you're going, and then, of course, there is the possibility of going higher or further. In the same way, the instructions are all there in these lists of stages and experiences, and it's quite useful to compare them sometimes with our own experiences, but I think we need not bother very much where we are, provided we know that we are going in the right direction and are doing what we have to do. Which milestone we've reached, I think we need not bother very much, if at all. I won't say it doesn't matter, but it doesn't help to think about it particularly. Otherwise you become like the athlete who's always measuring his biceps, and weighing himself. Your spiritual life becomes competitive, even if you haven't got other people in mind. It becomes ego-centred, ego-oriented. So press on. Make sure you make some progress every day, but don't bother too much exactly where you are. It sounds a bit paradoxical, but it is really like that. Sometimes you may feel you've made good progress throughout the last year, but you couldn't say whether you're now at stage 3 rather than stage 2. It might even seem that, in some odd manner, you've slipped back to stage 1; but on the whole it might be clear that progress had been made. At least so your friends tell you, and they can't be wrong, I suppose.

From a seminar on *The Endlessly Fascinating Cry* (1977, pp.178-9)

4. NO NEED TO WORRY ABOUT THE NEXT STEP

It's quite useful to have a theoretical idea of what lies ahead, but one doesn't need to bother about it too much.

Sometimes people wonder how, when you've got to a certain stage in meditation, you go about progressing to the next stage. But there's really no need to ask. If you get to a certain stage and you go on cultivating that, so that it becomes more and more full, more and more complete, then out of its very fullness it will move forward, under its own momentum, to the next stage. Similarly, as each stage of the path reaches a point of fullness, it gives birth to the next stage. We don't really have to worry about the next step; we just need to cultivate the stage we're at. It's quite useful to have a theoretical idea of what lies ahead, but one doesn't need to bother about it too much. Once one stage is fully developed it will automatically pass over into the next.

From *What is the Dharma?* (1998, p.124)

5. BEGINNER'S MIND

Everything you do is done for the first time, because you are different, the situation is different, the time is different, and perhaps even the place is different.

Sangharakshita: Beginner's mind is, I believe, a Ch'an or Zen expression. It is a mind which approaches even apparently familiar things in a fresh way, which sees them as it were for the first time. If you have ever meditated, you can probably remember your first experience of meditation: the first meditation class you attended; the first time you did the mindfulness of breathing or the *mettā-bhāvanā*. And that first experience, in many cases, is very strong, very fresh, just because it is the first. It makes a tremendous impact, a very deep impression on you – perhaps so deep that you never forget it. But after a while, what happens? I have known people who have told me that though they have been doing the *mettā-bhāvanā* or the mindfulness of breathing for, say, the last three years, their best experience of it was the first – presumably because they approached it with a beginner's mind. Perhaps when you do it for the second time, the third time, the fourth time, it is not quite so fresh. You don't appreciate it quite so much. If you are not careful, it becomes that old *mettā-bhāvanā* practice, that old mindfulness of breathing practice, or even that old meditation class. It all becomes rather dull and uninteresting and even unstimulating; you've done it all so many times before.

But you should try to think each time that you haven't done it before, because of course you *haven't* done it before. You don't step into the same river twice, as Heraclitus the Greek philosopher said. Everything you do is done for the first time, because you are different, the situation is different, the time is different, and perhaps even the place is different. You should keep alive that experience of freshness and newness, what one might call 'first-timeness', especially with regard to your meditation practice. Otherwise, you may start feeling that the whole idea of the spiritual life is a bit dull and a bit stale, and then you start becoming dissatisfied. You start looking out for something else, some distraction, usually; something that will give you a bit of a zip, a bit of stimulation, something that will make life seem interesting and exciting and make something happen. You might even start looking around for another spiritual practice. You might think, 'The mindfulness of breathing doesn't seem to be giving me very much; the *mettā-bhāvanā* doesn't seem to be giving me very much; my visualization practice doesn't seem to be giving me very much; maybe I made a mistake. Maybe it wasn't Mañjughoṣa after all, maybe it was Tārā; maybe it would be good if I changed my practice.' You start thinking in those terms. You start thinking: 'It might be good if I had a complete change. Maybe I'm being too spiritual. Maybe I ought to go back and have an experience of the world again.' You just give way to distractions or even start indulging in rather carping criticism of the Order or the spiritual community as an expression of your dissatisfaction and disgruntlement.

It is very important that you maintain that beginner's mind, that fresh approach, as though everything was happening for the first time;

because in truth it *is* happening for the first time. You are doing it for the first time. I remember when I was a child singing a hymn in church which began 'New every morning is the love'. The love, of course, is God's love, but ignore that! The morning is new, the day is new. It is not the same old day; it is not the same old sun. It is new every time. It is not the same old meditation. It is not the same old Buddhist centre. It is not the same old Bhante making his rather tiresome points again and again! It is all new; you have never heard it before. You approach it with a fresh mind, and therefore you appreciate it, and you enjoy it, and you rejoice in your own practice; you rejoice in the fact that you have the opportunity to practise the *mettā-bhāvanā* and the mindfulness of breathing, the opportunity to enjoy spiritual friendship. If you get into this state of losing your beginner's mind, you start not appreciating what you have got. You even start not appreciating the Three Jewels. Even they can start becoming dull and ordinary and uninteresting and uninspiring, just because you have lost that beginner's mind. So above all things, try to keep your beginner's mind with regard to everything that you do in the context of the spiritual life.

From concluding remarks at Guhyaloka
(15 points for Order Members, 1988, pp.12-3)

6. THE RHYTHM OF THE SPIRITUAL LIFE

It's your life, it's your development; nobody else can do it for you. You therefore have the responsibility of making your own decisions about priorities.

Q: I was just wondering if there are certain periods in your life when it's more suitable to do meditation, and others when it isn't – say when you've got a lot of work on, and your mind is so caught up in the working situation that you find it very difficult to meditate.

Sangharakshita: This raises the whole question of the rhythm of the spiritual life. There are various things, all of which are important for spiritual life, and for the development of the individual. There is meditation, there's study, there's work, there's all these things. Some people are so constituted that the best programme for them is something of each of these every day at certain stated hours: one hour's meditation in the morning before breakfast; then after breakfast, work for the rest of the morning; after lunch, some study; after tea, some more work, and then in the evening, another period of meditation – and so to bed. They thus have something of everything that is needed for the spiritual life every day. Others can't do it like that, for one reason or another, subjective or objective. They spend, perhaps, the whole day working, every day for a week or two, then they take two weeks off, and they spend all their time in meditation, then after that, they go off on a study retreat for a week, and do nothing but study. Or it may be that the rhythm, the wave is longer; you have a few months when you're completely into study, and then you have a few months when you're completely into meditation. The important thing is that, whether on a short-term basis or a long-term basis, provision is made for all these important aspects of spiritual life. How you do it depends on you. Everybody has to draw up his own list of priorities.

No one knows this better than me, because people are pressing me all the time to do this, that, and the other, and I can't fulfil all these requirements at the same time. Personally, I'd like to spend all my time writing books. But at the same time I'd like to spend all my time giving lectures. I can't do both, so I have to work out a scheme of priorities: that for a few months I'll give lectures, for a few months I'll write, and so on. Sometimes it's quite difficult, but you have to work out your own system of priorities. You may take the advice of your spiritual friends, but only you really know where the shoe pinches; only you really know what your needs are, or at least what your feelings are. So, after taking the advice of your spiritual friends, you have to decide whether to put work first, or meditation first. You have to make the decision. It's your life, it's your development; nobody else can do it for you. You therefore have the responsibility of making your own decisions about priorities. Sometimes it may be difficult, because you may be torn in different directions. But you have to try to work out your system of priorities.

Maybe it's best to try to work out what you can cut out, what isn't really necessary, and just reduce yourself to the few really necessary things – necessary in terms of your spiritual development – and then try to adjudicate, so to speak, between them, and spend more time on the things that are more important for you. That may change from time to time, from year to year, according to the way in which you are developing, and the kind of person you are. You might feel like spending week after week meditating; that might be your priority for the time being, or work might be. Nobody can quarrel with anybody else's list of priorities, provided each of us quite honestly make our own assessment, taking into account our own needs, the needs of others for whom we are responsible, and the needs of the overall situation.

One of the important things that everybody should realize in the broad sense is that we are all quite free to do whatever we want to do. Very often we don't realize this. Very often we say we can't do something when it's really an unacknowledged 'won't'. We disguise the 'won't' as a 'can't' to give ourselves a way out, so to speak, to let ourselves off the hook. But there's usually quite a lot that we can do if we only recognize the fact, and really want to do it.

From Q&A in Auckland (May 1979, pp.9-10)

7. WHEN MEDITATION BEGINS TO BITE

It's no longer just a pleasant comfortable sit where you float along quite happily and then go back to the pig trough, as it were. It's beginning to bite, it's beginning to take a hold, and you're beginning to be changed.

Q: Is it a common experience that when people start meditating they have a period of very successful meditations and then it seems to be quite difficult for quite a long time?

Sangharakshita: Yes, that's true. Occasionally it happens that somebody's first meditation is their best for a long time – months and months for some people. Even if that isn't the case, it's quite usual that for three or four months, maybe up to six months, after first coming along to meditation classes, everything goes quite well. People may not have a good meditation every time they sit, but they keep up a fairly steady level of progress. But after four to six months, in quite a number of cases, everything seems to go wrong. They can't meditate when they sit. They have lots of disturbing thoughts and start feeling rather churned up, day after day or even week after week. Sometimes they get quite upset. As far as I can see, what is happening is that the meditation is beginning to produce effects. They aren't just meditating with the surface of their minds, as it were. Something is percolating through, something is beginning to sink into the unconscious, and a sort of general upheaval is taking place, as a result of which for the time being they can't meditate. But usually if they stick with it and persist and don't force things, after a while they re-establish their meditation, in some cases on a better and more positive level, and in the meantime they may have sorted out a few personal problems, for want of a better term, or made some personal adjustments.

There can be a bigger and sometimes an even more traumatic upheaval after a couple of years, and quite often people stop meditating at that point. That seems to be a quite critical period. If you get through that, you're probably in it for good, as it were.

Q: I've been noticing a real difficulty in meditation, just when I was starting to get on better. I was wondering whether half the problem might be that I was getting fed up with it and getting annoyed, and whether that was holding me back from getting anywhere.

S: But why should one get fed up or annoyed with it if it's going well? Sometimes that does happen. Your meditation is going quite well and you're having a good positive experience, but for some reason or other you don't want to continue. It's as though there's something on a deeper level that is kicking against it – those unregenerate lower levels, as it were. So sometimes you might just have to persist gently. At other times it might be best to recognize your limitations, and just meditate for so long and no longer.

Q: It seemed as if one thing after another would come up. As soon as I'd get over coughing, I'd get tired, and after that there'd be something else. It would be just one thing after another, and I'd get really annoyed with it.

S: That suggests that your whole system is beginning to feel threatened. Your whole being, as it were, is beginning to think, 'My God, he's taking it all seriously!' It's no longer just a pleasant comfortable sit where you float along quite happily and then go back to the pig trough, as it were. It's beginning to bite, it's beginning to take a hold, and you're beginning to be changed. So of course there's a sharp reaction from that part of you – it's a very big part, obviously – which is not as yet involved. This definitely happens from time to time, on different levels.

There is another factor also, which is that meditation puts you in contact, very often, with feelings which are there, but which you haven't allowed yourself to experience. For instance, you might come along to a retreat, and you might be very tired without knowing it. You might have been working without any holiday or much of a rest for quite a few months, and you are really very tired; in your conscious mind you don't think you're tired, but actually your system is tired. When you get the opportunity to relax in meditation, you start coming into contact with that tiredness. So you mustn't think it's the meditation that has made you tired. You came along tired, or you came along angry or you came along resentful, and you've got in touch with that now, which is good. If you feel a real basic genuine tiredness, you need to rest, you need to take things easy. Or if you get in touch with anger or resentment, you need to find out where's it coming from, what's caused it. Is there anything that has to be changed in your life that is making you resentful, or is it just a purely basic resentment that you've got to get rid of?

When we come on retreat, especially when we come from a more or less normal life, we often come in a very battered state, psychologically, and we may have to experience that for a while. Everybody in this civilization is battered. You're being battered day and night, right and left. You go to work, you're battered, and you go home and you're battered there. Civilized man is a battered man. But you may only realize this when you come on a retreat or you start trying to meditate.

Another thing is the importance of keeping the beginner's mind. This is a Zen term but a very useful one. Why do you have such good meditation often when you begin? Because you don't know what's coming. You've no thoughts, no anticipations usually. You just do the practice. But after you've done it a few times and maybe had certain results from it, you start thinking and anticipating. You don't do it with a completely fresh mind, and that's why it becomes a bit stale or boring, because you think it's the same old meditation. But it isn't! Every time it's different. So every time you should approach it with a fresh mind, and do it as though for the first time. That's very, very important.

From a seminar on *Dhyana for Beginners* (1976, pp.5-7)

8. LETTING GO

You just have to accustom yourself to coming to the brink and then letting go.

Q: I find there's a tendency in meditation when I'm reaching a certain point when I begin to feel things moving, to stop, to hold back. Can you give some feedback on that?

Sangharakshita: This is something that happens for everybody. With practice you become accustomed to reaching a certain point, and the more often you reach that point, the easier it will be for you to go just a little bit further. So it is a question of bringing yourself to that point again and again, and sort of holding yourself there for as long as you can, and then of course, gradually – this will probably happen spontaneously – just going a bit beyond that point, and finding that you can go beyond and come back quite safely. Very often the feeling is that things are getting beyond your control, or you're sinking or sliding into some great gulf which will swallow you up and you won't exist any more. Of course that is exactly what happens! After a while you won't mind. You just have to accustom yourself to coming to the brink and then letting go. That's obviously what you do every night when you go to sleep, and you're not afraid of not coming back from that, so it might help to bring that to mind. You *can* come back. Of course, one day you won't! – but then ...

From the fourth seminar on *Precepts of the Gurus* (1980, p.11)

9. WITH MINDFULNESS, STRIVE (REVISITED)

One can make a great deal of effort, but if it does not include an effort to create more favourable conditions, one is almost wasting one's energy. On the other hand, one can be in the most favourable conditions imaginable, but if one is not making an effort, what use are those conditions?

Anyone who has tried to live a spiritual life knows how difficult it is to make even a little progress. We may look back somewhat sadly over the months or years, thinking, 'There hasn't been all that much change. I'm still more or less the same person I used to be.' Progress on the path is measured by inches, one might say. And even then, it is all too easy to slip by yards if one drops one's meditation practice or loses touch with one's spiritual friends.

When our meditation practice intensifies, it can take just a couple of days without meditating to put us – as it seems as soon as we sit down to meditate again – right back where we were months before. Of course, we have not literally gone back to where we were before – indeed it would be impossible for us to do so – and sometimes we may need to withdraw in order to move forward again more wholeheartedly. But anybody who meditates regularly will have this experience of finding that they have lost their 'edge' from time to time. The danger of falling back applies at all levels of the spiritual life. It is therefore crucial that we should reach a point beyond which we will be safe from backsliding. We need to reach firm ground.

Hence the importance of 'irreversibility'. It is found in the very earliest Buddhist texts – for example, in the *Dhammapada*, which says: 'That Enlightened One whose victory is irreversible [literally 'whose conquest cannot be conquered' or 'be made a non-conquest'] and whose sphere endless, by what track will you lead him astray, the Trackless One?'[98]

What does this mean? According to Buddhist tradition, our mundane experience naturally consists in action and reaction between opposite factors: pleasure and pain, love and hatred, and so on. Upon taking up the spiritual life, you get the same process of interaction between factors, but one factor augments rather than opposes the other. One traditional description of this process is in terms of the sequence of positive nidānas or links: awareness of the inherently unsatisfactory nature of existence, in dependence upon which arises faith, then joy, rapture, bliss, calm, meditative concentration, and 'knowledge and vision of things as they really are'. However, although this sequence is progressive or spiral rather than cyclical, it is reversible; you can revert back through the sequence until you are back where you started. It's a bit like playing snakes and ladders.

So the crucial point of the spiritual life is the point at which one passes from this skilful but reversible state to a state that is irreversible. This is the point of insight, the point at which one enters the Stream, the point at which – in terms of the sequence outlined above – one gains knowledge and vision of things as they really are. This is the real object of the spiritual life. There is no need to think in terms of Enlightenment or Buddhahood; that is simply the inevitable culmination of the irreversible sequence of skilful mental states that ensues from insight. Once you have entered the Stream, you are irreversibly bound for Enlightenment, one could say; you have sufficient spiritual momentum to take you all the way. You may still have a long way to go, but you are now safe from any danger of losing what you have gained.

It is therefore said of the Buddha's 'victory', his attainment of Enlightenment, that it is irreversible. It cannot be undone. There is no outside power that can make a Buddha no longer a Buddha. This applies not only to the Buddha, but also to the Arhant, the Once-Returner, and the Stream-entrant – and of course the irreversible Bodhisattva.

But until we have passed through that gate of irreversibility we are in a precarious position. This is why we need to make a constant effort in our spiritual life and also make sure that we are living and working in conditions that support our spiritual efforts. Until we have reached that point of no return, we need the most positive situation, the most helpful environment, we can possibly get.

This is what the Buddha was getting at in his last words, *appamādena sampādetha*, which can be translated 'with mindfulness, strive.' To reach the point of irreversibility one has to go on making an effort – including the effort to be mindful and aware enough to ensure that the conditions one lives in are conducive to one's making the best effort one possibly can. One can make a great deal of effort, but if it does not include an effort to create more favourable conditions, one is almost wasting one's energy. On the other hand, one can be in the most favourable conditions imaginable, but if one is not making an effort, what use are those conditions? Both are necessary.

Many people become aware of the effect of positive conditions when they go on retreat for the first time. The degree to which one can change in the course of just a few days is remarkable. Just leaving the city and staying in the country, being undisturbed by the pull of trivial distractions, and doing a bit more meditation and Dharma study than you usually have time for, can transform you into quite a different person – much happier, much more positive. So it isn't enough to try to change one's mental state through meditation; one needs the cooperation of one's environment. Without this it is very difficult, even impossible, to develop spiritually up to the point of irreversibility.

This fundamental concept of irreversibility – the point at which one's commitment to the spiritual path is so strong that no conditions can sway it – has been lost sight of to some extent, both in the Theravāda and in the Mahāyāna. This is a pity. No doubt it is good to have the concept of Enlightenment before us, but it needs to be brought down to earth; and thinking in terms of Stream-entry – in the broad sense, not in the narrow sense which opposes it to the Bodhisattva ideal – helps us to do that, reminds us that we cannot afford to slacken off our spiritual effort until we have reached the point of irreversibility.

From *The Bodhisattva Ideal* (1999, pp.184-6)

10. NEVER LOSE SIGHT OF YOUR OBJECTIVE

Those parts of you which don't want to change, which want to remain as they are, which don't want to come up into the open, don't want to be exposed, will start resisting, sometimes very strongly, and they will provide you with all sorts of excuses for not continuing.

Q: If one is moving into deeper states of meditation, is there anything beyond just trying to allow oneself to go deeper that one can usefully do?

Sangharakshita: There are several thing you can do. As with regard to mindfulness, and a number of other things, you must really *want* to go deeper. Otherwise you won't. You must want to go deeper, and you must take all the necessary steps to do so. You must avoid the hindrances and distractions. You must devote a sufficient amount of time to meditation so that you can develop a kind of momentum. And you must remain watchful and aware, and recognize that once you reach a certain point, or begin to reach a certain point, there's going to be a lot of resistance coming from deep down within you. Those parts of you, so to speak, which don't want to change, which want to remain as they are, which don't want to come up into the open, don't want to be exposed, will start resisting, sometimes very strongly, and they will provide you with all sorts of excuses for not continuing. So you must be on the alert and be able to recognize those factors within yourself at such times.

Q: That all sounds very complicated. You might get to a certain point and think, 'Well there's no point in going any further; maybe I'll go back and do something else.' You could be rationalizing, or on the other hand you could be right. Perhaps you might as well go back and do something else, or approach things from another angle completely.

S: Well, it isn't easy to approach deeper meditative experience from 'another angle'. I think the best way of going deeper is just to stick at what you're doing at that particular time. Don't switch to another practice, or go and have a cup of tea, or allow yourself to be distracted in that sort of way. Of course you must be sensible. If your knees are aching so badly that you can't concentrate, don't insist on sticking it out and just sitting there. Relax your limbs mindfully, perhaps even go and have a cup of tea, but be quite aware of what you're doing. You're only manoeuvring. You're only playing for time. You're keeping your meditative objective firmly in mind. You're not forgetting it; your aim is to sit down and get back into your practice as soon as you can, and you don't lose sight of that objective.

      From Q&A on the Bodhisattva Ideal (Tuscany 1984, pp.254-6)

Notes

1 *Satipaṭṭhāna Sutta*, verse 4, Sutta 10, *The Middle Length Discourses of the Buddha* (*Majjhima-Nikāya*), trans. Bhikkhu Ñāṇamoli and Bhikkhu Bodhi, Wisdom Publications 1995, p.145.

2 *Ibid.*, p.146.

3 From 'The Story of the Yak Horn' in *The Hundred Thousand Songs of Milarepa*, trans. Garma C.C. Chang, Shambhala, p.428.

4 John Dryden, *Absolom and Achitophel*, Pt. I lines 548-50.

5 *Meghiya Sutta, Udāna* 4.1.

6 *Hudibras* pt. 3, canto 3, line 547.

7 Wilhelm Reich (1897-1957) was a Viennese psychologist who, in treating patients, concentrated on their overall character structure rather than on individual symptoms.

8 John MacMurray, *Reason and Emotion*, Faber and Faber 1935.

9 *Karaniya Metta Sutta, Sutta Nipāta* 1.8, trans. H. Saddhatissa, Curzon Press 1994.

10 From 'The Story of the Yak Horn' in *The Hundred Thousand Songs of Milarepa*, *op.cit.*, p.428.

11 Śāntideva, *Bodhicāryāvatāra* or 'Guide to the Bodhisattva's Way of Life', chapter 6 ('The Perfection of Patience'), verse 24.

12 *Karaniya Metta Sutta, op.cit.*

13 Gampopa, *The Supreme Path of Discipleship: The Precepts of the Gurus*, 'The Ten Causes of Regret'; to be found in *A Buddhist Bible* edited by Dwight Goddard, published by Harrap, London, 1956; or *Tibetan Yoga and Secret Doctrines*, edited by W.Y. Evans-Wentz, Oxford University Press 2000.

14 *Karaniya Metta Sutta, op.cit.*

15 *Bodhicāryāvatara* chapter 8, verse 113.

16 Gampopa, *The Supreme Path of Discipleship: The Precepts of the Gurus, op.cit.*

17 *The Duties of Brotherhood in Islam*, translated from the *Ihyā* of Imām Al-Ghazāli by Muhtar Holland, The Islamic Foundation 1975.

18 Gampopa, *The Jewel Ornament of Liberation*, Rider 1970, chapter 7, 'Benevolence and Compassion'.

19 This is the first line of a traditional four-line prayer often included as part of a *sadhana* and expressing the profound wish that all beings may experience the *brahmavihāra*s, the 'four immeasurables':

May all sentient beings have happiness and its causes,
May all sentient beings be free of suffering and its causes,
May all sentient beings never be separated from bliss without suffering,
May all sentient beings be in equanimity, free of bias, attachment and anger.

20 *Samaññaphala Sutta* (Sutta 2, *Dīgha-Nikāya*), trans. Mrs A.A.G. Bennett, *Long Discourses of the Buddha*, Chetana Publications Ltd 1964, verse 81.

21 *The Tibetan Book of the Dead*, translated with commentary by Francesca Fremantle & Chogyam Trungpa, Shambhala 1987, p.13.

22 This may be the *Mahagovinda Sutta*, Sutta 20 of the *Dīgha-Nikāya*.

23 *Cūḷadukkhakhanda Sutta*, verses 20-2, Sutta 14, *The Middle Length Discourses of the Buddha (Majjhima-Nikāya)*, trans. Bhikkhu Ñāṇamoli and Bhikkhu Bodhi, Wisdom Publications 1995, p.189.

24 *Anguttara-Nikaya* 10.7, 'Lawfulness of Progress'.

25 Gampopa, *The Supreme Path of Discipleship: The Precepts of the Gurus, op.cit.*

26 Entering the *Path of Enlightenment*, Shantideva's *Bodhicaryāvatāra*, trans. Marion L. Matics, Allen & Unwin 1970, p.67.

27 T.W. and C.A.F. Rhys Davids (trans.), *Dialogues of the Buddha (Dīgha-Nikāya)*, Pali Text Society 1971, II, 82.

28 Trevor Ling, *The Buddha*, Temple Smith 1985, p.108.

29 Gampopa, *The Jewel Ornament of Liberation, op.cit.*, p.81.

30 *Samaññaphala Sutta* (Sutta 2, *Dīgha-Nikāya*), *op.cit.*, verse 77.

31 From 'Rechungpa's Journey to Weu' in *The Hundred Thousand Songs of Milarepa, op.cit.*, p.594.

32 *Mahaparinibbana Sutta* 2.25, *Dīgha-Nikāya*.

33 *Dhammapada* chapter 15, 'Happiness', verse 202.

34 *Dhammapada* chapter 15, 'Happiness', verse 200.

35 From 'The Story of the Yak Horn' in *The Hundred Thousand Songs of Milarepa, op.cit.*, p.436.

36 *Ibid.*, p.437.

37 Sangharakshita always uses the term Transcendental to refer to Enlightened states of consciousness, and mundane to refer to states of consciousness that are not Enlightened.

38 *Samaññaphala Sutta* (Sutta 2, *Dīgha-Nikāya*), *op.cit.*, verse 68.

39 *Ratana Sutta, Sutta Nipāta*, trans. H. Saddhatissa, Curzon Press 1994, p.24.

40 From 'Rechungpa's Departure' in *The Hundred Thousand Songs of Milarepa, op.cit.*, p.641.

41 From 'The Story of the Yak Horn' in *The Hundred Thousand Songs of Milarepa, op.cit.*, p.439.

42 'The Advice given to the Three Fortunate Women before the Departure', Canto 103, *The Life and Liberation of Padmasambhava*, Dharma Publishing 1987.

43 Gampopa, *The Jewel Ornament of Liberation, op.cit.*, p.178.

44 Śāntideva, *Śikṣa-Samuccayā*, trans. Cecil Bendall and W.H.D. Rouse, Motilal Banarsidass 1990, p.183.

45 Buddhaghosa's description of the practice is to be found in his *Visuddhimagga (The Path of Purity)*, trans. Bhikkhu Nanamoli, Buddhist Publication Society 1991, pp.288-90.

46 *Ibid.*, pp.173-90.

47 *Ibid.*, pp.337-43.

48 The Tibetan Wheel of Life depicts six realms of existence: the realms of human beings, gods, asuras or anti-gods, animals, hell-beings, and hungry ghosts. According to tradition, one can be born into any of these realms, but is not fated to stay in any of them for eternity; once the karma that resulted in one's birth into a particular realm is exhausted, one may be reborn into another. The teaching is taken literally by some Buddhists, metaphorically or psychologically by others.

NOTES

49 *Saṁyutta-Nikāya* xxii.49; *Aṅguttara-Nikāya* vi.49.

50 The six element practice is described by the Buddha in the *Mahārāhulovāda Sutta*, Sutta 62 of *The Middle Length Discourses of the Buddha (Majjhima-Nikāya)*.

51 The twelve links relating to the Wheel of Life are much better known than the twelve links of the spiral. It was Mrs C.A.F. Rhys Davids who first drew attention in modern times to the existence of the latter, and Sangharakshita has brought this teaching into greater prominence. For more on these two types of conditionality, see Sangharakshita, *What is the Dharma?*, Windhorse Publications 1998, chapter 7, 'The Spiral Path'.

52 *Satipaṭṭhāna Sutta*, Sutta 10 of *The Middle Length Discourses of the Buddha (Majjhima-Nikāya)*, trans. Bhikkhu Ñāṇamoli and Bhikkhu Bodhi, Wisdom Publications 1995, p.151.

53 Henry David Thoreau, *Walden*, chapter 2, section 19.

54 From 'Rechungpa's Journey to Weu' in *The Hundred Thousand Songs of Milarepa*, *op.cit.*, p.590.

55 *Samaññaphala Sutta* (Sutta 2, *Dīgha-Nikāya*), trans. Mrs A.A.G. Bennett, *Long Discourses of the Buddha*, Chetana Publications Ltd 1964, verses 69-74.

56 *Samaññaphala Sutta* (Sutta 2, *Dīgha-Nikāya*), *op.cit.*, verse 75.

57 *Vitakkasanthana Sutta*, Sutta 20, *Majjhima-Nikāya*.

58 Māra is a kind of Buddhist 'devil' figure who, among other things, personifies the forces of distraction and discouragement which impede spiritual practice. For an explanation of the different meanings of 'Māra', see, for example, Sangharakshita, *The Buddha's Victory*, Windhorse 1991, pp. 21-30.

59 Michael Carrithers, *The Forest Monks of Sri Lanka*, Oxford University Press 1983, p.245.

60 From 'Milarepa and the Novices' in *Buddhist Texts Through the Ages*, translated and edited by Edward Conze, I.B. Horner, David Snellgrove and Arthur Waley, Shambhala 1990, p.265.

61 Gampopa, *The Supreme Path of Discipleship: The Precepts of the Gurus*, 'The Ten Causes of Regret'; *op.cit.*

62 Sangharakshita, *The Three Jewels*, Windhorse Publications 1991, p.119.

63 'The Advice given to the Three Fortunate Women before the Departure', Canto 103, *The Life and Liberation of Padmasambhava*, *op.cit.*

64 *Samaññaphala Sutta* (Sutta 2, *Dīgha-Nikāya*), *op.cit.*, verse 83.

65 *Satipaṭṭhāna Sutta*, verse 5, Sutta 10, *op.cit.*

66 Gampopa, *The Supreme Path of Discipleship: The Precepts of the Gurus*, 'The Ten Causes of Regret', *op.cit.*

67 'The Advice given to the Three Fortunate Women before the Departure', *op.cit.*

68 From 'Heartfelt Advice to Rechungpa' in *The Hundred Thousand Songs of Milarepa*, *op.cit.*, p.576.

69 From 'Rechungpa's Journey to Weu' in *The Hundred Thousand Songs of Milarepa*, *op.cit.*, p.598.

70 See *Samyutta-Nikaya (The Connected Discourses of the Buddha)* 54.9.

71 *Entering the Path of Enlightenment*, Shantideva's *Bodhicaryāvatāra*, trans. Marion L. Matics, Allen & Unwin 1970, p.80.

72 'The dewdrop slips into the shining sea!' is the last line of Sir Edwin Arnold's epic poem about the Buddha, *The Light of Asia*.

73 *Dhatuvibhanga Sutta*, Sutta 140, *Majjhima-Nikāya*, sections 14-19. Section 19 begins 'Then there remains only consciousness, clear and bright'.

74 *Satipaṭṭhāna Sutta*, Sutta 10, *The Middle Length Discourses of the Buddha (Majjhima-Nikāya)*, verse 12.

75 *Satipaṭṭhāna Sutta*, Sutta 10, *The Middle Length Discourses of the Buddha (Majjhima-Nikāya)*, *op.cit.*, verse 10.

76 *Therigatha* 14.1.

77 *Udāna* III.2, *Nanda Sutta*.

78 *Entering the Path of Enlightenment*, *op.cit.*, p.81.

79 *Ibid.*

80 *Patika Sutta*, Sutta 24, section 2.21, *Dīgha-Nikāya*.

81 This meditation practice is a recapitulation of the process the Buddha describes himself as having followed just before his Enlightenment: 'I thought: What is there when ageing and death come to be? What is their necessary condition? Then with ordered attention I came to understand: Birth is there when ageing and death come to be; birth is a necessary condition for them.' In this way he traced back each of the links of conditioned coproduction. See *Samyutta-Nikāya* 12.65.

82 From 'Rechungpa's Third Journey to India' in *The Hundred Thousand Songs of Milarepa*, *op.cit.*, p.399.

83 From 'The Advice given to the Three Fortunate Women before the Departure', *op.cit.*

84 From the *Manjughosa-Stuti sadhana*.

85 These four factors are enumerated in the second chapter of Vasubandhu's *Bodhicittotpāda-sūtra-śāstra*.

86 According to Buddhist tradition, in this world-aeon – an unimaginably vast expanse of time – Śākyamuni, 'our' Buddha, was preceded by twenty-four other Buddhas, beginning with Dipaṅkara.

87 D.T. Suzuki, *Outlines of Māhayāna Buddhism*, Schocken 1970, p.304.

88 For a more detailed discussion of the faults, or marks, as they are often called, see Sangharakshita, *The Three Jewels*, Windhorse Publications 1991, chapter 11.

89 Tennyson, 'In Memoriam', LXXXV.

90 Gampopa, *The Supreme Path of Discipleship: The Precepts of the Gurus*, 'The Ten Things Not to be Avoided', *op.cit.*

91 This image was mentioned by Yogi C.M. Chen on an occasion at which Sangharakshita was present, and written down by Reverend B. Kantipalo in *Buddhist Meditation Systematic and Practical*; see www.yogichen/cw/cw35/bm13.html.

92 *The Buddha's Law Among the Birds*, trans. Edward Conze, Motilal Banarsidass 1986, pp.34-6.

93 Geshe Wangyal, *The Door of Liberation: Essential Teachings of the Tibetan Buddhist Tradition*, Wisdom Publications 1995, p.93.

94 Sir Edwin Arnold, *The Light of Asia*, Book 8.

95 'The Shepherd's Search for Mind', *The Hundred Thousand Songs of Milarepa*, *op.cit.*, pp.119-30.

96 Gampopa, *The Supreme Path of Discipleship: The Precepts of the Gurus*, 'The Ten Things to be Practised', *op.cit.*

97 Gampopa, *The Supreme Path of Discipleship: The Precepts of the Gurus*, 'The Ten Things to be Persevered In', *op.cit.*

98 *Dhammapada* 14.1.

Index

abhiṣeka 568-9
access/neighbourhood concentration 63, 85, 230, 249, 280, 453, 455, 564, 630
advanced practices 682-3
aesthetic appreciation 347-9, 591
aggression 287
Ajatasattu, King 292
ākāśa 475
Akṣobhya 605
alchemy 494
alienated awareness 30-1, 96-106, 210, 430, 453-5
   cause 101
altruism 16-7, 53-4, 187-9, 644
Amitābha 365-6, 546, 567, 572, 581, 605
ānāpāna-sati 26; *see also* mindfulness of breathing
anātman/anattā 143, 185, 442, 553
   misunderstanding 104-5
anger 141, 313, 314-5, 328, 350, 355, 513, 631-2, 666, 672
animism 493-5
antidotes to mental poisons 29-30, 313
anutpaticca-dharma-kṣānti 188
appamāda 322, 394
appanā-samādhi 64
Arhants 343, 432, 531
Aristotle 81
Arnold, Sir Edwin 651
arts/artists 16, 49, 240, 347-9, 420-1, 509, 592, 613, 635-7
arūpāloka 13, 276, 564
asubha 508
asubha bhavana 348, 501-10
Atīśa 638
attachment 170
Avalokiteśvara 193-4, 506, 531, 571, 580, 605, 620, 622, 641
Avataṁsaka Sūtra 485
avidyā 313, 512
awareness, *see* mindfulness

beauty 43, 347-9, 504-5, 506, 509, 579, 586, 595
beginner's mind 330-1, 685-7, 691
bhūmis 188
bīja mantra 32, 538, 573-4, 575
bliss 243-4, 257-60, 527
bodhi 355
Bodhicaryāvatāra 113, 141, 507
bodhicitta 34-5, 94, 190-1, 215, 552-6
   development of 533-6, 542, 543, 557
   and ordination 35
bodhipakṣya-dhammas 545
Bodhisattva 51, 54, 119, 168, 188, 314-5, 528, 554-5, 641, 694
   activity 641, 645
   archetypal 570-1, 580
   vow 255, 535
body 476, 493, 497-8
   awareness 68, 304-5; *see also* under mindfulness
   preciousness of 505-6, 532, 548
   speech and mind 529, 533
   unpleasantness of 499-509
brahmalokas 201, 218, 428
brahma-vihāras 31, 41, 113, 118-9, 166-7, 190-1, 192-220, 536, 542-3, 572-3, 586, 587, 646
   canonical sources 190-1, 217
   and the *dhyānas* 217-9, 276
   illimitable 219-20
   and Insight 212, 216-7, 218-9
Buddha, the 12, 29, 94, 133-4, 144, 217, 225-6, 270, 292, 317, 324, 418-9, 429, 592, 607, 639
   determination 393
   and the *dhyānas* 244-5, 254-60
   last words 394, 694
   mental activity 413-4
   and the natural world 491-2
   recollection of 551, 552-3, 555
   and the rose-apple tree 224, 395-6
   victory 693

THE PURPOSE AND PRACTICE OF BUDDHIST MEDITATION

why he meditated 253-60
Buddhas, female 494-5, 570
Buddhaghosa 36, 61, 120, 182, 197, 276, 315, 319, 320, 470, 489, 505, 561
Buddhism 12-3
  schools of 5
  and Western society 27-8
Buddhist scriptures 446
busyness 640-1, 647-8

cankamana, see walking meditation
characteristics of conditioned existence, *see lakṣaṇas*
chatter 308-12
Chen, C.M. 20, 29, 32, 38, 480, 573
Chenrezig 571
chöd practice 496-8
choice 323, 688-9
Christianity 168, 211, 259
cinta-maya-prajñā 404
cittadhārā 429
colours 303, 332, 559-60, 561-3, 565, 580-1, 611-2
comfort 336
commitment 34, 357-8
communication 263-4, 311, 388, 648
compassion 118, 144, 188, 194-5, 200-1, 203, 256, 527, 534-5, 551-2, 571, 575; *see also* karuna
compassionate activity 45
conceit 30, 313, 317, 477, 482-3
concentration 3-4, 8-9, 10, 18-21, 49-50, 58, 75, 223-9, 238, 243, 277, 335, 410, 431-2, 560, 649-51
  and emotion 248
  and Insight 406, 453
  objects of 20-1
  techniques 8
concepts 442-3, 458, 493, 517-20
conditionality 144, 267, 313, 317, 324-5, 404, 511, 513
conditioned coproduction 512
conditioned existence 549, 597
  faults 553
confidence 251, 330, 339, 447, 552-3, 556
Confucius 118, 175
consciousness 477, 481, 484, 512
  levels of 4, 9-10, 13-4, 52, 265
contemplation 4, 431; *see also* reflection
contentment 124-5

continuity of purpose 75
Conze, Dr Edward 51
corpse meditation 29, 347, 348, 469-71, 508; *see also* decay, contemplation of
craving 29, 259, 313, 315-7, 322, 507, 512
creativity 279, 678
criticism 210
cushions 305-6

ḍākas 530
ḍākinīs 497-8, 530
dāna, see generosity
dangers of meditation 370-2
death 33, 177, 180-3, 466-9, 476
  recollection of 32, 35, 316, 465
  spiritual 31-2, 44
decay, contemplation of 313, 316, 464-9
definitions of meditation 3-15, 649-52
deluded type 438
depression 351
depth of practice 608-9, 689, 695
desires 333-4
determination 330, 338-9, 392-3, 694-6
development 48-9, 54, 251-3, 517, 629, 656-7
devotion 288, 289, 370, 454, 555, 634, 658
Dhammapada 257, 259, 557
Dhardo Rimpoche 546
Dharmakāya 34, 429, 430, 591, 600
dharmapālas 530
dhyāna pāramitā 51
dhyānas 4, 22-3, 43, 52, 93, 231-80, 407, 630, 633-4, 651, 676
  arūpā 231, 236-7, 250-1, 266-7, 277-8, 445-6, 651
  and the *brahma-vihāras* 217-9
  and the Buddha 254-6
  and conceptual activity 410-1
  definition 231
  difference from *prajñā* 264-5
  effect on environment 241, 257
  balanced by energy 643
  and everyday life 261-4
  factors 238, 242-5, 251, 276-7
  first 229, 232-3, 235, 242, 247-9, 252, 262, 341
  fourth 233-4, 235-6, 266, 278, 433-4, 637
  indirect methods of attaining 630-8
  and Insight 427-60

702

INDEX

limitations 438
and mantra 625-6
methods of approach 265-6
mundane 261
natural state 232, 251, 284
obstacles to 325, 326-7, 328
other-regarding 269
rūpā 231-2
second 81, 229, 235, 252, 279-80, 677
third 233, 235, 247, 443
and thought 341
traditional similes 22-3, 234-6, 237-42, 243, 247-9, 250-1
and visualization 588, 625-6
and will power 270
dhyānāṅgas, see dhyānā factors
Diamond Sutra 496, 594
diary-keeping 359-62
difficulty 532
Dilgo Rimpoche 557
Dipankara 531
discipline 285, 321-2, 376-86
dislike 149-50, 208-10
distractedness/distraction 64-5, 74-5, 313, 314, 319, 320, 331, 332, 356, 398, 414-5, 649-50
doubt 7-8, 20, 283, 330, 336-8, 342-3, 686
dreams 51, 574, 653
drifting 391-2
drowsiness 331-3, 334-6, 673-5
drugs 51, 270-5
dualistic thinking/duality 493, 498, 522, 598-9, 601-2
Dudjom Rimpoche 557
dukkha 408, 505; *see also* unsatisfactoriness
misunderstanding 454-5
dzogchen 608

eating 286, 315; *see also* food
effort 45, 272, 280, 285, 300-3, 325, 338-9, 390-8, 421, 694
fourfold 319, 357
egalitarianism 317
ego 44, 264-5, 301-2, 496-7
eidetic image 564, 568, 592
ekāgratā (Pāli *ekaggatā*) 238, 243
emotions
alienation from 374, 561
engaged by visualization 595
negative 31, 116, 121-2, 131, 141-3,
145-6, 169, 351-2, 398, 426
positive 31, 44, 45, 93-4, 95, 112, 156, 164, 190, 200, 260, 370, 404, 417, 541, 612-4
and reason 248-9
reconnecting with 105, 183-4, 304, 430-1
repressed 102-3, 374-5, 653, 654
transformation 121-2
empathy 176
emptiness, *see* sunyata
ending meditation 66-7, 308-12
energy/energies 30, 43, 115, 279, 333, 335, 373, 375, 417, 451, 556, 646, 650, 675
balance with *dhyāna* 643
blocked 328-9
conserving 668
creative 678
release of blocked 243-4, 246, 483, 565
transformation 355
unification 50, 234, 238, 565
enjoyment 378-9, 380
Enlightenment 10, 12-3, 14, 24, 25, 35, 94, 224, 254, 257, 258, 265, 267, 313, 393, 468, 485, 495, 527, 541, 551, 552, 580, 656
aspiration for 47-8
embodiment of 607
glimpses 423-4
and *mettā* 189
envy 204
equanimity 234, 244-5; *see also upekkhā*
escapism 671
ethics 49, 96, 198, 285-6, 322, 363, 428, 630
everyday life 224, 261-2, 324, 424-5, 457-8, 631-3, 644-5, 647-8
exercise 288
experiment 672
external conditions for meditation 298-9, 320, 323, 332
extreme experiences 369-70

faith, *see śraddhā*
faith follower 458-60
fear 10, 32, 38, 366-70, 692
fetters 342-3
food 286, 315, 322; *see also* eating
contemplation of loathsomeness of 317, 505
formless meditation 608

703

foundation yogas 525-51
  'Hinayana' component 533
  Mahayana component 536
  relevance 544
four mind-turning reflections 392, 548-9
Four Noble Truths 112-3, 655-6
Francis, Saint 168
Freud, Sigmund 652-3
friendship 114, 129-31, 135-6, 162-3, 192, 367, 648-9
Fromm, Erich 660

Gampopa 185, 188, 250
Gandhi, Mahatma 527
gateways, three 452, 522
generosity 46, 347, 540-1, 557
getting up early 306-7
Goenka, S.N. 439
Going for Refuge 34, 349, 529, 533, 542-3, 557, 571-2
  as antidote to hindrances 357-8
  and prostration practice 529-33, 541-2
Going Forth 35
going through the motions 294, 338-9, 376
Govinda, Lama 211, 259, 273-4, 620
gratitude 154-5, 544, 557
gravitational pull 228, 363-6
greed 347, 513
greed type 436
grounding 67-8
group 675-6
growth 396-7
Guenther, H.V. 44
guilt 33, 102, 162, 185
guru 569, 572, 582
Guru Yoga 159, 557

habit 323-4, 336
happiness 119-20, 183-5, 192, 197-8, 202, 212-3, 225-6, 233, 239, 242-3, 259-60
hate type 437
hatred 29, 324; *see also* ill will
Heart Sutra 355, 443, 463, 521, 576, 598
healing 587
helping people 16-7, 44-5, 644
Higher Evolution 13, 649, 656, 659
Hīnayāna 527-8
hindrances, five 6-8, 19-20, 232, 242, 283-4, 313-58, 435
  antidotes 346-58

freedom from 344-5
  subtle 339-43
humanity 117-8

iddhi 237
ignorance 29, 313, 317, 343, 511, 512, 513, 514-5
ikebana 16
ill will 6, 20, 141-3, 145
illusion 596-7, 600-1
imagination 154, 175, 184, 619
impermanence 325, 403-4, 417-8, 480, 553
  and Insight 408
  reflection on 36, 70, 316-7, 424-5, 463-7, 480-1, 548-9, 579
impurities, ten 470-1
indecision 330
India 299
indifference 211, 244
indirect methods 14-5, 27, 390, 629-60
individuality 30, 75, 163, 260, 386, 651, 652, 662, 673-4
initiation 568-9, 582, 603, 622-3
initiative 260, 318, 323
innate purity 33
input 322-3
Insight 23-4, 85, 228, 401-60, 651-2; *see also vipassanā*
  cherish 398
  and devotion 634
  and dhyana 427-60
  'dry' 411-2, 452, 455-6
  instant 226-7, 406, 408-9
  and intellectual understanding 436
  and emotion 269, 404-5, 419, 430-1
  in everyday life 424, 631-3
  flashes 448-9, 611
  and *mettā* 118, 162, 173
  permanence of 434, 457-8
  preparing the mind for 402, 405-6, 413
  and study 448
  and thought 95, 269, 404-5, 419, 422, 430-1
  transformative effect 416
  and visualization 404, 595, 624
inspiration 239-40, 678
insubstantiality 71, 553
integration 4, 18-21, 30-1, 65, 96-7, 224, 237-9, 247, 367-8, 377, 386, 595, 650-1, 652

INDEX

horizontal 18-9, 238-9, 249, 633
integrated awareness 98, 100, 101, 105-6, 210-1
of reason and emotion 248-9
vertical 21-2, 238-9, 249
intellectual understanding 403, 412
and Insight 417-9, 430-1, 436, 443
intensity 543-4, 646
interconnectedness 71
interest 330, 333-4
interruptions 677
introversion 643-4
irreversibility 693, 694
iṣṭa devatā 581-3
Itivuttaka 115

Jaspers, Karl 652
jen 118, 175
jhāna, see dhyāna
jñānasattva 442, 610-1, 613
joy 162, 196, 345, 384
sympathetic, *see muditā*
Jung, Carl 659, 660
just sitting 29, 35, 204, 374, 424

kalyāṇa mitratā 17, 114, 162-3, 200, 557
kāmacchanda 326-7, 346-9
kāmaloka 13, 19, 256, 563-4
karma 144, 271-2, 317, 511, 514, 548, 637
weighty 64, 270-1
karuṇā 193, 214, 219; *see also* compassion
as motivation to relieve suffering 199-200
difference from *mettā* 172
karuṇā-bhāvanā 176, 199-203
Kashyap, Jagdish 640
kasiṇa practice 21, 36, 230, 559-64, 638
Keats, John 636
Kennett, Peggy 643
khandas 463-4
khemino 120
kindness 176
kleśa 164, 355, 356
Kurukullā 580

lakṣaṇas/lakkhaṇas 24, 70, 85, 88, 403, 408, 452, 522, 553, 608
Lawrence, D.H. 95
laziness 329, 641
length of meditation session 54, 378-9, 382-3

levitation 245-6
lifestyle 16, 49, 78-9, 290, 320-1, 323, 694
limitations of meditation 648-9
links, *see nidāna* chain
literal-mindedness 342, 416, 480
loathsomeness of the body 499-510
logic 92-4
love 115
falling in 589, 612-4
mode 163
mother's 161, 632
unconditional 144-5, 146-7

MacMurray, John 117
Machig Labdrön 497
Mādhyamikas 477, 485
madness 353-4, 366-7, 368
mahābhūtas 489, 490-1
mahaggata 52, 273
Mahāgovinda Sutta 190
mahāmaitrī 119, 175, 217
mahāsukha 527
Mahāyāna, the 32, 53-4, 119, 191, 194, 217, 257, 456, 528, 621
Maitreya 531
mandala
of the Five Buddhas 24, 494-5, 537, 590, 605
offering of the 539-41, 544-8
personal 65
Mañjughoṣa/Mañjuśrī 219, 442, 531, 571, 572, 580, 581, 582, 583-4
mano-niyama 637
mantra recitation 21, 69, 456, 575, 580, 584, 595, 602, 607, 620-6
Tārā 575, 576-7, 611-2, 621
Vajrasattva 538-9, 557
mantranaya 621
Māra 310, 324, 352-4, 398, 635
materialism 491
meaning of life 658-9
Meghiya 81, 82
memory 360, 361-2
mental illness 654-5
merit 540
transference 577
mettā (Skt *maitrī*) 29, 109, 111, 160-91, 192, 213-4, 614
basis of *brahma-vihāras* 196-7
and beauty 586

for the dead 180-3
difference from *karuṇā* 172
directing 149
for the dying 177
and erotic feelings 131-3
impartial/impersonal 137, 140-1, 152, 155-6, 165-6, 171, 186, 207-8
and Insight 118, 164, 173, 189, 405
misunderstanding 147-8
natural state 284
nature of 113-9
rational 117-8
reciprocal 171
translation 113-5
unlimited 219-20
mettā-bhāvanā 25, 29, 31, 40-1, 53, 69, 106, 193, 304, 313, 374, 466, 602, 609
antidote to anger and hatred 315, 328
basis of *brahma-vihāras* 196-7, 220
different from liking 142-3
drifting away from 138-9
effect on others 161, 178-80
and ghosts 242
how Sangharakshita learned 37, 40-1
method 109-11, 157, 159
for non-Buddhists 383-4
origin 36, 190-1, 217
progress in 680
stages
  first 123-8, 183-4
  second 129-34, 185
  third 135-9
  fourth 140-50
  fifth 151-9, 189, 211
suitable for everyone 395
Theravādin attitude to 40, 111, 189
undervalued 164, 189
variations 120
Mettā Sutta 111, 151, 315
Milarepa 64, 127, 253, 257, 260, 298-9, 372-3, 429, 452, 496, 516-9, 530, 663
mind
  Absolute 376
  blank 9, 11, 52, 228-9, 415
  preparation for Insight 402, 405-6, 453
  subtle mental activity 442
mindfulness 19, 28, 29-30, 39-40, 43-4, 45, 72-80, 95, 96, 98, 288, 319, 362, 394, 608
  of the body 19, 59-60, 67-8, 76-7

of breathing 8, 30-1, 53, 58-9, 106, 324, 602, 609
  antidote to distractedness 58, 313, 314
  counting, aids to 65-6
  fourth stage 66-8, 327
  how Sangharakshita learned 37
  and Insight 69-71, 405
  interest in 68-9
  method 60-4
  origin 36
  in Pāli canon 59
  outside Buddhist context 657-8
  and reflection 69-70
of emotions 19, 690-1
in everyday life 77, 85, 320-1, 382
excessive 98-9
four kinds/levels/foundations 72, 101
not exclusively Buddhist 30
identifying 128
of other people 78
of purpose 39-4075, 89
of thoughts 19
misunderstandings about meditation 9, 11-2, 52-3, 98, 106, 381, 646
Moggallāna 54
momentum 384-5, 406, 429
mothers 161, 632
motivations 47-8, 153-4, 223-4, 323, 333-4, 350, 377
muditā 118, 172-3, 196, 214
muditā-bhāvanā 204-6
mūla yogas, see foundation yogas
music 263, 302
mystical experience 240-1, 246
myth 492-5

Nāgārjuna 521
nāma-rūpa 512
Nanda 504
natural world 112, 119, 491-4
near enemies 197, 201, 203, 205
neighbourhood concentration, *see* access concentration
Nhamdog 428-9
nidāna chain, recollection of 29, 31, 313, 317-8, 511-5
nidānas, twelve positive 225, 227, 277, 345, 397, 511, 656, 693
Nirvāṇa, *see* Enlightenment
concept 517-20

INDEX

nīvaraṇas, see hindrances
Noble Eightfold Path 5, 46
non-Buddhists meditating 30, 383-4
non-duality 257, 343, 527, 551
non-violence 174-6
norm, the 117, 175-6
nostalgia 174

om mani padme hum 622
one-pointedness 238, 649
open air meditation 296-9, 320
openness 190
ordination 34, 35
origin of meditation practices 36
other-regarding attitude 111-3, 119-20, 269; *see also* altruism

Padampa Sangye 497
Padmasambhava 497, 530, 546, 605, 618
pain 258-60, 434
Pāli canon 634
pantheism 591
pāramitānaya 621
parents 534-5
Parinirvāṇa 259
Pascal, Blaise 470
path of regular/irregular steps 28, 34, 41-3, 45, 396, 487
patterns of meditation practice 361, 362
peace 196, 213-4
peak experience 398
pema (Skt *prema*) 132, 136-7, 170
Perfection of Wisdom sutras 491
physical activity 638-40, 647
physical effects of meditation 373-5
pity 202, 205
pleasure 258-60, 329
poetry 40, 92, 451, 635-7
poisons, mental 29-30, 313, 314-8
positivity, *see* emotions, positive
posture 287, 292, 304-5, 320
potential, spiritual 506, 584-5, 616-7, 618
power mode 161, 163
prajñā 264-5, 402, 408, 527; *see also* wisdom
prāṇa 62
prāṇāyāma 353, 372
prayer 178-9
preferences 208-10
prejudices 152

preparation for meditation 5, 50, 185, 227, 283-307, 321, 336, 338, 390, 466, 526-7, 577
pride, *see* conceit
priorities 687-9
prīti/pīti 232, 238, 243, 246, 277, 302
progress 41, 46, 54, 224, 251-3, 364, 419, 518-9, 680-96
prostrations 529, 532-3
psychic centres 375
psychology 47-8, 357-8
  difference from spiritual experience 403
psychotherapy 169, 649-60
puja 539, 555
puṇya 540
purification 33, 536-7, 557
purity 486, 538
purpose 3-4, 25, 46, 319, 321, 391-3, 415, 501, 658-9, 684, 696

quality of practice 338-9

Ratnasambhava 216
reactive mind 324, 513
reading 635
  about meditation 12, 288
reality 4, 44, 404, 579
  aesthetic aspect 590-1
reason 117, 493
  and emotion 248-9
rebirth 34, 153, 177, 428, 512, 534
  spiritual 32-3, 34, 44
receptivity 45, 190, 451
Rechungpa 64, 127, 296-9, 331, 516
reflection 21, 87, 88-9, 141, 316-7, 339-40, 404, 423, 424-6, 442-3, 451, 458, 459, 476, 520, 521, 549-56, 585, 588-9, 623
Refuge Tree 529-31
Refuges, Three 215; *see also* Going for Refuge
  esoteric 530-1
  Tantric 572
regularity of practice 378, 379, 381-2, 386
rejoicing in merits 167-8, 200, 205
relationships 136, 350, 351
relaxation 300-3, 374, 640
religion 658
repetition 535-6
resistance 335, 337-8, 365-6, 378, 385, 479, 675, 690, 695

707

responsibility for mental states 323, 324, 351-2, 688
rest 640-1
restlessness and anxiety 7, 20, 320, 330, 331, 342, 640
retreats 8, 15, 253, 301, 385-6, 420, 678-9, 691, 694
   solitary 301, 459, 631, 647, 661-79
   three-year 664-5
Rhys Davids, C.A.F. 117, 217
Right Livelihood 15-6
Rilke, Rainer Maria 167, 168
ritual 17, 498, 577
rūpā 464, 489-91
   and *śūnyatā* 355, 521, 576, 593, 598-9, 600-1
rūpāloka 13, 19, 564

sabbe sattā sukhī hontu 192
ṣaḍāyatana 512
sādhana 583, 609, 615-6
Śākyamuni 531; *see also* the Buddha
samādhi 223-9, 277, 402, 644-5
Samantabhadra 546
samāpatti 63-4
samatā-jñāna 216
samatha 32-3, 401, 404, 406-7, 409-13, 421, 423, 585
   relation to *vipassanā* 264, 401, 402, 405, 415-6, 418, 450, 456-7
samayasattva 442, 610-1, 613
sambhogakaya 600
samjñā 464
sampajañña, *see* mindfulness of purpose
saṁsāra 516-20, 548, 549, 596-7
saṁskāras 512
Sanankumara, Brahma 219
Sangha, the 98, 120, 162-3, 531, 675-6
   support of 253
Sangharakshita, meditation experience 37, 38-40, 41, 57, 80, 86, 352-3, 421-2, 465-6, 567, 578, 661
sankhārā 464
Śāntideva 113, 141, 315, 470
Sāriputta 54
satipaṭṭhāna, *see* mindfulness
Satipaṭṭhāna Sutta 59-62, 69-70, 112, 160-1, 467, 488, 491, 500
satsangh 17
seed syllable, *see bīja*

seeing 442-3
self 65, 97-8, 102-4, 264, 463, 518, 653
   fixed 468
self-other distinction 71, 187-9
self-view 343
selfishness 111-3, 444, 644
senses 51, 343, 441, 490, 512, 636-7
   withdrawal from 4, 5-6
sensuous experience, desire for 6, 19-20, 326-7, 346-9
sentimentality 203
sex 286
sexual desire 501-3, 508, 614, 671
Shakespeare 143
Shaw, George Bernard 202
Shelley, P.B. 592
siddhi 237
śīla, *see* ethics
silence 88-9, 309
sin 537
six element practice 29, 30, 31-2, 70, 185-6, 313, 472-95, 599, 602
   antidote to conceit 317, 483
   different forms of practice 482-4
   and Insight 405
   sources 36, 480-1
skandhas 463-4
skilful mental states
   definition 644
   intensity of 645-6
sleep 286-7, 294-5, 307, 333
sleepiness, *see* drowsiness
sloth and torpor 6, 20, 320, 321, 324-5, 331-3, 385
smṛti 73
solitude 291-2
Soma, Bhikkhu 57
Sona 82
sparśa 512
spiral path 42, 517
spiritual community, *see* Sangha
spiritual death 513
spiritual faculties, five 26, 46, 643
spiritual life 251-3, 517, 687-9
   stages 43-6, 363-6
śraddhā (Pāli *saddhā*) 31, 134, 157-9, 329, 504, 552-3
stopping 301, 6640-2
Stream-entry 187, 403, 419, 435-6, 440-1, 449, 631, 693, 694

INDEX

study, academic 95, 249
Dharma 49, 448, 458, 629, 635
stūpa 494, 546; *see also* under visualization
subha 508, 579, 586
Subhā 502-3, 504-5
Subhuti 217
subject-object distinction 112, 173, 180, 258, 343
suffering 53, 119, 172, 193, 198, 199-200, 201-2, 205, 259, 434, 535, 550-1, 554-5, 571, 634-5, 655-6
sukha 223, 225, 238, 242-3, 455
sukkha vipassanā 455
śūnyatā 32, 33, 44, 203, 398, 429, 482, 486, 527, 528, 573, 594
mantra 32, 486, 599
meditations 31-2, 516-22
and *rūpa* 355, 521, 576, 593, 598-9, 600-1
supernormal faculties 241
symbols 591-2
system of meditation 25-38, 43-6, 406, 482, 541-2, 602, 609
origin 38
and path of regular steps 41-2
summary 34-5

T'ai Chi Ch'uan 16, 68, 287, 629
talking about meditation 387-9, 603
tantien 68
Tantric Buddhism 372, 496-8, 525-8, 532, 568-70, 580, 621
refuges 572
Tārā 38, 194, 563, 581, 582, 605, 611-2
mantra 575, 576-7, 611-2, 621
visualization 570-8
Tathāgatas 555
tea ceremony 76
teacher, learning meditation from 288, 292
spiritual 157-9; *see also* guru
temperamental differences 15, 205, 394-5, 419, 437-8, 558, 560, 623
Tennyson, Alfred Lord 554
theoretical knowledge 42, 43, 45, 46, 424-6, 442
Theravāda tradition 36, 40, 215, 216-7, 256, 456, 506
Therīgāthā 502, 617
thīna-middha 6-7, 328

thought
associative 91-2
cessation of 228-9, 233, 243, 252, 263, 413-5, 431, 519, 560; *see also* mind, blank
clear 88-95, 338, 405
directed 89-91, 92, 142, 410-1, 414, 459
discursive 8-9, 233, 339-42, 422, 451
floating 339-41
lack of 103
wandering 9
Threefold Path 363-5
Tibetan Book of the Dead 33
Root Verses 392-3
Tibetan Buddhism 38, 153, 215, 317, 505-6, 526, 528-9, 532-3, 534, 570
Tibetan Wheel of Life 314, 317-8, 511, 512-3, 545
time of day to meditate 295, 306-7, 335-6, 354, 674
tiredness 284, 334-6, 392, 674
topsy-turvy views 503
transformation 45
Triratna Buddhist Community 220
tṛṣṇā 512
Tsongkhapa 37, 530

Udāna 504
uddhacca-kukkucca 330
unconscious, the 97, 110, 239, 575, 653
unfolding 224, 226
unsatisfactoriness 70, 227, 549, 553
unskilful mental states 364, 434-5
pandering to 670-2
unskilful/unwholesome roots, three 314, 350, 434, 513
upacāra-samādhi, *see* access concentration
upādāna 512
upekkhā/upekṣā 119, 173, 196, 207-14, 225
misunderstanding 211-2, 244
upekṣā-bhāvanā 205, 206-14, 216

Vairocana 572
Vajrapani 416, 571, 582
Vajrasattva 580, 581
mantra 538-9, 557
practice 33-4, 536-9, 542, 557, 563
Vajrayāna 33, 215, 257, 456, 525-8, 535, 557
approach to hindrances 355

Vasubandhu's four factors 549-56
vedanā 464, 480, 481, 512
vegetarianism 285, 287
vicikicchā 7, 330, 336-8
vigilance 322, 394
vimokṣa-dvaras 452, 522
viññāna/vijñāna 464, 512
viparyāsas 503
vipassanā (Skt *vipaśyanā*) 32, 69, 340, 403, 422-3; *see also* Insight
  practices 463-522
  relation to *samatha* 264, 401, 402, 405, 415-6, 418, 456-7
  and drugs 274-5
  'dry' 411-2, 455-6
  misunderstanding 412, 416, 440
  usage of term 481-2
  and visualization 585, 624-5
Vipassana Meditation teaching 25, 26, 86, 407, 439, 452, 453-5
vīrya 46, 643
vision 34, 44
visionary experiences 449
visualization 32-3, 40-1, 348, 442, 456, 459-60, 555-6
  'advanced' 683
  blue sky 482, 486, 573, 583, 598-9, 606
  of Buddhas and Bodhisattvas 538-9, 567-613, 616-7
  as concentration exercise 579, 585
  and *dhyāna* 588-9
  difficulty with 557-8, 606, 607, 623
  eidetic image 564, 586, 592
  emotions and 595

exercises 559-66
and healing 587
and Insight 404, 579, 585, 624
levels 574-5
preparation for 483, 542-3
stūpa 483, 485-6, 565-6
'Western' 604
Visuddhimagga 120, 197, 315, 320, 470, 505, 561
vitarka-vicāra 229, 238, 242, 633
vyāpāda 328

walking meditation 80-7, 454, 639
  purpose of 82-5
  and reflection 87
wilfulness 226-7, 270, 300-3, 371
will 272
wisdom 94, 117, 137-8, 363, 551, 651-2
Wisdoms, Five 24, 216, 355, 610
wongkur 568-9
wrathful forms 355-6
writing 249, 630-1
wrong views 373, 503
work 79, 261-2, 287-8, 290, 302-3, 631-2, 643; *see also* Right Livelihood

yidam 581-3, 607
  choosing 582-3, 615-6, 618
yoga 16, 287, 629
Yogācāra 481
yuga-nāda 527

Zen 5, 83, 330, 443, 594, 634, 637, 685
zest 156

Source Works

Published books

The Bodhisattva Ideal
Complete Poems
Creative Symbols of Tantric Buddhism
Facing Mount Kanchenjunga
A Guide to the Buddhist Path
Human Enlightenment
Living with Awareness
Living with Kindness
Moving against the Stream
The Rainbow Road
Tibetan Buddhism: an introduction
Vision and Transformation
What is the Dharma?
What is the Sangha?

Unpublished seminars

Pāli canon
The *Great Chapter* of the *Sutta-Nipāta*
Karaṇīya Mettā Sutta
Mahāparinibbāna Suttanta
Meghiya Sutta
Parabhava Sutta
Ratana Sutta
Samaññaphala Sutta

Mahayana texts
The Endlessly Fascinating Cry (Śantideva's *Bodhicaryāvatāra*)
The Precious Garland (Nāgārjuna)

Tibetan texts
The Life and Liberation of Padmasambhava
   Advice given to the three fortunate women before the departure
   Canto 37, Rivendell 1987
The Tibetan Book of the Dead
The Buddha's Law among the Birds
The Door of Liberation
The Jewel Ornament of Liberation (Gampopa)
   Tuscany 1985
   Benevolence and Compassion
   Ethics and Manners
   The Motive
   Patience and Strenuousness
Gampopa's *Precepts of the Gurus*, four seminars

Songs of Milarepa
Heartfelt Advice to Rechungpa
The Meeting at Silver Spring
Rechungpa's Departure
Rechungpa's Journey to Weu
Rechungpa's Third Journey to India
The Song of a Yogi's Joy
The Yak Horn

Zen texts
Dhyana for Beginners

Other texts and commentaries
Edward Conze's *Buddhism: its Essence and Development*
The Forest Monks of Sri Lanka, by Michael Carrithers

Abu Hamid Muhammad ibn Muhammad al- Ghazali's *The Duties of Brotherhood in Islam*
Hedonism and the Spiritual Life (review of Agehananda Bharati's *Light at the Centre*)
Trevor Ling's *The Buddha*
Manjughosa Stuti Sadhana retreat
A Survey of Buddhism, chapter 1
The Three Jewels
Stages of the Path Seminar

Order conventions
Western Buddhist Order First Convention, 1974
Western Buddhist Order Second Convention, 1975
Order Convention 1978
Men's Order Convention 1985
Women's Order Convention 1985

Ordination/pre-ordination retreats
Mitrata Omnibus q&a Tuscany 1981/2
Pre-Ordination Retreat, Padmaloka 1982
Noble Eightfold Path Tuscany 1982
Noble Eightfold Path q&a Tuscany 1983
Bodhisattva Ideal q&a, Tuscany 1984
Bodhisattva Ideal q&a, Tuscany 1986
Going for Refuge q&a Tuscany 1986
Guhyaloka 1988 q&a
Women's ordination retreat, 1988
Women's Ordination Retreat 1988
Women's Pre-Ordination 1988

Study group leaders events

The Higher Evolution of the Individual
The Higher Evolution of Man
Noble Eightfold Path q&a 1985
White Lotus Sutra

Other events
Auckland 1979, q&a
Question and Answer session in Christchurch, April 1979
Channel 4 Interview discussion
Conditions of the Stability of the Order
Mitra Retreat q&a 1985
New Zealand series of lectures Q&A 1975
Q&A Buddhist Soc. NSW 1979
Opening of Dhanakosa retreat centre q&a 1993
The past and future of the Order, 1985
Right Livelihood seminar, Windhorse Trading 1993
The Stability of Societies and the Order
Theris' q&a, Tiratanaloka 2002
Vinehall Men's Order/Mitra event 1981

Unpublished talk
Meditation versus Psychotherapy

All transcripts available at www.freebuddhistaudio.com.

Also from Ibis Publications

Beating the Drum: Maha Bodhi Editorials
Sangharakshita

Beating the Drum is a collection of editorials written between 1954 and 1964. The themes are diverse and surprising, and just as relevant to men and women of today. Whether pointing out the effects of horror comics (for which read computer games), bringing attention to the plight of animals, exposing Hindu casteism and unscrupulous Christian missionaries, or calling into question the apparent indifference of the Buddhist world, the voice of the Editor is one of sanity, clarity, humour, compassion and above all, challenge.

ISBN 978-1-291-10922-1

Dear Dinoo: Letters to a Friend
Sangharakshita

These letters are the product of a friendship between two very different people. Dinoo Dubash was the founder of one of the first Montessori schools in India. In her spare time she liked to paint, and to meditate, being keenly interested in things spiritual. She met Sangharakshita at a lecture he delivered in Bombay in 1955. She took a liking to him and immediately invited him round for tea. Soon afterwards they began to correspond – a correspondence which continued for nearly twenty years, spanning some of the most formative years of Sangharakshita's life.

ISBN 978-1-4478-5581-1

Triratna sources of meditation teaching

Most of Sangharakshita's works, including all the books quoted in *The Purpose and Practice of Buddhist Meditation*, are published by Windhorse Publications. Windhorse also publish books and CDs by many other Triratna meditation teachers. See www.windhorsepublications.com.

The website www.wildmind.org provides a whole range of meditation teaching, and another very useful website is freebuddhistaudio.com, on which can be found hundreds of talks on meditation and Buddhism, including the seminar transcripts quoted in this book.

There are Triratna Buddhist centres and retreat centres in many countries in the world, and all of them teach the meditation practices outlined in this book. See www.thebuddhistcentre.com for details of your nearest centre, and also see www.breathworks-mindfulness.org.uk and www.buddhafield.com.